H•O•T Credits

lynda.com Director of Publications: Tanya Staples

Editor: Karyn Johnson

Production Coordinators: Tracey Croom, Myrna Vladic

Compositors: Rick Gordon, David Van Ness, Myrna Vladic

Copyeditor: Darren Meiss

Beta Testers: Alex Marino, Scott Cullen

Proofreaders: Emilia Thiuri, Liz Welch

Interior Design: Hot Studio, San Francisco

Cover Design: Don Barnett, Owen Wolfson

Cover Illustration: Bruce Heavin (bruce@stink.com)

Indexer: Julie Bess, JBIndexing Inc.

Video Editors and Testers: Paavo Stubstad, Mike Harrison, Eric Geoffroy

H•O•T Colophon

The text in *Dreamweaver 8 H·O·T* was set in Avenir from Adobe Systems Incorporated. The cover illustation was painted in Adobe Photoshop and Adobe Illustrator.

This book was created using QuarkXPress and Microsoft Office on an Apple Macintosh using Mac OS X. It was printed on 60 lb. Influence Matte at Courier.

Table of Contents

Lynda Weinman's | Hands-On Training

Dreamweaver 8

Includes Exercise Files and Demo Movies

lynda.com

By Daniel Short & Garo Green

Dreamweaver 8 Hands-On Training

By Daniel Short and Garo Green

lynda.com/books | Peachpit Press
1249 Eighth Street • Berkeley, CA • 94710
800.283.9444 • 510.524.2178 •
510.524.2221(fax)
http://www.lynda.com/books
http://www.peachpit.com

lynda.com/books is published
in association with Peachpit Press,
a division of Pearson Education
Copyright ©2006 by lynda.com

ISBN: 0-321-29389-4

0 9 8 7

Printed and bound in the
United States of America

Introduction

A Note from Lynda Weinman

Most people buy computer books to learn, yet it's amazing how few books are written by teachers. Dan, Garo and I take pride that this book was written by experienced teachers, who are familiar with training students in this subject matter. In this book, you'll find carefully developed lessons and exercises to help you learn Dreamweaver 8—one of the most capable Web development tools available today.

This book is targeted at the beginning- to intermediate-level Web designers and Web developers who are looking for a way to get up to speed on the basics of Dreamweaver 8 quickly and easily. The premise of the hands-on approach is to get you up to speed quickly with Dreamweaver 8 while actively working through the lessons in this book. It's one thing to read about a program, and another experience entirely to try the product and achieve measurable results. Our motto is, "Read the book, follow the exercises, and you'll learn the program." I have received countless testimonials, and it is our goal to make sure it remains true for all our hands-on training books.

This book doesn't set out to cover every single aspect of Dreamweaver 8, nor does it try to teach you how to hand code a Web site from scratch. What we saw missing from the bookshelves was a process-oriented tutorial that teaches readers core principles, techniques, and tips in a hands-on training format.

I welcome your comments at **dw8hot@lynda.com**. If you run into any trouble while you're working through this book, check out the technical support link at **http://www.lynda.com/books/HOT/dw8**.

We hope this book will improve your skills in Dreamweaver 8 and Web design in general. If it does, we have accomplished the job we set out to do!

—Lynda Weinman

About lynda.com

lynda.com was founded in 1995 by Lynda Weinman and Bruce Heavin in conjunction with the first publication of Lynda's revolutionary book, *Designing Web Graphics*. Since then, lynda.com has become a leader in software training for graphics and Web professionals and is recognized worldwide as a trusted educational resource.

lynda.com offers a wide range of Hands-On Training books, which guide users through a progressive learning process using real-world projects.

lynda.com also offers a wide range of video-based tutorials, which are available on CD-ROM and DVD-ROM and through the **lynda.com Online Training Library**. lynda.com also owns the **Flashforward Conference and Film Festival**.

For more information about lynda.com, check out **http://www.lynda.com**. For more information about the Flashforward Conference and Film Festival, check out **http://www. flashforwardconference.com**.

Product Registration

Register your copy of *Dreamweaver 8 Hands-On Training* today and receive the following benefits:

- **FREE 24-hour pass to the lynda.com Online Training Library** with over 10,000 professionally

produced video tutorials covering over 150 topics by leading industry experts and teachers

- news, events, and special offers from lynda.com

- the lynda.com monthly newsletter

To register, visit **http://www.lynda.com/register/ HOT/dreamweaver8**.

Additional Training Resources from lynda.com

To help you master and further develop your skills with Dreamweaver 8, register to use the free, 24-hour pass to the lynda.com Online Training Library ™ and check out the following video-based training resources:

Dreamweaver 8 New Features
with Garrick Chow

Dreamweaver 8 Essential Training
with Garrick Chow

Studio 8 Web Workflow
with Abigail Rudner

Fireworks 8 Essential Training
with Abigail Rudner

Flash Professional 8 Essential Training
with Shane Rebenschied

Photoshop CS2 for the Web Essential Training
with Tanya Staples

Learning CSS 2
with Christopher Deutsch

Learning XHTML
with William E. Weinman

About Daniel and Garo

Daniel Short has been doing the Web gig since the end of 1998 and helps operate a successful Web development company, Site-Drive, Inc. He is also the Lead Developer for Cartweaver, driving the development of future versions of the shopping cart solution.

Dan is the author of several Dreamweaver video-based training titles for the lynda.com Online Training Library. Dan was also a co-author of *Macromedia Dreamweaver MX 2004 Magic* and contributing author to the previous edition, as well as a contributing author to the *Macromedia Dreamweaver MX 2004 Bible* and its previous edition. He has also written articles for several resource sites, such as AListApart.com and the Macromedia Developer Center.

Garo Green is the Chief Operating Officer for lynda.com, a leader in software books and video training for creative professionals. Garo has developed custom curriculum and courseware for software training, and has taught courses in hardware and software. Garo is the author of the *Dreamweaver Hands-On Training* books and many video training titles in the lynda.com Online Training Library.

Acknowledgments from Daniel

Believe it or not, we all started out without knowing a single thing about Web design. I was in that position when I decided that I wanted to take my fate into my own hands and do what I wanted to do, instead of whatever job happened to be paying my rent at the time.

When I made that decision, I met a slew of wonderful people that helped me get to where I am today. Through newsgroups, professional conferences, blogs, online tutorials, and even (can you imagine?) face-to-face cram sessions at 2 am, I built my skills and knowledge to a point where I can now "spread the love," and let you in on some of the wonderful techniques and technologies that make this business so exciting.

The individual that has most affected my career (and my life) is my partner Angela Buraglia, who has always pushed me to go the extra mile, and won't let me settle for just what "works." Thank you for everything you've done, and continue to do, to enrich my life and the lives of everyone you reach out to.

How to Use This Book

This section outlines important information to help you make the most of this book:

The Formatting in This Book

This book has several components, including step-by-step exercises, commentary, notes, tips, warnings, and video tutorials. Step-by-step exercises are numbered. Filenames, folder names, commands, keyboard shortcuts, and URLs are bolded so they pop out easily: **filename.htm**, **images** folder, **File > New**, **Ctrl+click**, **http://www.lynda.com**.

Commentary is in dark gray text:

This is commentary text.

Interface Screen Captures

Most of the screen shots in the book were taken on a Windows computer using Windows XP, as we do most of our design, development, and writing on Windows. We also own and use a Mac, and we note important differences between the two platforms when they occur.

HTM vs. HTML

All of the exercise files on the CD-ROM end with the .htm extension. As you design Web sites, you may see HTML files use the .html extension. You can name your files either way, and any browser will recognize the file.

What's on the HOT CD-ROM?

You'll find a number of useful resources on the HOT CD-ROM, including the following: exercise files, video tutorials, and information about product registration. Before you begin the hands-on exercises, read through the following section so you know how to set up the exercise files and video tutorials.

Exercise Files

The files required to complete the exercises are on the HOT CD-ROM in a folder called **exercise_files**. These files are divided into chapter folders, and you should copy each chapter folder onto your **Desktop** before you begin the exercise for that chapter. For example, if you're about to start Chapter 5, copy the **chap_05** folder from the **exercise_files** folder on the HOT CD-ROM onto your **Desktop**.

On Windows, when files originate from a CD-ROM, they automatically become write-protected, which means you cannot alter them. Fortunately, you can easily change this attribute. For complete instructions, read the "Making Exercise Files Editable on Windows Computers" section on the next page.

Video Tutorials

Throughout the book, you'll find references to video tutorials. In some cases, these video tutorials reinforce concepts explained in the book. In other cases, they show bonus material you'll find interesting and useful. To view the video tutorials, you must have QuickTime Player installed on your computer. If you do not have QuickTime Player, you can download it for free from Apple's Web site: **http://www.apple.com/quicktime**.

To view the video tutorials, copy the videos from the HOT CD-ROM onto your hard drive. Double-click the video you want to watch, and it will automatically open in QuickTime Player. Make sure the volume on your computer is turned up so you can hear the audio content.

If you like the video tutorials, refer to the "Product Registration" section earlier in this chapter and register to receive a free pass to the **lynda.com Online Training Library**, which is filled with over 10,000 video tutorials covering over 150 topics.

Making Exercise Files Editable on Windows Computers

By default, when you copy files from a CD-ROM to a Windows computer, they are set to read-only (write-protected). This will cause a problem with the exercise files because you will need to edit and save many of them. You can remove the read-only property by following these steps:

1 Open the **exercise_files** folder on the **HOT CD-ROM**, and copy one of the subfolders, such as **chap_02**, to your **Desktop**.

2 Open the **chap_02** folder you copied to your **Desktop**, and choose **Edit > Select All**.

3 Right-click one of the selected files and choose **Properties** from the contextual menu.

4 In the **Properties** dialog box, click the **General** tab. Deselect the **Read-Only** option to disable the read-only properties for the selected files in the **chap_02** folder.

Making File Extensions Visible on Windows Computers

By default, you cannot see file extensions, such as .htm, .fla, .swf, .jpg, .gif, or .psd on Windows computers. Fortunately you can change this setting easily. Here's how:

1 On your **Desktop**, double-click the **My Computer** icon.

Note: If you (or someone else) changed the name, it will not say **My Computer.**

2 Choose **Tools > Folder Options** to open the **Folder Options** dialog box. Click the **View** tab.

3 Deselect the **Hide extensions for known file types** option to make all file extensions visible.

Dreamweaver 8 System Requirements

Windows

- 800 MHz Intel Pentium III processor (or equivalent) and later
- Windows 2000, Windows XP
- 256 MB RAM (1 GB recommended to run more than one Studio 8 product simultaneously)
- 1024 x 768, 16-bit display (32-bit recommended)
- 650 MB available disk space

Macintosh

- 600 MHz PowerPC G3 and later
- Mac OS X 10.3, 10.4
- 256 MB RAM (1 GB recommended to run more than one Studio 8 product simultaneously)
- 1024 x 768, thousands of colors display (millions of colors recommended)
- 300 MB available disk space

Getting Demo Versions of the Software

If you'd like to try demo versions of the software used in this book, you can download demo versions as follows:

Firefox: **http://www.getfirefox.com**

Dreamweaver 8: **http://www.macromedia.com/go/dreamweaver**

Fireworks 8: **http://www.macromedia.com/go/fireworks**

1

Getting Started

We could start this book with lots of exercises, throwing you right into working with Dreamweaver 8 without any preparation. But then you would be flying blind, without understanding basic Web design funda-mentals such as XHTML, CSS, DHTML, XML, and JavaScript. Instead, we will start you off with some definitions, concepts, and guidelines to help with your hands-on Dreamweaver 8 training. Feel free to scan this chapter for information if you already know some of what is here, or jump right to the exercises in the next chapter.

What Is Dreamweaver 8?

At its roots, Macromedia Dreamweaver 8 is a WYSIWIG (what you see is what you get) XHTML generator. This means if you change something on the screen inside Dreamweaver 8, it will show you the results instantly and write the proper code for you. In contrast, if you were to code the XHTML by hand in a non-WYSIWIG editor, you would have to write the code and then view the results from inside a Web browser, write more code, and check again. The instant feedback of a live design environment such as Dreamweaver 8 speeds up your workflow tremendously, because you can see whether you like the results while you are working.

HTML vs. XHTML

We are at a rather interesting crossover point in the evolution of the World Wide Web. For many years, using HTML (Hyper Text Markup Language) was the only code you could use to create a Web page. Sure, there were other technologies such as JavaScript, Cascading Style Sheets, and server-side languages such as ASP, JSP, CFM, and such, but at the heart of every Web page was simple HTML. As of October 4, 2001, the W3C (the Web standards committee) decided to discontinue HTML. Taking its place is XHTML (Extensible Hyper Text Markup Language), a language almost identical to HTML with the exception that it has a stricter format and follows XML syntax rules. Does this mean that if you learned HTML you wasted your time? Heck no. You can still use HTML, as well as XHTML, to create Web pages. In fact, knowing HTML will help you make the transition to XHTML, so don't worry.

Over the last several years most Web designers have begun to embrace XHTML and have started using it to develop their Web pages. In an effort to ensure you learn the most up-to-date methods, you will see only XHTML code examples throughout this entire book. Even though you can still use HTML to create Web pages, not using XHTML would be a disservice to you, because it's the most current standard for creating Web pages. This chapter will give you more information on XHTML so you better understand the role it plays in Web design.

Roundtrip XHTML

Dreamweaver has gained and maintained a lot of great reviews and customer loyalty because of its use of Roundtrip XHTML, which lets you easily move between Dreamweaver and another text editor, such as FrontPage, BBEdit, or HomeSite with very little or no change to your code. Unless you are a programmer (and chances are you aren't if you are reading this book), this probably won't mean a whole lot to you right now. However, moving between different development tools can be very important when you are working with a programmer or in a team environment where everyone might not be using Dreamweaver. It's nice to know you can do this and not worry about Dreamweaver breaking your code by inserting unwanted and proprietary changes. Don't you wish all programs were so respectful?

A great many programmers have looked at WYSIWYG editors with dubious eyes because of their reputation for inflexibility and inclusion of nonstandard code. Dreamweaver 8 is one of the few WYSIWYG XHTML editors to win the approval of programmers and designers alike. Programmers like the product because they don't have to worry about their code being changed by Dreamweaver. Designers like it because it writes clean code without inserting a lot of proprietary and self-serving tags, and it lets them to do visual layout without touching a line of code. Hard to believe there is a tool that could please both of these divergent groups, but there is, and Dreamweaver 8 is it!

Now, truth be told, Dreamweaver can make some minor changes to a page once it's opened. Since the few changes it makes are usually cleaning up bad code, no one really frowns on these changes. In fact, Dreamweaver lets you control how code is rewritten (if at all) within the Preferences area of the program, so you still have full control over this feature. There is no reason to get into those issues now; these changes and how to turn them off (if you even want to do so) are covered in Chapter 12, *"XHTML."*

Do You Need to Learn XHTML to Use Dreamweaver?

Yes and no. If you use a WYSIWYG XHTML editor, then technically you can create an entire Web page without writing a single line of code. However, there may come a time when you will have to edit the code manually to troubleshoot a problem, such as when you encounter an incompatibility between browsers.

For some, XHTML can be quite intimidating at first glance—your first reaction may be to avoid it at all costs. After all, when you design pages using Photoshop, QuarkXPress, or InDesign, you don't need to look at raw PostScript code anymore. However, the early pioneers of desktop publishing had to know how to program in PostScript just to create a page layout! Designing for print also doesn't have the problem of multiple browsers and devices displaying the page; a printed page is a printed page, no matter who's viewing it.

In the past, if you didn't know some XHTML, you were at the mercy of a programmer, who might have more control over your design than you liked. With Dreamweaver 8, you can technically get by without understanding or writing a single

line of code. However, it won't be long before you need to look at the code and make some changes manually, especially if you long to be a true professional Web designer or developer. So we strongly recommend you take the time to learn XHTML. Most people who don't take the time to learn XHTML are at a disadvantage in the workplace, especially when they need to troubleshoot problems on their Web pages.

How do you learn XHTML? There are a lots of ways—you can take a class at school, take an online class, buy a training CD-ROM (we happen to know of a really good one!) or buy a book. An easy way to learn XHTML (and the way Dan personally got his start) is to view the source code of pages that you like. In XHTML, the code is visible to anyone who uses a Web browser. To view the source code of a page—whether it is in HTML or XHTML—in your browser, choose **View > Page Source** (FireFox) or **View > Source** (Explorer) or **View > View Source** (Safari). Once you get comfortable with some of the tags, you will likely be able to deconstruct how these pages were made.

What Does XHTML Do?

XHTML stands for Extensible Hyper Text Markup Language. It is a derivative of SGML (Standard Generalized Markup Language), an international standard for representing text in an electronic form that can be used for exchanging documents in an independent manner. XHTML is also the replacement for HTML.

At its heart, XHTML allows for the markup of text and the inclusion of images, as well as the capability to link documents together. Hyperlinks, which are at the core of any Web page's success, are what let you flip between pages in a site, or to view pages in outside sites. These hyperlinks are references contained within the markup. If the source of the link moves, or the reference to the link is misspelled, it won't work. One of the great attributes of Dreamweaver 8 is its many site-management capabilities, which will help you manage your internal links so they are automatically updated if the links are changed.

The last published version of HTML was 4.01. There will not be a version 5 of HTML. Instead, there is a newer standard: XHTML 1.0, which already exists as a formal recommendation sanctioned by the World Wide Web Consortium (the standards committee of the Web, otherwise known as the W3C). The next version of XHTML, version 1.1, is a formal recommendation, but still is more suitable for internal applications and isn't quite ready for mass public consumption.

So then how is XHTML different from its close companion HTML? The most visible difference between the two markup languages is in their syntax, with all opening tags requiring a closing tag. Here are some of the key differences:

- All element and attribute names are in lowercase. For example, **<P>** would not be valid, but **<p>** would be a valid XHTML element.
- All attribute values must be contained within quotes (single or double). For example, in HTML

you can write **<td nowrap>**, but in XHTML you have to write **<td nowrap="nowrap">**. Be consistent in the type of quotes you use; don't mix single quotes with double quotes, or vice versa.

- All nonempty elements must have a closing tag. For example, **<p>This is good text.</p>** is a valid XHTML element, but **<p>This is bad text.** would not be valid.
- All empty tags should be written with a space and a / symbol at the end of the tag. For example, **
** is a valid XHTML tag, but **
** is not. This method of closing empty tags ensures your pages are compatible with older browsers while honoring the XHTML specifications.

Before you panic, let's point out that Dreamweaver 8 will write all of the XHTML code for you. This gives you the freedom to create your Web pages in a visual way while letting Dreamweaver 8 create the code behind the scenes. So, if you don't have the patience or desire to learn XHTML, you really don't have to. Of course, we strongly suggest that you do take the time to learn XHTML because it will help you build and troubleshoot more complex pages.

XHTML follows the XML rules and syntax guidelines. Because XML has very rigid requirements for writing code, XHTML is a more structured markup language than HTML. This more structured approach to markup languages will enable one document to be viewed on multiple devices (Web browsers, cell phones, PDAs, and so on) by simply creating different style sheets for each device. (You will learn about style sheets later in the book.) In a nutshell, XHTML is basically HTML 4.01 reformatted using the syntax of XML, which is described later in this chapter. You will be glad to know Dreamweaver 8 has full support for XHTML. In fact, Dreamweaver 8 can even convert your existing HTML documents to XHTML. You will learn more about this in Chapter 12, *"XHTML."*

What Does XHTML Look Like?

If you have ever seen HTML code, you will find instant comfort in looking at XHTML code. Because XHTML is a reformatting of HTML, many things look the same or have minor differences. Although there are some distinct and critical differences between XHTML and HTML, they are both markup languages and share many common traits, which lessens the learning curve for those of you already familiar with HTML.

Here are some of the basic elements of an XHTML document written in correct syntax:

```
1.  <!DOCTYPE html PUBLIC "-//W3C//DTD XHTML
    1.0 Transitional//EN" "http://www.w3.org/
    TR/xhtml11/DTD/xhtml11-transitional.dtd">
2.  <html xmlns="http://www.w3.org/1999/xhtml">
3.  <head>
4.  <title>Untitled Document</title>
5.  </head>
6.  <body>This is where the content of your
    page will be placed.
7.  </body>
8.  </html>
```

Here is a breakdown of these XHTML code elements:

1. **Document Type Definition (DTD or DOCTYPE):** This URL points to a file outlining the available elements, attributes, and their appropriate usage.

   Three XHTML DTDs are available:

   - XHTML Transitional: This DTD lets you maintain backward compatibility with older browsers while still providing access to HTML 4.01 elements. (This is the DOCTYPE we'll be using throughout this book.)

   - XHTML Strict: This DTD removes many of the HTML elements that were designed to control the appearance of a page and how the user interacts with those elements. This is the truest form of XHTML elements.

   - XHTML Frameset: This DTD gives you access to the HTML elements needed to create framesets.

2. **XML namespace:** This URL points to a file that gives detailed information about the particular XML vocabulary used on the page, which is XHTML in this case.

3. The **<head>** tag contains all of the header information.

4. The **<title>** tag defines the page title, which appears at the top of the browser window and in a user's bookmark list.

5. All XHTML tags must be closed, so this is the closing **</head>** tag.

6. All of your visible content will be placed inside the **<body>** tag.

7. You guessed it! This is the closing **</body>** tag.

8. Last, but not least, is the closing **</html>** tag.

This example represents only a smidgen of the available XHTML tags, attributes, and values. But it covers the basics and is a great place to start your XHTML education. More examples of XHTML are covered in Chapter 4, *"Basics"* and Chapter 12 *"XHTML."*

File-Naming Conventions

Working with XHTML is much more restrictive than working with other types of computer media. One of the strictest parts about XHTML is its file-naming conventions:

- **Don't use spaces:** Save your files using no spaces between the filename elements. For example, the filename **about lynda.htm** is illegal because of the space between the words "about" and "lynda." Instead, write this filename as **about_lynda.htm** or **aboutlynda.htm.**

- **Avoid capital letters:** Avoid capitalization in your filenames. **AboutLynda.htm** will work as a filename, but any time you link to the file you will have to remember the correct capitalization. If you're using a Unix or Linux server, filenames are case-sensitive; if someone is typing the link directly into the browser, he or she will most likely type everything lowercase. It is far easier to simply use all lowercase letters.

- **Avoid illegal characters:** The following chart contains a list of characters to avoid when naming files.

File-Naming Conventions	
Character	**Usage**
. (dot)	Periods are reserved for filename extensions or suffixes, for example .gif and .jpg.
"	Quotes are reserved for HTML to indicate the value of tags and attributes.
**/ or **	Forward slashes (/) indicate files are nested in folders. If you include a forward slash in your filename, HTML may lose your references, thinking you are specifying a folder. A backslash (\) isn't allowed on Windows servers.
:	Colons are used to separate certain script commands on Mac and Windows computers. Avoid them in your filenames so not to confuse a filename with script command.
!	Exclamation marks are used in comment tags.

Filename Extensions

You may be curious about the many extensions used after the dot at the end of filenames. Here is a chart that lists the meaning of some extensions you'll run across during your development adventures:

Filename Extensions	
Extension	**Usage**
.htm, .html	These two extensions are commonly used to denote an HTML file. The three-letter extension works just as well as the four-letter version. Older DOS systems didn't allow for four-letter extensions, which is why you sometimes see .html abbreviated as .htm.

continues on next page

Filename Extensions *continued*	
Extension	**Usage**
.gif	GIF images
.jpg	JPEG images
.png	PNG images (also used for Macromedia Fireworks 8 source files)
.swf	Flash files
.mov	QuickTime movie files
.avi	AVI movie files
.aif	AIFF sound files

What Is CSS?

CSS stands for **C**ascading **S**tyle **S**heets. CSS is used for many different purposes, but its primary function is to separate the presentation from the structure of a page. **Presentation** has to do with the way a page "looks," whereas **structure** has to do with the "meaning" of the page's content. An **h1** tag defines that the text within is a header, and that the text carries some special meaning. Whether that header is blue, purple, big, small, italicized, or whatever, has to do with its presentation. It's important to separate the two so the structure of a page isn't compromised in order to make it look good. There are several other advantages to using CSS, which are discussed in Chapter 6, *"Cascading Style Sheets."*

CSS can be used to specify the font used for the text on the page, to lay out an entire Web page, and much more. CSS today plays a much more important role in the Web development process than it did just a few years ago. With better support for CSS between browsers, many developers use it on all of their pages. In fact, Dreamweaver 8 uses CSS by default for setting page properties, such as background color and image, default text colors, page margins, and such. Formatting and presentation that used to be done with HTML (which is considered improper usage of HTML), is now being done with CSS. Using CSS will help every Web designer in creating efficient and modern Web pages.

Dreamweaver 8 has incredible support for CSS, including creating complex and modern CSS layouts, which far exceed that of previous versions of the product. You will learn a lot of basic CSS in this book in Chapter 6, *"Cascading Style Sheets"* and Chapter 9, *"Layout."*

What Does CSS Look Like?

Unless you've already begun exploring CSS, you probably don't have any idea what CSS looks like. CSS is a deceptively simple language with very few pieces to the puzzle.

Here is a basic CSS rule written in correct syntax:

```
1.  body {
2.      font-family: Verdana, Arial, Helvetica,
        sans-serif;
3.      color: #000000;
4.      background-color: #FFFFFF;
5.  }
```

Here's a breakdown of these CSS elements:

1. **Selector and start of declaration block:** The selector tells the browser which element to style in the document. This can be an HTML element, an element with a specific class applied, or even an element with a specific ID. The text **body** is the selector and the left curly braces (**{**) is the start of the declaration block.

2. **Declaration:** A declaration consists of a property (in this case **font-family**) followed by a value (**Verdana, Arial, Helvetica, sans-serif**), followed by a semicolon to end the declaration. This declaration specifies the font for the entire document. You can specify as many declarations as you want inside the declaration block.

3. **Declaration:** This declaration specifies the color for the body text on the page to **#000000**, which is the hex value for black. Color declarations can use either hex colors or certain named colors, but it's always best to stick with hex.

4. **Declaration:** This declaration sets the background color of the page to white.

5. **End of Declaration block:** The right curly brace ends the CSS rule. Once you've ended on declaration, you're ready to start the next one.

What Is XML?

XML stands for E**x**tensible **M**arkup **L**anguage. XML is a set of guidelines for delimiting text through a system of tags so it can be read and processed by any device capable of reading a text file. You can think of it as a system for customizing Web content that must follow a set of specific syntax rules. Since XML is a text format that follows rigid guidelines, you can imagine why so many developers like to work with XML data; you can do just about anything with a text file, regardless of what computer and operating system you are using. For this reason, XML is used to move data between different computers and different operating systems, which makes it perfect for e-commerce solutions and sending and retrieving data from a database.

Dreamweaver supports templates, covered in Chapter 16, *"Templates and Library Items."* One of the advanced features of Dreamweaver 8 is the ability to export and import XML files through a template. Because XML is so complex and deep, and because the use of databases is outside the scope of this book, we don't include any XML exercises in any of the chapters. Here are some places you can go to learn more about XML:

- **World Wide Web Consortium:**
  http://www.w3.org/xml/

- **W3 Schools—XML:**
  http://www.w3schools.com/xml/

- **A List Apart:**
  http://www.alistapart.com/stories/usingxml

What Is DHTML?

DHTML (**D**ynamic **HTML**) is a collection of different technologies. This can include any combination of XHTML, JavaScript, CSS, and the DOM (**D**ocument **O**bject **M**odel). By combining these technologies, you can author more dynamic content than what basic HTML affords.

Some of the things possible with DHTML include animation, drag-and-drop, and complicated rollovers (buttons that change when a pointer moves over them). With Dreamweaver 8, you can create some fancy DHTML just by clicking a few buttons.

Just like with XHTML, DHTML effects in Dreamweaver 8 are coded behind the scenes. There are, however, some serious cross-platform issues with DHTML, because the behind-the-scenes code is supported quite differently between browsers. Fortunately, Dreamweaver 8 lets you target specific browsers, as well as test the compatibility of your DHTML effects.

DHTML uses a combination of XHTML, JavaScript, CSS, and DOM. The following table gives a short description of each:

DHTML Technologies	
Technology	**Explanation**
XHTML	**E**xtensible **H**yper **T**ext **M**arkup **L**anguage—the default markup for basic Web pages and the root of DHTML.
JavaScript	A scripting language used to manipulate Web pages.
CSS	**C**ascading **S**tyle **S**heets—a presentation language supported by version 4.0 and later Web browsers, which allows for better control over the appearance and positioning of elements on a Web page.
DOM	**D**ocument **O**bject **M**odel—the specification for how objects in a Web page are represented. The DOM defines what attributes are associated with each object, and how the objects and attributes can be manipulated.

What Is JavaScript?

JavaScript was developed by Netscape in 1995 and has become almost as popular as HTML. It actually has nothing to do with the Java programming language, but Netscape licensed the name from Sun Microsystems in hopes of increasing acceptance of the new scripting protocol. It's not certain if it was the name that did the trick, but JavaScript has become almost as widely adopted as HTML itself! The most common uses of JavaScript allow for rollovers, resizing browser windows, and checking for browser compatibility.

You can access most of the JavaScript routines through the Behaviors panel in Dreamweaver 8, which you will learn about in Chapter 11, *"Rollovers"* and Chapter 14, *"Behaviors."* This book covers many JavaScript techniques, including rollovers, browser sniffing, and external browser windows.

You will not have to learn to write JavaScript by hand in order to use it within Dreamweaver 8. This is very fortunate for anyone who's not a programmer, because JavaScript programming is far more complicated than XHTML.

What Is a Web Application?

In broad terms, a Web application is a Web site that delivers dynamic data instead of static data that has to be updated manually. (Amazon.com and eBay.com are great examples of a Web application.) Web applications have also been referred to as data-drive, database-driven, and dynamic sites. In almost all cases, a Web application involves a database and server-side scripting, such as ASP, ColdFusion, and PHP, and so on. Web applications aren't just one thing; they can take on many forms and serve many purposes. They can be used to handle e-commerce, inventory tracking, online auctions, and just about anything using a large amount of information. So what do Web applications have to do with learning Dreamweaver 8? First, Dreamweaver 8 can create complete Web applications, in addition to static Web sites. Although creating Web applications is outside the scope of this book, you should know that you can use Dreamweaver 8 to create them. As you advance your skills, you will find that you will not outgrow Dreamweaver—the sky's the limit as far as its capabilities are concerned.

Extending Dreamweaver

One of the greatest things about the Dreamweaver community is the way people share objects, commands, behaviors, and server behaviors, which are like plug-ins for Dreamweaver that let you add programming functionality without typing a single line of code. These prebuilt elements can be shared and distributed, much the way Photoshop plug-ins work. If you visit the Macromedia Dreamweaver Exchange (**http://exchange. macromedia.com/dreamweaver**) you'll find numerous ways to get more out of Dreamweaver 8 (and other versions of Dreamweaver) without having to learn a complex programming language. In addition, you'll find a collection of third-party sites that can help you extend the capabilities of Dreamweaver 8. There are tons of extension developers out there, so there's no way we could list them all. You can find a pretty comprehensive list at **http://www.dwfaq.com/Resources/ Extensions/**.

Now that you have a basic foundation in these key areas, you are ready to learn more about Dreamweaver 8 itself. The next chapter will introduce you to the Dreamweaver 8 interface and prepare you for the many step-by-step exercises throughout the rest of the book.

2

Interface

We love the Dreamweaver interface (let's not mince words here). No other HTML editor offers a robust editing environment with such an efficient and intuitive interface. Other HTML editors require you to open a lot of different-sized windows and panels in order to reach all of the features, requiring you to constantly hunt for the right tool at the right time. Dreamweaver 8, however, uses a system of adjustable panels and panel groups to suit your needs depending on the context of what you are doing. This saves screen real estate and makes learning the interface a lot easier. Although the Dreamweaver interface can be daunting at first, understanding the interface is probably one of the easier challenges ahead of you.

This chapter will take you through the basic concepts of the program's interface. In addition, we'll also share how to set up our favorite Dreamweaver 8 Preferences and configurations.

You might be antsy to start in on some of the step-by-step exercises contained in later chapters, but you should review this chapter first to identify the toolbars, panels, and windows you'll be using throughout this book.

Setting Up Your Workspace (Windows Users Only)

The first time you start Dreamweaver 8 (on a Windows system) you will be prompted to choose a workspace setup. This determines how the Dreamweaver 8 interface is initially set up. Don't be nervous about choosing one over the other. This simply determines on which side of the interface your panels are initially placed. (We've honestly never understood why they have this choice in there.)

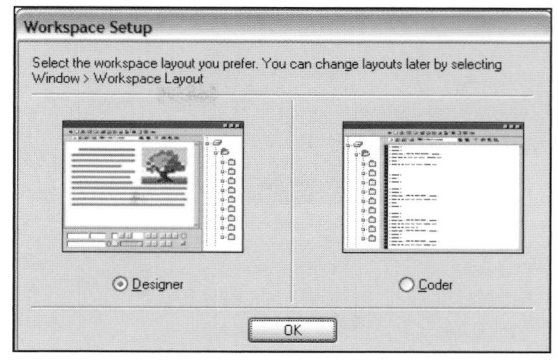

- **Designer:** This option sets up your workspace with all of the panel groups on the right side of the interface. The first document you open will be in Design view. During the course of this book, we use the Designer workspace, and suggest you choose the same workspace. However, when you are working on your own projects, be sure to choose the workspace you prefer.

- **Coder:** This option is the same as the Designer setup, except the panels are on the left side of the interface, and the first document you open will be in Code view.

The Macintosh Dreamweaver 8 interface is almost identical to the Windows Designer interface, except the various panels and windows float around the screen instead of being part of an integrated workspace. We point out the Mac and Windows interface differences throughout the book.

It can be a bit unnerving to decide which interface you want to use before you even have a chance to see the program. Don't worry, you can change your workspace at any time within Dreamweaver 8 by choosing **Window > Workspace Layout** and choosing **Coder**, **Designer**, or any of the other various options.

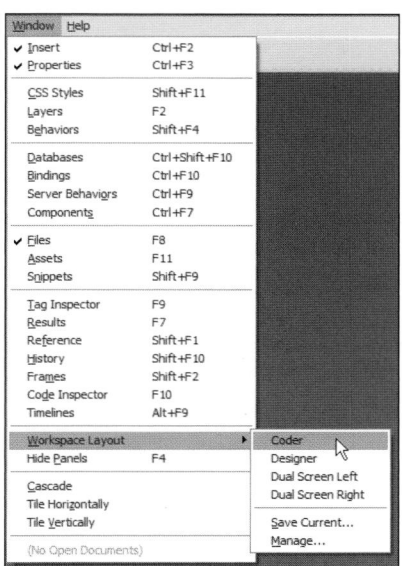

NOTE: | **Layouts for Mac Users**

If you're a Mac user, you don't get the choice of Coder or Designer layout, but you definitely get to save workspace layouts, so check your **Window** menu and have fun!

A Tour of the Interface

On Windows systems, the Dreamweaver 8 interface is contained within an integrated workspace, which means the Document window and all of the panels are positioned within a larger window. This layout can make working with multiple documents and panels easier because the panels don't float all over the screen as separate objects. The integrated workspace is available to Windows users only. Because there are significant differences between the Windows and Macintosh versions of Dreamweaver 8, we cover both interfaces in this section. Regardless of your operating system, there are six main parts to the interface.

Windows Interface

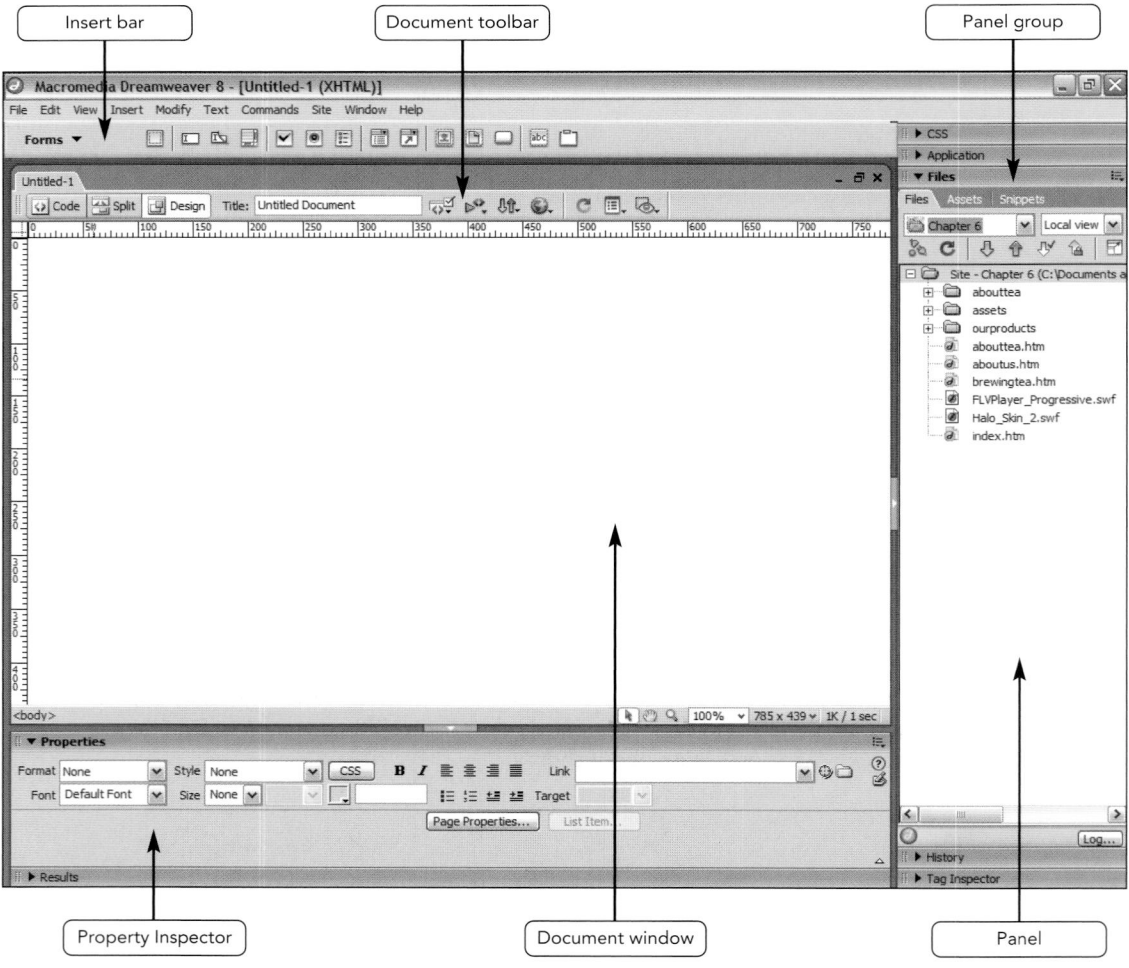

The six main elements of the Windows interface are as follows: the **Insert** bar, **Document** toolbar, Document window, **Property Inspector**, panels, and panel groups. By default, each time you open Dreamweaver 8, it opens with the Start page (which you'll see in just a bit).

Macintosh Interface

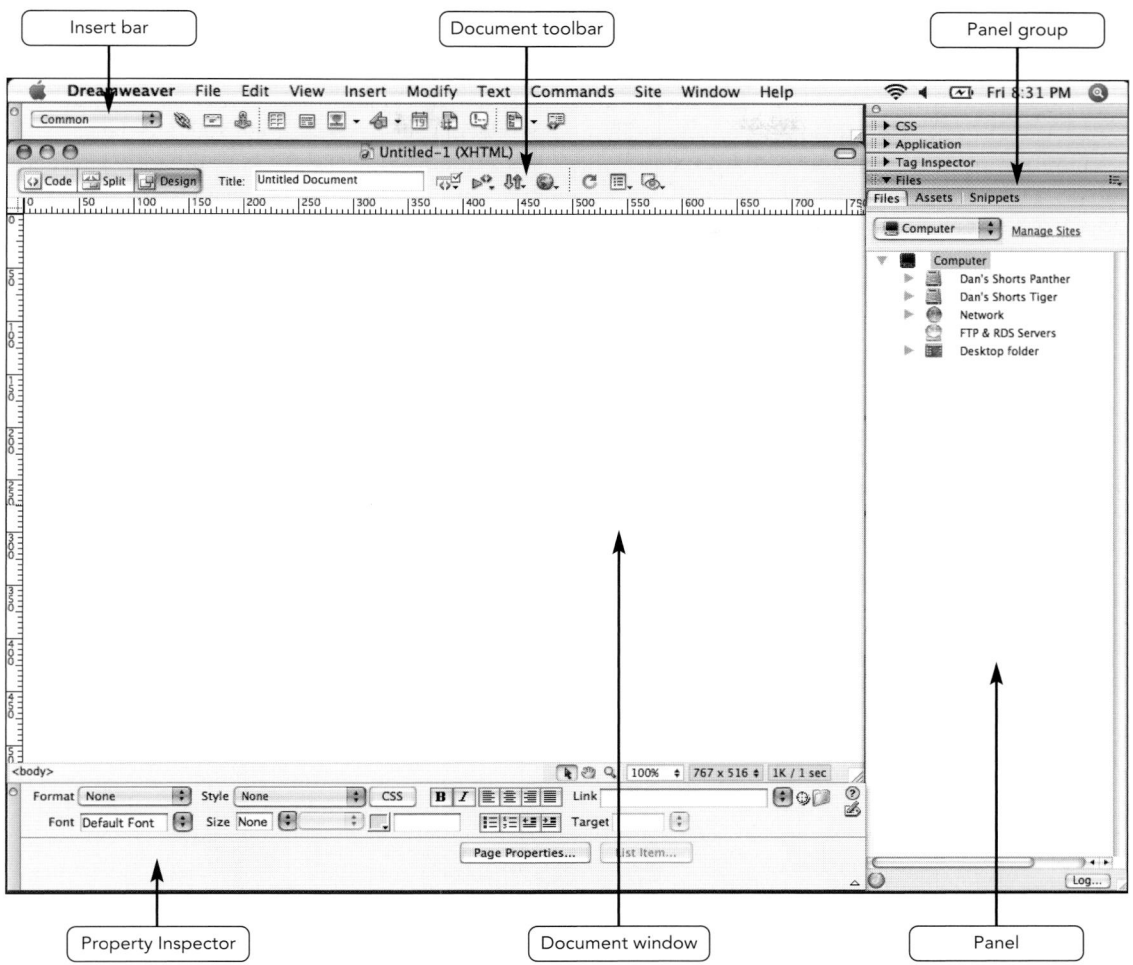

Insert bar

Document toolbar

Panel group

Property Inspector

Document window

Panel

The six main elements of the Mac interface are also as follows: the **Insert** bar, **Document** toolbar, Document window, **Property Inspector**, panels, and panel groups. By default, each time you open Dreamweaver 8, it opens with the Start page (which you'll learn about shortly).

The Start Page

The Start page offers a quick way to perform common tasks, such as opening recently viewed files, creating new documents, accessing templates, and more. You can even access some online tutorials and the Dreamweaver Exchange (you'll learn more about the Dreamweaver Exchange in Chapter 20, "*Getting Your Site Online*") by clicking its respective link. The Start page is a nice way to introduce you to Dreamweaver 8 by giving these common tasks a visual representation.

The Start page behaves and looks the same on both Mac and Windows, except the Mac Start page is a floating window, and the Windows Start page is part of the integrated workspace.

If, for whatever reason, you don't want to use the Start page, you can disable it by selecting the **Don't show again** check box in the lower-left corner of the **Start** page or by choosing **Edit > Preferences > General** (Windows) or **Dreamweaver > Preferences > General** (Mac) and deselecting the **Show start page** check box, as shown in the illustration here. Both options cause Dreamweaver 8 to open without the Start page showing.

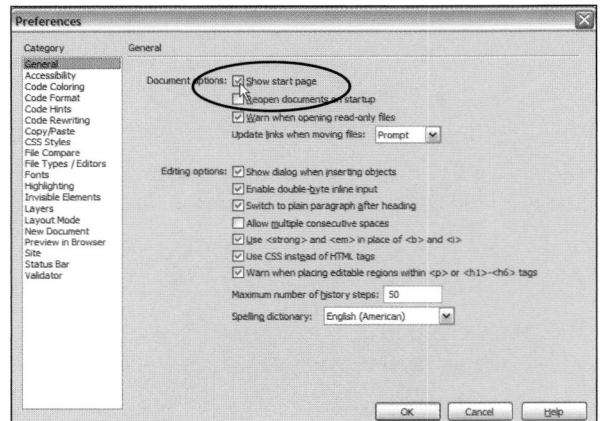

The Insert Bar

The Insert bar contains rows of object icons and is used as a one-click stop for many operations. If you move your mouse over the Insert bar and pause for a moment, you will see a tooltip appear, which explains what each of the icons does. This is the Windows Insert bar.

Many items that exist in the Insert bar also appear on the Insert menu in the top menu bar. The Insert bar provides one-click alternatives to using that menu bar. You may be comfortable clicking the icons, or you may prefer the menu access. There is no right or wrong way to do this; it's just a matter of personal preference.

If you preferred the tabbed-interface of the Insert panel that was available in Dreamweaver MX, you are in luck! Thanks to the clever people at Macromedia, you can change the interface of the Insert bar so it uses tabs instead of a pop-up menu. This is just another way you can modify Dreamweaver 8 to meet your individual needs. To switch to the tabbed interface, choose **Show as Tabs** from the **Insert** bar pop-up menu. To switch to the menu interface, choose **Show as Menu** from the **Insert** bar options menu.

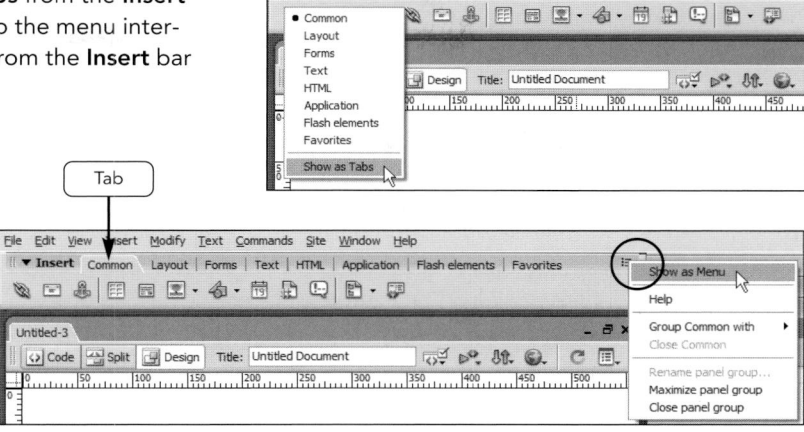

Types of Insert Bar Categories

The Insert bar is grouped into eight different categories. Each category contains a related set of objects. Here is a brief description of each of the Insert bar categories:

The Common group contains the most frequently used objects in Dreamweaver 8, including images, tables, layers, simple rollovers, Fireworks HTML, and so on. You will use this panel a lot.

The Layout group is really useful, and you will find yourself using this a lot as you build your pages. This panel lets you switch between editing modes, work with layout objects, and so much more. You'll learn about these items in Chapter 9, *"Layout."*

The Forms group contains all of the objects essential for creating forms for your Web pages. These objects include text boxes, buttons, menus, and so on. You'll learn about these items in Chapter 13, *"Forms."*

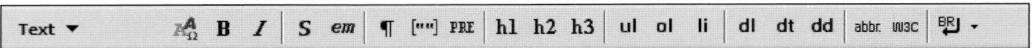

The Text group is an easy way to add formatting to text on your page. We don't think we've actually ever used this group (we generally use the Property Inspector and keyboard shortcuts), but you should at least know it's here in case you prefer using the Insert bar over other means of formatting text.

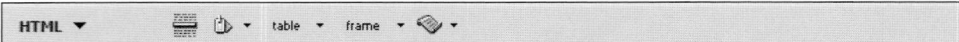

The HTML group contains objects useful for adding various HTML objects to your Web page, including horizontal rules, head content, scripts, and so on.

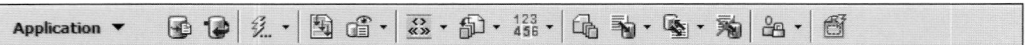

The Application group is designed for inserting dynamic objects on your page that interact with databases and middleware servers, such as ColdFusion, ASP, PHP, and .NET. Because of its advanced purpose, you will not be using this group in this book.

The Flash elements group contains one lonely item: a Flash Image Viewer. It's a neat little application, but we don't cover it in this book. It lets you to create a Flash image slideshow. You can find more information on Macromedia's Web site at *http://www.macromedia.com/support/documentation/en/dreamweaver/mx2004/flash_elements/*.

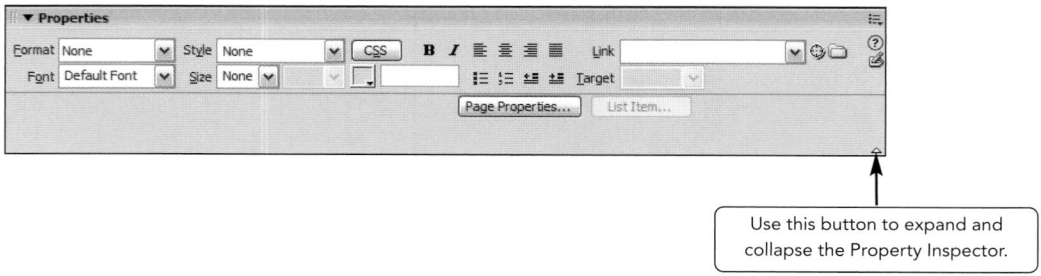

The Favorites group lets you create a custom group of objects you use most often. This is one of many ways Dreamweaver 8 lets you customize the interface to meet your individual needs.

Throughout the book, you'll learn how and when to use many of the objects in the Insert bar. For now, this is just a sneak peek to let you know they're there.

The Property Inspector

Like the Insert bar, the Property Inspector is context-sensitive, meaning it constantly changes depending on what type of element is selected. The Property Inspector controls many settings, including those for text, tables, alignment, and images. Because Dreamweaver 8 defaults to opening a blank page with the text-insertion cursor blinking, the Property Inspector defaults to displaying text properties, as shown in the screen shot here:

Use this button to expand and collapse the Property Inspector.

The Property Inspector changes depending on what is being edited in the current document. Because these elements change depending on context, future chapters will cover the various properties of this interface element in depth.

NOTE: | **Redundancy in the Interface**

Truth be told, there is some redundancy in the Dreamweaver 8 interface. For example, you can insert an image by clicking the **Image** button on the **Insert** bar or by choosing **Insert > Insert** Image. You can often align objects by using the **Property Inspector** or by using a command on a menu. Different options are convenient at times, but it can also be confusing to learn a program that has two or three ways to accomplish the same task. Throughout the book, we'll be citing our favorite ways to access features, but if you prefer an alternate method, don't let us stop you!

The Document Toolbar

You can access many of the options you need directly from the Document toolbar, which is attached to the top of each Document window. The Document toolbar contains a series of buttons and pop-up menus that let you change the document view, set the page title, preview the page in a browser, and interact with a server hosting your site.

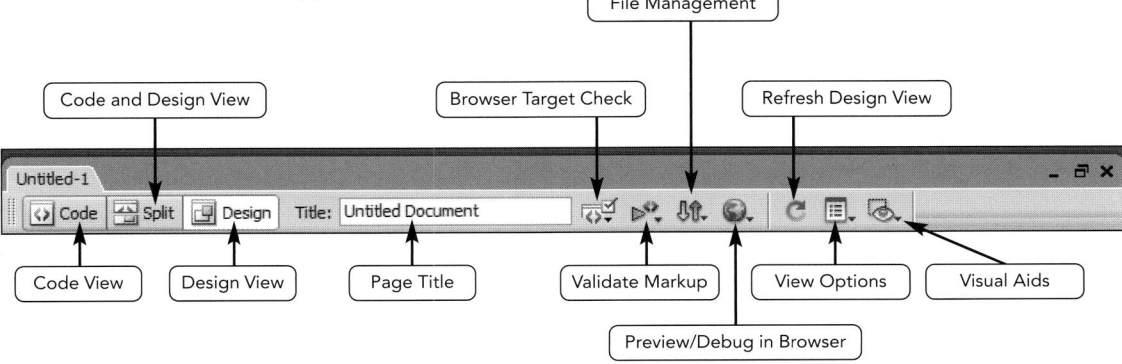

This is what the Document toolbar looks like in Windows.

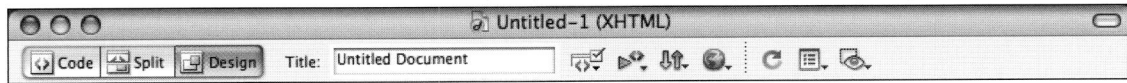

This is what the Document toolbar looks like on a Mac.

As you can see, the Mac Document toolbar is essentially the same as the Windows version. The following table describes what all of those buttons do:

Document Toolbar Features	
Feature	**Description**
Code View	Code view will display the code that creates your page. You can use this to edit the code directly and make changes without having to use a separate text editor, such as BBEdit or HomeSite. Code view is helpful if you are comfortable coding your pages or need to create or modify custom code, such as JavaScript, ASP, and so on. You'll have numerous opportunities throughout the book to learn to work with Code view.
Code and Design View	The Code and Design view will split your document in half, displaying both the code and the actual page layout. This view is helpful if you want to make some minor changes to the code and want to immediately see the visual effect they have on your page.
Design View	Design view is the default view for your Document window. This view will display your page in WYSIWYG (**w**hat **y**ou **s**ee **i**s **w**hat **y**ou **g**et) mode, which means you will see images, text, and other media as you add them to your page. This view is helpful if you aren't familiar with HTML or just don't want to take the time to type in all of the code yourself, plus it gives you a pretty accurate preview of what your page will look like in a browser as it's being designed.
Page Title	This text field lets you specify the title for your page. This text will appear at the top of the browser window and is used by some search engines to describe your site listing. It is also the name that identifies the page when you save it in a list as a bookmark or favorite in your browser. You can also set the title inside the Page Properties dialog box.
Browser Target Check	The Browser Target Check option gives you a quick way to check your code against various browsers and their different versions. From this pop-up menu, you can check your code and define which browsers and what versions your code is being checked against. You can also set an option so that your pages are automatically validated each time they are opened. You will learn more about this feature in Chapter 20, "*Getting Your Site Online.*"
Validate Markup	This pop-up menu lets you validate your code against various HTML and XHTML standards. You can validate the current document, a group of selected documents, or the entire site. You can also access various options to determine which items the validator will check against.
File Management	This pop-up menu lets you manage the files of your site by letting you upload/download files, unlock them, and check them in or out. It is great to have access to all of these options directly from the Document window. You'll learn how to upload and download files in Chapter 20, "*Getting Your Site Online.*"

continues on next page

Document Toolbar Features *continued*

Feature	Description
Preview/Debug in Browser	This pop-up menu lets you choose a browser to preview your page or debug the JavaScript. You can also access the Define Browsers dialog box, which will let you define new browsers or change references to existing browsers that have already been defined. We won't get into debugging JavaScript in this book, but at least you know where to find it should the mood strike you!
Refresh Design View	This button will let you refresh the contents of the Design view. This can be helpful if you make changes to your page in the Code view and don't immediately see the changes.
View Options	This pop-up menu lets you control several options that modify the appearance of the Code view. You can set the Code view to word-wrap, display line numbers, display syntax coloring, and so on. You can also set the Design view to be on the top of the Code and Design view and turn on rulers and guides. You'll get to put this view into practice in Chapter 12, *"XHTML."* This menu performs different functions based on whether you're in Code view or Design view so play a bit and have fun!
Visual Aids	This pop-up menu lets you turn many of the visual aids on and off in Design view. You can turn off invisible elements, template markup, CSS layout backgrounds, and some awesome new CSS rendering features, which you'll learn more about in Chapter 6, *"Cascading Style Sheets."*

The Document Window

The Document window is where all the action happens when you're creating a Web site. This is where you assemble your page elements and design your pages. The Document window is similar in appearance to a browser window. By default, the Document window will be in Design view, unless you have selected the Coder workspace, in which case the Code view will be used the first time you open a document.

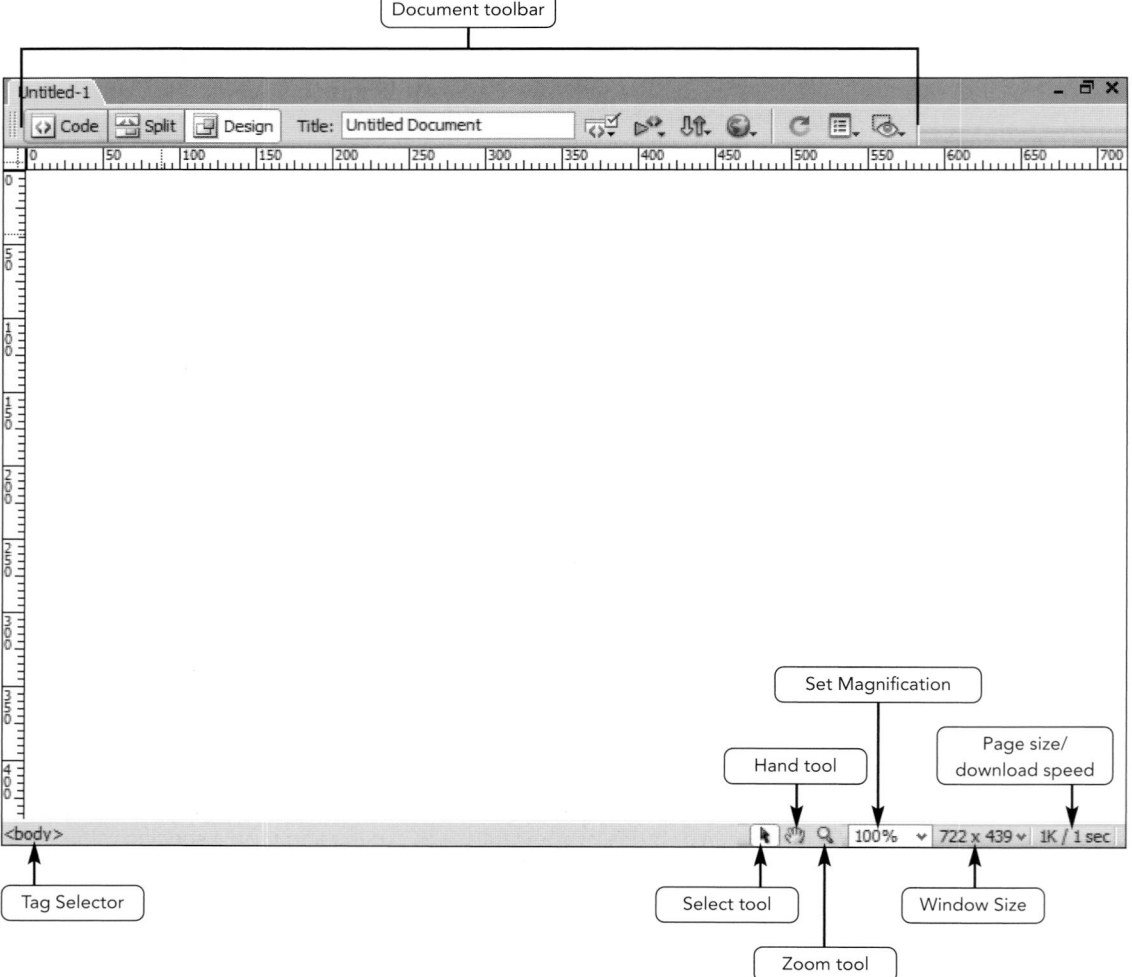

Document Window Features	
Feature	**Description**
Document toolbar	Each Document window has its own Document toolbar, which contains a series of buttons that let you do things like change the view of the Document window, change layout modes, add a page title, preview in a browser, and so much more. Earlier in this chapter, you'll find a detailed explanation of each function of the Document toolbar.
Tag Selector	If you select visual elements on your screen, the Tag Selector highlights the corresponding HTML code. It's a fast and easy way to select different items on your page. You'll learn how to use the Tag Selector in many chapters throughout the book.
Window Size	This pop-up menu lets you resize your window to various preset or custom pixel dimensions.
Page size/ download speed	This area gives you the approximate size (kilobytes) and download time for the current page. You can change this option to match the download speed of your typical user's computer.
Select tool	The Select tool is the default choice when editing a document. This lets you to place your cursor on the page to type, select images and tables, and interact with all of the elements on your page.
Hand tool	Use the Hand tool to move the Document view when you're at a magnification higher than 100%. If you're zoomed into Design view at 200%, you can use the Hand tool to move the document inside the Document window to view different areas of the page.
Zoom tool	Select this tool to quickly zoom into a specific area of the page. When you select the Zoom tool, your cursor will change to a magnifying glass, and you can click and drag an area to zoom in.
Set Magnification	This pop-up menu lets you to choose a predefined zoom level. The Document window will zoom in to whatever element is currently selected. You can also place your cursor inside the text half of the menu and type a specific value, then just press Enter (Windows) or Return (Mac) to zoom to whatever percentage you specified.

Document Window Views

Dreamweaver gives you the added control and flexibility of viewing your pages in one of three different views: Code view, Code and Design view, and Design view. By default, all new documents will open in the view of the current document, or the last document you had opened. So if the last document you worked on was in Code view when you closed it, the next new document will open in Code view. The three buttons in the left corner of the Document toolbar let you change between the three different views.

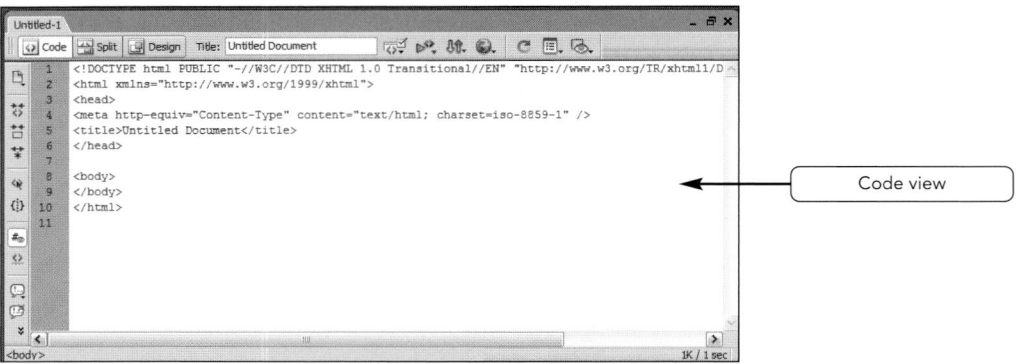

Code view

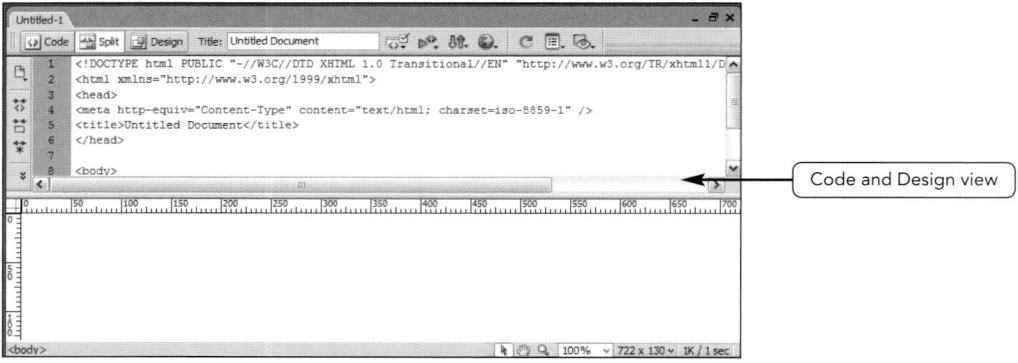

Code and Design view

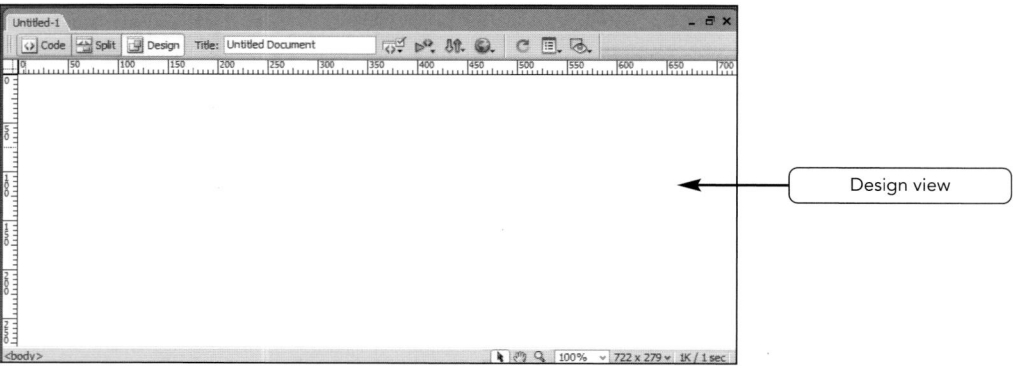

Design view

Multiple Document Windows

If you're working on a site of any size at all you're going to need to work with several documents open at the same time, which can be a pain to manage, even with a large monitor. Dreamweaver 8 makes it easy to work with multiple Document windows by placing a small tab for each open page at the top of the Document window. You can jump from one page to another by clicking a tab. **Note:** Your page must be maximized in order to see the tabs, otherwise the page will float around as a separate object.

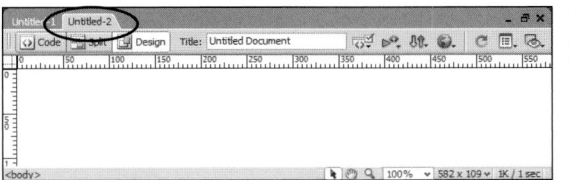
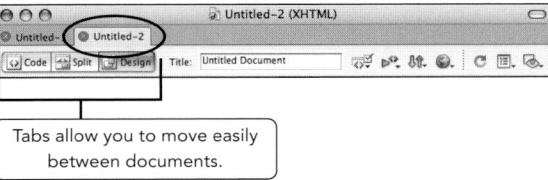

Tabs allow you to move easily between documents.

Panels and Panel Groups

Dreamweaver makes it easy to manage an otherwise complex interface through a system of panels and panel groups. These two interface elements work together to help you customize your workspace so you have open only the panels you need. Each panel group can contain several different panels, each identified by a tab. You can click each tab to quickly move between panels.

Panel groups contain two or more panels. The example shown in the illustration here shows the CSS panel group, which contains the CSS Styles and Layers panels. You can expand and contract panels by clicking the small black arrow in the upper-left corner of the panel group. All of the panels are accessible from the Window menu or by using a keyboard shortcut. You can customize panel groups or create your own by adding and removing panels by choosing the **Group with** and **Close panel** commands in the **Panel Options** menu.

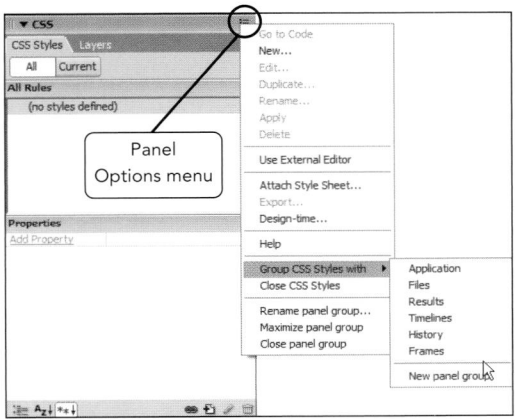

Panel Options menu

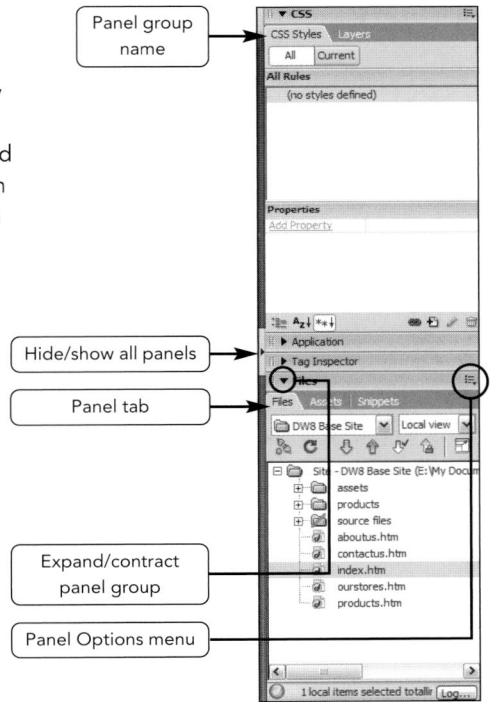

Panel group name

Hide/show all panels

Panel tab

Expand/contract panel group

Panel Options menu

You can rename panel groups by choosing **Rename panel group**, or you can make new panel groups by choosing **Group With > New panel group** from the **Panel Options** menu. This is a great way to customize the interface. **Note:** You cannot click and drag the panels to add or remove them from other panel groups; you must use the contextual menu or the Panel Options menu.

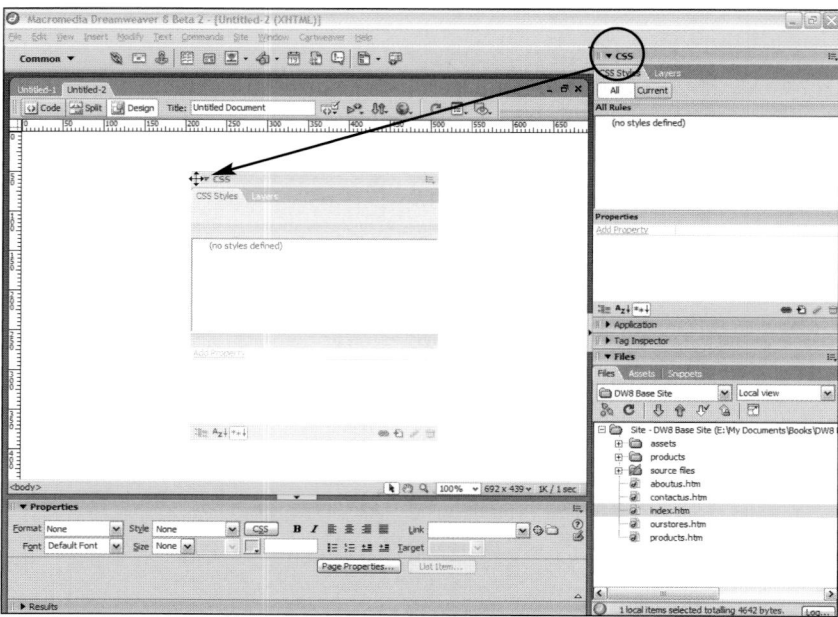

By default, all of the panel groups are docked along the right side of the screen. You can undock a panel group by clicking the small dots in the upper-left corner of a panel group (referred to as the *gripper*) and dragging to a new position.

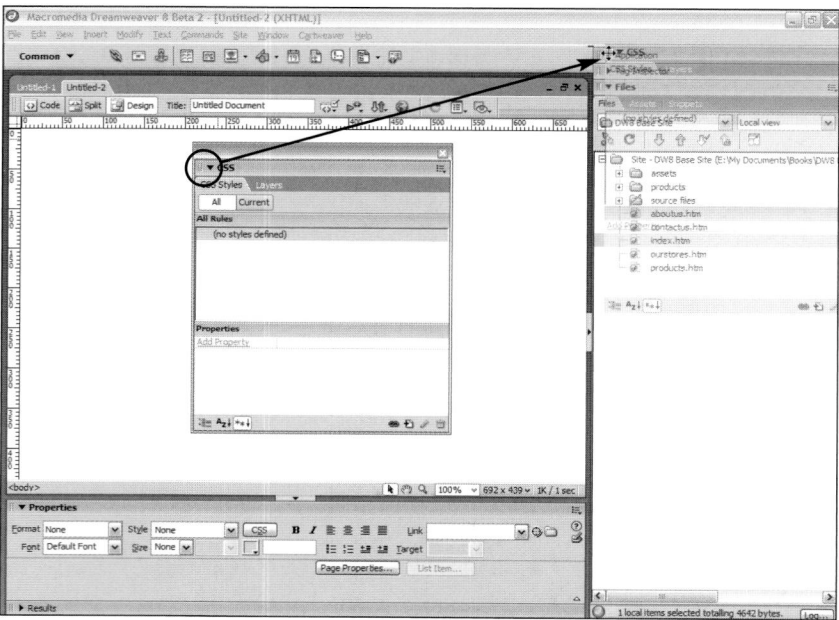

You can easily redock by clicking the gripper (upper-left area) and dragging over any of the other panels. When a dark line appears between the panel groups, you'll know where the panel group will appear when you release the mouse button.

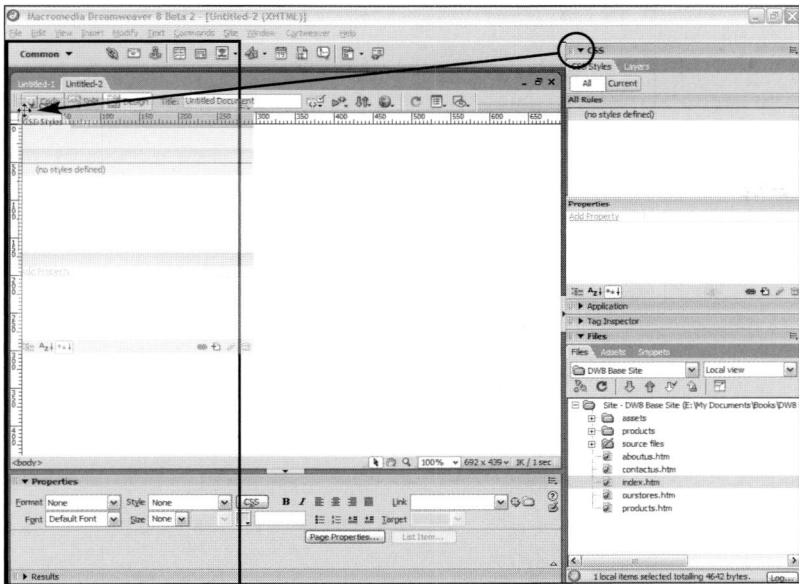

If you are using Windows, you can also dock panels along the left and right side of the Document window by clicking the upper-left area and dragging over any part of the right or left side of the Document window. A thick black line will preview where the panel will appear when you release the mouse button. If you are on a Mac, you can drag your panels and groups to the left side of the screen; they just won't dock and resize as nicely as they do in Windows.

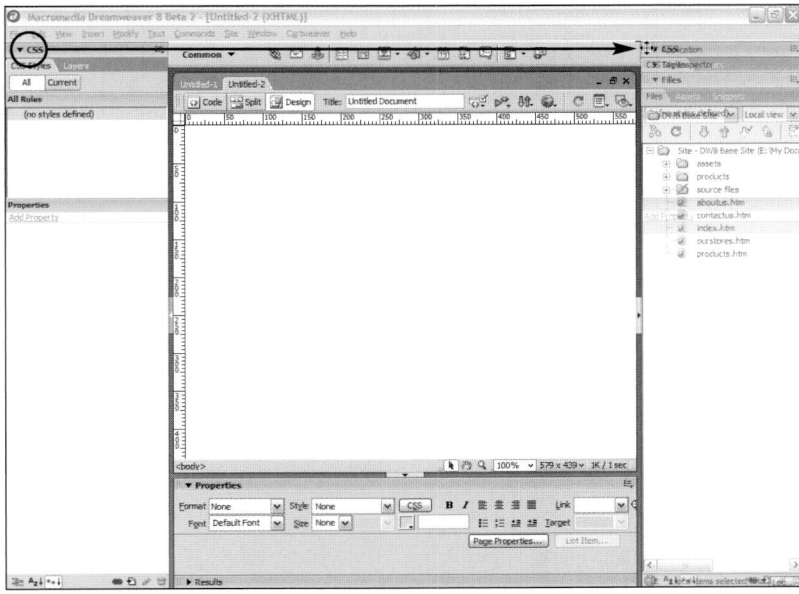

A lot of Dreamweaver developers like to arrange their panels along the left and right sides of the Document window. Of course, you really do need a large monitor to work effectively with your panels arranged this way. Remember, there is no wrong or right way to do this; it's simply a matter of personal preference.

Saving Workspace Layouts

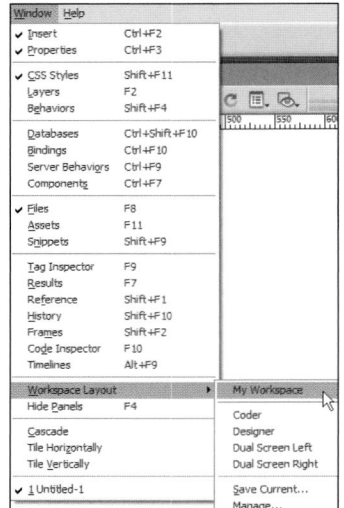

In Dreamweaver 8, you can save workspace layouts. Many developers work on several different types of sites. You might work on a dynamic site one day and need the Application panel and Tag Inspector, and work on a static XHTML site the next and need only the CSS panel. Saving workspace layouts lets you set up a layout for each workflow so you can and easily switch between the two (or three or four).

After you configure your panels and panel groups, choose **Window > Workspace Layout > Save Current** to open the **Save Workspace Layout** dialog box. Type a name for your saved workspace and click **OK**.

To access a custom workspace you created, choose **Window > Workspace Layout** and choose the custom workspace you want to use. Your panels will magically rearrange themselves!

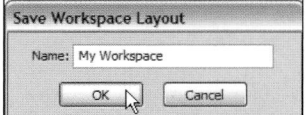

Preferences

There are many different preferences you can change to make Dreamweaver 8 your very own custom HTML/XHTML editor, such as code formatting, accessibility options, layers, and much more. You can change these settings at any time, and you will learn about most of them in later chapters.

To access the **Preferences** dialog box, choose **Edit > Preferences** (Windows) or **Dreamweaver > Preferences** (Mac). The next few pages will explore preferences you can set for external editors, file comparison utilities, preset window sizes, and browser choices.

External Editors

You can specify various file types and editors in Dreamweaver 8. You can specify another HTML editor, such as BBEdit or HomeSite, to edit the code Dreamweaver 8 generates. This book does not cover the use of external HTML editors; they are mostly used by programmers who are moving from another HTML editor they're already familiar with. If you set your preferences for an image editor, you can launch Fireworks or other image-editing applications from Dreamweaver 8 by right-clicking the image in the Files panel and choosing **Open with Fireworks**, or by clicking **Edit** in the **Property Inspector** with an image selected.

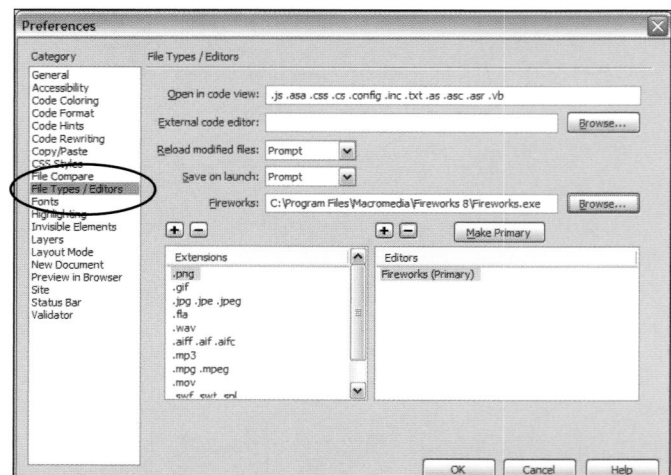

You can specify an external editor by choosing **Edit > Preferences** and clicking the **File Types / Editors** category. You can specify a separate editor for different types of files. For example, you can specify that GIFs or JPGs open in Fireworks or Adobe Photoshop, and that MOV files open in Adobe Premiere Pro or Apple QuickTime Player.

File Comparison Utilities

A handy new feature in Dreamweaver 8 is the file comparison utility integration. A file comparison utility (commonly referred to as a *diff utility*) compares two or more files and shows you the differences between them. This is particularly useful if you're working on a team with other developers and you need to know what they changed in a file.

You can specify a File Compare utility by choosing **Edit > Preferences** and clicking the **File Compare** category. Click **Browse** and browse to the executable file on your local hard drive for the application you want to use.

Once you define the File Compare application, highlight the local files you want to compare in the **Files** panel, **right-click** (Windows) or **Ctrl+click** (Mac) and choose **Compare Local Files**. The File Compare application you specified will open and compare the two selected files. You can also compare a local file against a file on a defined remote server.

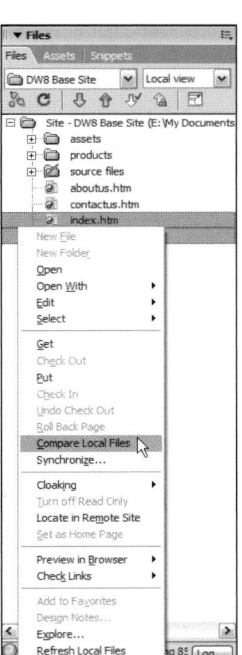

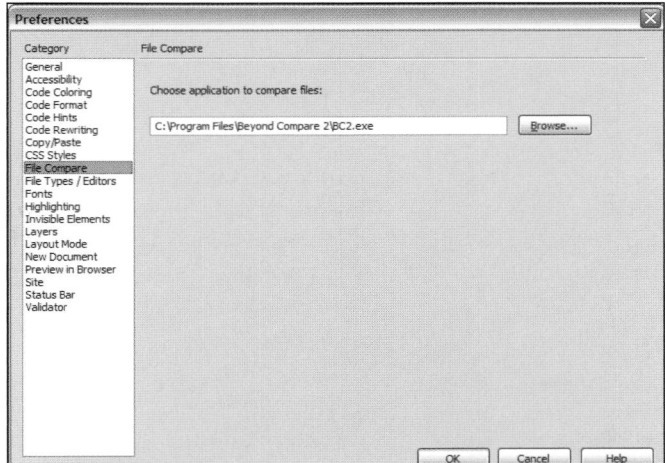

The Best $30 I Ever Spent

The best $30 Dan ever spent was for Scooter Software's Beyond Compare (**http://www. scootersoftware.com**). It lets you compare files and folders and move changes from file to file or directory to direc-
tory. You can even save com-
mon comparison sessions.
With the new File Compare
integration in Dreamweaver
8, the $30 has been even
more invaluable.

If you're on a Mac, you may
already have a file compar-
ing tool installed and don't
know it. Mac OS X includes
the graphical FileMerge
program from Apple in the
developer tools package.

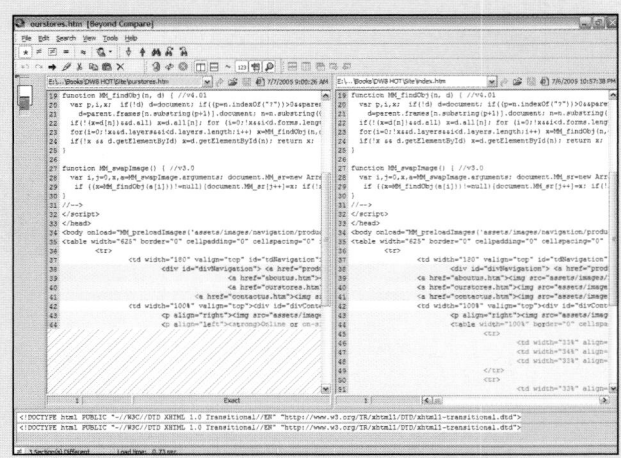

Preset Window Sizes

One of the pitfalls of Web design is that your page's look will change depending on the size of the monitor that displays it. Dreamweaver 8 has a handy feature—the Window Sizes option—to help you design more accurately for a specific monitor size.

The Window Sizes menu offers a variety of preset sizes for the Document window. For example, if you want to design for a 640 × 480 pixel screen, you can select this setting, and Dreamweaver 8 will automat-
ically resize the Document window to reflect this size setting. This option helps you visualize how your designs will look in browser windows of various sizes, but it doesn't physically change

the browser window size for your user. You will learn how to restrict the size of the browser window for your end user, should you choose to do so, by using a behavior in Chapter 14, "*Behaviors.*"

You can set your own window size settings by choosing **Edit > Preferences** and clicking the **Status Bar** category.

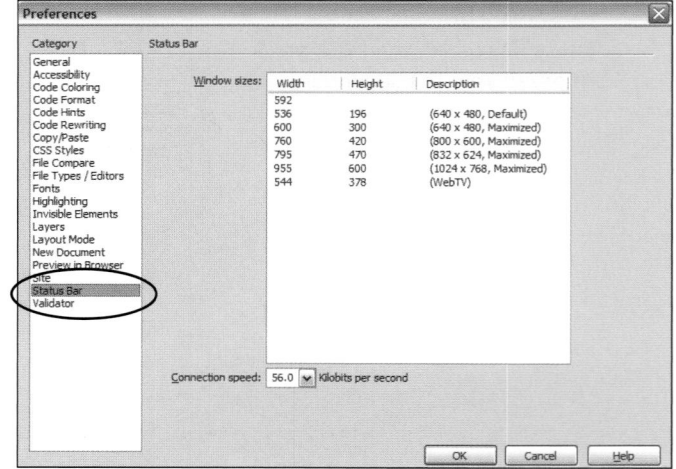

If your Document window isn't maximized, click the **Window Sizes** menu on the status bar to access the various default dimensions. If you choose **Edit Sizes**, you can add your own size presets.

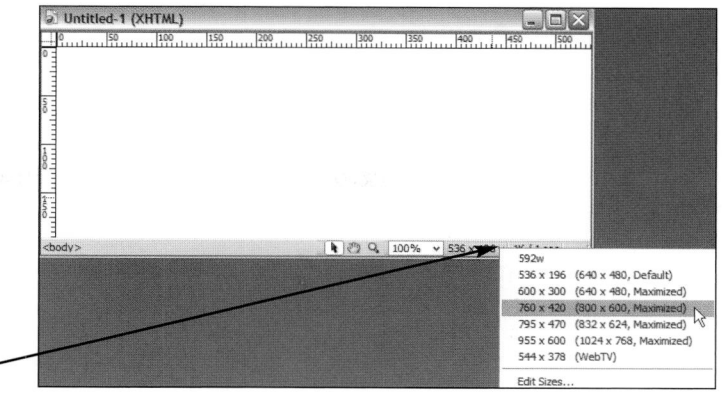

Click here

Defining a Default Browser

The screen captures in this book were created using Mozilla Firefox 1.0.4. You can download a copy of Firefox from **http://www.mozilla.org/products/firefox/**. You can use the browser of your choice for the exercises in this book. **Warning:** A few exercises may not work in earlier browser versions. To set up your browser preference, follow these steps:

1 Choose **Edit > Preferences** (Windows) or **Dreamweaver > Preferences** (Mac).

2 Under **Category**, click **Preview in Browser**.

3 Click the **plus** sign, **minus** sign, or the **Edit** button to add, remove, or change a browser from the list of choices.

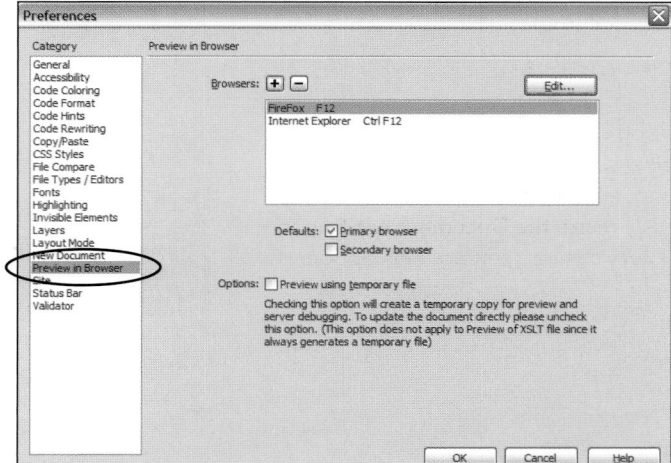

Note: The primary browser defines which browser launches when you press the **F12** shortcut key. The secondary browser defines which browser launches when you press **Ctrl+F12** (**Option+F12** on a Mac). Many designers like to preview in multiple browsers so they can ensure their work looks the same on all browsers. Using a primary and secondary setting will allow you to do so easily.

The Preview in Browser preference sets the primary browser to open with the **F12** shortcut key. You can add more than two browsers here, but you can only access the primary and secondary browsers using the shortcut keys. You can access the other browsers using the **Preview in Browser** button on the **Document** toolbar.

Shortcut Keys

Dreamweaver 8 has lots of shortcut keys. The following chart lists some favorites:

Shortcuts in Dreamweaver		
Command	Mac	Windows
New document	Cmd+N	Ctrl+Shift+N
Line break	Shift+Return	Shift+Enter
Page properties	Cmd+J	Ctrl+J
Select a word	Double-click	Double-click
Select a paragraph	Triple-click	Triple-click
Check spelling	Shift+F7	Shift+F7
Find and replace	Cmd+F	Ctrl+F
Layers	F2	F2
Insert bar	Cmd+F2	Ctrl+F2
Frames	Shift+F2	Shift+F2
Property Inspector	Cmd+F3	Ctrl+F3
Behaviors	Shift+F4	Shift+F4
Files	F8	F8
Results	F10	F10
History	Shift+F10	Shift+F10
CSS styles	Shift+F11	Shift+F11
Save	Cmd+S	Ctrl+S
Put	Cmd+Shift+U	Ctrl+Shift+U
Preview in primary browser	Cmd+F12	F12
Preview in secondary browser	Option+F12	Ctrl+F12
Hide/show all panels	F4	F4

TIP:

Customizing Keyboard Shortcuts

If you want to set up your own keyboard shortcuts, choose **Edit > Keyboard Shortcuts** (Windows) or **Dreamweaver > Keyboard Shortcuts** (Mac). You can change or add keyboard shortcuts to your heart's desire.

Dreamweaver 8 lets you define your own custom keyboard shortcuts and choose from several predefined sets of shortcuts; you can even save your own custom settings and export an HTML file for a handy reference.

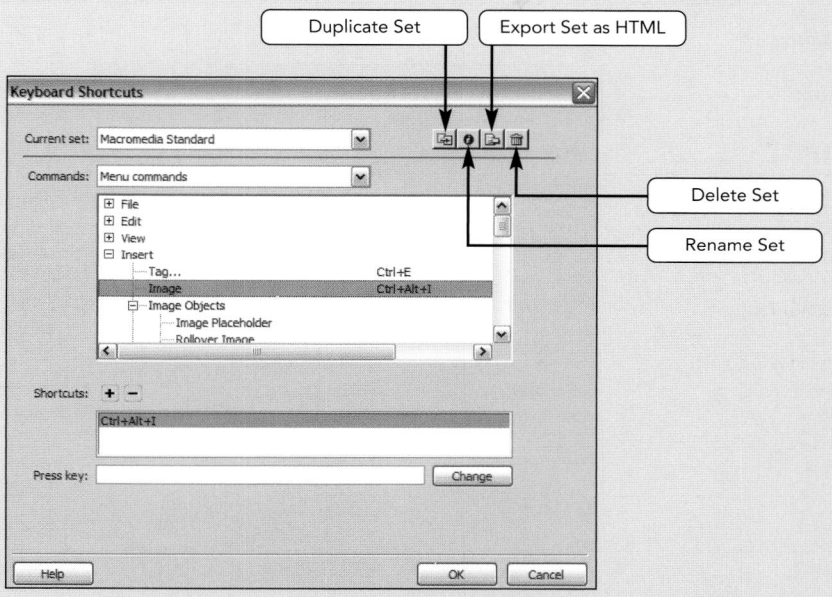

In this chapter, you got a quick tour of the Dreamweaver 8 interface and learned how to configure your Dreamweaver 8 preferences to your liking. Now that you know your way around Dreamweaver 8, it's time to start building some Web pages. In the next chapter, you'll learn how to define a site in Dreamweaver 8.

3

Site Control

Those of you who have built a Web page or two will likely agree that file management is one of the greatest challenges of this medium. For those of you who have yet to put up your first creation, you are probably wondering, "What is file management?" File management is the organization, folder structure, and naming conventions of all the pages and graphics in your Web site. Few other disciplines require the creation of so many documents at once, because every individual Web page is usually comprised of numerous CSS, media, and image files, not to mention all of the files linking back and forth to each other.

To compound the difficulty of managing numerous files, most people build Web sites from their hard drives, and when they've finished, they upload these files to a Web server so that the files can be viewed online. Let's say you created a folder on your hard drive and called it HTML and created another folder called graphics. If you put your HTML and graphics files inside those two folders, you would have to replicate this exact folder hierarchy when you uploaded those files to your Web server, or your links to those files would break. In this chapter, you will learn how to avoid such misfortune by building your Dreamweaver 8 site management skills.

What Is a Local Root Folder?

Dreamweaver 8 has a site management scheme that requires you to keep all your files within one main local root folder, so you can easily duplicate the folder hierarchy on your hard drive when you upload to a Web server. A local root folder is no different from any other kind of folder on your hard drive, except you have told Dreamweaver 8 that this is where all HTML and media files for your site reside.

If you think of the local root folder as the folder from which all other files stem, just like the roots of a tree, you will understand its function. A local root folder can contain many subfolders, but Dreamweaver 8 cannot keep track of elements unless they are stored inside the local root folder.

Taking the concept further, let's say you decide midstream to change the folder hierarchy of your site by adding a folder or changing a folder name. If you were hand-coding the pages, making these changes would be a hassle because you would need to change all references to that folder in every page of your site. Dreamweaver 8 makes this process painless, as long as you work within its site management structure.

By the time you are through with these exercises, you will have learned to define a site and a local root folder, create a site map, and reorganize files and folders. Not bad for a day's work!

WARNING:	**Don't Ignore Site Management**
	You might think site management in Dreamweaver 8 is a neat (but optional) feature, and you would rather skip it now and return to it later when you're in the mood. Don't do it! Site management is actually integral to Dreamweaver 8, and the program kicks up quite a fuss if you try to force it to work outside these boundaries. This book asks you to define a site with each new chapter, because if you have files outside your defined area, you will be constantly plagued by warnings that Dreamweaver is unable to find or link to files outside that defined site. So stick with it, and make sure you grasp the concepts in this chapter before moving on.

1 | Defining a Site

This exercise shows you how to define a site in Dreamweaver 8. You'll be working with a folder of HTML and image files from the **HOT CD-ROM** that you transfer to your hard drive. Once you've finished this exercise, the Dreamweaver 8 site management feature will catalog all the files inside this folder by building a site cache file—a small file that holds information about the location and name of all the files and folders in your site.

This exercise teaches you how to define a site from an existing Web site. You would use the same process if you wanted to use Dreamweaver 8 on a site that you or someone else had already created outside of Dreamweaver 8. At the end of the chapter, you'll complete an exercise that shows you how to define a site from an empty folder, which will more likely simulate your approach when you are starting a new site from scratch.

---

1 If you haven't already done so, copy the **chap_03** folder from the **HOT CD-ROM** to your **Desktop**. For clarity, leave this folder named **chap_03**.

The folder contains the required images and HTML files to complete the exercises in this chapter. You will be asked to add and change files, which requires you to have all of the files on your hard drive.

---

2 Open Dreamweaver 8 and choose **Site > New Site** to open the **Site Definition** dialog box.

---

3 In the **Site Definition** dialog box, click the **Basic** tab to display the basic mode of the **Site Definition** dialog box.

The basic mode guides you through the process of defining a site by asking a series of questions about your site. As you use Dreamweaver 8 more and more, you will find yourself using the Advanced tab—which you'll learn how to use later in this chapter—to define your sites.

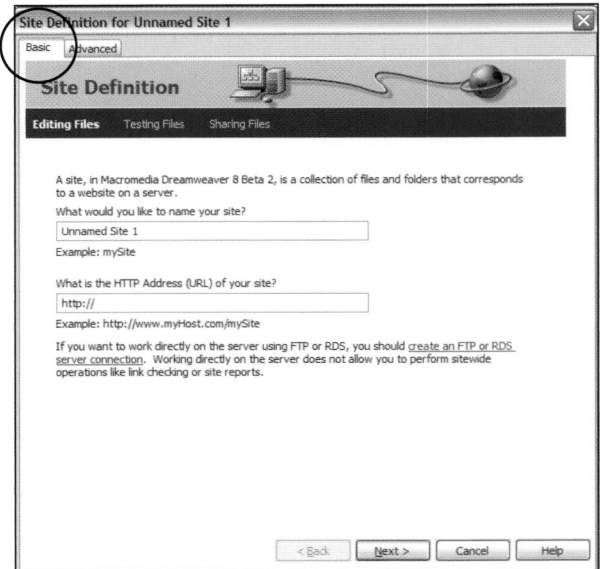

---

4 Type **Chapter 3** in the **What would you like to name your site?** field. Type the full URL of your site in the **What is the HTTP Address (URL) of your site?** field. (Leave it blank for now if you'd like.) Click **Next**.

The site name is an internal naming convention, so you can use any kind of name you want without worrying about spaces or capitalization. Think of it as your own pet name for your project, just like you give a folder or hard drive a custom name. The HTTP address you enter will be used by Dreamweaver 8 to manage root relative links in your site. You'll find out more about root relative links later in this chapter.

5 The next screen asks if you want to use a server technology for your site. Select the **No, I do not want to use a server technology** radio button and click **Next**.

If you're creating a Web application or a site connecting to a database, select **Yes...** to set up the proper options. However, a simple, static Web site, like the one you'll create in this book, does not require any special server technology setup.

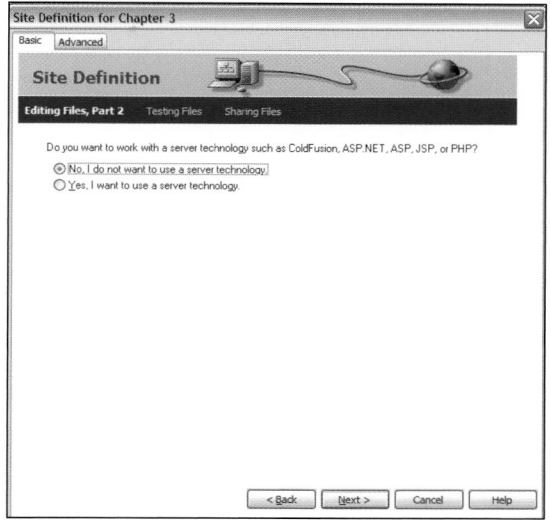

6 The next screen asks how you want to develop your pages. Select the **Edit local copies on my machine, then upload to server when ready (recommended)** radio button.

This option lets Dreamweaver 8 know you will create and edit the Web pages on your computer and then upload them to the Web when you are ready. The other radio button lets you edit your pages over a network and directly on a remote Web server.

Browse button

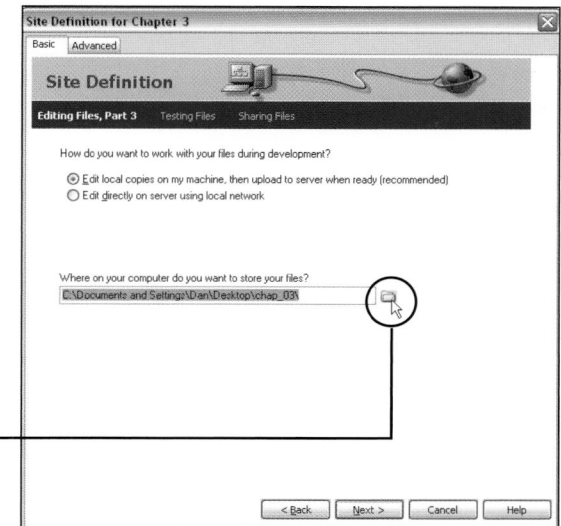

7 Click the **Browse** button (small folder icon) and browse to the **chap_03** folder on your **Desktop**. Select the **chap_03** folder and click **Select** (Windows) or **Choose** (Mac).

8 Click **Next**.

9 The next screen defines how you will connect to the remote Web server so you can upload your files. Make sure **None** is selected and then click **Next**.

Don't worry about this section for now—you'll learn more about connecting to a remote Web server in Chapter 20, *"Getting Your Site Online."*

Note: Changing the site definition settings is easy, even long after you've created them. Choose **Site > Manage Sites**, select the site you want modify, and click **Edit**.

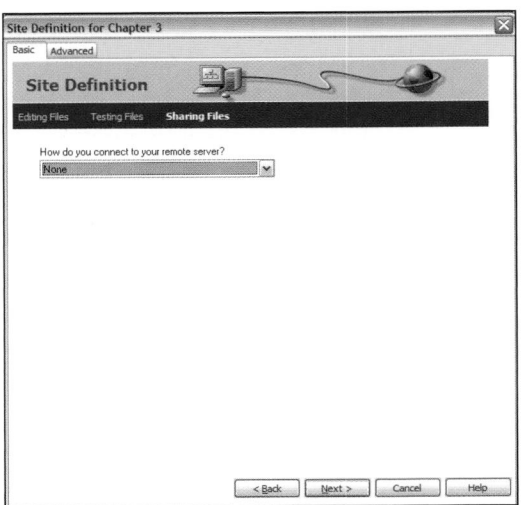

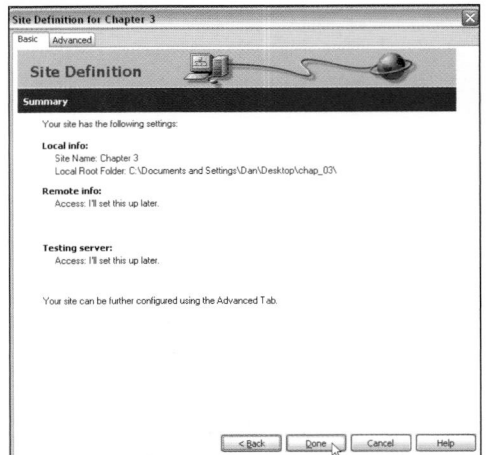

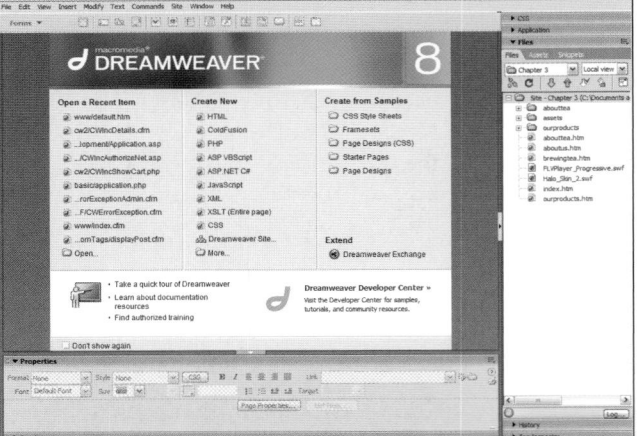

10 The next screen displays a summary of the settings you specified for your site. Take a moment to look over this screen to make sure you have everything set up properly. When you are ready, click **Done**.

The site is now defined as Chapter 3. The Files panel will display the contents of the **chap_03** folder on your Desktop. This is the folder that contains all of your HTML files and images, also referred to as your local folder. Although you might think very little has happened, you'll see the advantages of defining a site in upcoming exercises where you'll move files around and put this feature to the test!

Note for Windows Users: If you see locks next to the file or folder icons, refer to the Introduction to learn how to remove the locks before proceeding.

Local Root Folder, Root Folder, Root

As you work through Dreamweaver 8, you will notice references to a local root folder, a root folder, and root. All these terms are interchangeable. Each refers to a folder on your hard drive that contains all of the HTML, images, and so on for your Web site. This can be any folder on your computer. It can be empty, or it can have an entirely completed Web site. Don't be confused by this slight difference in terminology.

TIP:

Importing and Exporting Site Definitions

If you ever work with other developers on a project, you may both need the same settings in your site definitions, especially if you're working on a dynamic site. Going back and forth in email or on the phone trying to get things to match can be a pain. (What was the last octet of that IP address for the FTP server?) To take the pain out of setting up multiple copies of Dreamweaver with the same site setup, Dreamweaver 8 lets you import and export your site definitions.

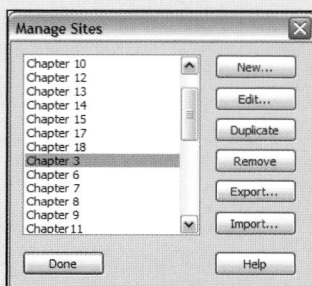

To export a site definition to share with someone else, choose **Site > Manage Sites** to open the **Manage Sites** dialog box. Select a defined site and click **Export**.

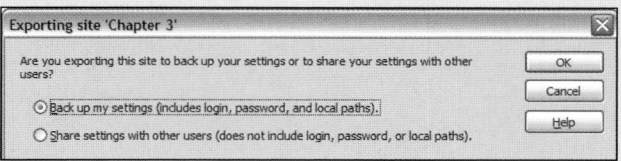

If you have any FTP settings defined for the site you selected in the Manage Sites dialog box, an **Exporting Site** warning dialog box will open asking if you want to back up your settings or share your settings with other users. Because you didn't define any FTP settings in the site definition you won't see this dialog box.

Choose **Back up my settings** if you want to export all of your login information, including user name and password. Remember, choosing this option shares your login and password, so make sure you're sharing it with someone you trust. If you'd rather not share your login and password, choose **Share settings with other users** to leave the sensitive information out. Click **OK** to close the **Exporting Site** dialog box.

Type a filename and click **Save** to create a **.ste** file containing your site definition. You can send this file as an email attachment to share it with any other Dreamweaver 8 user.

To import a site definition from another Dreamweaver 8 user, save the **.ste** file onto your computer. Choose **Site > Manage Site**s to open the **Manage Sites** dialog box, and click **Import**. Browse to the location where you saved the **.ste** file and click **Open**. The site will then be added to the list in the **Manage Sites** dialog box in Dreamweaver 8.

Understanding Relative and Absolute URLs

The term **URL** stands for **U**niform **R**esource **L**ocator. In plain English, URLs are the addresses you use when you go to a Web site. Some are simple, such as **http://www.lynda.com**, and others are more complicated and hard to remember, such as **http://www.lynda.com/info/books/dw8**. Regardless of whether a URL is short or long, there are two different types: **absolute** and **relative**.

An absolute URL looks like this: **http://www.lynda.com/index.htm**. A relative URL looks like this: **index.htm** or **pageone.htm** or **somefolder/pagetwo.htm**.

An absolute URL is a complete URL that specifies the exact location of a file on the Web, including the protocol (in this case, **http**), the host name (in this case, **www.lynda.com**), and the exact path to the file location (in this case, **/index.htm**). Use absolute URLs when you want to link to a site outside your own.

Relative URLs point to a page inside your Web site. For example, if you want to link from the Products page to the Home page, you don't need to include the full **http://www** information. Instead, you just include the file you want to link to. For example, you can just link to **index.htm** instead of **http://www.lynda.com/index.htm**.

You can use absolute URLs within your own site, but it's not necessary, and most Web publishers opt to use relative URLs instead. If you use relative URLs for internal documents, it's easier to move them if you change your domain name.

NOTE:

Never Trust Your Own Browser

If for some reason (and we can't think of any right now) you decide to work outside of the Dreamweaver site setup, never trust your own browser to let you know if a link is correct, especially if you're working locally. If you're working outside a defined site, Dreamweaver may write a link to an image, such as `src="file:///C|/MySite/someimage.gif`. If you check this page on your local machine, the image will appear in all its magnificent glory because it's located in that folder on *your* machine. As soon as Great Aunt Ruth looks at it on her machine across town, the image won't display correctly. Just one more reason to stick with those sites.

2 | Linking to Relative and Absolute URLs

Now that you have an understanding of the differences between relative and absolute URLs, it's time to learn how to identify them when you're working in Dreamweaver 8. Here's an exercise to show you how.

1 In the **Files** panel, locate the **index.htm** file and double-click to open it.

Although you can also open files by choosing File > Open and opening the file from your hard drive, train yourself to open HTML files from the Files panel instead. Opening files from the Files panel uses the site definition you specified and ensures you use the site management features in Dreamweaver 8.

2 Click the **teacloud** logo (**logo.png**) image to select it.

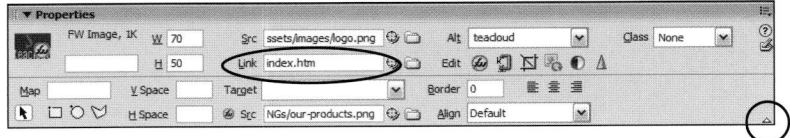

3 In the **Property Inspector**, take a look at the **Link** field. Notice it links to **index.htm**.

The link **index.htm** is a relative link. It does not have additional information in front of it, such as **http://www.teacloud.com/index.htm**. The file does not need that information because the filename is relative to other internal files in the site.

Tip: If the Property Inspector doesn't show as many features as the one shown here, click the arrow in the lower-right corner to expand it.

4 Scroll down to the bottom of the **index.htm** file and click anywhere in the **lynda.com** text link at the bottom of the Document window. (Click outside the table to get rid of the table width outlines if you can't see the link.)

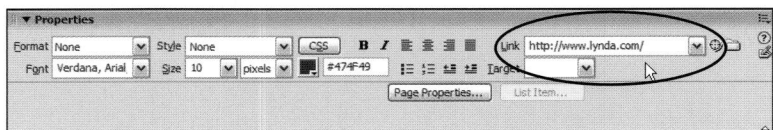

In the Property Inspector, notice this text links to **http://www.lynda.com**, which is an external link to another site on the Web. This type of link is referred to as an absolute link. It needs the additional information to specify its location because it is not relative to any internal documents, and it exists on its own server, separate from the site used in this book.

---

5 Close **index.htm**. You don't need to save your changes.

---

3 | Managing Files and Folders

From within the Files panel, you can create and move new folders and files from one directory to another. When you do this, you're actually adding folders and files to your hard drive, as you'll learn in this exercise. Accessing the files and folders directly from the Files panel in Dreamweaver 8 is essential to site management practices because Dreamweaver 8 can then keep track of where the files and folders have been moved, renamed, added, or deleted. This exercise shows you how to add folders and files to the Chapter 3 site you defined in Exercise 1.

1 In the **Files** panel, **right-click** (Windows) or **Ctrl+click** (Mac) the folder at the top of the local folder view. Choose **New Folder** from the contextual menu to add a new folder to the **chap_03** folder on your hard drive.

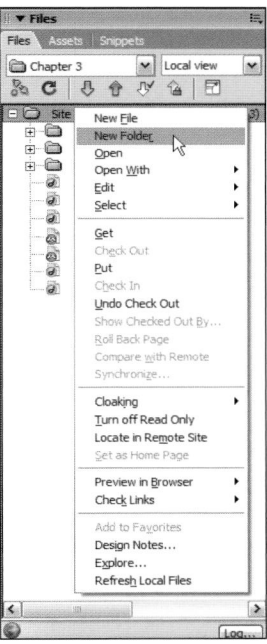

2 When the bounding box appears, type **html** for the folder name and press **Enter** (Windows) or **Return** (Mac).

Note: Before you continue, make sure you close all open files in Dreamweaver 8. If you have files open and you move their locations, Dreamweaver 8 may not be able to maintain the links and image paths in the file. So, as a rule of thumb, always make sure you close all of your files before you move them around in the Files panel.

Next, you'll learn to select files to move them into the folder you just created. Additionally, you'll learn how to select noncontiguous files—files that are not adjacent to one another.

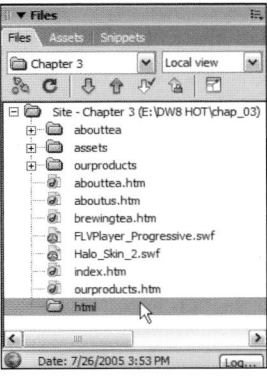

3   In the **Files** panel, click **aboutus.htm** to select it. Hold down the **Ctrl** (Windows) or **Cmd** (Mac) key and click **abouttea.htm** and **ourproducts.htm** to multiple-select the files.

4   With all three files selected, drag them into the **html** folder you created in Steps 1 and 2. The **Update Files** dialog box will open automatically.

Note: Don't worry if your **html** folder is in a slightly different location in the Files panel.

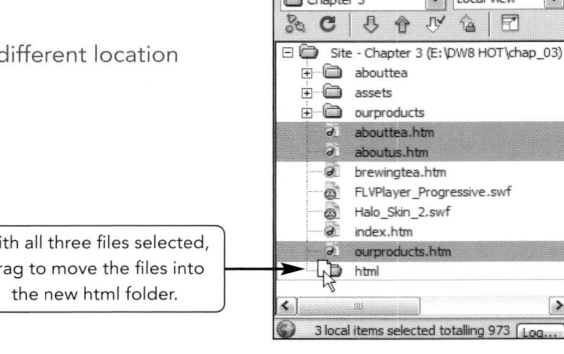

With all three files selected, drag to move the files into the new html folder.

5   In the **Update Files** dialog box, click **Update**.

When you move items in the Files panel, Dreamweaver 8 automatically prompts you to update their links by listing the files whose links were affected by the items you just moved. Once you click Update, Dreamweaver 8 rewrites these files automatically to reflect the change in file structure. If you moved the files directly on your hard drive instead of using the Files panel as you did in this exercise, you would not be prompted to update the affected links. Can you imagine how long it would take you to update the links manually?

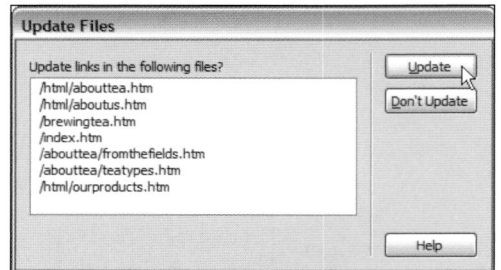

TIP: **Always Use the Files Panel**

If you want to add, modify, move, or delete files or folders in your Web site, always use the Files panel, as shown in this exercise. If you make these file or folder changes directly on your hard drive without using the Files panel in Dreamweaver 8, you'll have to manually repair the links by editing the links on each page. If you make your changes inside the Files panel, Dreamweaver 8 will keep track of them and automatically update your pages, as shown in this exercise.

EXERCISE

4 | Understanding Path Structure

This exercise shows how Dreamweaver 8 creates and alters path structures when you move files inside the local root folder. A path structure is how HTML represents the path to different files in your site, depending on where they are located. Relative and absolute URL paths can result in a variety of different path structures. In this exercise, you will move files around the local root folder in three distinct ways, each demonstrating a different type of path structure you might encounter.

1 In the **Files** panel, double-click **brewingtea.htm** to open it.

Notice the teacloud logo is missing from the upper-right corner of the site.

2 In the **Files** panel, click the **plus** sign (Windows) or **triangle** (Mac) to expand the contents of the **assets** folder and the **images** folder. (The **images** folder is inside the **assets** folder.)

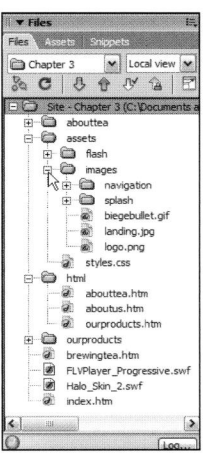

3 In the **images** folder, click **logo.png** to select it. Drag **logo.png** into the table cell in the upper-right corner of the page, as shown in the illustration here. When you release the mouse, the image is inserted on the page, and the **Image Tag Accessibility Attributes** dialog box opens automatically.

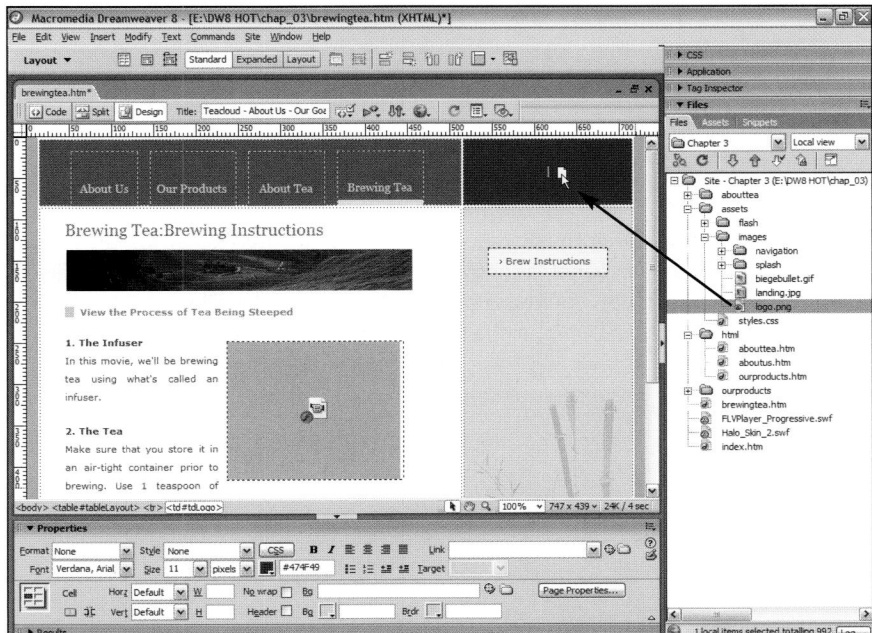

4 In the **Image Tag Accessibility Attributes** dialog box, type **teacloud logo** in the **Alternate text** field and click **OK**.

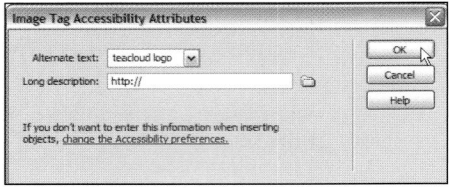

Specifying alternate text adds the necessary **alt** attribute to your image tag to ensure your images are accessible to those using screen readers or to those with images disabled in their browsers. As the dialog states, you can get rid of this dialog box in your preferences by clicking the link and deselecting the **Images** check box in the **Accessibility** category of the **Preferences** dialog box. We highly recommend leaving this feature turned on so you don't forget to add an **alt** attribute to all of your images.

---

5 After you insert the image, make sure it's selected (if not, just click the image in **Design** view), and take a look at the **Property Inspector**.

Notice the Src (source) field is set to **assets/images/logo.png**, which means the file is nested inside the **assets** and **images** folders—the same path as when you dragged the file from the Files panel.

Next, you'll insert the same image into a file inside a different folder.

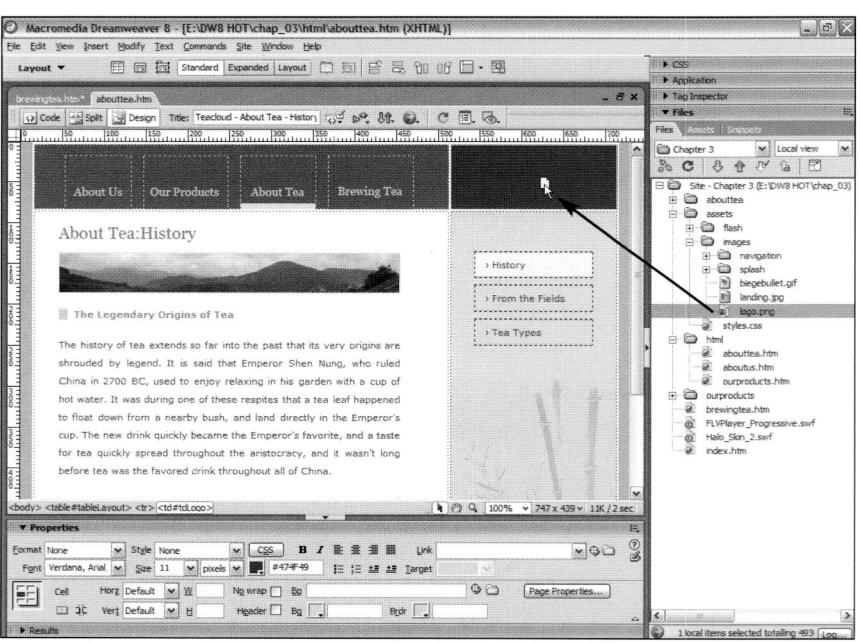

6 Open **abouttea.htm** from the **html** folder (which you moved here in Exercise 3). Using the same file and techniques you learned in this exercise, drag **logo.png** from the **Files** panel into the empty upper-right table cell, as shown in the illustration here. When the **Image Tag Accessibility Attributes** dialog box opens, type **teacloud logo** in the **Alternate Text** field and click **OK**.

---

7 Once you have inserted the image, make sure it's selected, and take a look at the **Property Inspector** again.

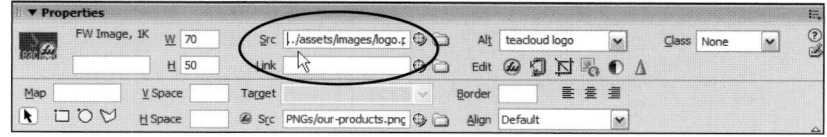

Notice the Src field is now set to **../assets/images/logo.png**. The **../** means the image file is up one folder level, and then nested inside the assets and images folders. The image is in the same folder that it was in Step 3, but the **abouttea.htm** file is at a different folder level than **brewingtea.htm**, so Dreamweaver 8 writes a different path to make sure the image displays correctly.

The purpose of this exercise was simply to show you how Dreamweaver 8 generates different path structures depending on the location of your files and folders in the Files panel. Path structures are something you'll encounter as you build HTML pages in Dreamweaver 8, and this exercise hopefully made them a bit less mysterious!

---

8 Close all open files. You don't need to save your changes.

Site Root and Document Relative Links

To confuse this discussion even further, there are two types of relative links—**site root** and **document**. In the previous exercise, you created document relative links to the teacloud logo image file. Document relative links are relative to a specific document. Site root relative links are relative to the *root* of a site.

So far you've looked only at document relative links (which you'll continue to use through the book). A typical link to your site's home page as a document

relative link would be **href="index.htm"**. A site root relative link to the same page would be **href="/index.htm"**. The forward slash at the beginning of the link tells the browser to go back to the root of your site and then start looking for the page requested.

The following table shows what different types of links resolve to, assuming the page you're on is at **http://www.mysite.com/somefolder/somepage.htm**:

Site Root vs. Document Relative Links	
Relative Link	**Description**
index.htm	This document relative link tells the browser to find a page named **index.htm** in the same folder as the current page, so this link would point to **http://mysite.com/somefolder/index.htm**.
/index.htm	This site root relative link tells the browser to go to the root of the site and then find a page named **index.htm**, so this link would point to **http://mysite.com/index.htm**.

continues on next page

Site Root vs. Document Relative Links *continued*

Relative Link	Description
foldername/page.htm	This document relative link tells the browser to find a folder named **folder name** at the same level as the current page and then find a page named **index.htm**, so this link would point to **http://mysite.com/somefolder/foldername/page.htm**.
../foldername/page.htm	This document relative link tells the browser to go up one folder level (**../**) and then find **foldername/page.htm**, so this link would point to **http://mysite.com/foldername/page.htm**.
/foldername/page.htm	This site root relative link tells the browser to go to the root of the site and then find **foldername/page.htm**, so this link would point to **http://mysite.com/foldername/page.htm**.

This table should clarify how these links work. Document relative links always start at the current page, and site root relative links always start at the root of the site. Why is this important? When you're testing locally, you should *always* use document relative links. If you try using root relative links, the browser would start looking at the root of your hard drive for all of your site files. (We're sure that's not where you store all of your files, right?) Using site root relative links makes far more sense once you start dealing with dynamic sites that use file includes and other dynamic tricks of the trade to generate pages on-the-fly. For now, just know that anytime you're creating links in Dreamweaver 8, they should be document relative links to keep your gorgeous head of hair from going gray.

VIDEO: | **understand_paths.mov**

To learn more about navigating the slippery slope of paths, check out **understand_paths.mov** in the **videos** folder on the **HOT CD-ROM**.

5 | Creating a Site Map

Creating a site map is a great way to examine the structure of your Web site because it lets you see the different levels of your Web site and the files and folders contained within those levels. Many people use site maps to show their client how the site looks from a structural viewpoint. You can easily create site maps in Dreamweaver 8, and you can even render the site map as a BMP or PNG file. Anytime you change the structure of the site, the site map updates automatically. This exercise shows you how easy it is to create and save a site map.

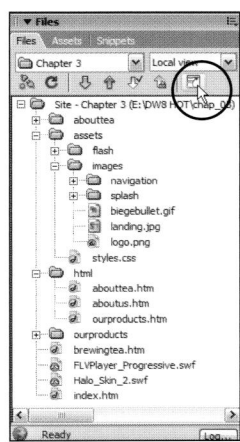
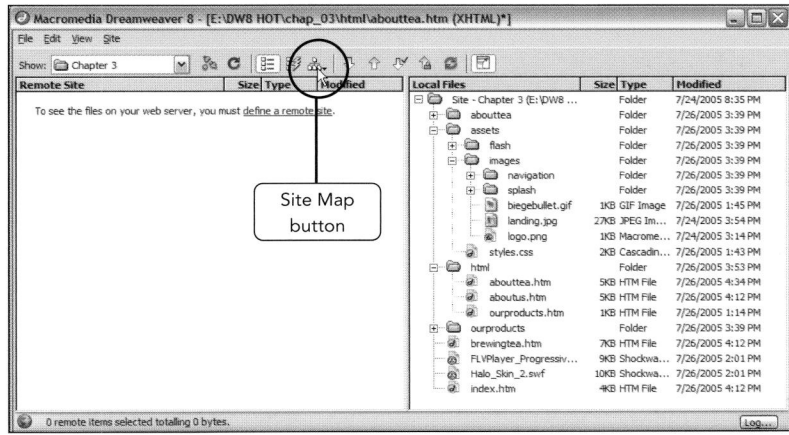

1 In the **Files** panel, click the **Expand/Collapse** button in the upper-right corner to expand the **Files** panel so it fills the entire screen.

By expanding the Files panel, you'll have access to the Site Map feature, which you'll use to create a site map.

2 Click and hold the **Site Map** button in the **Files** panel and choose **Map and Files** from the pop-up menu to display a site map of the **Chapter 3** site.

Dreamweaver 8 offers two ways to view a site map—**Map and Files** or **Map Only**. The illustration here shows the Site Map view. The Site Map view is great if you want to see the overall structure of your Web site and how the different pages link to each other. If you click

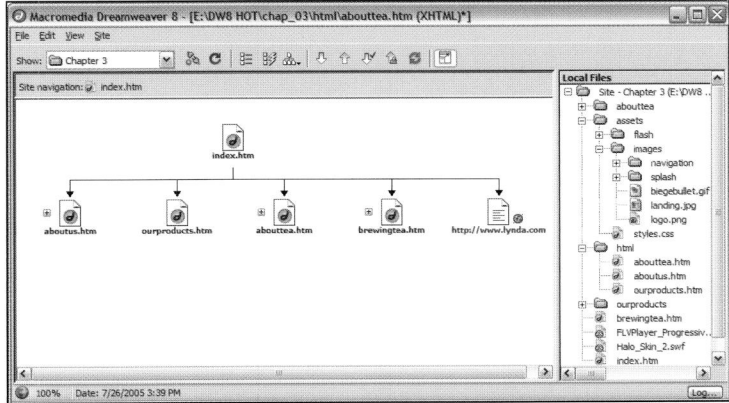

any of the plus signs, you will see the pages linked to that page.

Next, you'll take a look at the Chapter 3 site using the Map Only view.

3 In the **Files** panel, click the **Site Map** button and choose **Map Only**.

In the Map Only view, you can see the overall architecture of your Web site. Like with the Site Map view, if you click any of the plus signs, you will see the pages linked to that page.

Next, you'll learn how to save and print a site map.

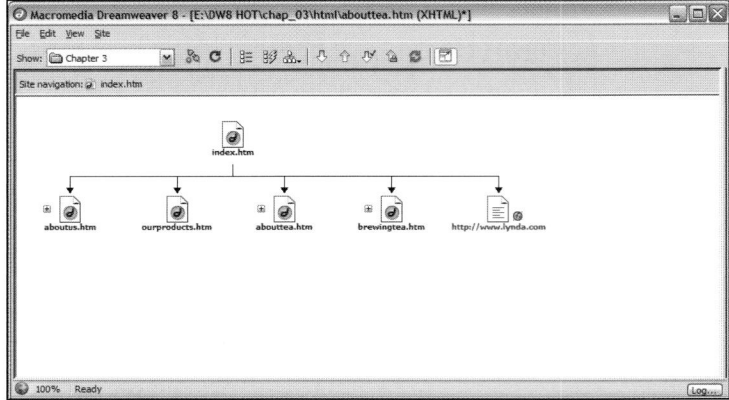

4 The process of saving the site map as an image, so you can view or print it later, is a bit different between the Windows and Mac systems:

- **Mac:** While viewing the site map, choose **File > Save Site Map.** In the **Save** dialog box, name the map by typing the filename for the site map (with the **.bmp** or **.png** file extension) and click **Save.**

- **Windows:** While viewing the site map, choose **File > Save Site Map** from the **Files** panel Option menu. In the **Save Site Map** dialog box, type the name for the site map in the **File name** field, choose the format from the **Save as type** pop-up menu, and click **Save.**

5 At the top of the window, click the **Expand/Collapse** button to return to the default Dreamweaver 8 interface.

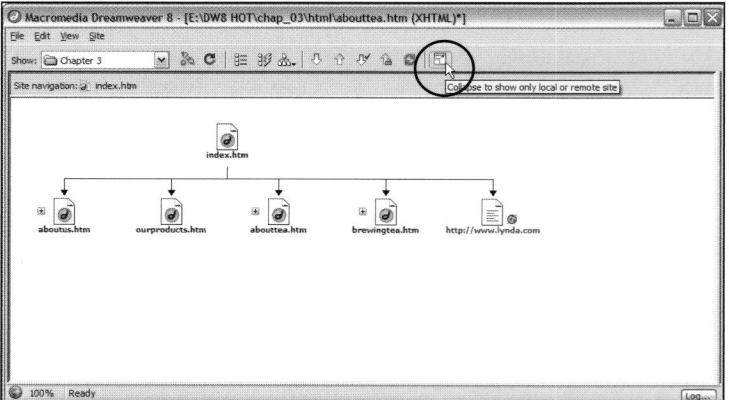

6 Close all open files. You don't need to save your changes.

VIDEO: | **site_maps.mov**

To learn more about creating site maps, check out **site_maps.mov** in the **videos** folder on the **HOT CD-ROM.**

EXERCISE

6 | Creating a Site from Scratch

So far, you've had a chance to work with the Dreamweaver 8 site management window by defining a site based on folders and files from the **HOT CD-ROM**. What about when you finish this book and go to create your own Web sites? You might know how to define a Web site that already exists, but you may not know how to go about creating a site from scratch. Fortunately, the process is exactly the same, but just in case, this exercise shows you how to define a site based on an empty folder and introduces you to the Advanced tab of the Site Definition window.

1 With Dreamweaver 8 open, navigate to the **Desktop** of your computer. Create a new empty folder on your **Desktop** and name it **mywebsite**.

2 Return to Dreamweaver 8 and choose **Site > Manage Sites** to open the **Manage Sites** dialog box, where you can define a new site or edit/remove an existing site. Click **New** and choose **Site** from the pop-up menu to open the **Site Definition** dialog box.

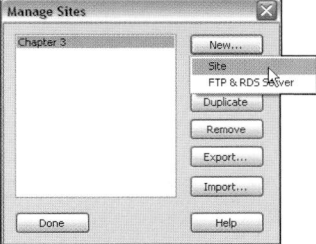

3 Click the **Advanced** tab. Fill in the **Site Name**. (We chose **My Website**, but you can name it anything you want.) Click the folder icon to the right of the **Local root folder** field and browse to the empty folder you created on your **Desktop** called **mywebsite**. Click **Select** (Windows) or **Choose** (Mac), then click **OK**. In the **Manage Sites** dialog box, click **Done**.

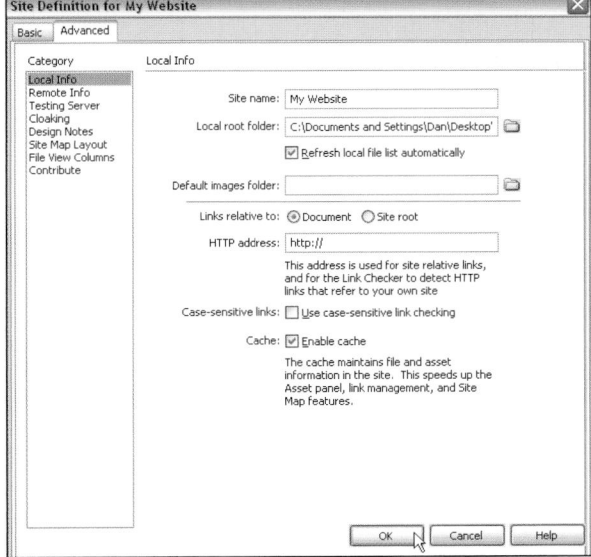

When you create a new site based on an empty folder, your Files panel will also be empty.

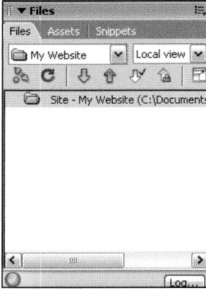

Next, you'll learn how to add files to your site. When you want to add, delete, or move files in your new site, make sure you use the Files panel, just as when you added, deleted, or moved files with an existing site earlier in this chapter. Using the Files panel ensures your files and links will be managed properly in Dreamweaver 8 and will save you many headaches down the road.

4 **Right-click** (Windows) or **Ctrl+click** (Mac) the local root folder at the top of the **Files** panel and choose **New File** from the contextual menu.

When you create a new file, Dreamweaver 8 automatically names the file **untitled.htm**, as shown in the illustration here.

5 Navigate to the **mywebsite** folder you created on your **Desktop** in Step 1.

Notice there is an HTML document called **untitled.html** in the **mywebsite** folder—it is the same HTML file you created and viewed in the Files panel in Step 4. It shows the Firefox logo because Firefox is our default browser. If you're using Internet Explorer as your default browser, you'll see the ubiquitous blue E instead.

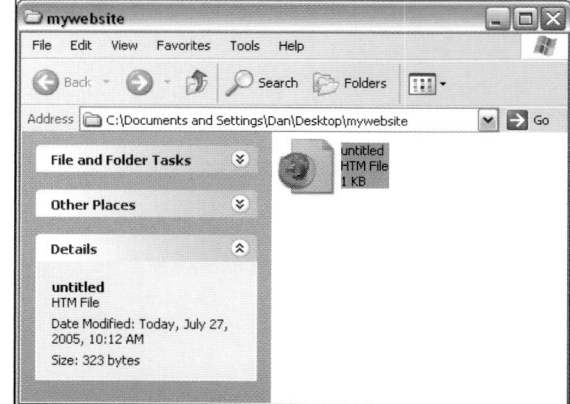

6 Close all open files. You don't need to save your changes.

As you can see from the exercises in this chapter, the site management capabilities in Dreamweaver 8 set it apart from every other Web development application available. Dreamweaver 8 remembers everything about your site for you, including rewriting links and taking care of image paths, which is a huge boon to your productivity. The ability to define sites for existing work, create sites from scratch, and import and export your site definitions with your colleagues makes it easy to work with other developers on a site. Many users think this type of information is easily disregarded, but you've seen just how powerful these tools really are. Next, you'll learn some basics to help you perform common tasks in Dreamweaver 8.

4

Basics

If you're the impatient type, this is the chapter you've been waiting for. The following exercises teach you how to get started with Dreamweaver 8, including creating and saving pages, inserting and aligning images and text, linking images and text, defining page properties with CSS, and inserting meta information, such as keywords and descriptions for search engines. The purpose of this chapter isn't to teach you everything about Web design or Dreamweaver 8; rather it is intended to get you comfortable with the application by building a simple page and performing other common Web development tasks. The rest of this book will focus on some of these areas in greater detail. Covering this much material may seem overwhelming, but fortunately Dreamweaver 8 makes most of these operations as simple as accessing a menu or clicking a button.

By the time you are done with this chapter, your Dreamweaver 8 feet will finally be wet, and you will be well on your way to understanding the program's interface for creating pages and sites. The exercises here will be your foundation for building more complex pages in future chapters.

1 | Creating and Saving a New Document

This exercise teaches you how to create and save a document in Dreamweaver 8. You will be saving this document as **index.htm**, which has special significance on the Web—it's almost always the beginning page of a site. Additionally, you will learn to set the title of the document—what users see at the top of their browsers while viewing the page.

---

1 Copy the **chap_04** folder from the **HOT CD-ROM** to your Desktop. Define your site as Chapter 4 using the **chap_04** folder as the local root folder. If you need a refresher on this process, visit Exercise 1 in Chapter 3, *"Site Control."*

---

2 If you already have documents open, save and close them as necessary. Each time you open Dreamweaver 8, by default it will open to the **Start** page, which lets you create a wide variety of documents by simply clicking a link.

You can disable the Start page in the preferences, which is explained in Chapter 2, *"Interface."*

---

3 On the **Start** page, click **More**, or choose **File > New** to open the **New Document** dialog box, which lets you choose a template for your new document.

Using the Dreamweaver built-in pages lets you get started quickly with new XHTML documents. When you use Dreamweaver 8 to create new files, it adds all of the basic structure for a new page so you don't have to do all of the repetitive work of adding **<head>**, **<body>**, **<title>**, and other tags to a new document.

The Start page is a quick and easy way to create new docu-

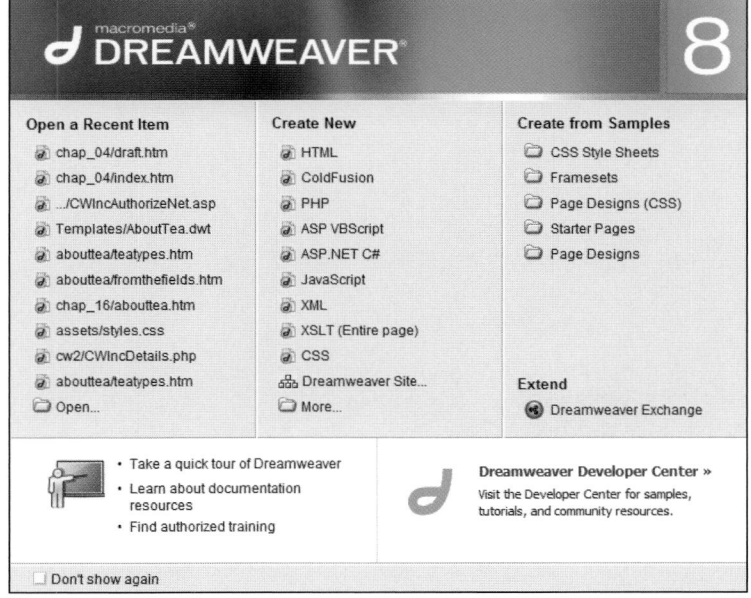

ments. However, it does not give you access to all of the new page templates inside Dreamweaver 8 or let you control some other options, such as creating a new page using XHTML instead of HTML. To access all of the new page templates, follow the next few steps.

---

4 Select **Basic page** from the **Category** list and select **HTML** from the **Basic page** list. Choose **XHTML 1.0 Transitional** from the **Document Type (DTD)** pop-up menu and click **Create**.

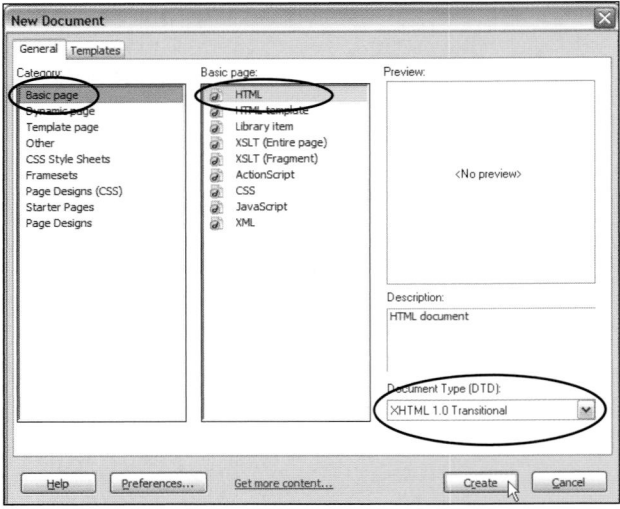

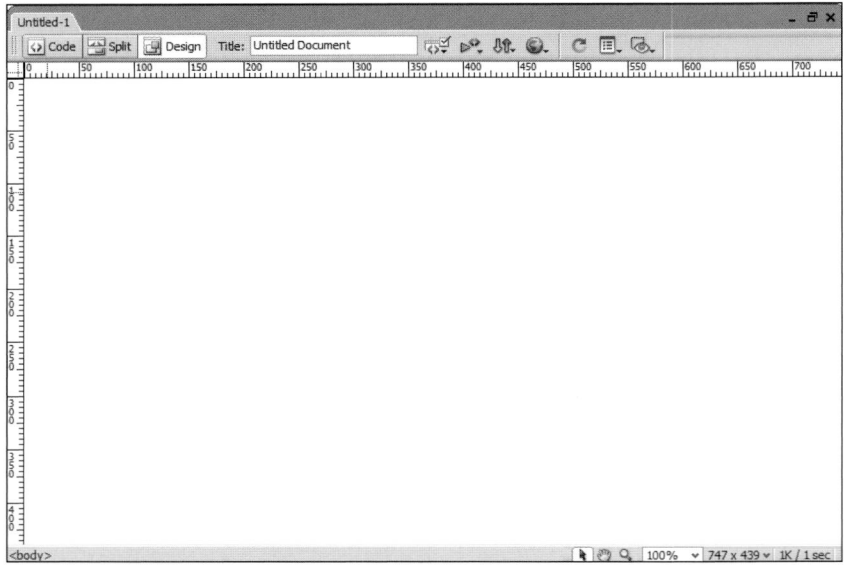

Dreamweaver 8 creates a new blank HTML/XHTML document. Notice the small tab (labeled "Untitled-1") in the upper-left corner; tabs appear for each open document when you maximize the Document window. If your Document window isn't maximized, these tabs will not be available.

These options instruct Dreamweaver 8 to create a basic HTML page. Only the New Document window lets you choose a specific Document Type (or DOCTYPE) for a new document, the Start page doesn't offer this option. Sure, you can add a DOCTYPE later (you will learn how to do this in Chapter 12, "*XHTML*"), but why not do it the correct way right from the start? You'll most likely stick with XHTML 1.0 Transitional, which is the default and what you'll use throughout this book. But if you work on a site that requires a different DOCTYPE, you can specify the default for all new documents in the New Document category of the Dreamweaver 8 preferences.

The New Document Dialog Box

The **New Document** dialog box gives you access to many templates, which help you create new pages in Dreamweaver 8. These templates—sorted by category—are designed to give you the necessary HTML code required to begin creating pages for specific purposes. For example, within the Starter Pages category, you'll find a number of different site designs ready to go. The templates are designed to save you time and get you started in the right direction. The Templates tab at the top is reserved for templates you create from scratch. You'll learn how to create templates in Chapter 16, *"Templates and Library Items."*

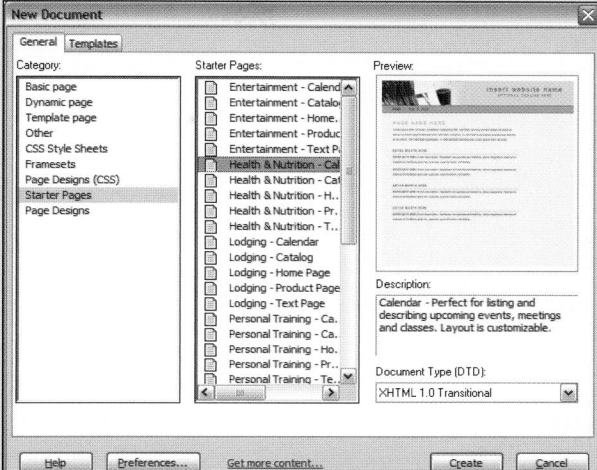

Choosing a DOCTYPE

The DOCTYPE tells the browser which version of HTML or XHTML it should use to render the page. In older browsers (Netscape 4 and the like), DOCTYPE was an unimportant part of the page. In modern browsers, the DOCTYPE you choose can determine how a page is rendered, which is why including a DOCTYPE at the top of every page is important.

Because XHTML is still being adopted across the Internet, you should probably still use the XHTML 1.0 Transitional DOCTYPE. This DOCTYPE includes support for older HTML attributes, such as table widths and targets on links, which lets you code newer documents using attributes from older specifications.

That's about all you need to know about DOCTYPEs for the moment. Just know you should have a DOCTYPE declaration at the top of every page in your site to ensure that browsers render each page in a predictable fashion.

Before you continue, make sure this page is in fact being created with the XHTML Transitional DOCTYPE you chose. You can't tell by simply looking at the page in Design view. To find out what's really going on, you need to open up the hood and look at the raw code of the page.

5 Make sure the **Document** toolbar is visible. If it's not, choose **View > Toolbars > Document**. In the **Document** toolbar, click the **Code** button to change to **Code** view.

As you probably guessed, the Code view displays only the code of your page. Some people find looking at all this code difficult or downright scary. Well, if you want to be a professional Web designer/developer, you really need to know code and feel comfortable working with it, and not limit yourself to just the visual editing environment of Dreamweaver 8. Consider this lesson "Code 101."

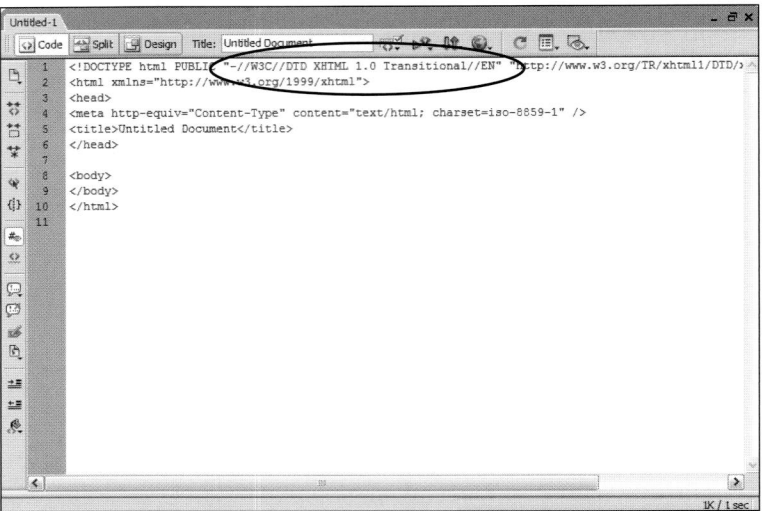

Take a look at the code in lines 1 through 3, which defines the DOCTYPE. As you can see, the DOCTYPE is set to XHTML 1.0 Transitional, just as you specified in Step 4. This code tells the Web browser (and the rest of the curious world) that this page is an XHTML page and not an HTML page. As long as you see this code, you can be assured your page is considered a true XHTML page.

---

6 In the **Document** toolbar, click the **Design** button to return to the default **Design** view of your page.

Before you go on, it is very important to save your file first. All of the site management benefits introduced in Chapter 3, *"Site Control,"* depend on Dreamweaver 8 knowing the physical location of your file. So, the program constantly notifies you if you are working on an unsaved document. Besides, no one wants to unexpectedly lose work, and this practice is good insurance against system crashes and/or a power outage. Anytime you see an asterisk (*) next to the filename of the page, you know you have made changes to your page and haven't saved them yet!

---

7 Choose **File > Save** or press **Ctrl+S** (Windows) or **Cmd+S** (Mac) to open the **Save As** dialog box. Type **index.htm** for the filename and click **Save**. Leave the file open for the next exercise.

Because you're currently on the Chapter 4 site, Dreamweaver 8 will automatically choose the file location based on the folder you specified during the site definition process. In this case, it defaults to the **chap_04** folder. You can change to a different folder if necessary.

The Significance of Default Documents

You just created a document called **index.htm**. What you may or may not appreciate is that this particular filename (along with a few others that we won't worry about at this point) has special significance. Most Web servers recognize the **index.htm** (or **index.html**) file as the default home page. (You can use **.htm** and **.html** interchangeably; both will be recognized by the Web server as HTML pages.) If you type the URL **http://www.lynda.com**, for example, what you will really see is **http://www.lynda.com/index.htm**, even though you didn't type it that way. The Web server knows to open the **index.htm** file automatically without requiring users to type the full URL. Therefore, if you name

the opening page of your Web site with the filename **index.htm**, the Web server will know to automatically display this file first.

This is why the filename index.html is so significant. It's also the reason most professional Web developers use it as the root filename, although on some servers a different name is used, such as **default.htm**. What you may not realize is you are not limited to just one **index.htm** file on your site. You can have an **index.htm** inside each folder that represents a category for your site, such as Company, Services, Store, and Products.

2 | Setting Page Titles

In this exercise, you'll learn how to set the page title of your documents. The page title appears at the top of users' browsers, and is also used for search engine listings and bookmark titles. Giving your page a good title is the first thing you should do before starting to work on the page.

---

1 If you just completed Exercise 1, **index.htm** should still be open. If it's not, double-click **index.htm** in the **Files** panel to open it.

---

2 Press **F12** to preview the page in your browser.

You can see from the figure that the title bar of the browser shows **Untitled Document**, which is not very meaningful. When you create Web pages, you need to give your page a meaningful title because the title is used by search engines to provide information about the page; the page title is used in users' bookmarks or favorites to name the page; and it gives users an easy way to figure out which page of a site they're currently viewing.

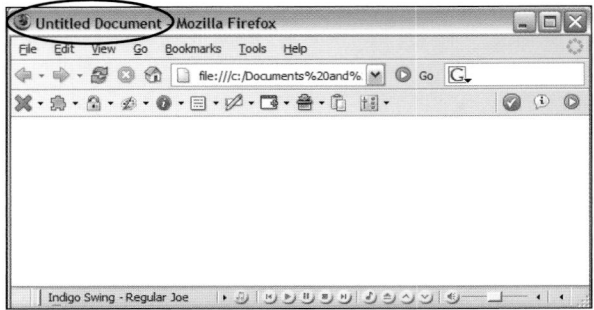

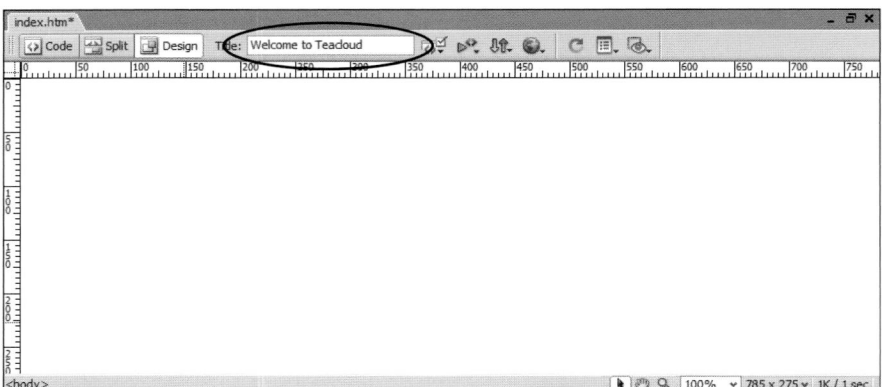

3 Return to Dreamweaver 8. If you look in the **Document** toolbar, you'll see **Untitled Document** in the **Title** field. Type **Welcome to Teacloud** in the **Title field** of the **Document** toolbar and press **Enter** (Windows) or **Return** (Mac) to define a page title.

N O T E :

Filenames vs. Titles

As you create Web pages with Dreamweaver 8, you will need to specify various names for your files, folders, sites, and so on. This might not seem tricky at first glance, but two different names are actually associated with XHTML files: the filename and the page title.

When you save a document, you will be assigning its filename. The filename must end with a valid document extension (**.htm** or **.html**). The other name associated with the document is called the page title. The file **index.htm** here, for example, has been assigned the page title "Welcome to Teacloud."

Filenames absolutely cannot contain spaces or special characters; if they do, the browser may not be able to request the correct file from the server. Page titles, however, are meant for public consumption, and you should make them as descriptive as possible. When users view the page in a browser, the title will be visible. Also, when users bookmark this page, the title will appear in their bookmark lists. When search engines index the page, it is often categorized by page title as well.

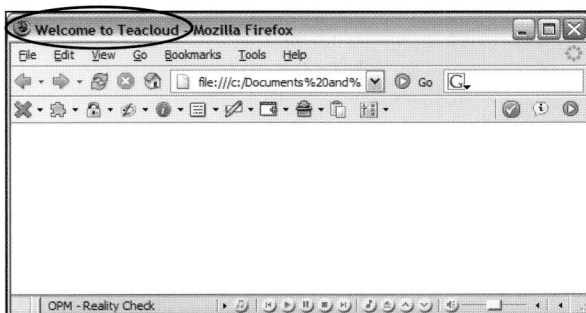

4 Press **F12** to preview the file again, and you'll see that the title bar now shows "Welcome to Teacloud."

Obviously, "Welcome to Teacloud" is a far more meaningful title than "Untitled Document." It gives your viewers an idea of what's on the page and makes it easy for them to figure out which page they're on.

---

5 Save and close **index.htm**.

In this exercise, you'll learn how to insert images for the site's home page image, logo, and navigation buttons.

---

1 In the **Files** panel, double-click **draft.htm** to open it. Make sure the **Assets** panel is visible. If it's not, choose **Window > Assets** or press **F11**.

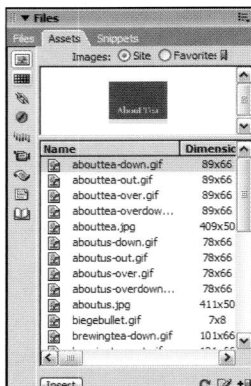

Inserting images from the Assets panel ensures you are working only with images from within your local root folder. This is a good practice, because inserting images from outside your local root folder will cause problems when you try to upload your page to the Web server—the images won't appear!

NOTE:

Working with the Assets Panel

The Assets panel is an incredibly powerful and useful feature in Dreamweaver 8; it's one of the panels you will use most often. The Assets panel maintains a listing of all the asset types (images, colors, links, movies, scripts, library items, and templates) within the current site. Each type of asset is separated into its own category so you can find what you are looking for quickly and easily. You can even designate an asset as a "favorite," which places the asset in the favorites group—a customized asset group containing items you use most often. This feature is really powerful when you have hundreds or thousands of assets within your local root folder. That might sound like a lot of assets, but you will be surprised how quickly they add up!

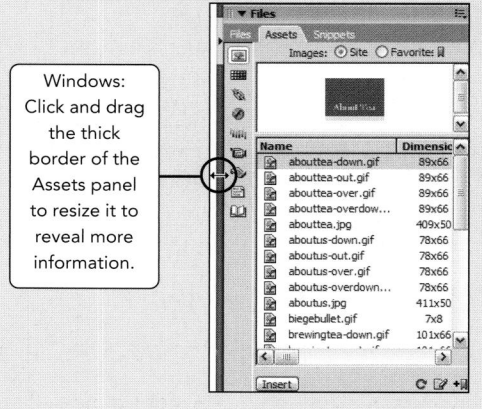

Windows: Click and drag the thick border of the Assets panel to resize it to reveal more information.

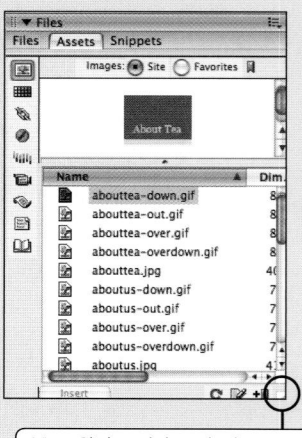

Mac: Click and drag the lower-right corner to resize it to reveal more information.

N O T E :

Working with the Assets Panel *continued*

The Assets panel is really small by default, and some of its features are hidden from view. In these images, you can see the Images group contains information about the file size, type, and path of the various images listed in the group. Each asset group has different columns relating to the specific type of assets. By default, the assets are listed in alphabetic order from A to Z. You can reverse the order by clicking the Name column at the top. In fact, you can rearrange all of the columns in ascending or descending order by clicking the column names—another handy-dandy feature of the Assets panel.

The Assets panel contextual menu lets you easily copy assets between the various sites you have defined. From this menu, you can also refresh the listing, which is sometimes helpful when you add new assets to a site and Dreamweaver 8 is already open.

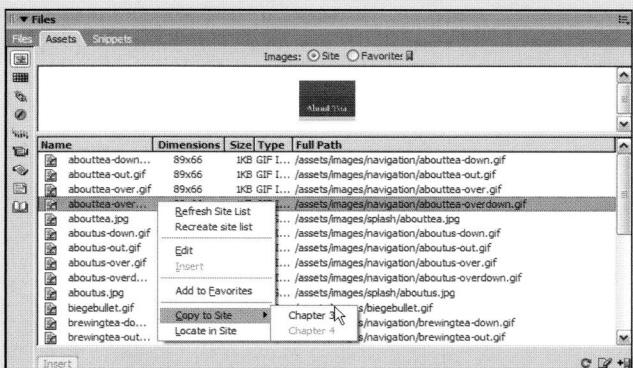

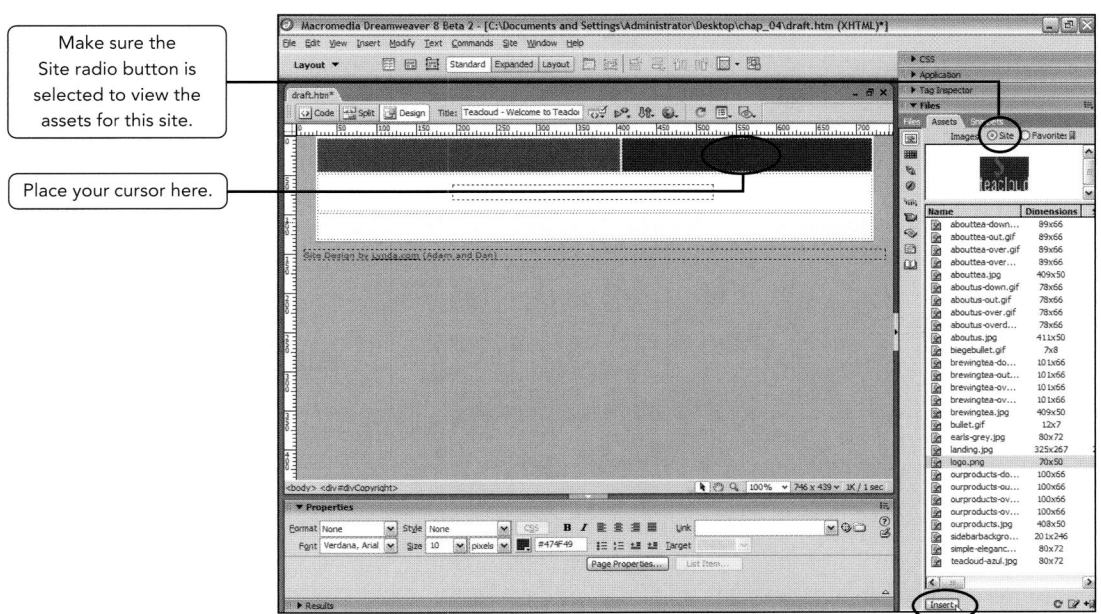

Make sure the Site radio button is selected to view the assets for this site.

Place your cursor here.

2 In the **Document** window, click to place your cursor inside the upper-right table cell. In the **Assets** panel, make sure the **Site** radio button is selected and click to select **logo.png**. Click the **Insert** button to insert **logo.png** into the table cell. When the **Image Tag Accessibility Attributes** dialog box appears, type **Teacloud Logo** in the **Alternate text** field and click **OK**.

When you're finished, the Teacloud logo populates the upper-right table cell of the page. Next, you'll apply the skills you learned and fill the rest of the page with images.

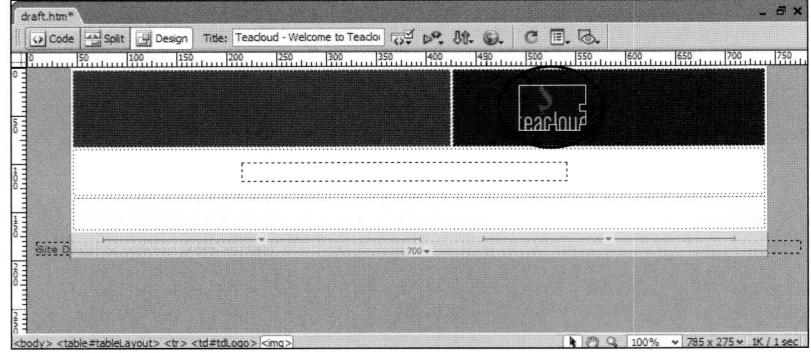

3 In the **Document** window, click to place your cursor in the upper-left table cell. In the **Assets** panel, click to select **aboutus-out.gif**. Click **Insert** to insert the selected image onto the page. When the **Image Tag Accessibility Attributes** dialog box appears, type **About Us** in the **Alternate text** field and click **OK**.

4 In the **Document** window, click to the right of **aboutus-out.gif** to deselect it. In the **Assets** panel, click to select **ourproducts-out.gif**. Click **Insert** to insert the selected image onto the page. When the **Image Tag Accessibility Attributes** dialog box appears, type **Our Products** in the **Alternate text** field and click **OK**.

5 In the **Document** window, click to the right of **ourproducts-out.gif** to deselect it. In the **Assets** panel, click to select **abouttea-out.gif**. Click **Insert** to insert the selected image onto the page. When the **Image Tag Accessibility Attributes** dialog box appears, type **About Tea** in the **Alternate text** field and click **OK**.

6 In the **Document** window, click to the right of **abouttea-out.gif** to deselect it. In the **Assets** panel, click to select **brewingtea-out.gif**. Click **Insert** to insert the selected image onto the page. When the **Image Tag Accessibility Attributes** dialog box appears, type **Brewing Tea** in the **Alternate text** field and click **OK**.

7 Click to place your cursor inside the dotted lines in the center of the page. In the **Assets** panel, click to select **landing.jpg**. Click **Insert** to insert the selected image onto the page. When the **Image Tag Accessibility Attributes** dialog box appears, type **Welcome to Teacloud** in the **Alternate text** field and click **OK**.

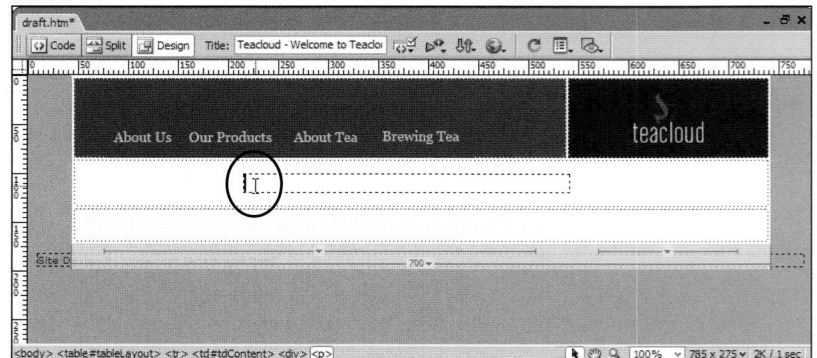

This is what your page should look like at this point. Not too bad for a day's work, wouldn't you say? As you can see, Dreamweaver 8 makes it really easy to insert images into your Web pages.

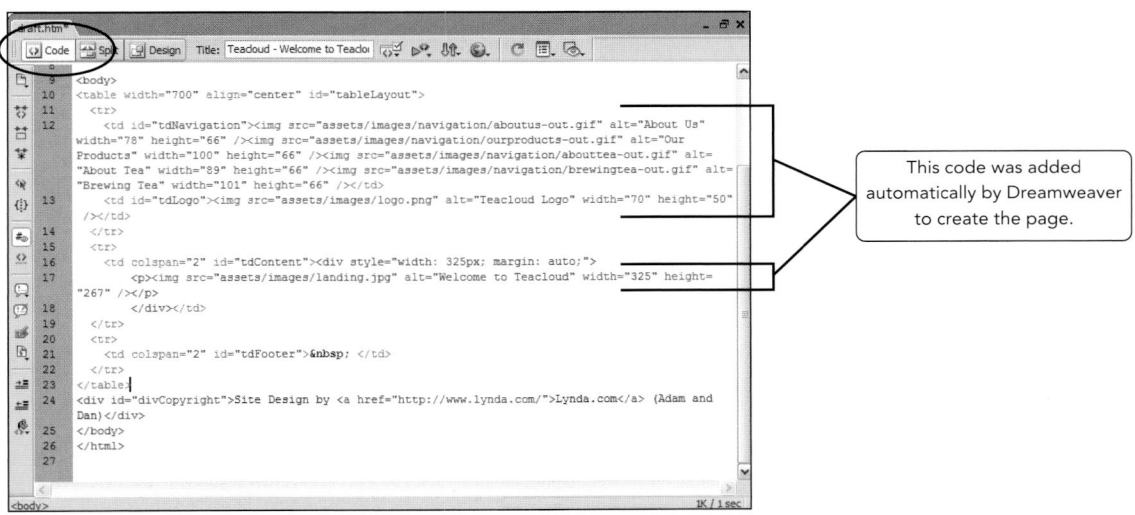

This code was added automatically by Dreamweaver to create the page.

8 In the **Document** toolbar, click the **Code** button to change the page view to **Code** view.

Even though you've added only a few images to the page, you can see that quite a bit of code is required. Dreamweaver 8 inserted an **<img>** tag for each of the images you inserted into the page. Imagine how long would it take you to type out all that XHTML code in Notepad or TextEdit!

Get into the habit of looking at the Code view of your page as often as possible. It's a great way to get more comfortable with what goes on behind the scenes in the XHTML code.

Note: If the code doesn't wrap to fit inside the Document window, choose **View > Code View Options > Word Wrap**.

9 In the **Document** toolbar, click the **Design** button to return to the **Design** view. Save **draft.htm** and leave it open for the next exercise.

TIP:

Other Ways to Insert Images

In this exercise, you learned how to use the Assets panel to insert images onto your page, which is the quickest and safest way to insert images onto your page. Why? First, only images within your site are listed in the Assets panel. Second, by inserting images from within your site, you ensure Dreamweaver 8 automatically creates the proper paths, so everything works when you upload your page to a remote Web server. But the Assets panel isn't the only way to insert images in Dreamweaver 8. Here are five other ways to insert images:

- Choose **Insert > Image**.
- In the **Insert** panel, click the **Image** button.
- Press **Ctrl+Alt+I** (Windows) or **Cmd+Option+I** (Mac).
- Click and drag the image from the **Assets** panel onto the page.
- Click and drag the image from the **Files** panel onto the page.

As you become more comfortable with Dreamweaver 8, you should use the method that fits best into your workflow.

---

4 | Inserting Text

Adding text to your Web page is simple in Dreamweaver 8. Just like with your favorite word processor, you can simply start typing text and the text will appear. In this exercise, you will add some text to the landing page you worked with in Exercise 3.

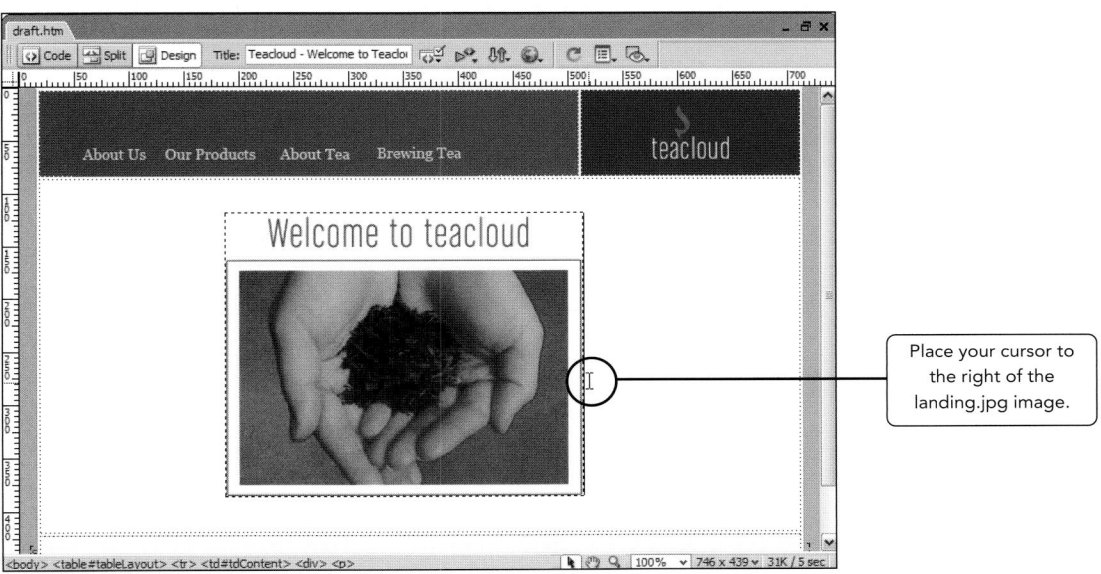

Place your cursor to the right of the landing.jpg image.

1 If you just completed Exercise 3, **draft.htm** should be open in Dreamweaver 8. If it's not, go back and complete Exercise 3. Click to the right of the **landing.jpg** file. Press **Enter** (Windows) or **Return** (Mac) to create a paragraph break and type the following text:

Brewing the finest loose leaf tea nature has to offer. We bring exotic and tantalizing teas from the fields to your cup. For over 15 years Teacloud has elevated the tea drinking experience and has provided tea lovers around the world with an unsurpassed quality.

2 Press **Enter** (Windows) or **Return** (Mac) to create another paragraph break and type the following text:

Please explore the rest of our site to learn more about the wonderful history, flavor, and fragrance of tea.

Your page should now match the page shown in the illustration here. Wondering why you didn't need to specify your fonts and font sizes? This page uses CSS to define the presentation of the page, and we've already taken care of all of that for you. You'll learn more about CSS in Chapter 6, *"Cascading Style Sheets"* and more about typography in Chapter 7, *"Typography."*

Next you'll add some text navigation to the bottom of the page.

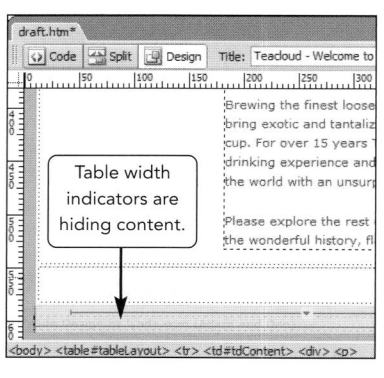

Table width indicators are hiding content.

Dreamweaver is being a little too helpful here and hiding the footer with the table widths.

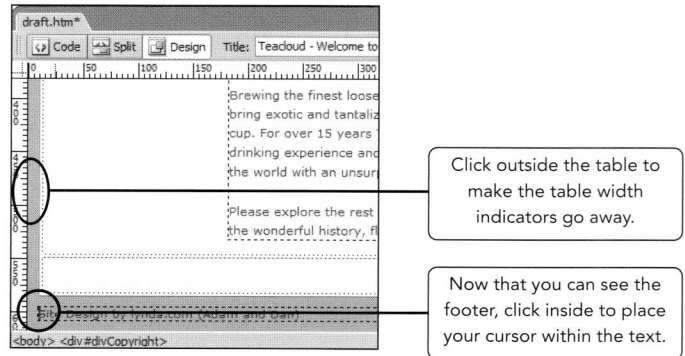

Click outside the table to make the table width indicators go away.

Now that you can see the footer, click inside to place your cursor within the text.

3 Position your cursor at the beginning of the text inside the footer at the bottom of the page. If the table width indicators are hiding the footer from you, click outside the table to remove the table width indicators, then click inside the footer.

4 Press **Shift+Enter** (Windows) or **Shift+Return** (Mac) to add a new line break and then press the up arrow to move your cursor up to the new line that was just inserted.

5 Type the following text on the new line to add some extra text navigation to the page (press **Shift+backslash** to add the pipe symbol [|]):

About Us | Our Products | About Tea | Brewing Tea

The pipe symbol is an effective and common way to separate characters in navigation bars.

Your page should now match the page shown in the illustration here.

6 Save **draft.htm** and leave it open for the next exercise.

Paragraph Breaks vs. Line Breaks

In the last exercise, each time you pressed **Enter** (Windows) or **Return** (Mac), Dreamweaver 8 skipped down the page two lines. Pressing this key inserts a single paragraph break (one line of blank space between paragraphs). The XHTML tag for a paragraph break is **<p>**. This is useful when you want to increase the space between different paragraphs. However, sometimes you may just want to go to one line directly below the one you are working on without introducing extra space. Pressing **Shift+Enter** (Windows) or **Shift+Return** (Mac) inserts a line break instead. The XHTML tag for a line break is **
. Knowing the difference between a **<p> and a **
** will give you more control over the spacing between lines of text.

This is where the closing paragraph tag, </p>, is located.

This is where the line break tag, <br />, is located.

The paragraph tag **<p>** creates an extra blank line between the closing paragraph tag **</p>** and the next line of content. The line break tag **
** places content on the very next line. You can see both of these here.

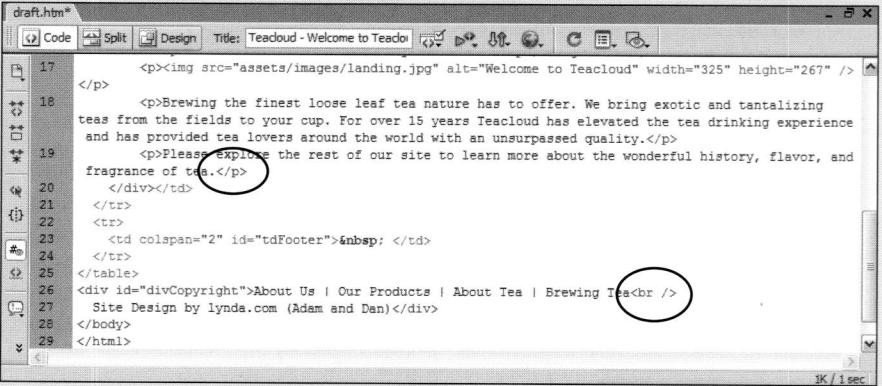

The illustration here shows what the closing paragraph **</p>** and the line break **
** tags look like in the XHTML code.

5 | Aligning Text and Images

Now that you have added some images and text to your page, it's time to learn how to align them. This section shows you how to use the Property Inspector to center and justify text and images. Keep in mind that this is the first alignment technique you are learning, and you will learn many other alignment techniques throughout this book.

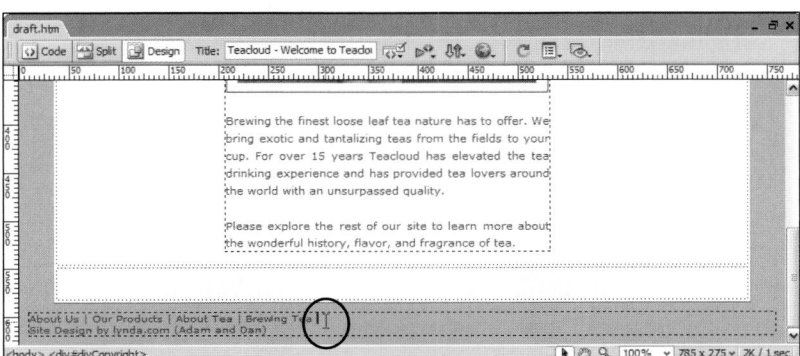

1 If you just completed Exercise 4, **draft.htm** should still be open. If it's not, go back and complete Exercise 4. Place your cursor inside the footer at the bottom of the page.

Note: If the table width indicators are hiding the footer, click outside the table to get rid of them.

2 In the **Property Inspector**, click the **Align Center** button to snap the text to the center of the screen.

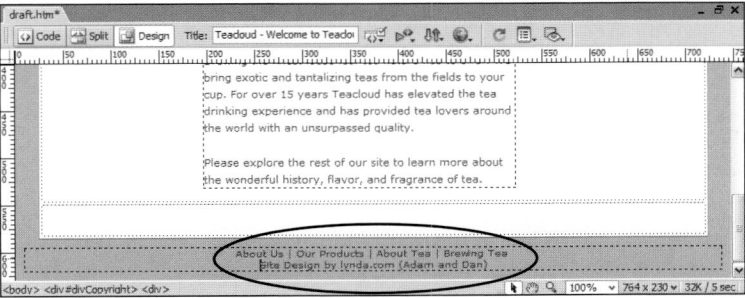

As you can see, the navigation text you created in Exercise 3, which was originally aligned to the left, is now aligned in the center of the page.

Next, you'll align the text for the navigation buttons at the top. Remember though, the navigation buttons aren't text like the navigation at the bottom—they are a series of images you inserted in Exercise 3.

3 Place your cursor anywhere inside the upper-left table cell containing the navigation buttons. In the **Property Inspector**, click the **Align Center** button.

Notice the navigation buttons are now centered! As you can see, you use the same technique to align images as you do to align text.

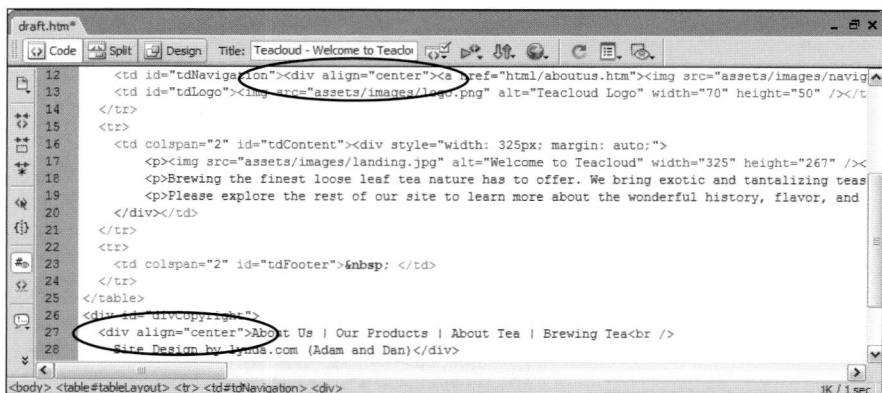

4 In the **Document** toolbar, click the **Code** button to view the code for this page.

Notice Dreamweaver added **<div>** tags with `align="center"` attributes around the footer and the navigation images. This tag and attribute are what instruct the text and images to align center, overriding the default alignment of the tag (which is left-aligned).

In addition to aligning left and center, you can also justify text. The text below the image in the middle of the page would look best justified so the right edge of the text lines up nicely with the right edge of the image above it. You'll learn how in the next steps.

5 In the **Document** toolbar, click the **Design** button to switch back to **Design** view. Click inside the first paragraph below the image and click the **Justify** button in the **Property Inspector**.

Wondering why only the first paragraph changed? Dreamweaver 8 applies alignment attributes to single paragraphs of text. Next, you'll justify the second paragraph of text. If you want to change the alignment of more than one paragraph at the same time, you can click and drag to highlight multiple paragraphs and then set the alignment properties in the Property Inspector.

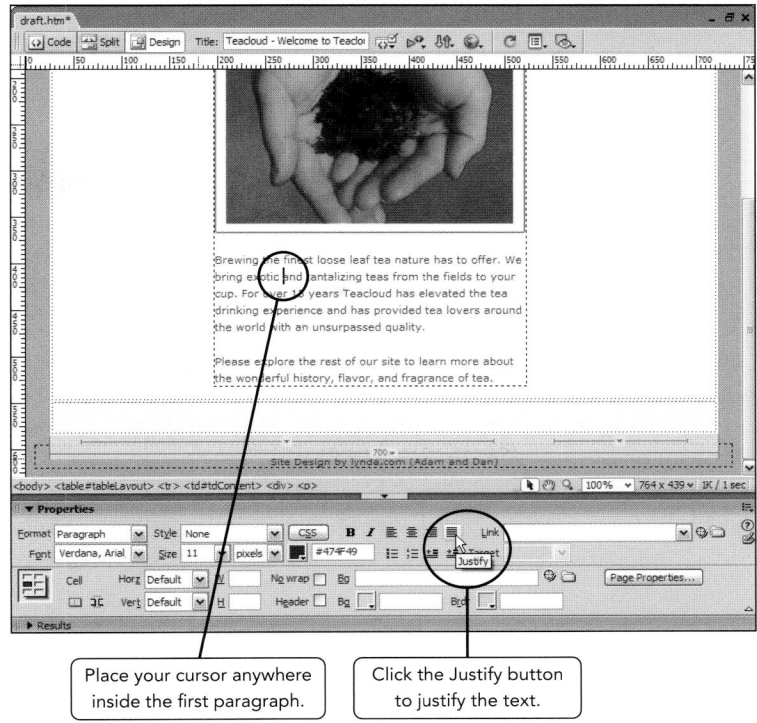

Place your cursor anywhere inside the first paragraph.

Click the Justify button to justify the text.

6 Place your cursor anywhere in the text of the second paragraph and click **Justify**.

As you can see, both paragraphs of text are now justified so the edges line up perfectly with the edges of the image. Very nice!

Although there are more efficient ways of aligning text (which you'll learn about later in this book), this is a great example of how quickly you can manipulate image and text alignment in Dreamweaver 8.

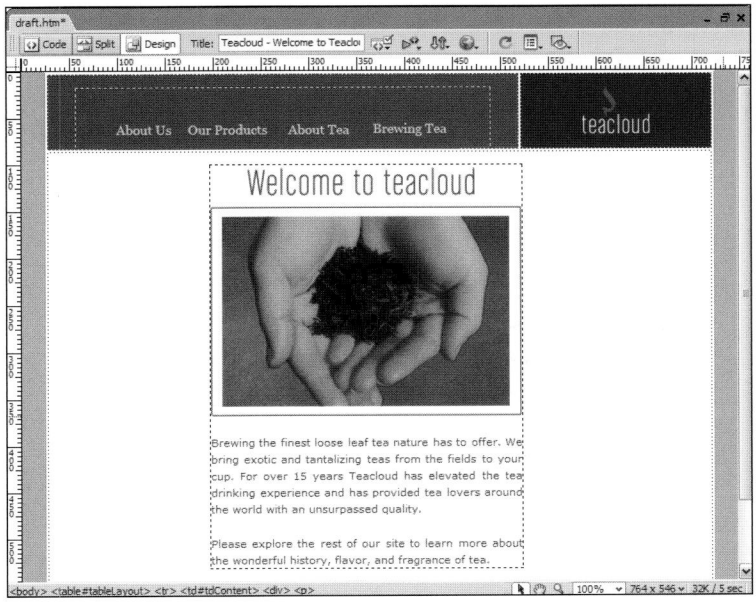

7 Save **draft.htm** and leave it open for the next exercise.

6 | Creating Links with Images and Text

Linking pages and sites is what makes the Web what it is. After all, what good is a page that doesn't link to somewhere else or doesn't have any other page linking to it? This exercise shows you how to set up links using the Property Inspector in Dreamweaver 8.

1 If you just completed Exercise 5, **draft.htm** should still be open. If it's not, go back and complete Exercise 5. Click to select the **aboutus-out.gif** (About Us) image.

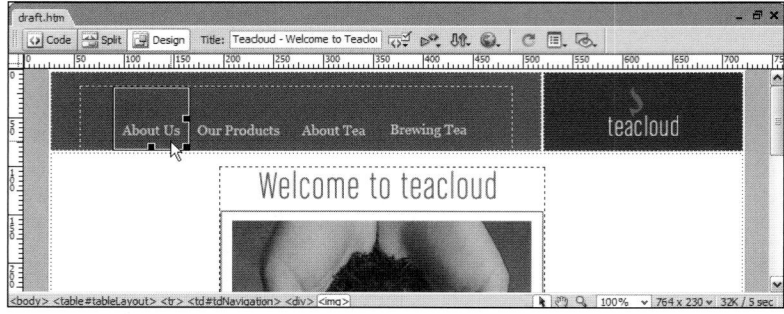

2 In the **Property Inspector**, click the **Browse for File** icon next to the **Link** field to open the **Select File** dialog box.

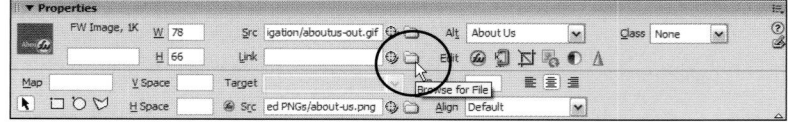

Note: If your Property Inspector panel is smaller than what is shown here, click the arrow in the lower-right corner to expand it.

3 Browse to the **chap_04/html** folder. Click **aboutus.htm** to select it and click **OK** (Windows) or **Choose** (Mac).

Congratulations, you have just created your first relative image link—you linked the About Us button to the **aboutus.htm** page in the **html** folder. Why is the link relative? As you learned in Chapter 3, *"Site Control,"* relative links link to files within the same site, not to an external Web site.

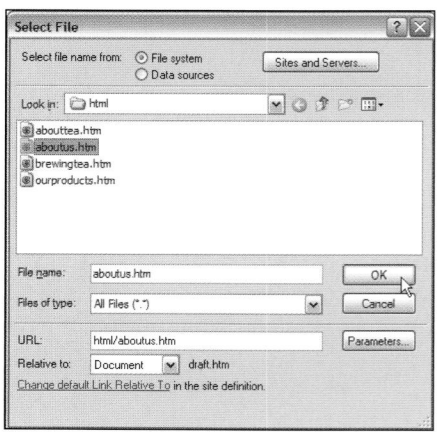

4 Click the **ourproducts-out.gif** (Our Products) image to select it.

5 In the **Property Inspector**, click the **Browse for File** icon next to the **Link** field to open the **Select File** dialog box.

6 Browse to the **chap_04/html** folder. Click **ourproducts.htm** to select it and click **OK** (Windows) or **Choose** (Mac).

You just linked the Our Products button to the **ourproducts.htm** page inside the **html** folder.

7 Repeat Steps 4, 5, and 6 to link the **About Tea** button to the **html/abouttea.htm** page and the **Brewing Tea** button to the **html/brewingtea.htm** page, respectively.

You have just successfully added links to the images on this page!

8 If you want to preview the links in a browser, press **F12** and click any of the images. Position your cursor over the navigation buttons. Notice the cursor changes to the hand icon, indicating it is a link.

Next, you will create links using text. The process is almost identical, except you will be selecting text instead of images.

9 Click and drag to highlight the words **About Us** at the bottom of the page.

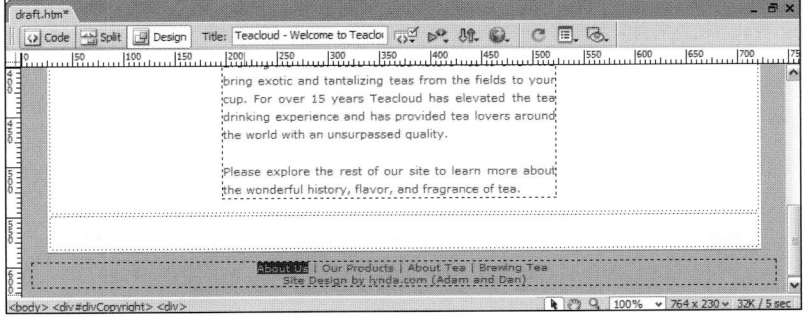

10 In the **Property Inspector**, click the **Browse for File** icon next to the **Link** field to open the **Select File** dialog box.

---

11 Browse to the **chap_04/html** folder. Click **aboutus.htm** to select it and click **OK** (Windows) or **Choose** (Mac).

---

12 Repeat Steps 9, 10, and 11 to link the **Our Products** text to the **html/ourproducts.htm** page, the **About Tea** text to the **html/abouttea.htm** page, and the **Brewing Tea** text to the **html/brewingtea.htm page**.

Wondering why the color of the links didn't change color? The style sheet applied to this page defines what color links should be. You'll learn all about style sheets in Chapter 6, *"Cascading Style Sheets."*

---

13 Click and drag to highlight the **lynda.com** text at the bottom of the page.

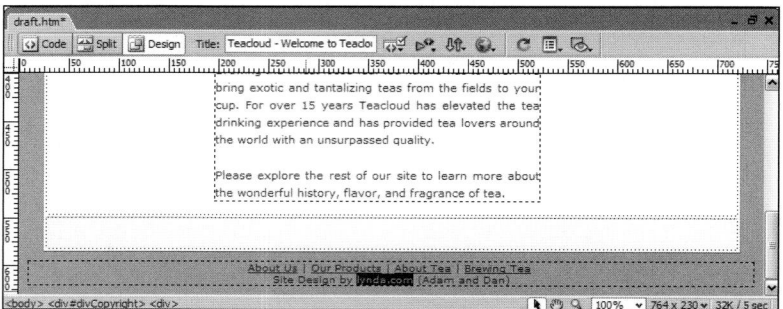

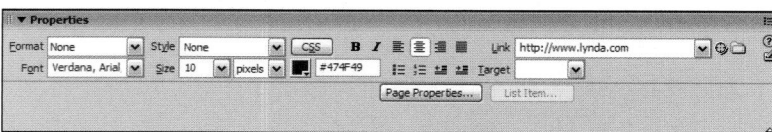

14 In the **Link** field in the **Property Inspector**, type **http://www.lynda.com** and press **Enter** (Windows) or **Return** (Mac).

Congratulations, you just created your first absolute link. It's an absolute link because it begins with an **http** header and includes the full address. As you know from Chapter 3, *"Site Control,"* any time you link to an external Web site, you must use an absolute link.

---

15 Press **F12** to preview the page in a browser so you can test the links you created in this exercise. When you're finished, close the browser and return to Dreamweaver 8.

---

16 Save **draft.htm** and leave it open for the next exercise.

---

7 | Inserting <meta> Tags

One of the big challenges of Web design (aside from designing and building a Web site) is letting the search engines know your site exists. There are two steps to getting your site listed: 1) list it with all the search engines out there; and 2) insert **<meta>** tags into your XHTML so the search engines can find and correctly index your site. Many search engines send robots (also called spiders) out to search the Web for content. When you insert certain **<meta>** tags into your document, you make it much easier for the search-engine robots to understand how to categorize your site. This exercise shows you how to add **<meta>** tags with specific attributes so you can make your Web page more search-engine friendly.

---

1 If you just completed Exercise 6, **draft.htm** should still be open. If it's not, go back and complete Exercise 6. Choose **Insert > HTML > Head Tags > Keywords** to open the **Keywords** dialog box.

Keywords reflect the content of specific pages. They're used by some (but not all) search engines to help provide accurate search results. You should always use short, relevant keywords and phrases that describe the content of the page.

---

2 Type **Tea, Brewing, Kettles, Teapots** and click **OK**.

When you define keywords for your Web pages, think about what keywords a user might type into a search engine to find your site.

---

3 Choose **Insert > HTML > Head Tags > Description** to open the **Description** dialog box.

Some (but not all) search engines use the description to describe the contents of a particular page in search listings.

---

4 Type **Teacloud brews the finest loose leaf tea nature has to offer. We bring exotic and tantalizing teas from the fields to your cup.** Click **OK**.

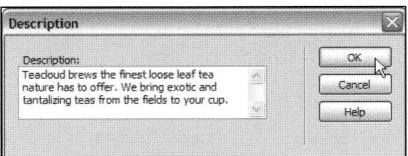

---

5 In the **Document** toolbar, click the **Code** button to view the code in this document.

Notice the **<meta>** information inside the **<head>** tag? Visitors to your site won't be able to see the **<meta>** tag information because it's only visible inside the XHTML code. It's a part of authoring the page, but it has nothing to do with appearance and everything to do with helping the search engines find and properly rank your site.

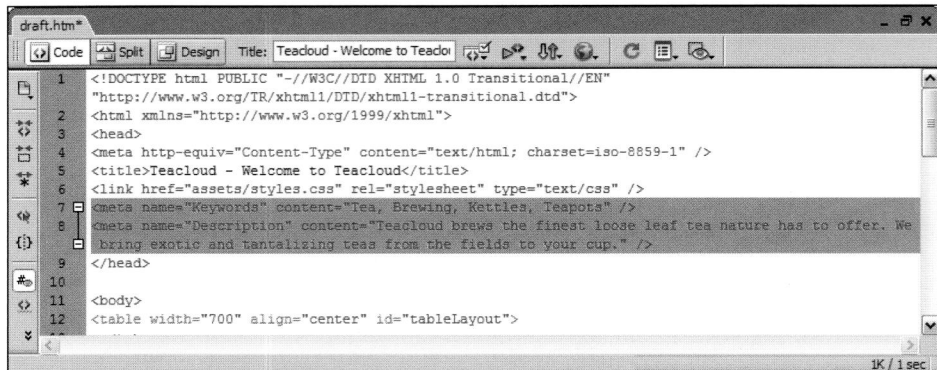

6 Close **draft.htm**. You don't need to save your changes.

Onward ho! You just built a page, set links, and added **<meta>** tags all in one chapter. Future chapters will reveal even more powers of Dreamweaver 8, so keep reading!

Keywords and Descriptions

Keywords are `<meta>` tag values that specify certain words to help Internet search engines index your site. Many search engines limit the number of keywords you can use. Choose your words wisely and use no more than 10 to 15 keywords that best describe the contents of your site.

Descriptions are `<meta>` tag values that also help Internet search engines index your site. Some search engines will use the description you create in their directory to describe your site. Again, some search engines limit the number of characters indexed, so keep it short and simple! If you would like more information about `<meta>` tags, check out these resources:

Web Developer: META Tag Resources

http://webdeveloper.internet.com/html/html_metatag_res.html

Search Engine Watch

http://searchenginewatch.com/webmasters/meta.html

5.

Linking

There are a few ways to create links that you haven't learned about yet. In this chapter, you'll learn about **Point to File**, which lets you point to a file inside your Files panel and create the link based on your selection. Another type of link is an **email link**. This special type of link launches your user's email program and automatically enters a recipient address. Another link you'll learn about here is called **named anchors**, which works in conjunction with links to let you jump to different sections of the same page. The final type of link this chapter demonstrates is a **file link**, which lets you link to files, such as PDFs, SIT and ZIP archives, and so on. If this all sounds abstract, dive into the chapter so you can get the hands-on experience that will make these new concepts understandable.

1 | Linking with Point to File

The Point to File feature is an alternate way to create links on your Web pages. This feature forces you to select files that are within your local root folder, eliminating the unwanted possibility of linking to files located outside of your defined site. Here's how it's done.

1 Copy the **chap_05** folder from the **HOT CD-ROM** to your **Desktop**. Define your site as **Chapter 5** using the **chap_05** folder as the local root folder. Make sure the **Files** panel is open. If it's not, choose **Window > Files** or press **F11**.

2 In the **Files** panel, double-click to open **index.htm**.

This file is complete but does not contain any links. You will create the links by using the **Point to File** feature in Dreamweaver 8.

3 Click the **aboutus-out.gif** (About Us) image to select it.

Before you can create a link, you select the image or text.

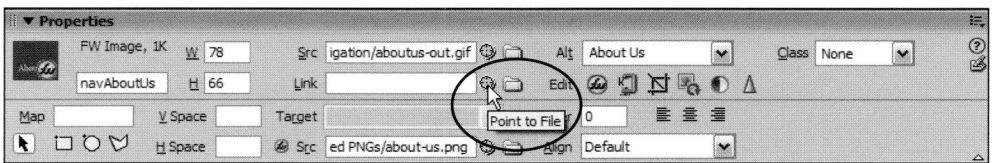

4 In the **Property Inspector**, click and hold the **Point to File** icon next to the **Link** field.

When you click and hold the Point to File icon, the Link field populates with text, telling you to point to a file to create a link.

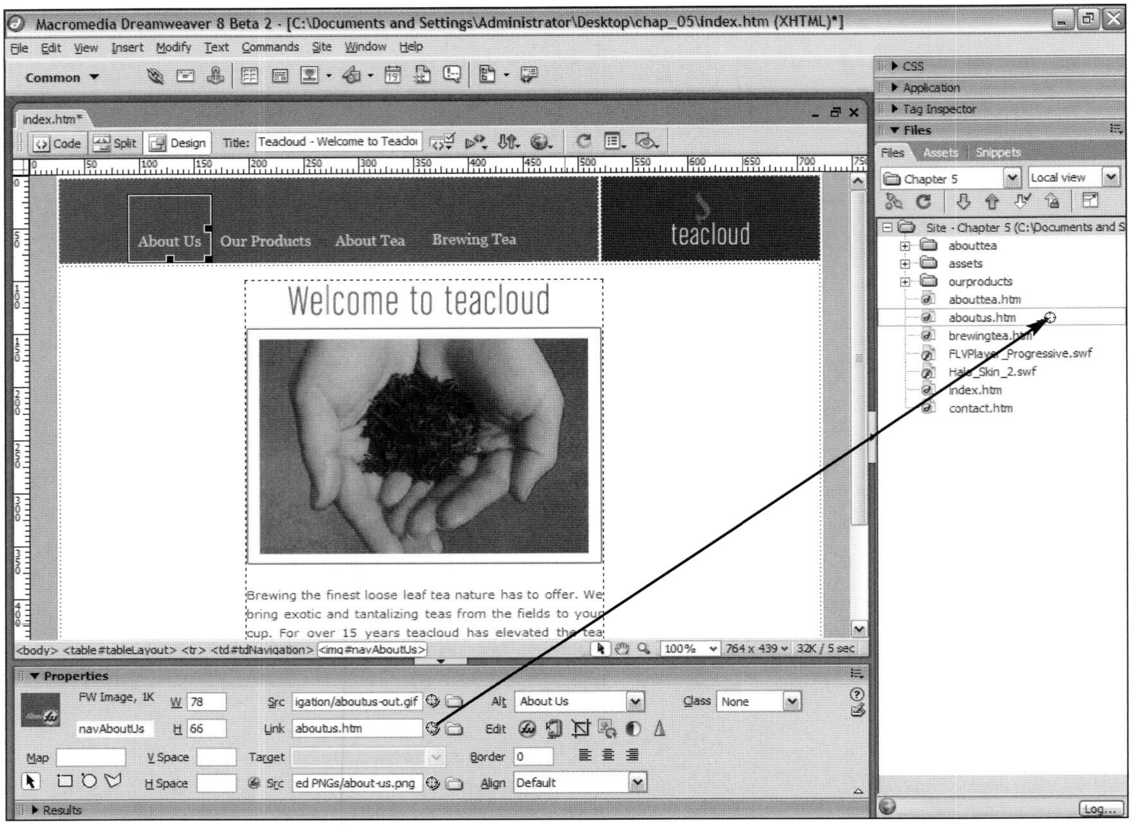

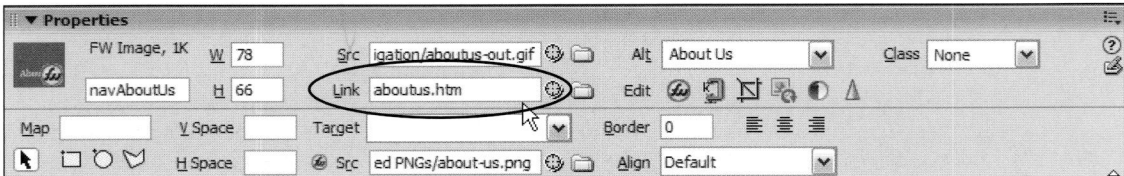

5 Click and drag the **Point to File** icon onto the **aboutus.htm** file in the **Files** panel and release the mouse.

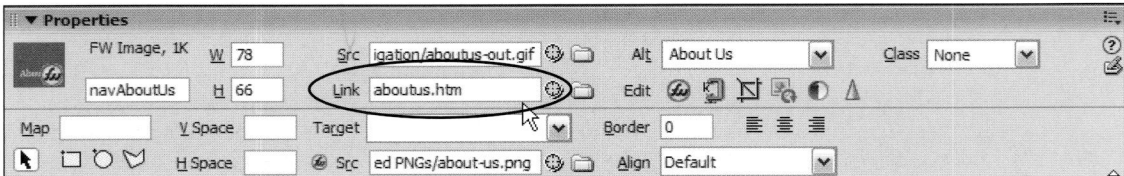

You've just successfully created a link to the **aboutus.htm** file. Notice the Link field displays the file you linked to in Step 5. This is a good place to look if you forget what file you linked to. The great thing about using this technique is that there's no possible way to accidentally set the link to a misspelled or missing file.

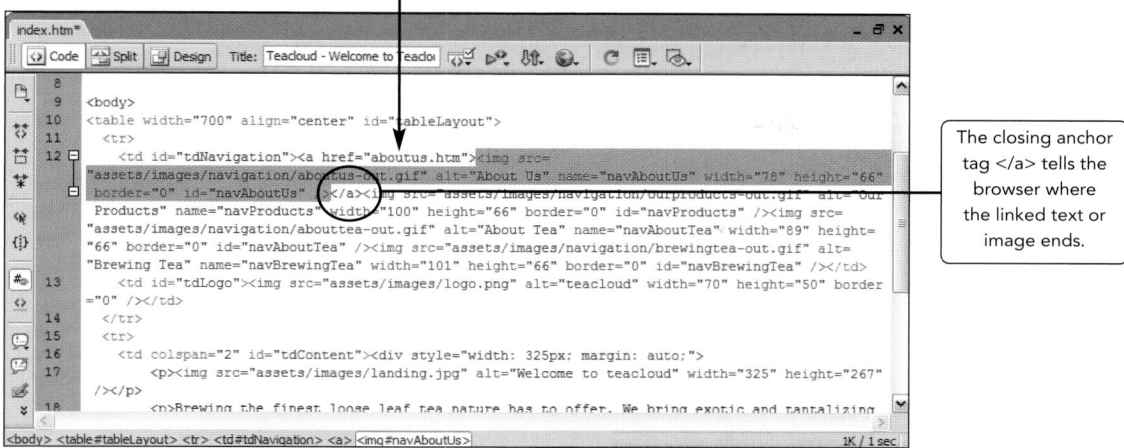

The opening anchor tag <a> combined with the href="aboutus.htm" attribute creates the link to the aboutus.htm page.

The closing anchor tag </a> tells the browser where the linked text or image ends.

6 In the **Document** toolbar, click the **Code** button to view the code for the **index.htm** page. Some of the code may be highlighted because the **aboutus-out.gif** image is selected in **Design** view.

This automatic highlighting of selected objects is one of our favorite features in Dreamweaver 8 because it lets you quickly see the relevant code for your selection in Design view. This feature will come in handy more and more as you design future pages.

The code shown in the screen shot was inserted into the page automatically by Dreamweaver 8 when you created a link to the **aboutus.htm** page. It's nice to know that you don't have to type all of this (and correctly) each time you want to add something as simple as a link to your page.

TIP: | **Learn As You Code**

If you are new to HTML/XHTML, we strongly urge you to get into the habit of flipping back and forth between Code view and Design view (or use the split view) so you increase your exposure to the raw code behind the visual design of your page. Doing this lets you instantly see the new code that Dreamweaver 8 creates as you perform various functions in the Design view. Being comfortable looking at and editing code is essential to every Web designer's success because there *will* come a time when you need to make a tweak here and there in your code.

---

7 In the **Document** toolbar, click the **Design** button to return to the **Design** view of the **index.htm** page.

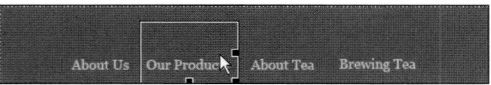

TOWER HAMLETS COLLEGE
Learning Centre
Poplar High Street
LONDON
E14 0AF

8 Click to select the **ourproducts-out.gif** (Our Products) image.

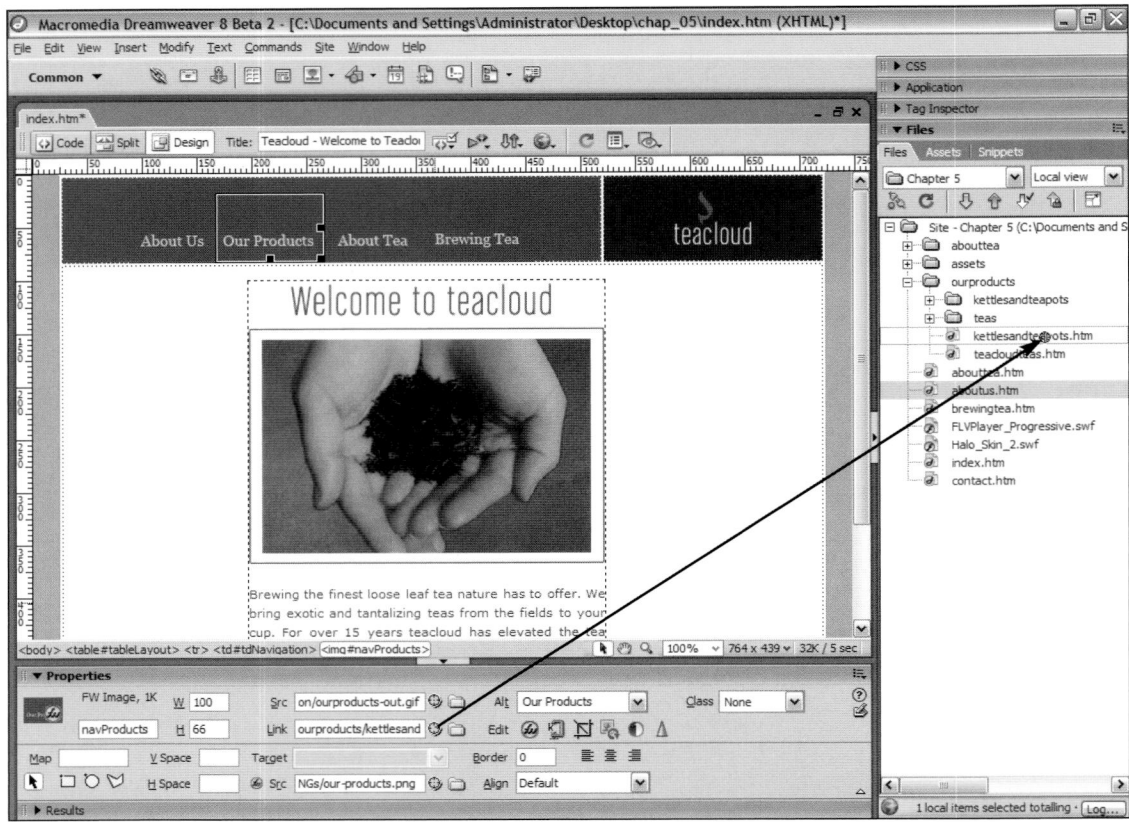

9 In the **Property Inspector**, click and drag the **Point to File** icon onto the **ourproducts** folder in the **Files** panel and hold it there until the folder expands. Position the icon over the **kettlesandteapots.htm** file. When you release the mouse, you'll create a link to **kettlesandteapots.htm** inside the **ourproducts** folder.

10 Repeat Steps 8 and 9 for the link from **abouttea-out.gif** (About Tea) to the **abouttea.htm** page and **brewingtea-out.gif** (Brewing Tea) to the **brewingtea.htm** page.

11 Press **F12** to preview the page in a browser so you can test the links. Click the navigation buttons to see if they work. When you are finished, return to Dreamweaver 8.

12 Close **index.htm**. You don't need to save your changes.

2 | Linking to New Source Files

In the last exercise, you learned how to use the Point to File feature to create links on your pages, which is the most common use of this feature. You can also use it other ways, such as quickly replacing images or placeholders on your page, as you'll do in this exercise. Placeholders let you to see what your page is going to look like before you insert actual source images—a useful feature if you're working with other developers or graphic designers who are supplying the artwork while you build the site.

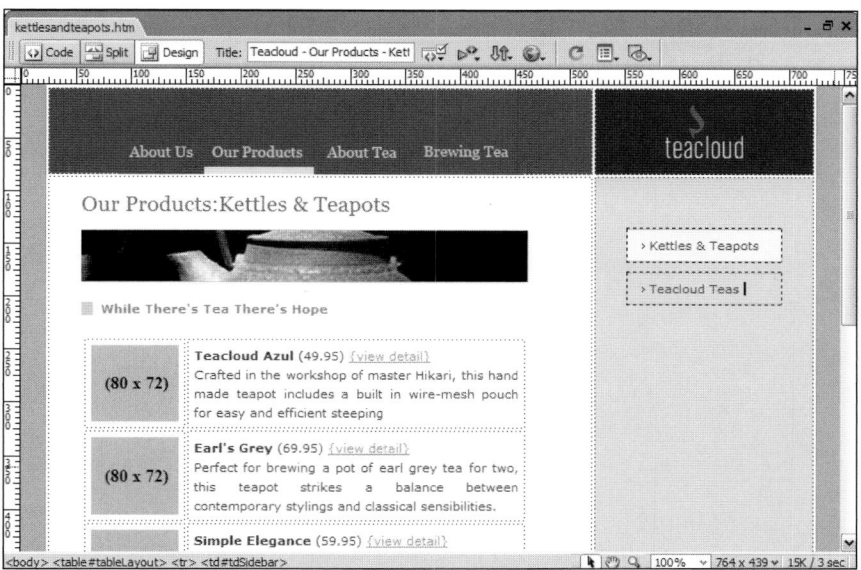

1 In the **Files** panel, double-click **kettlesandteapots.htm** in the **ourproducts** folder to open it.

This XHTML file contains a layout created with tables and several image placeholders.

N O T E : | ### What Is a Placeholder?

A placeholder is an object you can add to your page to represent where you'll insert final content. Placeholders are helpful in a workgroup where one person designs the page and another adds the content. You can add a placeholder by clicking the **Image Placeholder** button in the **Insert** panel or by holding down the **Ctrl** (Windows) or **Option** (Mac) key while clicking the **Insert Image** object in the **Insert** bar. You can resize the placeholder by selecting it and changing its height and width values in the **Property Inspector** so that it matches the dimensions of the image that will replace it. Resizing gives you a more accurate preview of your page layout and positioning. The height and width of the placeholder will be displayed in Design view, but you won't see any pixel dimensions in a browser, only a broken image.

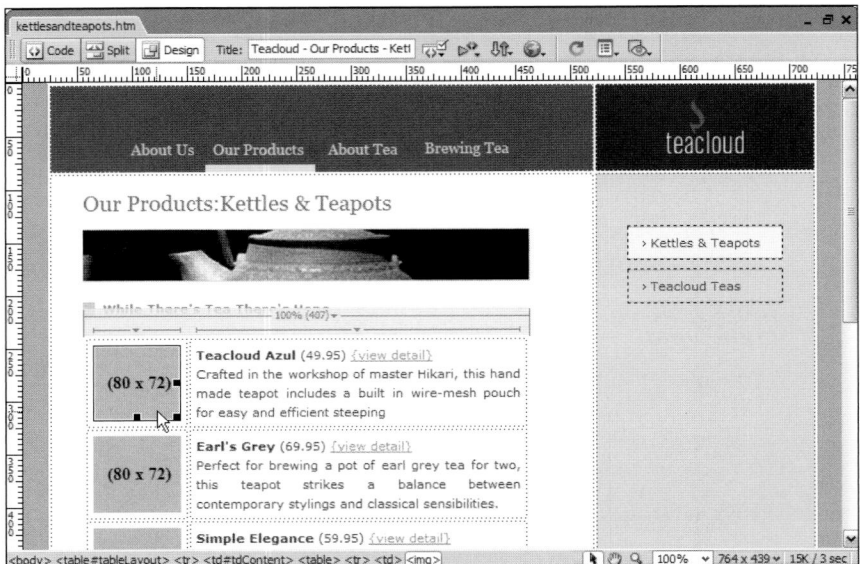

2 On the left side of the page, click the first image placeholder to select it.

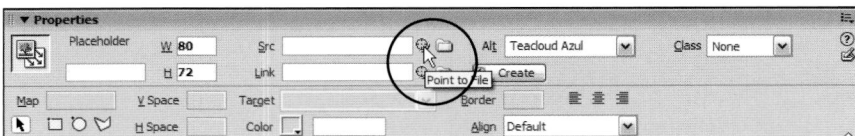

3 In the **Property Inspector**, click the **Point to File** icon next to the **Src** option and drag it over the **Files** panel. Hold the icon over the **assets** folder to expand it, and then hold the icon over the **images** folder, then the **products** folder, and finally the **kettles** folder to expand it so you can select one of the images inside. (Don't let go of that mouse button yet!)

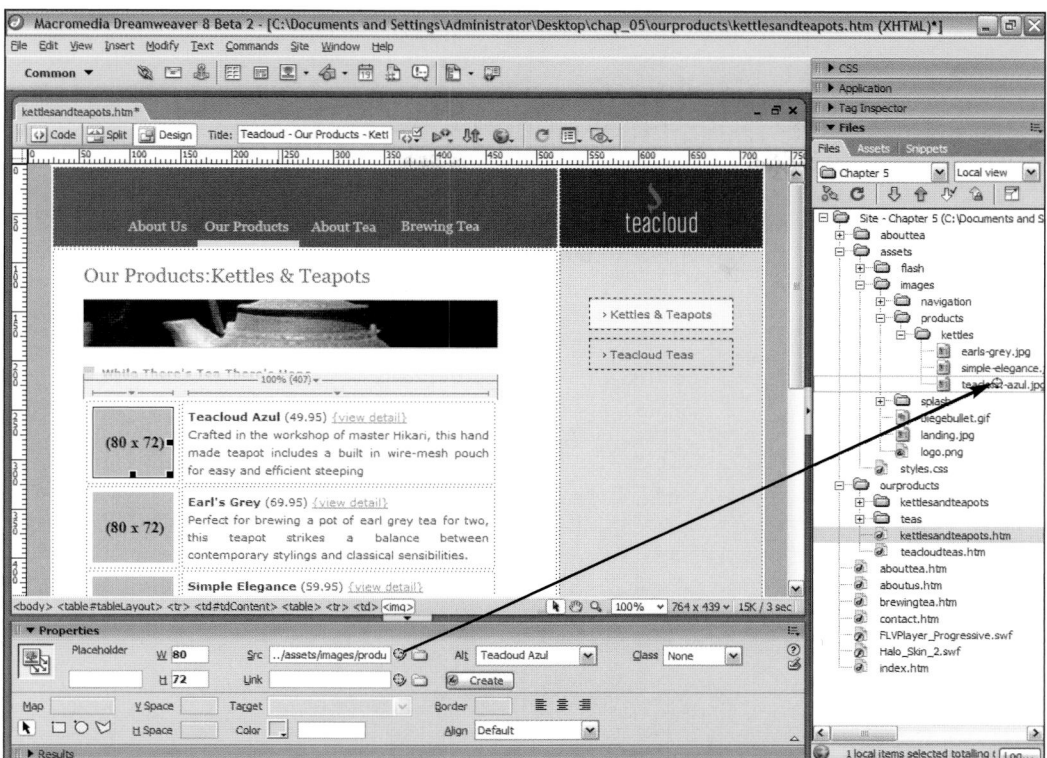

4 Position the icon over the **teacloud-azul.jpg** image and release the mouse button to replace the placeholder with **teacloud-azul.jpg**.

Notice the placeholder has been replaced with the selected image.

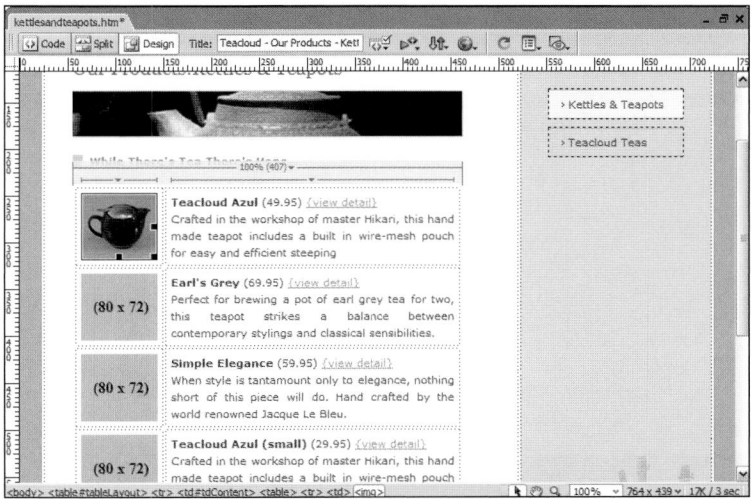

5 Click to select the image placeholder below the image you just replaced.

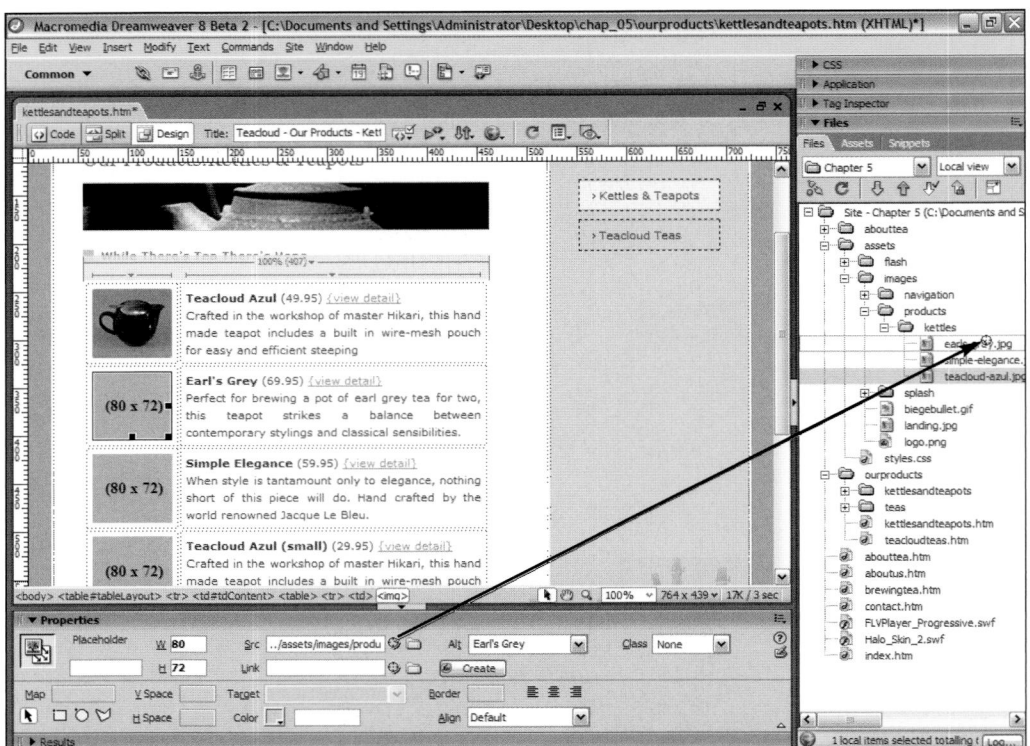

6 In the **Property Inspector**, click the **Point to File** icon next to the **Src** option. Drag it over **earls-grey.jpg** and release the mouse button to replace the placeholder with **earls-grey.jpg**.

Notice the second placeholder has now been replaced with the image.

7 Repeat Steps 5 and 6 to replace the next placeholder with **simple-elegance.jpg**.

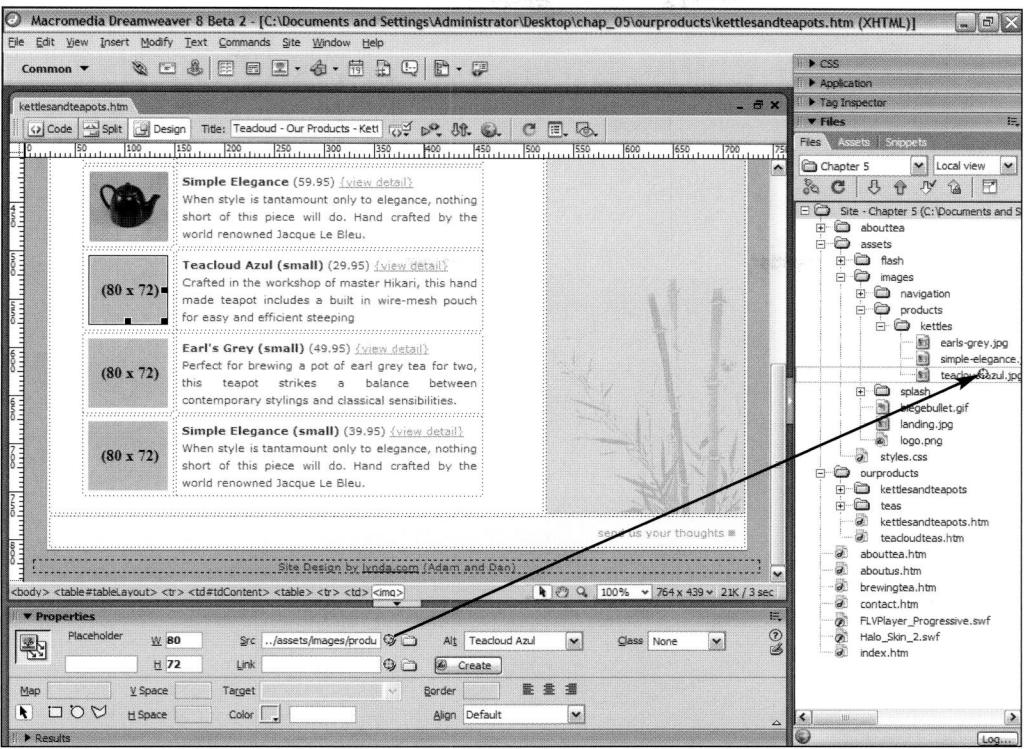

8 For a little extra practice, perform the same steps for the next three placeholders so that the "small" version of each teapot uses the same photo as their larger siblings. They're the same as the first three images, but a little target practice never hurt anybody.

When you're finished, your file should match the illustration here.

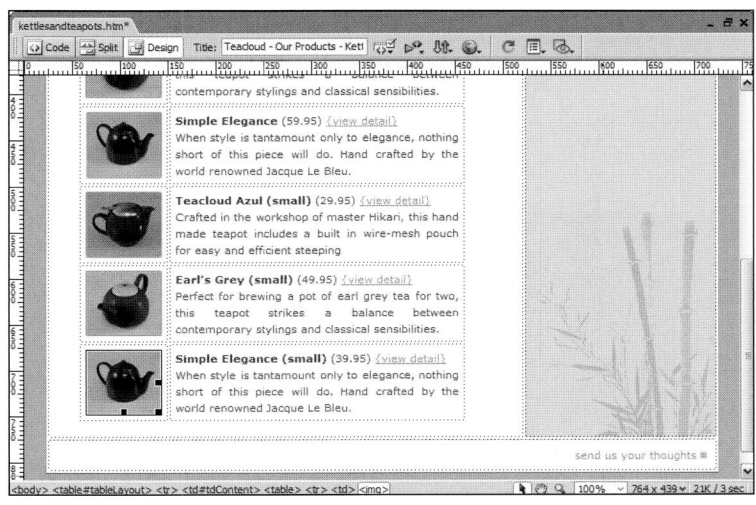

9 Save your changes and close **kettlesandteapots.htm**. You'll use this file again in Exercise 5 of this chapter.

An email link automatically launches a user's default email application and inserts the recipient's address into the To field. This process is convenient and doesn't require users to remember or copy and paste complex and lengthy email addresses. This exercise shows you how to create an email link.

1 In the **Files** panel, double-click **contact.htm** to open it.

This file contains descriptions of the different Teacloud customer service departments. Each department has its own email address for customers to contact them. You will create links to those email addresses in this exercise.

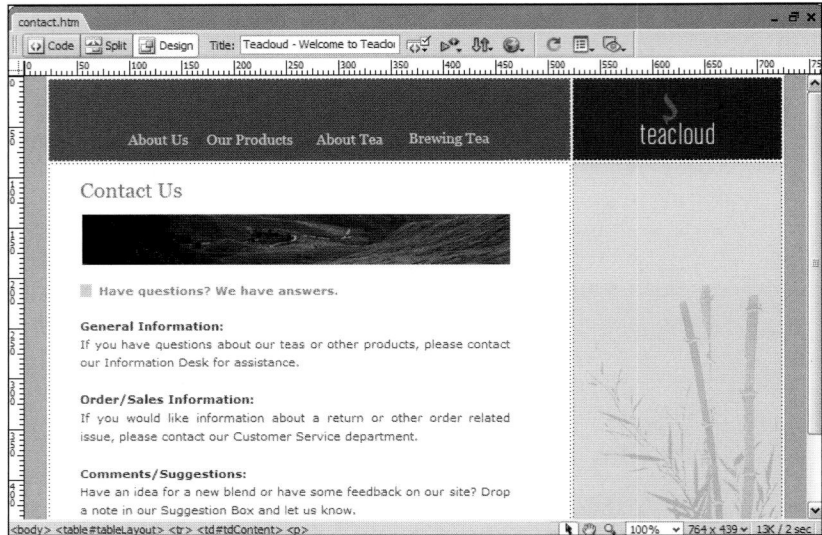

2 Click and drag to select the **Information Desk** text under the **General Information** section.

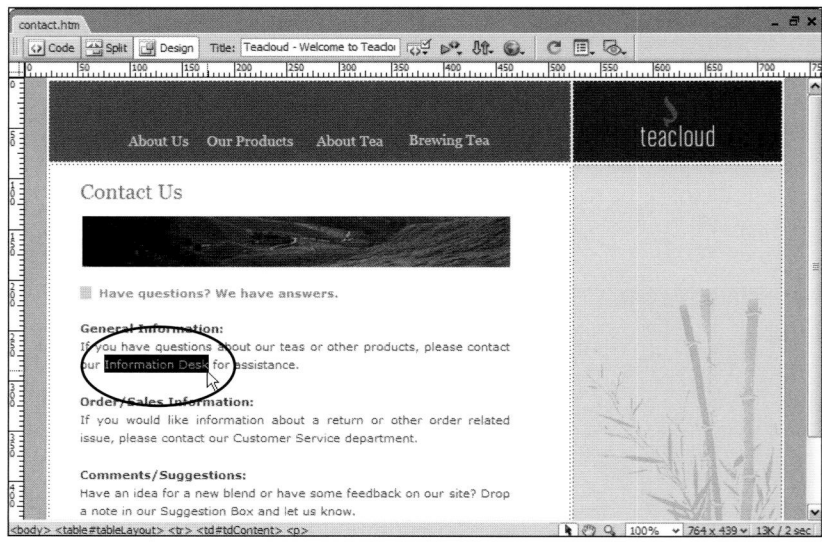

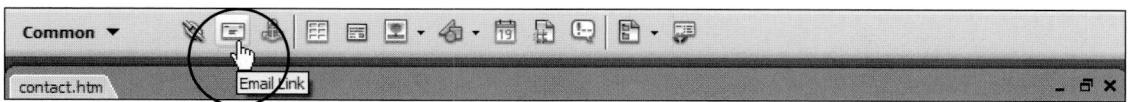

3 In the **Common** group of the **Insert** bar, click the **Email Link** icon to open the **Email Link** dialog box.

4 Notice the **Text** field populates automatically using your selected text. In the **E-Mail** field, type **info@teacloud.com**. Click **OK**.

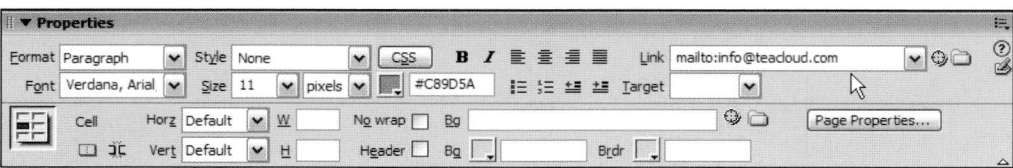

5 Click anywhere on the email link you created.

In the Property Inspector, notice the Link field reads **mailto:info@teacloud.com**. This is the correct format for creating email links.

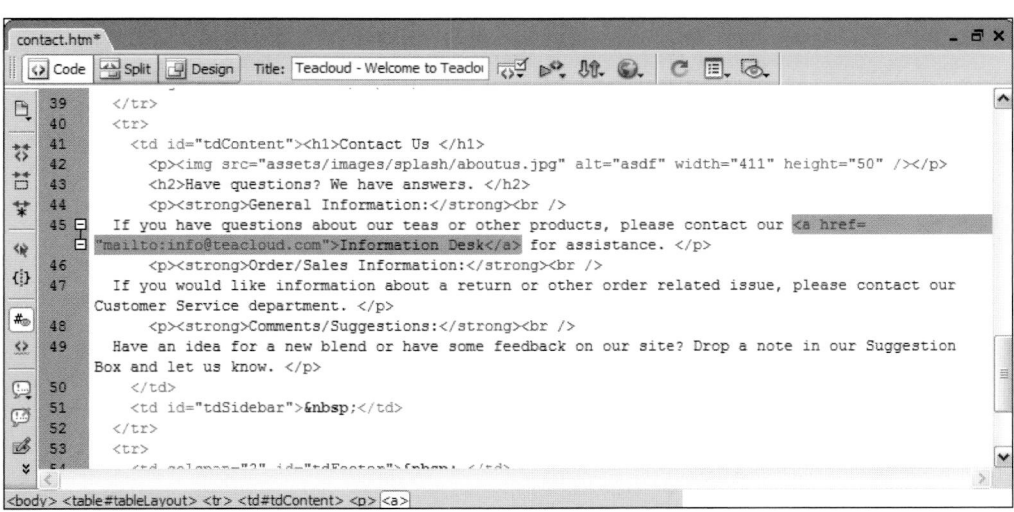

6 In the **Document** toolbar, click the **Code** button to view the code for this page.

The highlighted code shown here was added when you chose to insert an email link. Notice the similarity between an email link and other links you created in Exercise 1. They both start and end with the anchor tag **<a>**, and they both use the **href** attribute.

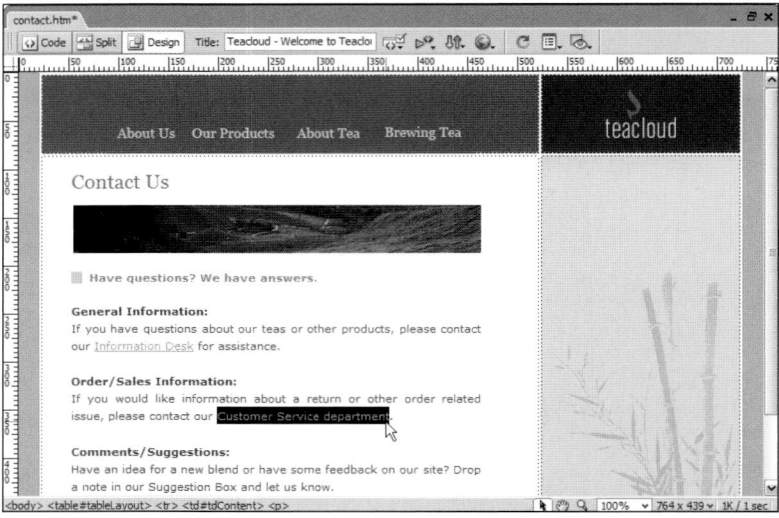

7 Click the **Design** button to return to the **Design** view of this page. Click and drag to select the **Customer Service department** text in the **Order/Sales Information** section.

---

8 Choose **Insert > Email Link** to open the **Email Link** dialog box.

As you can see, there are several ways to create email links—using the Insert bar as you did in Step 3, and using the menu as you did here.

9 Notice the text you selected appears in the **Text** field. In the **E-Mail** field, type **cs@teacloud.com**. Click **OK**.

Note: Because Dreamweaver automatically inserts any email address that you used in the previous steps, **info@teacloud.com** will automatically appear in the E-Mail field when you open in the Email Link dialog box. Not to worry, you can simply type another email address in the E-Mail field to specify a different email address.

Next, you'll learn how to create an email link without using the Email Link dialog box.

---

10 Click and drag to select the **Suggestion Box** text in the **Comments/ Suggestions** section.

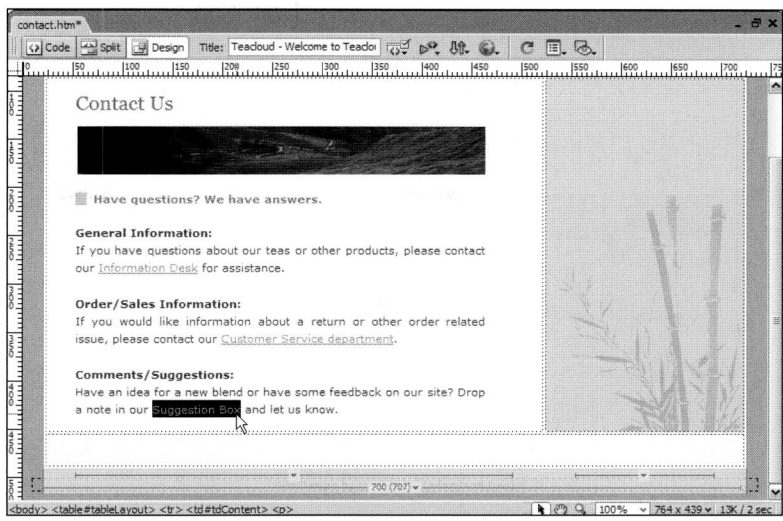

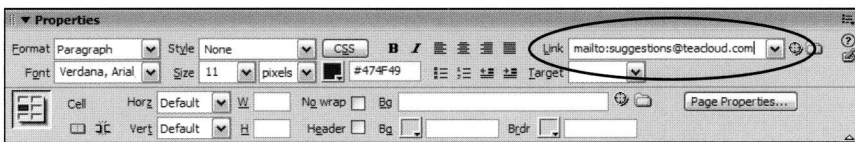

11 In the **Property Inspector**, type **mailto:suggestions@teacloud.com** in the **Link** field and press **Enter** (Windows) or **Return** (Mac) to create an email link from the selected text.

You see, there's yet another way to do the same operation. As you build your skills in Dreamweaver 8, you will develop your own personal preferences for creating email links, just as you will develop your own preferences for assigning links.

12 Press **F12** to preview this page in a browser. Click each of the email links to make sure they work. If you have a mail client installed locally it should open and create a new email message for you.

13 Close **contact.htm**. You don't need to save your changes.

WARNING:	**Browser Email Settings**
	Not all site visitors use a standard email program, such as Microsoft Outlook or Mac Mail. Many visitors use Web-based email programs, such as Hotmail or GMail. If visitors using a Web-based email program click an email link, they will get an error message asking them to set up an email account using a standard email program. There's not a lot you can do about this, so you might want to include the email address directly on the page (or simply use the email address on the page as the link) so visitors can copy and paste the address into their email programs.

4 Creating Named Anchors

Named anchors are a special type of link that let users jump to a specific section of a document. These links are particularly useful if you have large amounts of text on a single page that requires the user to scroll up and down through the document. Named anchors have two components—the anchor and the link. Working together, they make it easy to jump to specific areas of your page. This exercise shows you how to set up named anchors.

---

1 In the **Files** panel, double-click **teacloudteas.htm** in the **ourproducts** folder to open it. This file has a long list of teas separated by type. Scroll down to the bottom of the page to get a better idea of exactly how long this page really is.

As you can imagine, scrolling down a lengthy page can be annoying, and sometimes visitors to your site may not even realize you have additional content they're interested in near the bottom of the page. To help ease this annoyance (and make sure visitors get all the juicy bits from your site), named anchors make it possible to link visitors to a specific location on the same page with a single click.

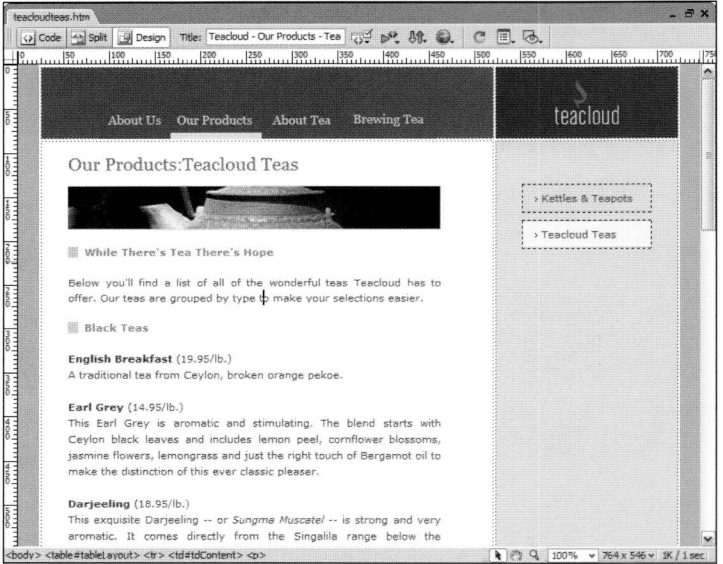

---

2 Click and drag to select the **Black Teas** text.

First, you'll learn how to wrap a named anchor around the text so users can easily jump to the Black Teas section farther down the page.

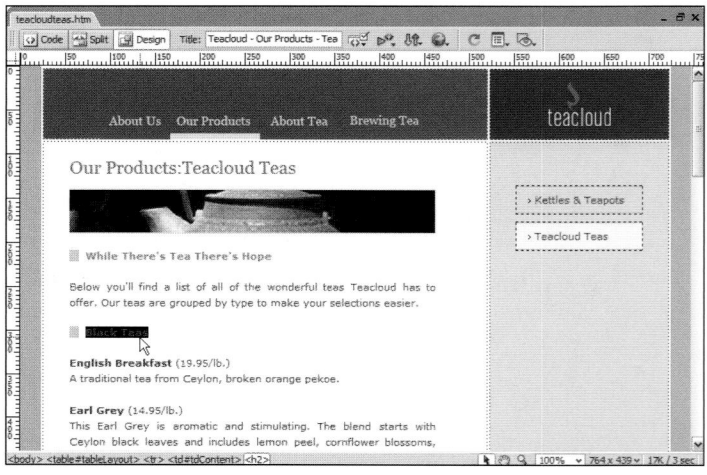

3 In the **Common** group of the **Insert** bar, click the **Named Anchor** button to open the **Named Anchor** dialog box.

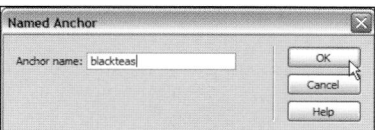

4 Type **blackteas** in the **Anchor name** field and click **OK**.

Tip: When you create anchor names, follow a few simple guidelines: use simple names without spaces or special characters, and don't use a number as the first character. Starting the anchor name with a number or including special characters or spaces can cause a browser to completely ignore the anchor.

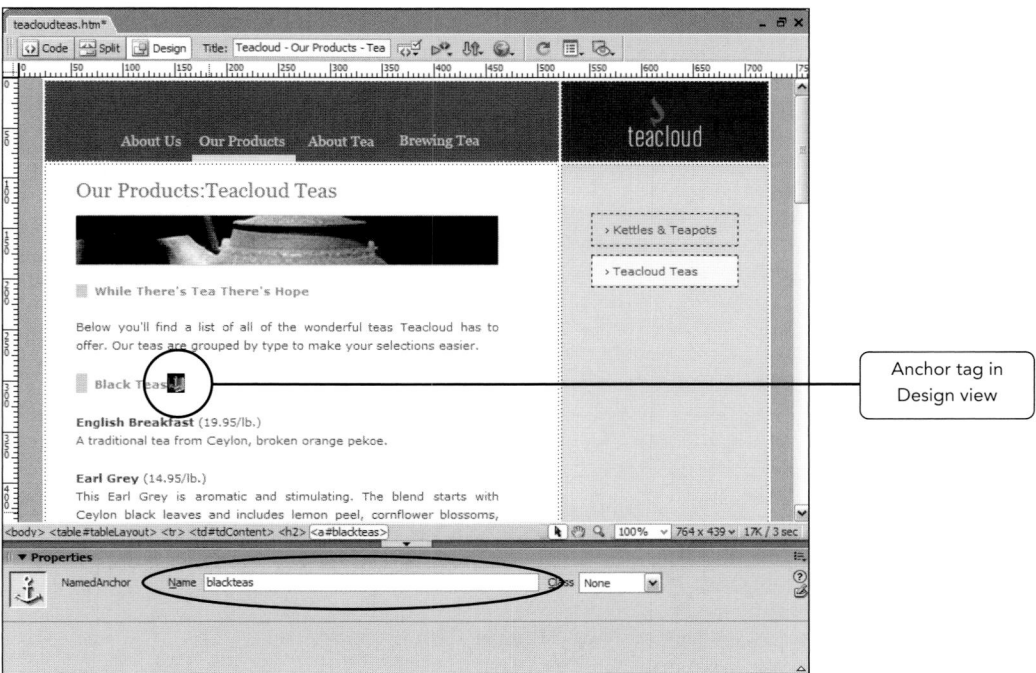

Anchor tag in Design view

Notice a small yellow anchor marker appears on your page where you insert the named anchor tag. Don't worry, no one but you will ever see the named anchor icon; it's there for your benefit as you create these types of links. When you preview the page in a browser, the icon will not be visible. **Note:** If your named anchor is selected, as it is in the illustration here, it will be blue, not yellow.

Tip: If you ever want to change the name you specified for a named anchor, click the yellow anchor marker and type a new name in the **Name** field of the **Property Inspector**.

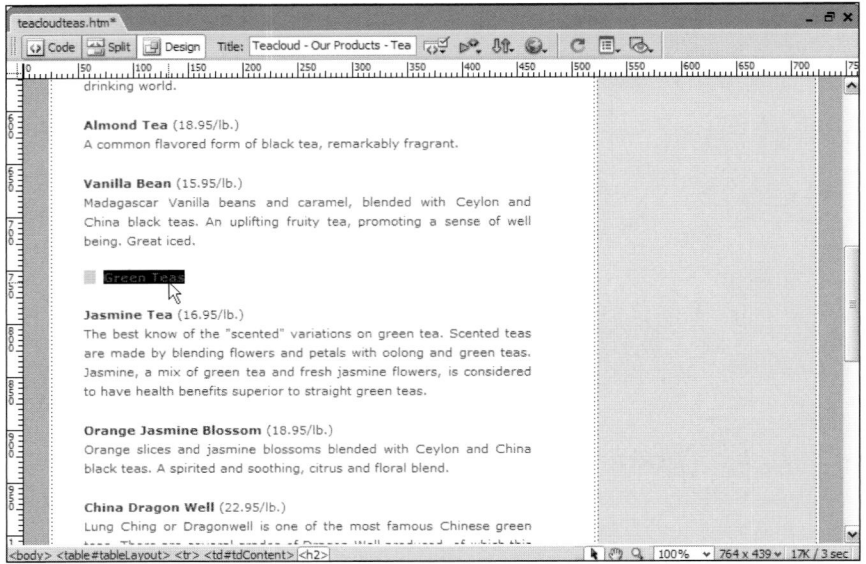

5 Scroll down the page until you find the **Green Teas** text. Click and drag to highlight the text.

You'll insert another named anchor here, so users can easily jump to the Green Teas section of the page.

---

6 Choose **Insert > Named Anchor** to open the **Named Anchor** dialog box. Type **greenteas** in the **Anchor name** field and click **OK**.

As you can see, there are several ways to create named anchors in Dreamweaver 8. You can use the Insert menu, as you did here, or you can use the Named Anchor button on the Insert panel as you did in Step 3.

---

7 Scroll farther down the page and find the **Oolong Teas** text. Click and drag to highlight the text and choose **Insert > Named Anchor** to open the **Named Anchor** dialog box. Type **oolongteas** in the **Anchor name** field and click **OK**.

Tip: Dreamweaver 8 also has a handy keyboard shortcut for inserting named anchors—**Ctrl+Alt+A** (Windows) or **Option+Cmd+A** (Mac). If you're creating a lot of named anchors, you'll find this keyboard shortcut very helpful!

Now that you've identified your named anchors, you need to create the sections of the page they will link to. You'll learn how in the next steps.

---

8 Scroll to the top of the page. Place your cursor at the end of the last sentence in the first paragraph and type **Feel free to browse our Black, Green, and Oolong teas.**

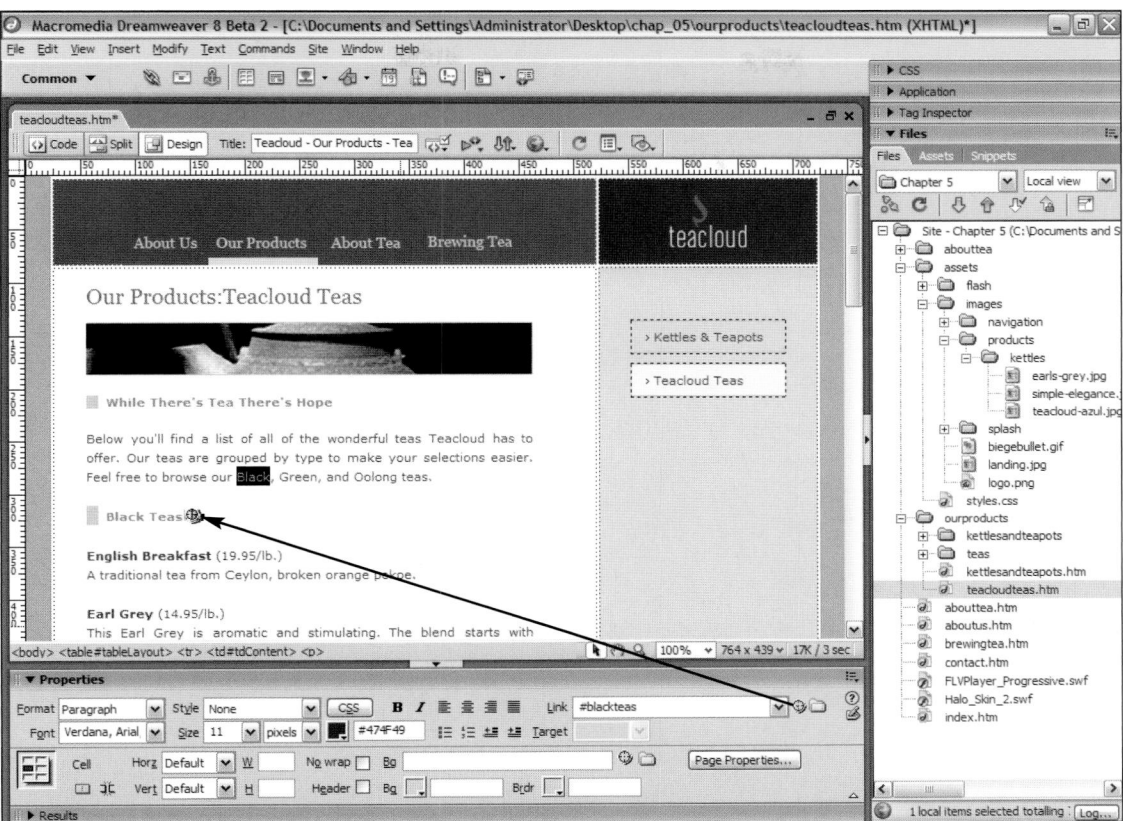

9 Click and drag to highlight the word **Black** in the line of text you typed in Step 8. In the **Property Inspector**, click and drag the **Point to File** icon onto the anchor marker after the **Black Teas** text. When you release the mouse, you'll automatically create the link between the text you highlighted and the **blackteas** named anchor you created in Steps 3 and 4.

Notice the link field in the Property Inspector has a pound sign (#) before the anchor name. Links to named anchors always begin with # to identify the link as a named anchor.

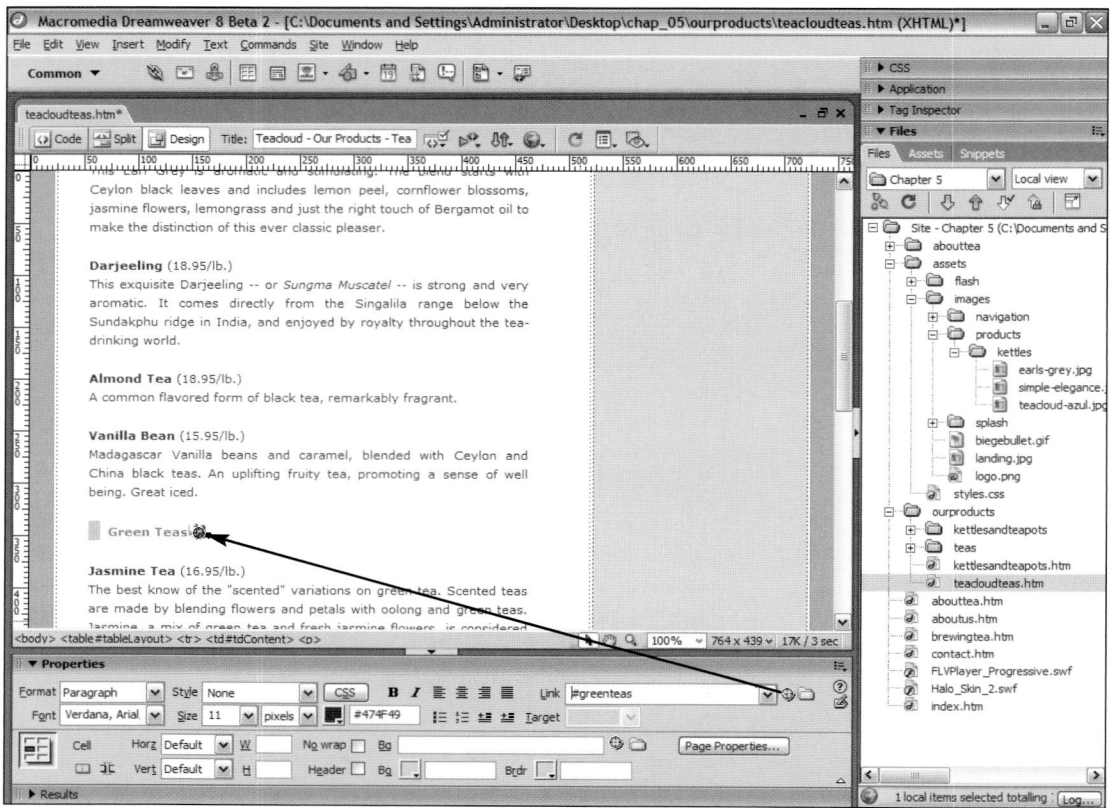

10 Click and drag to highlight the word **Green** in the text you typed in Step 8. In the **Property Inspector**, click and drag the **Point to File** icon onto the anchor marker after the **Green Teas** text. (If you can't see the anchor, just hold the mouse below the bottom of the document and Dreamweaver will scroll the document for you.) When you release the mouse, you'll automatically create the link between the text you highlighted and the **greenteas** named anchor.

---

11 Using the same technique, create a link from the **Oolong Teas** text to the **oolongteas** named anchor.

---

12 Press **F12** to preview the page in a browser. Click each of the links at the top to see how the named anchors work.

As you can see, named anchors are a nice way to jump to different sections within a single page. But wouldn't it also be nice if you had links to a named anchor that would take you back to the top of the page from anywhere else on the page? You will learn how in the next few steps.

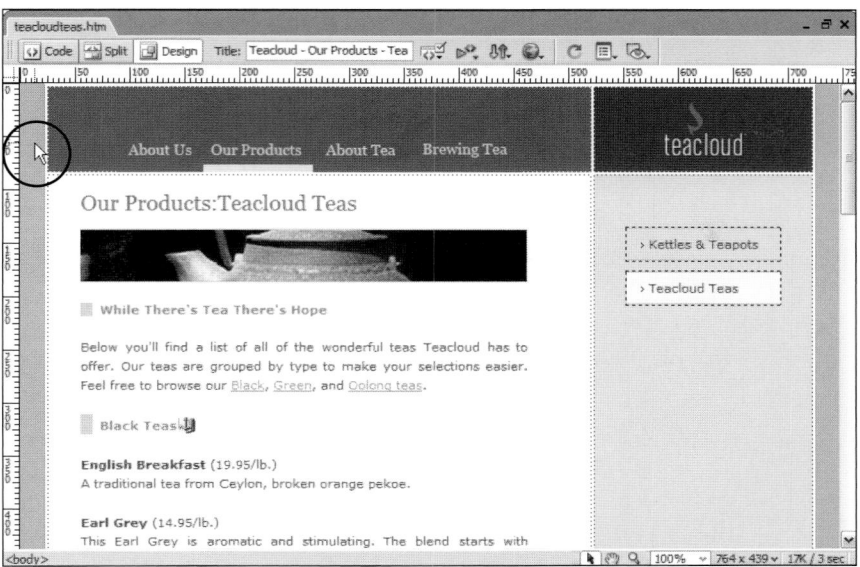

13 Close the browser and return to Dreamweaver 8. Click the upper-left corner of the document (to the left of the table containing all the content for the page) to place your cursor at the very beginning of the document.

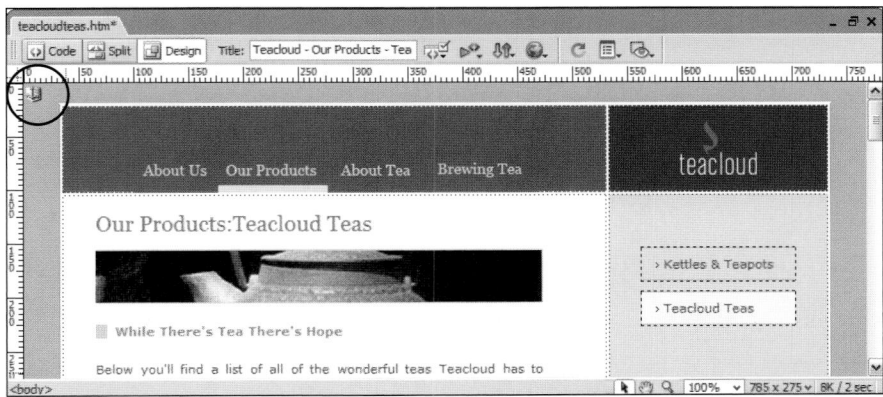

14 Choose **Insert > Named Anchor** to open the **Named Anchor** dialog box. Type **top** in the **Anchor name** field and click **OK**.

You now have a yellow anchor marker at the top of the page.

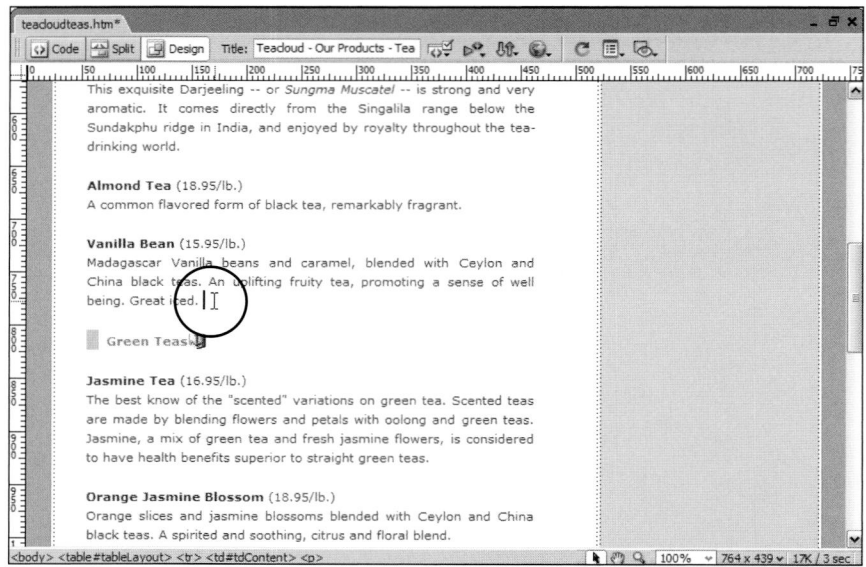

15 Scroll down the page until you find the **Vanilla Bean** text. Place your cursor at the end of the description and press **Enter** (Windows) or **Return** (Mac) to create a new paragraph.

16 In the **Common** group of the **Insert** bar, click the **Hyperlink** button to open the **Hyperlink** dialog box.

Using the Hyperlink dialog box is just another way to link to named anchors. Earlier in this exercise, you used the Point to File icon. The Hyperlink dialog box achieves the same result. As you've learned throughout this book, Dreamweaver 8 offers many ways to accomplish the same task!

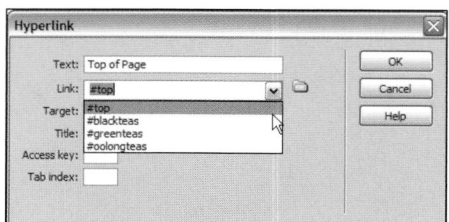

17 Type **Top of Page** in the **Text** field. Choose **#top** from the **Link** pop-up menu and click **OK**.

Because the Hyperlink dialog box shows you a list of all the named anchors in the current document, you can easily link directly to them. You can also easily create links in their entirety—text, **<a>** tags, the whole thing. The value in the Text field is added to the page with the **<a>** tag wrapped around it.

18 Using the techniques you learned in Steps 15, 16, and 17, create two more "top of page" links for the **Green Teas** and **Oolong Teas** paragraphs.

Adding these links will make it easy for visitors to move quickly between the different tea varieties, since they can click a link to jump directly to the section they're after.

---

19 Press **F12** to preview the page in a browser, and try clicking all of the links.

As you click each of the links, the browser will automatically scroll to the position of the anchor you clicked.

---

20 Return to Dreamweaver 8. Close **teacloudteas.htm**. You don't need to save your changes.

VIDEO: **anchor.mov**

To learn more about creating named anchors, check out **anchor.mov** located in the **videos** folder on the **HOT CD-ROM**.

5 | Linking to Files

In addition to creating links to XHTML pages, you may need to link to a file. For example, maybe you have a PDF (**P**ortable **D**ocument **F**ormat) brochure for users to download, or you want to let them download an entire folder of stuffed or zipped images. The possibilities are endless. The good news is that linking to files is just as easy as linking to other XHTML pages. This exercise shows you how.

---

1 In the **Files** panel, double-click **kettlesandteapots.htm** to open it. If you completed Exercise 2, the file should match the illustration here. If you haven't completed Exercise 2, not to worry, you can still follow along with the exercise. You'll just see placeholder graphics instead of the teapot images on the left side of the page.

This page contains a table with information about some of the kettles and teapots that are available from teacloud.com. You are going to create a link to a PDF file, containing similar information to what you see in the site. PDFs are a perfect format for printing.

---

2 At the top of the page, place your cursor after **While There's Tea There's Hope** and press **Enter** (Windows) or **Return** (Mac) to create a new paragraph.

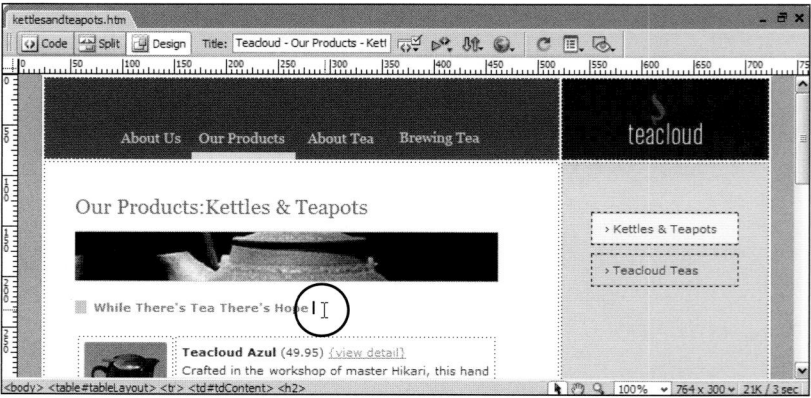

---

3 Type the text **View a PDF version of our Kettles & Teapots brochure.**

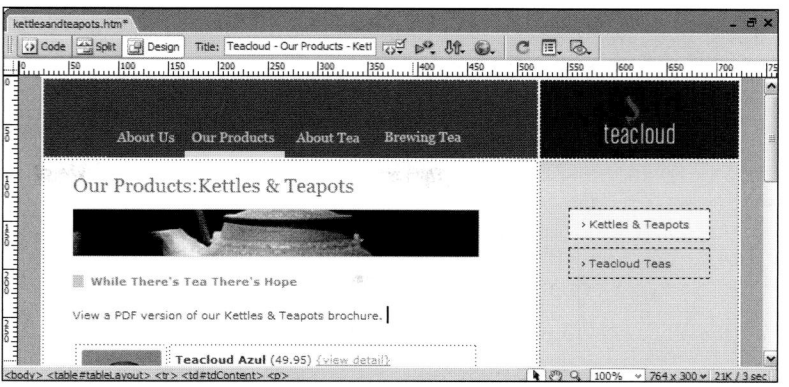

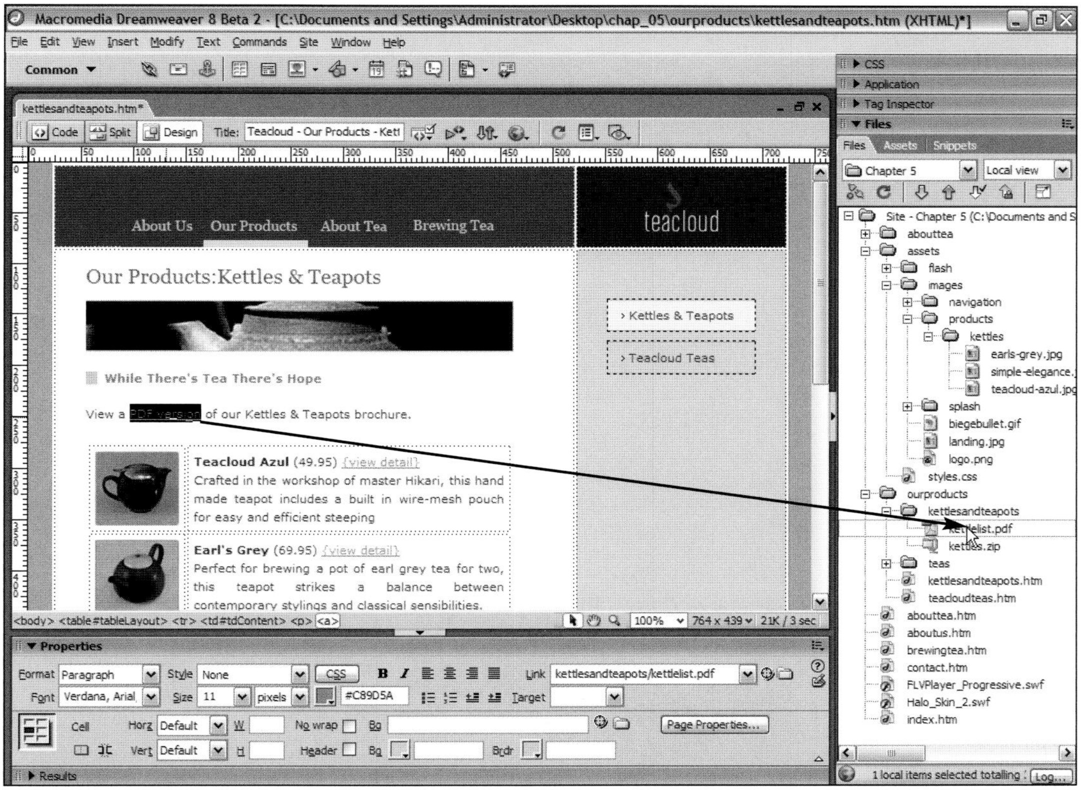

4 Click and drag to highlight the **PDF version** text you created in Step 3. Hold down the **Shift** key and click and drag the highlighted text onto the **kettlelist.pdf** file, which is located in the **ourproducts** folder in the **kettlesandteapots** folder. If the folders are not expanded, pause as you drag over each folder to expand the contents of the folder.

This linking method is identical to the one you learned earlier in this chapter with the Point to File option in the Property Inspector.

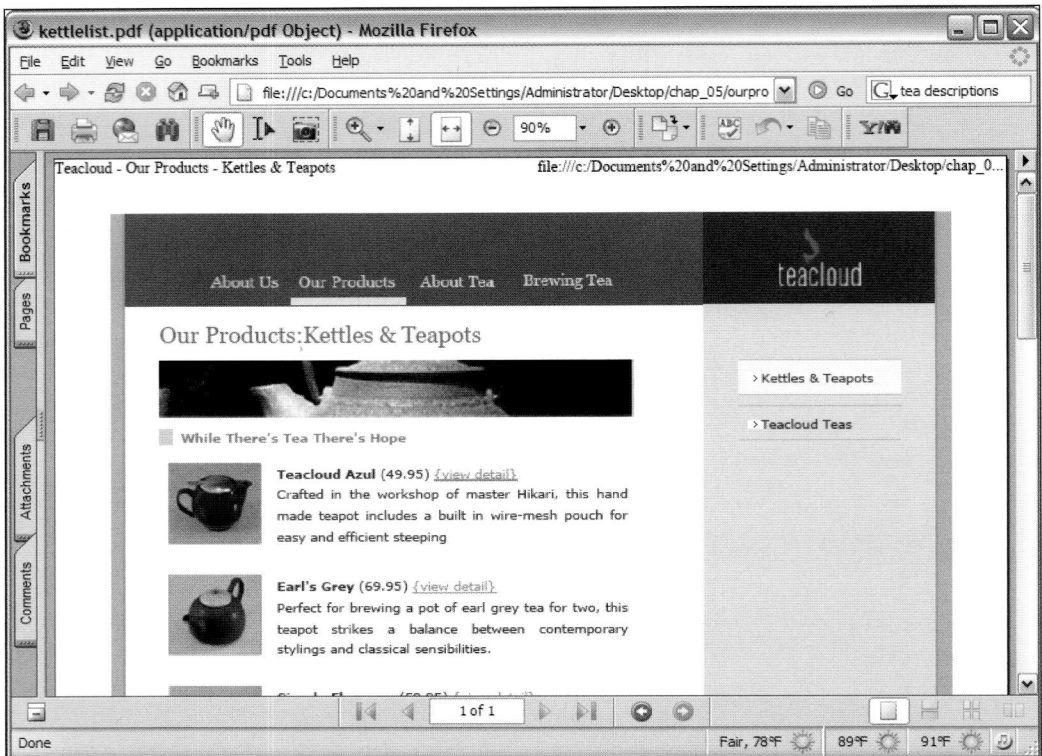

5 Press **F12** to preview this page in a browser. Click the link to the PDF.

Clicking a link that points to a PDF file automatically launches the Adobe Reader plug-in if it's installed in your browser. If it's not installed, and you get an error or the browser asks you where you want to download the file when you click the link, you'll need to download Adobe Reader from **http://www.adobe.com/reader** (it's free). You should also consider adding a link to the Adobe Reader download area to your page so users can download the plug-in if they don't already have it installed.

TIP:

Creating PDF Files

In this exercise, you have learned how to create and view a link to a PDF file, but you did not learn how to create the PDF file. Creating PDF files is a pretty easy process; you just need the right software.

If you think you'll create PDF files often, you might want to purchase the full version of Adobe Acrobat. Adobe Acrobat is a PDF authoring tool sold by Adobe; it lets you create PDF files from almost any application.

For more information about how to create PDFs from Adobe Acrobat, use the three-day pass to the lynda.com Online Training Library provided in the Introduction of this book and check out the following video-training resources:

Acrobat 7 Essential Training with Garrick Chow

New in Acrobat 7 with Garrick Chow

Learning Acrobat 6 with Garrick Chow

Or, you can create PDF files online for free at Adobe's Web site at **http://createpdf.adobe.com**.

For Mac OS X users, you can create PDFs from any application. Here's how:

1. Choose **File > Print** to open the **Print** dialog box.

2. Choose **Save as PDF** from the **PDF** button pop-up menu (Mac OS X 10.4 Tiger) or click the **Save as PDF** button (Mac OS X 10.3 Panther) at the bottom of the **Print** dialog box to open the **Save** dialog box.

3. Choose a location and type a filename in the **Save** dialog box. Click **Save**.

For more information about how to create PDFs from any application on Mac OS X, use the three-day pass to the lynda.com Online Training Library provided in the Introduction of this book and check out Mac OS X 10.4 Tiger Essential Training with Sean Collins.

In the following steps, you will learn how to create a link to a file of compressed images. Using a compressed file format lets you transfer large amounts of data, such as images, with a smaller file size. Two of the most common formats are SIT (StuffIt) files for the Mac, and ZIP files for both the Mac and PC. For this exercise, you'll use ZIP files, but the same concepts apply when you're working with SIT files.

6 Place your cursor at the end of the **View a PDF version of our Kettles & Teapots brochure** text you added earlier in this exercise. Press **Ctrl+Enter** (Windows) or **Ctrl+Return** (Mac) to create a new line break. Type **You can download images of all of our Teacloud teapots in a zip file.**

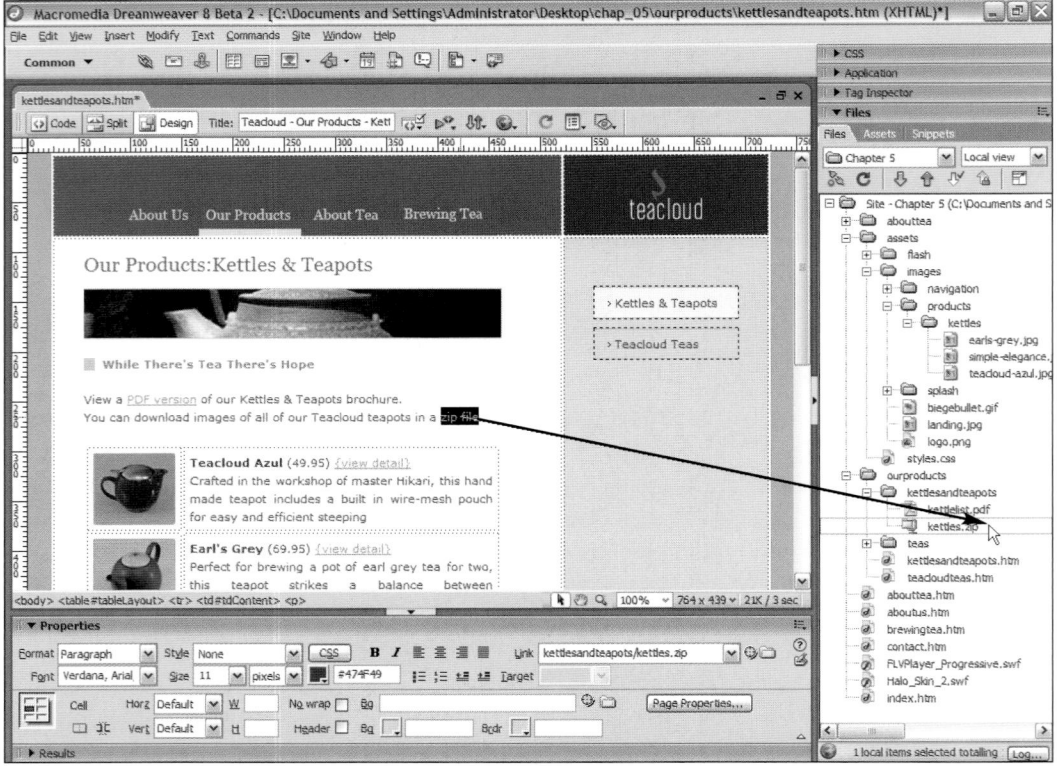

7 Click and drag to select the words **zip file**. Using any of the linking methods you learned in this chapter, create a link to the **kettles.zip** file located inside the **kettlesandteapots** folder.

8 Press **F12** to preview the page in a browser. Click the link to the **zip file**. You'll automatically be prompted to save the file on your hard drive. (For users visiting your site, they can simply click **Save** to save the file.) Click **Cancel** to abort the download.

TIP: | **Creating ZIP Files**

When you have a large file or a collection of files you want to share for download, compress the files so the download goes as quickly and smoothly as possible. Both Windows XP and Mac OS X natively support opening and creating ZIP files. If you're using Windows 2000, you can you can use WinZip (**http://www.winzip.com**) to open and create ZIP files. Here's how:

Windows: Right-click the file or folder of files you want to zip. Choose **Winzip > Add to zip file** from the contextual menu. In the dialog box that appears, give the Zip file a name and click **OK** to create your ZIP file.

Mac: Ctrl+click or **right-click** the file or folder of files you want to zip. Choose **Create Archive of** from the contextual menu. Mac OS X will automatically create a ZIP file for you!

---

9 Close **kettlesandteapots.htm**. You don't need to save your changes.

VIDEO: | **image_maps.mov**

One type of linking not covered in this chapter is image maps. Image maps let you link to multiple locations from a single image. For more information about how to create image maps, check out **image_maps.mov** in the **videos** folder on the **HOT CD-ROM**.

In this chapter, you learned how to link to files in numerous ways. You can use the Point to File feature in the Property Inspector, browse for files directly, or use the Hyperlink dialog box to create an entire link in one shot. In the next chapter, you'll begin learning about Cascading Style Sheets, the basis for any good site design.

6

Cascading Style Sheets

CSS (**C**ascading **S**tyle **S**heets) is a standard defined by the World Wide Web Consortium (W3C) that lets you separate the structure of your page from the presentation. As a result, you can develop an XHTML document that knows nothing about its colors, fonts, font sizes, or even where elements should be positioned. All of the styling and presentation information is handled by the rules defined in a CSS file. Why would you want to do this? If, for example, you want all the text in your document to be blue and all the headlines to be green, with standard HTML you would have to go through the elements on the page one-by-one and assign those colors to the text using **<font>** tags, which can clutter up your pages. Using style sheets, you can redefine all the elements in the entire document (or an entire Web site!) to turn blue with just one CSS rule and then perform the same single step for the headlines to turn green. You can even use CSS to control the color and background image for a page.

The CSS specification offers more control over type than XHTML tags do. With styles, you can specify the amount of space between lines of type (line height), and you can specify the size of the type in pixels, points, ems, or even inches. Anyone yearning for more control over typography is going to be drawn to using styles. (And an entire chapter on typography is coming up next.)

But CSS can help you do much more than just control type on your page. With CSS, you can create rollovers that would normally require a bunch of images and JavaScript. You will get a chance to do just that in the last exercise of this chapter. You can even use CSS to lay out entire Web pages. CSS has come a long way, and with much improved browser support today, you should definitely be using CSS on all your Web pages.

CSS Specifications

The W3C has released several recommendations for Cascading Style Sheets: CSS 1, CSS 2, and CSS 3. The CSS 1 recommendation was formalized December 17, 1996, and revised on January 11, 1999. It contains about 50 properties. The CSS 2 recommendation was formalized on May 12, 1998. It contains about 120 properties, including those from the CSS 1 recommendation. The CSS 3 specification isn't yet finished, and most browsers won't support the new properties created in the specification. You'll be using CSS 2 throughout this book, which is well supported by modern browsers and degrades quite gracefully in older browsers, meaning it won't cause an error even if it doesn't display as you'd like.

If you're interested, take the time to read the CSS 2 recommendations to learn what's possible with CSS, review CSS code examples, and learn about compatibility issues. However, we should warn you that these documents are very technical and make for boring reading. If you prefer something a bit more digestible, you should invest in a good CSS book, such as *Eric Meyer on CSS* and *More Eric Meyer on* CSS, both written by—you guessed it—Eric Meyer. Another great CSS book is *Cascading Style Sheets—Designing for the Web (Second Edition)*, written by Hakon Wium Lie and Bert Box.

You can find the CSS 2 recommendations online at **http://www.w3.org/Style/CSS/**.

The Cascading Part of Style Sheets

The term *cascading* in Cascading Style Sheets refers to how browsers interpret your style sheet. When you use multiple style sheets (such as inline and external, which you'll learn about later in this chapter) conflicts can arise, and the browser has to know which style sheet to honor. The *cascading* part of CSS refers to which rules the browser follows when it encounters conflicting CSS information. The rules are complex, and describing them here would require more space than we

have room for in this book. If you are interested in learning more about the rules for the cascading structure, visit **http://www.w3.org/TR/CSS21/cascade.html#cascade**. Understanding the cascade and specificity (how specific a rule is) can be a complicated and daunting subject. You'll get to work with it on a minimal basis in this book, but it's a subject well worth digging deeper into when you have the time.

Anatomy of a Style Sheet

The anatomy of a style sheet includes some terminology that is likely new to you, such as declarations and selectors. Here are some examples of how these terms relate to style sheet programming.

At the very core of CSS are **rules**. Here is an example of a simple CSS rule:

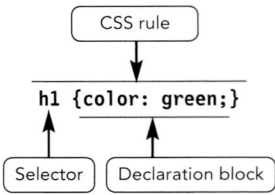

Rules consist of two parts: the **selector** and the **declaration block**. In this example, the **h1** (the Heading 1 tag) is the selector—it selects the **<h1>** elements on the page. The information contained in the brackets is the declaration—it modifies how the selector styles elements on a page. In this example, the selector selects all the Heading 1 elements on the page and modifies the color property of each to green, as specified in the declaration block.

A declaration block can contain multiple declarations, which are each made up of two parts: a property and a value, followed by a semicolon. Notice a colon separates the property from the value.

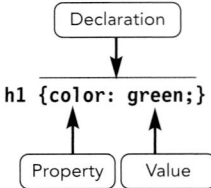

The **property** identifies what to change, such as color, and the **value** instructs the browser how to change it. In this example, the property identifies the **color** of the **<h1>** tag as the property to be changed, and the value instructs the browser to change the color to **green**.

This example is very simple but shows you the three basic parts of any CSS rule: the selector, the declaration block, and a series of declarations consisting of properties and values. You can add as many declarations inside a declaration block as you want. Here are some more-complex rules that set all of the properties for the **<h1>** tag in the Teacloud site.

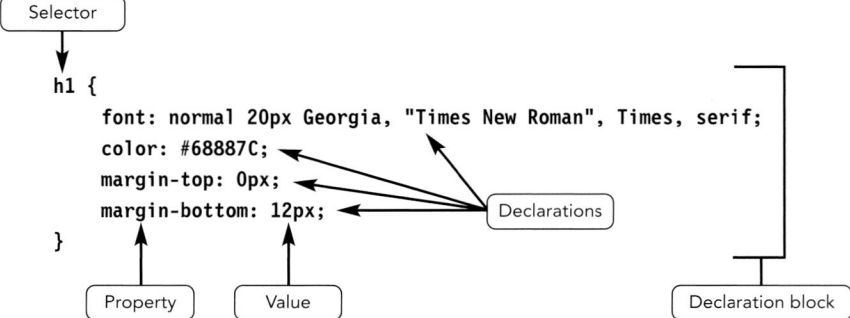

Even though the rules are far more complex, they still have the same basic parts: the selector, the declaration block, and the declarations. The declaration block simply has more declarations defined, each separated by a semicolon. Though it's helpful to use line breaks to separate the declarations, they're not required. You could have all of your declarations on the same line as long as they're separated by semicolons.

1 | Understanding CSS and Page Properties

This exercise gives you a gentle introduction to CSS in Dreamweaver 8. Although this exercise covers a lot of information, you will see how you can use CSS almost transparently to control the basic formatting of a Web page. For example, by simply setting the various page properties, Dreamweaver 8 automatically creates an embedded style sheet to handle formatting tasks, such as setting page background colors, font types and sizes, and page margins. As you will see in this exercise, it's very easy to separate the structure of a page from its presentation with CSS.

1 Copy the **chap_06** folder from the **HOT CD-ROM** to your **Desktop**. Define your site as **Chapter 6** using the **chap_06** folder as the local root folder. Make sure the **Files** panel is open. If it's not, choose **Window > Files** or press **F11**.

2 In the **Files** panel, double-click **abouttea.htm** in **chap_06** folder to open it.

This page contains the layout for the Teacloud site, but no other formatting, such as fonts, font color, background color, link color, or heading color, has been applied to the elements on the page. Unfortunately, this makes for a less than inspiring visual appeal. Not to worry, in this exercise you'll change these attributes using CSS.

3 In the **Property Inspector**, click the **Page Properties** button, or choose **Modify > Page Properties**, to open the **Page Properties** dialog box.

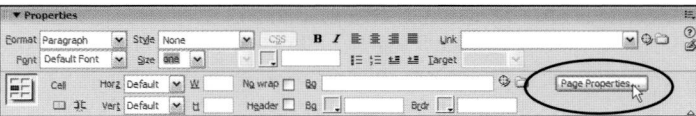

Before you start poking around the various Page Properties options, you need to understand exactly what you are about to do here. To the casual eye, it looks like you are doing nothing more than setting some very basic formatting options, such as background color, text color, background image, and so on. But, in fact, you are doing much more. By setting the page properties in this dialog box, you are asking Dreamweaver 8 to create an embedded style sheet and apply those styles to the various elements on the page.

Remember—an embedded style sheet sets options for the entire page. For example, if you choose a font list in this window (which you will be asked to do in the next step), such as Verdana, Arial, Helvetica, sans-serif, that font list will become the default font for all the text on your page. As you are about to see, with just a few clicks of the mouse you can create a rather complex and visually pleasing internal style sheet.

4 In the **Category** list, select **Appearance**. Choose **Verdana, Arial, Helvetica, sans-serif** from the **Page font** pop-up menu.

Specifying a page font determines the default font for the text on the page.

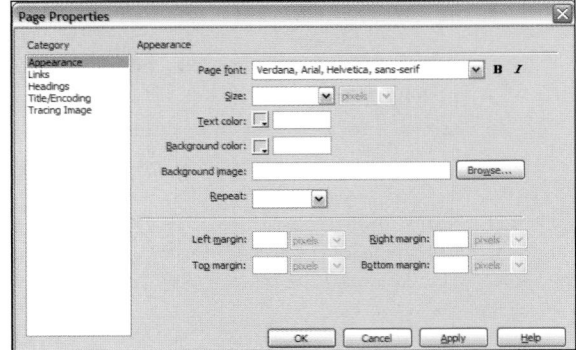

5 Type **11** in the **Size** field and make sure **pixels** is selected in the Size pop-up menu as shown in the illustration here.

Size sets the default size of the text on your page: 11 pixels is a nice size for most large bodies of onscreen text.

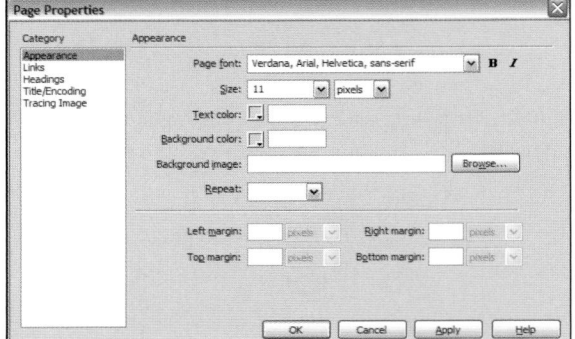

6 Type **#474F49**, which is the hexadecimal value for a dark green, in the **Text color** field. Type **#BEC2C2**, which is a light grayish color, in the **Background color** field.

7 Type **0** in the **Left margin**, **Right margin**, **Top margin**, and **Bottom margin** fields. Make sure **pixels** is selected in each pop-up menu as shown in the illustration here.

Setting the margins to 0 ensures the page is flush with all four edges of the browser. If you don't want the page flush with the browser, set the margins to a value higher than 0.

Tip: If you want to preview the changes you've made, click **Apply.** This lets you see the changes to your page without closing the Page Properties dialog box.

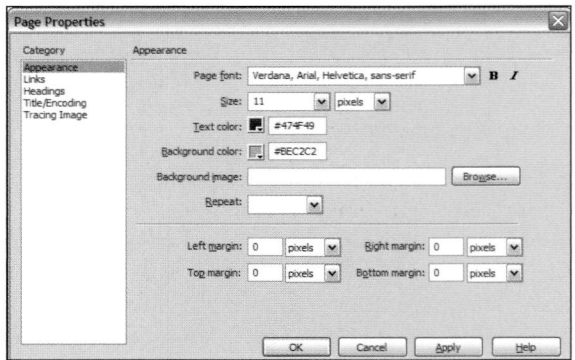

Now that you've finished specifying the Appearance attributes, next you'll set attributes for Links.

8 In the **Category** list, select **Links**.

Notice the contents of the Page Properties dialog box change so you can control how the links on your Web page appear. We like the way the Page Properties dialog box is organized into various categories—it gives you quick access to a lot of features without causing hysterical blindness.

---

9 Type **#C89D5A** in the **Link color** field, **#CFA970** in the **Visited links** field, **#9F7535** in the **Rollover links** field, and **#474F49** in the **Active links** field.

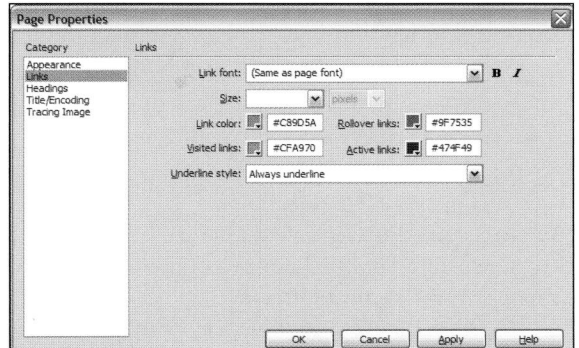

Link color specifies the color for all unvisited links on the page. Visited links specifies the color for any link a user has visited. Rollover links changes the link color when a user moves (or "hovers," in CSS-speak) his or her mouse over the link. Active links changes the link color as users click a link (with the mouse depressed), so it is less important than the Link color and Visited links color.

---

10 Choose **Hide underline on rollover** from the **Underline style** pop-up menu.

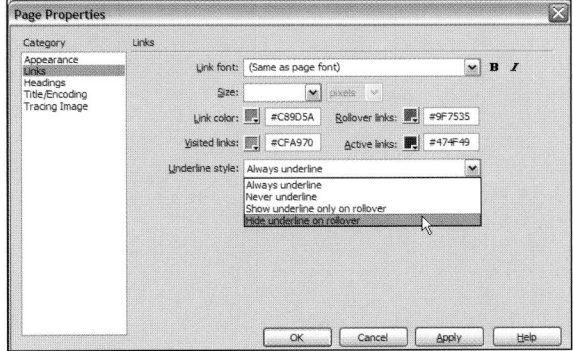

Underline style lets you control what happens to the line underneath the links when users move their mouse over the links on a page. By default, this option is set to Always underline, which causes the underline to be visible at all times. As you can probably guess, Hide underline on rollover, which you specified here, hides the underline when users move their mouse over a link.

Now that you've finished specifying the Link attributes, next you'll set attributes for Headings.

---

11 In the **Category** list, select **Headings**. Choose **Georgia, Times New Roman, Times, serif** from the **Heading font** pop-up menu. Type **20** in the **Heading 1** field, make sure **pixels** is selected in the size pop-up menu, and type **#68887C** in the **Heading 1 Color** field. Type **11** in the **Heading 2** field, make sure **pixels** is selected in the size pop-up menu and type **#949D87** in the **Heading 2 Color** field.

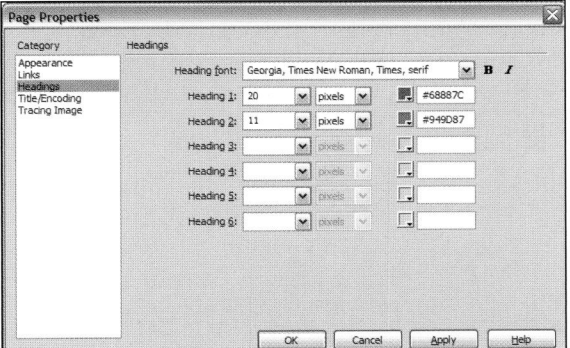

These options set the font, font size, and color for all headings in the document. Headings help identify and separate different areas of text on a page. As a result, you want to specify fonts and font sizes that are different, but still complementary to the ones you specified for the body text in the Appearance pane.

12 Click **OK** to accept these settings and close the **Page Properties** dialog box.

As you can see, the options you specified in the Page Properties dialog box have been automatically applied to the **abouttea.htm** page. With a single click, you now have the basic formatting for your page. It's not much to look at yet, but don't worry, you have still have lots to do.

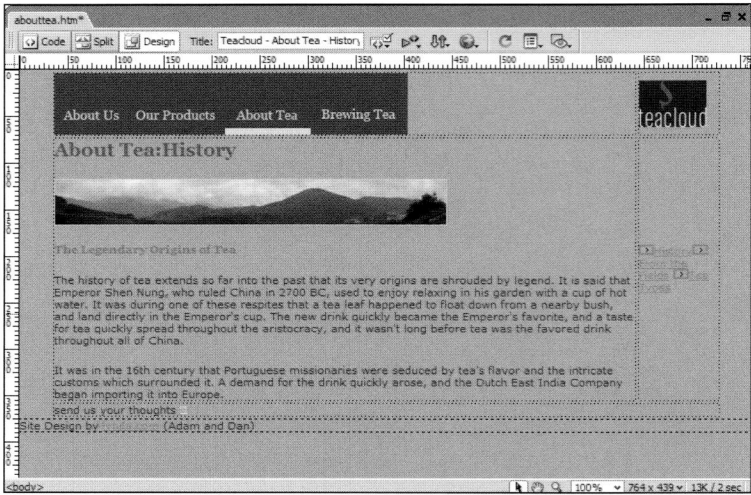

13 Press **F12** to preview the page in a browser.

Although Dreamweaver 8 does a great job at rendering CSS code within the Design view, there are some things it cannot render, such as the Rollover link color and underline effects. When you are done marveling at your hard work, exit the browser and return to Dreamweaver 8.

Even though you may not have been thinking about it or even aware of it, Dreamweaver 8 was building an embedded CSS style sheet as you changed the

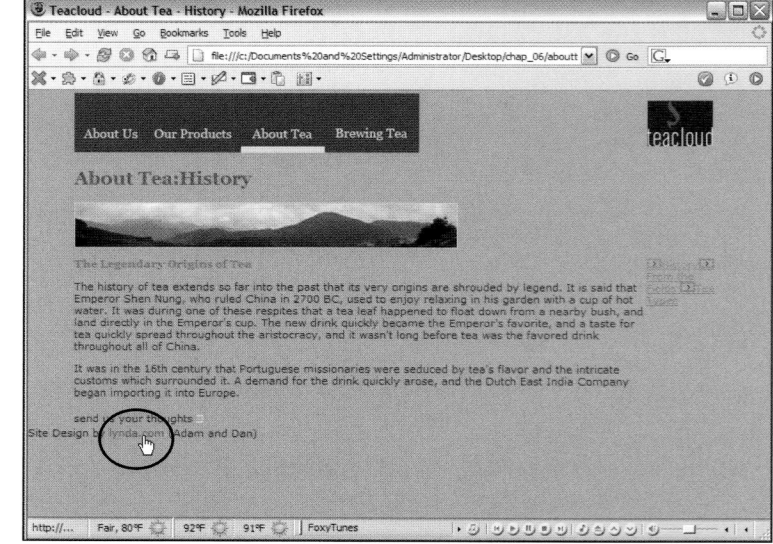

various page properties settings. Heck, you didn't even have to do anything except pick a few colors and options. This is a great example of how Dreamweaver 8 encourages you to use CSS to control the formatting and presentation of your Web pages.

14 In the **Document** toolbar, click the **Code** button to display the code for this page. If you have to, scroll to the top of the page (about line 32) so you can locate the embedded CSS code. Take a moment and read through the CSS code that was generated. As you can see, CSS pretty easy to read and follow.

All of this CSS code was created by Dreamweaver 8 automatically, and because it was placed inside the **<head>** tag of this document and affects only the formatting of this one document, it is referred to as an *embedded* style sheet. You'll learn about different types of style sheets, including embedded, inline, and external, later in this chapter.

```
32  <style type="text/css">
33  body,td,th {
34      font-family: Verdana, Arial, Helvetica, sans-serif;
35      font-size: 11px;
36      color: #474F49;
37  }
38  body {
39      background-color: #BEC2C2;
40      margin-left: 0px;
41      margin-top: 0px;
42      margin-right: 0px;
43      margin-bottom: 0px;
44  }
45  a:link {
46      color: #C89D5A;
47      text-decoration: underline;
48  }
49  a:visited {
50      text-decoration: underline;
51      color: #CFA970;
52  }
53  a:hover {
54      text-decoration: none;
55      color: #9F7535;
56  }
57  a:active {
58      text-decoration: underline;
```

TIP: | **Instant CSS Reference**

If you are new to CSS or just need a quick reference, Dreamweaver 8 includes a copy of the O'Reilly CSS reference guide (and a bunch of other O'Reilly guides). How convenient is that? No more lugging around fat books. Choose **Window > Reference** to open the **Reference** panel—go figure. You can also place your cursor inside any CSS rule or declaration and press **Shift+F1**—the CSS reference will go straight to the proper section.

---

15 In the **Document** toolbar, click the **Design** button to return to the visual editing environment.

There you go folks—you have made it through your first CSS lesson, and you didn't even have to type a single line of code—sweet!

---

16 Save your changes and keep **abouttea.htm** open for the next exercise.

Although this exercise was a great introduction to CSS in Dreamweaver 8, there is one potentially serious problem with using this workflow. Using CSS to set the page properties is a great thing to do, but the problem with this technique is that it forces you to create an embedded style sheet, which prohibits you from utilizing one of the most powerful features of CSS: applying the same styles to multiple pages. If you want all of the pages in your site to use the same page formatting options you set up in this exercise, you should use an external style sheet. Why? Because then you have to define the CSS just once and then apply it to other pages via a linked external style sheet. Using the workflow in this exercise would require that you repeat this process for every page in your site, which is a very inefficient way to work.

Don't panic! There's an easy solution! The next exercise shows you how to export the CSS code from this page to an external style sheet and then apply that style sheet to other pages. This will give you a real-world look at how things should really be done and still let you use this convenient workflow to get there.

The Page Properties Dialog Box

The Page Properties dialog box does more than just set the colors of the links and text. This handy chart provides an explanation of all the properties you can set for a page:

Category	Property	Description
HTML/XHTML Page Properties		
Appearance		
	Page font	Sets the font face for the entire document. By default, all elements in the page will be formatted with this font.
	Size	Sets the default font size for the entire document.
	Text color	Sets the default text color for the entire document. The values can be in hexadecimal format or by name, such as red, white, and so on.
	Background color	Sets the background color of the document. The values can be in hexadecimal format or by name, such as red, white, and so on.
	Background image	Sets a background image for your Web page. A background image can be any GIF or JPEG file. If the image is smaller than the browser panel, it will repeat (tile) by default.
	Repeat	Determines whether the background image specified for the page should repeat in a fashion other than the default. You can specify that an image not repeat at all, or that it repeat on either the x or y axis of the document.
	Left margin	Sets the left margin value for the document.
	Top margin	Sets the top margin value for the document.
	Right margin	Sets the right margin value for the document.
	Bottom margin	Sets the bottom margin value for the document.
Links		
	Link font	Sets the default font for all links in the document. You should generally leave this set to (Same as page font). You can also specify whether links should be bold or italic.
	Size	Sets the default size for all links in the document.

continues on next page

	HTML/XHTML Page Properties *continued*	
Category	**Property**	**Description**
	Link color	Sets the color for links.
	Visited links	A visited link color specifies how the link will appear after a visitor has clicked it.
	Rollover links	Sets the color for links when the user's mouse is hovering over the link.
	Active links	The active link color specifies how the link will appear while someone clicks it.
	Underline style	Determines how underlines are handled for all links in the document.
Headings		
	Heading font	Sets the font face for all headings in the document
	Heading 1–6	Sets the size and color for all headings in the document.
Title/Encoding		
	Title	Sets the title of your page that will appear in the title bar of the browser and when your page is bookmarked. This name can contain as many characters as you want, including special characters such as %(#*!.
	Document Type (DTD)	Sets the document type for the current document.
	Encoding	Specifies the language for the characters and fonts used in the document.
	Unicode Normalization Form	The setting determines how Unicode characters are handled in UTF-8 documents. You can find out more about Unicode Normalization at **www.unicode.org/ reports/tr15**.
Tracing Image		
	Tracing image	Creates guides to set up the layout of your page. Tracing images can be any GIF, JPEG, or PNG file.
	Transparency	Sets the transparency level of your tracing image.

Types of Style Sheets

In the previous exercise, you created an embedded style sheet using the Page Properties dialog box in Dreamweaver 8. This method is fine if you're working on a site with a single page, but, chances are, you're developing a number of pages that all need the same formatting. CSS offers three types of style sheets to style your documents, some more efficient than others. Knowing the difference between them is important so you can decide which one is best for your Web projects. The following table outlines the different types of style sheets:

Types of Style Sheets	
Type	**Description**

Embedded	Embedded style sheets are an internal part of the HTML document. All of the code is written inside the **`<head>`** tag of the document and affects only this one page. Some sample embedded CSS code looks like this:
	
	```<style type="text/css">```
	```<!--```
	```h1 {color: blue; font-family: Verdana;}```
	```-->```
	```</style>```
	
	Embedded style sheets are useful if you want to apply styles to a single page only.

External (linked)	External style sheets, also referred to as "linked" style sheets, are the most powerful type of style sheet because you can use a single style sheet to format hundreds, thousands, and even millions of pages. If you make a change to the external style sheet, all of the pages that link to the style sheet are instantly updated to reflect the new style(s). The contents of an external style sheet file looks just like the contents of an embedded style sheet, except they are not part of the HTML page. Instead, they are stored in a separate file with a .css extension instead of an .htm extension. The .css file simply contains a list of styles with no other XHTML code. Instead of embedding the code in the XHTML document, you make a link to the external CSS file. Here's an example: ```<link rel="stylesheet" href="mystyles.css" type="text/css />```

Inline	Inline styles are useful when you want to override some other style definition applied by an embedded or external style sheet, or if you have just one element in your site that's going to use this particular style and it doesn't need to be defined in your style sheet. Inline styles are similar to embedded styles, in that they are part of the XHTML document. However, they are written as an attribute of the tag you want to style. Here is an example of some sample code from an inline style:
	
	```<body>```
	```<h1 style="color: orange; font-family: Verdana">This is some sample text.</h1>```
	```</body>```
	```</html>```
	
	Inline styles are much less powerful than embedded and external style sheets, because if you ever want to change the style, you will have to do it every place the inline style appears in your document. Use inline styles for "one-off" styles that you won't use anywhere else in your entire site.

2 | Exporting and Linking External CSS Files

One of the most powerful features of CSS is linking a single external CSS file to multiple pages. This results in consistent formatting and an incredibly efficient and fast workflow. In the previous exercise, because of the Dreamweaver 8 defaults, you were forced to create an embedded style sheet when you set the various page properties. In this exercise, you will learn how to export the CSS from that page into an external CSS file and then apply the external CSS file to multiple pages. This exercise clearly shows you just how powerful external style sheets and CSS can be.

---

1 If you just completed Exercise 1, **abouttea.htm** should still be open. If it's not, go back and complete Exercise 1.

If a page already contains an embedded style sheet, the process of converting it into an external style sheet is pretty straightforward. Basically, you just export the CSS information into an external CSS file, remove the embedded CSS from the page, and then link the page to the newly exported CSS file. The next few steps walk you through this process.

---

2 Choose **File > Export > CSS Styles** to open the **Export Styles As CSS File** dialog box. Browse to the assets folder inside the **chap_06** folder. Save this file as **styles.css**.

You can save this file anywhere within the local root folder for the site, but it helps to keep all of your style sheets in one folder to keep things neat.

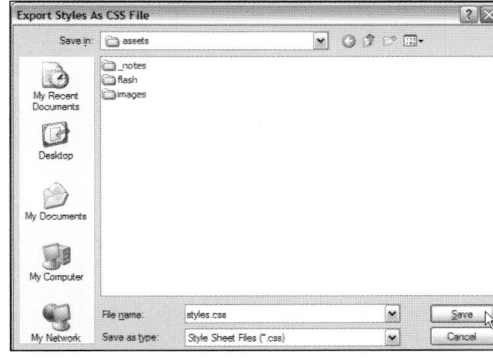

Even though you just exported the style sheet information to an external file, if you view the code for this page you'll find the embedded styles right where you left them. Since you just created an external CSS file and are going to link to that file to apply the formatting to this page and others, there is no need to have the embedded style sheet here. In fact, it can actually create problems later on by causing conflicts with the external style sheet. Get rid of it and use only the new external CSS file.

3 In the **Document** toolbar, click the **Design** button to return the visual editing environment.

---

4 Open the **CSS Styles** panel by choosing **Window > CSS Styles**. Click the **All** button to switch to **All** mode.

Make sure the CSS Styles panel is in All mode.

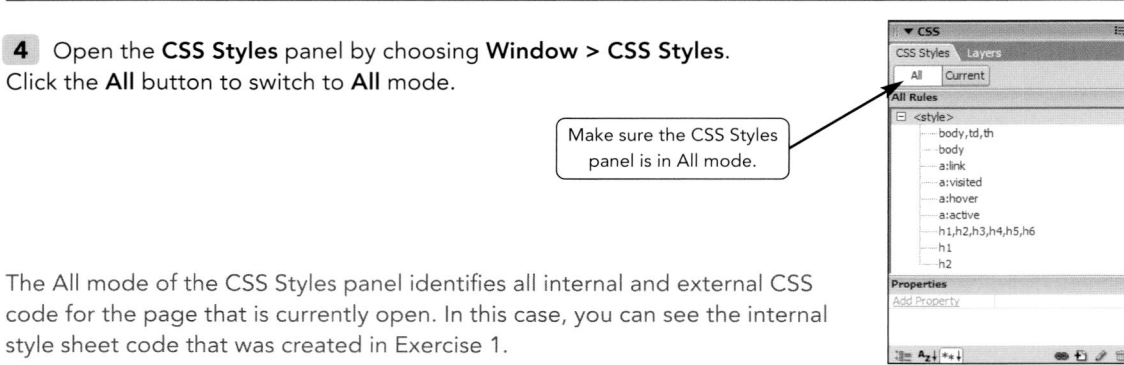

The All mode of the CSS Styles panel identifies all internal and external CSS code for the page that is currently open. In this case, you can see the internal style sheet code that was created in Exercise 1.

---

5 In the **CSS Styles** panel, click the word **<style>** and click the **Trash** icon to remove the internal CSS code from the page.

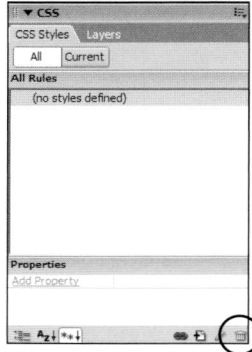

With all the internal CSS code removed from the page, you'll be left with a page that looks identical to the one you started with in Exercise 1—not terribly attractive!

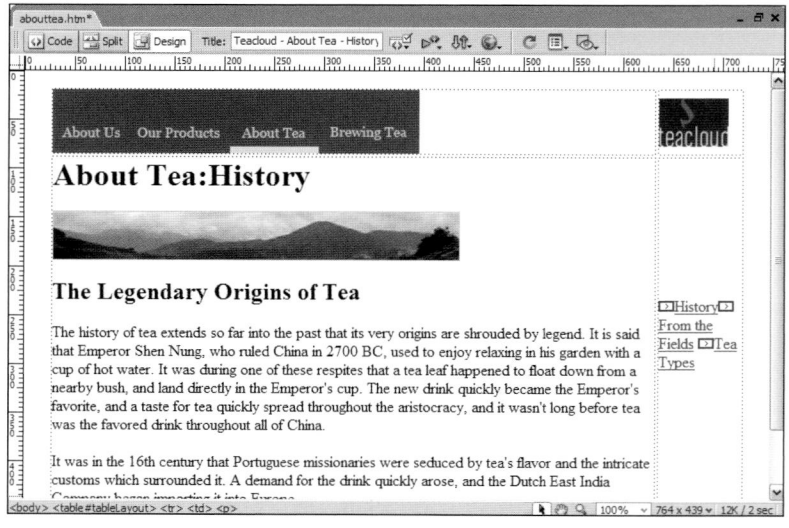

6 In the **CSS Styles** panel, click the **Attach Style Sheet** icon to open the **Attach External Style Sheet** dialog box.

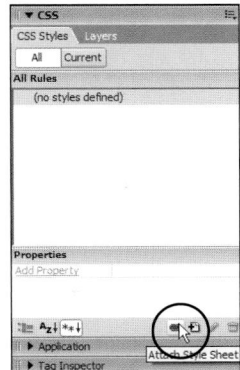

7 In the **Attach External Style Sheet** dialog box, click **Browse** to find and select the file you want to attach.

The Attach External Style Sheet dialog box lets you link to the external style sheet you created earlier.

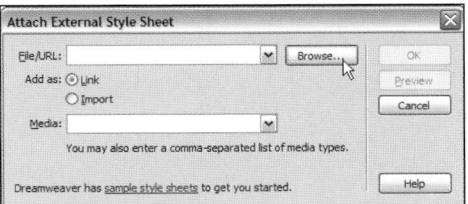

8 Browse to the **chap_06\assets** folder and select the **styles.css** file you exported in Step 2. This file contains all of the CSS you created in Exercise 1. Accept the defaults for the rest of the fields and click **OK** (Windows) or **Choose** (Mac) to select the file and to return to the **Attach External Style Sheet** dialog box.

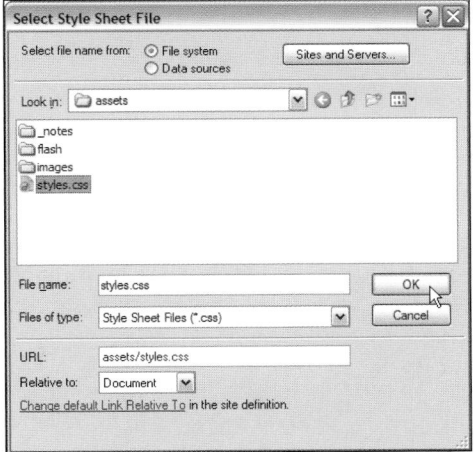

9 Select the **Link** option and leave **Media** blank.

The Import option uses a different syntax for linking to your external style sheets. The Import syntax isn't supported by older browsers, so it's a handy way to hide CSS code that older browsers (particular Netscape 4) don't support. The Media option lets you specify the style sheet for a particular type of media. You'll learn more about these options in Chapter 10, "Designing for Devices."

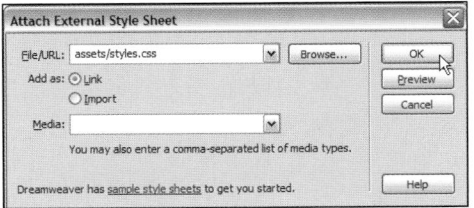

10 Click **OK** to attach the **styles.css** external style sheet to the page.

Your page now looks just like it did at the beginning of the exercise, with the major difference that you now have an external style sheet attached to your page instead of using embedded CSS. Next, you'll apply the **styles.css** external style sheet to other pages on the Teacloud site so you can see the true power of external style sheets.

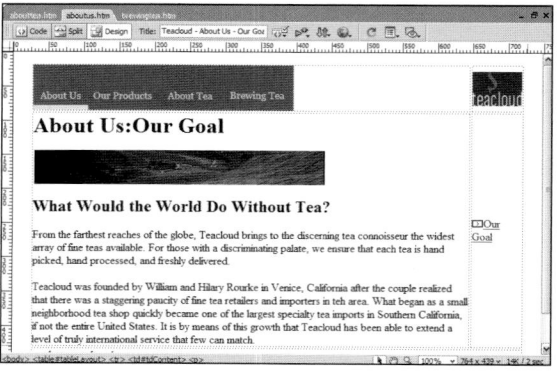 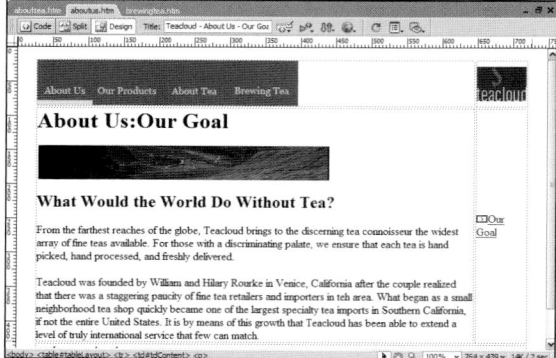

11 In the **Files** panel, double-click to open **aboutus.htm** and **brewingtea.htm**.

These pages are seriously lacking in some formatting. However, because they are part of the same site as the **abouttea.html** page, you'll want to apply the same formatting to these pages so all the pages on the Teacloud site have a consistent appearance. In the next few steps, you'll do just that!

12 Make sure **aboutus.htm** is the active document.

13 In the **CSS Styles** panel, click **Attach Style Sheet** to open the **Attach External Style Sheet** dialog box.

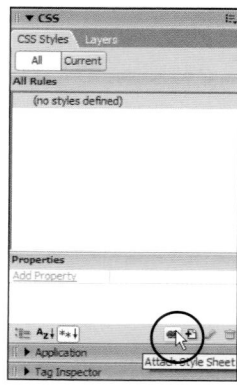

14 Because you already attached an external style sheet earlier, the path to it is already inside the **File/URL** field. Make sure the **Link** radio button is selected and click **OK**.

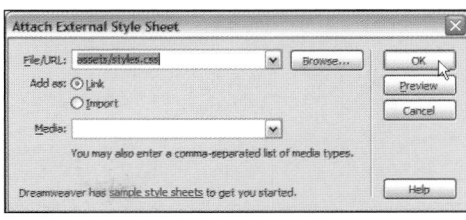

The Attach External Style Sheet dialog box remembers the most recently used external style sheets in the File/URL pop-up menu, which is helpful when you're working on multiple Web pages.

With the external style sheet attached to the **aboutus.htm** page, the page updates immediately and now perfectly matches the formatting of the **abouttea.htm** page. How cool—you just matched the formatting of the **abouttea.htm** page with the click of a button!

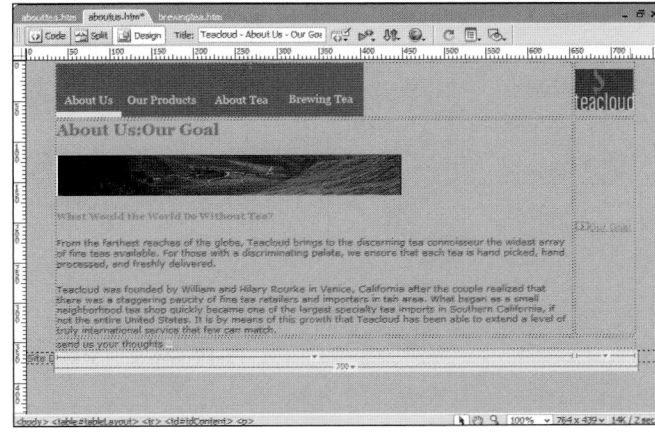

15 Repeat Steps 12, 13, and 14 to attach the **styles.css** external style sheet to **brewingtea.htm**.

As you can see, once you create an external style sheet, it's really easy to apply the same formatting to multiple pages. In fact, you could format hundreds of pages in minutes by simply attaching the external style sheet to each of those pages.

16 In the **CSS Styles** panel in *any* of the documents, click the **body** rule to select it. In the **Properties** pane of the **CSS Styles** panel, click the **color picker** next to **background-color** and choose white, **#FFFFFF**. You'll immediately see the background color change to white in all the documents that link to the **styles.css** external style sheet.

When you change a CSS rule in the CSS Styles panel from a page that links to the external style sheet, Dreamweaver 8 actually changes the code in the external style sheet. By default, it will automatically open the file for you and make the change.

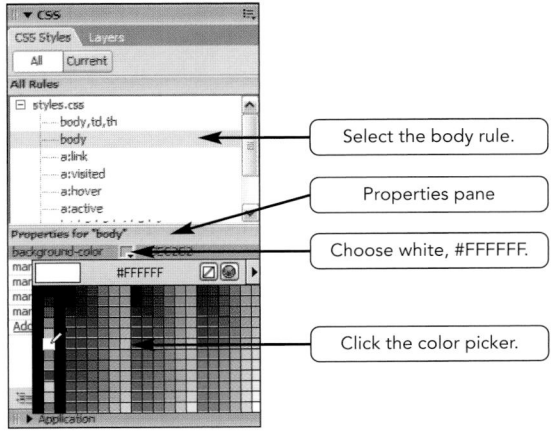

Select the body rule.

Properties pane

Choose white, #FFFFFF.

Click the color picker.

If you look at the top of the Document window, you'll see **styles.css** open and marked with an asterisk, which means that the file has changed. Dreamweaver 8 opens the style sheet for you by default so you can undo any changes you might accidentally make from an external file.

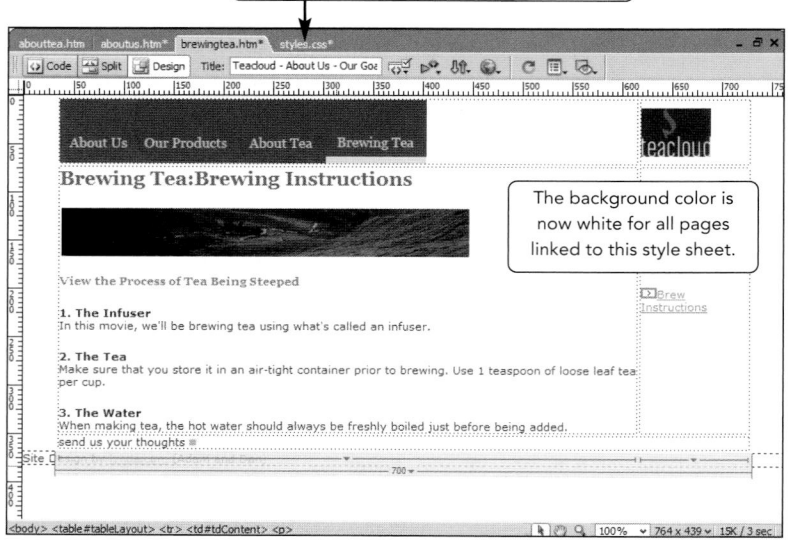

Dreamweaver has opened styles.css for you.

The background color is now white for all pages linked to this style sheet.

17 Choose **Window > styles.css** to switch to the CSS file. Scroll to the top and you'll see that Dreamweaver 8 changed the value for the back-ground color property to **#FFFFFF**.

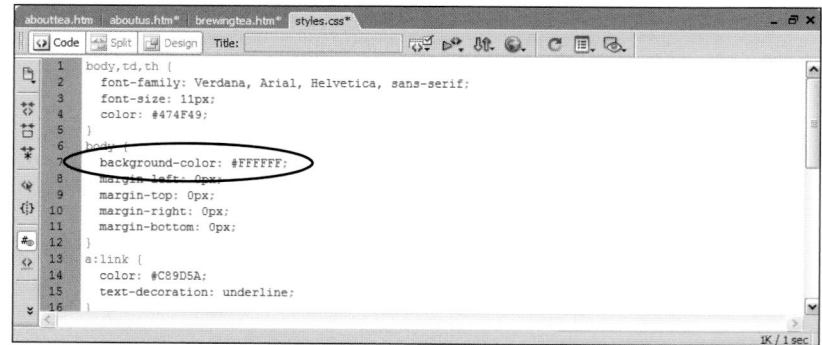

18 Close **styles.css** but don't save the changes; the background color reverts to the original gray color you chose in the last exercise.

Now that you've closed **styles.css** without saving your changes, all of the documents that are attached to this external style sheet have the gray background color restored. This is a great example of how power-ful external style sheets can be. With one change, you affected the appearance of three pages. Had the **styles.css** external style sheet file been linked to 100 pages, then all 100 pages would have been updated. Very powerful indeed!

19 Close **aboutus.htm** and **brewingtea.htm**—you don't need to save your changes. Keep **abouttea.htm** open for the next exercise.

The CSS Styles Panel

The CSS Styles panel received a serious makeover in Dreamweaver 8. It was already a powerful tool in Dreamweaver MX 2004, but Macromedia has put a lot more information into that one tiny panel. For that reason, we're going to take a bit of time and get more familiar with the CSS Styles panel. There are two modes for the CSS Styles panel: All (which you've already used a bit) and Current (which you'll learn about in more detail in this chapter).

The All mode shows you all of the style sheets that are linked to or embedded in the current document. It groups the rules by the style sheet they're defined in so you see a folder-like structure showing all of your CSS rules. The following illustration and chart provide an overview of the options in the All mode of the CSS Styles panel.

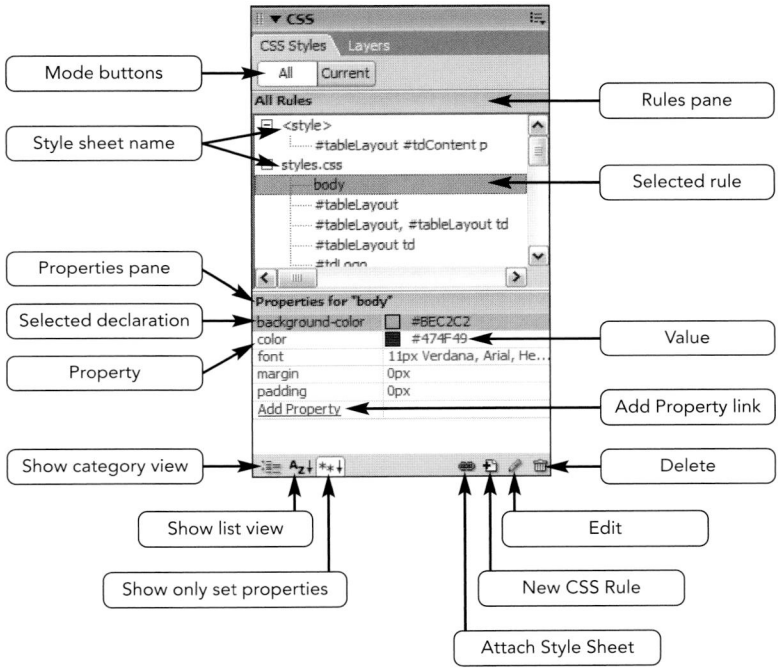

CSS Styles Panel All Mode

Item	Description
Mode buttons	Toggles between All mode and Current mode.
Rules pane	Contains all of the CSS rules that affect the current document.
Style sheet name	Lists the style sheet that affects the currently selected document. You can click the expand/collapse buttons to show or hide all of the rules for each style sheet.

continues on next page

CSS Styles Panel All Mode *continued*	
Item	**Description**
Selected rule	Highlights the currently selected rule in gray. All of the currently selected properties appear in the Properties pane.
Properties pane	Shows all of the declarations for the currently selected rule.
Selected declaration	Highlights the currently selected declaration in the Properties pane in gray.
Property	Contains all of the properties for the currently selected rule.
Value	Contains all of the matching values for the properties of the currently selected rule.
Add Property link	Adds a new declaration to the currently selected rule directly from the CSS Styles panel without having to go through the CSS Rule dialog boxes.
Show category view	Changes the Properties pane so it shows every possible CSS property, grouped by category.
Show list view	Changes the Properties pane so that it shows every possible CSS property in an alphabetical list with properties that already have a value listed at the top.
Show only set properties	Shows only the properties with valid values for the current selection. (This is the default, and what you'll use throughout the book.)
Delete	Deletes the currently selected rule from the style sheet, removes the style sheet from the current document if the style sheet name is selected, or deletes the currently selected declaration from a CSS rule if a declaration is selected.
Edit	Opens the currently selected rule in the CSS Rule Definition dialog box.
New CSS Rule	Opens the New CSS Rule dialog.
Attach Style Sheet	Attaches a style sheet to the current document.

The Current mode of the CSS Styles panel shows you all of the rules that apply to the currently selected element in Design view. An element's style in a document may be affected by 1 rule or 20, depending on how you have your styles defined. The Current mode of the CSS Styles panel makes it easy to see what rules affect which part of the document's display.

This information is a lot to digest, and you shouldn't expect to grasp it all at once. As you go through the rest of the exercises in this book, you'll become more familiar and comfortable with the CSS Styles panel, which is an integral part of doing any design work in Dreamweaver 8. The purpose of this information is to identify the elements that make up the CSS Styles panel so you're familiar with the terminology and controls as you work through the rest of the book.

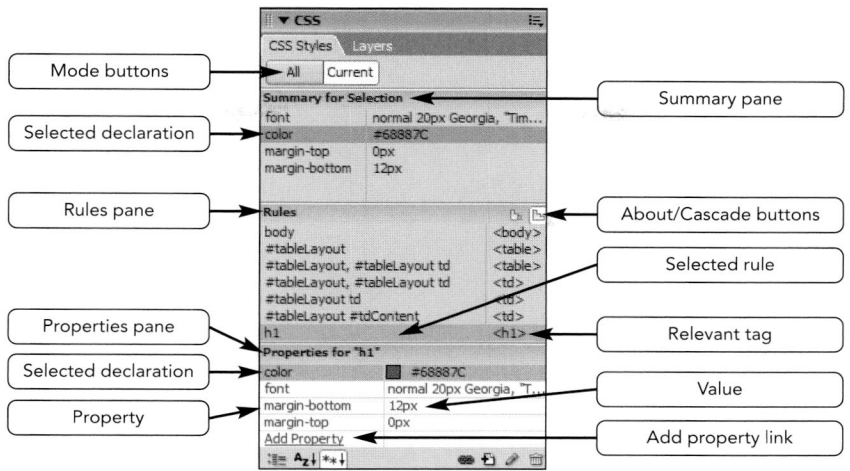

Mode buttons

Selected declaration

Rules pane

Properties pane

Selected declaration

Property

Summary pane

About/Cascade buttons

Selected rule

Relevant tag

Value

Add property link

CSS Styles Panel Current Mode

Item	Description
Mode Buttons	Toggles between All mode and Current mode.
Summary pane	Shows the end result of all of the styles applied to the current selection.
Rules pane	Shows all of the CSS rules that affect the current selection.
Selected declaration	Highlights the currently selected declaration in the Summary and Properties panes in gray.
About/Cascade buttons	Changes the display of the CSS Styles panel in Current mode. Choosing About shows a brief description of the currently selected declaration and states the rule that defines it. Choosing Cascade (the default, and what you'll use throughout the book) shows everything as it is in the screen shot.
Selected rule	Highlights the currently selected rule in gray. All of its properties are then displayed in the Properties pane.
Relevant tag	Shows the tag whose rule affects the display of the current selection.
Properties pane	Shows all of the declarations for the currently selected rule.
Property	Contains all of the properties for the currently selected rule.
Value	Contains all of the matching values for the properties of the currently selected rule.
Add Property link	Adds a new declaration to the currently selected rule directly from the CSS Styles panel without having to go through the CSS Rule dialog boxes.

CSS Selectors

Now that you're a bit more familiar with the CSS Styles panel, and you've created some rules for a document (even though it was through the Page Properties dialog box), it's time to start creating your own selectors. Before you can do that, you need to learn a bit more about all of the different types of selectors available.

A selector defines what a particular declaration block should be applied to. There are quite a few CSS selectors available, but you're only going to work with the most commonly used selectors: classes, type selectors, ID selectors, and a few pseudo-classes. Read on for a description of each of these selectors and an exercise on how to use each of them.

Selector Types		
Selector	**Example**	**Use**
Type	`p {color: green;}`	Type selectors are used to redefine all instances of a specific XHTML tag. For example, if you want to change the appearance of all the paragraphs in a document, you can create a type selector to change them all at once.
ID	`#myTag{color: green;}`	ID selectors are used to redefine one specific element, with an ID that matches the selector. In this example, any tag with an **ID** attribute equal to **myTag** would be styled with a green color: **<div id="myTag">**
Class	`.highlight {color: green;}`	Class selectors are used to style any element with a class attribute that matches the selector. Class selectors are the easiest type of selector to start using, but be careful not to litter your document with selectors that may be better suited to ID or Type selectors.
Pseudo-class	`a:hover {color: green;}`	Pseudo-class selectors are used to style an element when it's in a specific state. In this example, the rule will style an **<a>** tag when the user's mouse hovers over the link. Pseudo-classes are usually used to style links by changing the styling when a user interacts with a link.

Type Selectors

Type selectors are probably the most efficient way to declare CSS formatting rules. A type selector *redefines* how to render a particular XHTML tag. When I say "particular XHTML tag," I don't mean just one **<p>** tag on your page, but every single **<p>** tag on your page. One single type selector rule can affect thousands upon thousands of lines of code. These are mighty powerful indeed.

You may not realize it yet, but you've already written some CSS rules using type selectors. When you set the page font in the Page Properties dialog box, you were telling Dreamweaver 8 to create type selectors for you. Dreamweaver 8 created the following rules:

```
body,td,th {
    font-family: Verdana, Arial, Helvetica, sans-serif;
    font-size: 11px;
    color: #474F49;
}
body {
    background-color: #BEC2C2;
    margin-left: 0px;
    margin-top: 0px;
    margin-right: 0px;
    margin-bottom: 0px;
}
```

The first rule, which has the **body,td,th** selector, redefines the **<body>**, **<td>**, and **<th>** tags. Dreamweaver 8 grouped the three tags so all three have the exact same styles applied to them. This rule introduces you to the concept of grouping selectors. You can group as many selectors together as you'd like by separating the selectors with commas. Even though the **<td>** and **<th>** tags are inside the **<body>** tag, some browsers don't apply font sizes to table cells and headers properly, so Dreamweaver redefines all three tags for you.

The second rule redefines only the **<body>** tag to have a background color of **#BEC2C2** and margins of **0** all the way around. That's all there is to using type selectors. It's an awfully simple but powerful concept to grasp.

3 | Creating Type Selectors

This exercise walks you through creating and editing several type selectors to fine-tune the formatting of the pages you worked on earlier in this chapter. You'll move beyond the Page Properties dialog box to do some advanced formatting, and you'll get some face time with the CSS Styles panel so you can become more comfortable with how it behaves. Plus, you'll continue to explore the benefits of working with the external style sheet you attached in Exercise 2.

---

1 If you just completed Exercise 2, **abouttea.htm** should still be open. If it's not, go back and complete Exercise 2.

Although the formatting looks better than it did when you started back in Exercise 1, it could still use some more fine-tuning to make it a little more visually appealing.

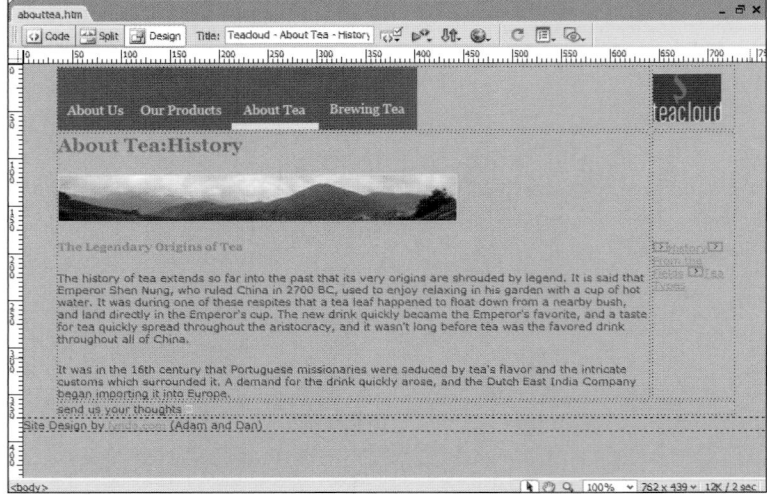

---

2 In the **CSS Styles** panel, click the **New CSS Rule** button to open the **New CSS Rule** dialog box.

First, you'll change the default style information for paragraph text in the document, specifically the line height (the space between the lines) and alignment of the text. The New CSS Rule dialog box lets you create new CSS rules or redefine existing rules. In this case, you're redefining an existing tag—the paragraph tag. If you're doing anything other than simple text formatting, you'll need to use the New CSS Rule dialog box.

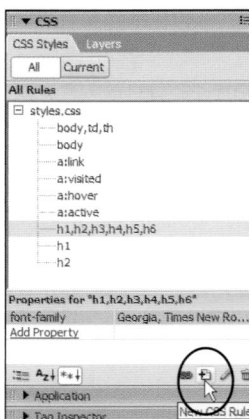

---

3 In the **Selector Type** section, select **Tag**. Type **p** in the **Tag** field. Make sure the **Define in** field is set to **styles.css**. Click **OK** to open the **CSS Rule Definition** dialog box.

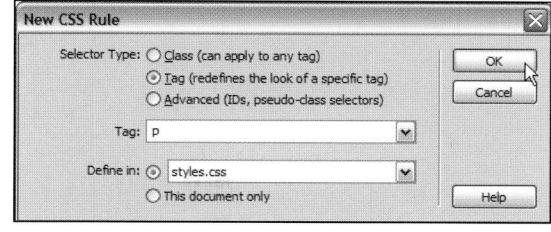

The three options for Selector Type are here simply for convenience. The Class option adds a period to the beginning of anything you specify in the Name field to make it into a class selector. The Tag option lets you type only tag names, and the Tag pop-up menu will show a list of all XHTML tags. I personally prefer to select Advanced, which lets you type anything you want into the Selector field.

The CSS Rule Definition dialog box lets you set almost every possible CSS property for your new rule. Because the text on the site is a little on the small side, it will look better if the lines in each paragraph are spaced farther apart.

---

4 Type **1.7em** in the **Line height** field. When you leave the field (by pressing **Tab** or clicking outside the field), Dreamweaver 8 will change the **Line height** field to **1.7** and automatically select **ems**.

Note: Don't worry too much about font measurements at this point. In the next chapter, you're going to learn all about the different font measurements.

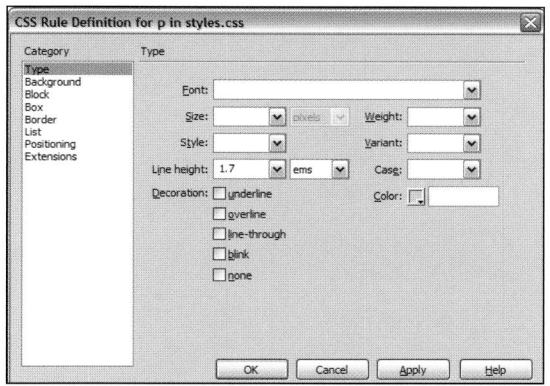

---

5 In the **Category** list, select **Block**. Select **justify** from the **Text align** pop-up menu to justify all of the paragraphs. Click **OK**.

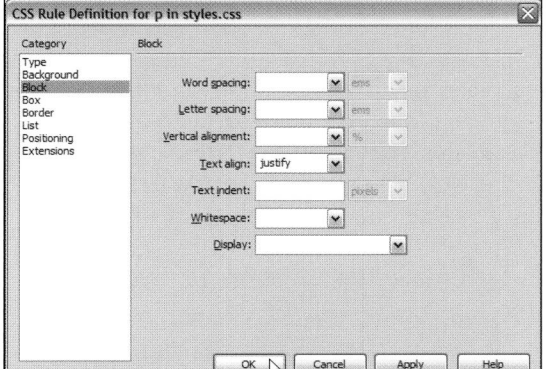

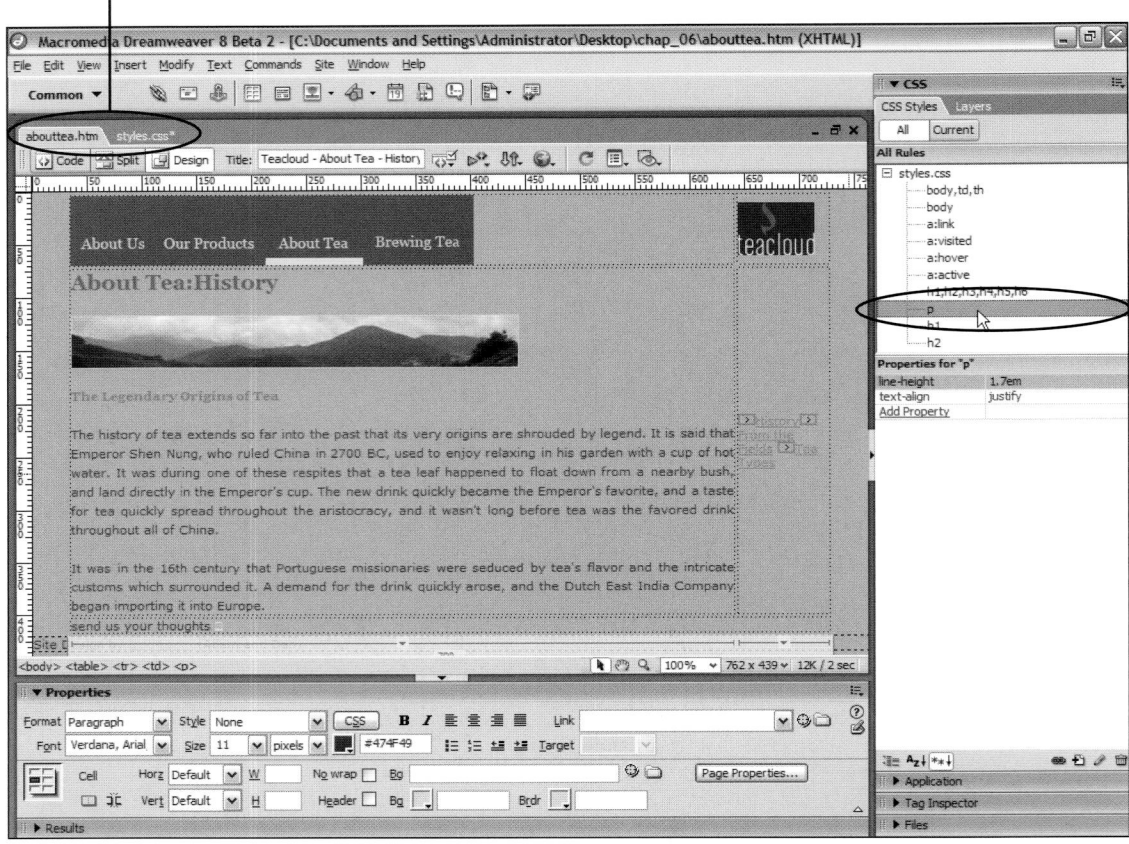

Styles.css has been opened and changed, but not a single line of code was changed in abouttea.htm.

With the new CSS style added, all the paragraph tags have some extra space between each line, and the text is nicely justified. You should also note that the **styles.css** file has been opened for you and is marked with asterisk on its tab, indicating it has changed. You should also see the new **p** rule in the CSS Styles panel.

Did you notice the **abouttea.htm** tab at the top of the Document window is *not* marked as changed? Even though the display of the file is markedly different, not a single line of code was changed in the file; only the style sheet you attached in Exercise 2 has changed. Again, this is the true benefit of working with CSS—the presentation is separate from the content. If you had other pages in the site using this style sheet, they would also update with each change.

Next, you'll make some changes to the headings used on the page. Although the **<h1>** tag looks fine in the serif font you specified in the Page Properties dialog box, the rest of the headings are smaller, and serif fonts can be difficult to read at smaller sizes.

6 **Right-click** (Windows) or **Ctrl+click** (Mac) the **h1,h2,h3,h4,h5,h6** rule in the **CSS Styles** panel and choose **Delete** from the contextual menu.

Did you catch what just happened? The **h1,h2,h3,h4,h5,h6** rule declared the font for all headings should be **Georgia, Times New Roman, Times, serif**. Because you deleted the rule, all the headings are now styled with the font specified for the **<body>** tag, which is **Verdana, Arial, Helvetica, sans-serif**. By default, if you remove or choose not to specify a rule for the headings, the style sheet will use the same rule as the **<body>** tag if one is defined.

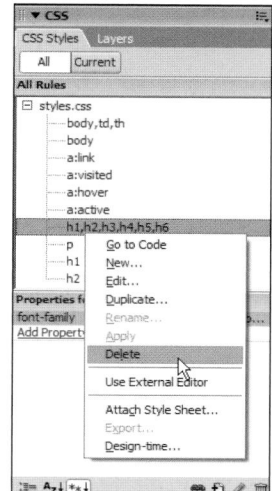

If you switch to the Current mode of the CSS Styles panel and place your cursor inside the **<h1>** tag, you'll see the font is now **Verdana, Arial, Helvetica, sans-serif**. If you position your mouse over the font-family declaration in the Summary pane, you'll see the property is set in the **body,td,th** rule in **styles.css**. Now that's one handy panel.

In order to change the font for the headings below Heading 1, you had to remove the CSS rule for all headings, including Heading 1. What if you want Heading 1 to continue using the same font? Not to worry, you can go back and change Heading 1, which you'll do in the next steps. Because all the headings were grouped together in a single rule, changing that one rule changed the font for all the headings at the same time.

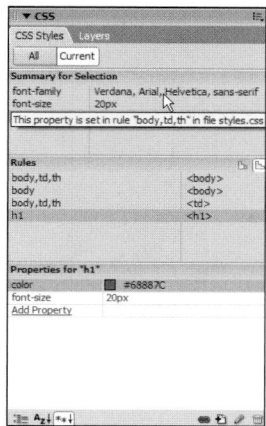

7 Select the **h1** rule from the **Rules** pane of the **CSS Styles** panel. Click the **Edit Style** button to open the **CSS Rule Definition** dialog box, which shows all the declarations for the rule.

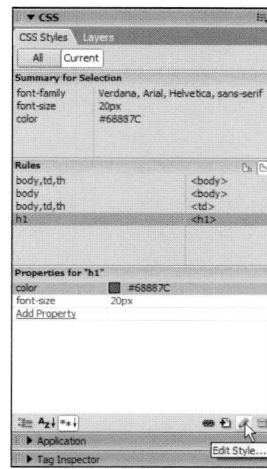

8 Choose **Georgia**, **Times New Roman**, **Times**, **serif** from the **Font** pop-up menu and click **OK**.

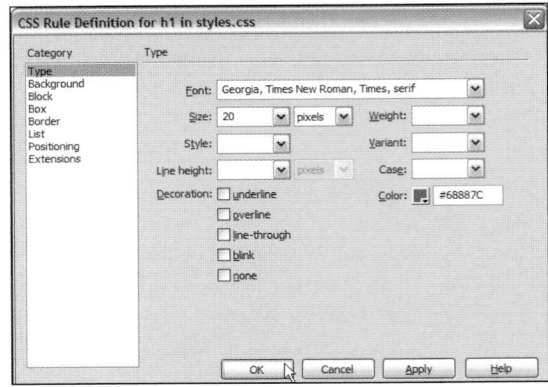

The **<h1>** tag is back to using a serif font while the other headings continue to use the sans serif font. Also note the **abouttea.htm** file still hasn't changed a bit. All the editing you've done is part of the style sheet, not the **abouttea.htm** file, which means if you had multiple pages linked to the style sheet, all the pages would update automatically. Once again, you're seeing firsthand the power and efficiency of using CSS to separate the presentation from the content of pages.

The last thing that's not quite right with this page is that the arrow images in the right side-bar have borders around them. Browsers, by default, add borders around any image tag that's located inside an anchor tag (**<a>**). These images serve as anchors to navigate to other sections on the About Tea page. Without CSS, you'd have to edit each image individually and set its border to 0 in the Property Inspector (which is how the navigation images are defined). Fortunately, there is an easier way—with a CSS rule.

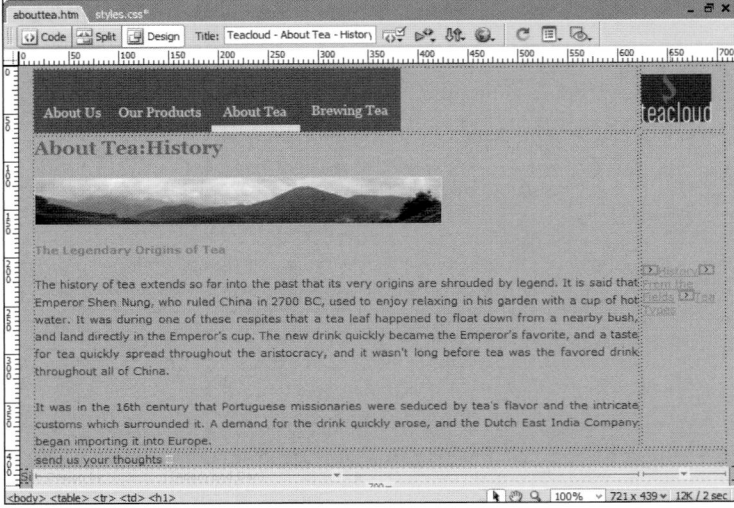

---

9 In the **CSS Styles** panel, click the **New CSS Rule** button to open the **New CSS Rule** dialog box.

---

10 In the **New CSS Rule** dialog box, select **Advanced** in the **Selector Type** section. In the **Selector** field, type **a img**. Make sure the **Define in** field is set to **styles.css**. Click **OK**.

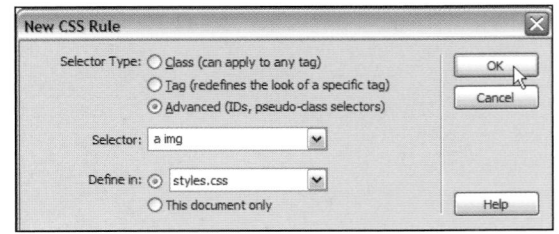

You've just created a descendent selector. A descendent selector contains any number of regular selectors separated by spaces. What this particular rule means is "find any **img** tag that's a *descendent* of (or inside of) an **a** tag." Any image that is inside an anchor in the document will be affected by the rule you're about to create.

---

11 In the **CSS Rule Definition** dialog box select **Border** from the **Category** pane and type **0 pixels** in the **Width** field. Leave the **Same for all** box checked to set all the borders for the image to **0** and click **OK**. You can leave the **Style** and **Color** blank.

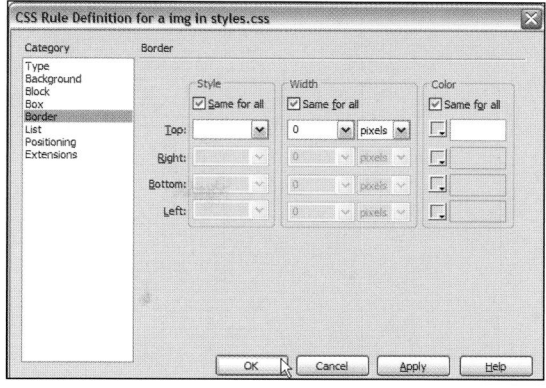

The borders are now gone from the images in the sidebar. Do we need to even mention **abouttea.htm** still hasn't changed? Just as with the other steps in this exercise, the changes you made are to the style sheet, not to **abouttea.htm**, which means the change would automatically update in any other file the style sheet was linked to.

The last rule you're going to edit is the **h2** rule. In order to set the **<h2>** tags off a bit more, it would be nice to have a colored box next to each **<h2>**. You can do this with an image, but you'd need to add that image in front of every single **<h2>** tag in the site. How about using a border instead?

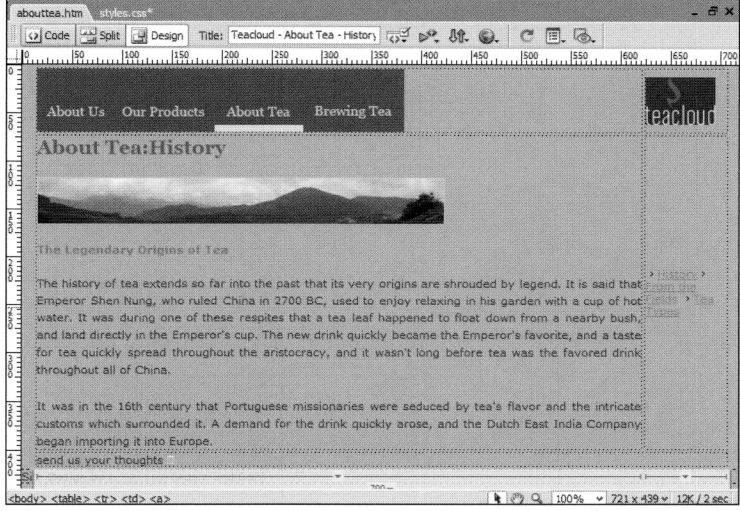

12 Click anywhere inside the **<h2>** tag on the page and select the **h2** rule in the **CSS Styles** panel.

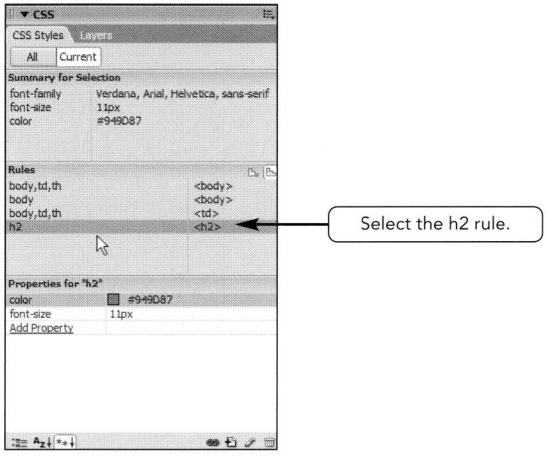

Select the h2 rule.

13 Click the **Add Property** link and choose **border-left-color** from the pop-up menu.

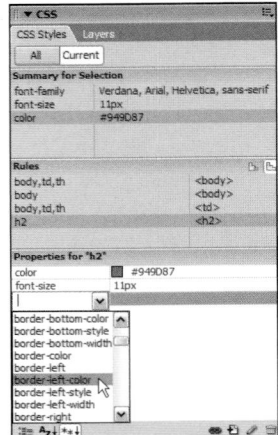

14 Click the **color picker**. Position your pointer over the color swatch for the **color** property. The pointer automatically changes to the eyedropper. Click the color swatch to sample the color—**#949D87**.

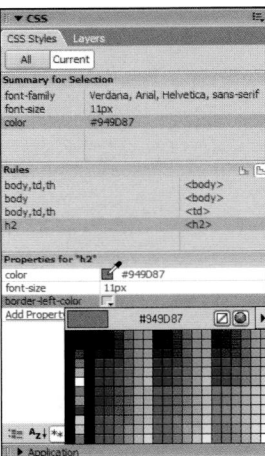

15 Click the **Add Property** link and choose **border-left-width** from the pop-up menu. Type **11px** for the value.

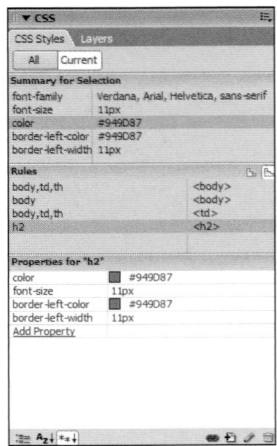

16 Click the **Add Property** link, choose **border-left-style** from the pop-up menu, and choose **solid**.

17 Click the **Add Property** link, choose **padding-left** from the pop-up menu, and type **7px**.

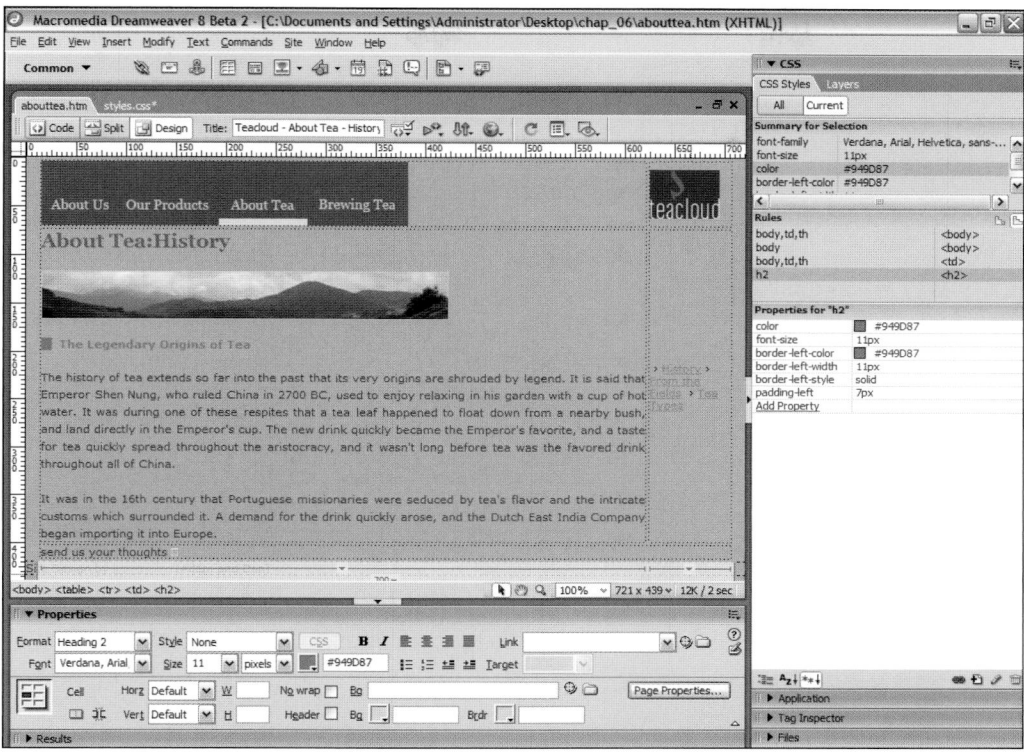

When all is said and done, you should have four new declarations in the CSS Styles panel, and the **<h2>** tag now has a nice square "bullet" next to it, all without adding an image to the page and (do we really need to say it?) without changing **abouttea.htm**. The changes are all part of the style sheet.

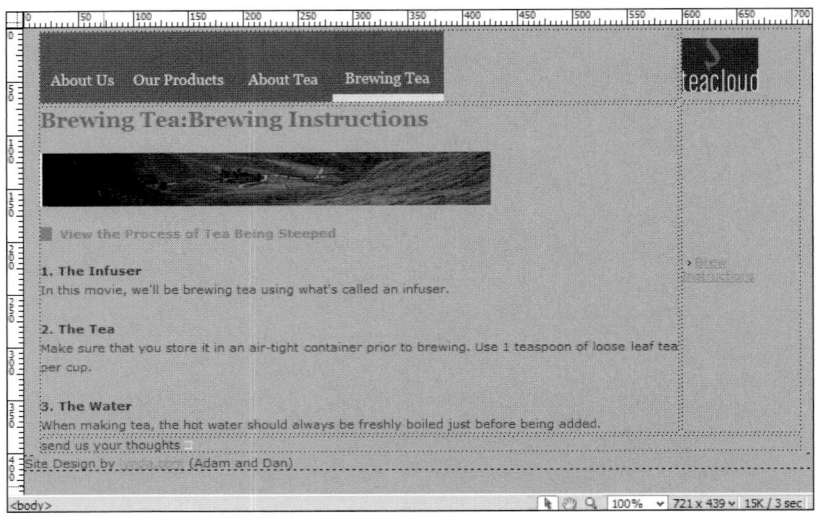

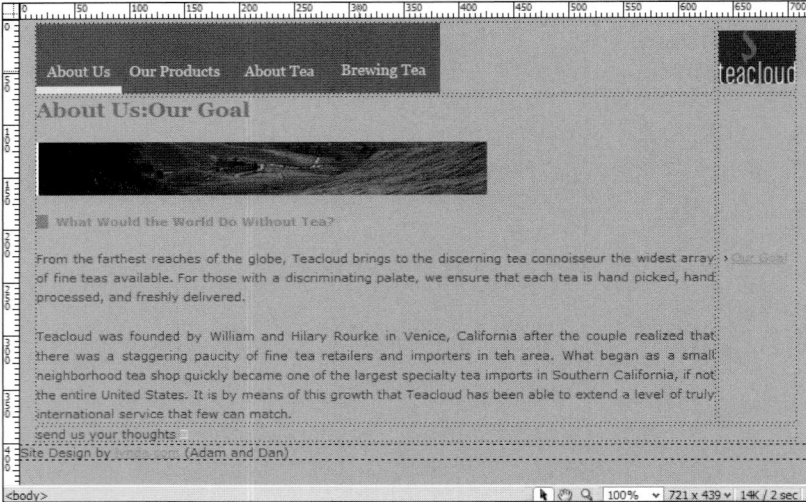

18 In the **Files** panel, double-click **aboutus.htm** and **brewingtea.htm** to open both files.

Notice the changes you made throughout this exercise are reflected in these pages as well. In Exercise 2, you linked the same style sheet to **abouttea.htm** as well as the two files you opened here. Because the changes you made in this exercise were to the style sheet, not **abouttea.htm**, the changes were automatically applied to **aboutus.htm** and **brewingtea.htm**. Are you seeing the power of CSS?

In this exercise, you learned how to modify CSS rules using type selectors. The next exercise walks you through setting up ID selectors.

---

19 Since you didn't actually change anything in the file, go ahead and leave **abouttea.htm** open for the next exercise. Save the changes to **styles.css** and leave it open for the next exercise as well.

ID Selectors

There will come a time when you want to style one specific element on a group of pages, such as a navigation bar, a background color, a logo, or even a footer that's displayed on every page of the site. This one element should be treated differently than anything else in the site. Your immediate solution would probably be to create a class selector and apply that class to the footer inside each page. A more elegant (and semantically correct) approach is to give that element a unique ID and then style just that specific element. The more specific you are with your rules, the less likely you are to have issues with something getting incorrectly styled. Take this example:

```
#divCopyright {
    font-size: 10px;
    margin: 1em;
    text-align: center;
}
```

The pound symbol (#) identifies this selector as an ID selector. The text following the pound symbol is the ID of the element that should be styled. So the following **<div>** would have a font size of 10 pixels and a margin of 1em, and it would be centered:

```
<div id="divCopyright">This is the site Copyright</div>
```

No other element in the page will have this same style applied to it, since ID selectors should be unique in each document. You should never have more than one element with the same ID. Although it's possible, it will work, and the browser won't crash on you, it's technically incorrect.

4 | Creating ID Selectors

ID selectors are one of the most powerful tools available when you're working on the layout of your pages. They let you target specific areas of your page for styling. This exercise shows you how to set the necessary IDs on the elements you want to style as well as define the ID selectors to do the actual styling.

1 If you just completed Exercise 3, **abouttea.htm** should still be open. If it's not, go back and complete Exercise 3.

In this exercise, you're going to style each of the table cells for the layout. Each table cell will have an ID that uniquely identifies it on the page, and then each table cell will get its own style. This ensures only one specific element gets styled.

2 To begin using ID selectors, you need to add some IDs to the document. Click anywhere inside the table on the page and then click the **<table>** tag in the **Tag Selector**.

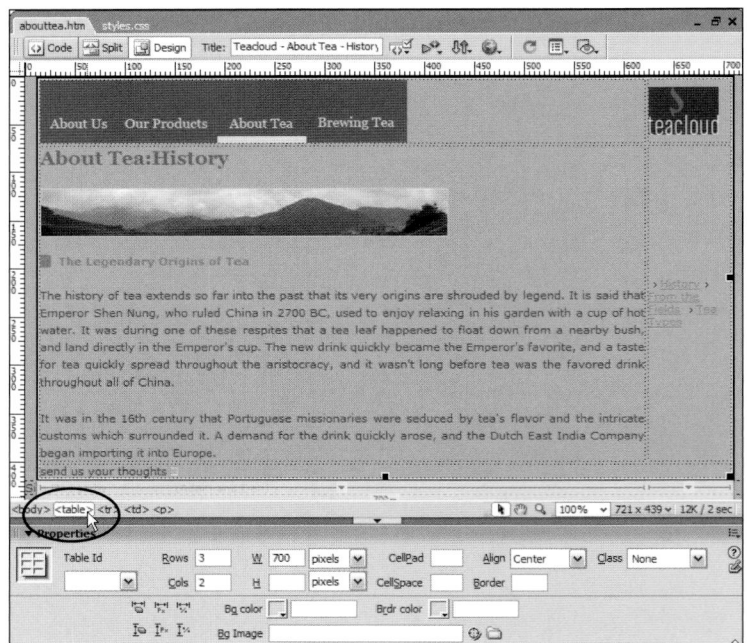

3 In the **Property Inspector**, type **tableLayout** in the **Table Id** field.

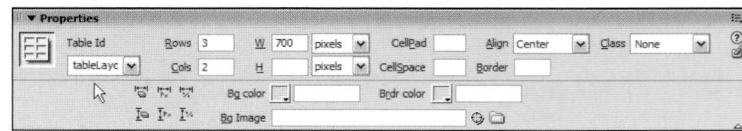

The Table Id pop-up menu identifies all the ID selectors defined in the style sheet. which is helpful because if you create your ID selectors first, you can simply choose them from the pop-up menu. Since ID selectors are case-sensitive, choosing them from the pop-up menu means you don't have to worry about typing them in incorrectly.

NOTE: | **Naming ID Selectors**

As a general rule, it's best to name your ID selectors with the tag first, and then the purpose for that particular tag. In the previous step, you redefined the table that contains the layout for the entire page, so **tableLayout** is a very descriptive and useful name for the selector. Using descriptive names makes it easy to tell which styles affect which elements just by looking at the style sheet itself.

4 In the **CSS Styles** panel, click the **New CSS Rule** button to open the **New CSS Rule** dialog box.

5 Match the settings to the ones shown in the illustration here and click **OK** to open the **CSS Rule Definition** dialog box.

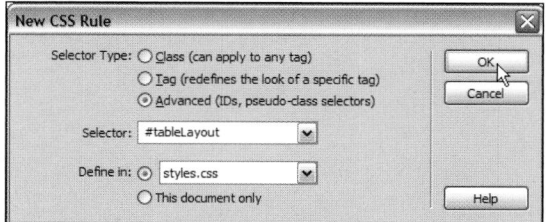

Because you had an element with an ID of **tableLayout** currently selected in the document, Dreamweaver 8 automatically added the ID selector to the Selector field. You can change the Selector if necessary, but in this case Dreamweaver 8 got it right.

6 In the **Category** list, select **Background**. Type **#FFFFFF** in the **Background color** field. In the **Category** list, select the **Border** category. Uncheck the **Same for all** option for **Style**, **Width**, and **Color**. Type **solid**, **1 pixels**, and **#B0B0B0** for the **Right** and **Left** borders. Click **OK** to add the new rule.

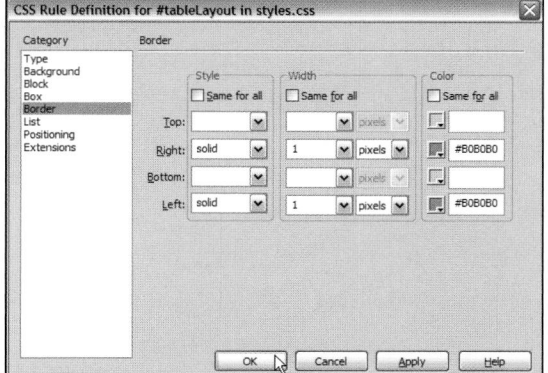

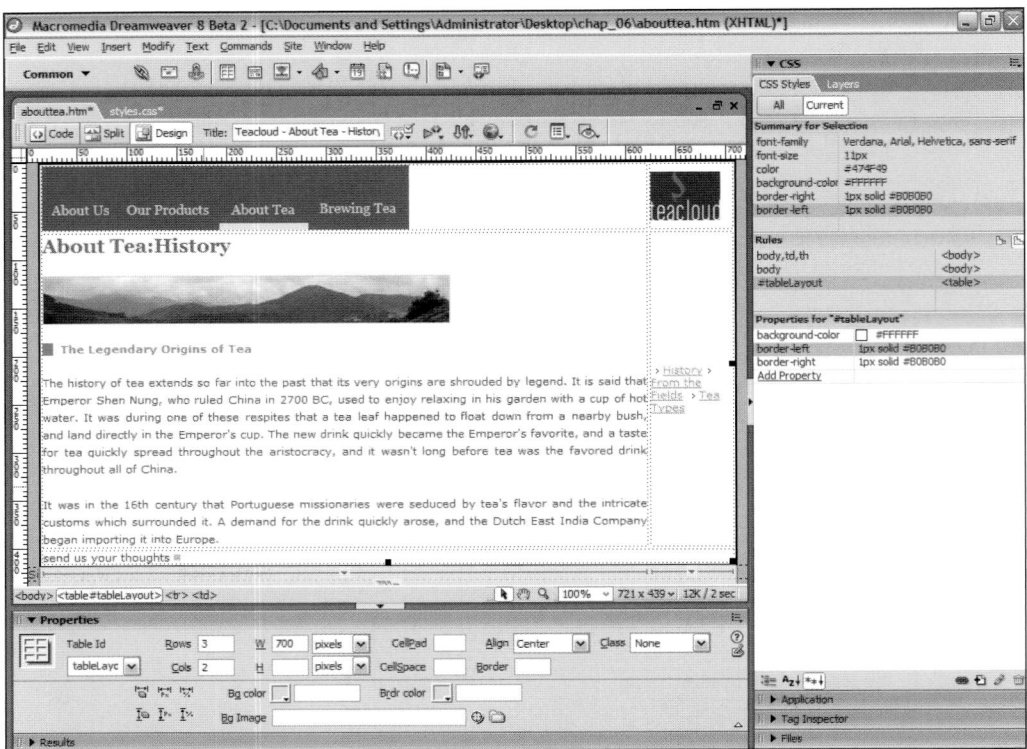

You just created an ID selector to change the background of the page from gray to white, which radically transforms and improves the appearance of the site. The #tableLayout selector you just created affects only the element with that specific ID—in this case the background color for the table.

Next, you'll make some changes to the styling of the navigation bar at the top of the page. You're going to define this style in the opposite order you defined the style for the background color. This time, you're going to create the ID selector first, and then apply it to the table cell.

---

7 In the **CSS Styles** panel, click the **New CSS Rule** button to open the **New CSS Rule** dialog box.

---

8 In the **Selector Type** section, select **Advanced**. Type **#tdNavigation** in the **Selector** field. Make sure the **Define in** field is set to **styles.css**. Click **OK** to open the **CSS Rule Definition** dialog box.

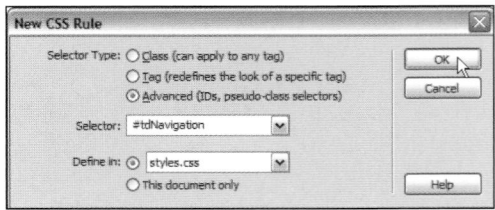

---

9 In the **Category** list, select **Background** and type **#6E7970** in the **Background color** field. In the **Category** list, select **Block** and select **Center** from the **Text align** pop-up menu. In the **Category** list, select **Box**. Uncheck the **Same for all** box in the **Padding** section and type **0** in the **Bottom** field. Click **OK**.

The 0 bottom padding ensures the navigation images are flush with the bottom of the table cell. You'll learn more about dealing with table margins and padding in Chapter 8, "*Tables.*"

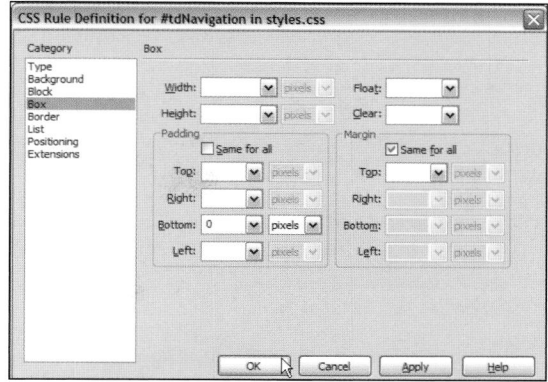

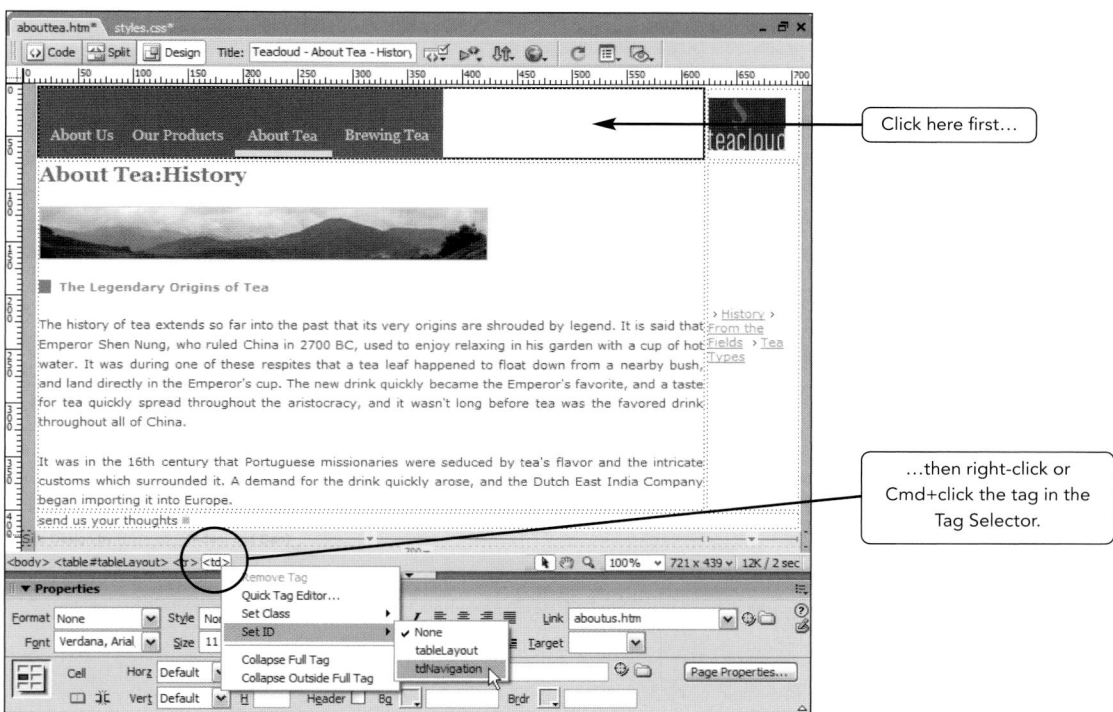

10 In the **Document** window, click anywhere inside the table cell containing the navigation. In the **Tag Selector**, **right-click** (Windows) or **Cmd+click** (Mac) the **<td>** tag. Choose **Set ID > tdNavigation** from the contextual menu.

That's just another way to make sure that the IDs on your XHTML elements actually match the ID selectors in your CSS file. There isn't always a way to set an ID from the Property Inspector like you can with **<table>** tags, so using the contextual menu in the Tag Selector can save you a lot of time and headaches trying to figure out why an element isn't getting styled correctly when you may have just got the capitalization wrong.

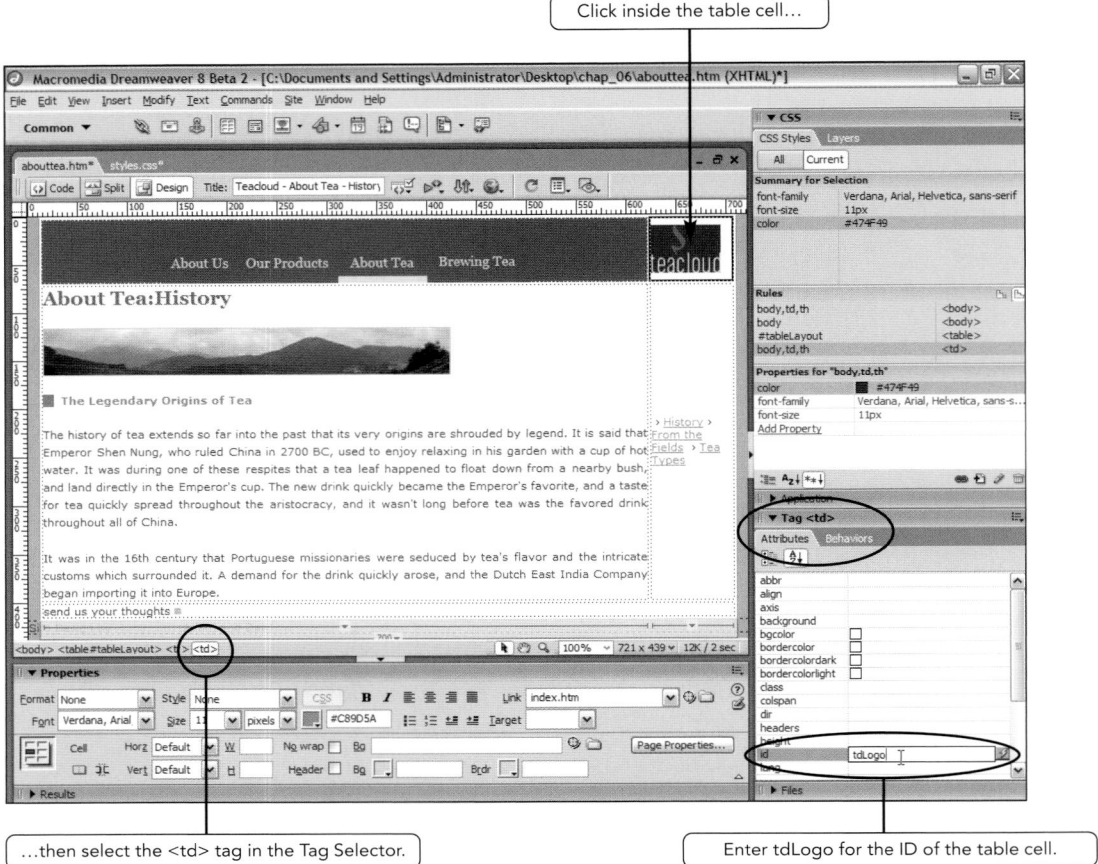

Click inside the table cell...

...then select the <td> tag in the Tag Selector.

Enter tdLogo for the ID of the table cell.

11 Click inside the table cell containing the Teacloud logo. Select the **<td>** tag in the **Tag Selector** and then choose **Window > Tag Inspector** to open the **Tag Inspector**.

The Tag Inspector lets you see (and edit) all of the attributes of a particular XHTML tag. Since there is no way to assign an ID to a table cell from the Property Inspector, you're going to use the Tag Inspector to do it this time.

---

12 In the **Tag Inspector**, make sure the **Attributes** tab is selected. Click to the right of the **id** attribute, type **tdLogo**, and press **Enter** (Windows) or **Return** (Mac).

---

13 In the **CSS Styles** panel, click the **New CSS Rule** button to open the **New CSS Rule** dialog box. In the **Selector Type** section, select **Advanced**. Type **#tdLogo** in the **Selector** field and make sure the **Define in** field is set to **styles.css**. Click **OK** to open the **CSS Rule Definition** dialog box.

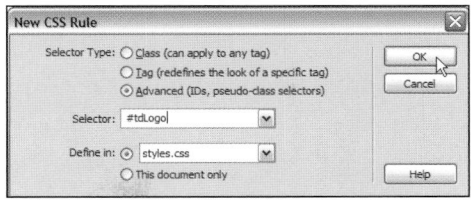

14 In the **Category** list, select **Background** and type **#474F49** in the **Background color** field. In the **Category** list, select **Block** and choose **Center** from the **Text align** pop-up menu. In the **Category** list, select **Box** and set the **Width** to **140 pixels**. Click **OK**.

The text-align property aligns everything in the element the style is applied to. When the rule is applied to a table cell (as it is in this case), all elements inside that table cell will be centered. The text-align property isn't just for text.

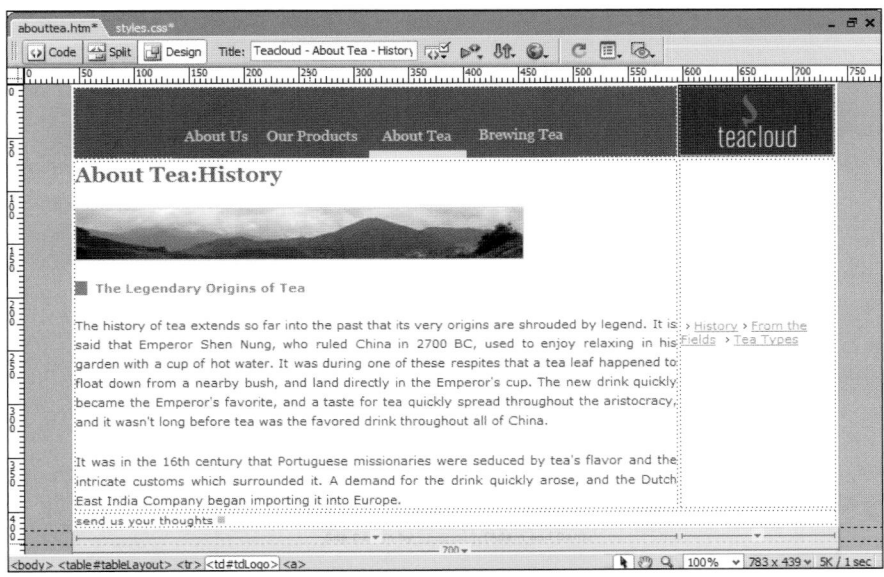

The table cell containing the logo now has the same background color as the logo image, and the logo is nicely centered in the table cell.

The last table cell you're going to style is the sidebar on the right side.

15 Click inside the table cell below the Teacloud logo and select the **<td>** tag in the **Tag Selector**.

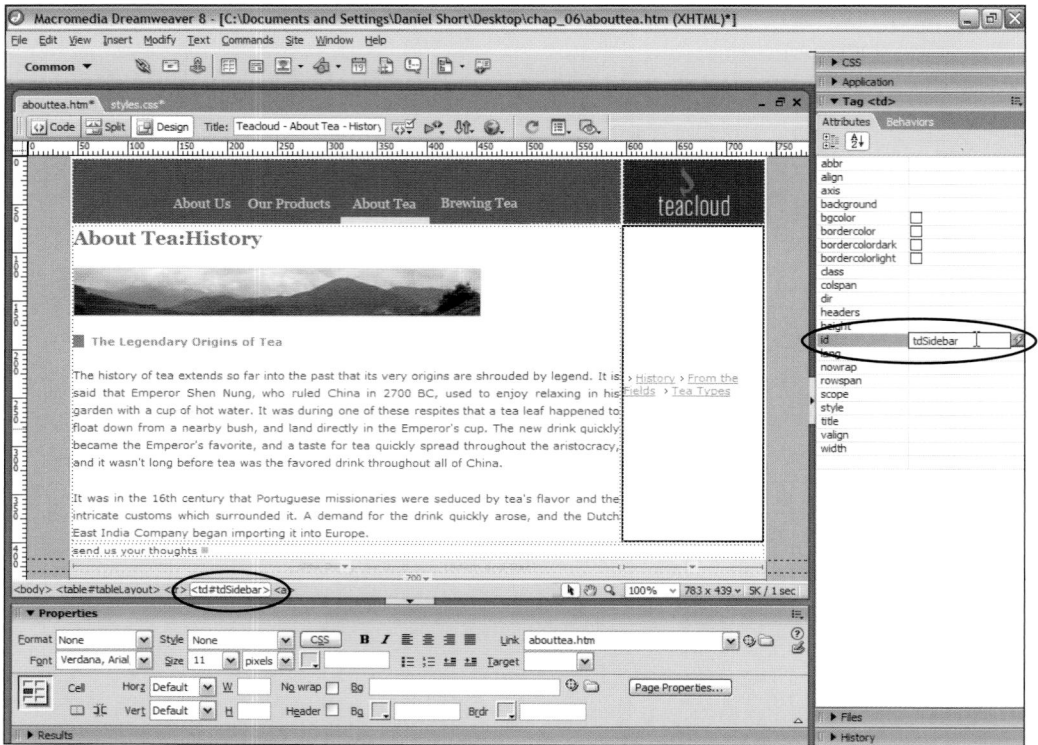

16 In the **Attributes** tab of the **Tag** panel, set the **id** to **tdSidebar**.

17 In the **CSS Styles** panel, click the **New CSS Rule** button to open the **New CSS Rule** dialog box.

18 In the **Selector Type** section, select **Advanced**. Type **#tdSidebar** in the **Selector** field and make sure the **Define in** field is set to **styles.css**. Click **OK** to open the **CSS Rule Definition** dialog box.

19 In the **Category** list, select **Background** and type **#E3E5DC** in the **Background color** field. Click **Browse** for the **Background Image** and select the **sidebarbackground.gif** file in the **images/navigation** folder. Choose **no-repeat** from the **Repeat** pop-up menu. Choose **bottom** from the **Vertical position** pop-up menu. In the **Category** list, select **Block** and choose **top** from the **Vertical alignment** pop-up menu to ensure the content is always aligned with the top of the table cell.

Setting the background image to no-repeat and aligning it to the bottom of the sidebar ensures the image doesn't repeat at all inside the table cell, and that it always displays at the very bottom of the sidebar table cell.

20 Click **OK** to create the new style.

21 Press **F12** to view the page in a browser. Dreamweaver 8 prompts you to save **abouttea.htm**. Click **Yes** to save the changes. Dreamweaver 8 then prompts you to save the CSS file that's attached to

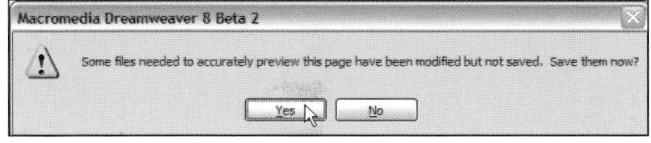

this document. Because you made changes to **styles.css**, Dreamweaver 8 has to save the file before the browser will properly render the page. Click **Yes** to save the changes.

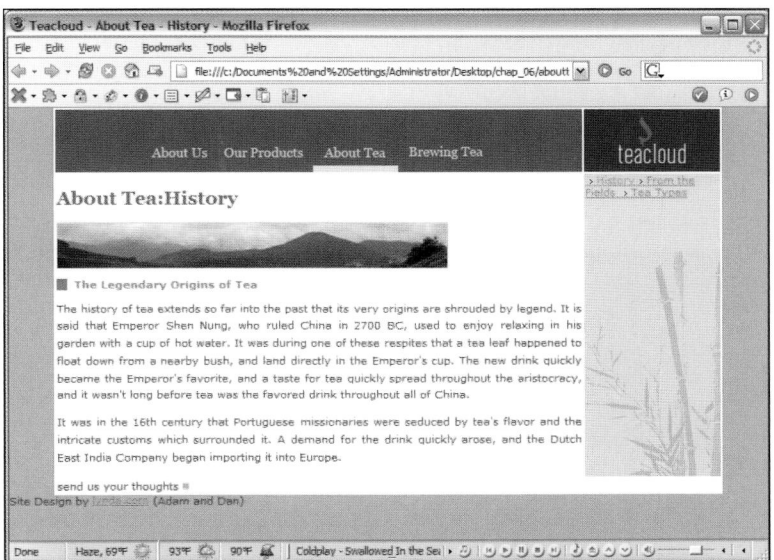

The page is starting to look pretty good at this point. All of the table cells are properly styled using a minimum of CSS rules. Giving each of the table cells an ID ensures they're the only table cells that are affected by the new styles.

This exercise showed you how to specify ID selectors to affect a specific element on the page. You won't be finishing the entire page at this point—you'll have time for that in Chapter 8, "*Tables.*" Now it's time to cover class selectors.

---

22 Return to Dreamweaver 8. Keep **abouttea.htm** and **styles.css** open for the next exercise.

VIDEO: | **idselectors.mov**

For more information about ID Selectors, check out **idselectors.mov** in the **videos** folder on the **HOT CD-ROM**.

Class Selectors

The class selector lets you specify a custom selector name and apply that style to an XHTML element using the **class** attribute. A class selector should start with a period (.) and be followed by the class name, which can't contain any special characters or spaces and can't start with a number. Here's an example of a class selector:

```
.smallprint {font-size: 10px;}
```

You could apply this rule to a paragraph with the following code:

```
<p class="smallprint">This is some small text.</p>
```

You could also apply the rule to a **<div>** or a table cell (**<td>**) just as easily:

```
<div class="smallprint">This is also some small text.</div>
```

Class selectors can also start with a tag name if the class should only be applied to particular elements. Let's assume you want small print text in paragraphs to be 10 pixels, but you want small print inside **<div>** tags to be 12 pixels. You would use the following class selectors:

```
p.smallprint {font-size: 10px;}
div.smallprint {font-size: 12px;}
```

Using these two class selectors, any paragraph with a class attribute of **smallprint** will be 10 pixels and any **<div>** with a class attribute of **smallprint** will be 12 pixels.

Class selectors are one of the easiest selectors to wrap your head around, and at first glance they seem like an easy and efficient way to start formatting a page, and that's how most people get started. But I caution you to take it easy with class selectors. It's entirely possible to become "class-happy," applying classes all over your page to get the formatting you desire. Although this seems like a good idea in the beginning, it can often lead to pages that are difficult to manage and update. A common mistake is to define a class for the body text of a document and then apply that class to every **<p>** tag on the page. Many new CSS users end up with something like this:

```
<p class="bodytext">A paragraph with lots of text…</p>
<p class="bodytext">Another paragraph with lots of text…</p>
<p class="bodytext">Yet another paragraph with lots of text…</p>
<p class="bodytext">The last paragraph with lots of text…</p>
<p class="smallprint">A paragraph with small text</p>
```

This accomplishes little in the way of separating out presentation information, because every paragraph has to be told how it should be styled. It's far more efficient to simply redefine the **<p>** tag using a type selector, which you learned about earlier. So be careful with your classes, and try to use them as a last resort. Use classes for exceptions to the other CSS rules you define. This code looks much more efficient and easy to read:

```
<p>A paragraph with lots of text…</p>
<p>Another paragraph with lots of text…</p>
<p>Yet another paragraph with lots of text…</p>
<p>The last paragraph with lots of text…</p>
<p class="smallprint">A paragraph with small text</p>
```

5 | Creating Class Selectors

Class selectors are probably the most common selector (and the most often abused). They let you define a class that you can apply to multiple elements using a class attribute on the XHTML tag. This exercise shows you how to create and apply class selectors in Dreamweaver 8.

---

1 If you just completed Exercise 4, **abouttea.htm** should still be open. If it's not, go back and complete Exercise 4.

As a general rule, sites tend to have their copyrights and less important text in a smaller font than the rest of the site. You're going to create a class to make text smaller on the site.

---

2 In the **CSS Styles** panel, click the **New CSS Rule** button to open the **New CSS Rule** dialog box.

---

3 In the **Selector Type** section, select **Class**. Type **smallprint** in the **Name** field and make sure the **Define in** field is set to **styles.css**. Click **OK**.

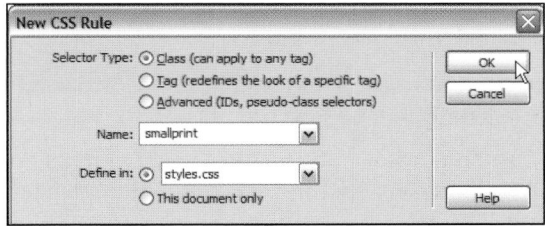

---

4 In the **CSS Rule Definition** dialog box, set the **Size** to **10 pixels** and click **OK**.

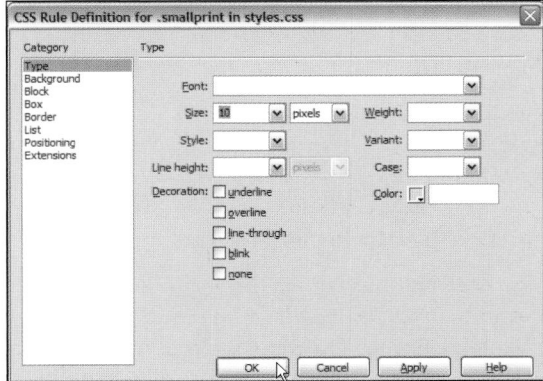

---

5 If you didn't already have it open, **styles.css** will open. It will be marked with an asterisk to indicate that the document has changed. Switch to the **All** mode in the **CSS Styles** panel. Scroll to the bottom of the **Rules** pane, and you'll see the new class selector has been added to the style sheet.

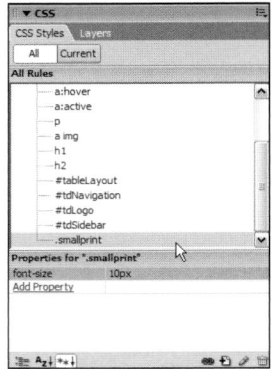

6 Click inside the table cell at the bottom of the layout containing the text **send us your thoughts**. In the **Property Inspector**, choose **smallprint** from the **Style** pop-up menu.

When your cursor is inside a tag and there is no text selected, the Property Inspector will apply the class to the first tag it finds. If you have a block of text selected and choose a style from the Property Inspector, Dreamweaver will wrap the selected text with a **<span>** tag with the class applied to it.

Click inside the table cell first.

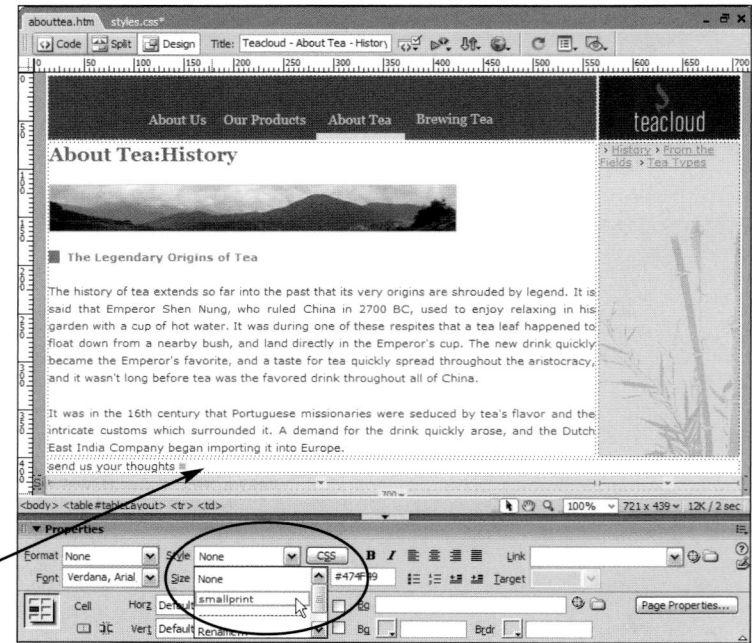

N O T E : | **Span, the All-Purpose Container**

The **<span>** tag is a generic container that doesn't have any default styling. It's used to wrap text or other objects with a tag that can be easily styled. It's easy to get carried away with **<span>** tags, and Dreamweaver makes it a little too easy sometimes by wrapping just about anything in a **<span>**. Pay careful attention to what Dreamweaver is doing, and try to avoid the **<span>** tags by applying classes to tags that are already on the page (such as the **<td>** you just applied a class to).

You should notice
Dreamweaver has added
the class attribute to the
<td> tag, and the Tag
Selector now shows the
smallprint class applied.
The *send us your thoughts*
text is also just a tad
bit smaller.

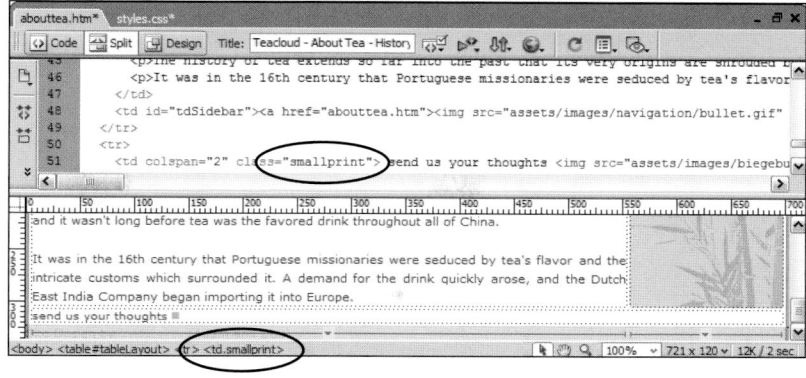

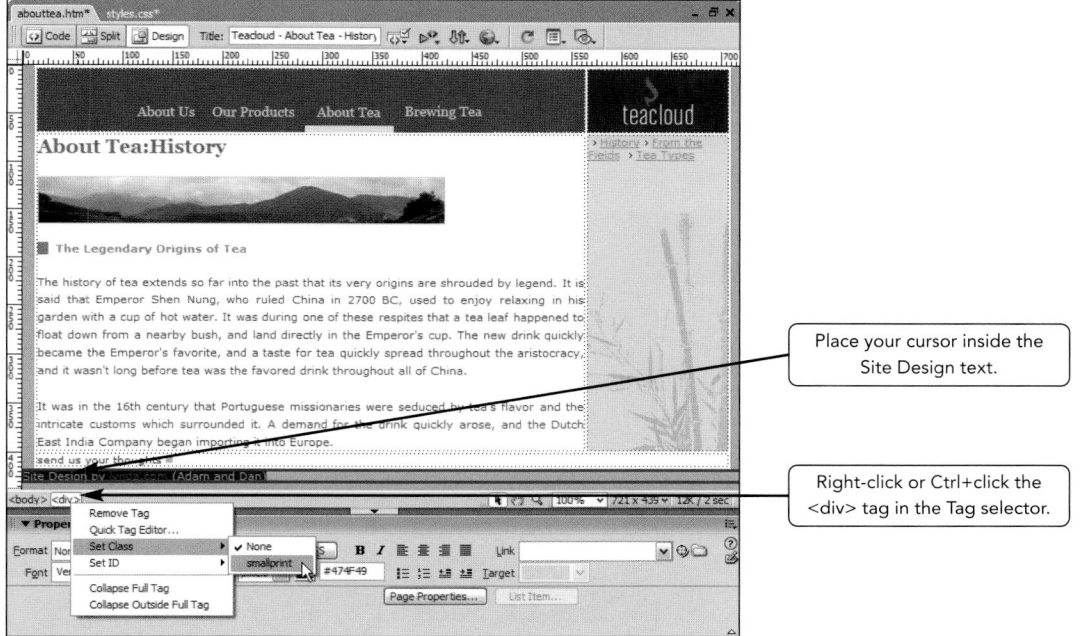

Place your cursor inside the
Site Design text.

Right-click or Ctrl+click the
<div> tag in the Tag selector.

7 If you can't see the text at the bottom of the screen because of the table width indicators, choose
View > Visual Aids > Table Widths to turn them off. Click inside the **Site Design by lynda.com** text.
Right-click (Windows) or **Ctrl+click** (Mac) the **<div>** tag in the **Tag Selector** and choose **Set Class >
smallprint** from the contextual menu.

8 The **Site Design by lynda.com** text is now 10 pixels as well. Unfortunately, it doesn't look very good aligned to the left of the screen. You need to create a new rule to center any text inside a `<div>` that has a class of `smallprint`. In the **CSS Styles** panel, click the **New CSS Rule** button to open the **New CSS Rule** dialog box.

9 In the **New CSS Rule** dialog box, select **Advanced** in the **Selector Type** section. Type **div.smallprint** in the **Selector** field. Make sure **styles.css** is selected in the **Define in** field. Click **OK** to open the **CSS Rule Definition** dialog box.

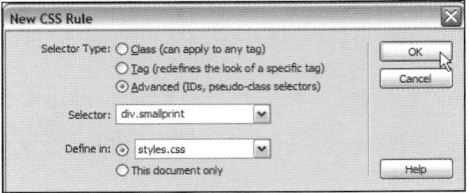

10 In the **CSS Rule Definition** dialog box, select **Block** in the **Category** list and choose **Center** from the **Text align** pop-up menu. Click **OK** to create the style.

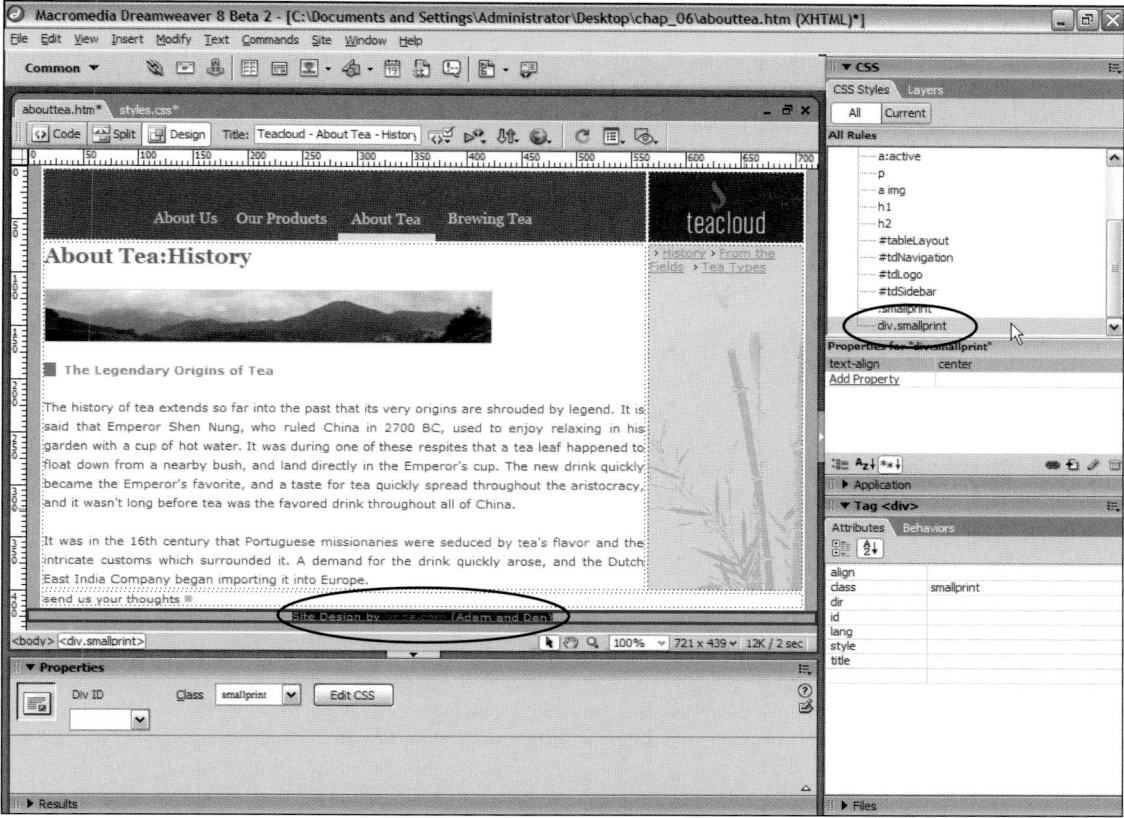

You should now see the new div.smallprint class in the Rules pane of the CSS Styles panel. The text in the <div> is now centered. You've just created a complex CSS class selector that states that any <div> tag with a smallprint class should not only be 10 pixels tall, but should also be centered.

11 Save your changes and keep **abouttea.htm** and **styles.css** open for the next exercise.

Pseudo-Class Selectors

The last type of selector you'll learn about is called a pseudo-class. A pseudo-class describes the *state* of a particular element and isn't based on something that can be determined by looking at the source code of a document. Pseudo-classes are tacked onto the end of other selector types to assign a style that happens only when an object is in a certain state. The most common pseudo-classes, and the ones you'll use more often than any other, are `:link`, `:visited`, `:hover`, and `:active`. These pseudo-classes are most often applied to links, or `<a>` tags. A common rule using a pseudo-class is to remove underlines from links when a user holds his or her mouse over the link. Dreamweaver 8 automatically wrote a rule for this when you used the **Page Properties** dialog box and chose **Hide underline on rollover** back in Exercise 1:

```
a:hover {
    text-decoration: none;
    color: #9F7535;
}
```

This rule redefines the `<a>` tag using a type selector, but because it has the `:hover` pseudo-class on the end, the rule is activated only when the user's mouse hovers over the link. Here's a description of the four pseudo-classes you'll be using most often:

Common Pseudo-Classes	
Pseudo-Class	**Description**
`:link`	This style is applied to elements that have not yet been visited.
`:visited`	This style is applied to elements that have been visited.
`:hover`	This style is applied when the element is underneath the user's mouse.
`:active`	This style is applied when the user clicks, or activates, the element.

TIP: | **LoVe HAte Relationship**

Generally speaking, you should apply pseudo-class selectors in a specific order to ensure links display properly. The mnemonic LoVe HAte can help you remember to define them in the following order: `:link`, `:visited`, `:hover`, then `:active`. Because of the cascading nature of style sheets, these classes will be applied to elements in the order in which they are defined.

EXERCISE 6 | Creating CSS Rollovers with Pseudo-Classes

Pseudo-class selectors are one of the more powerful selectors. Not only can they style an element, but they can change an element's style based on user interaction. In this exercise, you'll learn how to create some sophisticated navigation using nothing but a few pseudo-class selectors.

1 If you just completed Exercise 5, **abouttea.htm** should still be open. If it's not, go back and complete Exercise 5.

If you've been watching closely in the previous chapters, you would have noticed the sidebar navigation was far more attractive than what is in the current chapter. You're going to style the links in the sidebar to make them match what you've seen in the other chapters.

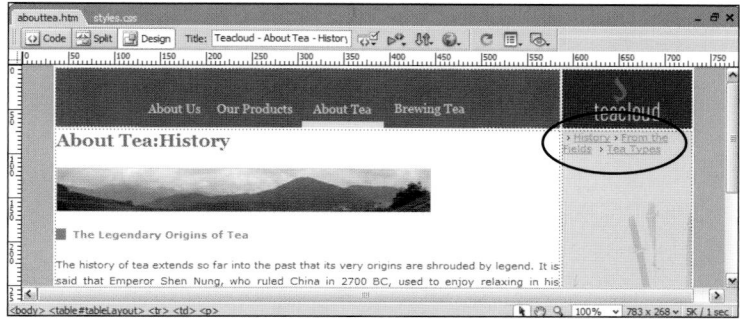

2 The first thing to do is give the links their default style. In the **CSS Styles** panel, click the **New CSS Rule** button to open the **New CSS Rule** dialog box.

3 In the **Selector Type** section, select **Advanced**. Type **#tdSidebar a** in the **Selector** field, and make sure the **Define in** field is set to **styles.css**. Click **OK**.

Notice you're creating another descendent selector, just like you did in Exercise 3 when you defined a border for all images inside an anchor. In this rule, you're selecting all anchors that are inside the sidebar table cell.

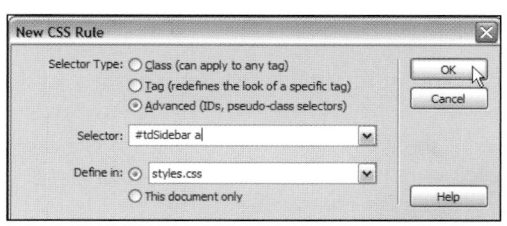

4 In the **CSS Rule Definition** dialog box, select **Type** in the **Category** list and select the **none** check box. Type **#474F49** in the **Color** field.

Choosing none for the text decoration ensures that the links in the sidebar don't have underlines.

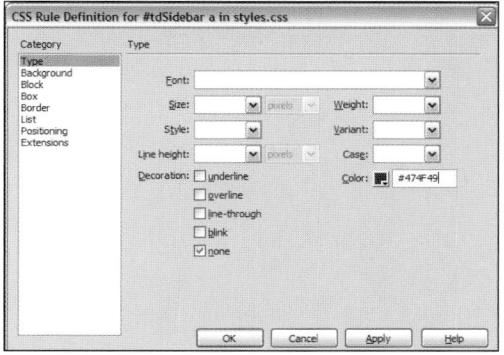

5 In the **Category** list, select **Block** and choose **block** from the **Display** pop-up menu.

Setting the links to be block-level elements ensures that each anchor reserves space in the document and all of the anchors will stack up on top of each other. If the anchors were left as inline elements, they would all line up in a row, which isn't the effect you're after.

NOTE:

Block Level Elements vs. Inline Elements

One of the most powerful capabilities of CSS is to change the way an element is treated by browsers. We're not talking about just changing colors, but actually changing the fashion in which an element is handled. There are two types of elements: block and inline.

Block-level elements "reserve space," which means that with a block-level element, nothing can sit to the left or right of the element, because it reserves that space for itself. In the previous step, you defined the anchor tag as a block-level element so that each anchor would reserve the space to the left and right of it and each element stacks up nicely below the one before it.

Inline elements don't reserve any more space than it takes to display them. Other inline elements line up nicely to the left and right of other inline elements, and they display in a line, just like a row of text.

---

6 In the **Category** list, select **Box** and type **8** in the **Padding Top** field. Leave the **Same for all** box selected to ensure that all sides of the anchor have the same padding. Type **10** in the **Margin Top** field and leave the **Same for all** box selected.

Setting a value for the padding adds some space around the text inside the anchor, which will make it look more like a button. Adding a margin around each anchor ensures they're nicely spaced out and their borders (which you'll add next) butt up against each other.

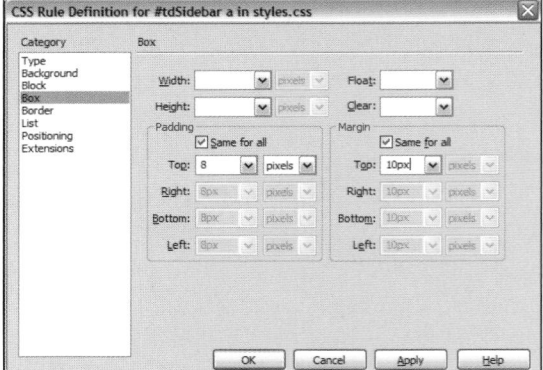

7 In the **Category** list, select **Border**. Deselect all of the **Same for all** boxes, and choose **solid** from the **Style Top** and **Style Bottom** pop-up menus. Type **1px** in the **Width Top** and **Width Bottom** fields. Type **#CED2B6** in the **Color Top** and **Color Bottom** fields. Click **OK** to add the rule to your document.

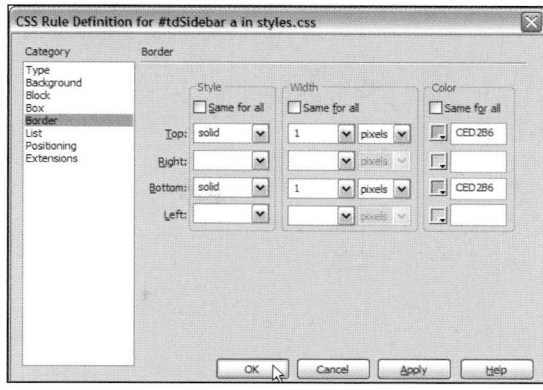

The border settings add a top and bottom border to each link in the sidebar, which adds some visual separation between the buttons and lets the user know where the "hot spots" are (where they're able to click).

When the first rule is complete, the buttons in the sidebar look fantastic. Each of the links is surrounded by a dotted line because Dreamweaver 8 now sees them as block-level elements. When you preview the page in your browser (almost there, we promise), you won't see the dotted line around the links.

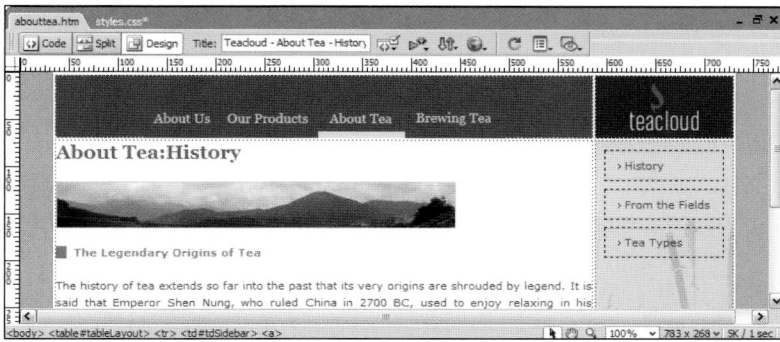

8 In the **CSS Styles** panel, click the **New CSS Rule** button. In the **New CSS Rule** dialog box, select **Advanced** in the **Selector Type** section. Type **#tdSidebar a:hover** in the **Selector** field. Make sure the **Define in** field is set to **styles.css**.

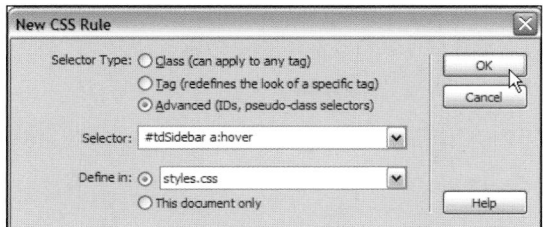

This rule, which includes the :hover pseudo-class, is going to change the background color of the links when the user hovers his or her mouse over the link.

9 In the **CSS Rule Definition** dialog box, select **Background** in the **Category** list. Type **#FBFCF9** in the **Background color** field. Click **OK**.

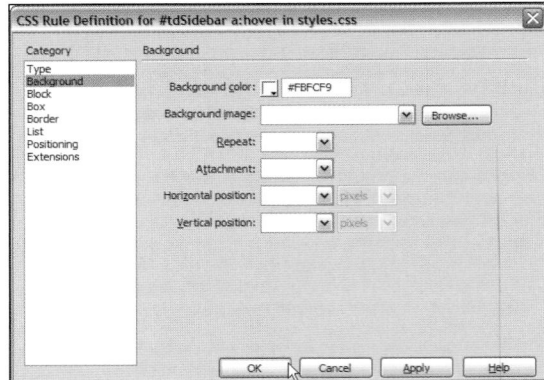

10 Press **F12** to preview the page in your browser, and when prompted, save all of the necessary documents. Move your mouse over each of the links, and you'll see the background color change for each link.

That's all there is to CSS rollovers. The process is simple, but the payback is amazing. You can create complicated navigation without using a single image, which cuts down on bandwidth and page load time, and also makes your pages much easier to maintain. If you decide to add a new link or change the text of a link, there's no need to create or edit image files.

Ask the SelectOracle

One of the most confusing parts of working with CSS is figuring out what those darned selectors actually mean. Well, the easiest way is to simply ask the SelectOracle. You can type any number of selectors or put in the full URL to a CSS file online into the Oracle, and it will give you a plain English (or Spanish) description of exactly what that selector matches.

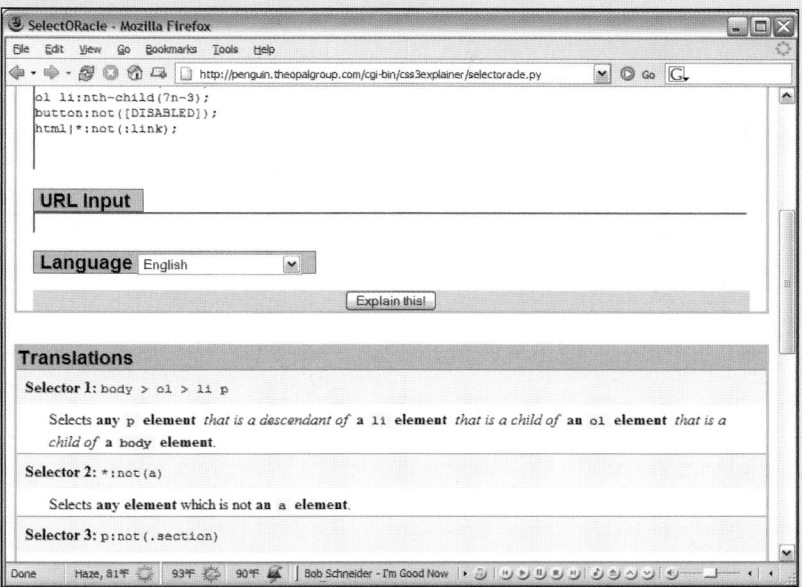

You can find the SelectOracle at **http://gallery.theopalgroup.com/selectoracle/**. It's the first place to turn to if you're looking at a site that's doing something you don't quite understand, or if you need to write a particularly complex rule and can't seem to get it right on your own.

You covered a lot of material in this chapter, and hopefully we've stretched your boundaries a bit. You should now have a pretty good understanding of how to apply styles to your pages and how to work with the powerful CSS Styles panel. In the next chapter, you'll expand your CSS knowledge and learn how to do more with the typography of your site.

7

Typography

In the past few years, there has been a tremendous push to separate the structure on a Web page from its presentation. Part of this separation movement has caused the **<font>** element to be left behind in favor of using CSS (**C**ascading **S**tyle **S**heets) in its place. CSS offers a more precise and flexible alternative to the **<font>** element. You won't find any **<font>** tags in any of the code in this book for that reason.

This chapter will show you how to control your site's typography using CSS and basic XHTML formatting tags (except for **<font>**). You'll learn how to set font styles, such as bold, italics, and underlined; font sizes; colors; and faces, such as Times Roman, Helvetica, Arial, and so on. You'll also learn about how to create bulleted lists, definition lists, and unordered lists. If you haven't heard those terms before, they will also be explained in detail in this chapter. Also, you'll learn about a great feature in Dreamweaver 8—Flash Text, which lets you use any font or style you want without worrying about how it will appear on other platforms.

Leaving the <font> Tag Behind

The World Wide Web Consortium (**http://www.w3.org**) has eliminated the **<font>** tag from the formal XHTML specification. If you're not familiar with the **<font>** tag (or as some like to call it, the *evil* **<font>** tag), it lets you change the font characteristics of a block of code. Unfortunately, the **<font>** tag affects only the code it's wrapped around. Take this for example:

```
<p><font face="Verdana, Arial, Helvetica, sans-serif">This is a paragraph full of text.</font></p>
```

This looks all well and good, right? The text *This is a paragraph full of text.* would be displayed in the desired font without any problem. What if you want every paragraph on a page to have the same font? You'd need to do something like this:

```
<p><font face="Verdana, Arial, Helvetica, sans-serif">This is a paragraph full of text.</font></p>
<p><font face="Verdana, Arial, Helvetica, sans-serif">This is another paragraph full of text.</font></p>
```

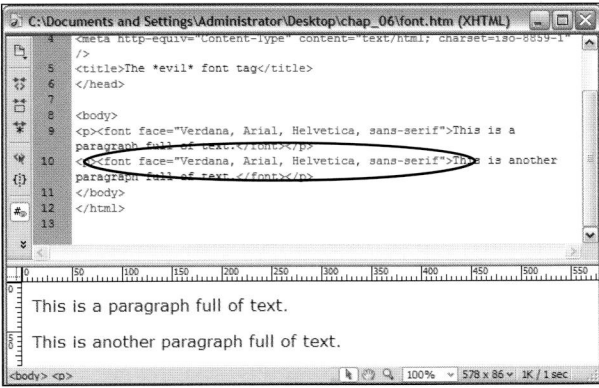

Just multiply that by roughly 20 pages in a site, with every paragraph in the site requiring the same font formatting. Now imagine, if you will, your client suddenly decides the text should use the Georgia font instead—oh, and *red*, too. You now need to change *every single* **<font>** tag in the *entire site* to this:

```
<p><font color="#FF0000" face="Georgia, Times New Roman, Times, serif">This is a paragraph full of text.</font></p>
```

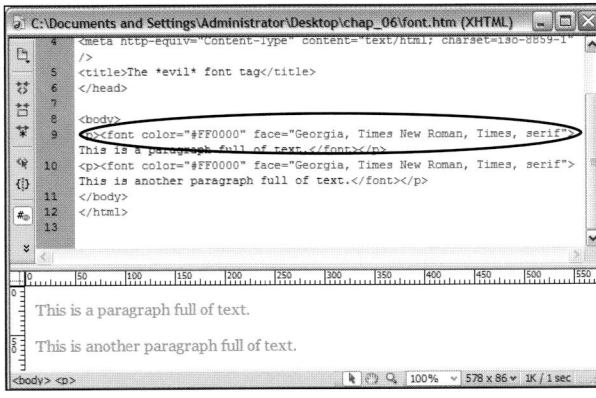

Again, multiply that by 20 pages in a site, and you have a couple of hours of work ahead of you manually changing **<font>** tags, double-checking to make sure everything is correct, and generally working up an ulcer. Imagine a client with a penchant for changing their minds and you'll soon be at the funny farm.

Let's look at the same problem, but solve it with CSS. Here's our XHTML code:

```
<p>This is a paragraph full of text.</p>
<p>This is another paragraph full of text.</p>
```

First, notice the code is much easier to read than the code samples shown earlier with the **<font>** tag. It's not cluttered up with display information, but it also doesn't have any formatting. You can add that formatting by creating a new CSS rule that redefines how all **<p>** tags should be rendered by the browser. Here's what the code looks like:

```
<style type="text/css">
p {
   font-family: Verdana, Arial, Helvetica,
sans-serif;
}
</style>
<p>This is a paragraph full of text.</p>
<p>This is another paragraph full of
text.</p>
```

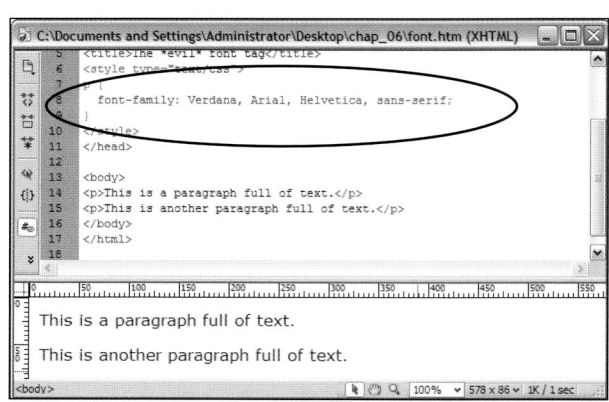

As you can see, this code sample is much easier to read than the **<font>** mess you saw first. Now if your client with the commitment problem comes back with the same request, "Make it red and Georgia!"—no problem, just change that one rule:

```
<style type="text/css">
p {
   font-family: Georgia, "Times New Roman",
Times, serif;
   color: #FF0000;
}
</style>
<p>This is a paragraph full of text.</p>
<p>This is another paragraph full of
text.</p>
```

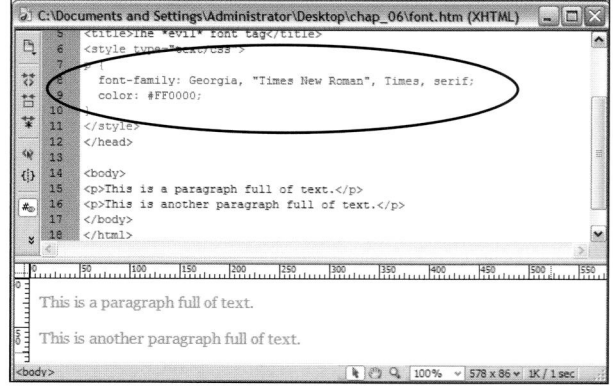

As you can see, that single change modified the font for every **<p>** tag on the entire page. If that style declaration was in an external file attached to every page in your site (which you learned about in the previous chapter), you'd only have to change the font and color for **<p>** tags in *one* spot. Think of all the money you'll save on antacids!

Valid XHTML Typographic Elements

With all the hubbub surrounding the use or misuse of the **<font>** tag combined with all kinds of conflicting information on the Web, we figured it would be a good idea to give you a listing of some of the more common XHTML 1.0 elements that relate to Web typography. The purpose of this list is to identify the XHTML elements that relate specifically to typography, not to list all of the elements that will work in modern and older browsers. These elements are used to identify the structure of the text on the page, though some browsers will apply some default formatting to the elements. By using only these XHTML elements to control the type in your pages, you will ensure that your pages are XHTML-compliant and that you truly separate the structure of your page from its presentation.

XHTML 1.0 Typographic Elements	
XHTML Element	**Description**
<p>	The paragraph tag is used to define paragraphs on a Web page. You will get to work with the paragraph element in Exercise 1 of this chapter.
<h1> through **<h6>**	The heading tags are used to define various levels of importance on a page and have a range from 1 to 6, with 1 being the most important. You will learn more about heading elements in the "The Importance of Headings?" sidebar later in this chapter.
<ul>	The unordered lists tags are used to create lists with bullets (or other characters). You will get to work with them in Exercise 5.
<ol>	The ordered lists tags are used to create lists with numbers (or other characters) that follow an ascending order. You will get to work with them in Exercise 5.
<li>	The list items tags are used to define items within an ordered or unordered list.
<dl>	The definition lists tags are used to identify a list of words that are being defined, much like you would find in an ordinary dictionary.
<dt>	The definition term tag is used to identify a word that is going to be defined on a page. This is similar to looking up a specific word in a dictionary.
<dd>	The define definition tag is used to identify text that is being used to define the word within a definition term element. This would be similar to identifying the definition in a dictionary.
<hr />	The horizontal rule tag is used to add a horizontal divider on a page.
<pre>	The preformatted tag is used to add text to a page that maintains the exact formatting applied in Code view. Text within this tag can contain as many spaces or tabs as desired and is typically formatted using a monospaced font, such as Courier.

continues on next page

XHTML 1.0 Typographic Elements *continued*	
XHTML Element	**Description**
<em>	The emphasis tag is used to add emphasis to text on a page. Most browsers render text wrapped with **<em>** tags as italic by default. Although this sounds like its affecting presentation, it's really identifying text that will be read with emphasis by screen reader programs for the sight-impaired.
<strong>	The strong element is used to add additional emphasis to text on a page. Most browsers make text wrapped with **<strong>** tags bold by default.

Please remember that this list is not complete and represents only the XHTML 1.0 elements that we think you will encounter most often. For a complete listing of all valid XHTML 1.0 elements, please visit the following links:

XHTML 1.0—Transitional
http://www.w3.org/TR/xhtml1/DTD/xhtml1-transitional.dtd

W3 Schools
http://www.w3schools.com/xhtml/xhtml_reference.asp

XHTML 1.0—Frameset
http://www.w3.org/TR/xhtml1/DTD/xhtml1-frameset.dtd

XHTML 1.0—Strict
http://www.w3.org/TR/xhtml1/DTD/xhtml1-strict.dtd

Formatting Text with the Property Inspector

In this exercise, you will learn how to format text by modifying the typeface, size, and color. When you change font styling with the Property Inspector, Dreamweaver 8 writes a series of styles for you so you don't have to define any CSS styles at all. As you will see, creating and formatting text with Dreamweaver 8 is just as easy as working with any word processing application.

1 Copy the **chap_07** folder from the **HOT CD-ROM** to your **Desktop**. Define your site as **Chapter 7** using the **chap_07** folder as the local root folder. Make sure the **Files** panel is open. If it's not, choose **Window > Files** or press **F11**.

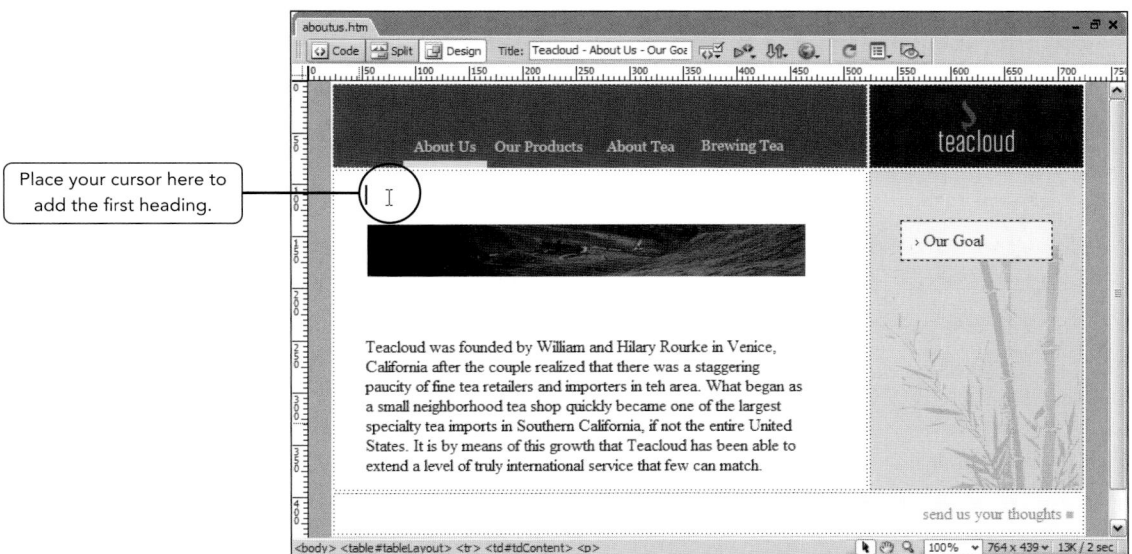

Place your cursor here to add the first heading.

2 In the **Files** panel, double-click **aboutus.htm** to open it. Place your cursor above the image in the center of the page, and type **About Us:Our Goal**.

This is a version of the About Us page used throughout this book, but it's missing a few key pieces of text, which you get to add throughout this exercise.

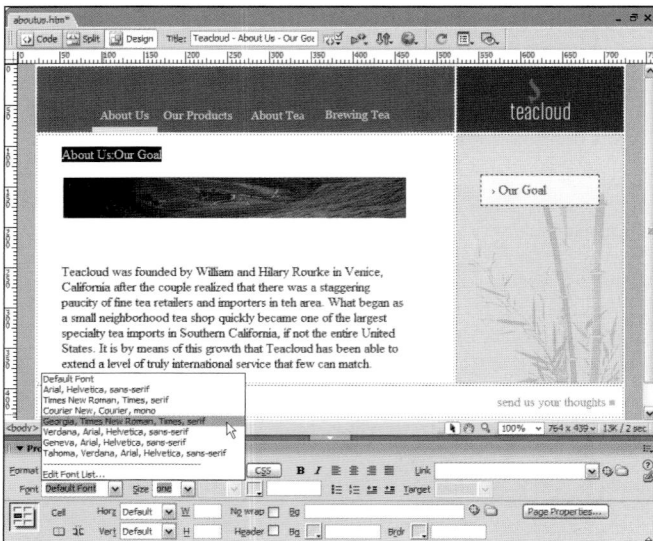

3 Click and drag to select the text you just typed. In the **Property Inspector**, choose **Georgia, Times New Roman, Times, serif** from the **Font** pop-up menu.

Unless you have the Georgia font installed on your computer, you probably didn't notice any change at all, because the font was already styled with Times New Roman to begin with.

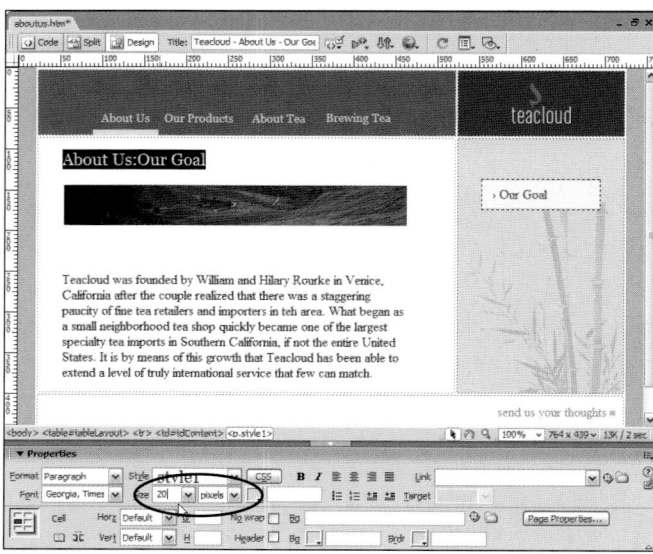

4 With the text still selected, type **20** in the **Size** field. The pop-up menu right next to **Size** will then show **pixels**, which means the text is set to be **20 pixels** tall. Press **Enter** (Windows) or **Return** (Mac) to commit your changes.

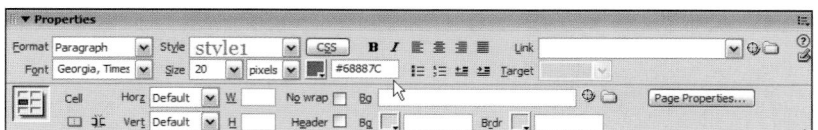

5 With the text *still* selected, type **#68887C** in the **Color** field.

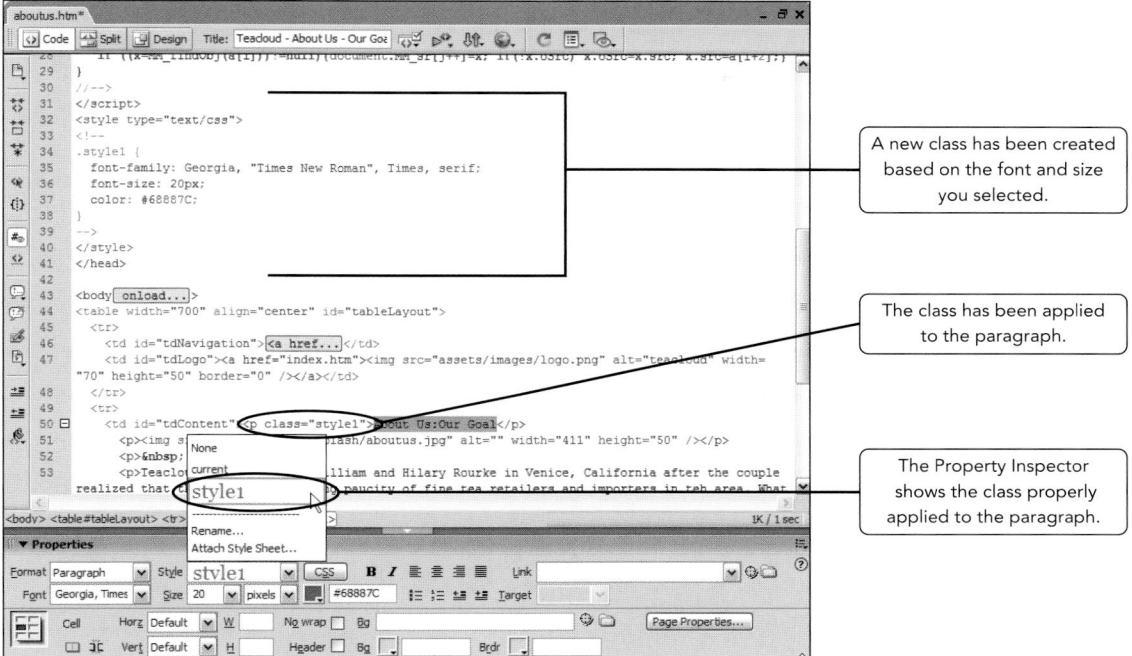

A new class has been created based on the font and size you selected.

The class has been applied to the paragraph.

The Property Inspector shows the class properly applied to the paragraph.

If you switch to Code view, you'll notice several changes to your page. First, Dreamweaver 8 added a **<style>** tag with a class defining the formatting you just specified. That class has also been applied to the **<p>** tag surrounding the *About Us:Our Goal* text. And finally, the Property Inspector now shows style1 has been applied to the text. **Note:** We collapsed a few blocks of code to make the screen shot easier to understand. You'll learn about collapsing code in *"Chapter 12, XHTML."*

6 Switch back to **Design** view. This text seems to hold some special meaning to this page, it's the first item on the page, and it's larger than the remaining text in order to stand out. This text seems like a good candidate for a heading. With your cursor anywhere inside the block of text, choose **Heading 1** from the **Format** pop-up menu in the **Property Inspector**.

The text is now surrounded by an **<h1>** tag instead of a **<p>** tag, indicating the text is a heading, not just regular paragraph text.

N O T E :

The Importance of Headings

In the last step, you formatted some text using headings. The tags look like this: **<h1>**. They range from 1 to 6 and change the size of the text they're wrapped around. Most browsers will display them in a decreasing font size as the numbers get larger. (An **<h1>** tag is rendered larger than an **<h2>**, and so on.)

Headings don't just make text larger, they also serve a very noble and useful purpose: giving your pages *structure*, which accomplishes several things:

- **Readability:** Headings make the page easier to read by breaking things into smaller digestible pieces. People reading online are more likely to skim through a long page of text instead of reading the entire article line by line. Providing occasional headings makes it easier for viewers to get right to the text they want.

- **Accessibility:** If sight-impaired users access your Web page, they might not "see" your Web page, but will instead have a reading device "read" it aloud. Heading tags can be used by screen readers to make it much easier for visually impaired people to navigate through a Web page. You might not imagine that your site has much of a sight-impaired audience, and perhaps do not think this information applies to your site design strategy. In many cases, however, making your site accessible is not an option, but a requirement (especially if you work for a company or organization that must meet Section 508 accessibility standards (**http://www.section508.gov**).

- **Findability:** Search engines *love* headings because they represent text of some increased importance. If something is a heading, it must be relevant to what immediately follows it, so search engines will give more weight to text in a heading than they will to text in the rest of a document. So make your headings useful and relevant, and the search engines will love you.

Our advice is to use heading tags instead of increased font sizes for headlines. Give your page structure in order to make it meaningful.

7 By default, heading tags are bold, but for the Teacloud layout, this particular heading shouldn't be. If the **CSS Styles** panel isn't already open, choose **Window > CSS Styles** to open it. The screen shot describes the main sections of the panel.

If you haven't already, make sure you go through Chapter 6, *"Cascading Style Sheets"* to learn more about the CSS Styles panel.

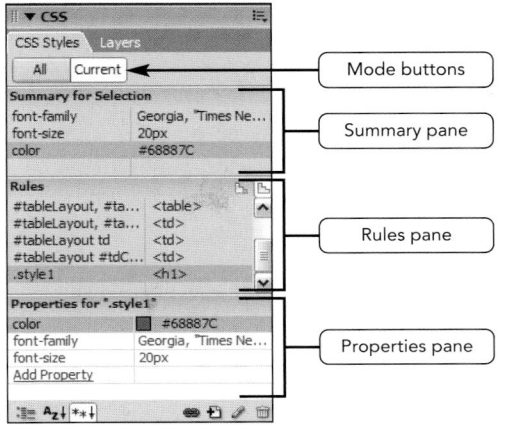

8 **Right-click** (Windows) or **Ctrl+click** (Mac) **.style1** in the **Rules** pane and choose **Edit** from the contextual menu, or click **.style1** and click the **Edit Style** button. The **CSS Rule Definition** dialog box appears.

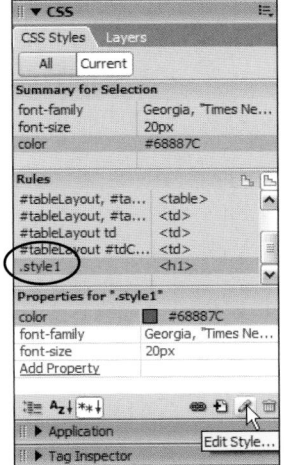

9 Choose **normal** from the **Weight** pop-up menu and click **OK**.

You just changed the style definition for the class applied to the **<h1>** tag.

What you've just done is alright, but anytime you want an **<h1>** tag to look like the one you just set up, you need to apply the **style1** class to it. If you have 50 **<h1>** tags in your site, you need to apply the class to every single one of them. It's far better to use a type selector to redefine how all the **<h1>** tags are displayed; you just have to update the type selector, and all 50 **<h1>** tags will update automatically. Using a type selector in this case is far more efficient.

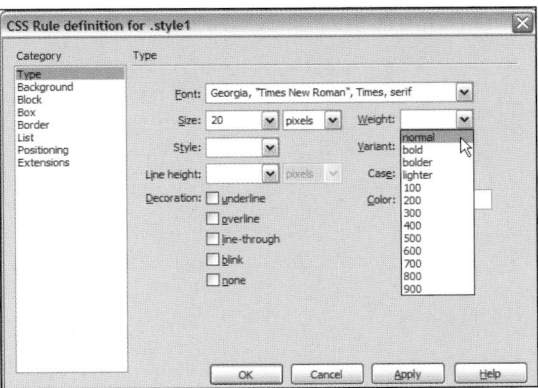

The Property Inspector Can Make You Class Happy

If you recall from the previous chapter, we warned you about becoming class happy, where you apply classes all over the place in order to format your documents. Dreamweaver's Property Inspector makes it far too easy to become class happy (and with badly named classes at that). Every time you change a font setting in the Property Inspector, you run the risk of Dreamweaver creating another class, such as .style2, .style3, and so on. Class names should be descriptive, and all style2 and style3 tell you are that they're the second and third styles Dreamweaver wrote for you. For that reason, you'll be using the CSS Styles panel to set all font formatting from here on out so that you have more control over your code. It's a bit more work up front, but in the end your pages will be easier to maintain.

10 The only way to change a CSS selector from one type to another is to switch to **Code** view and change it manually. In the **Document** toolbar, click the **Code** button to switch to **Code** view.

11 Scroll up to line 33 and find the **.style1** CSS rule. Highlight the text **.style1** and press **Delete** to remove the selector, and then type **h1** in its place.

Replace the .style1 class selector with an h1 type selector.

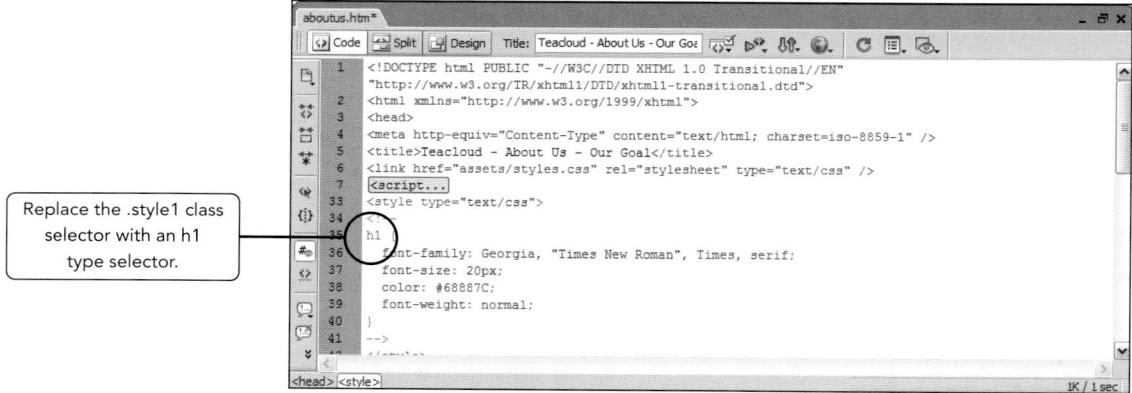

When you're finished, the CSS rule should look like the code in the illustration here.

12 Switch back to **Design** view. Notice the text looks the same. The rule still applies to the **<h1>**, it's just using a type selector instead of a class selector. Now you can remove the class. Place your cursor anywhere inside the **<h1>** and choose **None** from the **Style** pop-up menu in the **Property Inspector**.

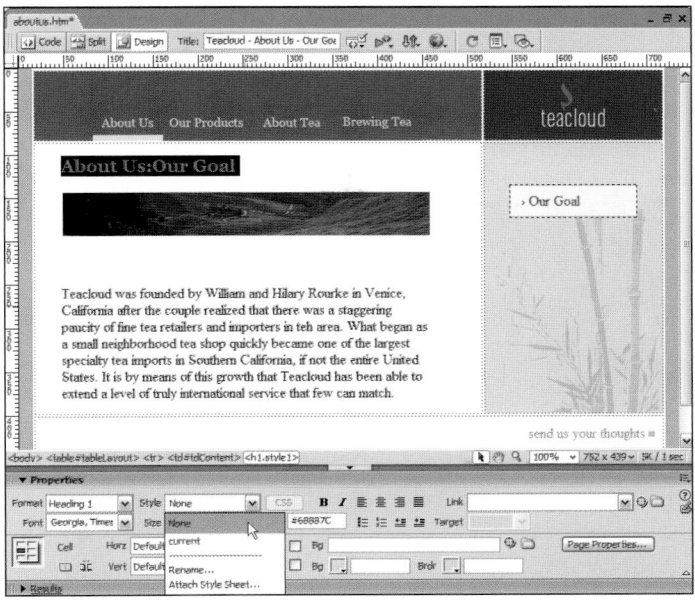

13 Place your cursor in the blank space below the image on the page and type the eternal question on everyone's mind: **What Would the World Do Without Tea?**

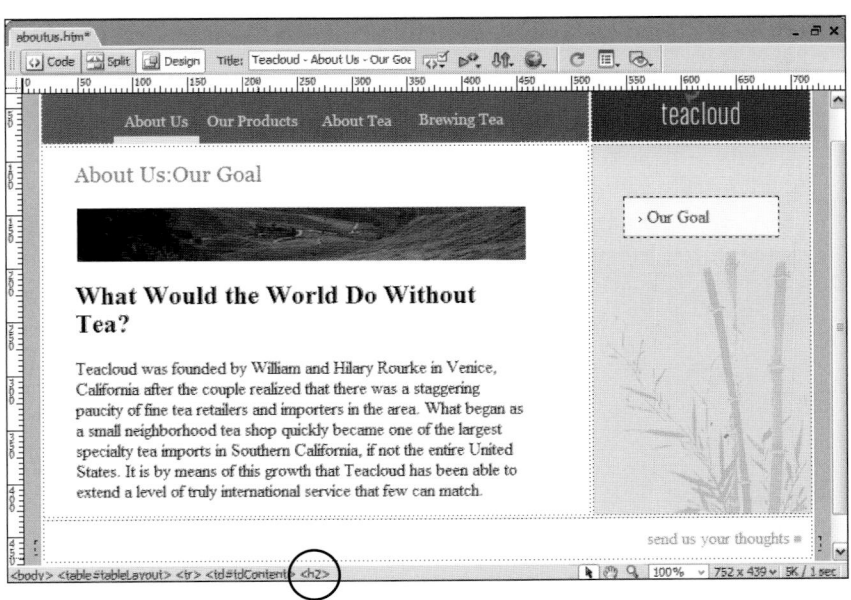

14 With your cursor still in that paragraph, press **Ctrl+2** (Windows) or **Cmd+2** (Mac) to wrap the text in an **<h2>** tag instead of a **<p>** tag.

15 In the **CSS Styles** panel, click the **New CSS Rule** button. In the **New CSS Rule** dialog box, select **Tag** from the **Selector Type** list and type **h2** into the **Tag** field. Make sure **styles.css** is selected in the **Define in** list and click **OK**.

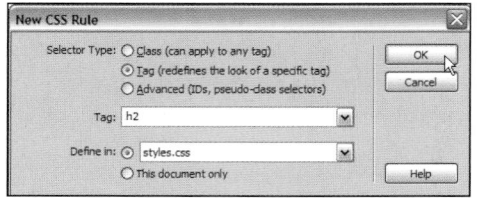

16 In the **CSS Rule Definition** dialog box, set the **Size** to **11 pixels**, choose **bold** from the **Weight** pop-up menu, and type **#949D87** in the **Color** field. Click **OK** to add the style to **styles.css**.

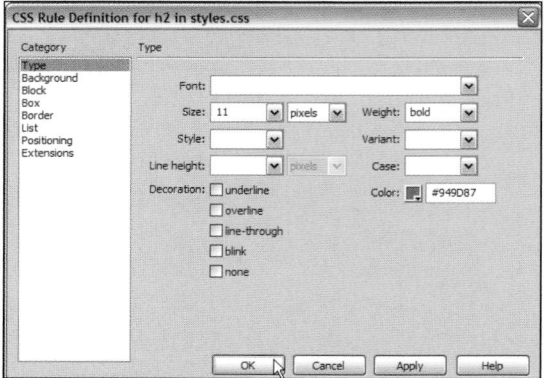

You're almost there. The last thing to do to get all of the type correct is to redefine the font family for the body of the document. The **<h2>** you created and the paragraph below it definitely don't look right in the default serif font. Notice **styles.css** has also been opened for you since changes have been made to the file.

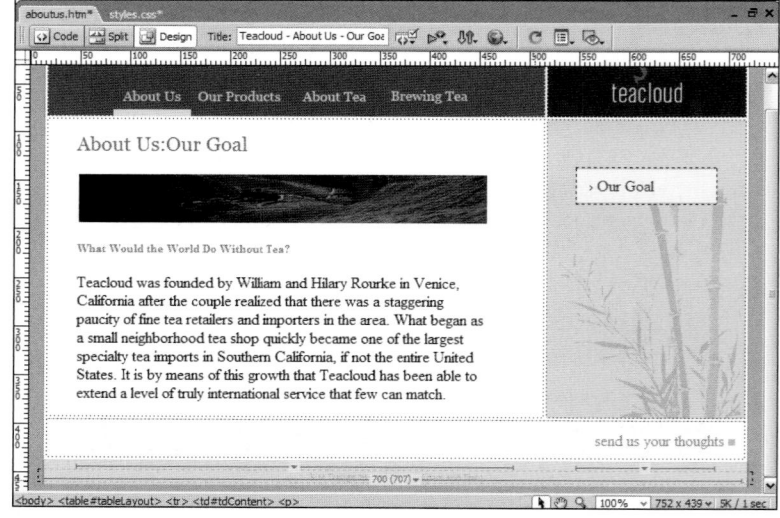

17 In the **CSS Styles** panel, click the **New CSS Rule** button. In the **New CSS Rule** dialog box, select **Tag** from the **Selector Type** list and type **body** into the **Tag** field. Make sure **styles.css** is selected in the **Define in** list and click **OK**.

Redefining the style of the body tag affects everything in the entire document. This is a great way to set some default styles for every element on the page; then you only need to code for the *exceptions*, such as changing the font face for the **<h1>** or the font size of the **<h2>**.

18 In the **CSS Rule Definition** dialog box, choose **Verdana, Arial, Helvetica, sans-serif** from the **Font** list and set the **Size** to **11 pixels**. Click **OK** to add the new rule.

The page is definitely looking better. However, there's not quite enough white space on the page, so things still look cramped. In the next exercise, you'll learn how to use margins, padding, and line-height to improve the readability of your pages.

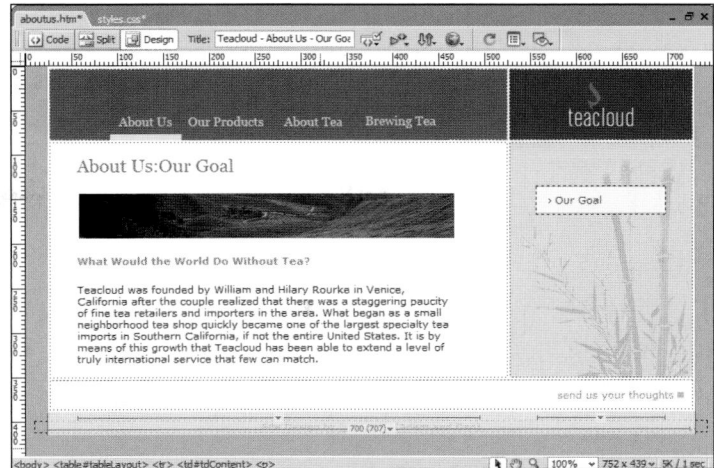

19 Save your changes, and keep **aboutus.htm** open for the next exercise.

This exercise showed you how to use the Property Inspector to apply font settings to the text on your page, and how to define the default font style for the entire document the "right" way. Unfortunately, the Property Inspector has the tendency to create class-happy pages, which makes your projects harder to manage in the long term, so throughout the rest of this chapter you'll be using the CSS Styles panel to create your styles.

What Measurement Should I Use?

If you've played with the CSS Rule Definition dialog box at all, you probably noticed there are quite a few different units of measurement for sizing text, some of which you'll use on a daily basis, others you'll probably never touch in your design career. The following table describes each of the measurement units:

CSS Measurement Units	
Measurement Unit	**Description**
Screen Measurements: pixels	Pixel refers to the actual pixels of the device viewing the content. If a font size is set to 12 pixels, its height will be 12 pixels on the device viewing the content. Pixel measurements are the most reliable between different operating systems and devices.
ems	The em size is a relative measurement, which means it can change based on the context it's used in. One em is equal to the current size of the text. If you set a font to be 1.5 ems, it will be 1.5 times its default size, whether that's generated by another CSS rule or the browser default.

continues on next page

CSS Measurement Units	*continued*
Measurement Unit	**Description**
Screen Measurements: **exs**	The ex measurement is similar to the em, but its height is based on the height of the lowercase *x* in the current font. We've never personally had a use for this particular measurement.
%	Percentage measurements will render exactly the same as em measurements. If you set a font size to be 150%, it will be rendered 1.5 times its default size, whether that's generated by another CSS rule or the browser default.
Print Measurements: **points**	Point measurements are used for printing, and each point is equal to 1/72nd of an inch.
in, cm, mm	You can also size print content by inches, centimeters, and millimeters.
picas	A pica is equal to 12 points.

Well, now that you know what the different CSS measurements are, which one should you use? That depends completely on what you're after as a designer. Pixel measurements give you the most control over how your text will appear, but if you're serving your site to a Windows majority using Internet Explorer, you're taking away some of their choices. If your site has font sizes set in pixels, it's impossible for a Web user to resize the text on your page. Most designers' initial reaction to that is "Great! I don't want them destroying my layout by resizing the text anyway." Unfortunately, many people have pretty bad eyesight, and some sites are simply unusable if the font is too small, so allowing users to increase the font size helps them get the information they need. All other browsers we're aware of allow a user to resize the text regardless of the font size used, but Internet Explorer is still the majority.

So what measurements do I use? As a general rule, you might consider setting a default font size for the body of your document in ems, and then size everything based on that default measurement. So the rule for the body of the document would be something like this:

```
body {
    font-size: 0.8em;
}
```

That rule sets all of the text on the entire page to 0.8 em. Then all further measurements are based off of that measure, so an h1 would be styled like this:

```
h1{
    font-size: 1.5em;
}
```

Using ems allows you to have fine control over your sizes, but still lets users resize their text. In order to avoid confusion and skip the whole "which to use" discussion, you're going to be using pixels to size the text throughout this book. As you become more familiar with CSS and start developing your own development style, pick what works best for you and your visitors.

2 | Managing White Space with Margins, Padding, and Line Height

If we could give you only one piece of advice for styling your text, it's "use white space." The Web is full of text, and the devices that we have to read text aren't suited for the job. The typical desktop printer prints text at over 600 dpi (dots per inch), whereas the monitor sitting on your desk can't show more than 72 dpi. Reading text on a screen is far more difficult than reading it on paper. Because of this low resolution, use lots of white space in order to make your pages easier to read. In this exercise, you'll learn how to manage the white space of your text using margins, padding, and line height.

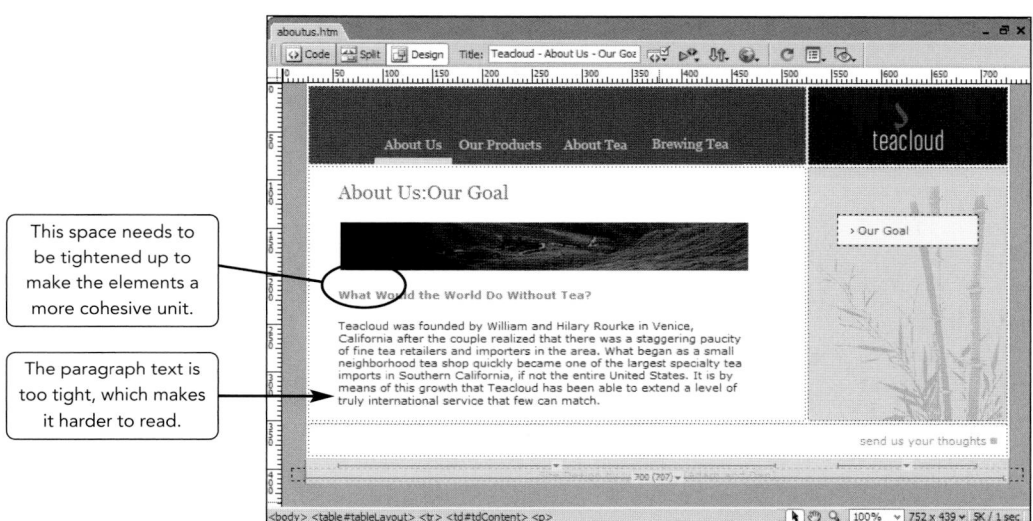

This space needs to be tightened up to make the elements a more cohesive unit.

The paragraph text is too tight, which makes it harder to read.

1 If you just completed Exercise 1, **aboutus.htm** should still be open. If it's not, go back and complete Exercise 1.

In this exercise, you'll tighten up the space around the headings and create more space between the text in the paragraphs.

2 The first thing to do is adjust the line height of the paragraphs on the page. In the **CSS Styles** panel, click the **New CSS Rule** button to create a new rule.

3 In the **New CSS Rule** dialog box, choose **Tag** from the **Selector** pop-up menu, type **p** in the **Tag** field, and click **OK**.

4 Set the **Line height** to **1.7ems** and click **OK** to add the new rule.

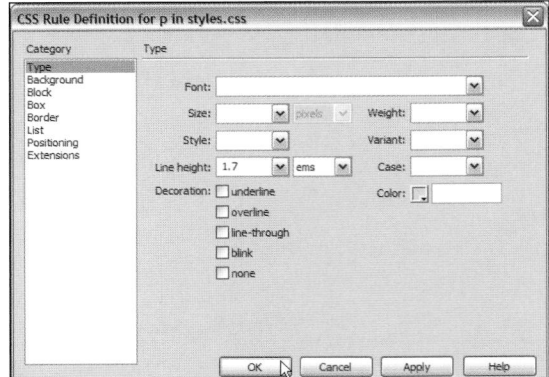

The line height makes an immediate difference in the display of the page. The text in the paragraph now has more space between the lines of text, which makes it easier for a reader to scan from line to line without getting lost.

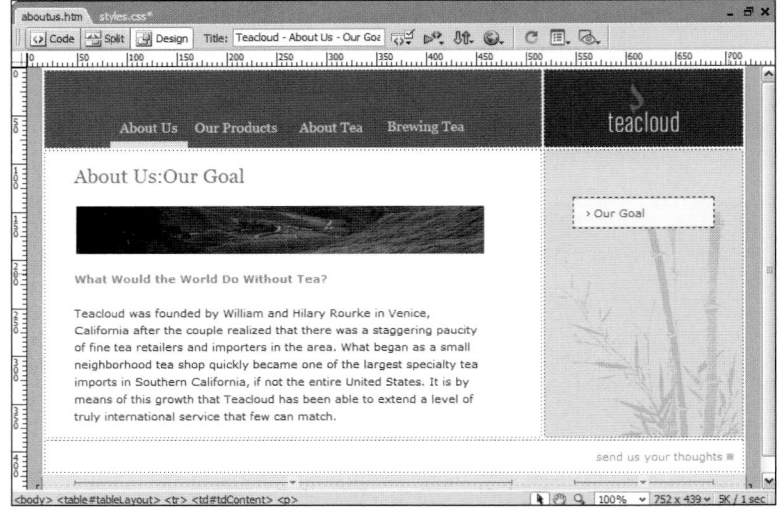

Now it's time to tighten up the space between the **<h1>** and the image immediately following it by changing the margins on the **<h1>** tag.

5 In the **CSS Styles** panel, **right-click** (Windows) or **Ctrl+click** (Mac) the **h1** rule and choose **Edit** from the contextual menu to open the **CSS Rule Definition** dialog box.

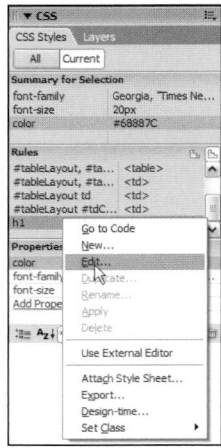

Understanding Line Height

Line height, by definition, is the total height of a line of text, including the white space above and below the actual characters. The following illustration should make this more obvious:

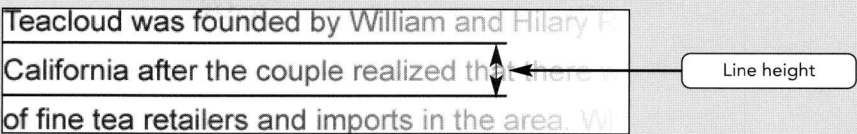

Line height

If you set the font size of a paragraph to 10 pixels, and then set the line height to 20 pixels, you can calculate the amount of white space above and below the line of text with the following equation:

(line height − font size) ÷ 2 = white space above and below text

So with a font size of 10 pixels and a line height of 20 pixels, the math looks like this:

(20 − 10) ÷ 2 = 5 pixels

This means that a line height of 20 pixels on a paragraph with a font size of 10 pixels would have 5 pixels of white space above the characters, and 5 pixels of white space below the characters. Setting the line height to twice the font size is the same as setting a paragraph to be double-spaced in your favorite word processing program.

If you're anything like us you'd rather not deal with math when it comes to formatting your text, so as a general rule just use whatever looks good to you and skip the math altogether. The mathematical rules simply make it a little easier to understand what's happening when you format your sites.

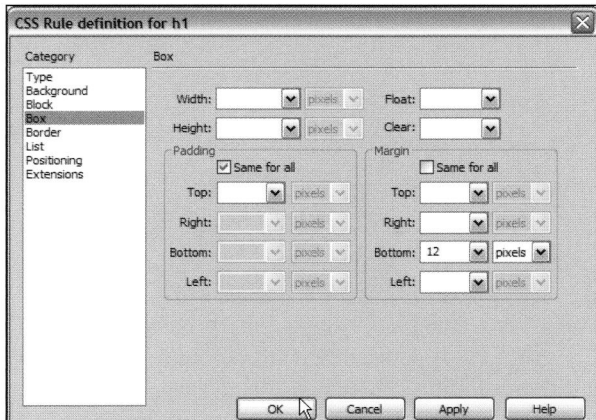

6 In the **CSS Rule Definition** dialog box, select **Box** from the **Category** pane. You want to change only the space below the **<h1>** tag, so deselect the **Same for all** check box in the **Margin** section and set **Bottom** to **12 pixels**. Click **OK** to apply the rule.

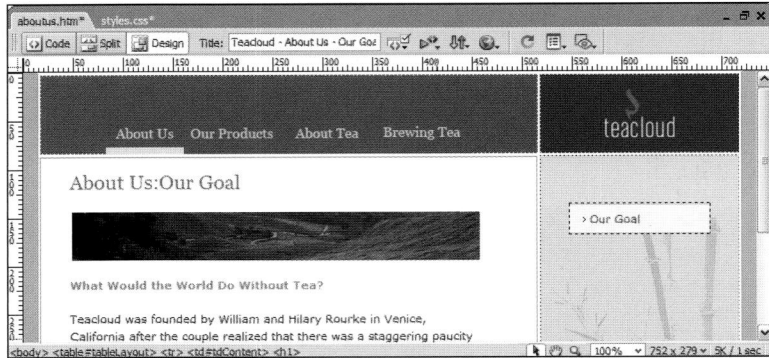

The last change made to the h1 rule didn't affect the display of the document at all. The reason that nothing changed is due to the way margins are calculated.

NOTE:

Understanding How Margins Are Calculated

The last change you made to the h1 rule didn't affect the display of the document because of the way margins are calculated. Every element on the page has a margin, and text elements (headings and paragraphs) have built-in margins. Two adjacent elements share their margins, and the larger of the two margins is used to separate the two elements. Take the **<h1>** on the page and the following image (which is in a **<p>** tag) as an example:

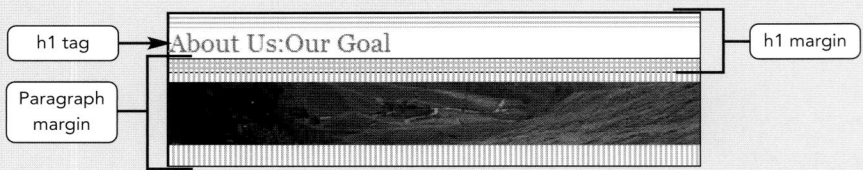

The **<h1>** tag has 12 pixels of bottom margin, shown by the horizontal lines above and below it. The paragraph containing the image has a default margin of about 20 pixels, shown by the vertical lines, which is roughly twice the font size of the paragraph. We say "about 20 pixels" because this is the browser default margin that's being drawn, which can be quite different between browsers. When the browser decides how far to space the two elements apart it *collapses* the margins, placing them on top of each other so that the space between the two elements is equal to the *larger* of the two margins. In the page you're working on, the larger margin on the **<p>** tag is the one that's honored, which is why there was no visual change to the display of the document when you set the bottom margin of the **<h1>** to 12 pixels; the **<p>** tag still had a margin greater than 12 pixels, so the **<p>** tag's margin was used to separate the two elements.

7 To finish collapsing the space between the header and paragraph, double-click the **p** rule in the **CSS Styles** panel to edit it. In the **CSS Rule Definition** dialog box, select **Box** from the **Category** pane. In the **Margin** section, set **Top** to **0 pixels**. Click **OK** to apply the rule.

Now that the top margin of all **<p>** tags is set to 0, the **<h1>** tag and the following paragraph are spaced 12 pixels apart. Because of the collapsing margin calculations, the browser determines that 12 is greater than 0, and so it sets the margin between the two elements to 12 pixels.

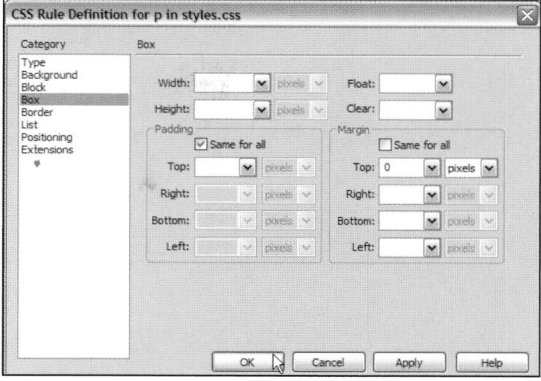

8 To tighten up the space around the **<h2>** tag, double-click the **h2** rule in the **CSS Styles** panel to edit it. In the **CSS Rule Definition** dialog box, select **Box** from the **Category** pane. In the **Margin** section, set **Top** to **0 pixels**, and set **Bottom** to **12 pixels**. Click **OK** to apply the rule.

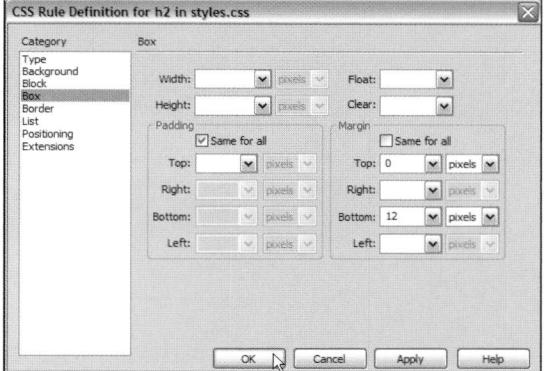

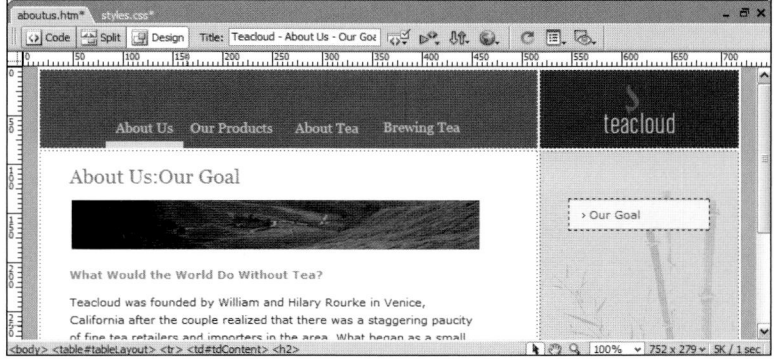

The page is looking pretty good now. The headers are spaced nicely around the image and the paragraph of text is much easier to read with the line height. The last thing to do is to differentiate the **<h2>** tag by adding a small colored border on the left side of the text. Adding the border will simulate the appearance of a square and will help make the heading stand out from the rest of the text. Sound strange? Follow the next few steps, and you'll see what a useful trick this is!

9 Double-click the **h2** rule in the **CSS Styles** panel again to open the **CSS Rule Definition** dialog box. Select **Border** from the **Category** pane and deselect **Same for all** in the **Style**, **Width**, and **Color** sections. Choose **solid** from the **Left** pop-up menu and set **Size** to **11 pixels**. Type **#D7DACE** in the **Color** field. When you're finished, make sure your settings match the ones shown in the illustration here. Click **OK** to apply the rule.

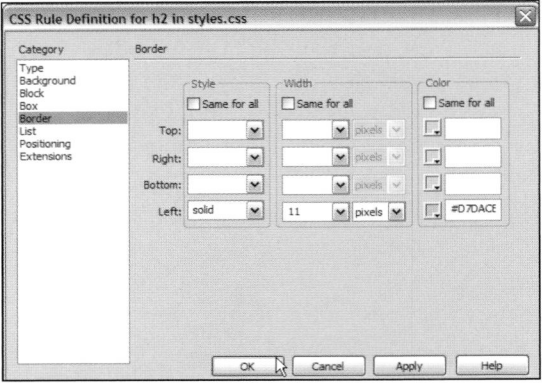

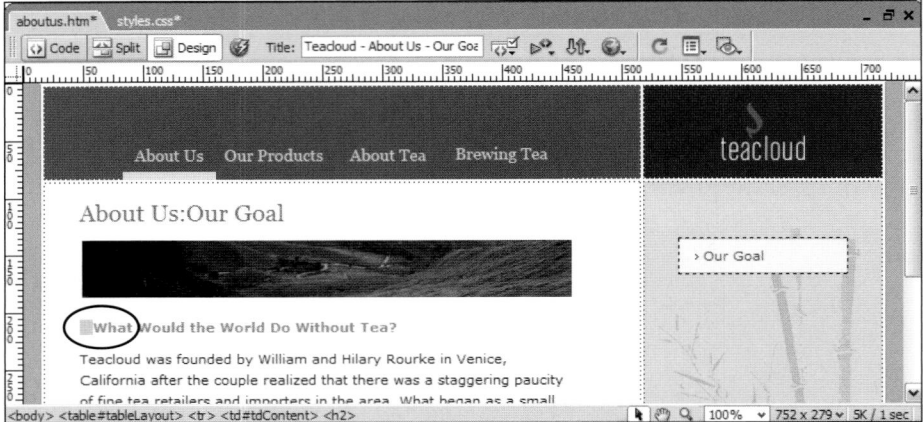

The **<h2>** now has a border to the left of it, which looks like a square icon. Pretty cool trick, huh? Unfortunately, it's *still* not looking quite right—the border is right up against the first letter of the **<h2>** tag, which makes things a little crowded. Not to worry, you can get rid of the crowding inside the **<h2>** tag by adding some padding. You'll learn how in the next step.

---

10 Double-click the **h2** rule in the **Styles** panel one last time, and select **Box** from the **Category** pane. Deselect the **Same for all** box in the **Padding** section and set **Left** to **7 pixels**. Click **OK** to apply the rule.

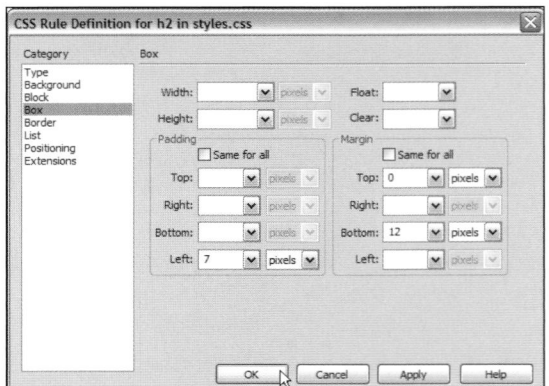

With the seven-pixel padding added, the border on the `<h2>` tag is nicely separated from the text.

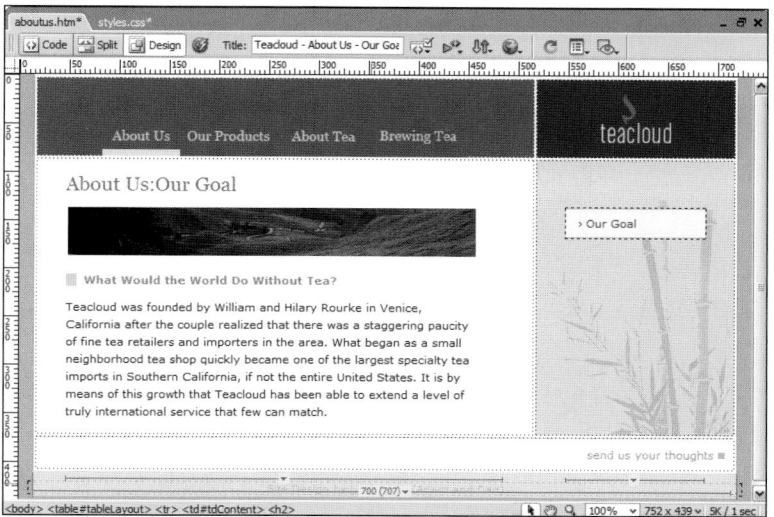

 NOTE:

Understanding Padding

Margins control the space outside a block of text; padding controls the spacing inside a block of text. The following illustration shows the anatomy of a block of text (or as the CSS specification likes to call it, a box):

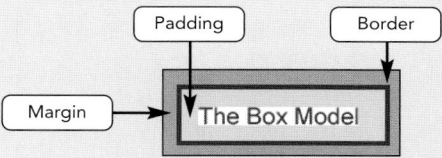

As you can see, the padding for a box of text is added between the text and the border applied to the box, whereas the margin is drawn outside the box. In the example you're working with here, adding seven pixels of left padding to the `<h2>` tag moves the text seven pixels from the left border of the box, thus giving you that little extra space necessary to finish off the formatting.

11 Close **abouttea.htm**. You don't need to save your changes.

In this exercise, you learned how to use line height, margins, and padding to control the white space in your documents. Properly managing your white space can greatly increase the readability (and usability) of your Web sites.

3 | Using Font Lists

Now that you've played with setting font faces, you may be wondering why you're limited by the default font choices Dreamweaver offers. Dreamweaver 8 offers the most common collection of fonts that users viewing your site will have installed on their computers. In this exercise, you will learn how to add and modify the font lists that come with Dreamweaver 8. You will learn how to modify what typefaces are in the existing font lists and how to create your own custom font list.

1 In the **Files** panel, double-click **fontlists.htm** to open it.

This page contains a list of the default font lists provided by Dreamweaver 8. The last paragraph, however, isn't a standard Dreamweaver 8 font list. In this exercise, you'll learn how to create this font list.

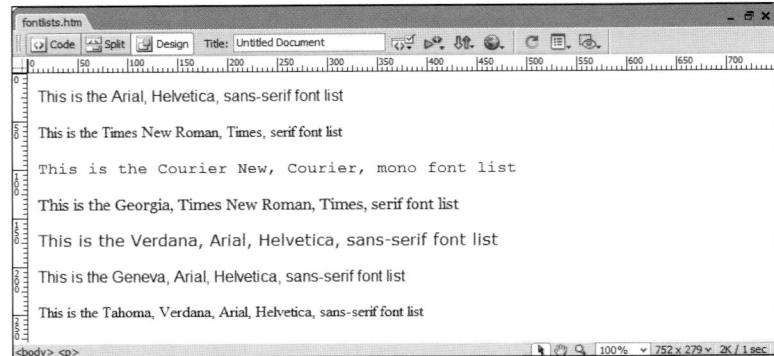

NOTE:

How Font Lists Work

Font lists are a very useful way of ensuring the text on your Web page is viewed the way you intended. When users load a Web page, the browser searches for each font in the list until it finds one that is installed. Once the browser finds a font in the list, it will use that font to display the text on the Web page. For example, if you apply the "Arial, Helvetica, sans-serif," font list to a piece of text, the browser will try to use Arial first to display text. If the user does not have Arial installed, the browser will then try to display Helvetica. If the browser cannot not find Helvetica, it will display the default sans-serif font on the user's computer. The goal of font lists is to create sets of fonts that have similar structure and characteristics, so the contents of your Web pages appear the same from viewer to viewer.

2 Place your cursor anywhere in the document. In the **Property Inspector**, choose **Edit Font List** from the **Font** pop-up menu to open the **Edit Font List** dialog box.

The Edit Font List dialog box lets you create and edit existing font lists, which you'll learn how to do in the following steps.

3 In the **Available fonts** list, click **Tahoma** to select it, and click the **<<** button to add it to the **Chosen fonts** list.

If you don't have Tahoma installed on your local machine, it won't be in the list. Don't worry if it's not there, just type **Tahoma** into the field below the **Available fonts** list. This field lets you to add fonts that you don't actually have installed on your local machine.

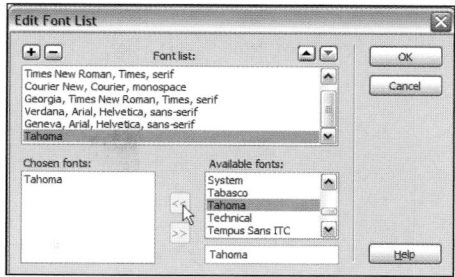

4 In the **Available fonts** list, click **Verdana** to select it, and click the **<<** button to add the font to the **Chosen fonts** list.

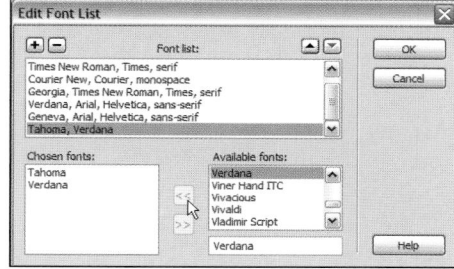

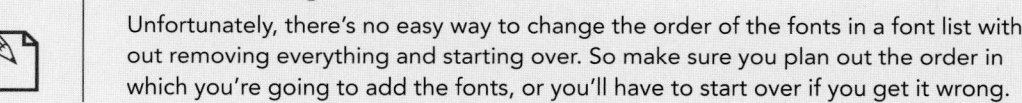

NOTE:

Add Them Right the First Time

Unfortunately, there's no easy way to change the order of the fonts in a font list without removing everything and starting over. So make sure you plan out the order in which you're going to add the fonts, or you'll have to start over if you get it wrong.

5 In the **Available fonts** list, click **Arial** to select it, and click the **<<** button to add it to the **Chosen fonts** list.

6 In the **Available fonts** list, click **Helvetica** to select it, and click the **<<** button to add it to the **Chosen fonts** list.

7 Finally, at the bottom of the **Available fonts** list, click **sans-serif** to select it, and click the **<<** button to add it to the **Chosen fonts** list.

8 When you're all done, the **Edit Font List** dialog box should match the illustration here. Click **OK** to add the new list to the font list.

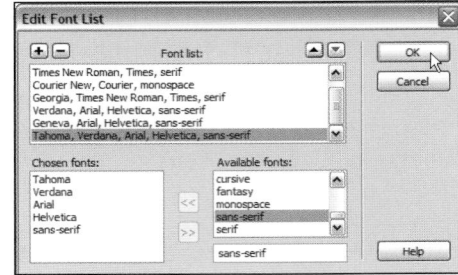

TIP: | **Always Provide an Alternative**
You should always have a generic font type as the last item in your font list. If users don't have any of the fonts in the list, they'll at least see a font of the type you're after. Valid generic font types are as follows: cursive, fantasy, monospace, sans-serif, and serif.

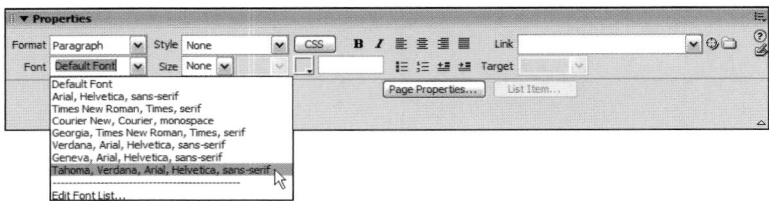

9 Highlight the **This is the Tahoma, Verdana, Arial, Helvetica, sans-serif font list** text in the document. In the **Property Inspector**, choose the **Tahoma, Verdana, Arial, Helvetica, sans-serif font list** from the **Font** pop-up menu.

Notice the text automatically changes to reflect the font choice you just made. This exercise gives you an example of how these font lists will display on your computer. What you see might appear differently in other people's browsers, because they might have different fonts installed on their computers than you do, so the second, third, or even fourth font on the list might be displayed instead of the first one.

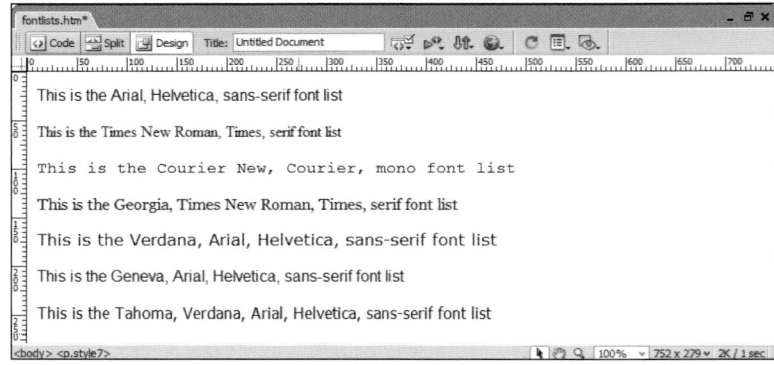

---

10 Close **fontlists.htm**, You don't need to save your changes.

---

4 | Aligning Text

In this exercise, you will learn how to align text on the page. You have four options for aligning text: Left Align, Center Align, Right Align, and Justify. You do have some extra options when you align text next to images, which you will also explore in this exercise.

---

1 In the **Files** panel, double-click **brewingtea.htm** to open it.

Notice the text on the page is aligned to the left. This is the default alignment setting for text.

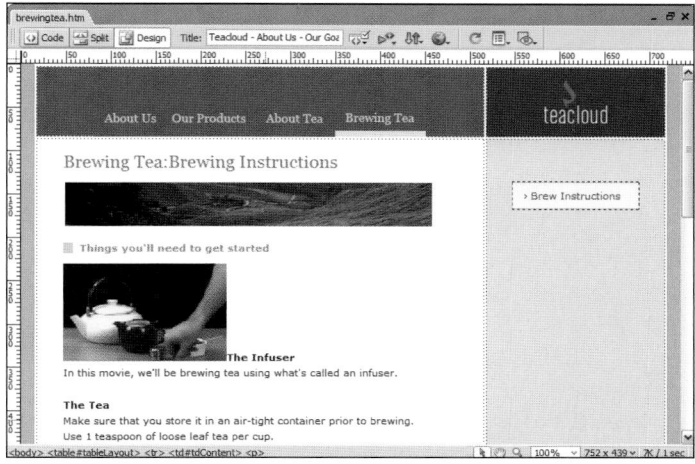

---

2 Click anywhere in the line of text that reads **Brewing Tea:Brewing Instructions**.

3 In the **Property Inspector**, click the **Align Center** button to center your text on the page.

Clicking the Align Center button in the Property Inspector added the **align** attribute to the **<h1>** tag. Although this is alright for single elements, if you want all **<h1>** tags to be centered, you should edit the h1 rule in the CSS Styles panel and set the Text Align property to the desired alignment.

> The align attribute has been added to the <h1> tag.

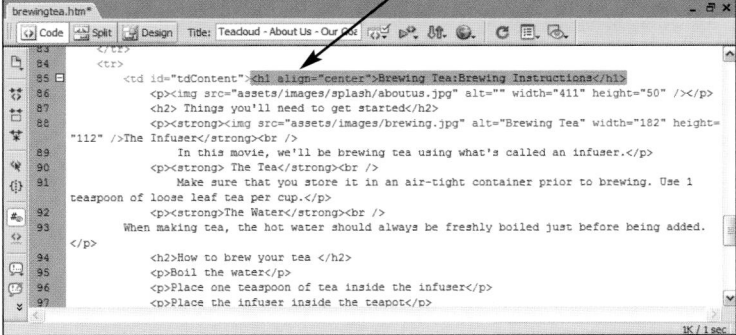

---

4 In the **Property Inspector**, click the **Align Right**, **Justified**, and **Align Left** buttons to see how each of them affects the alignment of this line of text.

---

5 Click the photo of the teapot and the hand reaching for the tea infuser to select it. Take a look at the contents of the **Align** pop-up menu.

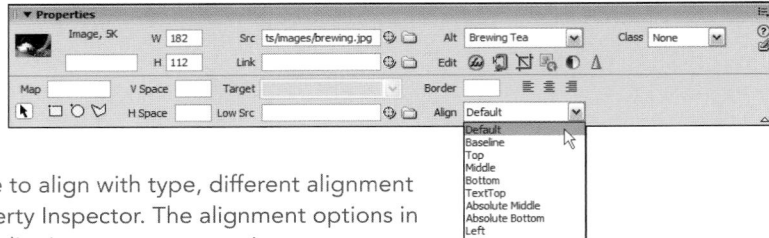

Notice when you select an image to align with type, different alignment options are available in the Property Inspector. The alignment options in this menu are strictly used when aligning text next to an image.

---

6 In the **Property Inspector**, choose **Left** from the **Align** pop-up menu.

Notice the text moves to the top-right of the image. The image has been "floated" to the left, so the text flows along the right side of the image.

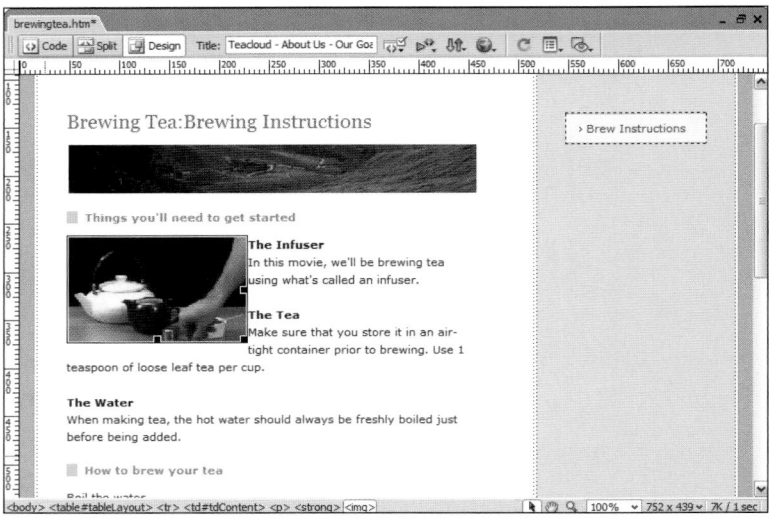

Aligning Text and Images

Dreamweaver 8 offers many alignment options for text and images. The following chart defines all the alignment terms, so now you will know what you are requesting when you select one:

XHTML Text and Image Alignment Options

Alignment	Description
Default	Varies between browsers, but usually uses Bottom alignment as the default
Baseline	Aligns the baseline of the text to the bottom of the image
Bottom	Aligns the baseline of the text to the bottom of the image (same as Baseline)
Absolute Bottom	Aligns text, including descenders (letters such as g and j), to the bottom of the image
Top	Aligns the image to the tallest part of the object (image or text)
TextTop	Aligns the image with the tallest character in the line of text
Middle	Aligns the baseline of the text to the middle of the image
Absolute Middle	Aligns the middle of the text to the middle of the image
Left	Left-aligns the image and wraps text to the right
Right	Right-aligns the image and wraps text to the left

7 With the image still selected, choose **Right** from the **Align** pop-up menu.

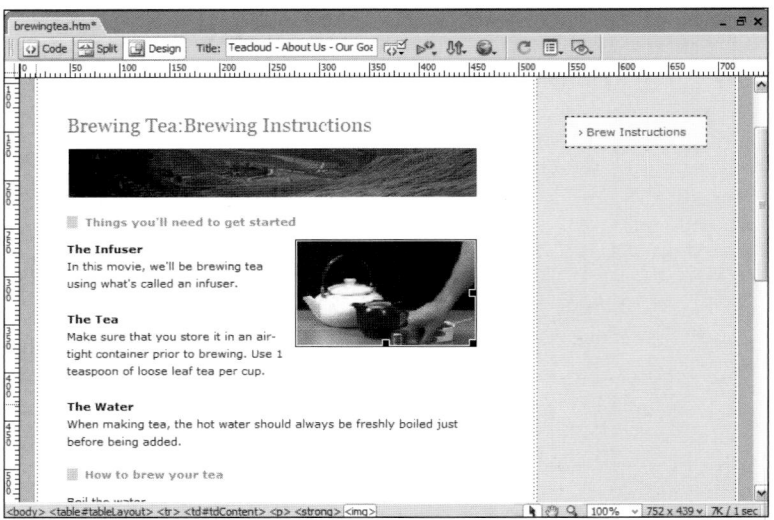

Now that the image is aligned to the right, the text flows nicely down the left hand side of the image. This lets you to make better use of the space on your page and add some visual interest to your text. Just remember the text will be on the opposite side of the image's alignment. This means that if you align an image to the left, the text will flow to the right; if you align an image to the right, the text will flow to the left.

8 Save your changes, and keep **brewingtea.htm** open for the next exercise.

EXERCISE
5 | Using Ordered, Unordered, and Definition Lists

In this exercise, you will learn how to create a variety of lists—an ordered list, an unordered list, and a definition list. You can generate these lists from existing text or from scratch, and as a general rule they behave just like a list in a word processing application.

1 If you just completed the last exercise, **brewingtea.htm** should still be open. If it's not, go back and complete Exercise 4.

2 Click and drag to highlight the text beneath the **Things you'll need...** heading.

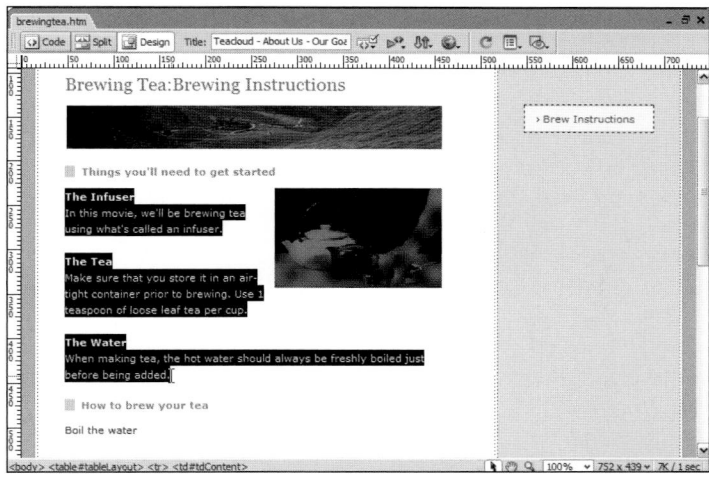

3 In the **Property Inspector**, click the **Unordered List** button.

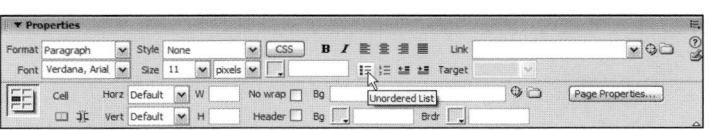

You just created an unordered list! Unordered lists are great for items that don't require a specific order.

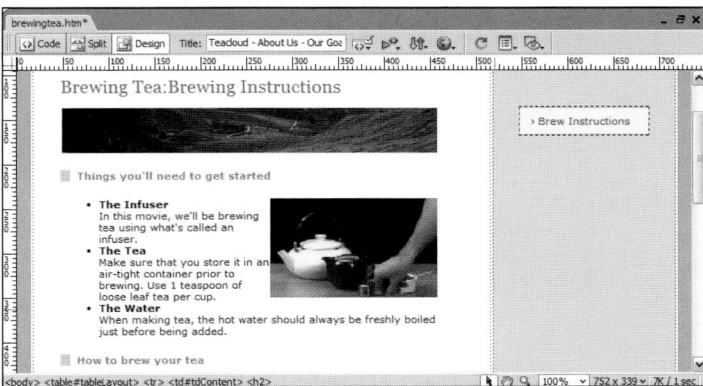

4 Click and drag to highlight the text beneath the **How to brew...** heading.

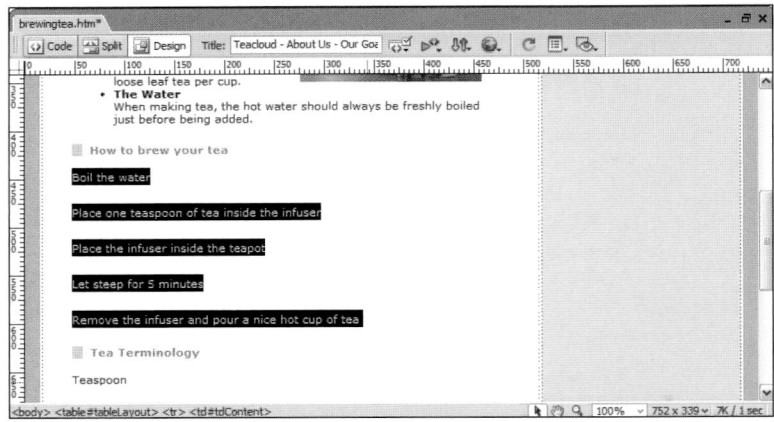

5 Choose **Text > List > Ordered List**, or click the **Ordered List** button in the **Property Inspector**.

You just created an ordered list using numbers to number each item in the list. Use ordered lists when your list requires a specific order. In this case, users should follow the steps in numerical order to make a tasty cup of tea.

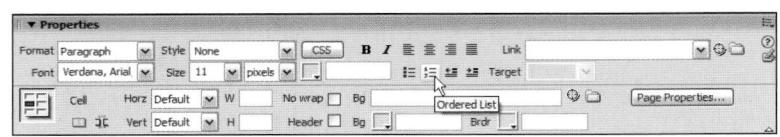

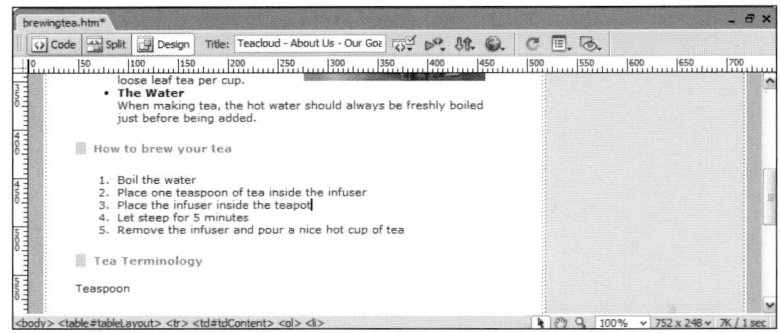

6 Click and drag to highlight the text beneath the **Tea Terminology** heading.

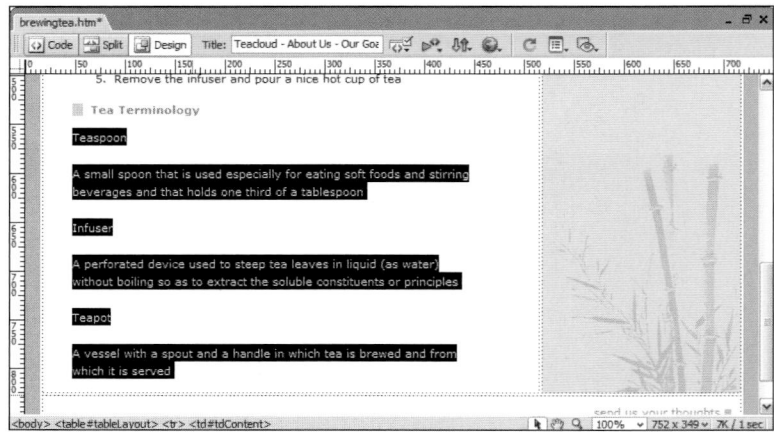

7 Choose **Text > List > Definition List**.

You just created a definition list. Definition lists are great for giving people more information about a particular term. The use of a definition list makes it obvious which text goes with which item.

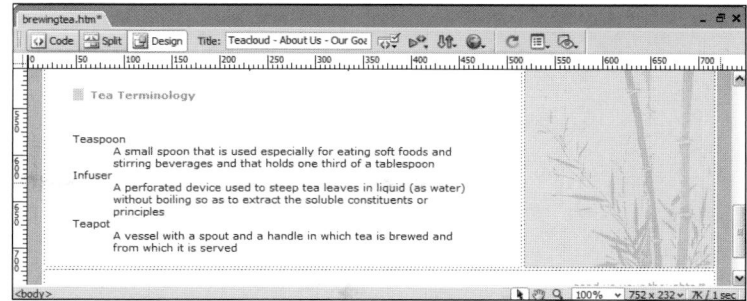

NOTE:

What's in a List?

The previous steps were pretty short and simple. However, what goes on behind the scenes is a bit more involved. When you define a list, Dreamweaver 8 wraps each selection in a tag that defines the list, and then wraps each item in the list with tags showing that they're a member of the list. Take the **How to brew your tea** list as an example. Before you defined it as an ordered list, the code looked like this:

```
<p>Boil the water</p>
<p>Place one teaspoon of tea inside the infuser</p>
<p>Place the infuser inside the teapot</p>
<p>Let steep for 5 minutes</p>
<p>Remove the infuser and pour a nice hot cup of tea</p>
```

After you made it into an ordered list, the code was changed to this:

```
<ol>
    <li>Boil the water</li>
    <li>Place one teaspoon of tea inside the infuser</li>
    <li>Place the infuser inside the teapot</li>
    <li>Let steep for 5 minutes</li>
    <li>Remove the infuser and pour a nice hot cup of tea </li>
</ol>
```

In this code, the **<ol>** tag tells the browser that what's inside those **<ol>** tags is in fact a list. Each item in the list is wrapped with an **<li>** tag, which defines it as a list item.

The benefit of this structure is that if you want to change the **How to brew your tea** list to an unordered list, which shows bullets instead of numbers, you'd simply change the **<ol>** tag to a **<ul>** tag, and it will automatically change the unordered list to an ordered list.

8 Close **brewingtea.htm**. You don't need to save your changes.

In this exercise you learned how to create the most basic of lists. Lists are an *incredibly* powerful way of organizing information, and the very brief overview you've received here doesn't really do them justice. Because they're so powerful, they can also be quite difficult to wrap your head around. If you'd like, do some of your own research to learn more about how to use host lists. For more information, check out Listamatic at **http://css.maxdesign.com.au/listamatic/**.

What Is Flash Text?

It's pretty hard to be involved in Web design today and not hear the word "Flash." It has become widely adopted in the Web design industry as an alternative and/or adjunct to XHTML formatting. Macromedia Flash 8 is a vector-based drawing, animation, interactivity, and application development program. You can use it to create something as simple as a button for a Web page or as complex as an entire video game that can be played on the Web. Flash 8 uses a proprietary file format called SWF (pronounced "swiff"). Flash content that gets uploaded to the Web always ends in the .swf suffix.

In order to view Flash content on the Web, you must have the Flash Player installed in your browser. If you don't have this plug-in, you can download it for free at **http://www.macromedia. com/software/flashplayer**, though the majority of browsers have some version of Flash already installed.

The **Flash Text** feature in Dreamweaver 8 lets you create text and text rollovers for your Web pages, using any font on your system, in the SWF file format. Flash Text is a great feature for creating text rollovers and small lines of text, such as headlines for your body text, because it lets you use exactly the font you want without having to worry if users viewing the site have it installed on their computers. As a result, you can have full control over the appearance of the text. Unfortunately, Flash Text is not searchable by search engines and, as a result, you should not use it for large bodies of text. Before you move on to the exercise and learn the nuances of Flash Text, here's a handy list that outlines some of the pros and cons of this feature:

Using Flash Text	
Pros	**Explanation**
Font integrity	With Flash Text, you can use any font installed on your system, and the visitors to your page don't need to have that font installed, as they do with regular XHTML text. This feature gives you much more flexibility when you are designing your pages.
Text rollovers	Creating text rollovers usually requires that you use a separate image-editing program to create the necessary images. With Flash Text, you can create text rollovers without ever leaving Dreamweaver 8.
Cons	**Explanation**
Plug-in required	To be viewed properly, all Flash content on the Web requires a plug-in. Flash Text is no different and requires that the Flash plug-in be installed in the browser.
Not accessible	Flash, as a general rule, is not accessible. Individuals with disabilities have a hard time dealing with Flash content because browsers don't know what's inside Flash files, so they can't let users know where buttons and text exist. Recent versions of Flash have improved this problem, but there's still a long way to go. If you're concerned about accessibility, you should only use Flash Text for items that aren't integral to the functionality of your site.

6 | Creating Flash Text

In this exercise, you'll create Flash Text. Flash Text lets you use any font you want without worrying whether the visitors to your site will have it installed on their computers. It also lets you easily create rollovers without using any JavaScript. It's really easy to learn and use—read on and try it out to see what we mean!

1 In the **Files** panel, double-click **index.htm** to open it.

This page is almost identical to the **index.htm** files in other exercises, except it's missing the Welcome to teacloud text above the image. You're going to create that text using Flash Text.

2 Click the hand image to select it and press the **left arrow** key to move the cursor before the image.

3 Choose **Insert > Media > Flash Text** to open the **Insert Flash Text** dialog box.

4 Choose a font for your text from the **Font** pop-up menu. Type **30** in the **Size** field to set the size of your text in points.

I am using a font called ChantillyLH, which is similar to the font used for the Teacloud logo. If you don't have ChantillyLH installed, use whatever font you have available.

5 Click the **Color** box. Position your pointer over the gray background in the navigation bar. Notice the pointer changes to the eyedropper, indicating you can sample color. Click to sample color from the gray area.

Select the dark navigation background color.

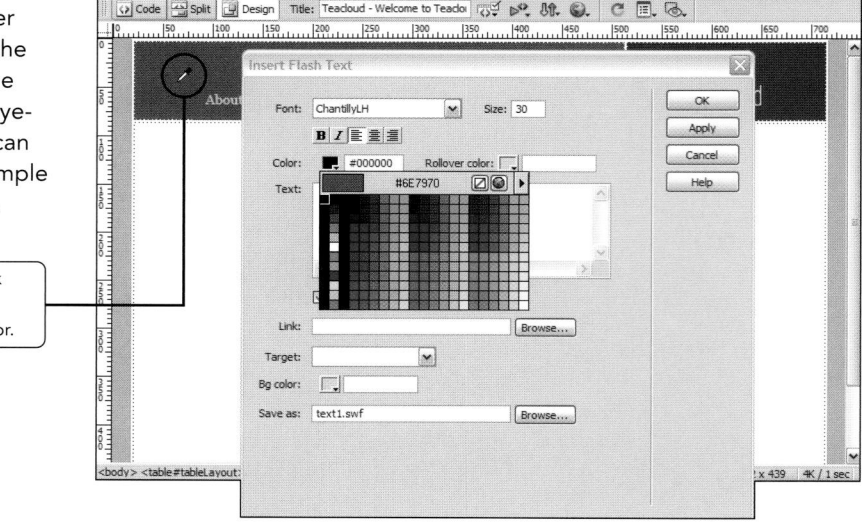

6 Click the **Rollover color** box. Position your pointer over the dark gray background behind the Teacloud logo. Click to sample color from the dark gray area.

Setting this color will automatically create a rollover effect for the Flash Text.

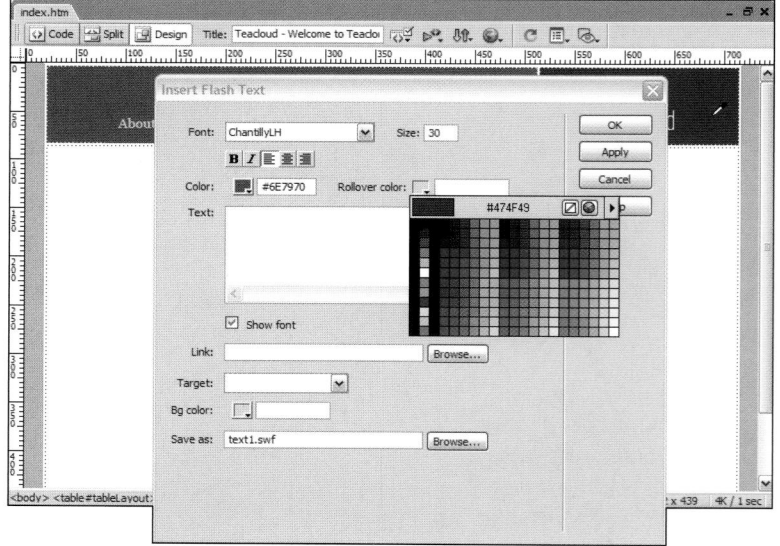

7 In the **Text** field, type **Welcome to teacloud**.

By default, the Show Font check box is selected, giving you a preview of the text in the font you selected.

Warning: This dialog box will not give you a preview of the size you specified; you can only see the actual size in the document itself.

8 Type **#FFFFFF** in the **Bg Color** field to set the background color to white.

---

9 In the **Save as** field, type **welcome.swf**. Click **OK** to open the **Flash Accessibility Attributes** dialog box.

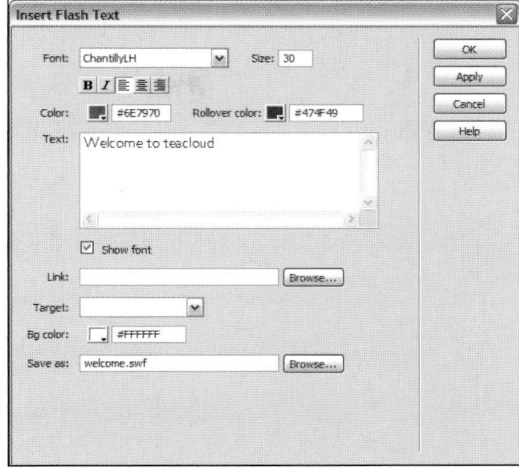

---

10 Type **Welcome to teacloud** in the **Title** field and click **OK**.

At minimum, you should always add a title to the Flash Text so users who don't have the Flash Player installed can see what the Flash Text should be.

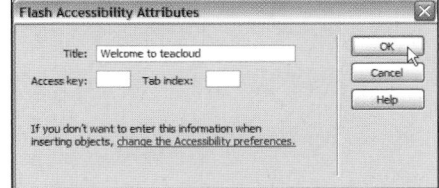

When you're finished, your page should match the illustration here.

As you can see, you just successfully added a *Welcome to teacloud* title using Flash Text. Next, you'll learn how to preview the Flash Text.

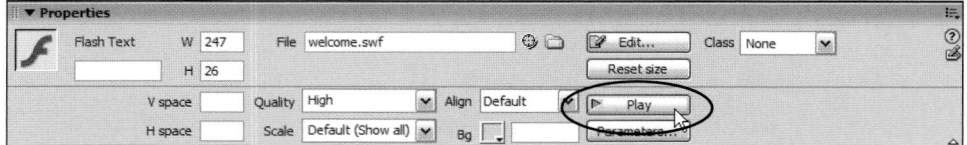

11 With the **Flash Text** selected, click the **Play** button in the **Property Inspector**. Move your mouse over the **Flash Text** to preview the rollover effect. Click the **Stop** button to turn off the preview.

12 Press **F12** to preview your page in a browser. Take a look at the **Flash Text**. Position your mouse over the text to see the rollover.

You should see your *Welcome to teacloud* text in the font you specified. When you move your mouse over the text, it will change to the darker color you specified in the Flash Text dialog box.

13 Return to Dreamweaver 8. Close **index.htm**. You don't need to save your changes.

TIP: | **Preview All Flash**

You can quickly and easily way preview all of the Flash content on your pages by simply pressing **Ctrl+Alt+Shift+P** (Windows) or **Shift+Option+Cmd+P** (Mac). You will get an instant preview of all the Flash files on your page.

In this chapter, you learned about the basics of typography. A lot of this was review from Chapter 6, *"Cascading Style Sheets,"* but you should have picked up some new tips for your text formatting arsenal, including how to take care of that all-important white space in your documents. In the next chapter, you'll learn how to work with tables, which you've been dabbling with throughout the entire book as you worked through the exercises. Now it's finally time to get serious with them.

8

Tables

For many years, tables have been the de facto way to create the layout for Web pages. Despite never being intended for this purpose, tables control the layout on many Web sites to this day. Tables consist of rows and columns that intersect to create cells and were originally designed to give Web designers a way to display and organize charts and data. The authors of the original HTML specifications who created tables for the Web did not predict developers would use tables to build entire layouts instead of just displaying text and numbers. You'll learn about both uses for tables: a formatting device for data and a layout device for custom positioning of various page elements. Though CSS offers new (and more semantically correct) ways to lay out your sites, which you'll learn about in Chapter 9, *"Layout,"* tables still serve a very real need for quick and easy layouts that display well across multiple browsers.

This chapter shows you how to create custom tables, insert rows and columns, manipulate borders, and handle formatting and sorting tasks. You will also learn how to use tables to align and position images. Tables are a critical item in your Web design toolbox, and Dreamweaver 8 gives you great control and techniques for mastering them.

What Is a Table?

A table is a highly versatile feature in XHTML. It can be useful for organizing data or positioning page elements. What does a table look like under the hood of Dreamweaver 8? It is composed of a combination of XHTML tags.

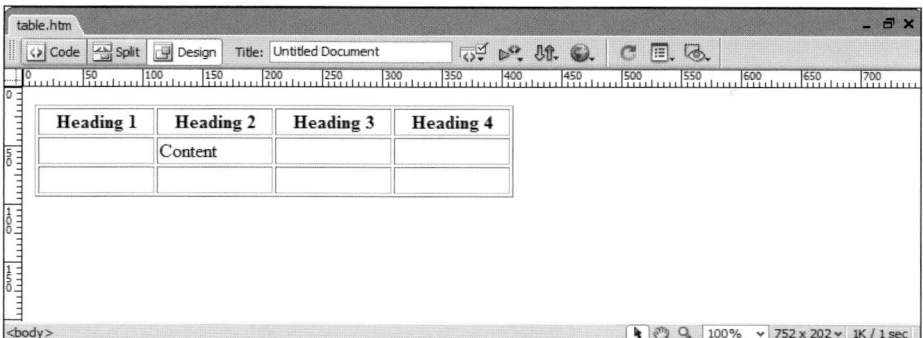

The most basic of tables in Dreamweaver 8. This table consists of four columns and three rows.

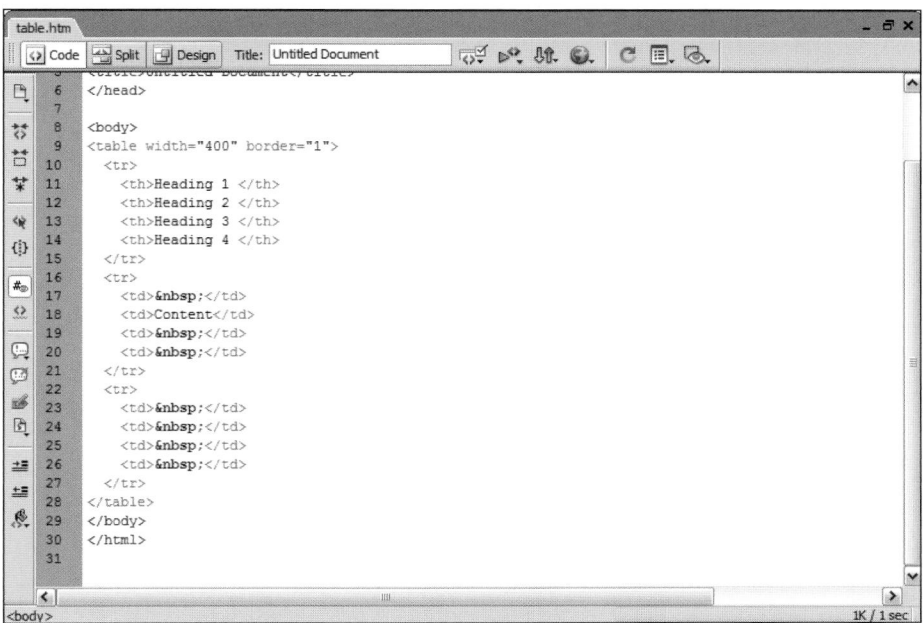

Here's the XHTML code for the table. Tables always begin with a **<table>** tag. The **width** and **border** elements are attributes of the **<table>** tag. The **<tr>** tags define the start and end of each table row, and the **<td>** and **<th>** tags define each individual table cell.

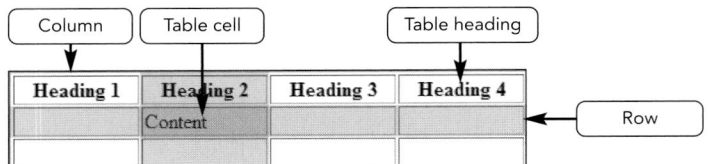

A table contains rows, columns, and cells. Each row in the table is defined by a **<tr>** tag. Each **<tr>** tag can have any number of **<td>** and **<th>** tags, which define the table cells. The browser will line up each of the cells in the table rows in order to create the table columns; you don't have to define table columns with XHTML tags.

The **<th>** tag defines a special kind of table cell: a table header. Table headers should be used in the first row of a table to define the contents of that column. Screen readers and other software used by disabled viewers can tell the difference between a header and a regular table cell and can give the user more information about the table they're "looking" at.

There are more tags related to tables, but you won't be using them all in this book. Here's a list of the most common table tags:

Table Tags	
Tag	**Use**
<table>	The **<table>** tag determines the start and end of a table. You can specify the entire width of the table, whether or not the table has a border, and the spacing to place between table cells.
<caption>	The **<caption>** tag places a text heading above the table, which labels the table for reference. For instance, a table containing the third quarter financial report might have a caption of *Q3 Financials*.
<tr>	The **<tr>** tag defines the start and end of a table row.
<th>	The **<th>** tag defines a table header, which acts as a label for a group of table cells, whether they're in a row or a column.
<td>	The **<td>** tag defines a standard table cell.

EXERCISE

1 | Creating and Adding Content to a Table

What better way to get started with tables than by creating one from scratch? This exercise shows you how to create and add data to a table from scratch. You will learn to work with a combination of the Insert Table object, the Modify > Table menu, and the Property Inspector. You'll also build a simple listing table for the Teacloud teapot collection.

1 Copy the **chap_08** folder from the **HOT CD-ROM** to your **Desktop**. Define your site as **Chapter 8** using the **chap_08** folder as the local root folder. Make sure the **Files** panel is open. If it's not, choose **Window > Files** or press **F11**.

2 In the **Files** panel, **right-click** (Windows) or **Ctrl+click** (Mac) the local root folder and choose **New File** from the contextual menu to create a new document. Save it as **teapots.htm**. In the **Files** panel, double-click the file you just created to open it. Set the title of the document by typing **Teacloud Teapots** into the **Title** field of the **Document** toolbar.

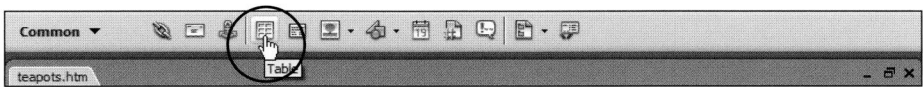

3 In the **Common** group of the **Insert** bar, click the **Insert Table** button, or choose **Insert > Table**, to open the **Table** dialog box.

Using the Table dialog box, you can create and format a table exactly how you want it from the very beginning. The most important sections are Table size and Header, which control how many rows and columns the table has, how wide it is, how thick the borders are, how table cell spacing is handled, and which rows or columns contain **<th>** tags. The Accessibility section lets you add a caption for the table, as well as a complete summary of what the table contains (which is not displayed in the browser). You'll certainly become more familiar with this dialog box as you work with tables more and more.

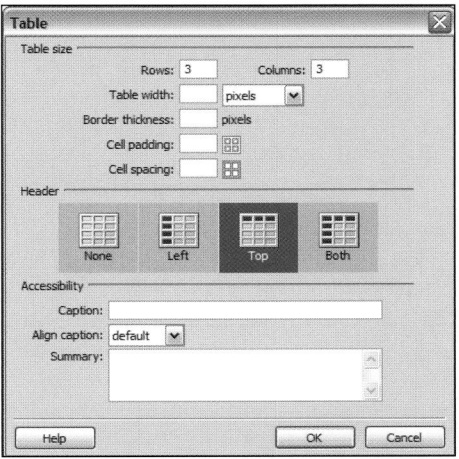

The table you're going to create will have information for three products, which includes a photo, a description, and a price, so you need four rows (don't forget the header row) and three columns.

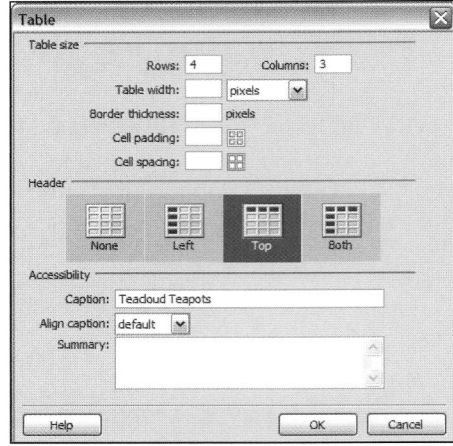

4 Type **4** in the **Rows** field, type **3** in the **Columns** field, click **Top** in the **Headers** section, and type **Teacloud Teapots** in the **Caption** field. Click **OK** to create the table using the criteria you specified.

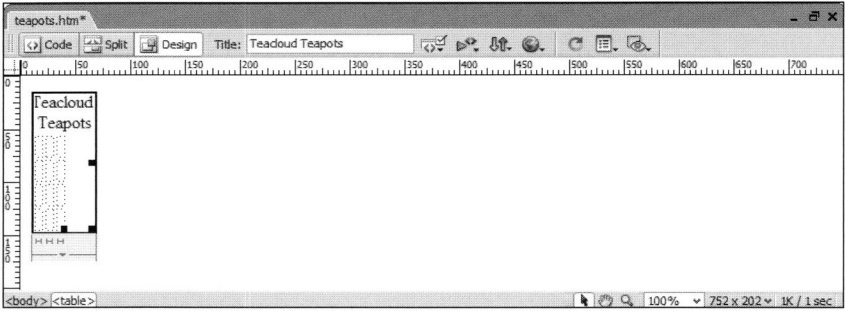

Your first exposure to tables doesn't look very exciting does it? When you completed the Table dialog box, you didn't supply any value for the width of the table, so Dreamweaver 8 collapses the table to the smallest size necessary to fit its contents. Since this table doesn't yet have any contents, it's been collapsed to its smallest size. The dotted lines you see around each cell are just table border guides; they won't be visible in a browser.

5 To make the table easier to work with, press **F6** or choose **View > Table Mode > Expanded Tables Mode**. The **Getting Started in Expanded Tables Mode** dialog box will appear if this is the first time you've used this mode. Select the **Don't show me this message again** check box and click **OK**.

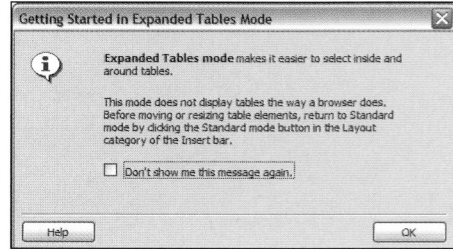

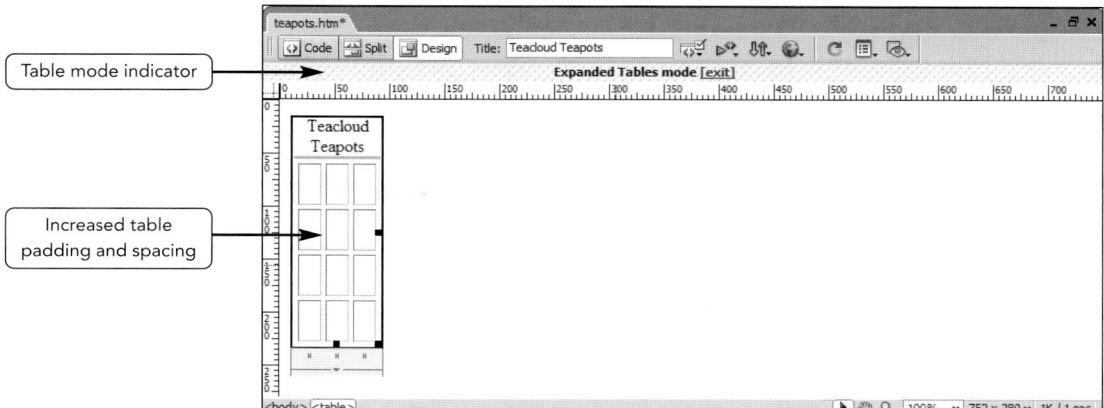

Expanded Tables mode increased the cell padding and cell spacing of the table (which you'll learn about in a bit), which makes it easier to select the table cells and insert content. The table mode indicator at the top of the document lets you know what table mode you're in, and provides a link to exit the Expanded Tables mode.

NOTE:

Understanding Table Modes

Dreamweaver 8 has three different table modes: Standard view (default), Expanded Tables mode, and Layout view. You can switch between these various modes by choosing **View > Table Mode** and selecting the appropriate mode. Throughout this chapter, you will work mostly in Standard mode. In the next chapter, you will get a chance to work with the Layout view. The Expanded Tables mode is similar to Standard view except extra cell padding and table borders are used to make table editing easier.

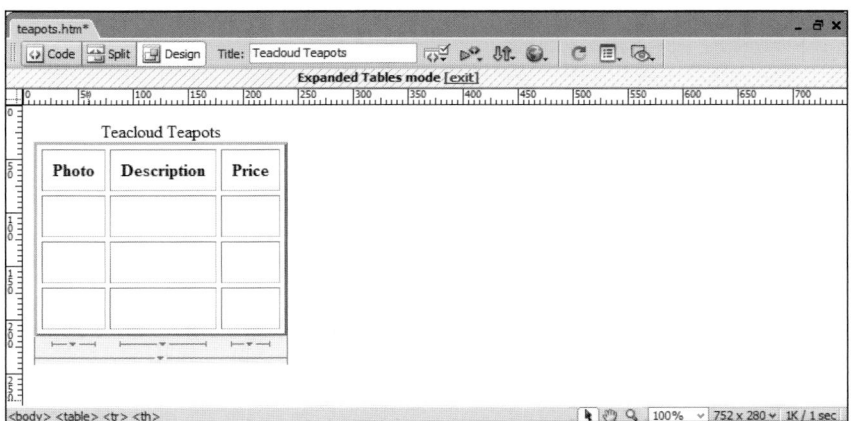

6 Place your cursor in the first table cell in the upper-left corner and type **Photo**. Press the **Tab** key to move the cursor to the next table cell and type **Description**. Press **Tab** once more and type **Price** into the last cell in the first row.

Moving Through Tables

The Tab key lets you to quickly move through a table, both forward and backward. Pressing the Tab key moves your cursor to the next cell in the table, even if it's in the next row. Pressing Shift+Tab moves your cursor to the previous cell. If you're in the very last cell of the table and press the Tab key, a new row is added to the bottom of the table, and your cursor will be placed in the first cell of the new row.

7 Now that you have some content to hold the table cells open, click the **exit** link in the table mode indicator to get out of **Expanded Tables** mode.

8 Place your cursor in the first cell in the **Photo** column. Choose **Insert > Image**. Browse to **assets/images/ products/kettles**, select the **teacloud-azul.jpg** image, and click **OK**. If the **Image Tag Accessibility Attributes** dialog box opens, type **Teacloud Azul** in the **Alternate text** field and click **OK**.

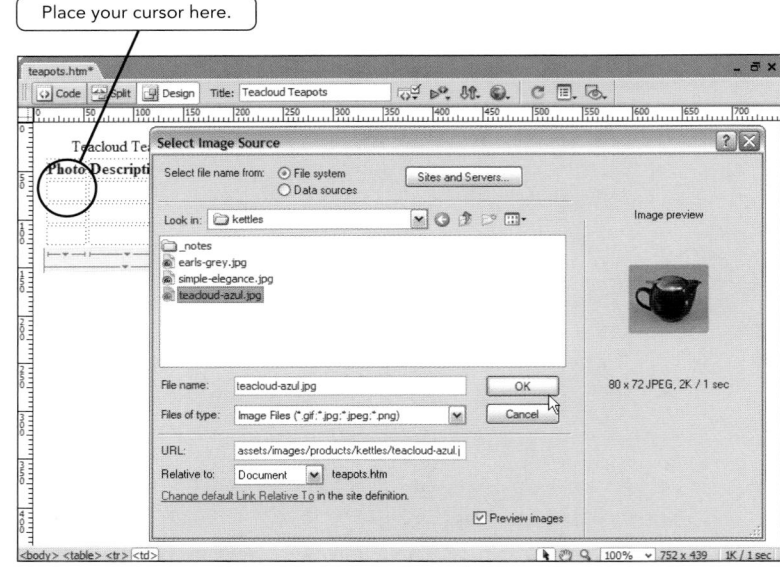

Place your cursor here.

This is what your table should look like with the new image inserted.

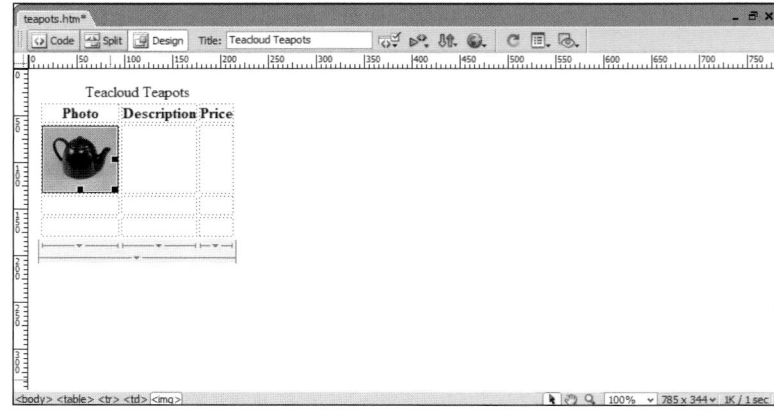

9 Press **Tab** to move the cursor to the **Description** cell and type the following text:

Teacloud Azul
Crafted in the workshop of master Hikari, this hand made teapot includes a built in wire-mesh pouch for easy and efficient steeping.

If the text starts to get cramped while you're typing, simply click anywhere outside the table cell, or press **F5**, to refresh the Design view. Dreamweaver 8 holds off updating tables as you type in order apply the text to the page faster.

---

10 Press **Tab** again and type **$49.95** in the **Price** column.

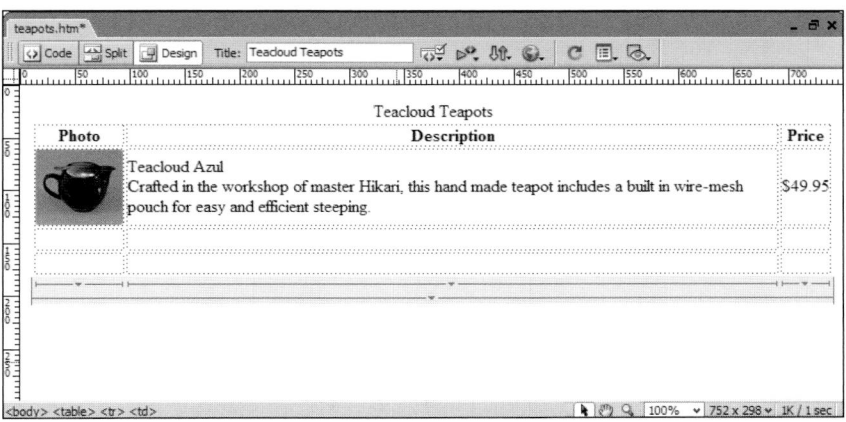

You've now finished adding your very first row of table data.

---

11 Now it's time to complete the information for the next two teapots. Press **Tab** to move your cursor to the **Photo** cell in the third row. Using the techniques you learned in Step 8, insert the **earls-grey.jpg** image from the **assets/images/products/kettles** folder. If the **Image Tag Accessibility** dialog box appears, type **Earls Grey** for the alternate text and click **OK**.

---

12 Press **Tab** and type the following text in the **Description** column:

Earl's Grey
Perfect for brewing a pot of earl grey tea for two, this teapot strikes a balance between contempo-rary stylings and classical sensibilities.

---

13 Finally, press **Tab** and type **$69.95** in the **Price** column.

The table is starting to look a little better now that it's got content. One more row to go!

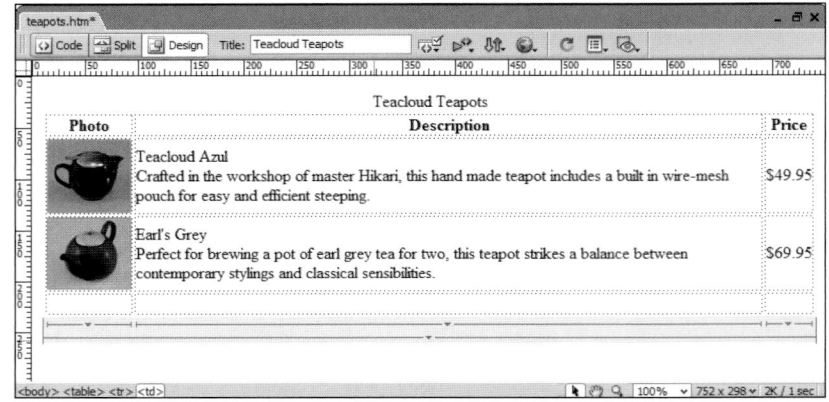

---

14 Press **Tab** to move your cursor to the **Photo** cell in the fourth row. Insert the **simple-elegance.jpg** image from the **assets/images/products/kettles** folder.

---

15 Press **Tab** and type the following in the **Description** column:

Simple Elegance
When style is tantamount only to elegance, nothing short of this piece will do. Hand crafted by the world renowned Jacque Le Bleu.

---

16 Press **Tab** and type **$59.95** in the **Price** column.

The table is finally complete, nicely laid out in columns and rows.

In this exercise, you learned how to insert a table into the document and navigate through the table cells. The next exercise will teach you how to manipulate the display of your tables.

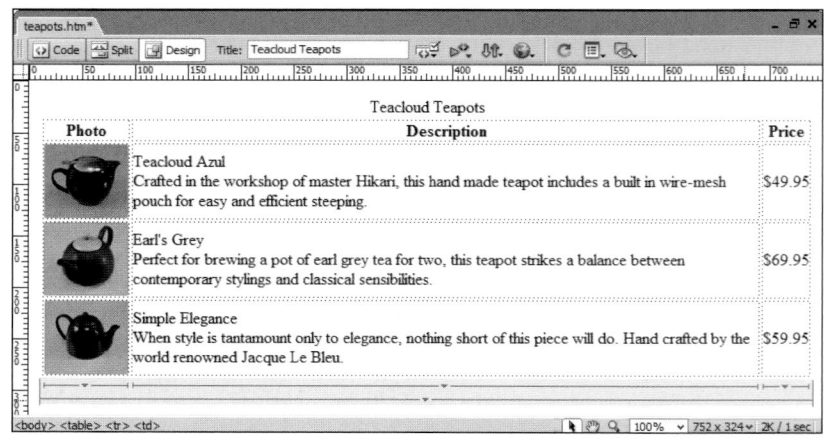

---

17 Save your changes and keep **teapots.htm** open for the next exercise.

---

2 | Changing the Border of a Table with XHTML

This exercise helps you build your table formatting skills using the table you created in Exercise 1. It also alerts you to a common XHTML problem relating to empty table cells. You see, even if a table cell is empty, you have to put something in it to preserve the table formatting. That "something" can be a single-pixel transparent GIF, which is a small image file set to be fully transparent, invisible, or preferably just a non-breaking space. It serves as a placeholder to keep the table formatting from collapsing with empty cells.

1 If you completed Exercise 1, **teapots.htm** should still be open. If it's not, go back and complete Exercise 1.

2 Press **F12** to preview the file in your browser.

Notice how the dotted lines don't appear in the browser? In this file, you haven't set the border yet, so it defaults to 0. Also, the table displayed in the browser doesn't have any borders to separate the content.

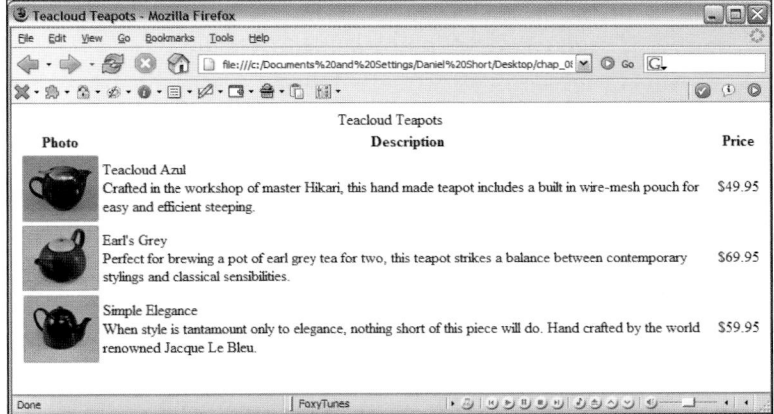

3 Return to Dreamweaver 8. Select the entire table by moving your pointer over the edge of the table until you see a thin red outline, and the pointer changes to show a small table. With the red line visible, click to select the table.

Note: You can also select a table by using the Tag Selector at the lower left of the document window. Here's how: Click anywhere inside the table. You should see the word **<table>** appear in the Tag Selector. Click it to select the table.

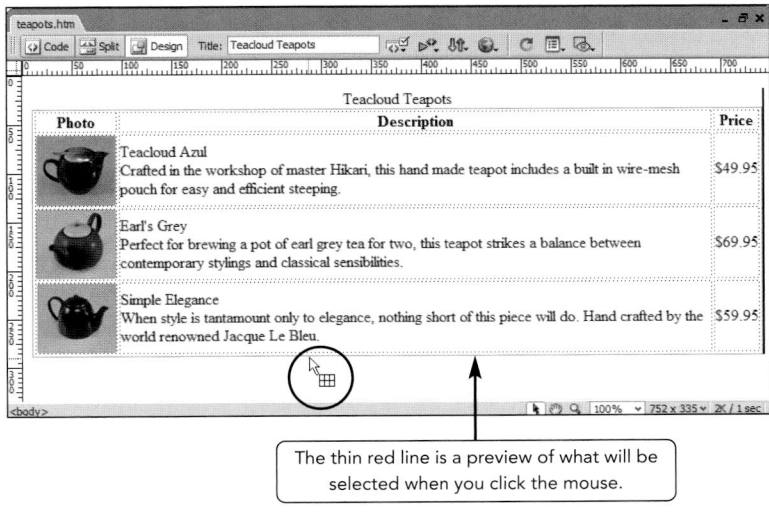

The thin red line is a preview of what will be selected when you click the mouse.

When the table is selected, you'll see a thick black line around the outside of the table.

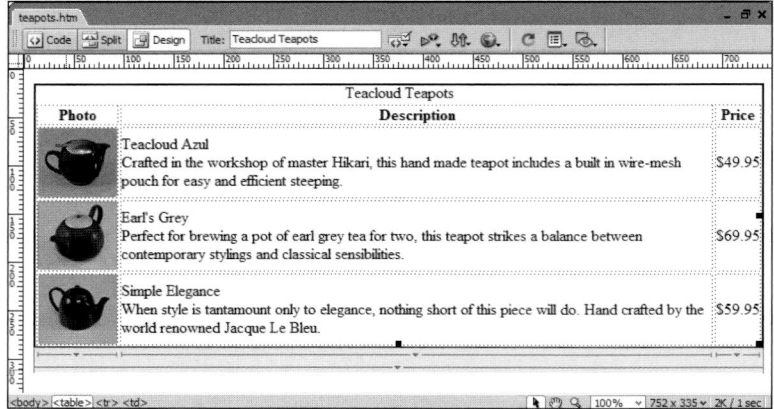

4 In the **Property Inspector**, type **1** in the **Border** field and press **Enter** (Windows) or **Return** (Mac).

Notice the border is now drawn around the table and each table cell.

5 Press **F12** to preview the results in a browser.

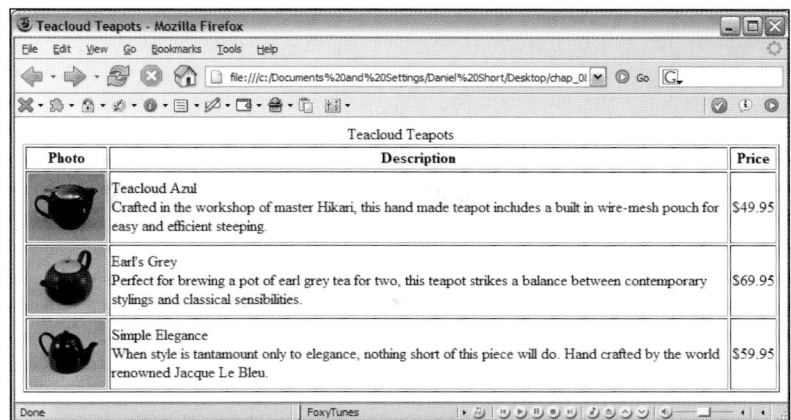

Notice how the border value affected the appearance? Borders are one of the most basic controls you have over the appearance of tables. It's not the prettiest border in the world though, so in the next exercise you'll learn how to use CSS to spiff it up.

6 It's fairly obvious that the first column of the table contains a photo, so the heading in that first column is pretty redundant. With your mouse over the **Photo** text, hold down the **Ctrl** (Windows) or **Cmd** (Mac) key and click the table cell to select the entire cell.

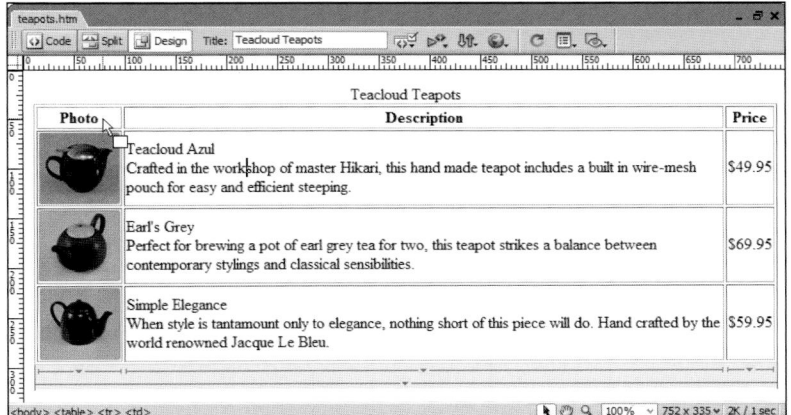

You'll notice the mouse cursor changes to show a small box (representing a single table cell), and the table cell has a red outline to indicate that clicking the mouse will select the entire table cell.

7 Press **Delete** to delete the text in the table cell.

8 In the **Document** toolbar, click the **Code** button to display the code for this page.

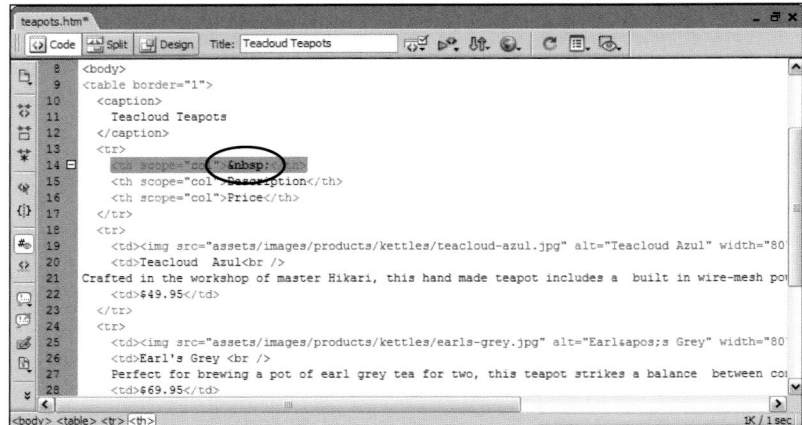

This is the code required to display the table you just modified. Notice the first **<th>** element contains a nonbreaking space element (** **), even though you just deleted the *Photo* text from the table cell. Dreamweaver 8 automatically inserts the ** ** element into every empty table cell, whether it's a newly created cell or one that's been emptied by having its content removed. Some browsers require that every cell contain some content; cells that don't contain content will collapse, and borders around those cells won't be displayed—Internet Explorer is one of the largest culprits here. The nonbreaking space is the perfect solution because it qualifies as content to the browser and is invisible to the person viewing your page, so nobody ever knows it's there (except the browser, of course). The next few steps will show you why this is important.

NOTE:

Scope Attributes

You may have noticed the **<th>** tag has a **scope** attribute applied to it. Dreamweaver automatically adds the **scope** attributes if you specify headers when the table is created. The **scope** attributes tells screen readers and other accessibility devices what the **<th>** tag applies to either a column (**scope="col"**) or a row (**scope="row"**).

---

9 While still in **Code** view delete the ** ** from the **<th>** tag, so that the table cell is completely empty.

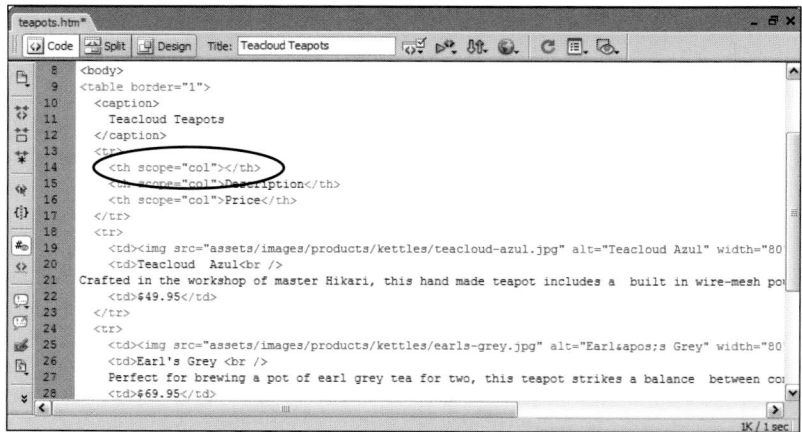

10 Switch back to **Design** view.

Notice the upper-left table cell now has a dashed border around it instead of a solid border.

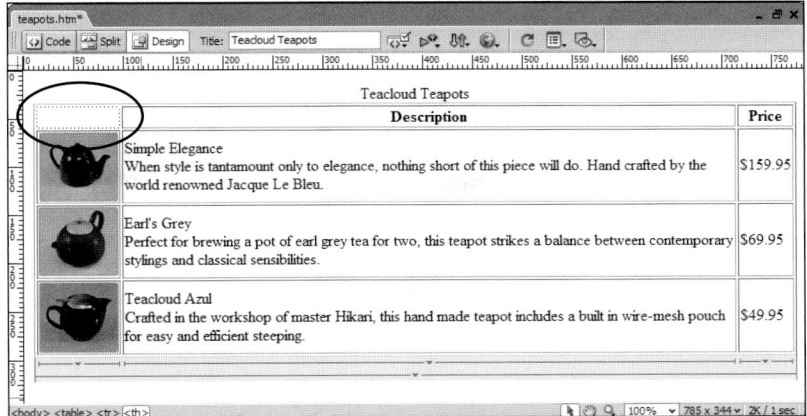

11 Press **F12** to preview the page in Internet Explorer. (If you're using FireFox, you won't see the same problem.)

In Internet Explorer, a table cell without any content will not display a border.

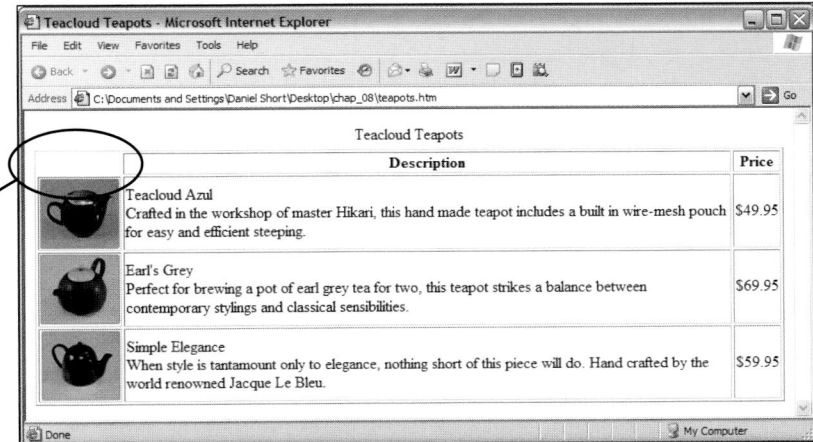

Notice the upper-left cell no longer has a border around it. Without a nonbreaking space, Internet Explorer 6 in Windows and Internet Explorer 5 on the Mac will not properly render the table cell.

12 Return to Dreamweaver 8 and make sure your cursor is still positioned inside the **<th>** tag. Choose **Insert > HTML > Special Characters > Non Breaking Space**, or press **Ctrl+Shift+spacebar** (Windows) or **Cmd+Shift+spacebar** (Mac) to replace the nonbreaking space you deleted earlier. Press **F12** to preview the page again, just to make sure everything is OK.

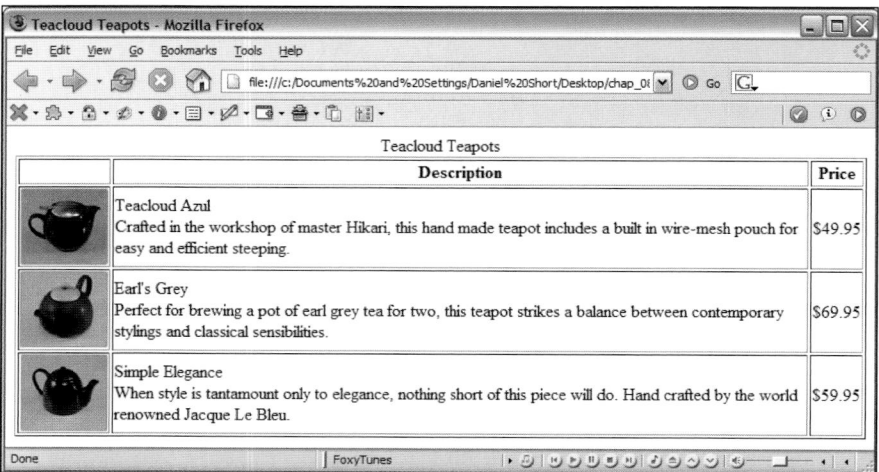

Your page should now look the same as it did in step 5 of this exercise.

WARNING: | **Special Characters Warning**

If you receive a warning stating that special characters may not appear in all browsers, click OK. The nonbreaking space is actually an encoded character and will display just fine in any browser.

---

13 Save your changes and keep **teapots.htm** open for the next exercise.

In this exercise, you learned how to apply a border to a table using the standard attributes of the **<table>** tag. In the next exercise, you'll learn how to take finer control of your table borders using CSS.

3 | Changing the Border of a Table with CSS

The previous exercise showed you how to create a border on a table using standard XHTML attributes. Although the border is functional, it's certainly not very easy on the eyes. This exercise will show you how to use CSS to take control of your table borders, allowing you to create fine line borders of any color.

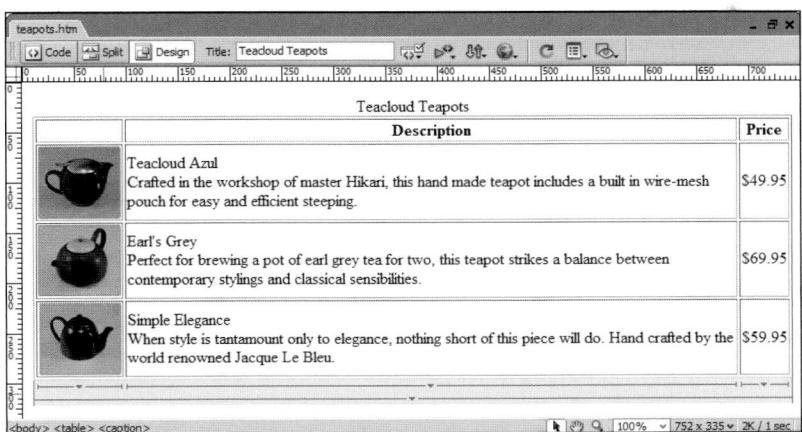

1 If you just completed Exercise 2, **teapots.htm** should still be open. If it's not, go back and complete Exercise 2.

The borders on the table—created with standard XHTML attributes—aren't very nice to look at.

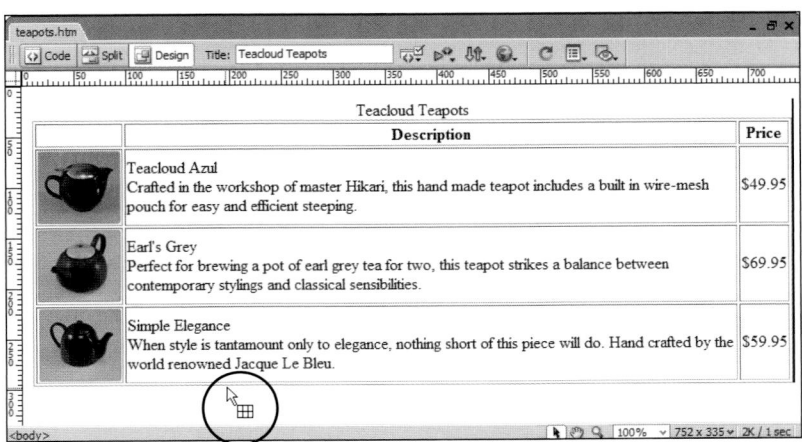

2 Select the table by clicking the **<table>** tag in the **Tag Selector** or by clicking the edge of the table (remember to wait until you see the red border).

3 In the **Property Inspector**, delete the value from the **Border** field and press **Enter** (Windows) or **Return** (Mac) to commit the changes.

Now it's time to start setting borders with CSS.

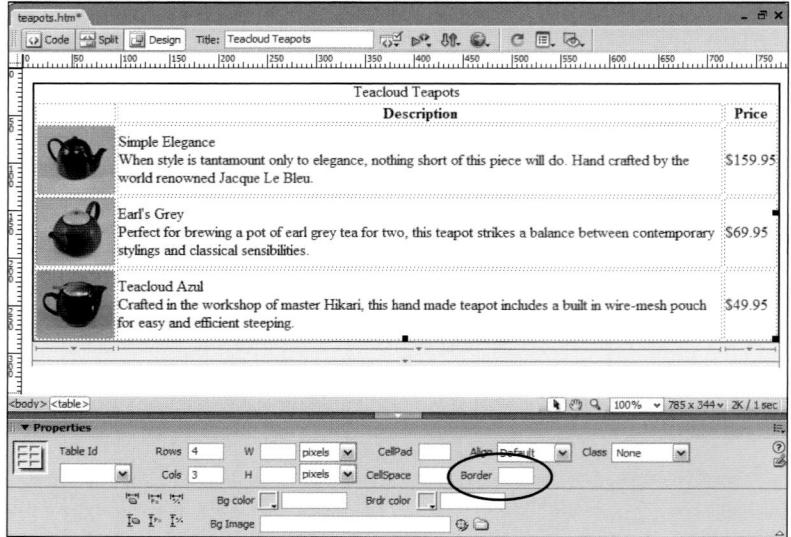

4 In the **CSS Styles** panel, click the **New CSS Rule** button. Select **Tag** in the **Selector Type** section, choose **table** from the **Tag** pop-up menu, and select **This document only** in the **Define in** section. Click **OK** to start defining the rule.

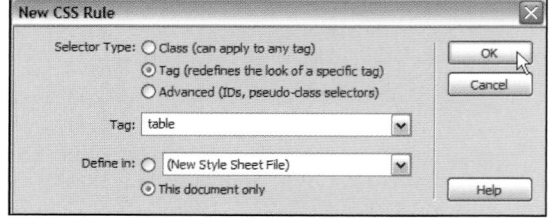

5 Select **Border** from the **Category** pane. Leave the **Same for all** options selected. Choose **solid** from the **Top** pop-up menu in the **Style** column and set **Width** to **1 pixels**. Type **#000000** in the **Color** field. Click **OK** to create and apply the rule.

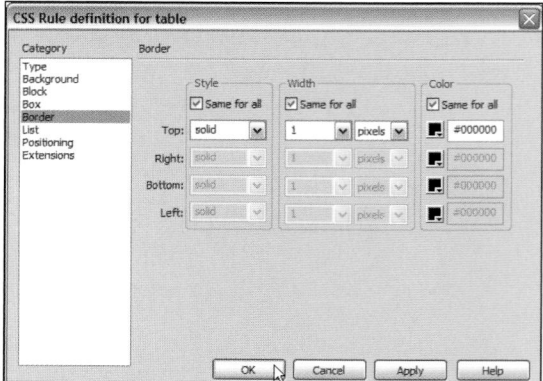

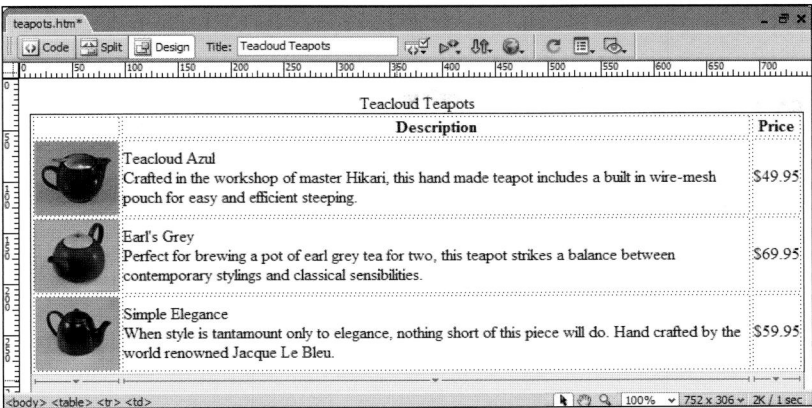

You should now see a thin black border around the table on the page. You were probably expecting borders around all of the table cells, but the rule you created applies *only* to the `<table>` tag itself. The `<table>` tag affects only the border around the perimeter of the table. To apply the same borders to the entire table, including the dividing lines between the cells, you must redefine the styles for the `<table>`, `<th>`, and `<td>` tags. You'll learn how in the next steps.

---

6 Choose **Edit > Undo Edit CSS Style** to undo the rule you just created. In the **CSS Styles** panel, click the **New CSS Rule** button.

---

7 In the **New CSS Rule** dialog box, select **Advanced** in the **Selector Type** section and type **table, th, td** in the **Selector** field. Leave **Define in** set to **This document only**. Click **OK** to define the style.

In this case, you're using a group of selectors to define not only the `<table>` tag, but the `<th>` and `<td>` tags as well.

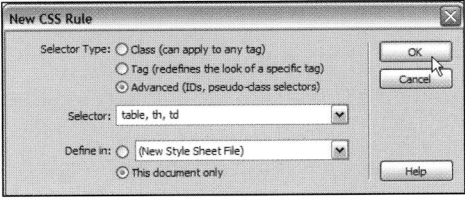

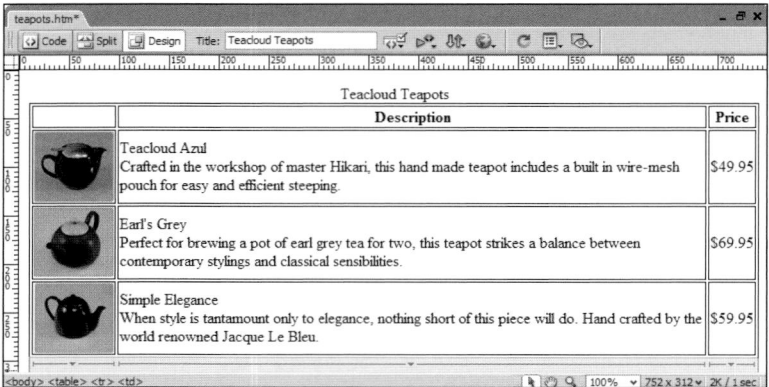

8 In the **CSS Rule Definition** dialog box, select **Border** from the **Category** pane. Leave the **Same for all** options selected. Choose **solid** from the **Top** pop-up menu and set the **Width** to **1 pixels**. Type **#000000** in the **Color** field. Click **OK** to create and apply the rule.

This looks a little more like it, but there's some space showing between each table cell.

---

9 Press **F12** to preview your page in the browser.

As you can see, the same space appears between the table borders. By default, table cells have some spacing around them, very similar to the margins around paragraphs. To fix this problem, you'll need to add another property to the CSS rule that's not in the **CSS Rule Definition** dialog box like all of the other border settings.

---

10 In the **CSS Styles** panel, click the **table, th, td** rule to select it. Click the **Add Property** link.

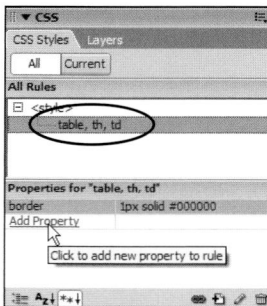

11 Type **border-collapse** in the field. Click in the second column and choose **collapse** from the value pop-up menu.

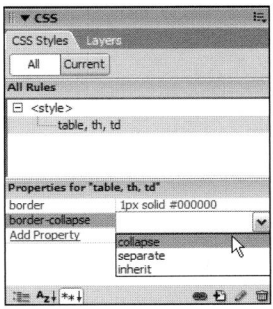

The Design view updates automatically. Unfortunately, nothing changed. This view does not support the border-collapse attribute, so it still shows the table borders separated.

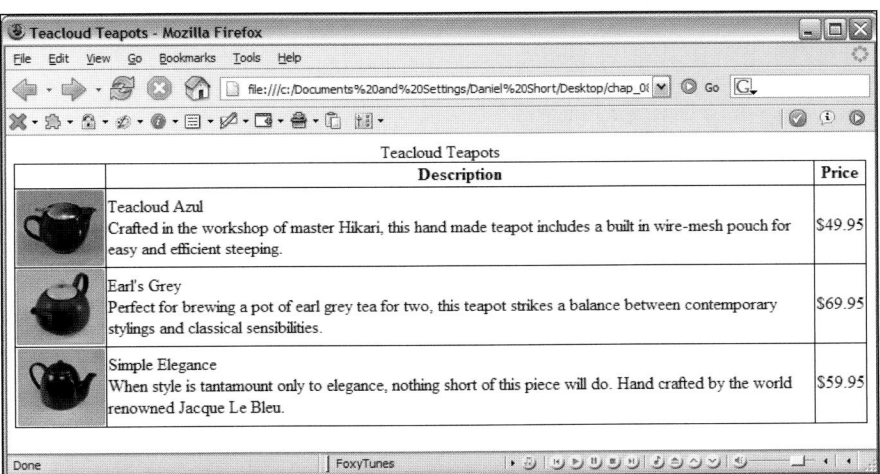

12 Press **F12** to preview your page in the browser.

The borders are now nice and tight. You'll agree this is a much better look than the bulky beveled borders the XHTML border attribute provided.

13 Save your changes and keep **teapots.htm** open for the next exercise.

In this exercise, you learned how to add table rows to your table using CSS instead of XHTML. CSS gives you a much finer level of control over your table borders. In the next exercise, you'll start adding color to the table.

4 | Adding Color to Tables

Next on the list of table building skills is learning how to apply color formatting. When it comes to coloring your tables, you may use the automatic color features or set whatever custom colors you desire. In this exercise, you will learn how to manually apply color to the background of tables, columns, rows, and cells by using the Property Inspector, and, of course, you'll learn some CSS as well.

---

1 If you just completed Exercise 3, **teapots.htm** should still be open. If it's not, go back and complete Exercise 3.

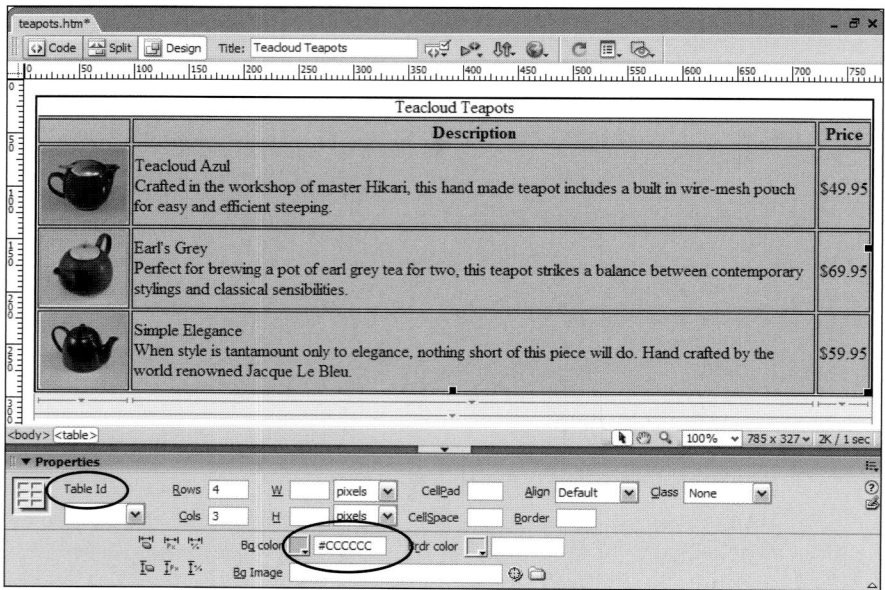

2 To begin coloring the table, select the entire table by clicking anywhere inside the table and clicking the **<table>** tag in the **Tag Selector**. In the **Property Inspector**, type **#CCCCCC** in the **Bg color** field to set the background color for the entire table.

As you can see, the table background immediately changes to a grey.

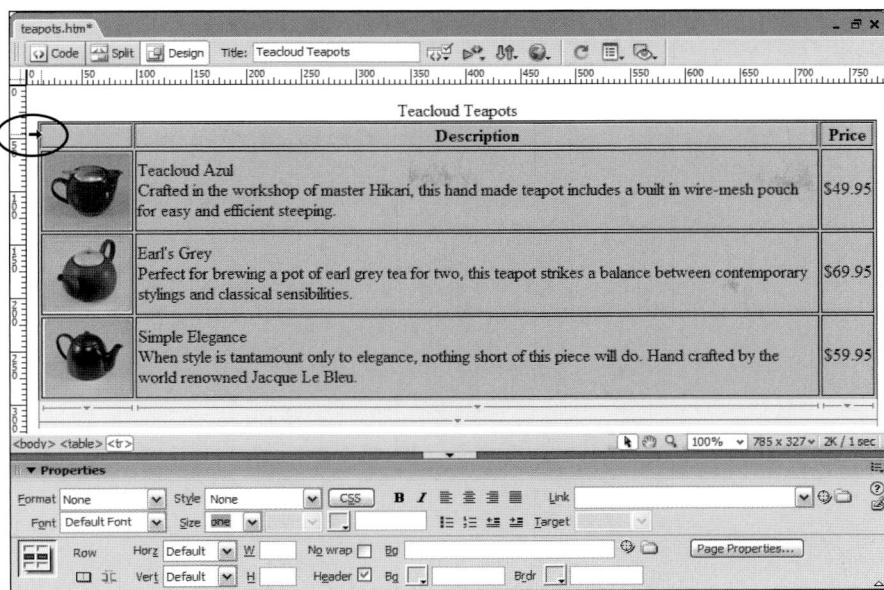

3 Move your pointer to the left of the upper-left table cell until it changes into a right-facing arrow. Click to select the first table row. You'll know the row is selected when you see the thin red line.

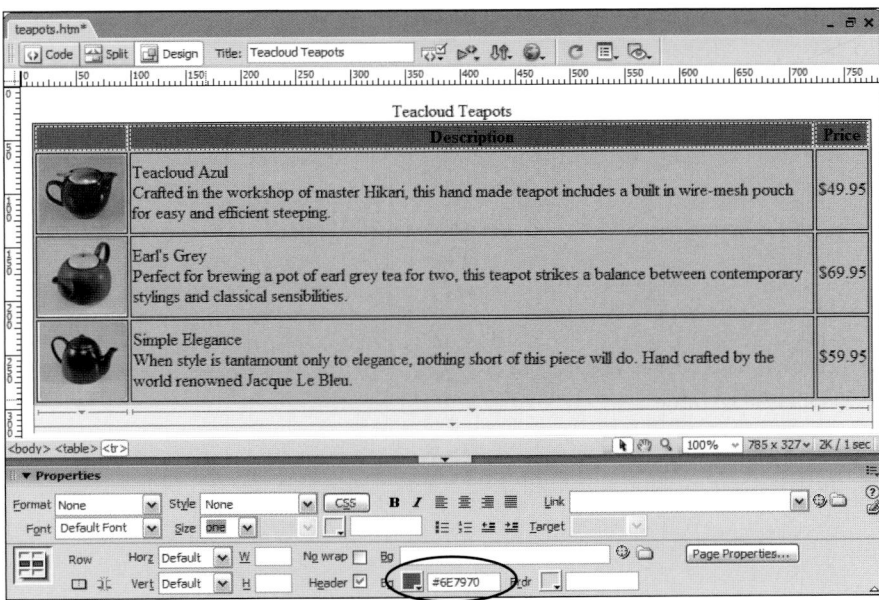

4 In the **Property Inspector**, type **#6E7970** in the **Bg** field and press **Enter** (Windows) or **Return** (Mac) to commit the changes.

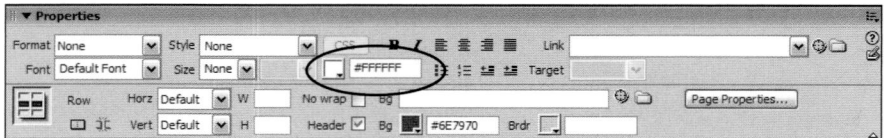

5 The black headings are now a little difficult to read over the dark background color. In the **Property Inspector**, type #FFFFFF in the **Font Color** field and press **Enter** (Windows) or **Return** (Mac) to commit the changes.

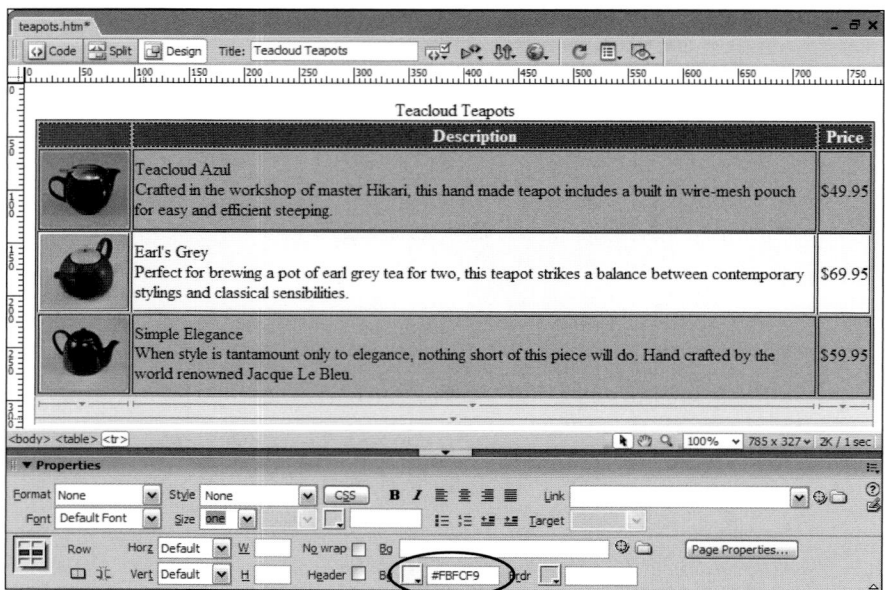

6 To make the rows of the table stand out a little more, it's always nice to use alternating row colors. Select the third row of the table, which contains the Earl's Grey teapot. In the **Property Inspector**, type #FBFCF9 in the **Bg** field and press **Enter** (Windows) or **Return** (Mac) to commit the changes.

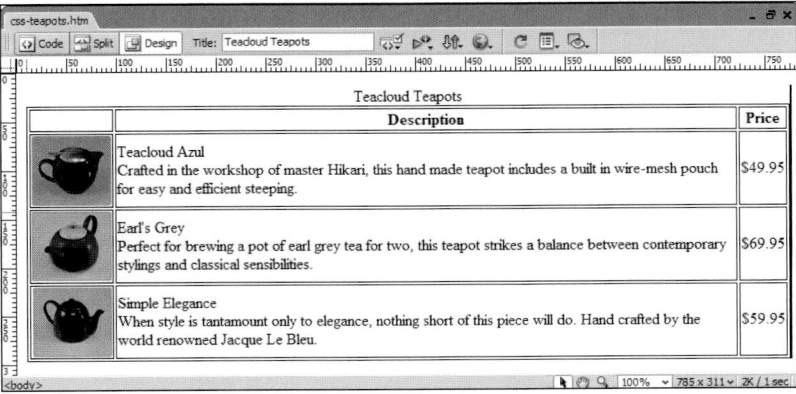

```
teapots.htm*                                                              _ ⊡ ×
  ◇ Code  ⊟ Split  ◻ Design  Title: Teacloud Teapots      ⊙⊽ ⚲ ⚙ ⊙.  C ▤ ⭕.
  18  <table bgcolor="#CCCCCC">
  19    <caption>Teacloud Teapots</caption>
  20    <tr bgcolor="#6E7970">
  21      <th scope="col"><span class="style1"></span></th>
  22      <th scope="col"><span class="style1">Description</span></th>
  23      <th class="rightAlign style1" scope="col">Price</th>
  24    </tr>
  25    <tr>
  26      <td><img src="assets/images/products/kettles/teacloud-azul.jpg" alt="Teacloud Azul" width="80" hei
  27      <td>Teacloud Azul<br />
  28        Crafted in the workshop of master Hikari, this hand made teapot includes
  29        a built in wire-mesh pouch for easy and efficient steeping.</td>
  30      <td class="rightAlign">$49.95</td>
  31    </tr>
  32    <tr bgcolor="#FBFCF9">
  33      <td><img src="assets/images/products/kettles/earls-grey.jpg" alt="Earl's Grey" width="80" height="
  34      <td>Earl's Grey <br />
  35        Perfect for brewing a pot of earl grey tea for two, this teapot strikes
  36        a balance between contemporary stylings and classical sensibilities.</td>
  37      <td class="rightAlign">$69.95</td>
  38    </tr>
  39    <tr>
  40      <td><img src="assets/images/products/kettles/simple-elegance.jpg" alt="Simple Elegance" width="80"
  41      <td>Simple Elegance <br />
  42        When style is tantamount only to elegance, nothing short of this piece will do.  Hand crafted by
  43      <td class="rightAlign">$59.95</td>
  44    </tr>
  45  </table>
<body> <table> <tr> <td.rightAlign>                                     2K / 1 sec
```

This is the new code for your table. You can see that the **<table>** tag has a **bgcolor** attribute, each of the **<th>** tags now has a **<span>** tag wrapped around the text (even the empty table cell), and the third row also has a **bgcolor** attribute.

You've now seen how to work with colors using XHTML attributes, but the deep inner geek inside can't stand to see you use XHTML attributes where you can use CSS. So it's time to start over with this table and do the same formatting using CSS instead. This will allow you finer control over the colors and make it easy to style hundreds of tables with the same colors by using an external style sheet. Using CSS to style tables has all of the benefits of styling regular text that you learned about in previous chapters.

---

7 Save and close your file, and then open **css-teapots.htm** from the **Files** panel. This file has the same table and formatting your page had at the beginning of this exercise.

```
css-teapots.htm                                                           _ ⊡ ×
  ◇ Code  ⊟ Split  ◻ Design  Title: Teacloud Teapots      ⊙⊽ ⚲ ⚙ ⊙.  C ▤ ⭕.
```

Teacloud Teapots		
	Description	**Price**
	Teacloud Azul Crafted in the workshop of master Hikari, this hand made teapot includes a built in wire-mesh pouch for easy and efficient steeping.	$49.95
	Earl's Grey Perfect for brewing a pot of earl grey tea for two, this teapot strikes a balance between contemporary stylings and classical sensibilities.	$69.95
	Simple Elegance When style is tantamount only to elegance, nothing short of this piece will do. Hand crafted by the world renowned Jacque Le Bleu.	$59.95

Notice the file looks the same as it did when you opened it in Step 1. First, you'll set the background color for the table.

8 In the **CSS Styles** panel, double-click the **table, th, td** rule to open the **CSS Rule Definition** dialog box. Select **Background** in the **Category** pane and type **#CCCCCC** in the **Background color** field. Click **OK** to update the rule.

Next, you'll create a new rule for the **<th>** tag.

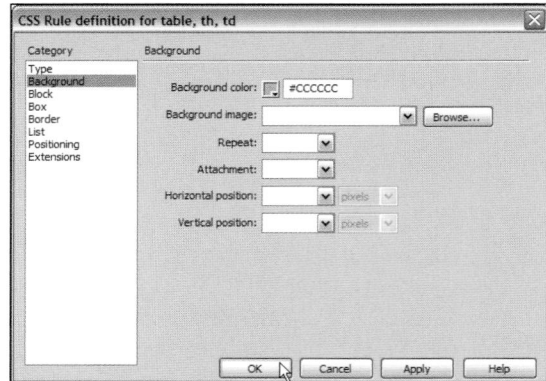

9 in the **CSS Styles** panel, click the **New CSS Rule** button. In the **New CSS Rule** dialog box, select **Tag** in the **Selector Type** section, type **th** in the **Tag** field, and leave the **Define in** option set to **This document only**. Click **OK**.

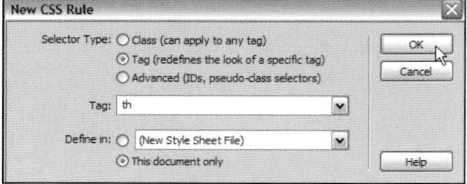

10 In the **CSS Rule Definition** dialog box, select **Type** in the **Category** pane. Type **#FFFFFF** in the **Color** field. Select the **Background** color from the **Category** pane and type **#6E7970** in the **Background color** field. Click **OK** to apply the rule.

In this step, you're using the "cascade" of Cascading Style Sheets to override the color of the **<th>** tag defined in the **table, th, td** rule. Because you defined the **th** rule after the **table, th, td** rule, it's lower in the cascade, so it takes precedence, and the **<th>** tag will have a background color of #6E7970.

From a display perspective, there's no difference in the look of the CSS-styled table versus the HTML-styled table. If you look at the code though, there's not been any change to the **<table>** or **<th>** tags, just a few new styles.

The last thing you need to do is set the alternating row color, which you'll do next.

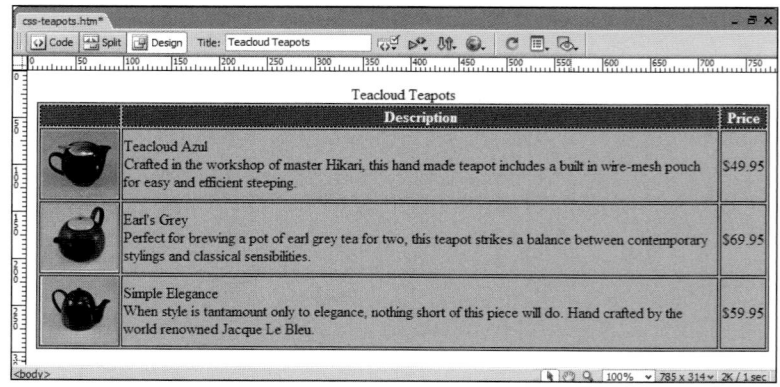

11 In the **CSS Styles** panel, click the **New CSS Rule** button. In the **New CSS Rule** dialog box, select **Advanced** in the **Selector Type** section, type **tr.altRow td** in the **Selector** field, and leave the **Define in** option set to **This document only**. Click **OK**.

This new rule will be applied to a table row. The new rule, **tr.altRow td**, states that any **<td>** tag inside a **<tr>** tag with a class of **altRow** will be styled using this new rule.

---

12 In the **CSS Rule Definition** dialog box, select **Background** from the **Category** pane. Type **#FBFCF9** in the **Background color** field. Click **OK** to add the new rule.

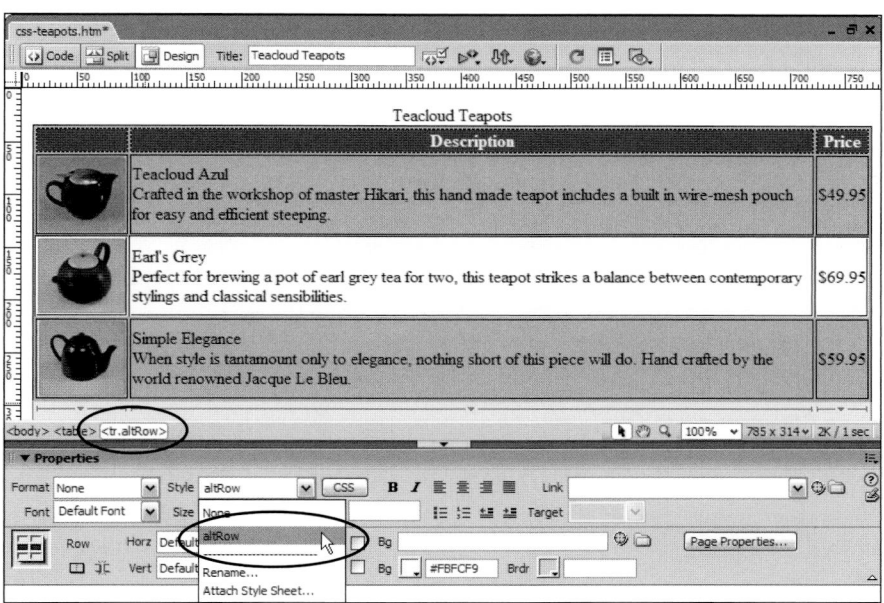

13 Select the table row containing the Earl's Grey teapot. In the **Property Inspector**, choose **.altRow** from the **Style** pop-up menu.

The table now looks exactly as it did when you styled it using the Property Inspector. However, you've made minimal changes to the table at this point, only adding a simple class to control the alternating row color. If you decide to change the color of the headings, or the color of the alternating row color, you could now change it in one place. Imagine a site with dozens of tables that need to be styled, and you'll agree that going the CSS route is definitely preferred.

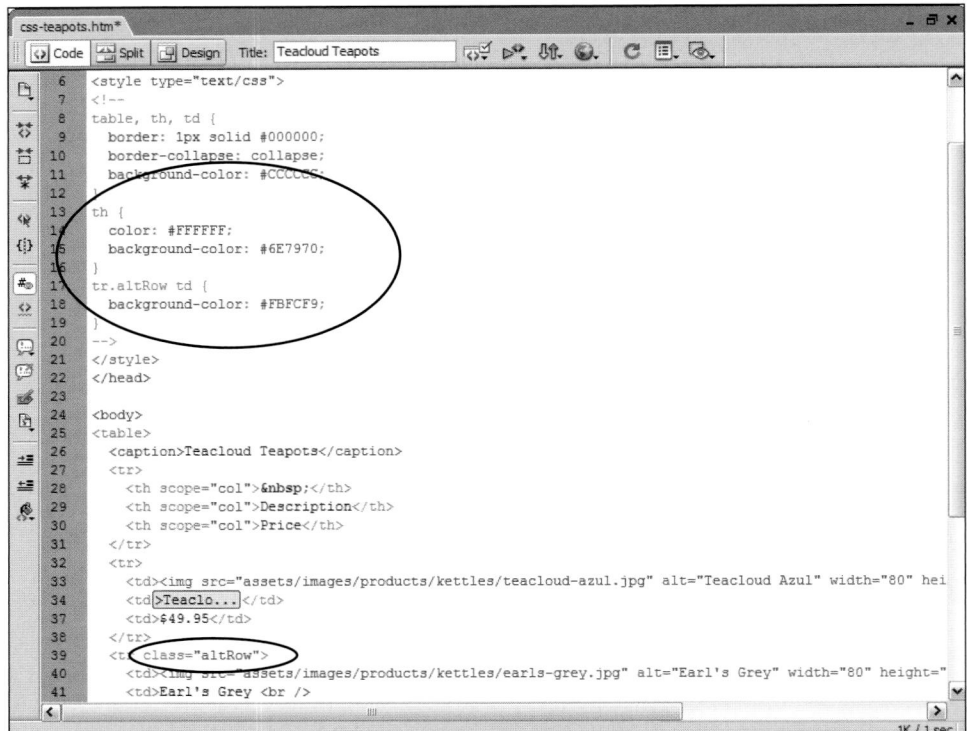

```
6    <style type="text/css">
7    <!--
8    table, th, td {
9       border: 1px solid #000000;
10      border-collapse: collapse;
11      background-color: #CCCCCC;
12
13    th {
14       color: #FFFFFF;
15       background-color: #6E7970;
16    }
17    tr.altRow td {
18       background-color: #FBFCF9;
19    }
20    -->
21    </style>
22    </head>
23
24    <body>
25    <table>
26      <caption>Teacloud Teapots</caption>
27      <tr>
28        <th scope="col"> </th>
29        <th scope="col">Description</th>
30        <th scope="col">Price</th>
31      </tr>
32      <tr>
33        <td><img src="assets/images/products/kettles/teacloud-azul.jpg" alt="Teacloud Azul" width="80" hei
34        <td>Teaclo...</td>
37        <td>$49.95</td>
38      </tr>
39      <tr class="altRow">
40        <td><img src="assets/images/products/kettles/earls-grey.jpg" alt="Earl's Grey" width="80" height="
41        <td>Earl's Grey <br />
```

Title: Teacloud Teapots

css-teapots.htm*

1K / 1 sec

Notice the differences in the CSS-based code compared to the code you created earlier in this exercise. There are a few new CSS rules, but the table code itself hasn't changed at all, except for the class now applied to the Earl's Grey table row. The **<th>** tags are much more efficient using this method, because you don't have to apply a bunch of **<span>** tags to change the color of the text. The code is far cleaner and easier to maintain using CSS to format your tables.

---

14 Save your changes and keep **css-teapots.htm** open for the next exercise.

In this exercise, you learned how to change the colors of your table, both with XHTML and CSS. In the next exercise, you'll learn how to change the alignment of the text and images in the table cells.

The Format Table Command

You can do even more with formatting tables than what you just learned in these exercises. You can use the Format Table command to quickly and easily customize your table's color settings; plus, it is great if you have trouble with, or plain don't like, choosing colors. By choosing **Commands > Format Table**, you can open the Format Table dialog box. (You'll need to remove any captions in your table, unfortunately.) If you want to use the Format Table command, you must select the entire table or click inside one of the table cells before you choose the command from the menu.

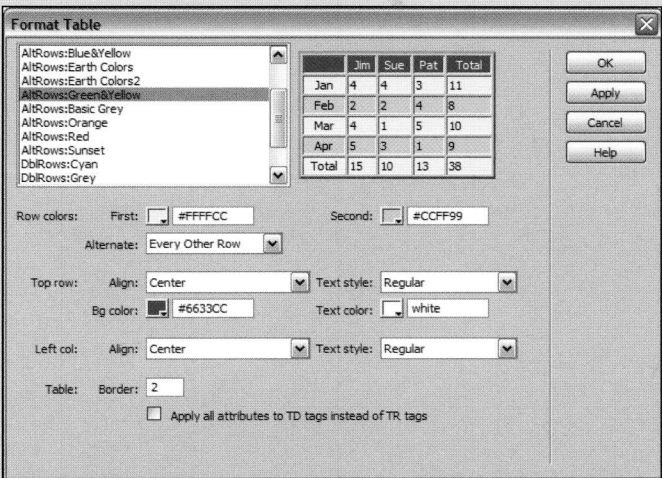

The Format Table dialog box gives you access to a long list of preset color themes you can apply to your tables. As you click through the various themes, notice how the preview in the middle changes so you can preview that theme. These color combinations are part of Dreamweaver 8, and you can apply them to any table. Additionally, you can customize the color theme by clicking any of the color boxes and selecting a color from the picker.

The only gotchas here are that you can't use the command on tables with captions, and the dialog box uses standard XHTML attributes for the style and not CSS. If you want to use it on a table with captions, simply remove the caption, run the command, and then add the caption back to your table.

Tables handle alignment a little differently than other XHTML tags. You can use the standard alignment buttons in the Property Inspector to align something inside a table cell, but it's usually a better idea to let the table cell itself actually handle the alignment. This exercise will show you how to change the alignment of table cells.

---

1 If you just completed Exercise 4, **css-teapots.htm** should still be open. If it's not go back and complete Exercise 4.

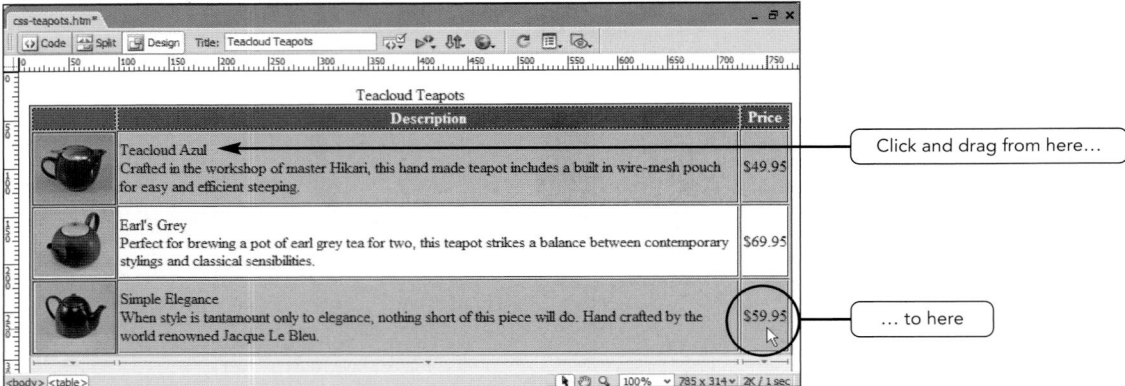

By default, content inside table cells is centered vertically inside the cell, which, 99 percent of the time is not what you'll want for your tables. Changing this behavior is pretty simple.

---

2 Click and drag from inside the **Description** column for **Teacloud Azul** to the **Price** column for **Simple Elegance** to select all six of the table cells.

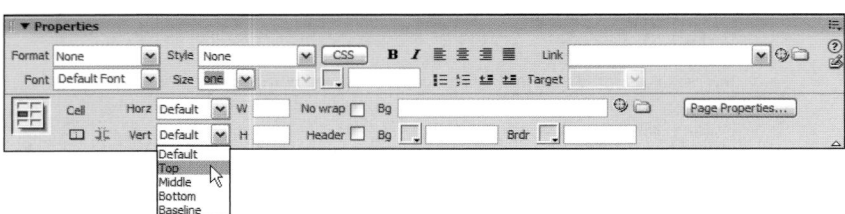

3 In the **Property Inspector**, choose **Top** from the **Vert** pop-up menu (which handles vertical alignment).

The contents of the
selected cells move to the
top of the table cell so that
it lines up nicely. You can
also see that a **valign** attribute has been added to the
<td> tags, with a value of
top. This is how XHTML
handles table cell align-
ment. As usual, it's time to
give this a try with CSS.

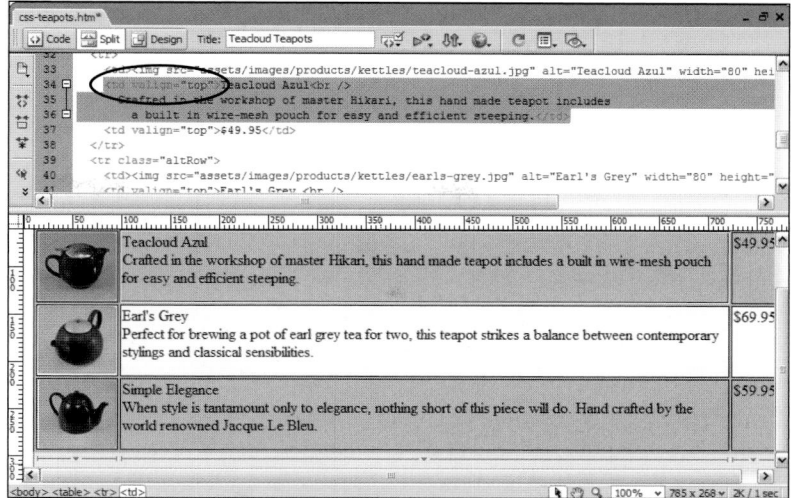

4 Choose **Edit > Undo Set Attribute** to undo the table
alignment changes. You're going to set the same alignment using CSS this time. In the **CSS Styles** panel, click
the **New CSS Rule** button. In the **New CSS Rule** dialog
box, select **Advanced** in the **Selector Type** section, type
th, td in the **Selector** field, and leave the **Define in** option
set to **This document only**. Click **OK** to define the rule.

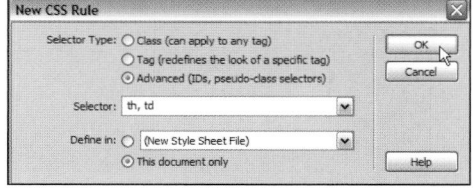

5 In the **CSS Rule
Definition** dialog box,
select **Block** from the
Category pane and set
the **Vertical alignment**
property to **top**. Click **OK**
to apply the rule.

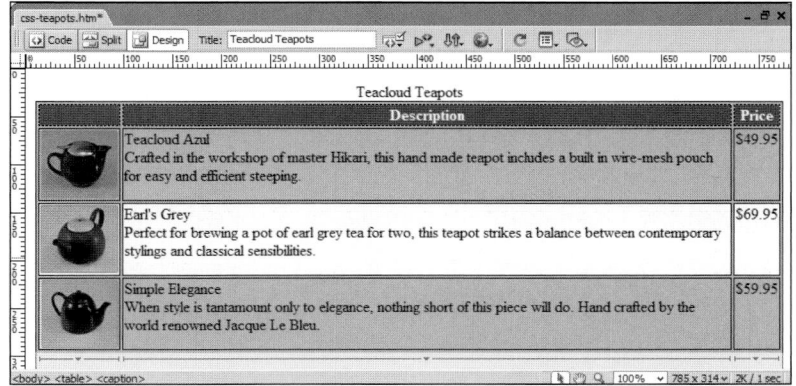

The table doesn't look any different than it did when you used the table cell's **valign** attribute. However,
using CSS to control the cell alignment means that the alignment applies to *every* cell of the table, so
that you don't have to manually set the alignment on every table cell.

6 It's time to do some horizontal alignment. Change the price of the Simple Elegance teapot to **$159.95**.

Notice the prices are lined up along the left side of the table cell. As a general rule, prices should line up on their decimal places (by aligning them to the right) so they're easier to read.

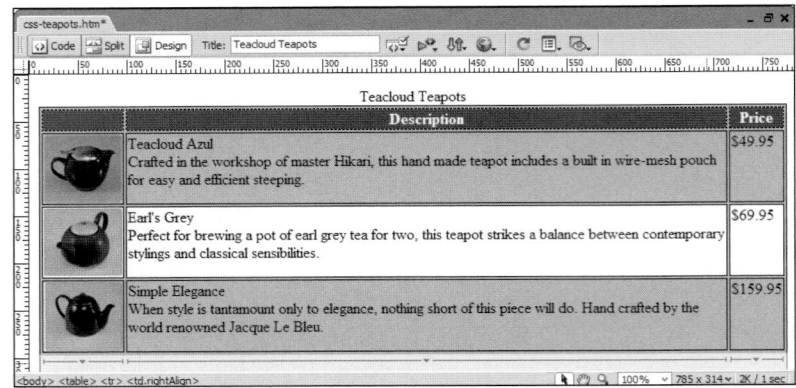

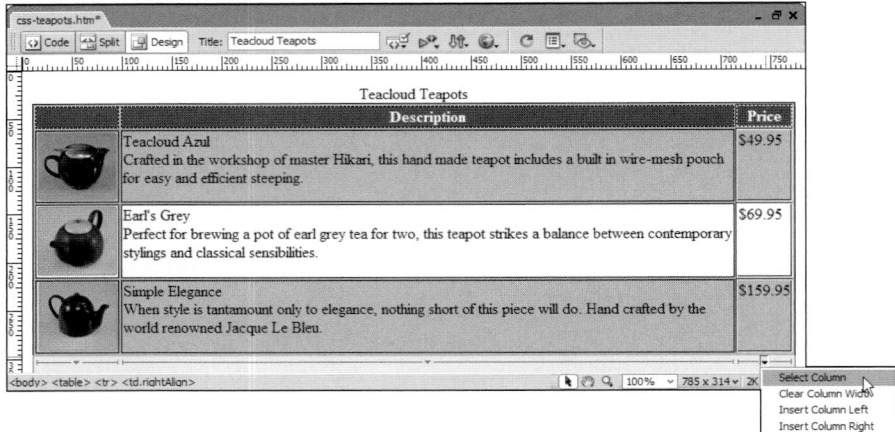

7 If you can't see the column header menus below the table, choose **View > Visual Aids > Table Widths**. At the bottom of the **Price** column, click the column header menu and choose **Select Column**.

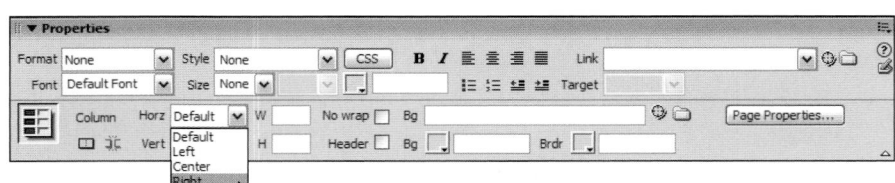

8 In the **Property Inspector**, choose **Right** from the **Horz** pop-up menu.

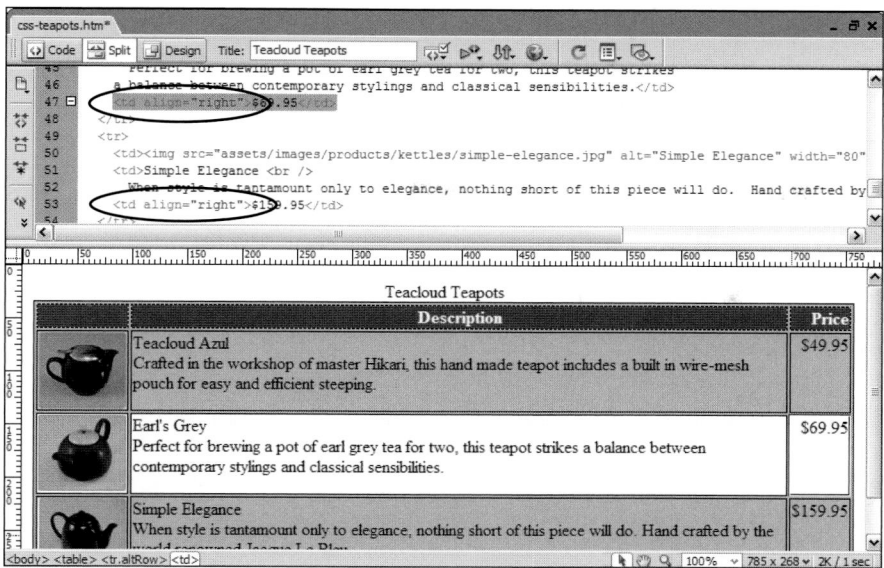

The Price column is now nicely aligned to the right. If you take a look at the code, you'll see an `align` attribute added to each table cell with a value of `right`. But, you guessed it—it's time to do the same thing with CSS.

9 Choose **Edit > Undo Set Alignment** to remove the changes you just made.

NOTE:

Table and Column Header Menus

When you select a table in Dreamweaver 8, you'll notice a bunch of green lines and little arrows at the bottom of the table and each of the columns. These **column header** menus give you quick access to some table features. The options on the bottom-most menu affect the *entire* table, such as clearing all heights and widths, making all widths consistent, and even hiding the table widths.

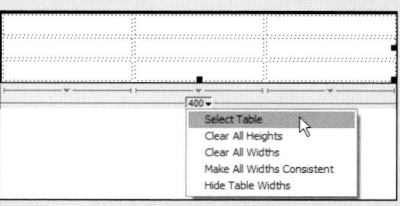

The column header menus for the individual columns offer different options, such as clearing the width of an entire column and inserting a new column to the right or left. These menus are visible only in the Dreamweaver 8 interface and never in a browser. If you deselect the table, the menus will disappear. **Note:** You can turn off the column header menus by choosing **View > Visual Aids > Table Widths**.

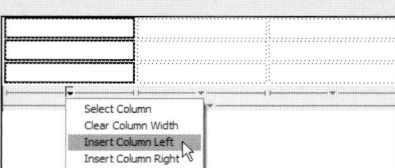

10 In the **CSS Styles** panel, click the **New CSS Rule** button. You're going to define a class that will be applied to any table cell you want to right-align. In the **New CSS Rule** dialog box, select **Class** in the **Selector Type** section, type **.rightAlign** in the **Name** field, and leave the **Define in** option set to **This document only**. Click **OK** to define the rule.

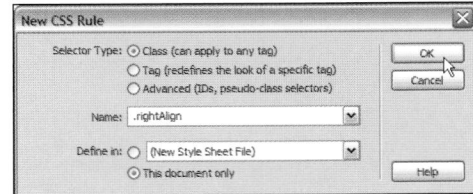

---

11 In the **CSS Definition** dialog box, select **Block** in the **Category** pane, and choose **right** from the **Text align** pop-up menu. Click **OK** to apply the rule.

---

12 Select the **Price** column again. In the **Property Inspector**, choose **rightAlign** from the **Style** pop-up menu.

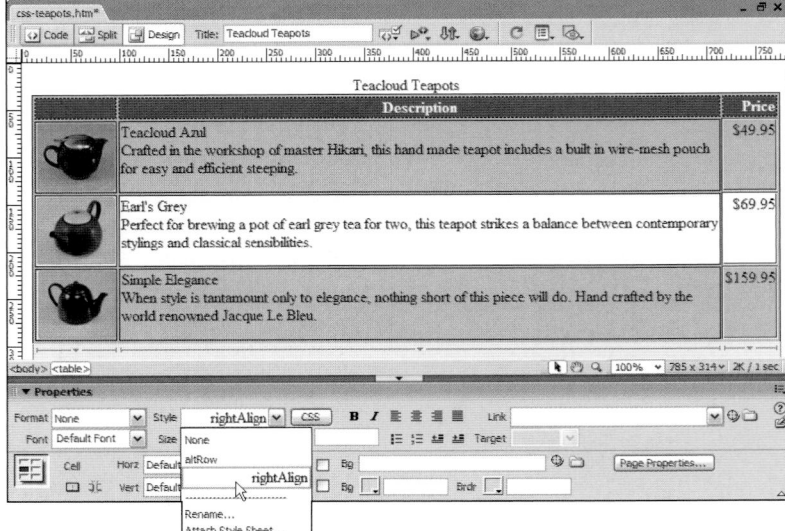

Once again, the table looks the same, but you're now using a method that's far easier to maintain than a bunch of XHTML attributes on your table.

The next thing to do is to get the content away from the edges of the table a bit. Having the text too close to the borders often makes it difficult to read.

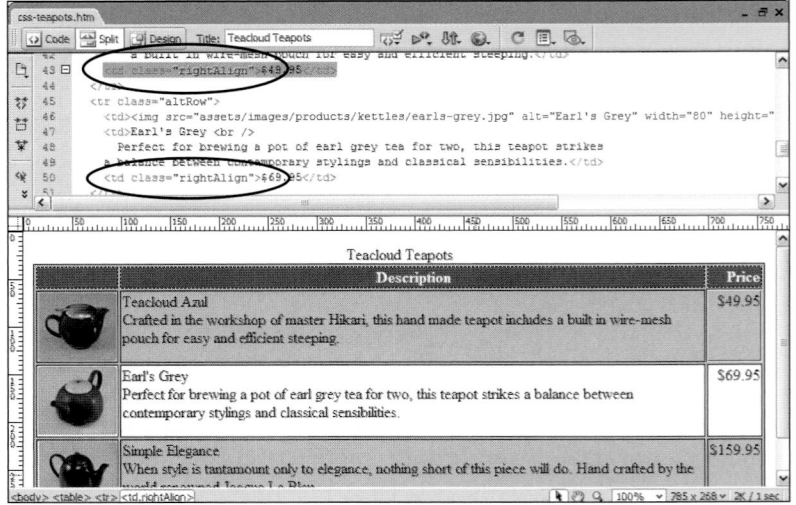

13 In the **CSS Styles** panel, double-click the **th, td** rule to edit it.

14 In the **CSS Rules Definition** dialog box, select **Box** in the **Category** pane. Type **5** in the **Padding** field and click **OK** to apply the rule.

NOTE:

Table Cell Padding

Cell padding in tables works just like padding on standard typographic elements, which you learned about in Chapter 7, "*Typography.*" Padding is added to the inside of the table cell, and it controls the distance of the text from the border.

15 Press **F12** to preview the page in a browser.

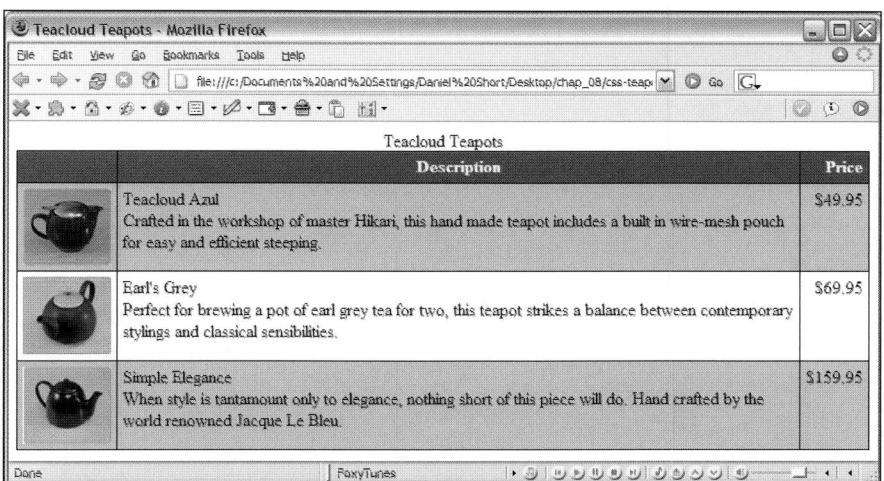

The table looks much better now that the alignment has been taken care of and the text has a little more room to breathe in the table cells.

16 Save your changes and keep **css-teapots.htm** open for the next exercise.

6 | Sorting a Table

Way back in Dreamweaver 2.0, Macromedia introduced the capability to sort table content both alphabetically and numerically. Before this feature existed, if you wanted to sort a table, you had to copy and paste each row or column manually. Thankfully, sorting table content is only a simple dialog box away.

1 If you just completed Exercise 5, **css-teapots.htm** should still be open. If it's not go back and complete Exercise 5.

2 Make sure your cursor is somewhere inside the table. Choose **Commands > Sort Table** to open the **Sort Table** dialog box.

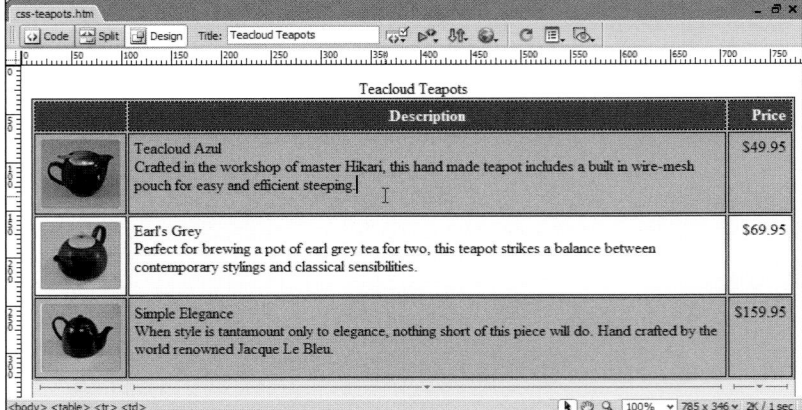

3 Choose **Column 2** from the **Sort by** pop-up menu and choose **Alphabetically** and **Ascending** from the **Order** pop-up menus. Click **OK**.

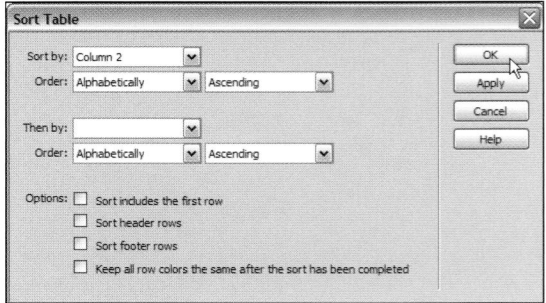

As you can see, the table contents have been sorted according to the product name. The images and prices stayed with their appropriate descriptions, and the alternating row colors were maintained.

Next, you'll sort the table by price (most expensive first).

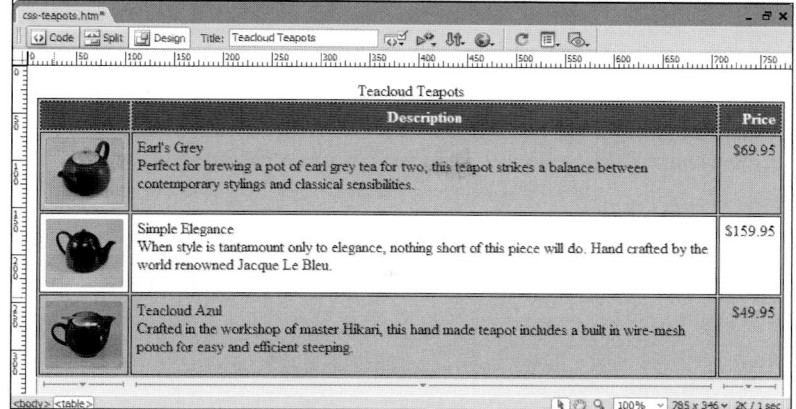

4 With the table still selected, choose **Commands > Sort Table** to open the **Sort Table** dialog box.

5 Choose **Column 3** from the **Sort by** pop-up menu and choose **Numerically** and **Descending** from the **Order** pop-up menus.

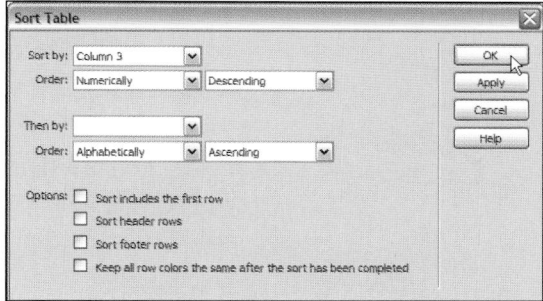

As you can see, the table is now sorted by price, with the most expensive item first.

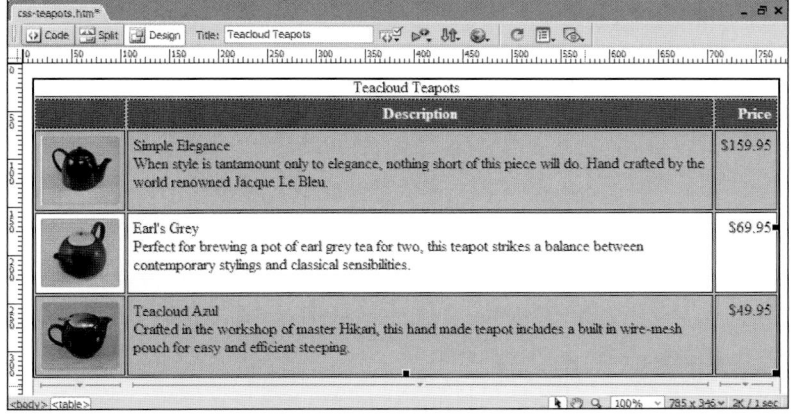

NOTE:

Sort Table Command Options

The Sort Table dialog box has a variety of options to help you modify the appearance of tables. See the following chart for an explanation of all its features:

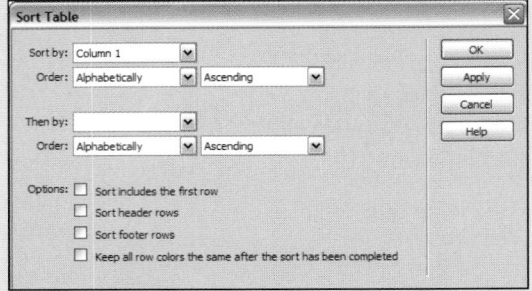

Sorting Features

Feature	Definition
Sort by	Use this option to select which column you would like to use to sort the table.
Order	Use these two pull-down menus to choose **Alphabetically** or **Numerically** and **Ascending** or **Descending**.
Then by	Use this option to sort multiple columns in your table.
Sort includes the first row	If this box is selected, the first row in your table will be sorted. This option is off by default because most often the first row is used as a header for the table.
Sort header rows	If this box is selected, all the rows in the table's headers (if any) will be sorted using the same criteria as the body rows.
Sort footer rows	If this box is selected, all the rows in the table's footers section (if any) will be sorted using the same criteria as the body rows.
Keep all row colors the same after the sort has been completed	If this box is selected, all of the row colors will remain associated with their content, even if the rows are rearranged after the sorting is completed. Leave this box deselected to keep alternating table rows in their rightful place.

6 Save your changes and keep **css-teapots.htm** open for the next exercise.

7 | Setting Table Widths

When you created the table for this exercise, you didn't explicitly declare any width for the table, so the browser determines the width for you by stretching out the table as wide as it can in order to accommodate the table's content. As a result, your tables will change based on the size of the browser window. Although many times this functionality is what you're looking for, other times you'll want to specify the exact width. In this exercise, you'll learn how to take control of your table widths by specifying widths in both pixels and percentages. You're going to learn about controlling table size with pixels first, and then after that you'll switch to percentages.

---

1 If you just completed Exercise 6, **css-teapots.htm** should still be open. If it's not go back and complete Exercise 6.

First, you'll set the table width to 500 pixels, which means no matter what size your browser is, the table will always remain fixed at 500 pixels wide.

---

2 Select the entire table. In the **Property Inspector**, type **500** in the **W** (width) field and press **Enter** (Windows) or **Return** (Mac) to commit your changes to the table.

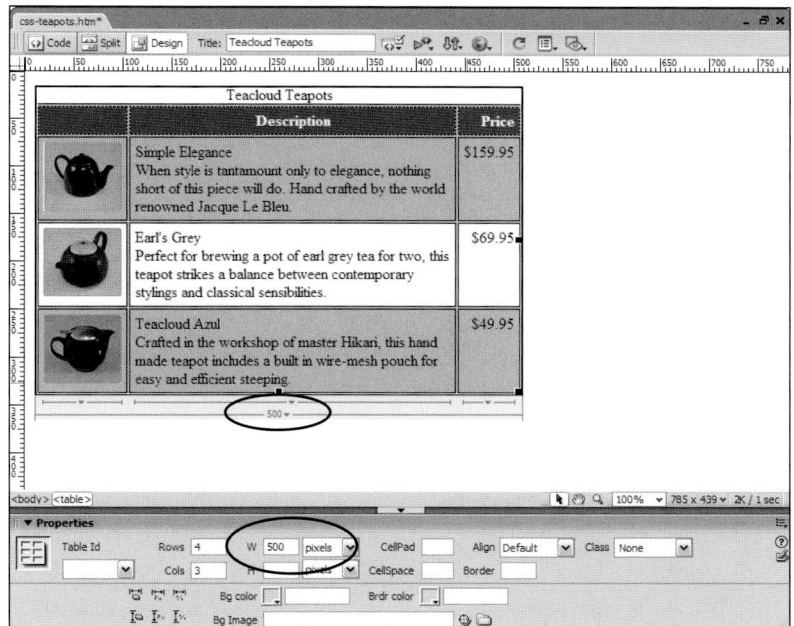

After you change the table width, the table column header at the bottom of the table shows the width of the entire table. With the column headers, you can easily see your column and table widths without selecting the appropriate cell or table and checking the Property Inspector.

With a fixed table width of 500 pixels, the Price column is a bit narrow. Next you'll make it wider to give it a bit more space.

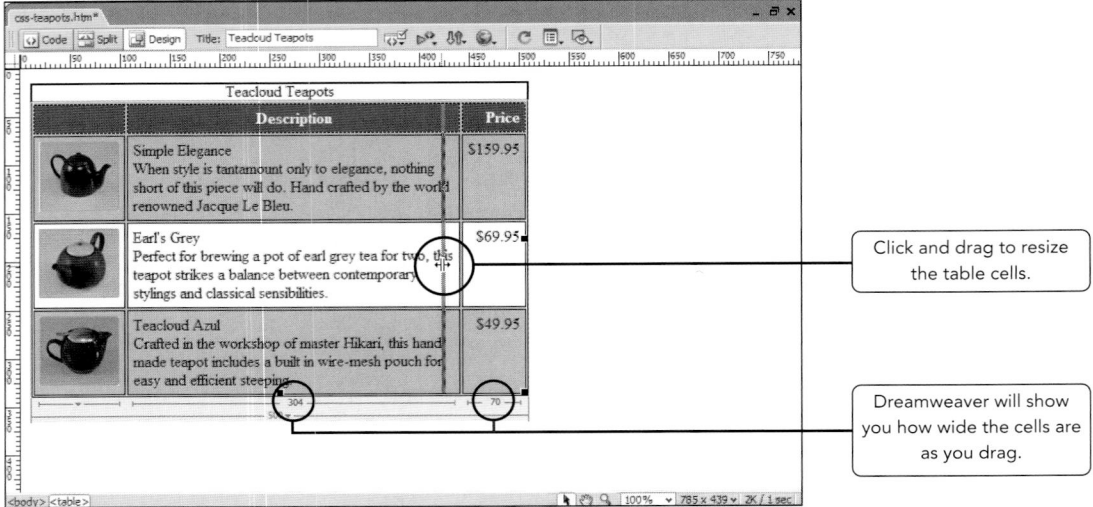

Click and drag to resize the table cells.

Dreamweaver will show you how wide the cells are as you drag.

3 Position your pointer over the divider between the **Description** and **Price** columns and click and drag to resize the columns. Make the **Price** field about **70** pixels and then release the mouse button.

Clicking and dragging the column widths is a quick and easy way to adjust pixel-based column widths. Dreamweaver 8 will set the width of the columns on either side of the line you're dragging.

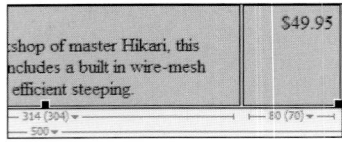

The table widths at the bottom of the table give you more information than you probably suspected. If, for whatever reason, Dreamweaver can't draw the table cell at the width you specified, it will give you the width that's specified in the XHTML, and then the width that it's actually rendered in parentheses.

Next, you'll learn how to create percentage-based table widths. You can use the table column header menu to quickly remove all of the sizing information from the table.

NOTE:

Calculating Table Cell Widths

Having rendered table cell widths that aren't the same as the widths in the XHTML isn't always a bad thing. In Step 3 of this exercise, Dreamweaver tells you that the table cells are being drawn 58 pixels wide, even though you specified that the cell should be 70 pixels wide. Let's do a little math to figure out why this is happening.

If you recall in previous exercises, you added 5 pixels of padding to the **<th>** and **<td>** tags using CSS. When padding is added to a table cell, it's added all the way around. So Dreamweaver added 5 pixels of padding to the left of the table cell and 5 pixels to the right of the table cell, for a total of 10 pixels of padding as far as the width of the cell goes. You also added a border around the table cells. A border on the left and one on the right adds up to 2 pixels. Let's use this formula to calculate the width:

Cell width – (left padding + right padding + left border + right border) = actual width

If you use the values you defined in the CSS, the formula looks like this:

$$70 - (5 + 5 + 1 + 1) = 58$$

So the effective width of the contents of the table cells turns out to be 58, just like Dreamweaver 8 said. If, for whatever reason, you had content that was wider than the table cell, such as an extra large image that stretched out the table cell, Dreamweaver 8 would list the larger table cell size in parentheses to let you know your table is getting stretched out.

That's just one more thing Dreamweaver 8 does to make your table formatting life easier.

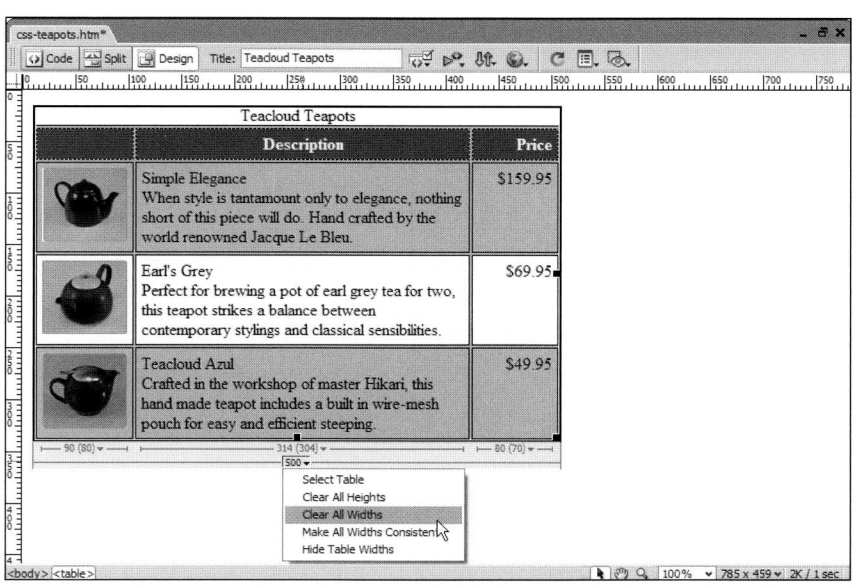

4 Click the column header menu for the table width and choose **Clear All Widths**.

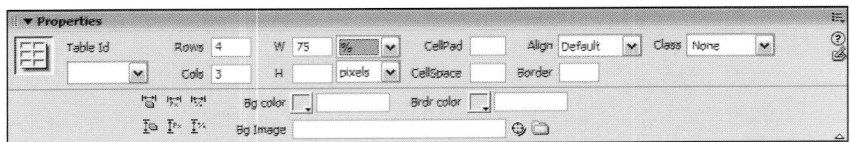

5 With the table still selected, type **75%** in the **W** field in the **Property Inspector**.

Percentage width tables can be handy if you're trying to create a fluid layout, which adjusts with the user's monitor. If your layout is flexible enough, it will display nicely on any screen resolution.

The table width markers work essentially the same for percentage-based table widths. The percentage is listed, and then the actual rendered width of the table or table cell is listed in parentheses. Yours may not match the illustration depending on how wide your document window is.

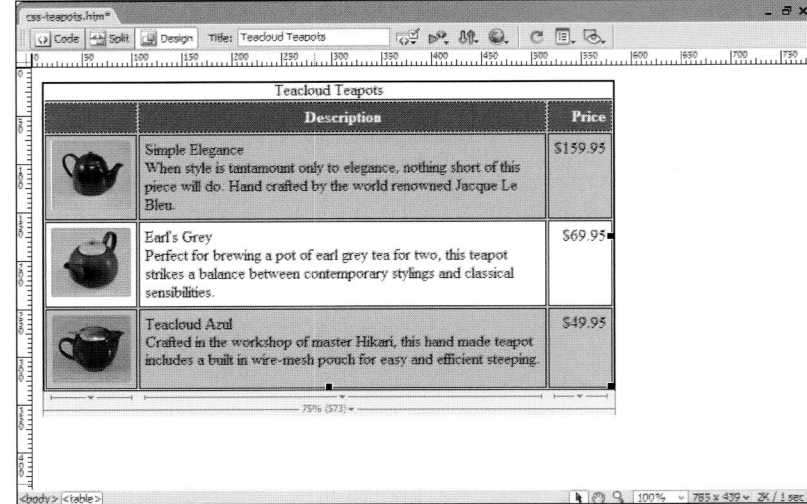

6 Click and drag the divider between the **Description** and **Price** columns to **70** pixels again.

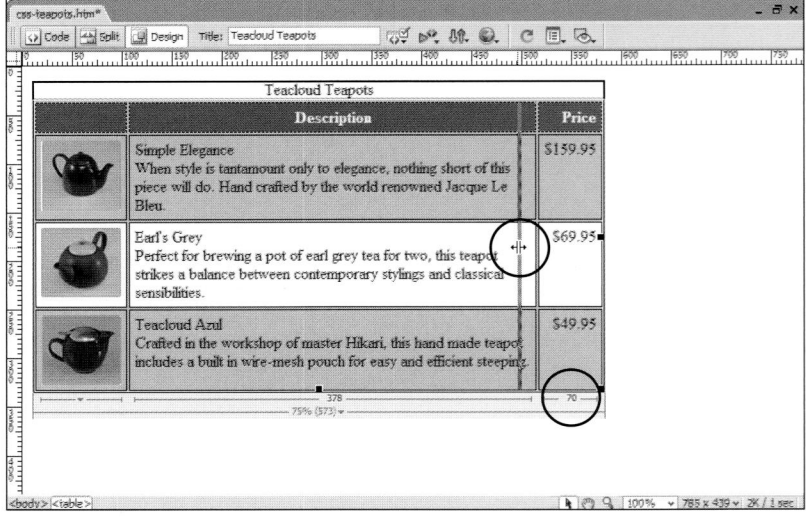

Notice that all of the table cells received a percentage width this time. Dreamweaver 8 knew that the table itself was set to a percentage, so it set each of the columns to be a percentage as well.

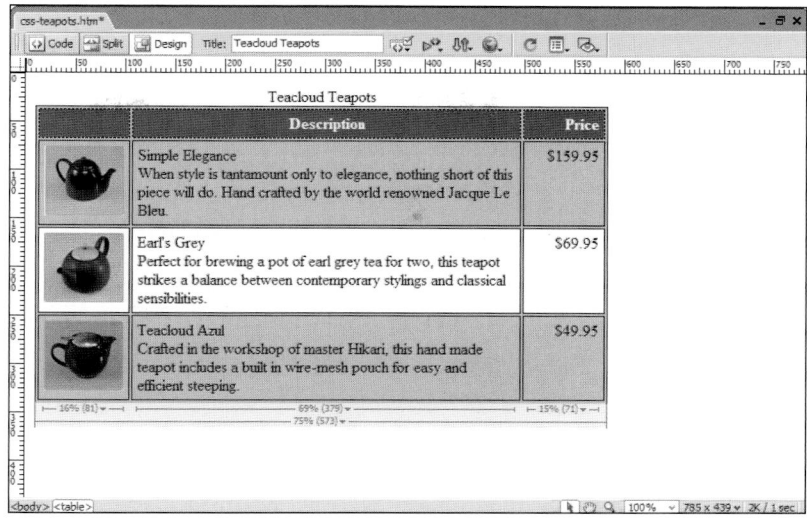

7 Press **F12** to preview the page in your browser, and click and drag to change the browser width to see the table flex.

Because all of the table cells have percentage widths, every table cell changes width as the browser window is resized. Even the photo column is resized, which isn't desirable in this particular layout.

Because you probably don't want to have the photo column of the table resize with the browser width, you can set that column to use a pixel-based width instead of a percentage width.

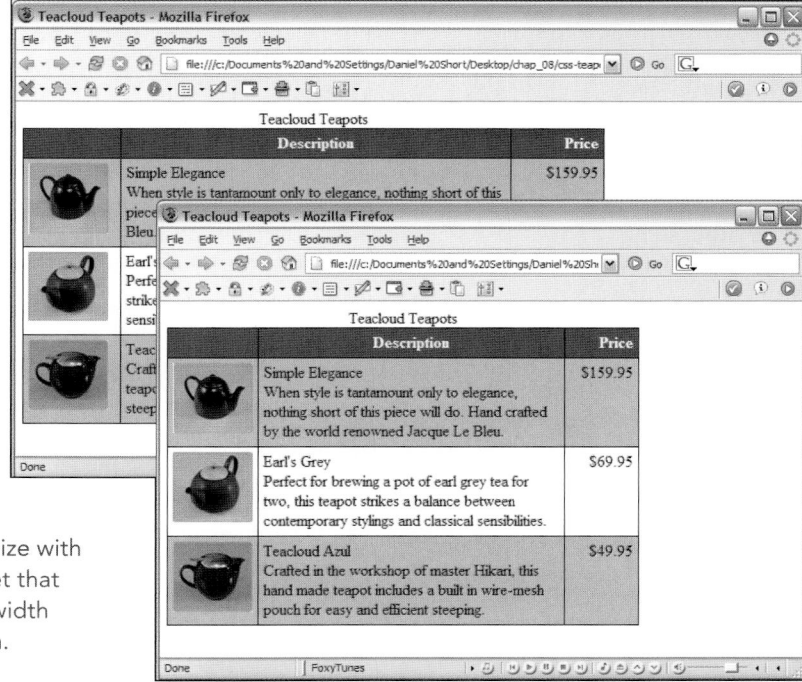

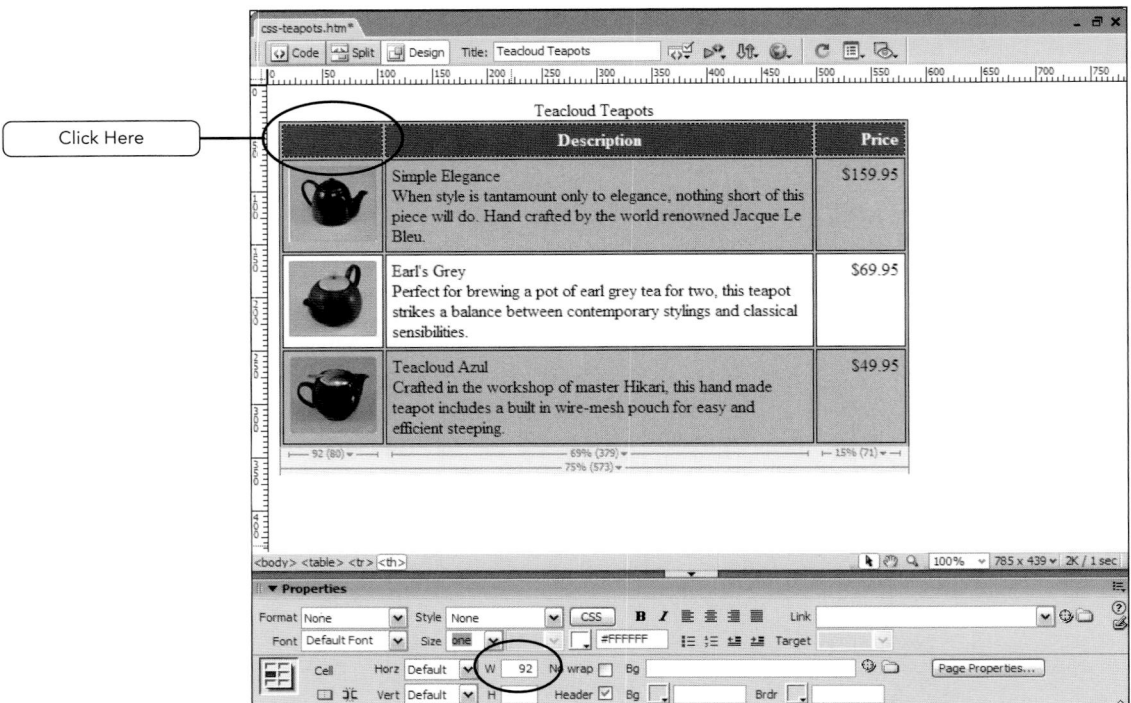

Click Here

8 When Dreamweaver 8 writes table widths after you click and drag a column divider, it sets only the first row of the table to have a width. Only one cell in any column needs a width in order to force the entire column to have that same width. In order to change the width of the photo column, click in the upper-left table cell. In the **Property Inspector**, type **92** in the **W** field.

When specifying widths on individual table cells, you don't need to specify pixels. Simply enter a number, and pixels are the assumed measurement. If you want a table cell to have a percentage-based width, just enter the % symbol after the number. We specified the value 92 because the images are each 80 pixels wide. Add 10 pixels of padding and 2 pixels for borders, and you get 92 pixels.

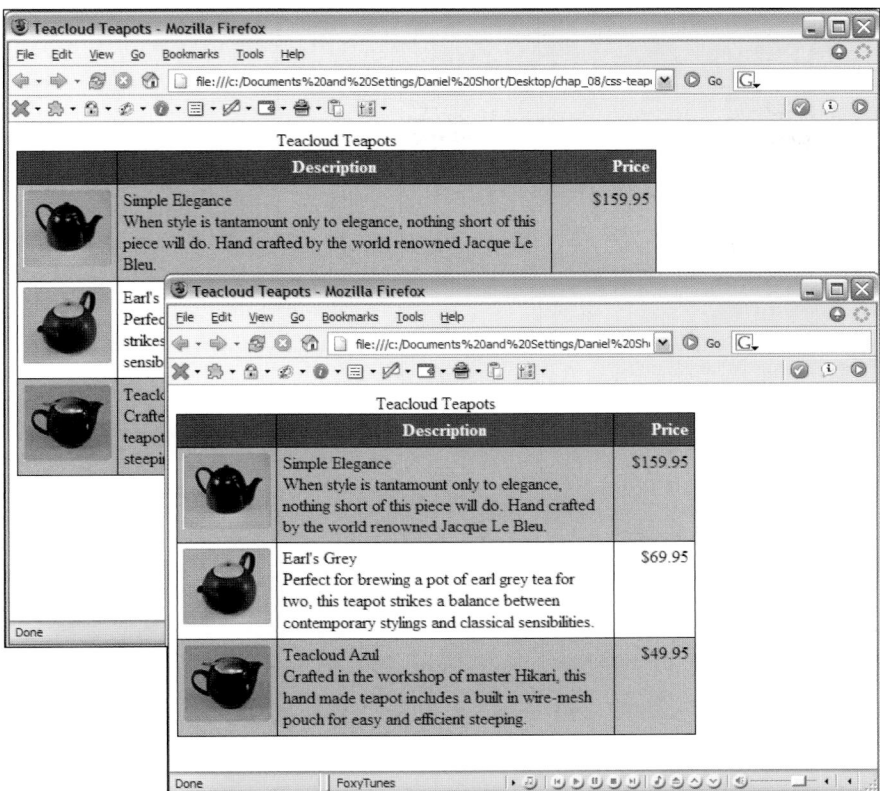

9 Press **F12** to preview the page in your browser. Resize the browser a few times, and you'll see that the second and third columns flex with the browser, but the first column stays rock solid at 92 pixels wide.

10 Close **css-teapots.htm**. You don't need to save your changes.

VIDEO: | **tablewidths.mov**

To learn more about managing table widths, check out **tablewidths.mov** in the **videos** folder on the **HOT CD-ROM**.

8 | Creating Rounded-Corner Tables

Tables, like most things on the Web, are square. Images are square, frames are square, the browser window is square, and CSS uses the "box model"; everything about how the Web is constructed consists of boxes. It's no wonder Web designers are always looking for ways to make things look less square. It's impossible for a table to have rounded corners, plain and simple. The nature of the Web is boxes, and we'll most likely never get away from that. So instead, you're going to use images to give the user the illusion of rounded table corners.

---

1 In the **Files** panel, double-click **rounded.htm** top open it.

This file just has a bit of text and an image that you're going to place into a table with rounded corners.

---

2 Place your cursor at the beginning of the document and choose **Insert > Table**. In the **Table** dialog box, type **3** in the **Rows** field, type **3** in the **Columns** field, and set the **Table width** to **400 pixels**. Type **0** for the **Border thickness**, **Cell padding**, and **Cell spacing**. In the **Header** section, click **None**. Click **OK**.

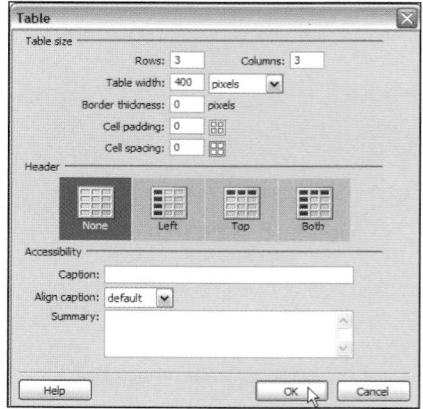

Notice the table already has a background color. We took the liberty of defining a style to redefine the table's background color for you.

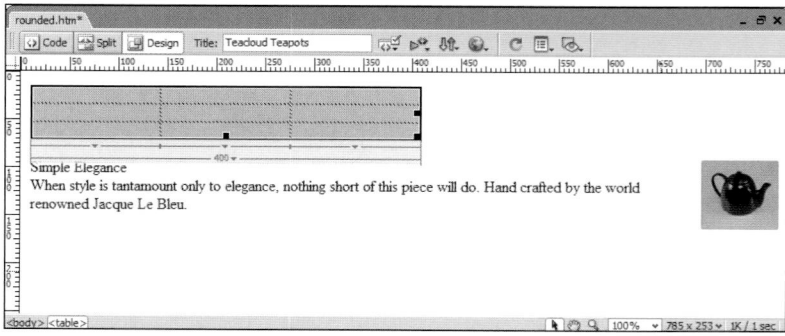

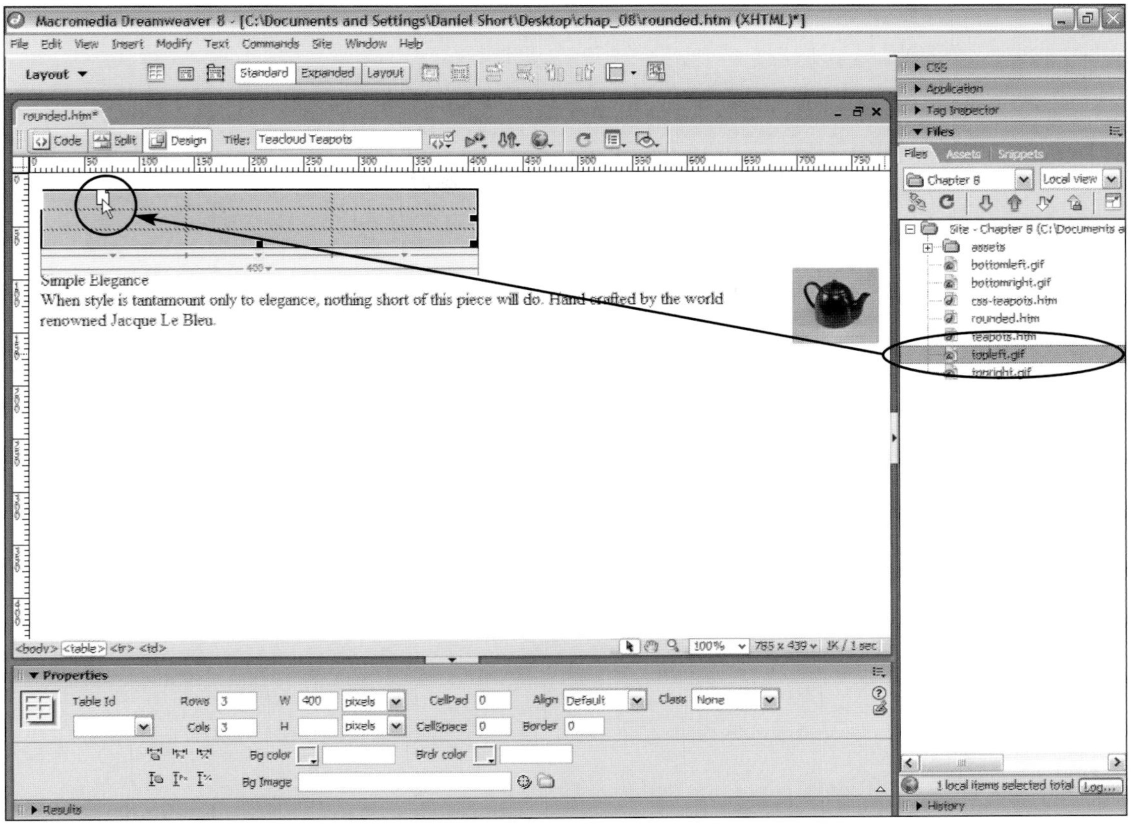

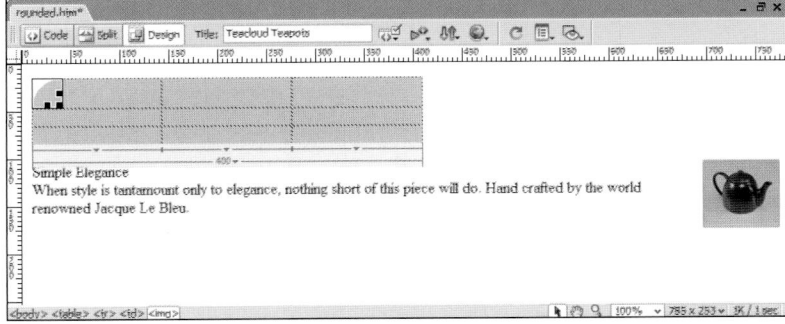

3 Click and drag the **topleft.gif** file from the root of your site to the upper-left table cell. If the **Image Tag Accessibility Attributes** dialog box appears, choose **<empty>** from **Alternate text** pop-up menu and click **OK**.

You can see that the image inserted into the upper-left corner of the table has the same background color as the table itself, and it has a white matte around it to match the page background color.

4 Click and drag the **topright.gif** file from the root of your site to the upper-right table cell. If the **Image Tag Accessibility Attributes** dialog box appears, choose **<empty>** from **Alternate text** pop-up menu and click **OK**.

5 Click and drag the **bottomleft.gif** file from the root of your site to the lower-left table cell. If the **Image Tag Accessibility Attributes** dialog box appears, choose **<empty>** from **Alternate text** pop-up menu and click **OK**.

6 Click and drag the **bottomright.gif** file from the root of your site to the lower-right table cell. If the **Image Tag Accessibility Attributes** dialog box appears, choose **<empty>** from **Alternate text** pop-up menu and click **OK**.

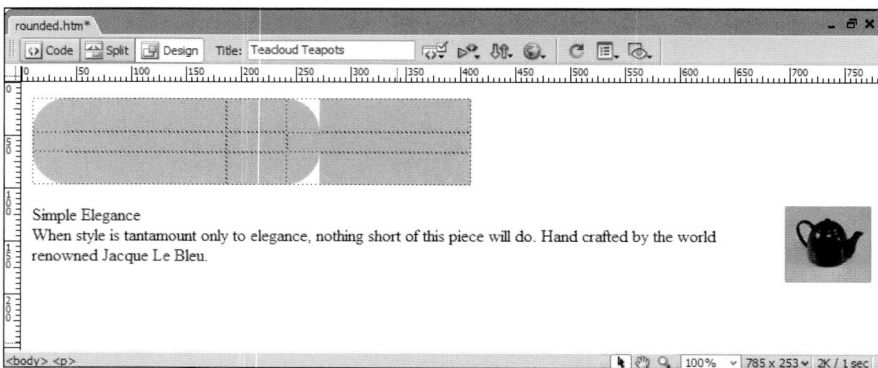

With all of the images are inserted, you can see how things are coming together. Unfortunately, the images aren't being rendered like they should be because of the lack of widths on the table cells.

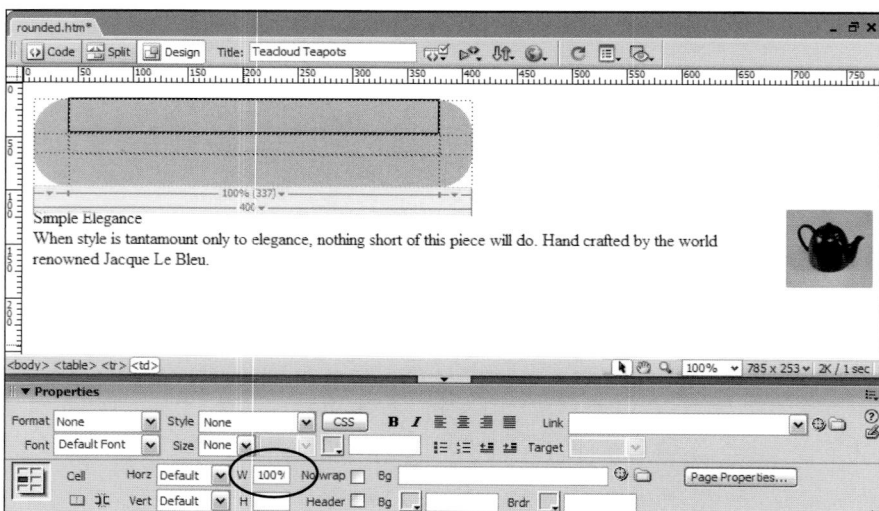

7 Click inside the top middle table cell, and type **100%** in the **W** field in the **Property Inspector**.

Setting the width of the center column to 100% means the center column will take up as much space as it can, forcing the first and third columns to collapse tightly around the contents of their cells.

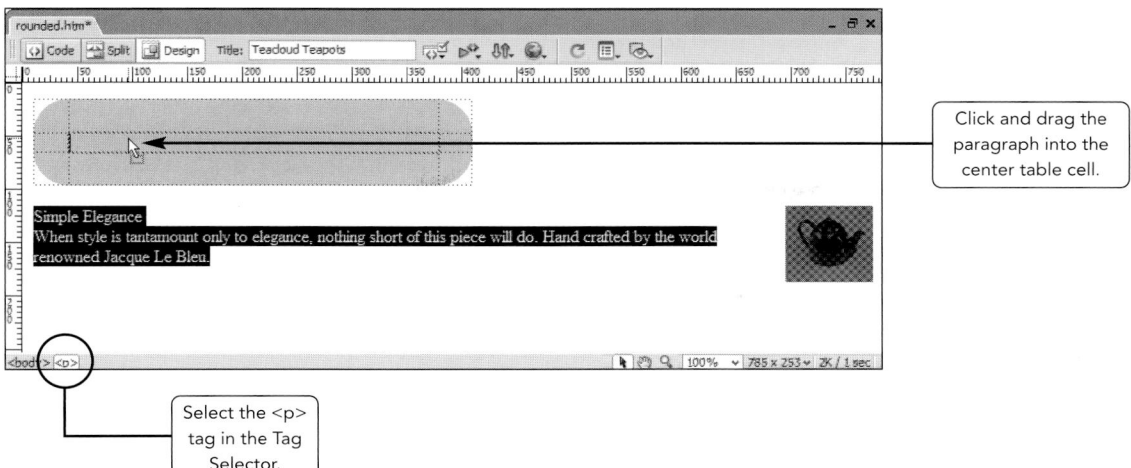

Click and drag the paragraph into the center table cell.

Select the <p> tag in the Tag Selector.

8 Click inside the text at the bottom of the page and select the **<p>** tag in the **Tag Selector**. Once the contents of the paragraph are highlighted, click and drag the entire paragraph into the center table cell.

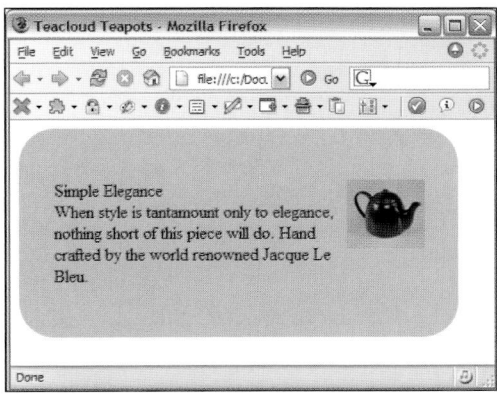

9 Press **F12** to preview the file in your browser.

You now have a table with nicely rounded corners. All of the table cells collapse tightly around the four corner images.

Round Corner Construction

The four images used in this exercise were created in Fireworks by drawing a square with rounded corners and exporting each corner of the square as a different GIF file. You can find this Fireworks PNG file (**rounded-corners.png**) in the **assets** folder.

When working with rounded table corners, you should make sure the background color of your images is the same as the page you're going to be using them on to make sure that the images blend in seamlessly with the background color of the page. You can see where the images are being placed by changing the border of the **<table>** tag to 1.

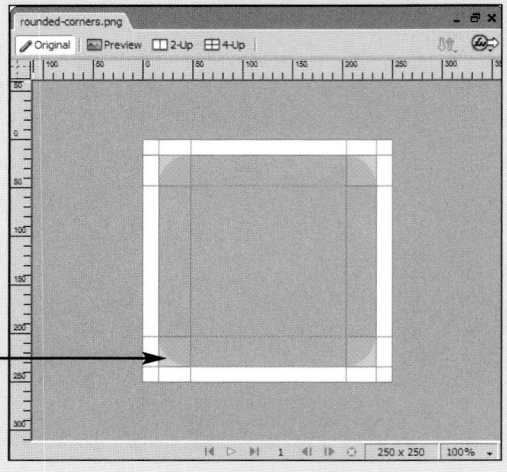

Each corner of the square was exported as a separate GIF file.

You can then clearly see how each of the table cells collapses around its rounded corner image.

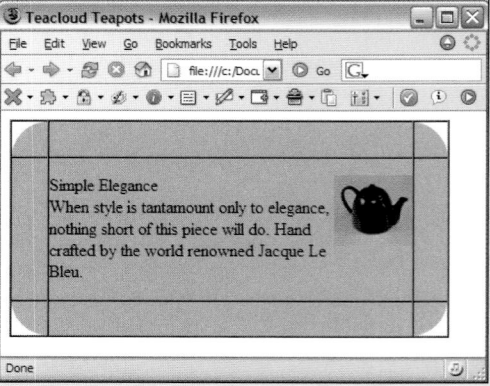

10 Close **rounded.htm**. You don't need to save your changes.

In this chapter, you learned how to create and edit tables, as well as how to format them using both XHTML and CSS. You also learned how to align text neatly, and how insert images into a table to eliminate some of the boxy-ness inherent in Web design. Tables will be a part of your daily development, so it definitely pays to spend some time learning the intricacies of table manipulation. In the next chapter, you'll learn more about laying out entire Web pages, including more fun with tables.

Layout

In traditional layout programs, such as Adobe PageMaker, Adobe InDesign, and QuarkXPress, most people take it for granted that they can move blocks of text and images around almost anywhere on the screen. Unfortunately, standard XHTML doesn't contain any tags that let you position elements easily. You've learned how you can use tables to position your elements both horizontally and vertically on your Web pages with table settings, but creating a basic table still doesn't give you the precision you get in traditional print layout programs. This problem has caused considerable frustration among Web page designers.

Fortunately, Dreamweaver 8 has built-in functions to help you work in a visual mode to create precise alignment for your text and images. You'll learn how to align your images using tracing images and layers, which you can then convert into tables that can be viewed on nearly any browser. Dreamweaver 8 has an alternative layout feature called layout cells, which gives you the freedom of absolute positioning while still conforming to XHTML table guidelines! You'll learn several techniques that let you position elements anywhere on your Web page, such as tracing images and layers, converting layers to tables, and working with layout tables and layout cells. After completing these exercises, you can decide for yourself which method you prefer when building your own pages.

Tracing Images, Layers, and Tables for Layout

This chart outlines the concepts behind tracing images, layers, and tables, which you will learn about in the exercises that follow:

Tracing Images, Layers, and Tables Defined	
Item	**Definition**
Tracing image	An image (GIF, JPEG, or PNG) that you can load into the background of the Design view in Dreamweaver to serve as a reference for layout. Consider this the blueprint you follow to build your pages.
Layer	Layers are just absolutely positioned `<div>` tags. You can place them anywhere on the page, and they are completely self-contained. They aren't affected by other elements, and they don't affect the position of other elements on the page.
Table	Tables can hold images and text in place, but they are not intuitive or flexible when it comes to positioning them on the screen. However, Dreamweaver 8 offers some helpful features that give you more flexibility, including innovative table drawing tools, and the capability to convert layers to tables.

1 | Applying a Tracing Image

Imagine you have mocked up a wonderful layout for a Web page in Photoshop, Fireworks, Illustrator, or any drawing or painting program of your choice. The next step is getting the layout into Dreamweaver 8. The Tracing Image feature in Dreamweaver 8 lets you export an image of that layout (as a GIF, JPEG, or PNG) and place it in the background of your page, which you can then use as a reference to align your XHTML elements to match up to it perfectly. In this exercise, you will learn how to apply a tracing image to your Web page, as well as how to change its transparency and position on the page.

---

1 Copy the **chap_09** folder from the **HOT CD-ROM** to your **Desktop**. Define your site as **Chapter 9** using the **chap_09** folder as the local root folder. Make sure the **Files** panel is open. If it's not, choose **Window > Files** or press **F11**.

---

2 In the **Files** panel, double-click **index.htm** to open it. This page is empty except that its **Title** is **Welcome to Teacloud**. Choose **Modify > Page Properties** to open the **Page Properties** dialog box. Select **Tracing Image** from the **Category** list.

---

3 Click **Browse**.

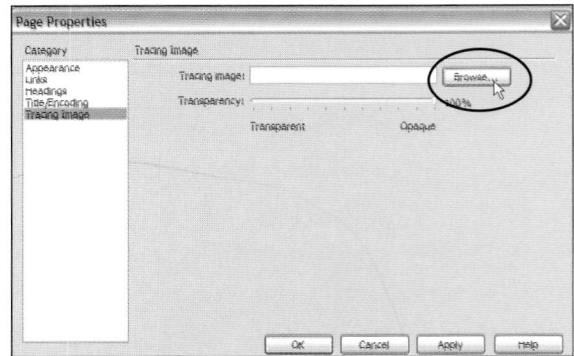

---

4 Browse to the **assets** folder and select **landing.gif**. Click **OK**.

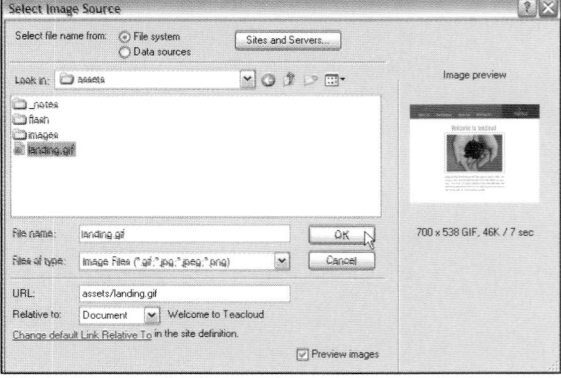

---

5 Leave the **Transparency** slider at **100%**. Click **OK** to close the **Page Properties** dialog box.

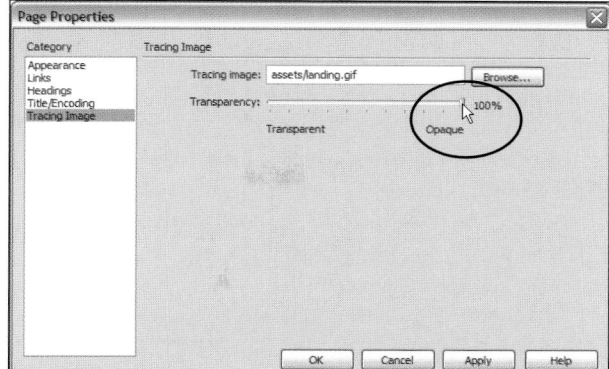

This is what your page should look like with the tracing image applied. It was inserted at 100% opacity in the Page Properties dialog box, which makes it opaque.

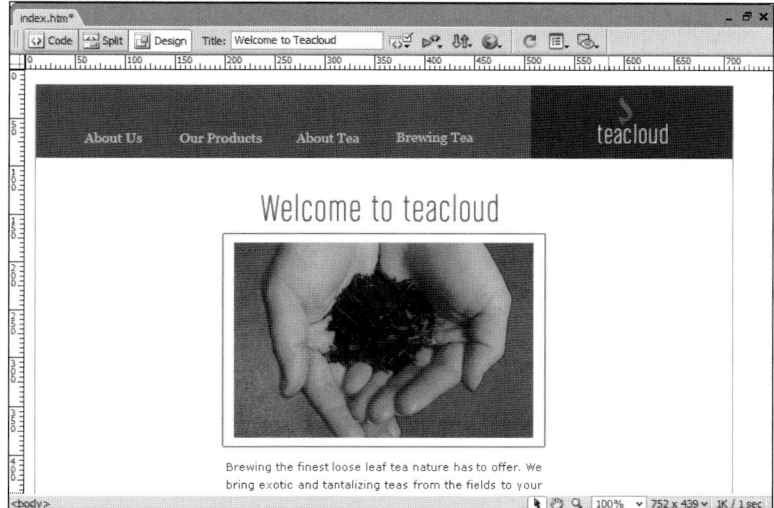

NOTE:

Browser Offset

The white space you see above and to the left of the tracing image is the result of Dreamweaver 8 honoring the default margins that browsers add to your documents. By default this offset is X:10 Y:15, which means the image is offset 10 pixels from the top and 15 pixels from the left of the document. You can modify this offset by choosing **View > Tracing Image > Adjust Position**.

Dreamweaver 8 offsets tracing images from the upper-left corner to emulate an offset that exists in Web browsers. You can get rid of this offset by setting the margin settings in the Page Properties window. You'll want to leave the offset alone—it

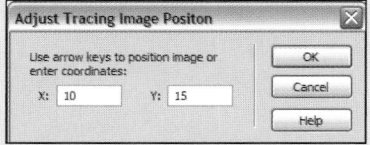

represents what will happen in a browser, anyway. If you haven't accounted for this offset in the design of your tracing image, we suggest you don't change this setting.

6 Press **F12** to preview this page in a Web browser.

Notice that the page appears completely blank. The tracing image appears only in Dreamweaver 8, and it won't be visible to your end user.

---

7 Return to Dreamweaver 8 and choose **Modify > Page Properties** to access the tracing image settings again.

---

8 Drag the **Transparency** slider down to **50%** and click **OK**.

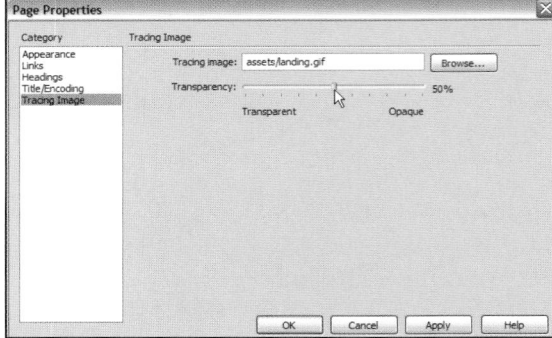

With the opacity reduced, it's much easier to use the tracing image as a guide because it doesn't compete with foreground images and text.

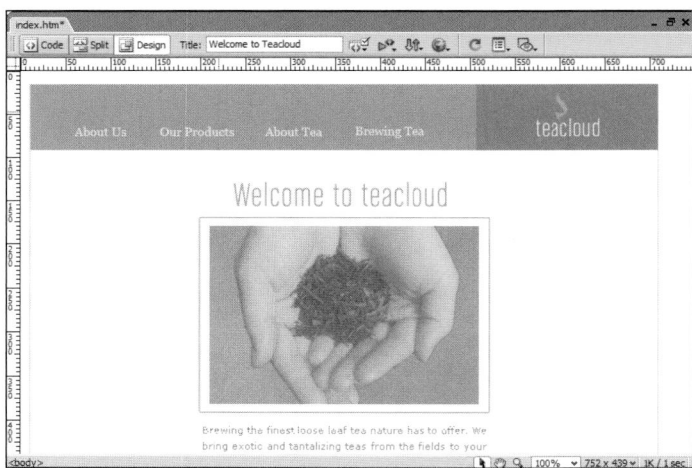

9 Save your changes and keep **index.htm** open for the next exercise.

NOTE: | **Tracing Image and Background Images**

Once you apply a tracing image to your page, it will hide any background images applied to the document while you are editing the document inside Dreamweaver 8. However, if you view the page that contains the tracing image in a browser, the background image will be visible and the tracing image will not. In other words, tracing images are only visible to you while you're working in Dreamweaver 8.

2 | Adding Layers

In previous chapters, you placed artwork and text directly on your page or inside tables. With that method, you can right-, left-, or center-align elements, and that's the end of the story. This is frustrating because it would be much easier if you could stick that artwork or text anywhere you wanted on the page and have it stay there. Layers are your friends because you can position them anywhere without restriction. Rather than simply placing artwork and text on a page, as you have been doing so far, you can put your content into layers and move it anywhere you want, even using the new guides in Dreamweaver 8 to make sure they're lined up nice and neat. In this exercise, you will learn how to create layers on your page and insert images and text inside them.

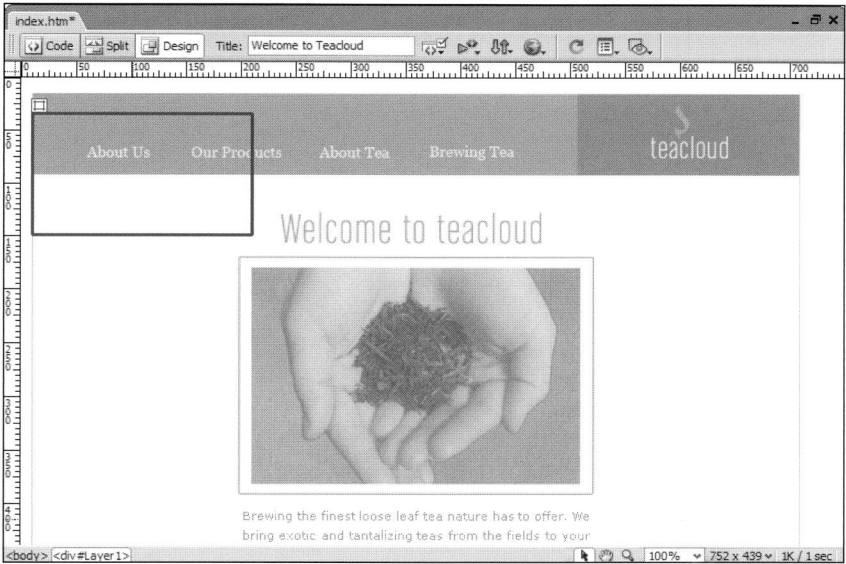

1 If you just completed Exercise 1, **index.htm** should still be open. If it's not, go back and complete Exercise 1.

2 Choose **Insert > Layout Objects > Layer**.

With the Layer object, you can click and drag to draw a layer anywhere you want on the page.

3 Move your cursor over the **layer handle** (the box on the upper left of the layer) and click and drag to move the layer so the upper-left corner aligns with the **teacloud** logo in the tracing image. Using the **resizing handles**, resize the layer so that it fits around the edges of that image.

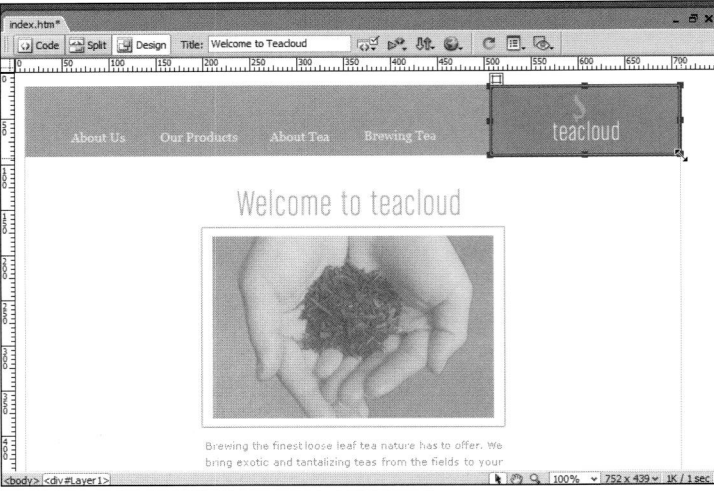

NOTE:

The Zoom Tool

If you have a hard time getting your layers lined up just right (and we never get them right the first time), Dreamweaver 8 now lets you zoom in Design view. All you need to do is click the magnifying glass icon in the Tag Selector and then click and drag a box around the area you want to zoom into.

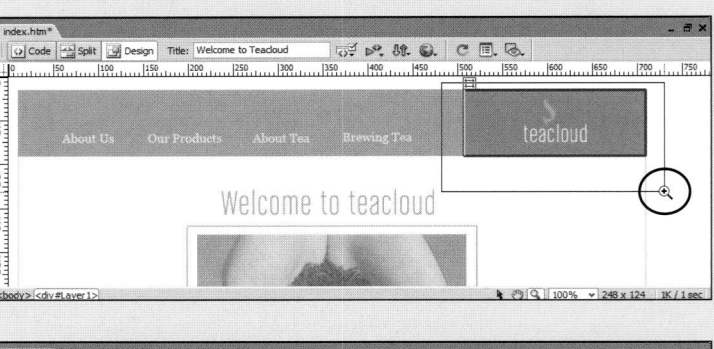

The list pop-up menu next to the magnifying glass offers you a quick way to zoom to a predefined zoom percentage, or just to get back to the 100% view.

4 Click inside the layer and choose **Insert > Image**. Browse to **assets/images** and select the **logo.png** file. Click **OK**. If the **Image Tag Accessibility Attributes** dialog box appears, type **Teacloud Logo** in the **Alternate text** field and click **OK**.

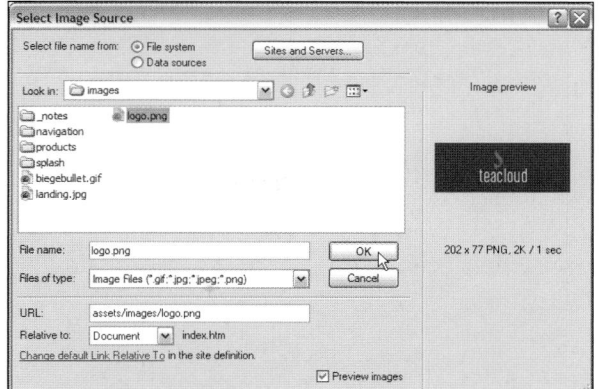

An image is now inside the layer. Notice how this image is darker, whereas the tracing image is screened back? That's because you set the tracing image's opacity to 50% in the last exercise, which makes it easy to distinguish between the tracing image and the final artwork.

Click anywhere inside the top ruler.

Drag the ruler down until it snaps into place on top of the Teacloud logo layer.

5 Next you're going to draw the layer for the navigation area, but to make sure everything gets lined up correctly, use the guides, which are a new feature in Dreamweaver 8. To place a guide at the top of the **Teacloud** logo layer, click inside the ruler at the top of the document and drag a guide to the top of the logo layer; it should snap nicely into place when you get close enough to the layer.

6 Do the same for the bottom of the **Teacloud** logo: drag a guide from the top ruler until it snaps into place at the bottom of the layer.

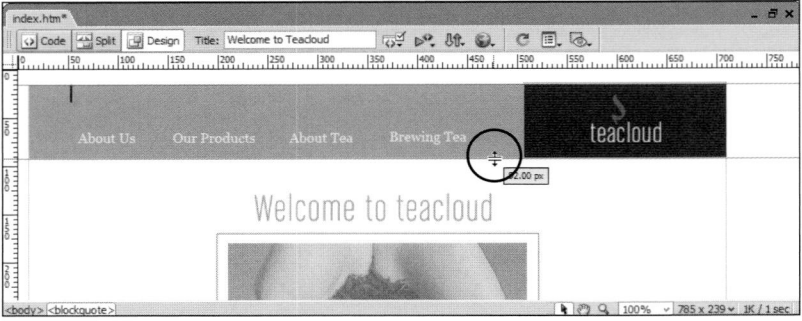

7 Finally, drag a guide from the left ruler so that it lines up with the left of the navigation bar in the tracing image.

Now that you have guides for the navigation layer, it will be a "snap," quite literally, to draw the navigation layer. As you draw a layer, your cursor

will snap to each of the guides to ensure that you get the layer in just the right spot.

8 In the **Common** group of the **Insert** bar, click the **Draw Layer** object.

This is just another way to access the Draw Layer object. If you're drawing a large number of layers, it's definitely quicker to access the Draw Layer object via the toolbar than the menu.

9 Before you draw the layer, choose **View > Guides > Lock Guides** so you don't accidentally move a guide while you're working. With the **Draw Layer** tool selected, draw a layer around the navigation area of the tracing image.

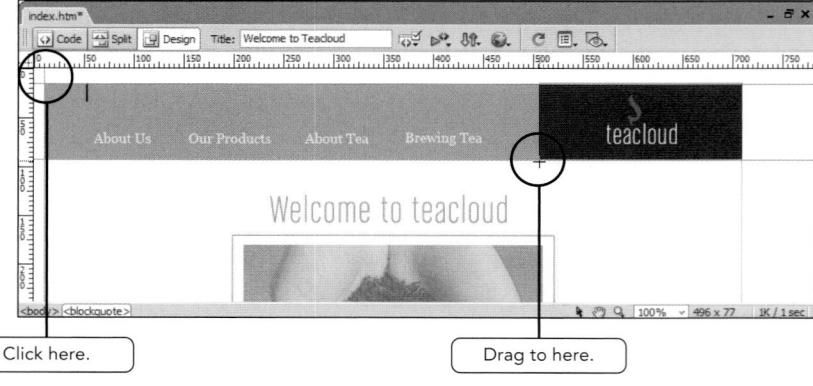

Click here.

Drag to here.

10 Insert **aboutus-out.gif**, **ourproducts-out.gif**, **abouttea-out.gif**, and **brewingtea-out.gif** from the **assets/images/navigation** folder into the new layer you just created. If the **Image Tag Accessibility Attributes** dialog box appears, type an appropriate description in the **Alternate text** field for each image and click **OK**.

Unfortunately, this layer doesn't have any styling that defines how the images should be aligned inside the layer. In the next step, you'll determine how everything should be aligned.

11 Open the **CSS Styles** panel by choosing **Window > CSS Styles**. Switch to the **All** mode of the panel and expand the **<style>** group.

Notice there are two styles in here that you didn't write. Each time you draw a layer using the layer tools, Dreamweaver 8 automatically gives the layer a name and creates a style, which defines how to position the layer on the page. This is a good thing because it gives you a quick and easy hook into the layers you just created.

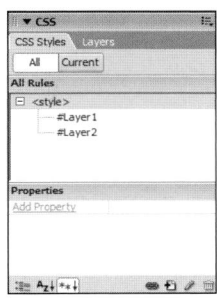

12 In the **CSS Styles** panel, select the **#Layer2** style (for the second layer you drew). In the **Properties** pane, click the **Add Property** link. Choose **text-align** from the **Property** pop-up menu and choose **center** from the **Value** pop-up menu.

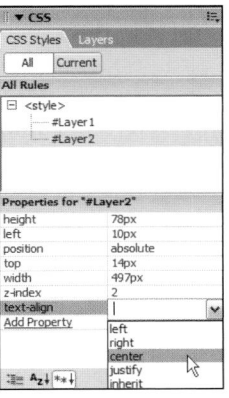

Notice the navigation images are now centered in the layer.

13 Click the **Add Property** link again. Choose **background-color** from the **Property** pop-up menu and type **#6E7970** in the **Value** field.

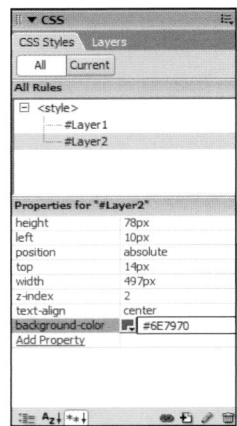

Notice the navigation now has a solid background color matching the images.

---

14 Press **F12** to preview the page in your browser.

As you can see, both layers are positioned right where you wanted them. Unfortunately, the Teacloud layout calls for an extensive use of borders and the design is supposed to be centered. With layers, it's nearly impossible to get a good centered layout, and it's completely impossible

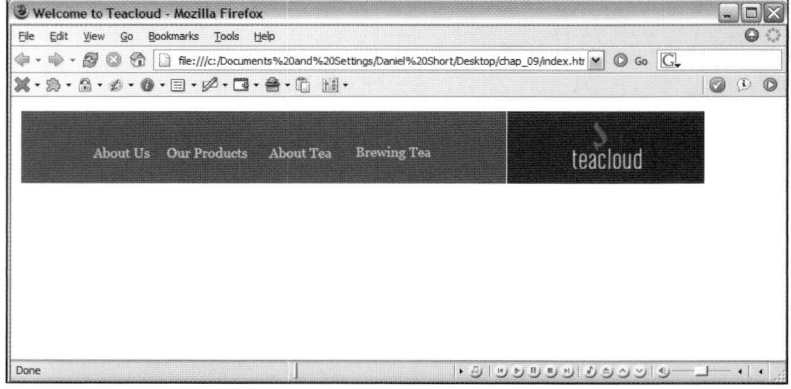

to do it with the design tools alone. That's one reason we prefer to do most of my layouts with tables, and only use the occasional layer here and there as required. In the next exercise, you'll start working with layout tables.

---

15 Close **index.htm**. You don't need to save your changes.

VIDEO: | **layers.mov**

To learn more about using layers, check out **layers.mov** in the **videos** folder on the **HOT CD-ROM**.

What Makes a DIV a Layer?

If you watched the code as you worked through the last exercise, you may have noticed that each of the layers was actually a `<div>` tag with an ID CSS selector applied to it. The CSS rules for each `<div>` tag look something like this:

```
#Layer1 {
    position:absolute;
    left:507px;
    top:15px;
    width:202px;
    height:76px;
    z-index:1;
}
```

The most telling part of that CSS rule is the first item, `position:absolute`. That property tells the browser to put the element exactly where you tell it to, using the top and left properties that immediately follow. As far as Dreamweaver 8 is concerned, that's what makes a `<div>` tag a layer. The term *layer* in Dreamweaver 8 simply refers to an element that has a position property set to absolute. In fact, any element (an `<img>` tag, a paragraph, you name it) will be treated as a layer if Dreamweaver 8 finds the `position:absolute` declaration.

WARNING: **What About Converting Layers to Tables?**

You may have heard that Dreamweaver can convert layers to tables, and tables to layers. Although this is true (check out the **Modify > Convert** menu), we highly discourage it. The conversion process can create some difficult-to-maintain code, and as a general rule does more harm than good. Feel free to experiment with this feature, but we caution you to steer clear from using it for your site designs.

What Is the Layout View?

Dreamweaver 8 contains an alternate way to create the layout for your Web pages called Layout view. The Layout view feature lets you create layout cells and tables by drawing them exactly where you need them, at exactly the size you want. This technique was introduced in Dreamweaver 4 as a more visual way to design your layouts while creating table code behind the scenes. Although converting from layers to tables is convenient and easy, it produces table code that is not as "clean" or as optimized as possible. Layout cells and tables, on the other hand, produce far better code.

3 | Using Layout Tables and Layout Cells

This exercise shows you how to use layout cells and layout tables to create a table for the layout of a Web site. It won't be exactly the same as the table layout you've worked with throughout this book, since those were created by hand, but it will be similar and will show you another way to quickly put together a table-based layout.

---

1 In the **Files** panel, double-click **layout.htm** to open it.

This page is completely blank except for a tracing image so you can see the layout you're going to create.

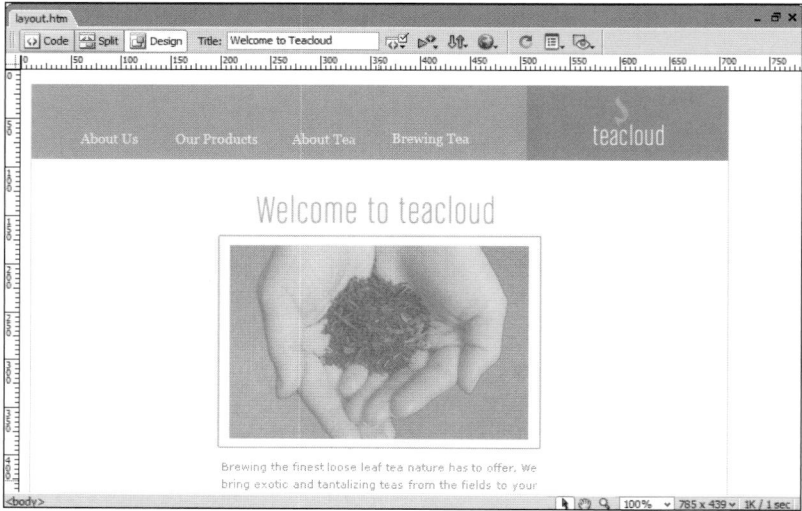

---

2 Choose **View > Table Mode > Layout Mode** to switch to Layout mode. When you see the **Getting Started in Layout Mode** dialog box, click OK.

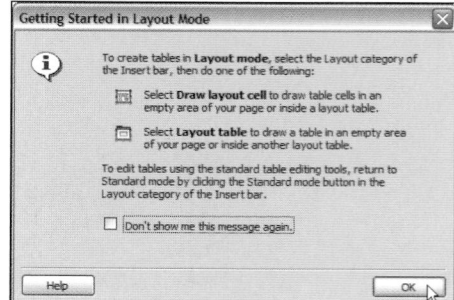

Layout Table objects

Layout mode indicator

You'll notice several changes when you switch to Layout mode. You'll see a hashed border above and below the top ruler, as well as an exit link to get out of Layout mode. You should also notice a few new objects enabled in the Insert bar, which you'll use to begin drawing your tables.

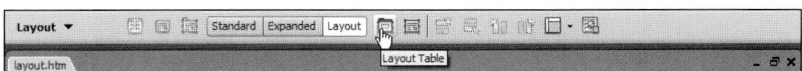

3 In the **Insert** bar, click the **Layout Table** object so you can begin drawing a table.

Click here.

Drag to here.

4 In **Design** view, click and drag to draw the table, as shown in the illustration here.

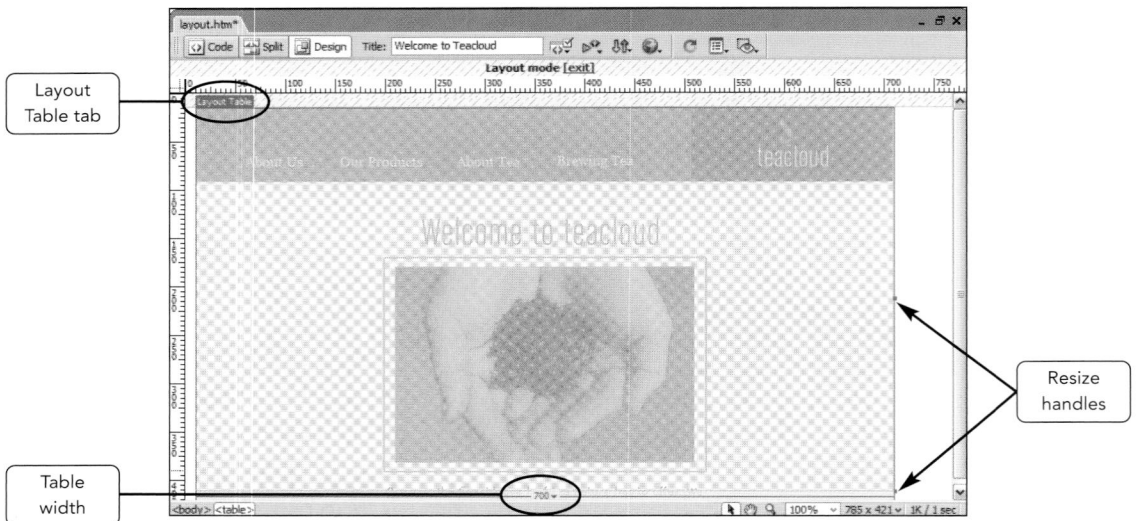

After drawing the table border, Dreamweaver 8 adds a gray translucent background where the table should be, and adds a Layout Table tab to the top of the table so you know what you're working with. You should also notice resize handles all the way around the table, and the table width is displayed at the bottom of the table.

5 Now it's time to draw the actual table cells. In the **Insert** bar, click the **Draw Layout Cell** object, which will let you draw individual cells inside the table.

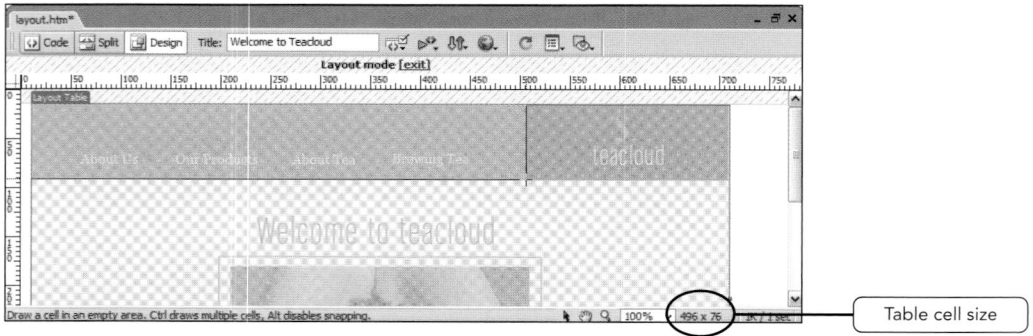

6 Starting in the upper-left corner of the layout table, draw a table cell the size of the navigation bar, which should be 496 pixels by 76 pixels.

You can check to see how large the cells are as you draw them by watching the status bar.

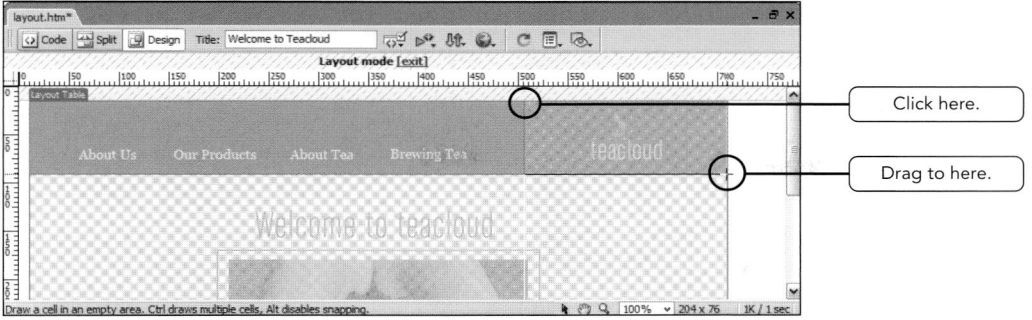

Click here.

Drag to here.

7 Click the **Draw Layout Cell** object again, and beginning in the upper-right corner of the last cell you drew, draw a table cell covering the **Teacloud** logo, which should be 204 pixels by 76 pixels. Because you're drawing to the edge of the table, it will snap to the edge of the table border.

8 Click the **Draw Layout Cell** object again, and draw a table cell to hold the **Welcome to teacloud** image, which should be 324 pixels by 320 pixels.

Don't worry if you don't get it just right the first time—you can always adjust the table cells using the resize handles or adjust the width manually through the code or Property Inspector.

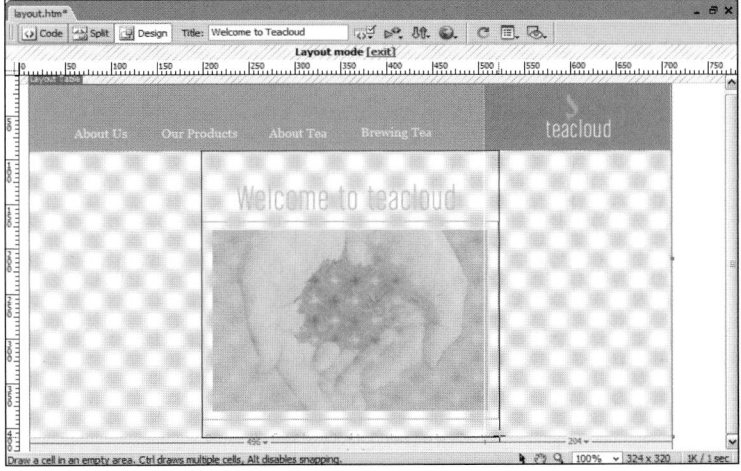

When you're finished drawing the layout cells, the contents of the **layout.htm** file should match the illustration shown here.

Drawing Multiple Layout Cells

As you work with the layout cells feature, you will find yourself creating several cells at once. However, each time you draw a cell, you need to reselect the Draw Layout Cell object before you can create another one. This can get annoying and slow down your workflow quite a bit. If you hold down the **Ctrl** (Windows) or **Cmd** (Mac) key while you draw a layout cell, you can draw as many cells as you want without having to reselect the object each time.

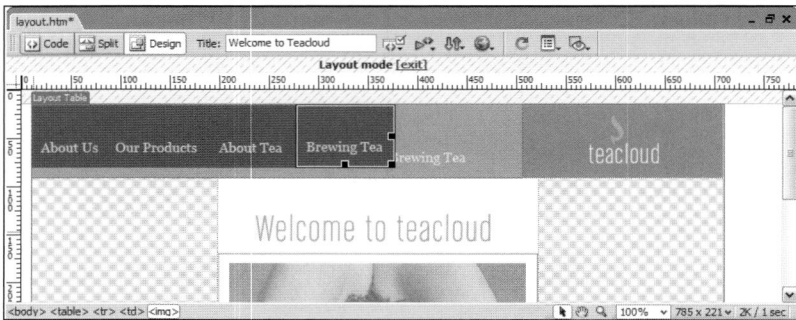

9   It's now time to fill the table with content. First, insert **aboutus-out.gif**, **ourproducts-out.gif**, **abouttea-out.gif**, and **brewingtea-out.gif** from the **assets/images/navigation** folder into the upper-left table cell. If the **Image Tag Accessibility Attributes** dialog box appears, type an appropriate description in the **Alternate text** field for each image and click **OK**.

10   Click the edge of the table cell to select it. In the **Property Inspector**, choose **Center** from the **Horz** pop-up menu and choose **Bottom** from the **Vert** pop-up menu. Type **#6E7970** in the **Bg** field to set the background color of the table cell.

Notice the Property Inspector is a little different for table cells when you're in Layout mode versus the Standard mode you used in Chapter 8, "*Tables.*" You get a few extra options, and quite a few (background image, header options, and so on) have been removed. For this reason, it's not really possible to work only in Layout mode since you don't get access to all of the table and table cell properties.

11 Insert the **logo.png** image from the **assets/images** folder into the upper-right table cell. If the **Image Tag Accessibility Attributes** dialog box appears, type **Teacloud Logo** in the **Alternate text** field and click **OK**.

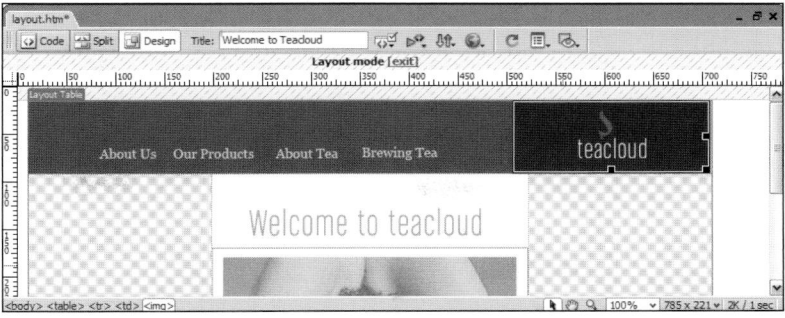

12 Insert the **landing.jpg** image from the **assets/images** folder into the center table cell. If the **Image Tag Accessibility Attributes** dialog box appears, type **Welcome to Teacloud** for the **Alternate text** and click **OK**.

Unfortunately, the image isn't lining up nicely with the tracing image. You'll need to adjust the center table cell to bring the image down in line with the tracing image.

13 Click the border of the center table cell to select it and click and drag the top-center resizing handle to bring the top of the image down in line with the tracing image.

> Grab the resizing handle and drag the top of the table cell down.

Again, don't worry about getting it right on the first try; just keep adjusting until you get the image where you want it.

14 Press **F12** to preview the file in your browser.

Everything is now right where you placed it in Layout view. In the next exercise, you'll start working with table and cell widths in Layout mode.

---

15 Save your changes and keep **layout.htm** open for the next exercise.

Working with Layout Table Widths

It may not seem like something as simple as setting table widths deserves an exercise all its own, but layout tables handle things a little differently than table widths in Standard mode (which you used in Chapter 8, "*Tables*"). In this exercise, you'll work with autostretch layout cells and learn how to manage the ebb and flow of your table cells in percentage-based layouts.

---

1 If you just completed Exercise 3, **layout.htm** should still be open. If it's not, go back and complete Exercise 3.

---

2 Select the navigation table cell. In the **Property Inspector**, select the **Autostretch** radio button.

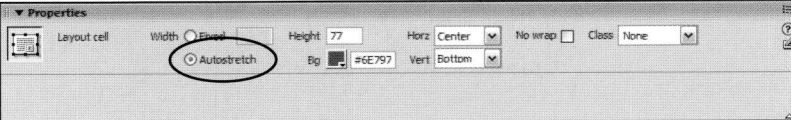

Setting this table cell to autostretch means that as the browser window expands and contracts, the navigation table cell with always fill up as much of the available width as it can.

---

3 When the **Choose Spacer Image** dialog box appears, select the **Create a spacer image file** option to instruct Dreamweaver 8 to create a single-pixel transparent GIF file, in case you don't already have one available. Click **OK**.

---

4 In the **Save Spacer Image File As** dialog box, browse to the **assets/images** folder and click **Save**. The file will be named **spacer.gif** automatically.

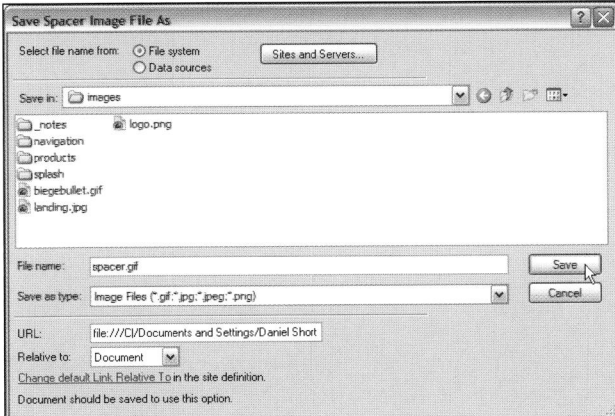

You should notice quite a few changes to your document. The table now fills the entire width of the screen (and then some). The column header menus at the bottom of the screen have also changed to indicate which cells are autostretch cells and which are fixed width.

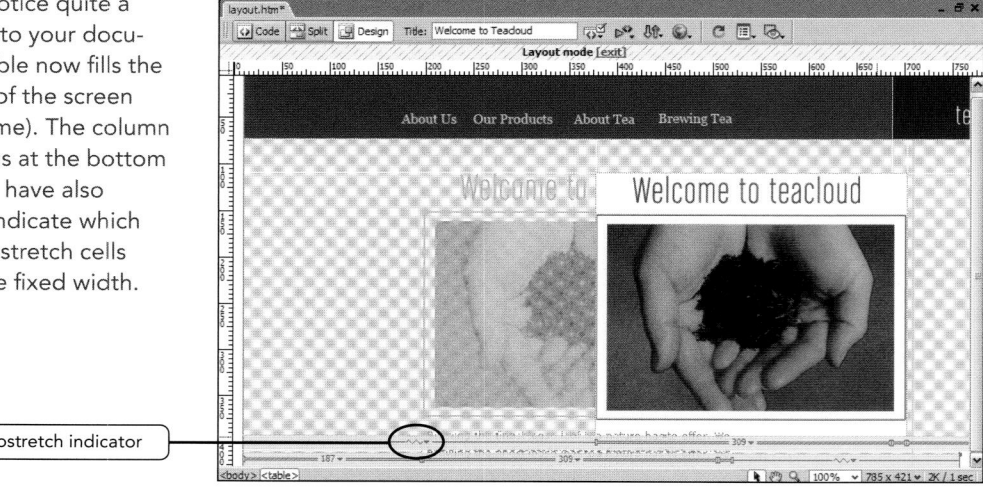

Autostretch indicator

NOTE:

Understanding Spacer GIF Options

In order to prevent the table from collapsing in some browsers, Dreamweaver 8 will insert an invisible GIF inside the cells without content. If you're not overly concerned with older browsers, you can choose **Don't use spacer images for autostretch tables** in the **Choose Spacer Image** dialog box, but you may end up with odd results in some table layouts.

NOTE:

Understanding the Anatomy of Layout Cells

Notice the bottoms of the cells have changed. The following chart explains what each of these visual cues mean:

Layout Cell Display	
Item	**Description**
242 ▾	A layout cell with a numeric value displayed at the bottom means that the cell has a specific width value set in pixels. You can change this value with the resize handles or in the Property Inspector.
242 ▾	A layout cell with a numeric value and thick double lines is an indication that the cell is set to a specific pixel value, and it also contains a **spacer.gif**. This occurs when another column has been set to autostretch.
～▾	A layout cell with a little squiggle at the bottom is an indication that the column has been set to autostretch, which means it will stretch to fill the remaining horizontal space in the browser window. You can change this setting to a fixed-pixel value in the Property Inspector.

5 Press **F12** to preview the page in your browser.

Resize the browser and you'll see the navigation always fills the available width. However, the Welcome to teacloud graphic doesn't stay centered in the document. To get things to stretch the way they should, you need to do a little more work.

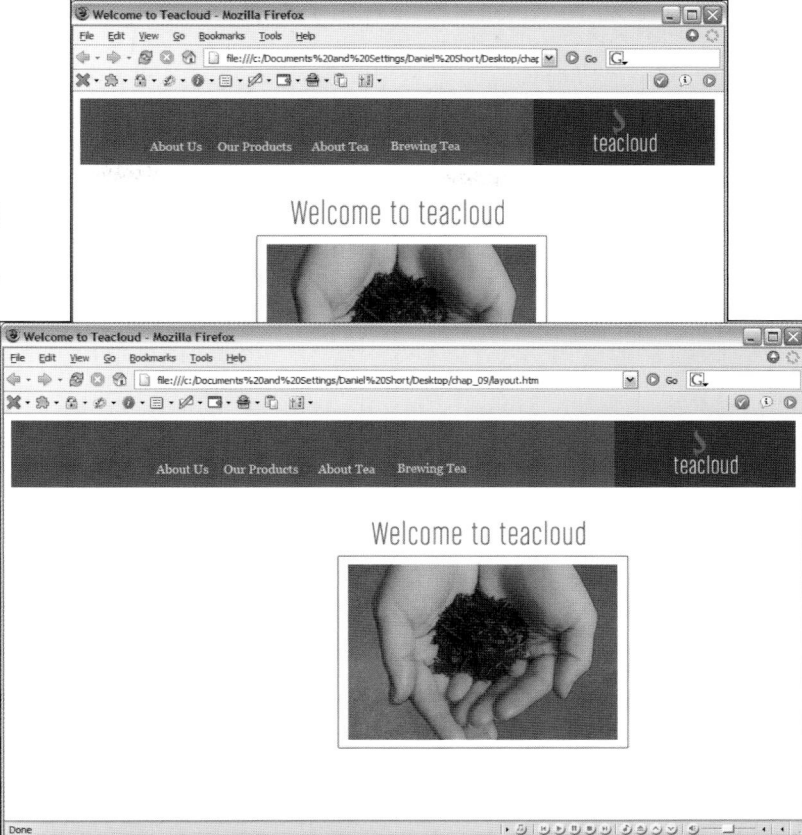

6 Return to Dreamweaver 8. Select the center table cell and click and drag the left and right resize handles to make the center table cell as wide as the entire table.

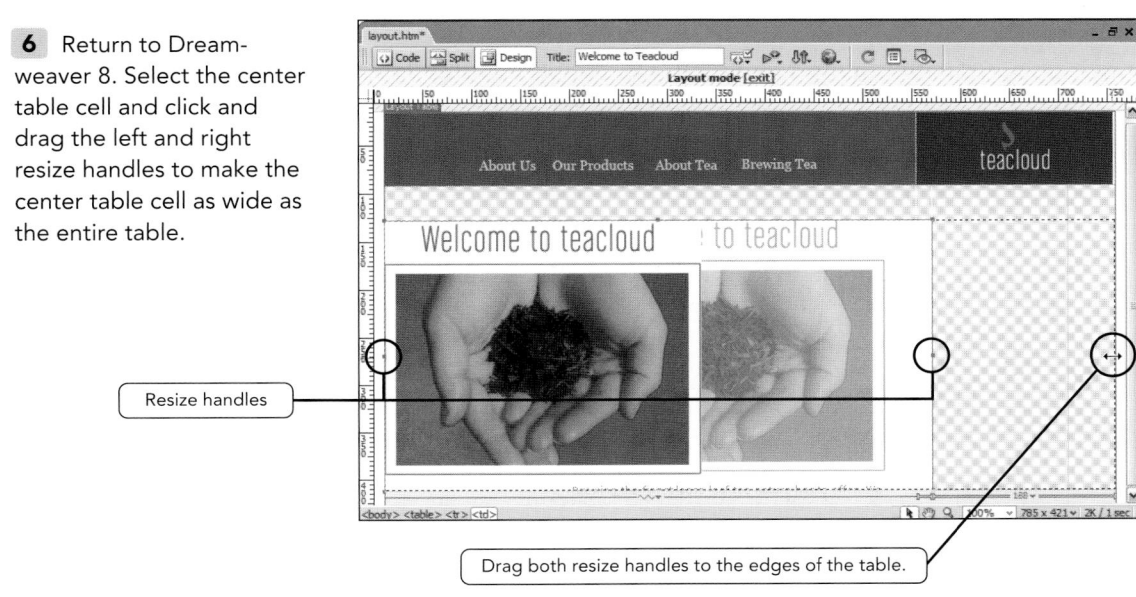

Resize handles

Drag both resize handles to the edges of the table.

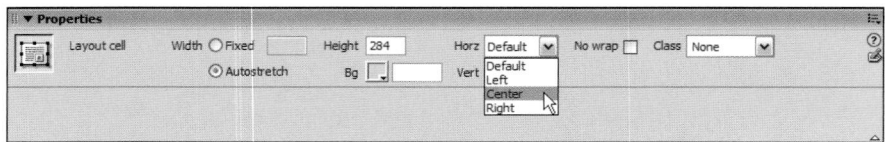

7 With the table cell still selected, choose **Center** from the **Horz** pop-up menu in the **Property Inspector**.

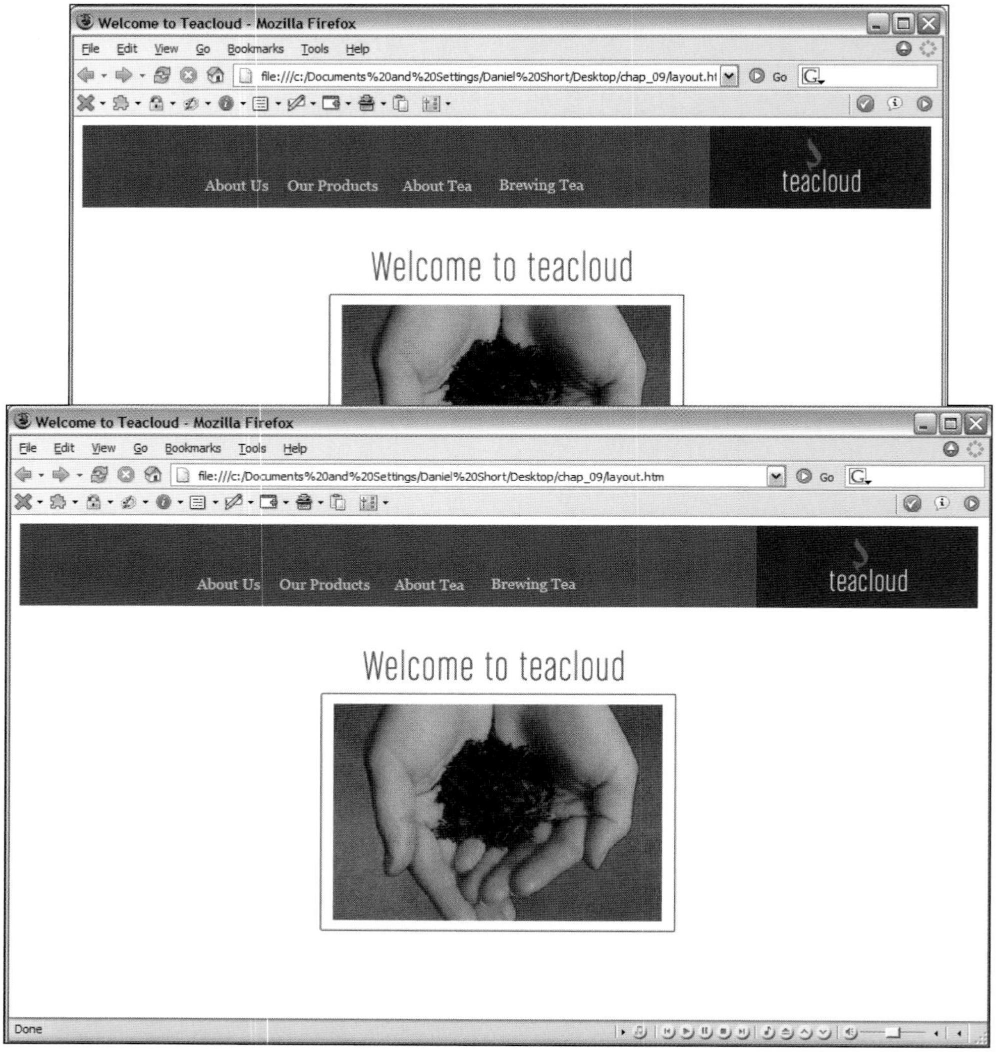

8 Press **F12** to preview your page in the browser again.

Now, no matter how much you resize the browser window, the navigation always stays where it's supposed to be, and the Welcome to teacloud image is locked into the center of the page.

9 Close **layout.htm**. You don't need to save your changes.

VIDEO: | **layoutview.mov**
To learn more about working with Layout view, check out **layoutview.mov** located in the **videos** folder on the **HOT CD-ROM**.

You're all finished with another chapter. In this chapter, you learned how to draw and manipulate layers, how to use the Zoom tool and guides to make it easy to draw your layers, and how to use Layout mode to quickly develop complicated table structures. In the next chapter, you'll learn how to get your pages ready for print.

10

Designing for Devices

In the past, if someone was looking at your Web site, you knew they were looking at it from a computer somewhere. They had at least a 15-inch monitor, and they were using one of four or five Web browsers. They either used a Mac or a Windows PC, and that was it. As a result, it was "easy" to develop a site to fit these fairly narrow parameters. As the world becomes increasingly connected, users are accessing the Internet with smaller and more diverse devices. Your site may be accessed by a Mac, a PC, a PDA, a mobile phone, or even a refrigerator (and no, we're not kidding). This change in the Internet landscape is just now starting to creep into the everyday life of a Web designer. As this change increases, you'll be required to design for something other than the computer screen we've all become accustomed to.

In this chapter, you'll learn how to use CSS to design for a printer by creating a print media style sheet; after all, a printer is just another device you can accommodate through your designs. Once you learn the concepts of using a CSS media style sheet for one type of device, you can easily apply the principles you've learned to other media style sheets and devices; you just need to learn which rules and concepts work on the particular type of device you're designing for. At the end of this chapter, you'll find some additional resources for designing for mobile devices.

What's a Device?

A device (in Web terms) is any electronic widget a user uses to view a Web page. This can be a computer (the default device we all design for), a PDA (such as a Palm or Pocket PC), a mobile phone, a TV, or the printer attached to your desktop at home. Cascading Style Sheets provides the flexibility to render pages differently, depending on the type of device that's accessing a particular Web page. The following list shows all of the different device types CSS accounts for:

SS Media Types	
Media Type	**Description**
all	Used as the default media type by CSS if nothing else is specified. As a result, any device accessing the site will use this style sheet to render the contents of the page.
braille	Used for Braille tactile feedback devices.
embossed	Used for Braille printers.
handheld	Used for handheld devices, such as PDAs and mobile phones.
print	Used for printing and print previews.
projection	Used for projectors.
screen	Used for computer displays.
speech	Used for speech synthesizers. There is a complete section of the CSS specification intended for aural representation of data.
tty	Used for teletypes and other devices intended for the hearing impaired.
tv	Used for television displays, such as Microsoft's WebTV.

1 | Attaching a Printer-Friendly Style Sheet

The easiest device to design for is the printer. Nearly everyone has one, and in order to see what your page will look like on a printer, you simply need to use your browser's print preview options. In this exercise, you'll link your page to a print media style sheet so users can effectively print the Teacloud site.

1 Copy the **chap_10** folder from the **HOT CD-ROM** to your **Desktop**. Define your site as **Chapter 10** using the **chap_10** folder as the local root folder. Make sure the **Files** panel is open. If it's not, choose **Window > Files** or press **F11**.

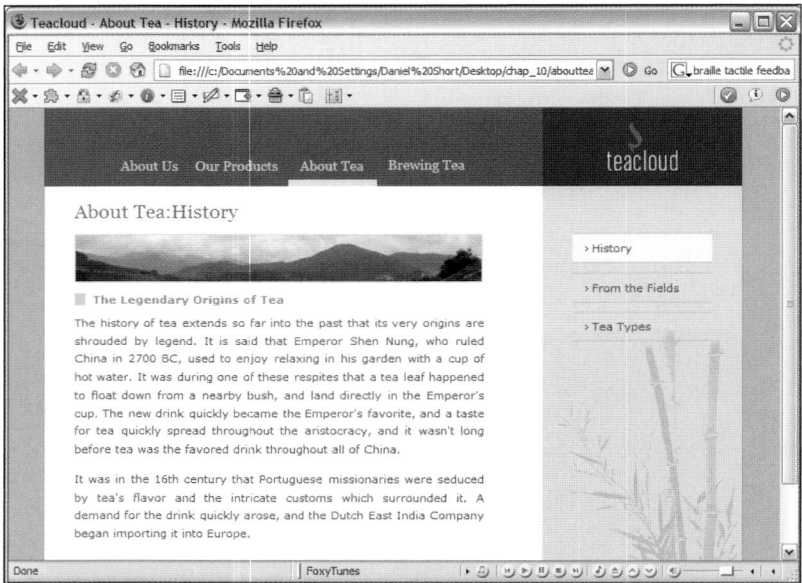

2 In the **Files** panel, double-click **abouttea.htm** to open it. Press **F12** to preview the file in your browser.

3 If you're using Firefox or Internet Explorer, choose **File > Print Preview**. If you're using Safari, choose **File > Print** and click **Preview**.

As you can see, the printed version of this page isn't very compelling. The navigation doesn't provide any help to a user when the page prints, and the logo looks terrible without its background color.

---

4 Return to Dreamweaver 8. If it's not already open, open the **CSS Styles** panel by choosing **Window > CSS Styles**. Click the **Attach Style Sheet** button to attach a new style sheet.

We've created a blank style sheet file for you (**print.css**) that you're going to attach. There aren't any styles defined, but you'll need to follow a few extra steps to make sure the style sheet is attached correctly.

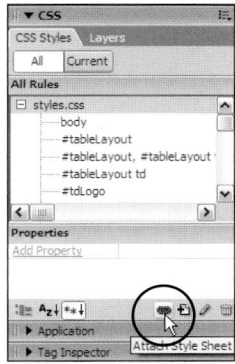

---

5 In the **Attach External Style Sheet** dialog box, click the **Browse** button and locate the **print.css** file in the **assets** folder. Select **Link** as the **Add as** option, choose **print** from the **Media** pop-up menu, and click **OK**.

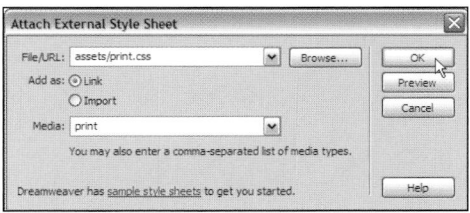

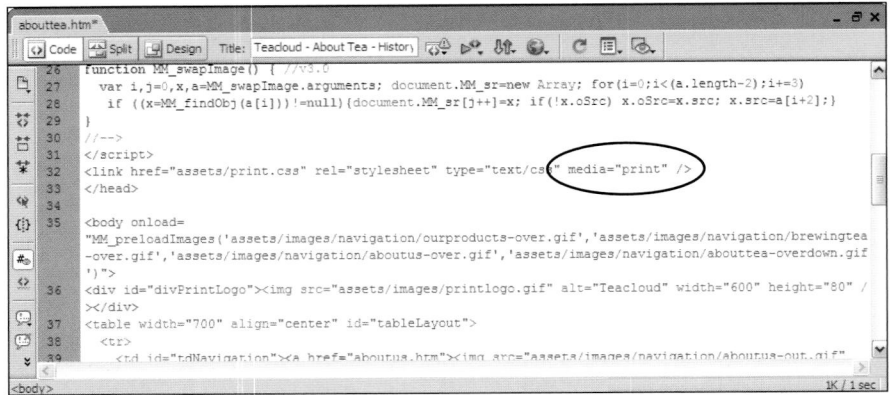

6 Switch to **Code** view. Scroll up to line 32 and find the **<link>** tag that attaches the **print.css** file.

Notice the **<link>** tag has a **media** attribute of **print**. Adding the **media** attribute declares the style sheet should be used only for a specific type of media, in this case, print.

---

7 Save your changes and keep **abouttea.htm** open for the next exercise, where you'll actually start creating the print styles.

---

2 | Styling for Print

Now that you've attached a print media style sheet to your page, it's time to actually start creating the rules. One of the new features in Dreamweaver 8, the Style Rendering toolbar, makes it easy to design for devices, including printers, by allowing you to switch back and forth between style sheets when working in Design view. As you'll see, the Style Rendering toolbar has some quirks, but this exercise gives you an idea of what to expect as you style your pages.

---

1 If you just completed Exercise 1, **abouttea.htm** should still be open. If it's not, go back and complete Exercise 1.

---

2 If it's not already open, open the **CSS Styles** panel by choosing **Window > CSS Styles**. Click the **New CSS Rule** button to open the **New CSS Rule** dialog box.

First, you're going to hide the navigation table cell.

---

3 In the **New CSS Rule** dialog box, select **Advanced** for the **Selector Type** and type **#tdNavigation** in the **Selector** field to create a CSS rule that applies only to the navigation table cell. In the **Define in** pop-up menu, choose **print.css** and click **OK** to open the **CSS Rule Definition** dialog box.

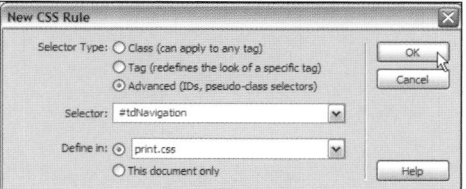

Choosing **print.css** ensures this change will only apply to the print media style sheet, not the style sheet, so these changes will only affect the site when users choose to print the contents of a page.

---

4 In the **CSS Rule Definition** dialog box, select **Block** in the **Category** list and set the **Display** property to **none**. Click **OK** to create the rule.

Setting the Display property to none will essentially "turn off" the navigation, so it does not display when users print the page.

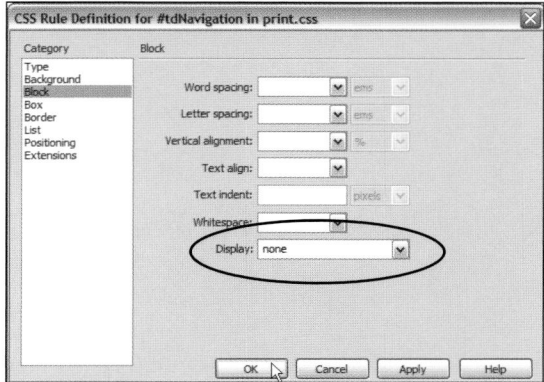

5 You won't see any change in **Design** view, but press **F12** to preview the page in your browser. Again, you don't see any changes. Open the print preview. If you're using Firefox or Internet Explorer, choose **File > Print Preview**. If you're using Safari, choose **File > Print** and click **Preview**.

The display in the browser isn't quite what you were after. The navigation is now hidden, but the logo still needs some work. You should notice, however, that the navigation displays just fine when viewing it in the browser; it disappears only when you choose Print Preview. Again, the changes you made are only to the print media style sheet.

6 Return to Dreamweaver 8 and switch to the **print.css** file. The logo, the side navigation, and the footer should also be hidden. Change the **#tdNavigation** rule to **#tdNavigation, #tdLogo, #tdSidebar, #tdFooter** by simply typing the new selectors directly into the CSS file. When you're finished, your CSS file should look like the illustration here.

Changing the rule to include the additional table cells ensures they're also hidden when users attempt to print the page.

7 Switch back to **abouttea.htm** and press **F12** to preview the file again. If you're using Firefox or Internet Explorer, choose **File > Print Preview**. If you're using Safari, choose **File > Print** and click **Preview**.

As you can imagine, the process of editing a style sheet, saving the document, opening it in the browser, and opening the browser's print preview can be a tedious process. The Style Rendering toolbar makes this a far less painful process.

8 Return to Dreamweaver 8 and switch back to **Design** view. Choose **View > Toolbars > Style Rendering** to open the **Style Rendering** toolbar.

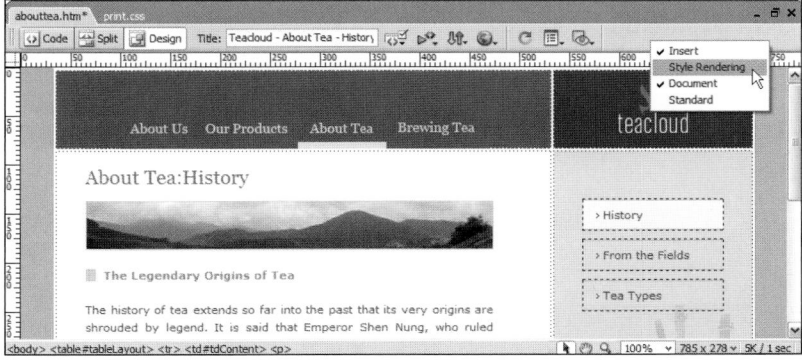

Understanding the Style Rendering Toolbar

The Style Rendering toolbar lets you switch the display to different media style sheets directly in Design view. Each of the buttons on the Style Rendering toolbar relates to a specific media type.

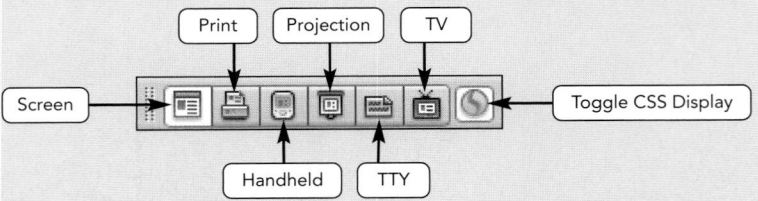

Each button, except for the last, causes Dreamweaver 8 to render the document with a different type of media style sheet. The last button, Toggle CSS Display, actually turns all CSS rendering on and off. This lets you see what your document will look like if it's viewed by a device that doesn't support CSS.

Although style rendering in Dreamweaver 8 for other media types isn't perfect (which you'll discover in a moment), it definitely helps you get close to your final design when designing a particular media style sheet.

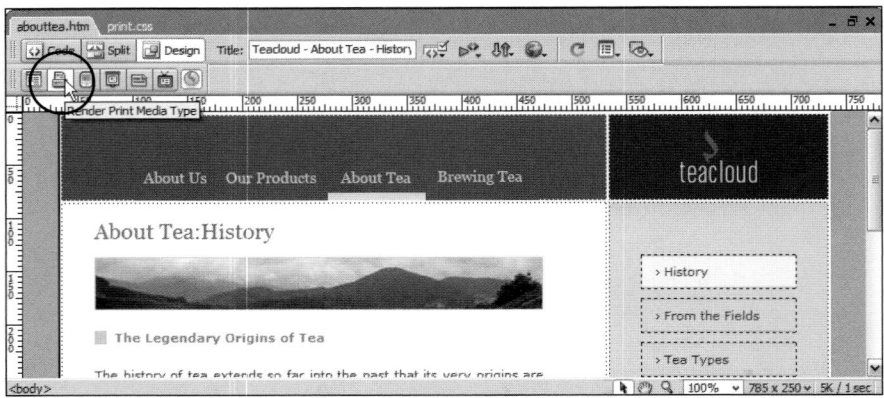

9 In the **Style Rendering** toolbar, click the **Render Print Media Type** button.

Unfortunately, the `display:none` style on table cells happens to be one of the styles Dreamweaver 8 fails to render, so at this point the Style Rendering toolbar isn't terribly exciting.

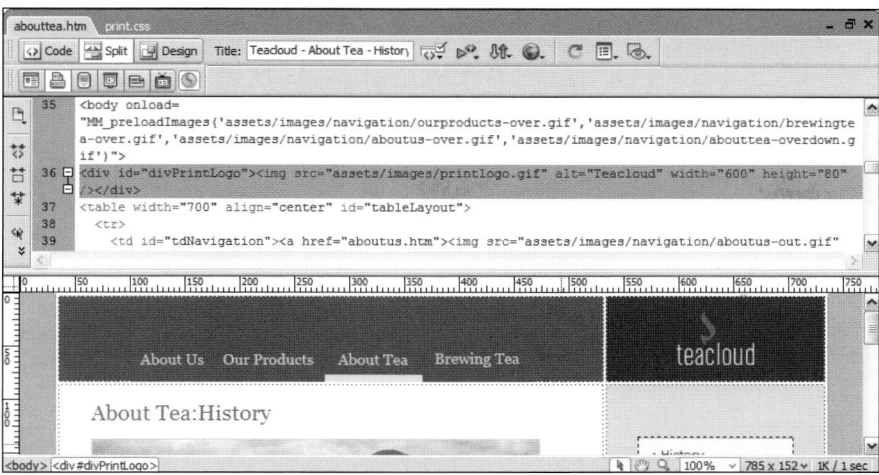

If you take a peek at the code of **abouttea.htm**, you'll notice a **<div>** that's hidden. This **<div>** contains a logo specifically for printing, but its **display** property is set to **none** in the **styles.css** file, which is used for the screen.

---

10 In the **CSS Styles** panel, click the **New CSS Rule** button so you can define a rule to display the print logo.

---

11 In the **New CSS Rule** dialog box, select **Advanced** for the **Selector Type** and type **#divPrintLogo** in the **Selector** field. In the **Define in** pop-up menu, choose **print.css**. Click **OK**.

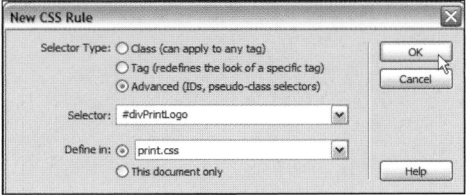

12 In the **CSS Rule Definition** dialog box, select **Block** from the **Category** list. Set the **Text align** property to **center** and set the **Display** property to **block**.

The **styles.css** file sets the display property of **divPrintLogo** to none, which hides it from the browser. Setting the Display property to **block** in the print style sheet ensures the image displays when users print the page.

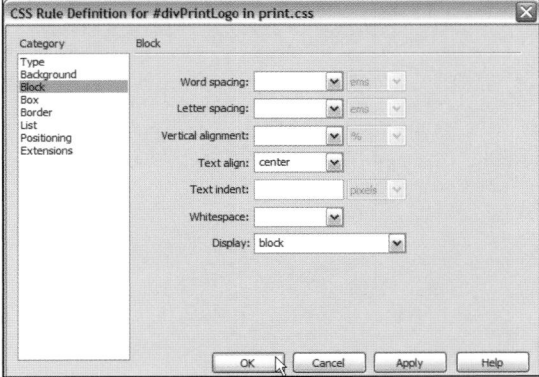

Now that the print logo `<div>` has been set to display as a block, it shows up in Design view when you select Print in the Style Rendering toolbar.

13 In the **Style Rendering** toolbar, click the **Render Screen Media Type** button. The print logo disappears again.

Now that you're showing the screen media style sheet, the print logo is hidden. The `display:none` rule in the **style.css** file now takes precedence over the `display:block` style you added to **print.css**.

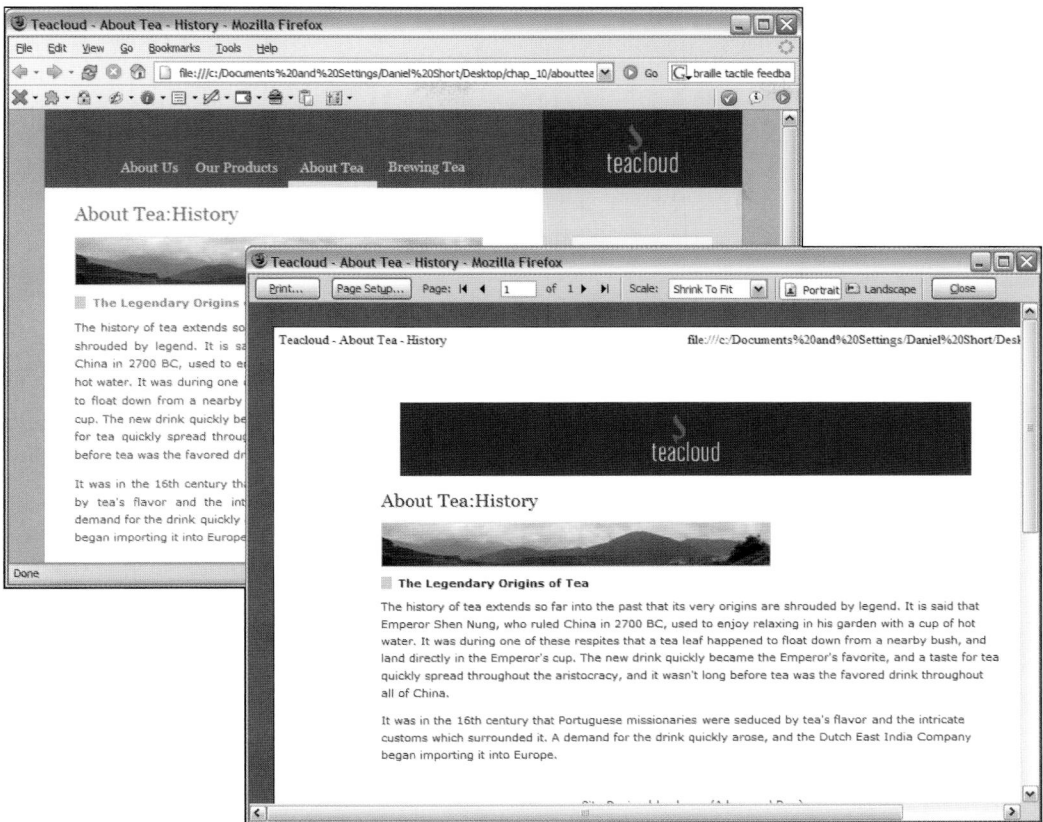

14 Press **F12** one last time to preview the page in your browser. The browser now shows the design as it's always been. If you're using Firefox or Internet Explorer, choose **File > Print Preview**. If you're using Safari, choose **File > Print** and click **Preview**.

Notice the new print logo displayed with the navigation stripped from the document, just as intended. As you can see, using CSS and the new Style Rendering toolbar in Dreamweaver 8 makes it easy to design for different devices. Although you learned how to design for a printer in this exercise, you can apply the skills you learned when designing for any device, including PDAs, mobile phones, and so on.

---

15 Return to Dreamweaver 8 and save and close all open files.

Testing in Multiple Devices

Unfortunately, designing for mobile devices is nearly another book unto itself. For that reason, we don't cover designing for other devices, such as PDAs, mobile phones, or refrigerators (still not kidding). You can, however, find myriad resources online for developing for and emulating other device types. Here's a short list of sites that offer emulators to help you develop for other devices:

Palm OS Emulator
http://www.palmos.com/dev/tools/emulator/

PocketPC Emulator
http://www.microsoft.com/downloads/details.aspx?FamilyID=57265402-47a8-4ce4-9aa7-5fe85b95de72&displaylang=en

SmartPhone 2003 Emulator
http://www.microsoft.com/downloads/details.aspx?FamilyID=791bae52-b057-4d72-b263-105534825ca5&displaylang=en

YoSpace PDA Emulator
http://www.yospace.com/pdaemu.html

This chapter showed you how to specify a print media style sheet, as well as how to use the Style Rendering toolbar to toggle individual style sheets on and off. Unfortunately, Dreamweaver 8's rendering of other media styles isn't an exact science, but as you begin to learn more about the inner workings of Dreamweaver 8 and the limitations of the devices you're designing for, using the Style Rendering toolbar will speed up your development immensely. In the next chapter, you'll learn how to create rollovers and navigation bars to spice up your sites.

11

Rollovers

One of the key challenges in Web development is to produce artwork that clearly communicates how to navigate through your site. Rollover graphics, which change when the user's mouse moves over them, are great for adding visual cues that ensure your audience knows an image has special meaning or that it is a link. Rollovers are also great if you have limited space because you can put extra information within the changing graphic. For example, you can make a button that says *Services*, and when a visitor places his or her mouse over the word, it can change to list the services you offer.

What you might not realize is that rollovers aren't just XHTML. Instead, rollovers are a combination of XHTML and JavaScript. JavaScript allows you to manipulate the user's browser to perform actions not possible with simple XHTML code.

Dreamweaver 8 automatically writes all of the necessary JavaScript code without your ever having to write the scripts or even understand how they are constructed. Once you get more familiar with JavaScript, you'll most likely continue using the rollover capabilities in Dreamweaver 8 because it can literally save days of programming work. For this reason, the Dreamweaver 8 rollover feature is helpful to both designers and programmers.

Rollover Rules

Although this book provides many exercises that teach you how to implement rollovers, it is our hope that you'll move beyond the exercises to create your own custom rollover graphics once you get the hang of this feature. If you plan to make your own rollovers from scratch, you should be aware of a few important concepts.

Rollovers require a minimum of two graphics—an "off" state and an "on" state. Because this is a book on Dreamweaver 8, it doesn't cover how to make the graphic component of rollovers. You would need an imaging program, such as Fireworks or Photoshop, to make the images.

You'll learn more about creating graphics in Fireworks in Chapter 15, *"Fireworks Integration."*

If you are going to make your own rollover graphics in an image editor, one important rule to understand is that the graphics for the "off" state and "on" state for each of your rollover images must have the same dimensions, or they might look distorted. If you have two different-sized pieces of artwork, the JavaScript will scale both to the same width and height, causing distortion. For this reason, all the images provided in this chapter's exercises share the same dimensions.

NOTE:

Designing Graphics for the Web

For more information about designing rollovers and other graphical content for the Web using image-editing programs, such as Fireworks and Photoshop, sign up to use the free 24-hour pass to the **lynda.com Online Training Library** provided in the Introduction to this book and check out the following video-based training resources:

Adobe Photoshop CS2 for the Web
with Tanya Staples

Macromedia Fireworks 8 Essential Training
with Abigail Rudner

Or, check out the following books, also available from **lynda.com**:

Adobe Photoshop CS2 for the Web Hands-On Training
by Tanya Staples
lynda.com and Peachpit Press
ISBN: 0321331710

Designing Web Graphics 4: The Definitive Guide to Web Design and Development
by Lynda Weinman
lynda.com and New Riders
ISBN: 0735710791

---

1 | Creating a Simple Rollover

This first exercise shows you how to create a simple rollover. These types of rollovers involve two pieces of artwork. The first graphic—the original state—appears on the screen initially; the second graphic—the over state—appears when a user rolls his or her mouse over it. In JavaScript terminology, this is called a swap image. But you will not be writing any JavaScript from scratch because Dreamweaver 8 makes creating a simple rollover as easy as a few button clicks.

1 Copy the **chap_11** folder from the **HOT CD-ROM** to your **Desktop**. Define your site as **Chapter 11** using the **chap_11** folder as the local root folder.

The original state before the mouse rolls over the graphic in the Web browser

The over state after the mouse rolls over the graphic in the Web browser

The two images you see here are what you'll be using to create the rollovers in this exercise. The image on the left will be inserted directly into the page, and the image on the right is what will be displayed when the user moves his or her mouse over the image.

2 In the **Files** panel, double-click **index.htm** to open it.

This is the same design you've been using throughout the book, but we've removed the navigation from the top of the page. You'll get to add that navigation back in the following steps.

3 Click inside the table cell in the upper left of the page.

This is where you'll insert the navigation buttons, which will include rollovers with an over state.

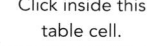

Click inside this table cell.

4 In the **Common** group of the **Insert bar**, choose **Rollover Image** from the **Image** pop-up menu to open the **Insert Rollover Image** dialog box.

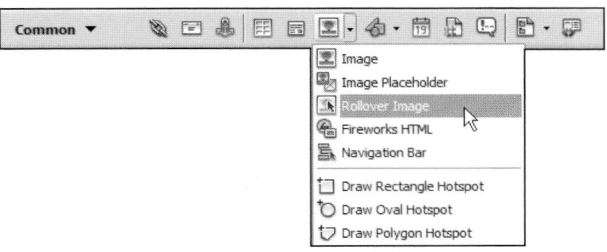

5 Type **aboutus** in the **Name** field. For the **Original image**, click **Browse** and select **aboutus_out.gif**, which is located in the **assets/images/navigation** folder. For the **Rollover image**, click **Browse** and select **aboutus_over.gif**, which is located inside the same folder. Type **About Us** in the **Alternate text** field. Type **aboutus.htm** in the **When clicked, Go to URL** field. Click **OK**.

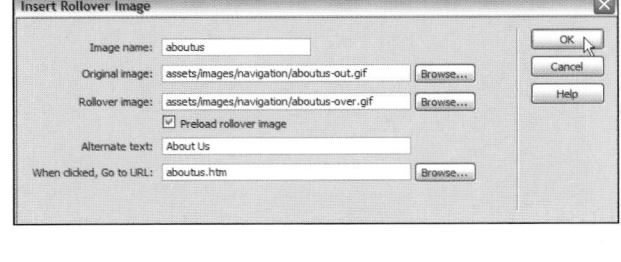

The image has been added to the page. If you look at the Tag Selector, you can see that the image has been wrapped in an **<a>** tag, and the image has been given the ID **aboutus**.

NOTE:

Understanding the Insert Rollover Image Options

The Insert Rollover Image dialog box contains a number of options, and you need to understand each option and its role in the creation of rollovers:

Insert Rollover Image Options	
Field	**Description**
Image name	The image name field specifies the ID that will be applied to the `<img>` tag so the JavaScript code Dreamweaver 8 inserts can properly identify the image. The image name should be alphanumeric with no special characters, and it should start with a letter, not a number.
Original image	The original image is the image that will be displayed when the page first loads; it continues to appear until a user rolls his or her mouse over the hot spot.
Rollover image	The rollover image is the image that will be displayed when the user moves his or her mouse over the original image or hot spot.
Preload rollover image	Select this box to ensure the rollover image graphic is loaded as soon as the page loads. If this option isn't selected, the browser won't actually grab the rollover image from the server until after the user moves his or her mouse over the image. It's best to leave this option turned on, otherwise users can see a delay waiting for the rollover image to download while rolling over a hot spot.
Alternate text	This field adds the `alt` attribute to the image.
When clicked...	This field specifies the location the users will be sent to when they click the image. For example, if the rollover is for a navigation bar, insert the page you want to link to when users click the navigation button.

6 Press **F12** to preview the rollover. Position the mouse over the image you just inserted.

Notice as you roll over the image, the corresponding "over" image appears.

7 Return to Dreamweaver 8, and place your cursor directly after the **About Us** image. Choose **Insert > Image Objects > Rollover Image**.

8 In the **Insert Rollover Image** dialog box, type **ourproducts** in the **Name** field. For the **Original image**, click **Browse** and select **ourproducts_out.gif**, which is located in the **assets/images/navigation** folder. For the **Rollover image**, click **Browse** and select **ourproducts_over.gif** located inside the same folder. Type **Our Products** in the **Alternate text** field. Leave the **When clicked, Go to URL** field blank. Click **OK**.

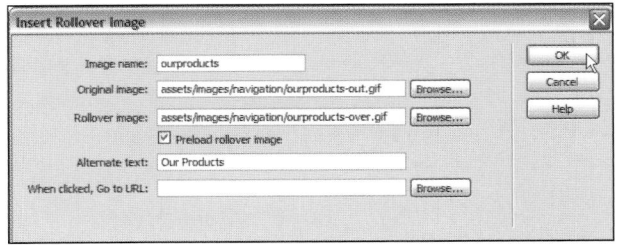

9 Use the techniques you learned in Steps 7 and 8 to create navigation buttons, complete with over states, for the **About Tea** and **Brewing Tea** buttons. You'll find their corresponding out and over images in the **assets/images/navigation** folder.

NOTE:

Null Links and Rollovers

You may have noticed when you inserted the last three images that the Link for the **<a>** tags was set to a hash mark (#). Dreamweaver 8 inserted this symbol in order to create a link, even though you didn't specify one.

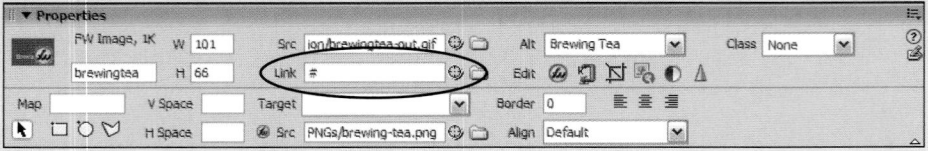

This link was added because it is necessary for the JavaScript rollover to work. Inserting a hash mark in the Link field inserts a stand-in link that doesn't actually take the user anywhere. It simply acts as a placeholder so the user can see the rollover. Once the rest of the pages are in place, you can then link them to the correct page.

10 Press **F12** once more to preview all of the rollovers.

Move your mouse over each of the buttons, and you'll see the over state displayed.

---

11 Save your changes and keep **index.htm** open for the next exercise.

Inserting Rollovers

As you'll see later in this chapter, there are other ways to insert rollovers. Using the Insert Rollover feature, in our opinion, is certainly the most efficient. In addition to inserting both image states, you also get to name the image, give it an **<alt>** tag, and set your link, all in one dialog box.

Creating Animated Rollovers

Throughout this chapter, you'll learn different methods to insert and work with rollovers. In addition to what you're learning here, you should experiment with rollovers to examine new ways users can interact with your pages. One such technique is an **animated rollover**. An animated rollover is exactly the same as a static-image rollover, but it uses an animated GIF in one, or both, of the rollover states. Although this can add a nice touch to any page, you want to be careful not to overdo it. In the case of animated GIFs, a little goes a long way. If your animated GIF is set to loop, that is, play continuously, preloading the image is fine. If it is only supposed to play once, make sure the **Preload Rollover Image** check box is deselected when importing the image. If the animated GIF preloads, the animation will play when preloaded, and by the time your user ends up rolling over the image, it will no longer animate!

2 | Creating Disjointed Rollovers

Disjointed rollovers aren't really as painful as they may sound. A disjointed rollover happens when a user moves his or her mouse over one image and another image on the page changes. The "disjoint" happens because you're affecting a different image than the one the user is interacting with. This exercise shows you how to create a disjointed rollover and introduces you to the Swap Image behavior, which was added for you automatically in the previous exercise.

1 If you just completed the Exercise 1, **index.htm** should still be open. If it's not, go back and complete Exercise 1.

It's always nice to give users some additional information about where they're going to end up when they click a link. You're going to add a bit of "hint" text for each of the navigation buttons on your page.

2 Place your cursor directly above the **Welcome to teacloud** image.

3 Choose **Insert > Image** and browse to **blank.gif** in the **assets/images/hints** folder. If the **Image Tag Accessibility Attributes** dialog box appears, choose **<empty>** for the **Alternate text** and click **OK**.

It may not seem that you've done much at this point— you've just inserted a plain blank image. However, this image will serve as the placeholder for the hint images you're about to add when the user moves his or her mouse over each of the images in the navigation bar.

4 With the image still selected, type **hintimage** in the **ID** field of **Property Inspector**.

As mentioned in the previous exercise, each image that has a rollover attached to it must have a valid ID in order for the JavaScript Dreamweaver 8 inserts to find it.

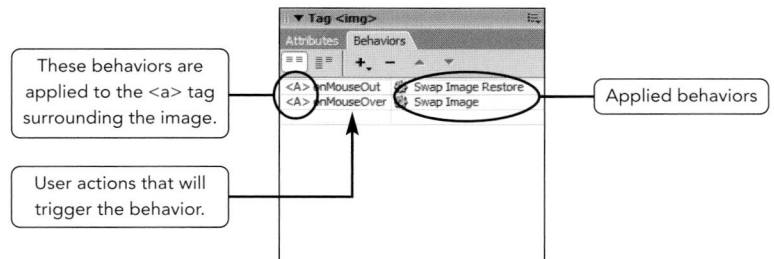

These behaviors are applied to the <a> tag surrounding the image.

User actions that will trigger the behavior.

Applied behaviors

5 Select the **About Us** image in the navigation bar, and switch to the **Behaviors** panel by choosing **Window > Behaviors**.

The Behaviors panel shows you each of the JavaScript behaviors attached to the selected element on the page. You can see that the About Us image has a Swap Image behavior and a Swap Image Restore behavior applied. The left column shows you the event the behavior is attached to; notice that it's actually applied to the **<a>** tag and not the **<img>** tag itself.

6 Click the **plus** (+) button to add a new behavior and choose **Swap Image** from the pop-up menu.

7 In the **Swap Image** dialog box, select **image "hintimage"** from the **Images** list. Click **Browse** and select **aboutus.gif**, which is located in the **assets/images/hints** folder. Leave the **Preload images** and **Restore images onMouseOut** options selected and click **OK**.

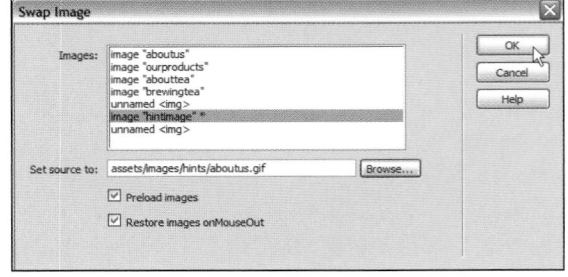

The Images list shows all the images on your page, even images without IDs. Any image without an ID shows as **unnamed <img>**. All images that have valid IDs are listed with their associated ID so you can easily find them. Leaving the two check boxes selected ensures the images get preloaded by the browser, and that the image you're swapping is restored to its original state when the user moves his or her mouse off of the image (the Swap Image Restore behavior is added automatically).

Notice the behavior you just added doesn't look the same as the one you applied in Step 5 because the Swap Image behavior has been added to the **<img>** tag, and not the **<a>** tag. Some browsers (especially older version of Netscape) don't honor behaviors on **<img>** tags.

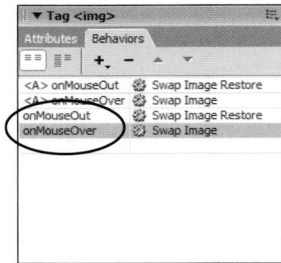

8 In the **Behaviors** panel, click the **onMouseOut** event to select it. Open the events pop-up menu and scroll up until you find **<A> onMouseOut**, then select it.

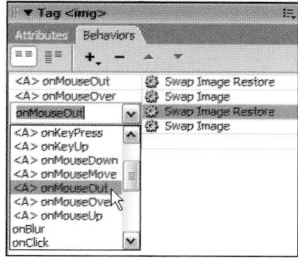

9 Perform the same actions for the **Swap Image** behavior applied to **onMouseOver**. After you're all done, your **Behaviors** panel should match the illustration shown here.

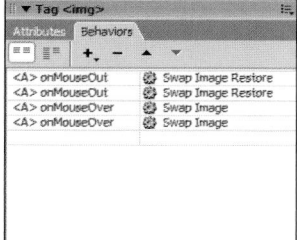

You just applied an additional Swap Image behavior to an existing image, but if you already have one Swap Image behavior, it's easier to just edit the one that's already there.

10 Select the **Our Products** image, and in the **Behaviors** panel, double-click the **Swap Image** behavior.

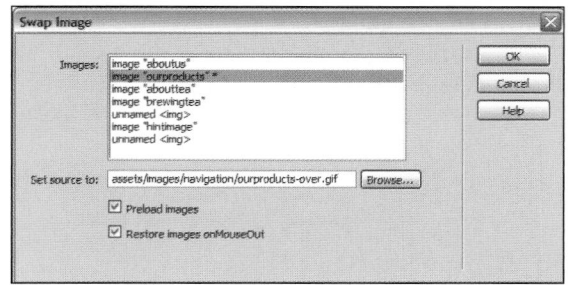

Notice that the ourproducts image is already selected, and it has an asterisk next to it. The asterisk indicates there is already a swap image for that particular image. The great thing is you can add more.

11 In the **Swap Image** dialog box, select **image "hintimage"** in the **Images** list. Click **Browse** and select **ourproducts.gif**, which is located in the **assets/images/hints** folder. Click **OK**.

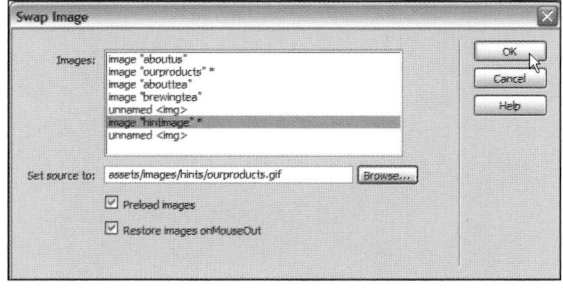

Now there is an asterisk next to both **ourprod-ucts** and **hintimage**, which means the Swap Image behavior will now swap *two* images instead of one.

12 Use the techniques you learned in Steps 10 and 11 to create the rollovers for the **About Tea** and **Brewing Tea** navigation images, setting the **hintimage** to **aboutea.gif** and **brewingtea.gif**, which are both located in the **assets/images/hints** folder.

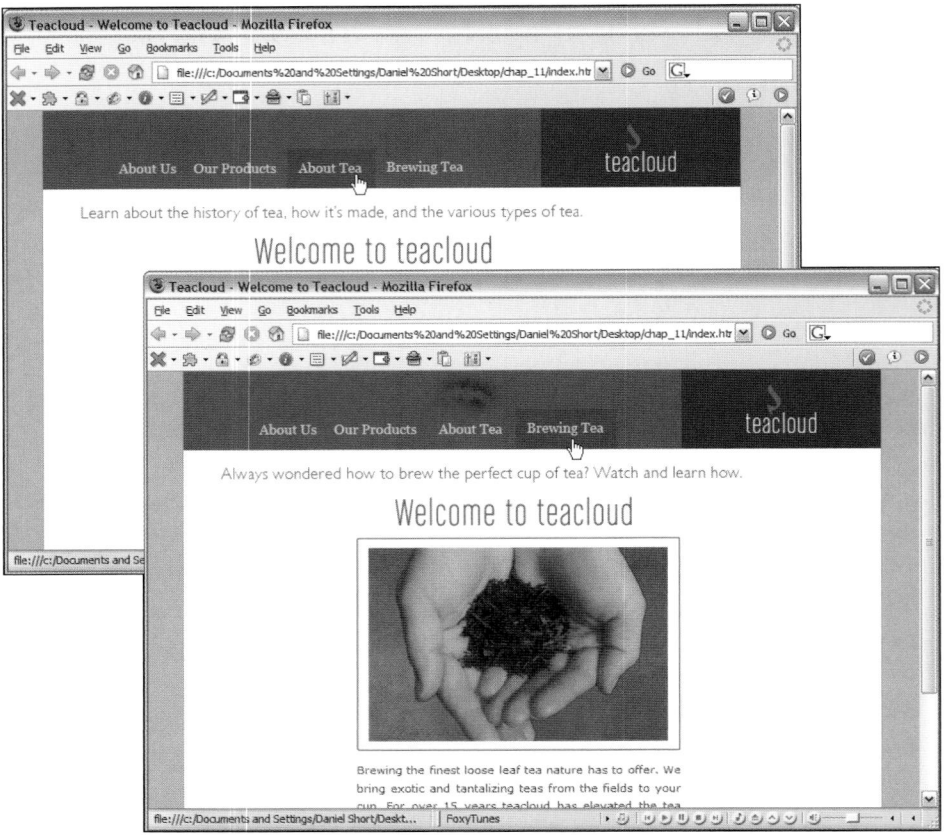

13 Now that all of the **Swap Image** behaviors have been updated, press **F12** to preview your page in the browser. Each of the navigation images now shows a hint about what users will see when they click the button.

14 Close **index.htm**. You don't need to save your changes.

VIDEO: | **swapimages.mov**

Adding Swap Image behaviors can sometimes be a confusing prospect, dealing with image IDs, multiple behaviors, and an oftentimes less-than-intuitive Behaviors panel. To learn more about Swap Image behaviors, check out **swapimages.mov** in the **videos** folder on the **HOT CD-ROM**.

Creating Navigation Bars with Multiple Rollover States

So far, you have created simple rollovers and disjointed rollovers. You have one more type of rollover to learn before you get to play with a bit of Flash—the navigation bar. A navigation bar allows each button to display four states: **up**, **over**, **down**, and **over while down**. Instead of working with two images for each rollover, this type of rollover requires that you work with four—one for each separate state. This might sound intimidating, but the Dreamweaver 8 navigation bar feature makes it much easier than you might imagine.

| Out | Over | Down | Over while down |

1 To begin with, take a look at the **aboutus-out.gif**, **aboutus-over.gif**, **aboutus-down.gif**, and **aboutus-overdown.gif** images in this illustration. Each of the navigation buttons has the same style of images, one for each of the states that will be defined using the Dreamweaver 8 navigation bar feature.

NOTE:

Understanding Rollover States

Keeping track of the different types of rollover states can be a little tricky. This chart outlines what the different states mean:

Rollover States	
State	**What It Does**
Up	The graphic that appears on the Web page when it is loaded. This is also referred to as the "out" or "off" state.
Over	The graphic that appears when the user's mouse moves over the image. Most often, this image will revert back to the Up state when the mouse is moved off of the image. This is sometimes referred to as the "on" state.
Down	The graphic that will appear after the user clicks on the over state. This state will not change again until the user's mouse moves over this image or clicks on another image.
Over While Down	This appears when the user's mouse moves over the down state. It works just like the over state, except that it works on the down state only.

2 In the **Files** panel, double-click **aboutus.htm** to open it.

This file is missing the navigation bar that you set up on **index.htm**. Instead, you're going to set up the entire navigation in one fell swoop.

3 Place your cursor in the cell in the upper-left corner of the page.

This is the cell where you'll insert the navigation bar, which will contain rollovers with multiple states.

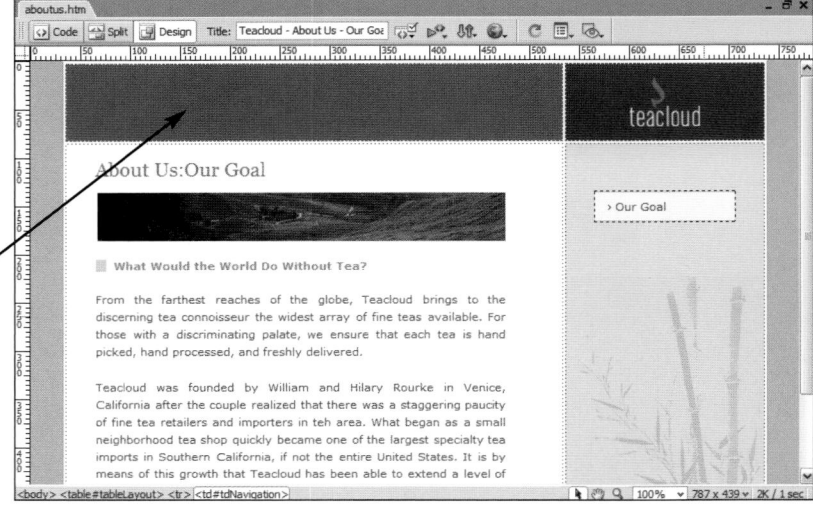

Place your cursor here.

4 Choose **Insert > Image Objects > Navigation Bar** to open the **Insert Navigation Bar** dialog box.

The Insert Navigation Bar dialog box can be a bit intimidating at first, but you'll get used to it quickly.

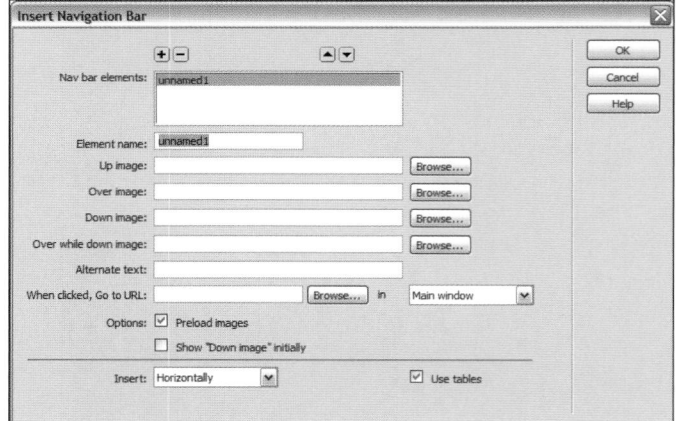

5 Type **aboutus** in the **Element name** field.

This is the same as the image name you provided when you used the Insert Rollover Image behavior. This will be used as the ID for the `<img>` tag.

6 Click **Browse** next to the **Up image** field. Select the **aboutus-out.gif** file, which is located in the **assets/images/navigation** folder.

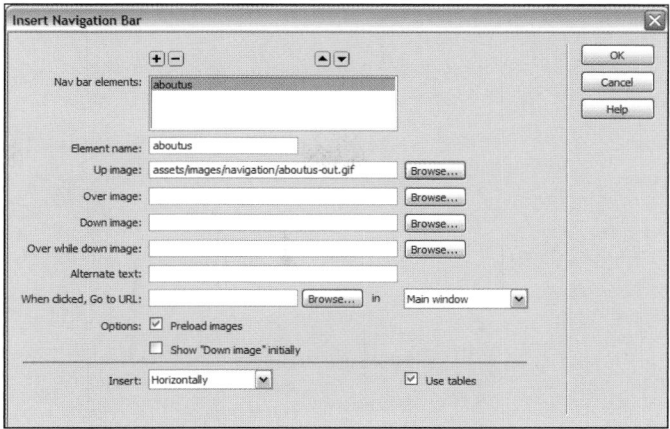

---

7 Click **Browse** next to the **Over image** field. Select the **aboutus-over.gif** file, which is located in the **assets/images/navigation** folder.

---

8 Click **Browse** next to the **Down image** field. Select the **aboutus-down.gif** file, which is located in the **assets/images/navigation** folder.

---

9 Click **Browse** next to the **Over while down image** field. Select the **aboutus-overdown.gif** file, which is located in the **assets/images/navigation** folder.

---

10 Type **About Us** in the **Alternate text** field.

---

11 Leave the **When clicked, Go to URL** field blank, since you're already on the **About Us** page.

---

12 Because you're adding this navigation bar to the **About Us** page, select the **Show "Down image" initially** option.

---

13 Deselect the **Use tables** option.

Leaving this box checked would place each of the navigation buttons in its own table cell; however, you don't need this option in the design you're working on.

When you're finished, the options in the Insert Navigation Bar dialog box should match the illustration shown here.

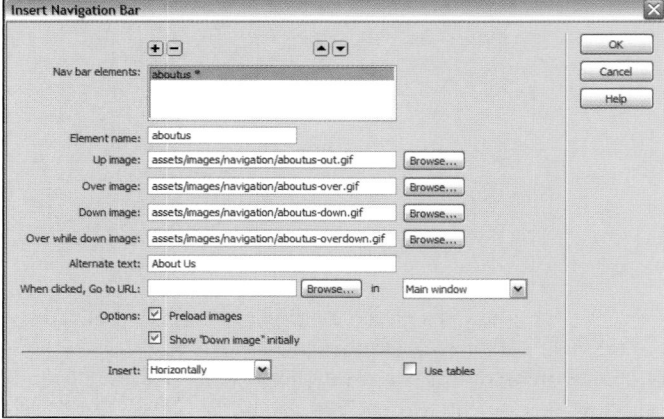

14 At the top of the **Insert Navigation Bar** dialog box, click the **plus** (+) sign to add the next image in the navigation bar. A new unnamed element is added to the **Nav bar elements** list.

15 In the **Insert Navigation Bar** dialog box, match the settings to the ones shown in the illustration here to create the rollover states for the **Our Products** image.

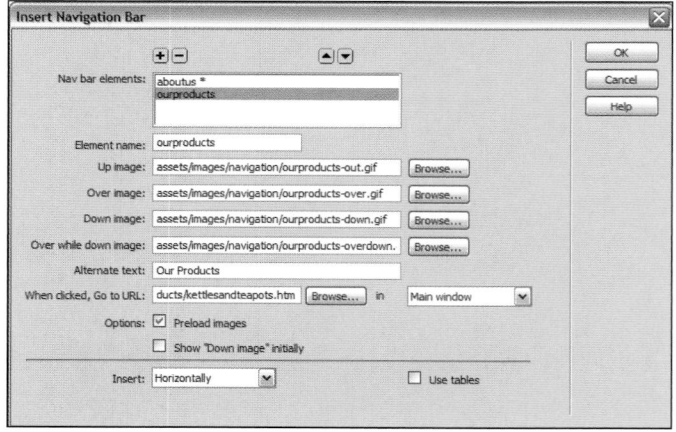

16 Click the **plus** (+) sign to add the next image in the navigation bar. A new unnamed element is added to the **Nav bar elements** list. Match the settings to the ones shown in the illustration here to create the rollover states for the **About Tea** image.

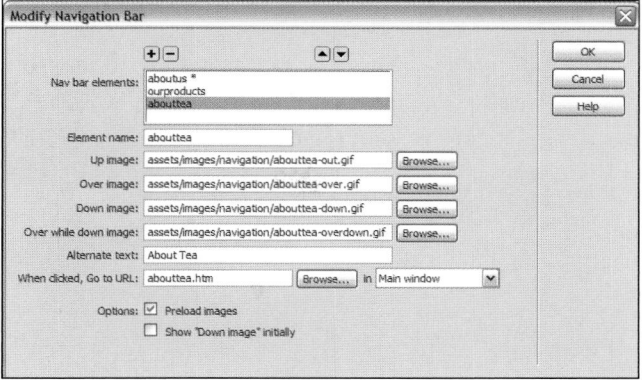

17 Click the **plus** (+) sign to add the next image in the navigation bar. A new unnamed element is added to the **Nav bar elements** list. Match the settings to the ones shown in the illustration here to create the rollover states for the **Brewing Tea** image.

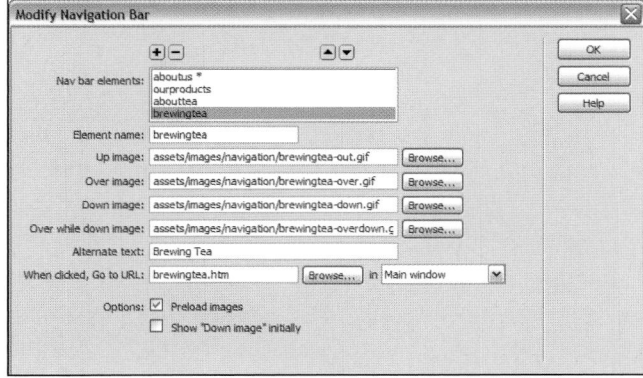

This is what the dialog box should look like when you're finished. Notice that the **aboutus** entry in the **Nav bar elements** list has an asterisk next to it, which tells you that that particular element is set to show the down image initially. This gives you a quick indication of the state that each button will be in when the page loads.

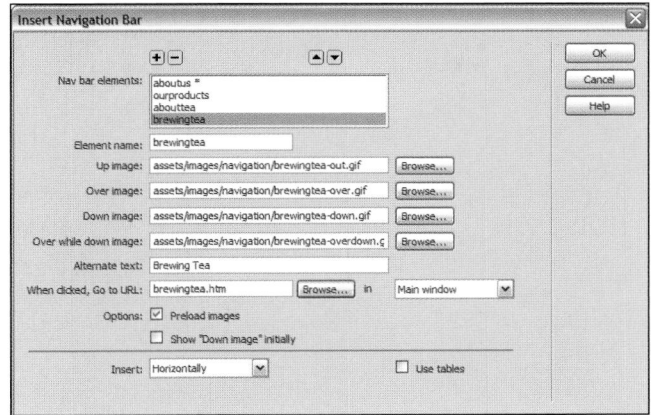

18 Click **OK** to close the **Insert Navigation Bar** dialog box.

Dreamweaver 8 automatically creates a table, inserts the images you specified, and creates all of the complex JavaScript necessary for the rollovers to function—all in about a half a second.

19 Press **F12** to preview the page in the browser. Move your mouse over the buttons to see how they behave.

If you click any of the other navigation buttons, you'll find that those pages are missing the navigation bar. Luckily, Dreamweaver 8 makes it easy to move your navigation bars from page to page.

20 In **aboutus.htm**, hold down the **Ctrl** key (Windows) or the **Cmd** key (Mac) and click the navigation table cell to select it. Choose **Edit > Copy** to copy the navigation bar to the **Clipboard**.

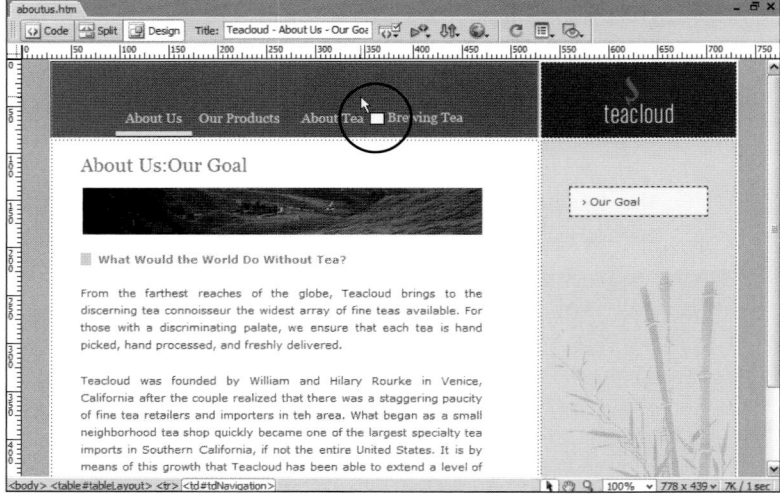

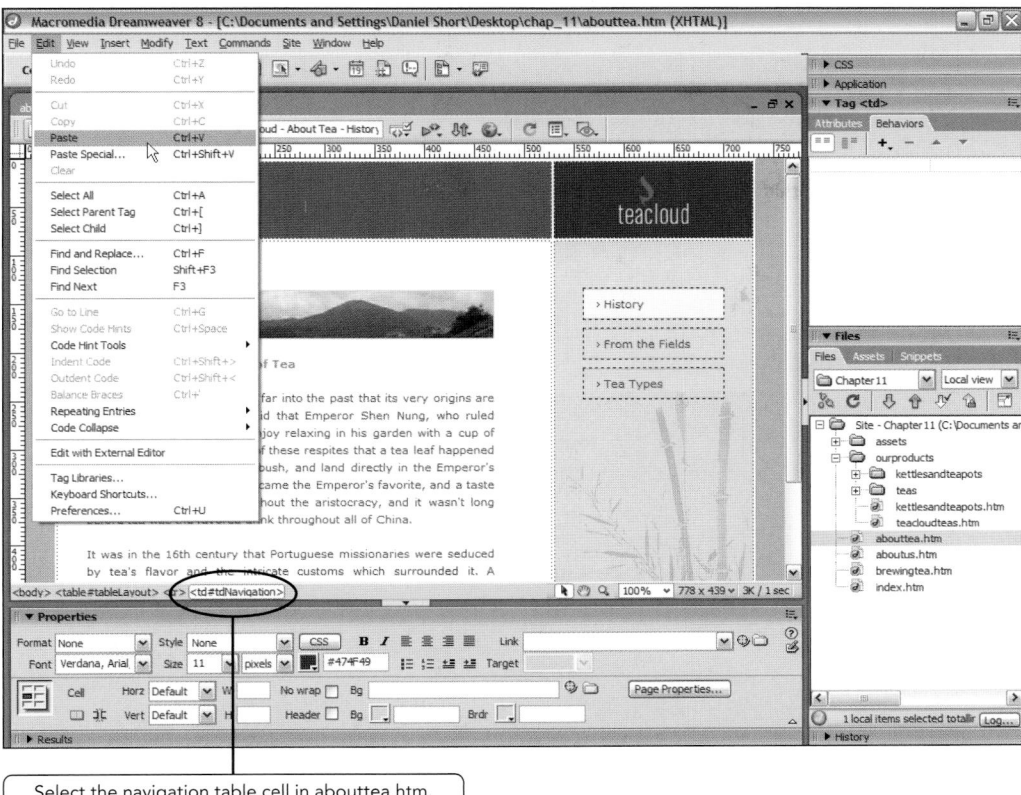

Select the navigation table cell in abouttea.htm.

21 In the **Files** panel, double-click **abouttea.htm** to open it. **Ctrl+click** (Windows) or **Cmd+click** (Mac) the navigation table cell to select it, and choose **Edit > Paste** to paste the navigation bar into the table cell.

The navigation bar is now inserted into **abouttea.htm**, but the wrong image is in the down state.

22 Choose **Modify > Navigation Bar** to edit the navigation bar on the page.

---

23 With **aboutus** selected in the **Nav bar elements** list, set the **When clicked, Go to URL** field to **aboutus.htm** and deselect **Show "Down image" initially**.

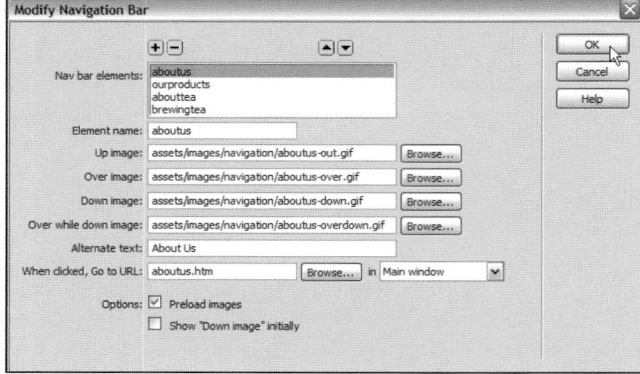

---

24 Select **abouttea** from the **Nav bar elements** list and select the **Show "Down image" initially** check box. Click **OK**.

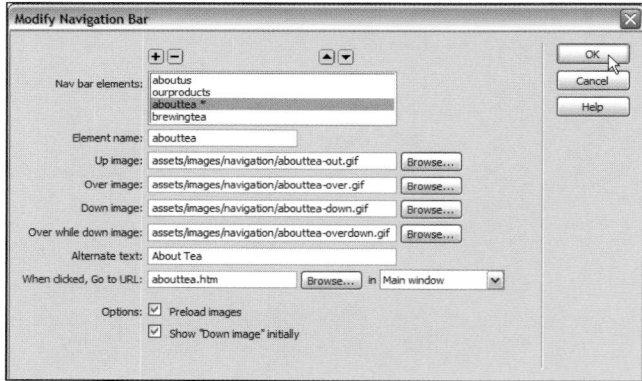

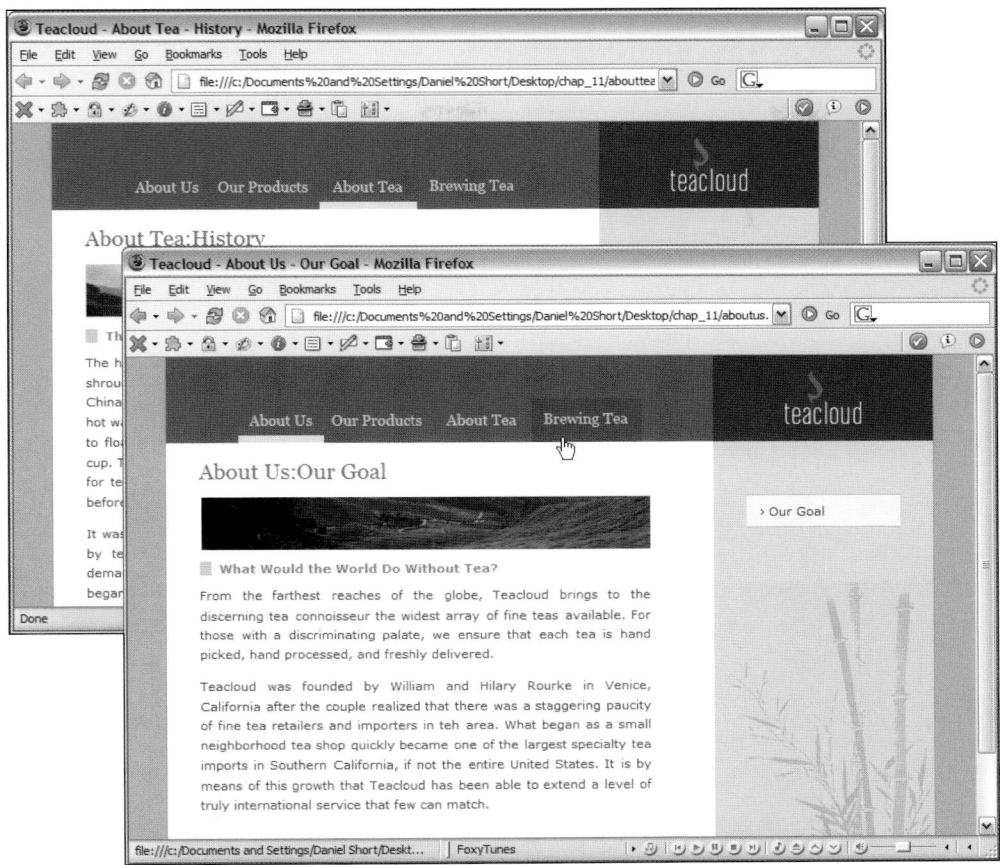

25 Press **F12** to preview the page in a browser, and browse back and forth between **About Us** and **About Tea** to see how the states change for each of the images.

26 Close all open files. You don't need to save your changes.

In this exercise, you learned how to use the Dreamweaver 8 navigation bar behaviors to set up a complicated navigation bar on multiple pages. At this point, you're finished learning about standard rollover images, and in the next exercise you'll start inserting Flash Buttons directly inside Dreamweaver 8.

What Are Flash Buttons?

Dreamweaver 8 lets you create Flash Buttons, which have very similar characteristics to other rollovers you have worked with in this chapter. For example, Flash Buttons have an up state and over state and you can set them to link to other pages. However, unlike with other buttons, you create them from within Dreamweaver 8, which means you can quickly change them with just a few clicks, which can save time. You don't need to use an image editor such as Fireworks or Photoshop to work with Flash Buttons.

Creating Flash Buttons is fairly simple, as you will see in the next exercise. What is different is that

Dreamweaver 8 creates the rollover in the SWF file format, instead of GIF or JPG. In other exercises, you have simply worked with existing images designed in an image-editing program and set the behavior to write the necessary JavaScript to enact a rollover. With Flash Buttons, you create actual Flash files in Dreamweaver 8, which can be wonderfully convenient!

In order to view Flash content on the Web, you must have the Flash plug-in installed in your browser. If you don't have this plug-in, you can download it for free at **http://www.macromedia. com/software/flashplayer/**.

Creating Flash Buttons

Pros	Explanation
Font integrity	With Flash Buttons, you can use any font installed in your system, and the visitors to your page don't need to have that font installed. This gives you much more flexibility when you are designing your pages.
Easily updated	With just a few clicks, you can change the text and entire look of your Flash Buttons, which can save a lot of time when you need to make changes to your site.
Complex animations	Some of the Flash Buttons in Dreamweaver 8 have more complex animation than you could easily achieve with animated GIF files.
Design consistency	Because you can set up a navigation system that uses Flash Buttons in minutes, it's easy to get a consistent look and feel to your site without spending a lot of time designing your own rollover graphics. This helps to bring consistency to the overall design of your site.
Cons	**Explanation**
Plug-in required	Users need a plug-in to properly view Flash content on the Web. Flash Buttons are no different and require that the Flash plug-in be installed in the user's browser.
Limited linking	Site-root relative links don't work with Flash Buttons. If you're not sure what a site-root relative link is, don't worry, plenty of Web designers go their whole careers without using them. Just be aware that they don't work with Flash Buttons.
Fixed button sizes	Although Flash Buttons allow you to use any font installed in your system and choose the font size, the buttons themselves don't change to fit the text. Often you'll find your text too big for the button you've chosen. Usually a small modification to your text will make it fit, but you need to design with this in mind.

4 | Creating Flash Buttons

Flash Buttons are quick and easy to create and offer more variety than your plain vanilla image rollovers. This exercise shows you how to insert Flash Buttons into your site designs. Keep in mind, you may find Flash Buttons difficult to work with because the text you plan to use for the button may not fit.

---

1 In the **Files** panel, double-click **teacloudteas.htm** from the **ourproducts** folder to open it.

This file is just like the ones you started with in earlier exercises—it's just missing its navigation bar.

---

2 Place your cursor in the empty navigation table cell.

Place your cursor here.

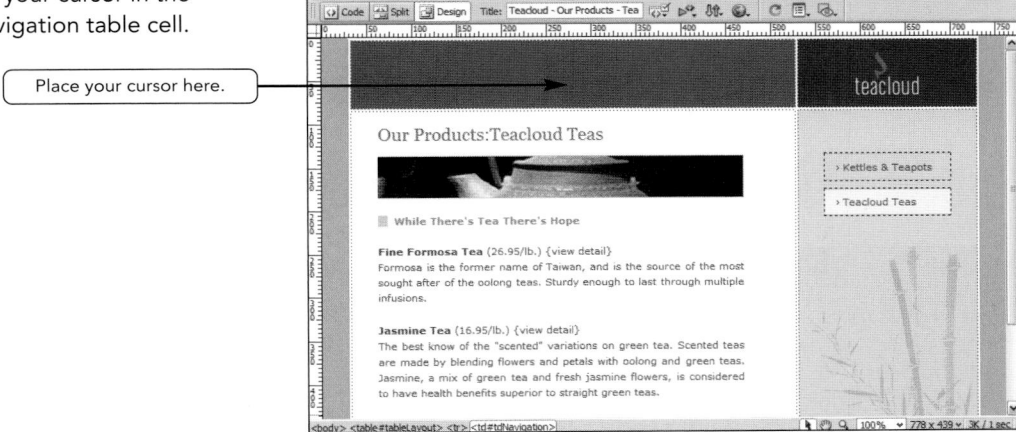

---

3 Choose **Insert > Media > Flash Button** to open the **Insert Flash Button** dialog box.

---

4 Select **Beveled Rect-Green** from the **Style** list.

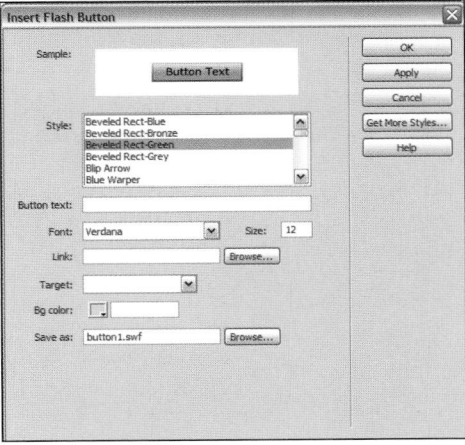

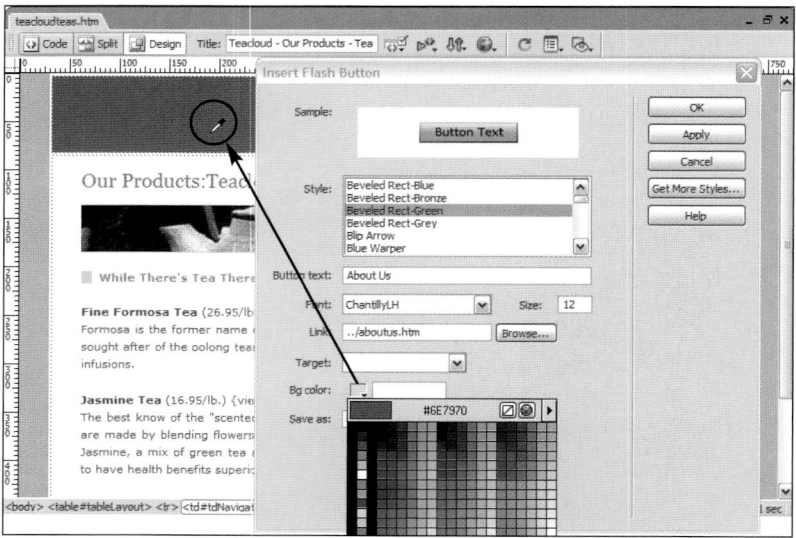

5 Type **About Us** in the **Button text** field, and choose a font you'd like to use from the **Font** pop-up menu. (In this case, we chose **ChantillyLH**.) Leave the **Size** set to **12**. Click **Browse** and select the **aboutus.htm** file at the root of the site. Finally, click the **color picker** and click to sample the background color of the navigation cell.

Always make sure you specify the background color the Flash movie is going to be on top of. Otherwise, you may end up with a white box around a button on top of a dark green background.

---

6 Choose a **Target**. In the **Save as** field, keep the filename **button1.swf**. Click **OK**. If the **Flash Accessibility Attributes** dialog box appears, type **About Us** in the **Title** field and click **OK**.

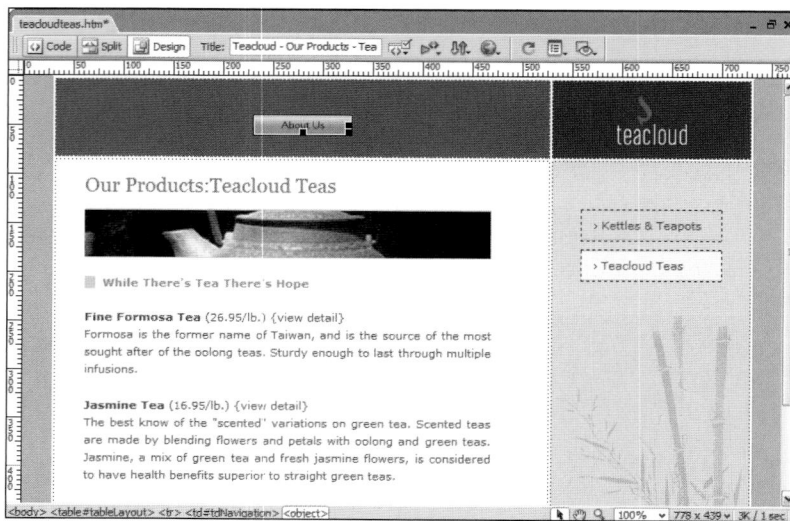

This is what your page should look like with the Flash Button inserted. Notice it's not quite as elegant as the rollovers you worked with in the past three exercises. When you work with Flash Buttons, you're limited to the predesigned buttons created by the designers at Macromedia. As a result, the buttons don't look as visually compelling as they would if you designed them yourself or had a graphic designer design them for you.

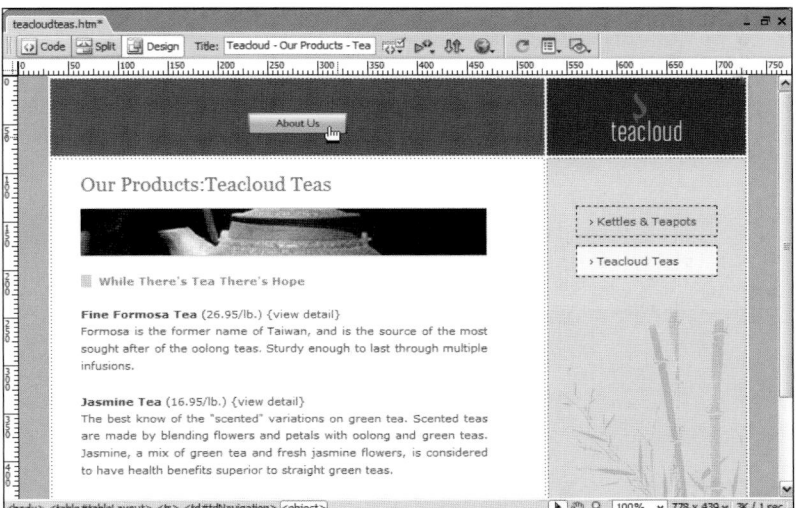

7 With the **Flash Button** selected, click the **Play** button in the **Property Inspector** and then move your mouse over the **Flash Button** while in **Design** view in Dreamweaver 8.

With the Flash Button playing in Design view, you can see the rollover state of the button. Click the button to get a glimpse of the down state. If you want to create the rest of the buttons, simply place your cursor after the **About Us** button, choose **Insert > Media > Flash Button**, and complete the dialog box for each of the other three buttons.

8 Close **teacloudteas.htm**. You don't need to save your changes.

In this chapter, you learned about different types of rollovers. You learned how to create simple rollovers and disjointed rollovers, how to apply multiple rollovers to a single anchor, how to create complex navigation bars, and even how to insert Flash Buttons with just a few clicks. Mastering rollovers will give you a definite advantage when it comes to designing effective navigation. In the next chapter, you'll dig into the code behind all of this wonderful work Dreamweaver 8 does for you, and you'll become intimately familiar with the Dreamweaver 8 Code view.

12

XHTML

Beginners often wonder whether it's necessary to know XHTML to be a successful Web designer. Several years ago, the answer was a resounding "yes," because there were no alternatives to writing XHTML/HTML to create Web pages. However, since the introduction of WYSIWYG editors such as Dreamweaver 8, Web developers are shielded from writing the markup and can create Web pages in a completely visual environment. The invention of the WYSIWYG editor brought Web page publishing within the reach of almost anyone. However, it's still our belief that a basic understanding of XHTML is beneficial to *anyone* planning to work in this field professionally. This book doesn't teach XHTML, but you can teach it to yourself by looking at the markup while building pages visually within Dreamweaver 8.

Dreamweaver 8 gives you three ways to view the Document window, combining the best of both the visual and the code environment. The Design view is the visual WYSIWYG editing environment where you will do most of your work. The Code view lets you use Dreamweaver 8 like other full-featured text editors that specialize in XHTML, such as BBEdit or HomeSite. The Split view lets you work with both the code and the visual elements of your page within the same Document window.

1 | Viewing the Markup

The Dreamweaver 8 interface has three extremely useful buttons: the Code View button, the Split View button, and the Design View button. The ability to toggle quickly between editing your code and working in the visual editing environment makes working with XHTML intuitive for anyone. For those of you who are familiar with XHTML, you won't feel so far from home when using Dreamweaver 8. Those of you who are less familiar with markup will find that you can watch Dreamweaver 8 create that markup as you use the visual editing environment. Observing this process is actually a great way to teach you good authoring techniques.

This first exercise exposes you to all three views to show you how to edit your XHTML effectively. Even if you don't know a whole lot about XHTML, you should still work through this exercise.

1 Copy the **chap_12** folder from the **HOT CD-ROM** to your **Desktop**. Define your site as **Chapter 12** using the **chap_12** folder as the local root folder. Make sure the **Files** panel is open. If it's not, choose **Window > Files.**

2 Create a new blank file by choosing **File > New**. Select **HTML** from the **Basic page** category. Choose **XHTML 1.0 Transitional** from the **Document Type (DTD)** pop-up menu and click **Create**.

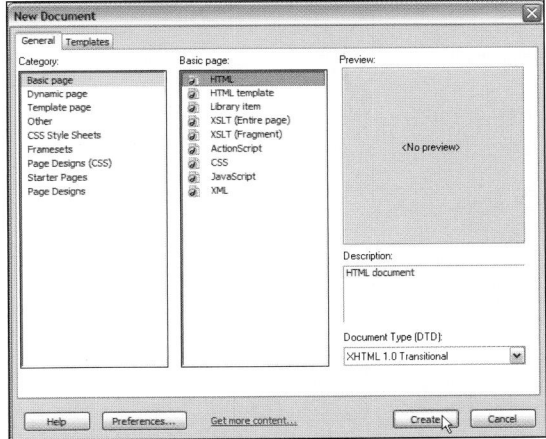

3 Click the **Code View** button to view the XHTML of your **Document** window. Even though the page looks empty in the **Design** view, some important XHTML already exists in the **Code** view.

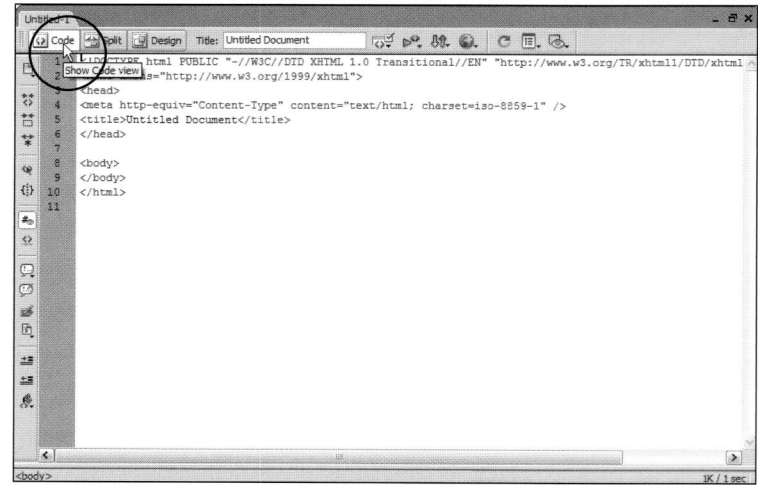

4 Click the **Design View** button to return to the **Design** view.

As you can see, switching between these different views is really easy.

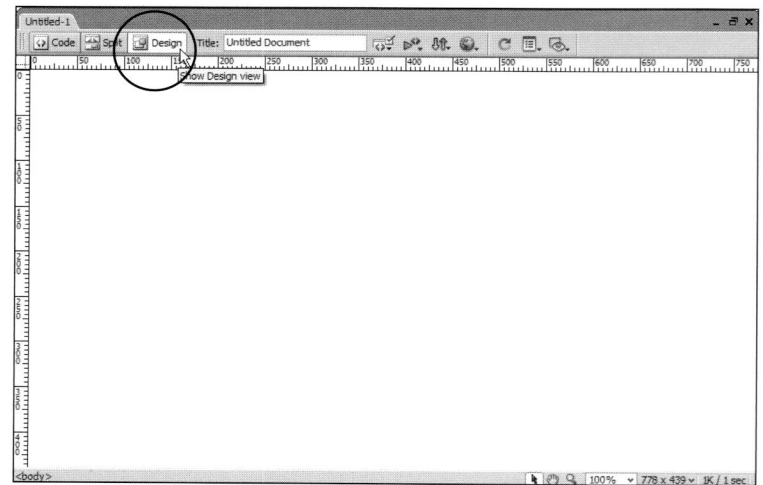

5 Choose **Insert > Table** to open the **Table** dialog box. Make sure the settings match those shown here, and then click **OK**.

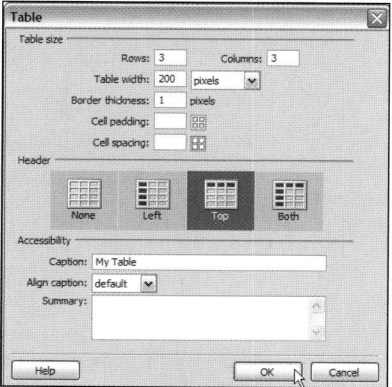

6 Click the **Code View** button.

You can see Dreamweaver has written a large amount of XHTML code for you. Because you selected the table in Design view, when you switch to Code view all of the necessary XHTML to create that table is also selected.

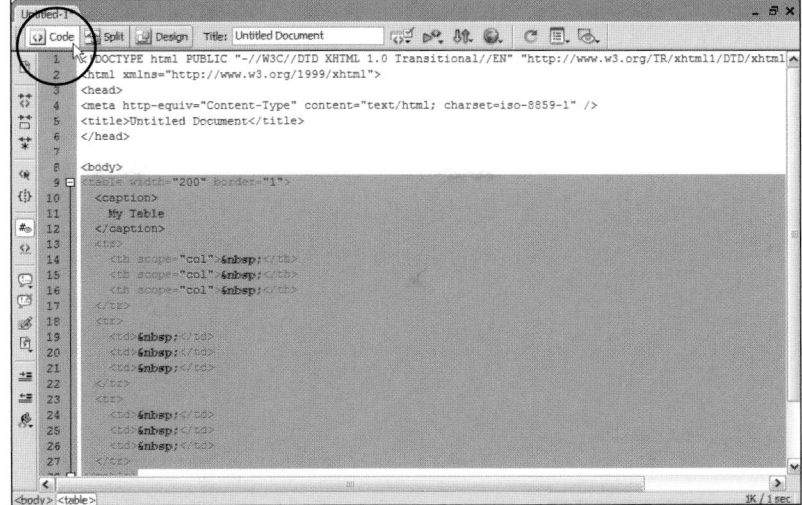

7 Click the **Split View** button to split your **Document** window so you can see the markup and the table on your page at the same time.

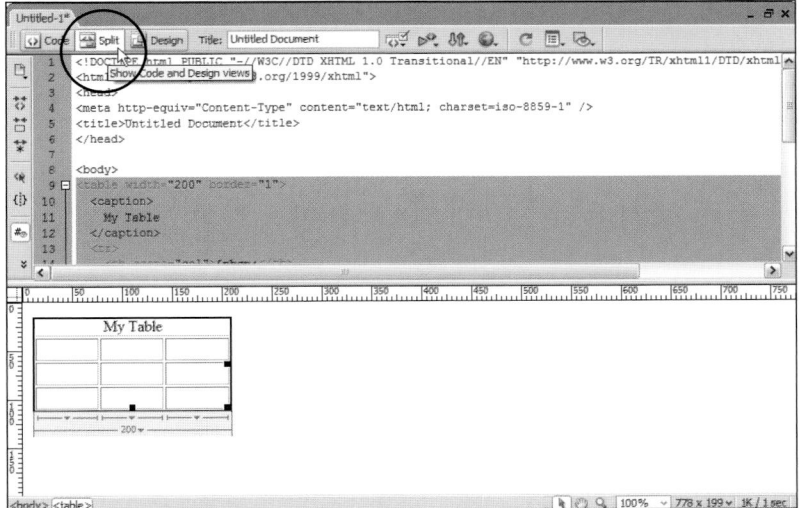

8 Hold your mouse to the left of the first table row until it displays a right-facing arrow. Click to select the entire row.

Notice the relevant XHTML to create that row is also selected. This level of visual feedback makes it easy to identify how the markup and the visual display are related.

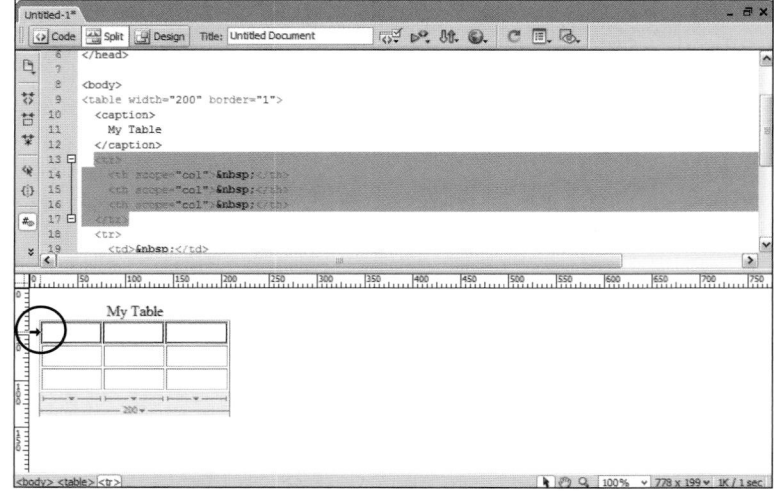

9 In the **Property Inspector**, click the **Bg** color swatch and choose any color you'd like for the background color of the selected row. (we're partial to purple.)

Notice how the background color was applied to the **<tr>** attribute rather than each **<td>** tag? Applying the background attribute to one tag rather than three tags is an example of learning efficient coding.

Look at the Code window. See how the XHTML is updated to reflect the changes you just made? This is a great way to learn XHTML. You can literally

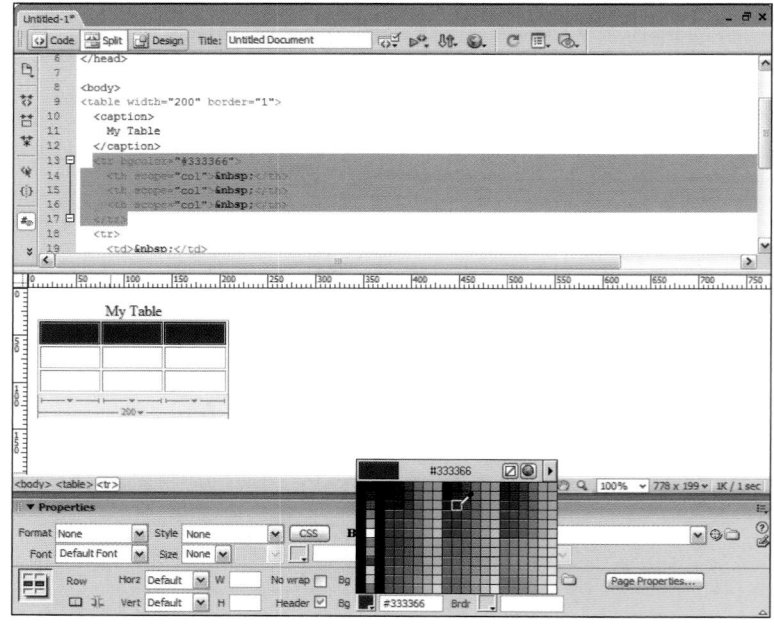

watch Dreamweaver 8 generate the markup as you add, modify, and remove content from your page. Go ahead and make some more changes to your page, but leave the Code window open so you can watch Dreamweaver 8 create all the XHTML.

10 Save the file as **xhtml.htm** and keep it open for the next exercise.

Options in Code View

Several options are available to customize how you work in Code view. The following table outlines each of these options:

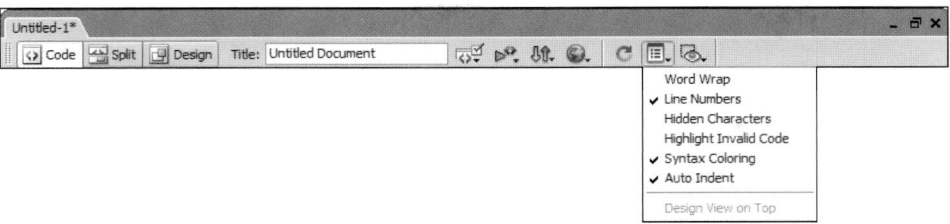

Code View Options	
Option	**Description**
Word Wrap	Wraps code within the window so you don't have to scroll to the left and right, making large amounts of code easier to see.
Line Numbers	Adds line numbers along the left side of the window. This is especially helpful when you need to identify a specific line of code, such as when you're troubleshooting an XHTML error. The numbers won't appear in the final XHTML output; they're just there for your reference.
Hidden Characters	Shows all hidden characters in the document, including tabs, spaces, and line breaks. This makes it easier to identify where you might have any rogue characters that are affecting the display of your page.
Highlight Invalid Code	Highlights invalid HTML code in yellow. This is really helpful when you are looking for errors in your code. When bad code is selected, look in the Property Inspector for ways to correct the problem.
Syntax Coloring	Color-codes parts of your XHTML based on your code color preferences. This helps you quickly spot the different elements of code.
Auto Indent	Automatically indents code, which helps with readability.
Design View on Top	Available only in Split view, this option inverts the positioning in the Document window.

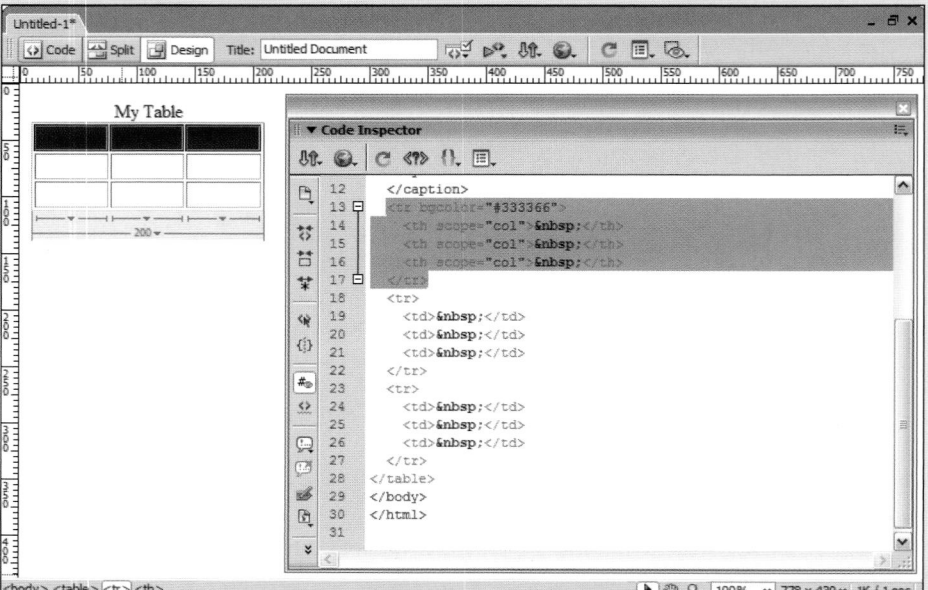

Although the three document views are very useful, there is one more way to view the markup in your pages. The Code Inspector is identical to the Code view, except the Code Inspector is a floating window above the Document window. You can access the Code Inspector by choosing **Window > Code Inspector** or by pressing **F10** (Windows) or **Shift+F10** (Mac). You can resize this floating window and move it around the screen without affecting the main Document window, which can be nice if you have a large monitor (or multiple monitors) and want to see the markup next to the visual editing environment.

2 | Editing in Code View

Now that you have an idea of how the Code window works, you will learn how to use it to modify your page. In fact, if you wanted to build a page by hand, you could create your entire page right within the Code window.

In this exercise, you will use the Code window to add content to your page and then make modifications to it. The purpose of this exercise is to help you become more comfortable with the Code window.

1 If you just completed Exercise 1, **xhtml.htm** should still be open. If it's not, go back and complete Exercise 1. Click anywhere below the table and press **Enter** (Windows) or **Return** (Mac) to create a new paragraph. Type **Dreamweaver 8 Hands On Training**. Look inside the **Code** window and watch as your text is created.

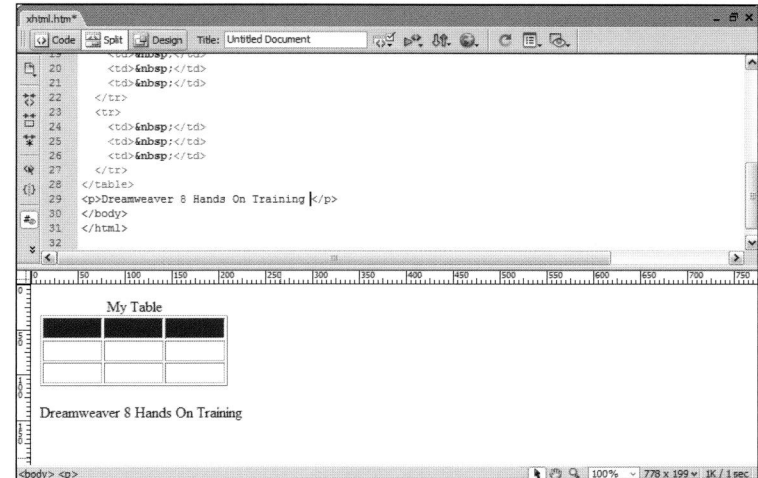

2 Inside the **Code** window, place your cursor before the word **Dreamweaver** and type **Macromedia**. When you are done typing, press **Ctrl+`** (that's the tilde symbol, to the left of the number 1 on your keyboard) to switch to **Design** view to see the changes updated.

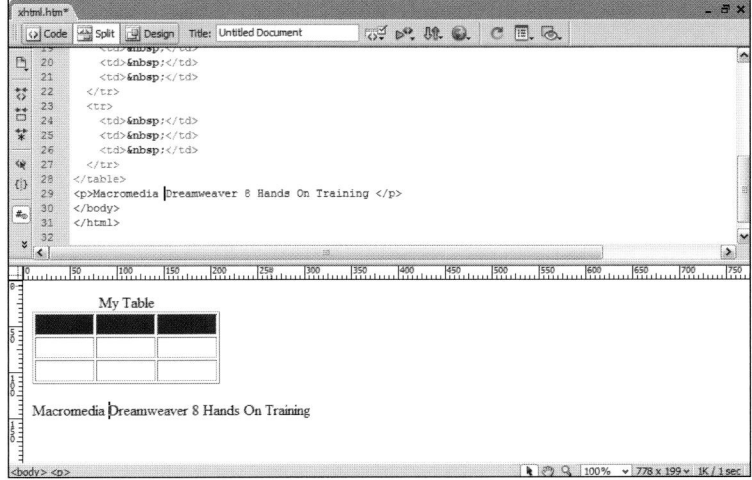

3 In the **Design** window, click and drag to highlight the text **Hands On Training**. With the word highlighted, click the **Bold** button in the **Property Inspector**. Notice that the **<strong>** tags were added around the word in the **Code** window.

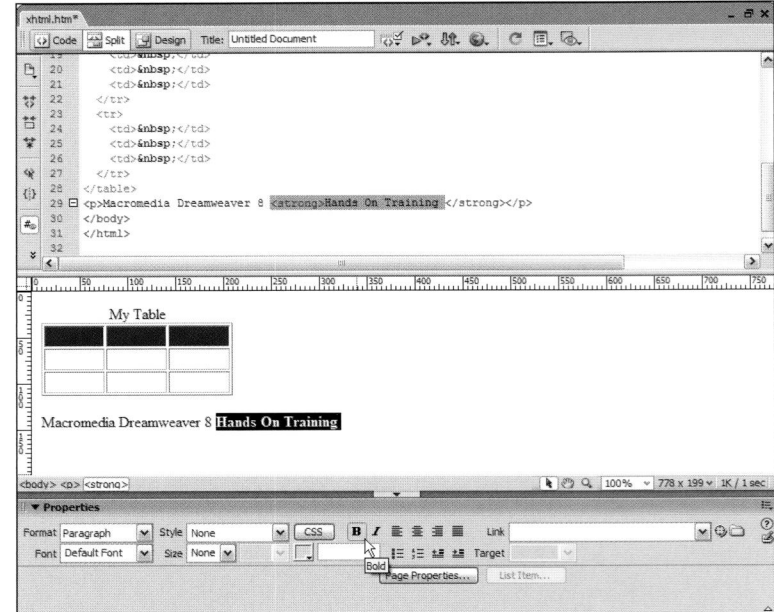

4 In the **Code** window, manually change the **<strong>** tags to **<em>** tags. The **<em>** tag will format the text in italics instead of bold, whereas the **<strong>** tag was used to bold the text.

You don't have to know HTML tags, such as **<strong>** and **<em>**, but if you do know them, you can type them right into the code. It's easier to use the Property Inspector for this type of formatting. This exercise is here simply to show you that you can edit the code directly if you want to, which achieves the same result as if you had used the Property Inspector.

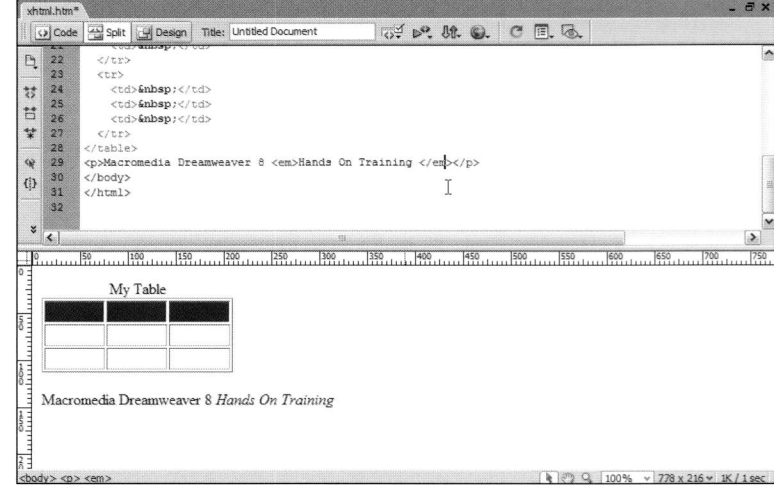

Code Formatting Preferences

Dreamweaver 8 gives you several ways to control the view and behavior of the Code view. In the Preferences window, you can use the Code Coloring, Code Format, Code Hints, and Code Rewriting options to set everything from how the XHTML code appears to how it is formatted. So if you find yourself working in the Code view a lot, be sure to look over these different options.

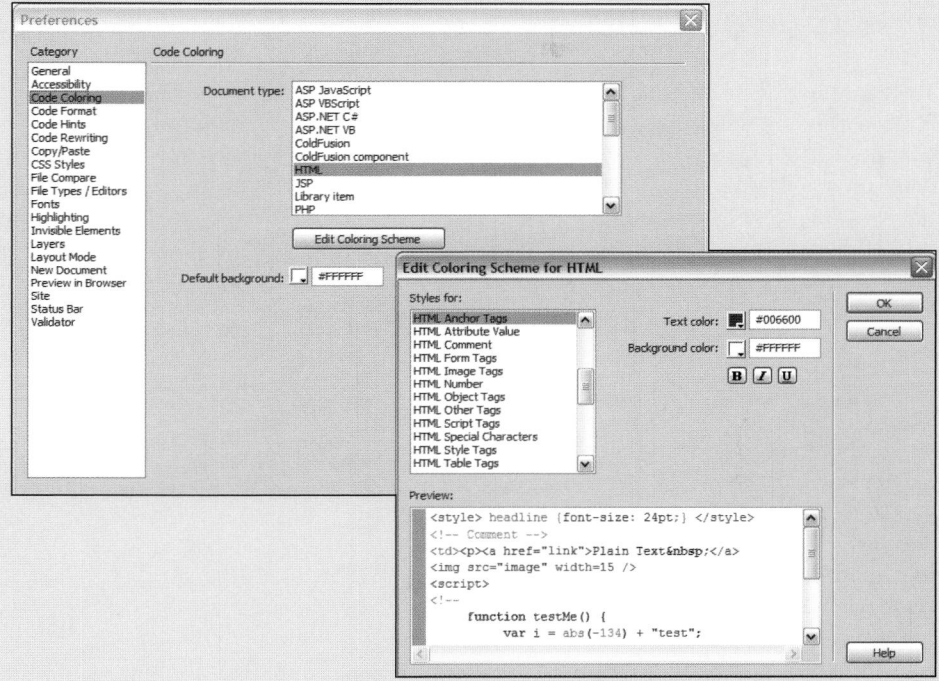

5 Close **xhtml.htm**. You don't need to save your changes.

You can begin to see how you can use the Design window and the Code window in tandem to create and modify your documents.

VIDEO: | **codeview.mov**

Working with Code view is far more powerful than a few simple exercise can really demonstrate. To learn more about working with Code view, check out **codeview.mov** in the **videos** folder on the **HOT CD-ROM**.

The Code Toolbar

The Code toolbar is one of the best new features in Dreamweaver 8. Once you become familiar with XHTML, and Web development in general, you'll most likely start spending more and more time in Code view. The Code toolbar makes your life much easier by giving you quick access to the most common tasks you need to perform while working in Code view. The following diagram tells you what each button is, and the table afterwards describes what each button does:

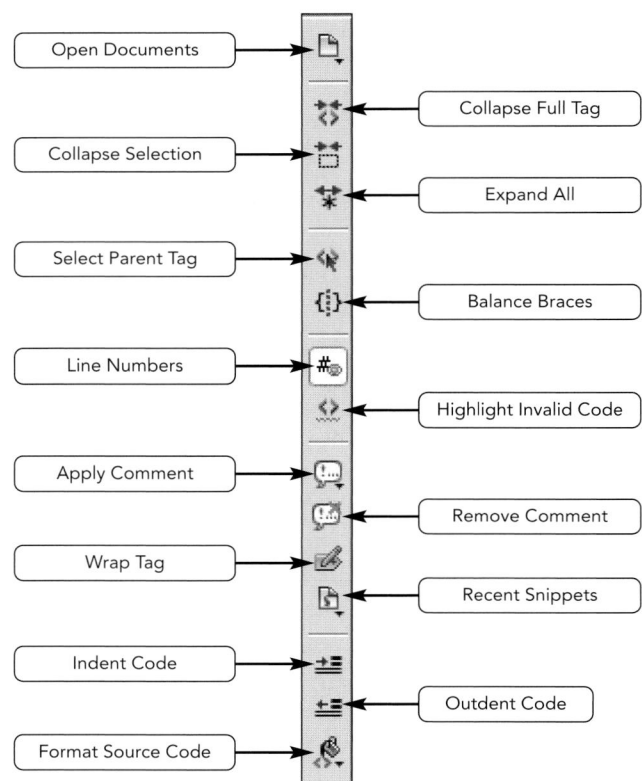

Code Toolbar Functionality

Button	Description
Open Documents	Opens a pop-up menu, which lists the full file path of all open documents. If you're working on a large number of open documents, use this button to quickly find the document you need.
Collapse Full Tag	Collapses the entire tag that currently contains the cursor. You'll learn more about this button in Exercise 3.
Collapse Selection	Collapses the currently highlighted selection. You'll learn more about this button in Exercise 3.
Expand All	Expands all currently collapsed blocks of code.
Select Parent Tag	Selects the parent tag of the current selection. If your cursor is inside a table cell, clicking this button will select the **\<td\>** tag. Clicking the button again will select the **\<tr\>** tag, which is the **\<td\>** tag's parent.
Balance Braces	Selects all of the code between the enclosing parentheses, braces, or square brackets. If you have the code **(some text)** in your document, and your cursor is between the words *some* and *text*, clicking this button will select the words *some text*. This function is particularly useful when working with JavaScript since it's dependent on where braces and parentheses start and end.
Line Numbers	Turns the line numbers on and off in Code view.
Highlight Invalid Code	Highlights any invalid XHTML in yellow so it's easy to find.
Apply Comment	Wraps the current selection in a comment, or inserts a blank comment. You can apply multiple different comment styles from this button.
Remove Comment	Removes a comment wrapped around the current selection.
Wrap Tag	Opens the Quick Tag Editor in Wrap Tag mode, which you'll learn more about in Exercise 4.
Recent Snippets	Displays a list of recently used snippets. You'll learn more later in this chapter.
Indent Code	Adds a single tab to the beginning of each line in the current selection.
Outdent Code	Removes a single tab from the beginning of each line in the current selection.
Format Source Code	Reformats the source code of the current document, resetting all of the tabs to make it easier to see the tag nesting structure.

3 | Using Code Collapse

Once you start developing more complicated sites, the XHTML to create those sites also becomes more complicated. If you start working on dynamic sites using a server language like ASP, .NET, or ColdFusion, your code becomes even more complicated. You'll oftentimes need to reference multiple parts of a page at a time, but when your files start reaching more than 100 lines of code, referencing other parts of your page's code starts to become difficult because you have to scroll back and forth to check the relevant lines. Dreamweaver 8 can collapse blocks of code to get them out of your way to make it far easier to manage large files. In this exercise, you'll learn how to use our new favorite feature in Dreamweaver 8.

1 In the **Files** panel, double-click **abouttea.htm** to open it. If you're not already in Code view, choose **View > Code**.

The first thing you'll probably notice is the JavaScript that Dreamweaver 8 has inserted to handle the image rollovers for the navigation. This code starts at line 7 with an opening **<script>** tag and ends on line 32, below the edge of the screen. Considering that Dreamweaver 8 manages the JavaScript for you, you may prefer not to see it in your code.

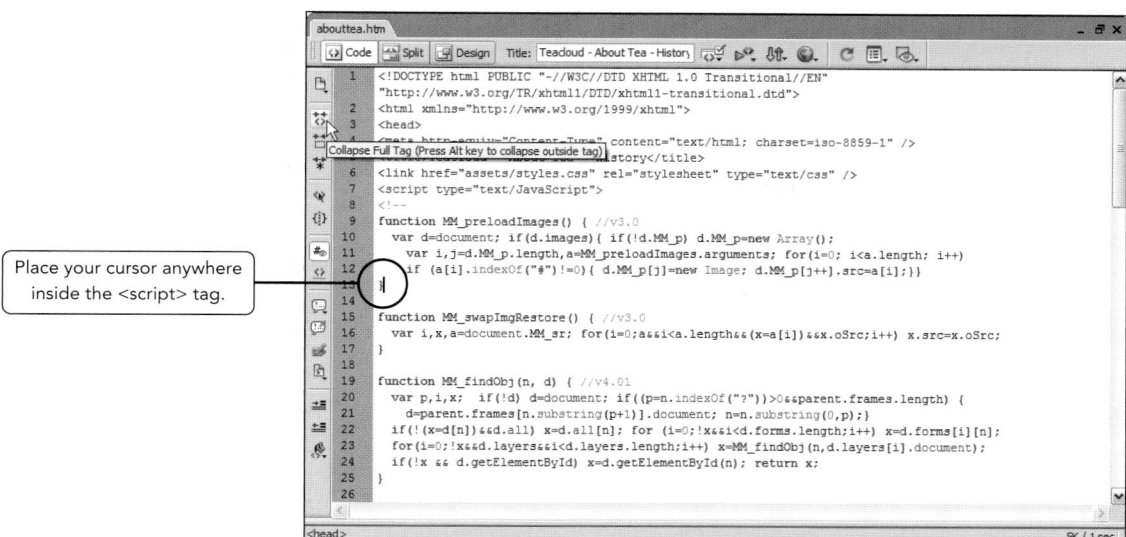

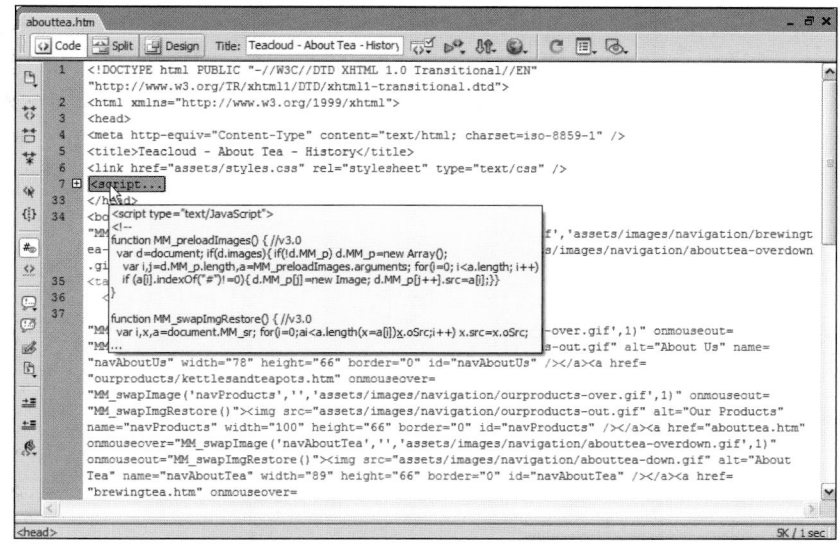

Place your cursor anywhere inside the <script> tag.

2 Place your cursor anywhere inside the **<script>** tag and click the **Collapse Full Tag** button in the **Code** toolbar.

The Collapse Full Tag button in the Code toolbar collapses the entire tag currently surrounding the cursor. In this case, it will collapse the entire **<script>** tag.

After you collapse the **<script>** tag, it is displayed with a gray background and a plus symbol next to it. If you hold your mouse over the collapsed code, Dreamweaver 8 shows you the first 10 lines of code inside the collapsed area to give you an idea of what's inside.

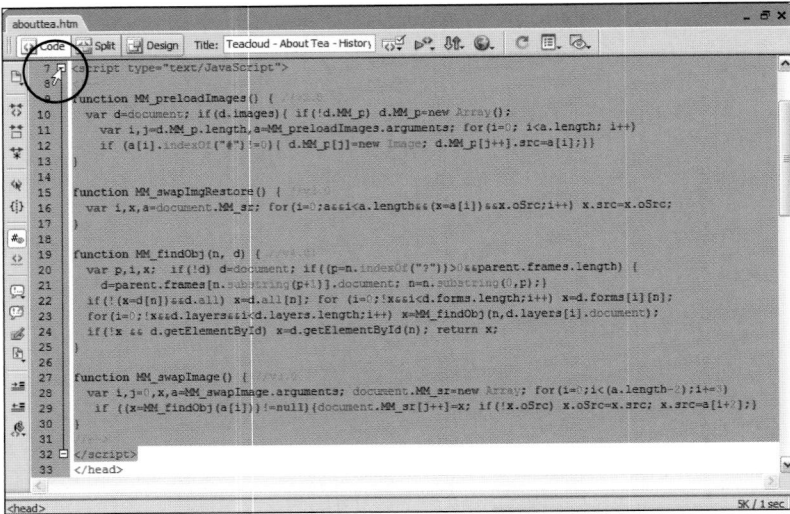

3 If you need to edit any of the code inside the collapsed block, click the **plus** symbol (Windows) or the **triangle** (Mac) to the left of the collapsed block or double-click the collapsed block.

When you expand a block of code, Dreamweaver 8 expands it and then immediately selects the entire block for you. This makes it easy to look inside a block of collapsed code and then immediately collapse the code again.

---

4 With the **<script>** tag and its contents still selected, click either of the **minus** symbols at the beginning and the end of the selected code (Windows) or click the **triangle** (Mac).

The code collapse indicators (the plus and minus symbols) will display any time you make a selection inside Code view in Dreamweaver 8. This lets you collapse any piece of code on the page, whether it's a few words of text or an entire tag.

---

5 Scroll a little farther down the page until you get to line 41, which is where the table cell containing all of the content for the page is located.

When working on a site that has the design completed, you may care only about the content that's unique for the current page, which is almost always contained in either a single table or a **<div>** tag. You may find it helpful to collapse everything but the content area of the page to keep from getting distracted by all of the code surrounding the section you need to work on.

---

6 **Right-click** (Windows) or **Ctrl+click** (Mac) the **<td>** tag that contains all of the content for the page. From the contextual menu, choose **Selection > Collapse Outside Full Tag**.

You can also hold down the **Alt** (Windows) or **Option** (Mac) key and click the **Collapse Full Tag** button in the **Code** toolbar if you prefer.

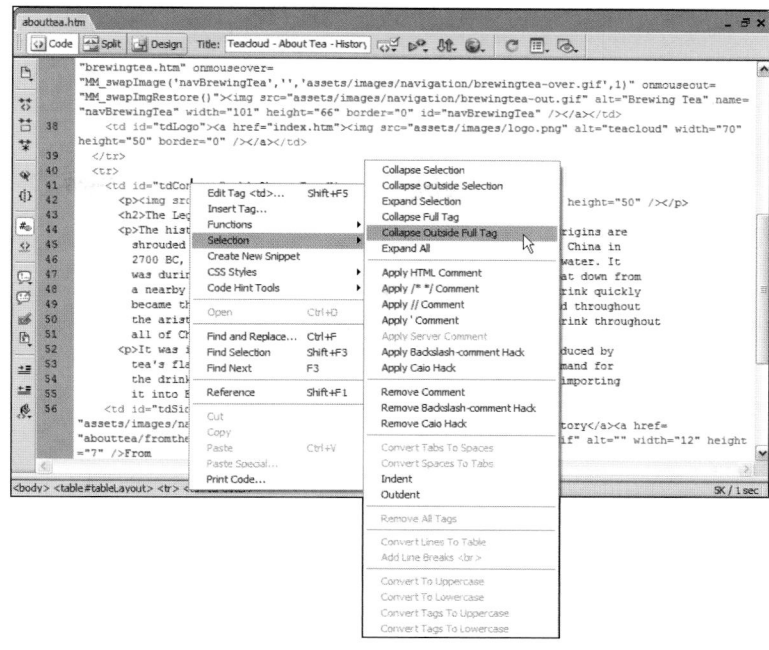

Now that you've collapsed everything outside the content table cell, you won't have any distractions while you're working on your code. Everything outside that **<td>** tag has been completely collapsed.

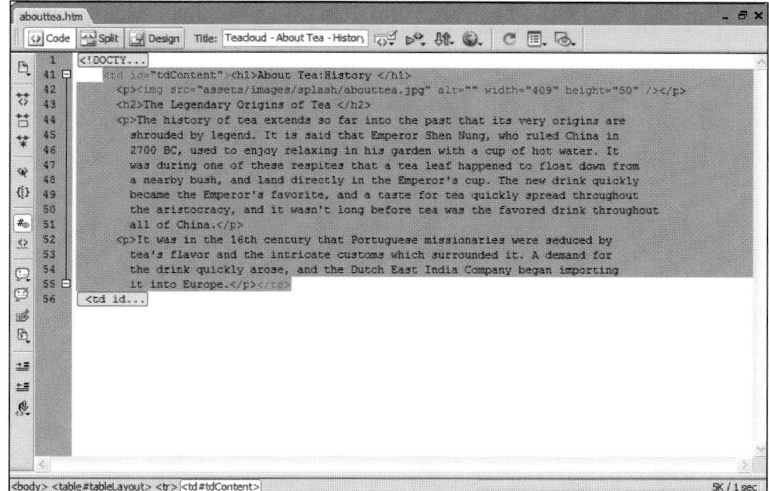

WARNING:

Code Collapse and Undo

When first working with code collapse, you might feel compelled to treat it like any other edit to your code—collapse a block of code, decide you really didn't want to, and press **Ctrl+Z** to undo the change. Unfortunately, attempting to undo a code collapse action doesn't work, you just end up undoing the last actual change to the code you made. If you're an undo-aholic, this is going to throw you the first few times, but once you get used to it, you'll remember to just double-click the collapsed block to expand it.

7 Choose **View > Code and Design**.

You can see that the collapsed code is still rendered in Design view in Dreamweaver 8. Collapsing blocks of code doesn't have any effect on the display of the document in Design view.

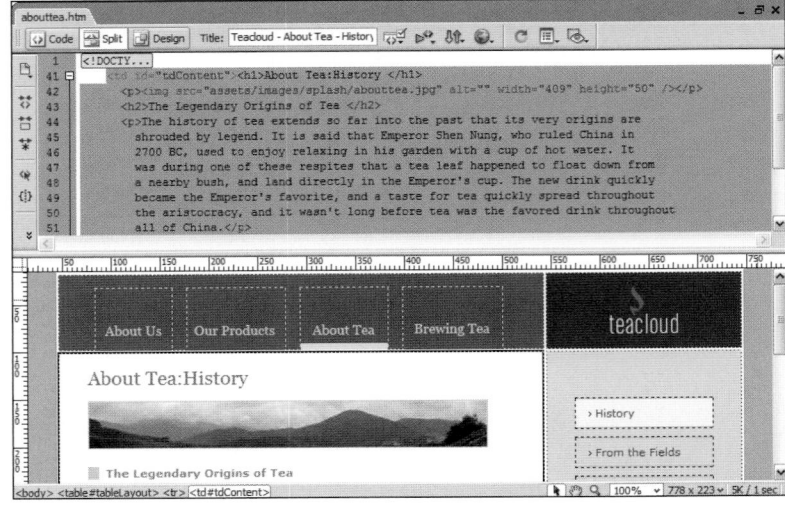

8 If you've been collapsing a large number of code blocks, you might have some difficulty finding a line of code that could be causing a problem. To get rid of all collapsed blocks of code, click the **Expand All** button in the **Code toolbar** to expand every collapsed block of code in the document.

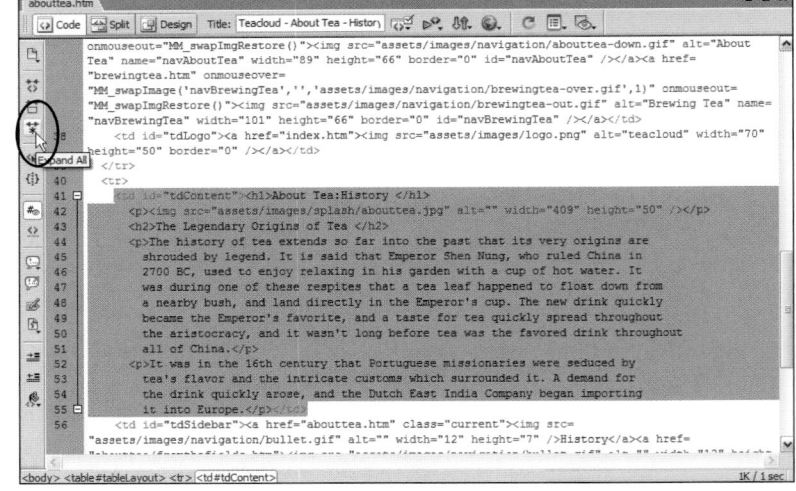

9 Leave this file open for the next exercise. You don't need to save it, because collapsing code doesn't have any effect on the actual code of your page, so there are no changes to save.

Note: Code Collapse Doesn't Forget. Dreamweaver 8 will remember what blocks of code were collapsed in a document, even after you close it. If you reopen a document that had a block of code collapsed, that code will still be collapsed, which makes it easy to start right back where you left off.

4 | Using the Quick Tag Editor

The Quick Tag Editor gives you instant access to the XHTML on your page without requiring you to switch to Code view, which is great if you want to make a quick change to a tag or attribute. This exercise shows you how to use the Quick Tag Editor to quickly edit the XHTML behind your pages without leaving Design view.

---

1 In the **Files** panel, double-click **aboutus.htm** to open it.

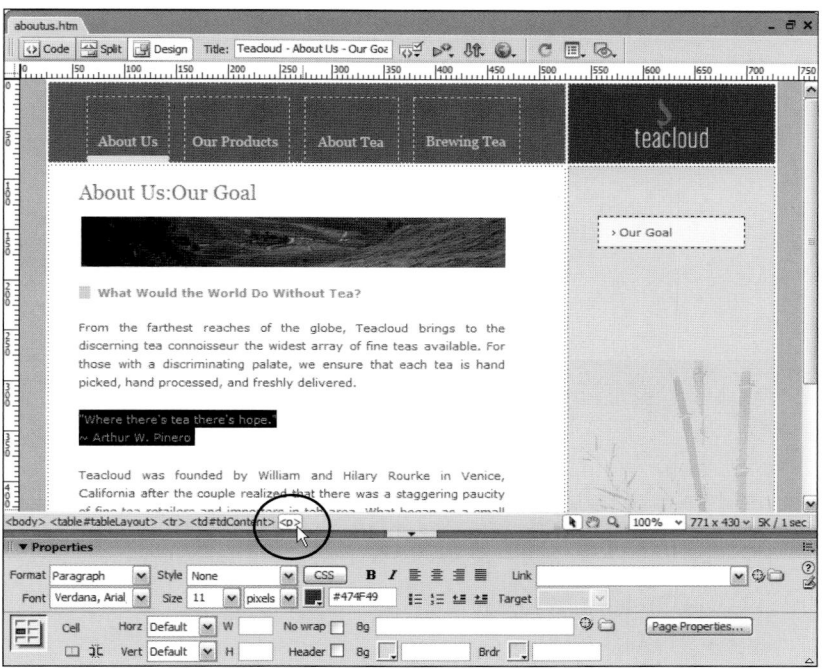

2 Place your cursor inside the quote in the center of the page, and then select the **<p>** tag surrounding it in the **Tag Selector**.

---

3 Press **Ctrl+T** (Windows) or **Cmd+T** (Mac) to open the **Quick Tag Editor**, which appears directly above the selected tag.

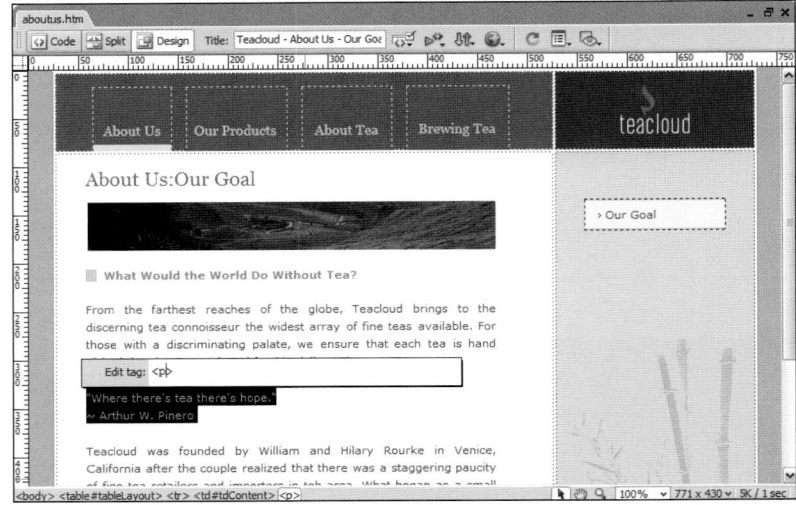

4 Press the **spacebar** to add a space after the **p** and type **style="background-color: #CCCCCC;"** and press **Enter** (Windows) or **Return** (Mac) to commit the changes.

You just directly edited the **<p>** tag surrounding the quote without ever switching to Code view. There's more to the Quick Tag Editor though.

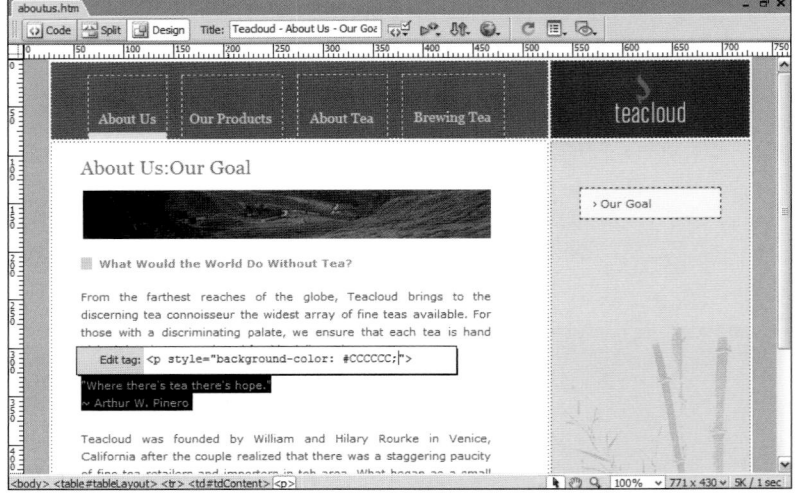

5 With the text still selected in **Design** view, press **Ctrl+T** (Windows) or **Cmd+T** (Mac) *twice* to set the **Quick Tag Editor** to **Wrap Tag** mode.

The Wrap Tag mode of the Quick Tag Editor lets you quickly wrap the current selection in another tag. In this case, you're going to wrap the paragraph in a `<blockquote>` tag to indent the content.

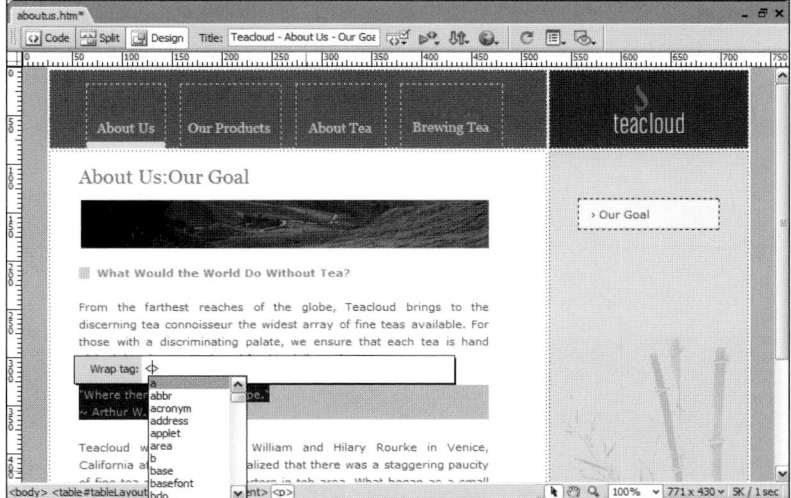

6 Type **blockquote** (or choose it from the tag list) and press **Enter** (Windows) or **Return** (Mac) to commit the changes.

In the Tag Selector, notice the `<p>` tag is now wrapped in a `<blockquote>` tag.

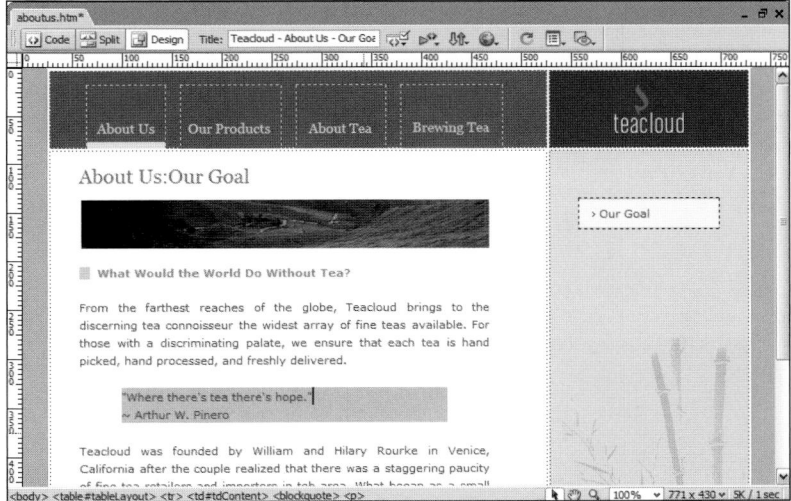

7 Save your changes and keep **aboutus.htm** open for the next exercise.

The Quick Tag Editor is a great tool if you want quick access to the XHTML. As you just saw, you can make changes to the XHTML without ever leaving the visual environment.

5 | Using the Tag Editor and Tag Chooser

Another way to add markup to a document is to use the Tag Editor and Tag Chooser. The purpose of this exercise is to show you alternate ways to add and modify the markup code on your page. Whichever method you choose depends on what your workflow and personal preferences are.

---

1 If you just completed Exercise 4, **aboutus.htm** should still be open. If it's not, go back and complete Exercise 4.

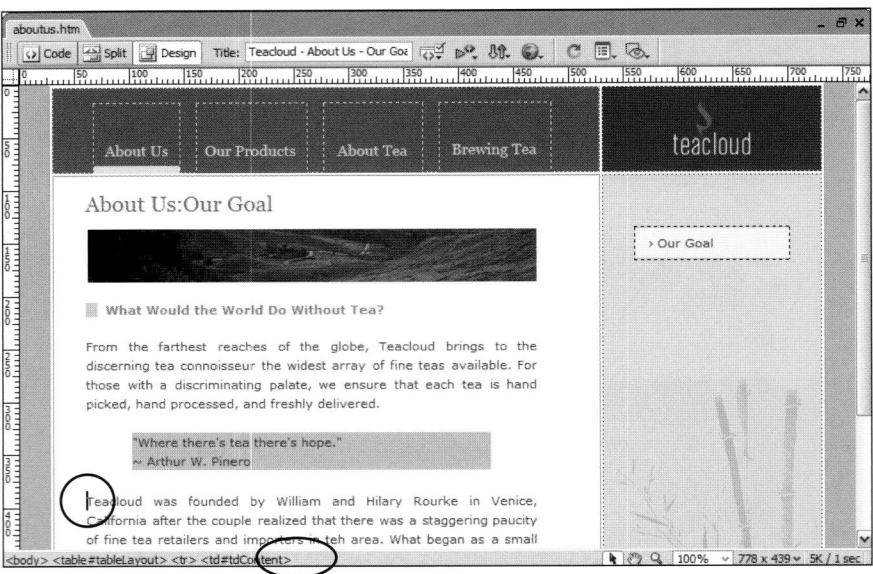

2 Place your cursor at the beginning of the paragraph following the quote. In the **Tag Selector**, click the **<p>** tag and press the **left arrow** key to move your cursor position before the opening **<p>** tag of the paragraph.

It sometimes takes a bit of manipulation to get your cursor in the right spot when working in Design view. If you followed the steps correctly your cursor should be at the beginning of the paragraph, and you *should not* see a **<p>** tag in the Tag Selector.

---

3 Choose **Insert > Tag** to open the **Tag Chooser** window.

---

4 In the left pane, highlight **HTML tags**.

The right pane loads all of the available XHTML tags.

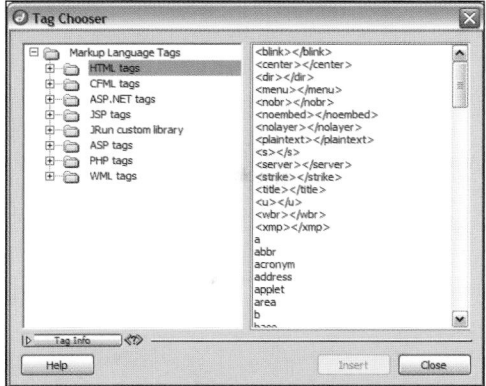

5 Scroll down until you find **h2**. Select it and click **Insert**.

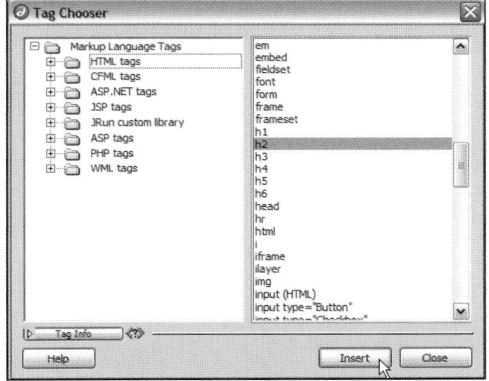

6 The **Tag Editor** for the **h2** element opens. In the **Header** field, type **The Teacloud Founders**. To learn more about the tag you've chosen, click the **Tag info** triangle. Click **OK**.

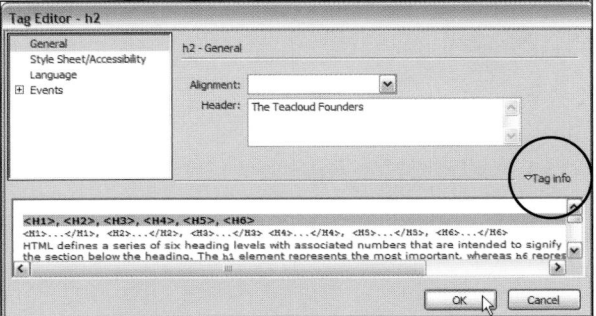

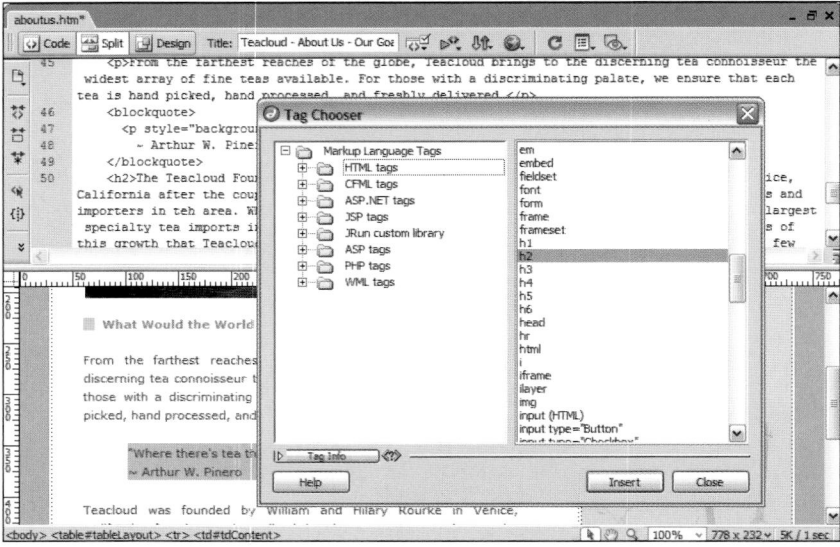

7 In the **Tag Chooser**, click **Close** to close the dialog box.

8 The document goes automatically into **Split** view, and the cursor's focus is in the **Code** window. Click inside the **Design** view or click the **Design View** button in the **Document** toolbar to see the new **<h2>** added to the design.

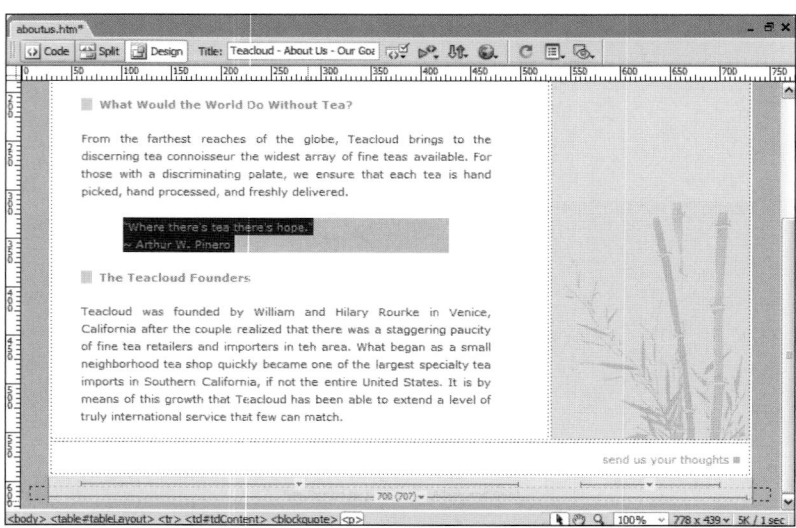

9 Click inside the quote above the new **<h2>** and select the **<p>** tag from the **Tag Selector**.

10 Choose **Modify > Edit Tag** to open the **Tag Editor** for the **<p>** tag.

11 Select the **Style Sheet/Accessibility** category and remove the background color property from the **Style** field. Click **OK**.

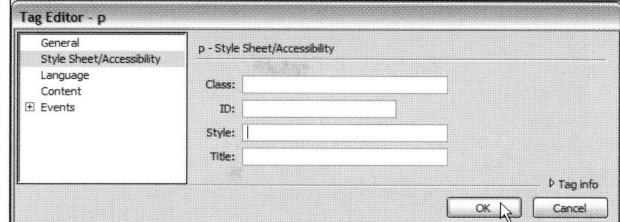

The changes in the Tag Editor are now reflected in Design view.

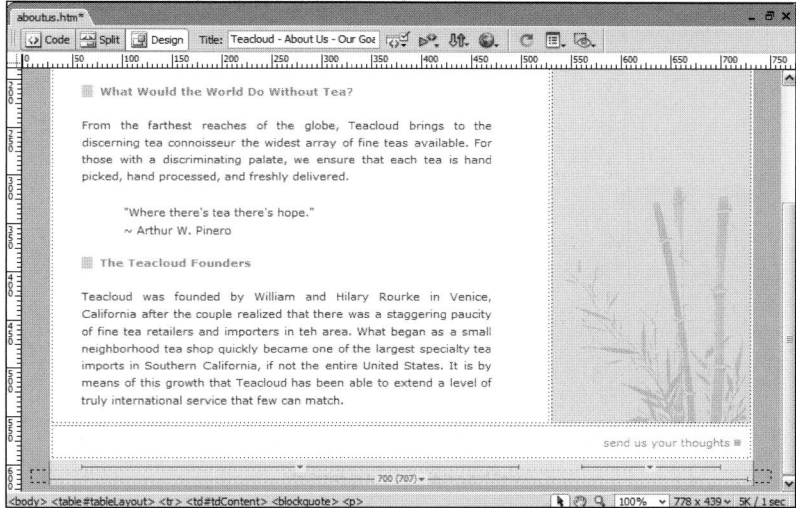

12 Save your changes and keep **aboutus.htm** open for the next exercise.

The Tag Chooser and Tag Editor are an easy way to edit the properties of a tag directly in Design view. Because all of the attributes are nicely categorized, you can easily change what you need to without worrying about the necessary syntax.

Code Validation

Code validation is a way for you to ensure you're writing the correct code. Dreamweaver 8 lets you validate your code against the XHTML specifications so that you can check your code for potential problems, which is very helpful for two reasons. First, you'll find any errors you've made that could cause problems with your page; and second, you can ensure your documents conform to Web standards, which in turn means the markup you're using will work in the largest number of browsers possible. You can access the **Code Validator** by choosing **File > Check Page > Validate Markup**. A listing of errors (if there are any) will appear in the Results panel, which identifies the problem and the exact line of markup where the error occurs.

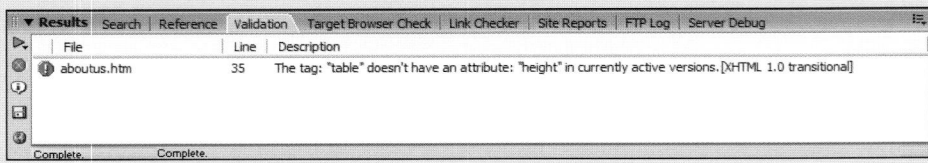

The Validator Preferences let you choose how your markup is validated if there is no **DOCTYPE** associated with your page. For example, you might choose to use very strict forms of HTML or XHTML, and you can set this up in the Dreamweaver 8 preferences. This flexibility makes the validation process more efficient by letting you exclude languages or language versions you're not using.

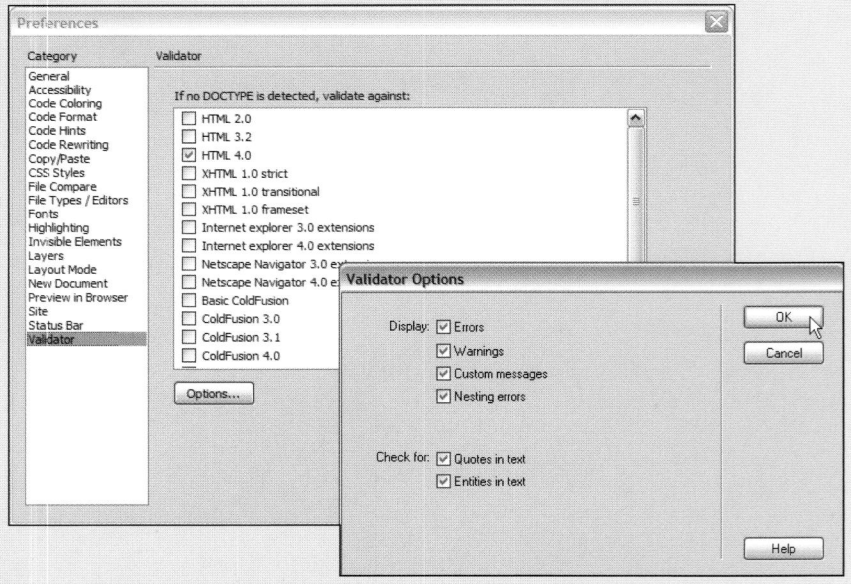

EXERCISE

6 | Working with Snippets

No one can remember every piece of useful code they've ever used. Dreamweaver 8 offers a way to store all of those small bits of code you use every day, and they're called snippets. These are pieces of code (XHTML, JavaScript, CSS, server-side code, you name it) you can add to your documents with the click of a button. Dreamweaver 8 comes complete with its own set of predefined snippets, and you can even create your own. This exercise shows you how to add one of the predefined code snippets to your page and how to add your own snippets to Dreamweaver 8.

---

1 If you just completed Exercise 5, **aboutus.htm** should still be open. If it's not, go back and complete Exercise 5.

---

2 Place your cursor before the **About Us:Our Goal** text at the top of the page.

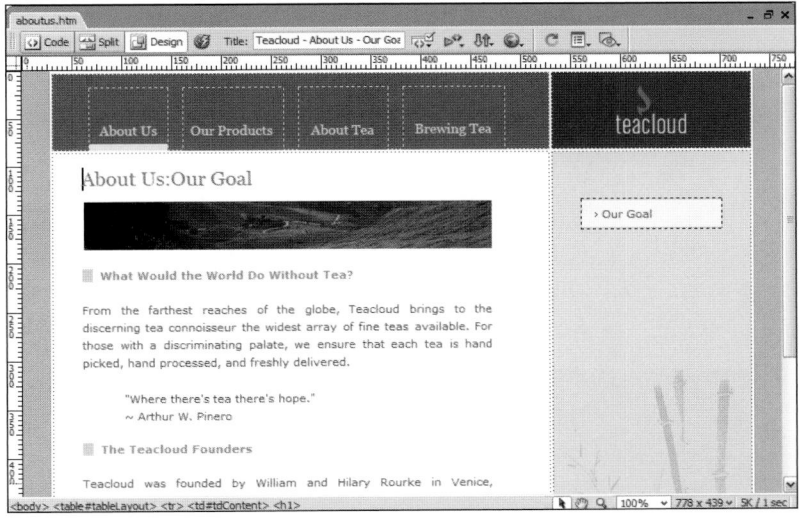

---

3 Choose **Window > Snippets** to open the **Snippets** panel.

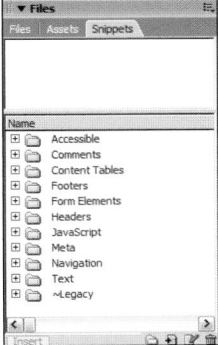

---

4 Open the **Navigation** folder, then open the **Breadcrumb** folder and select **Colon as Separator**. Click the **Insert** button to insert the code snippet into the page.

As you select each snippet, you'll see a preview of the code it will insert inside the preview window at the top of the Snippets panel.

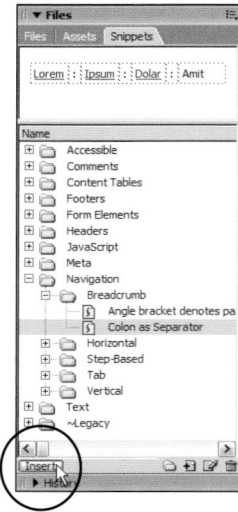

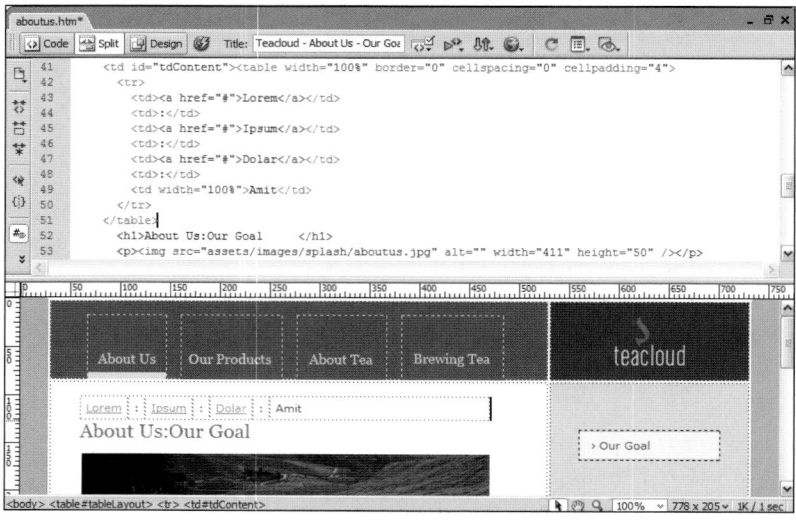

If you switch to Split view, you can see that Dreamweaver 8 has inserted an entire table, complete with placeholder links for adding your own breadcrumb-style navigation.

---

5 If you're not already in **Split** view, switch to **Split** view. Choose **Edit > Undo Insert Snippet** to remove the table you just inserted.

Simple breadcrumb-style navigation doesn't really require an entire table.

---

6 Place your cursor before the **<h1>** tag in **Code** view and type the following:

```
<p><a href="#">Lorem</a>
: <a href="#">Ipsum</a>
: <a href="#">Dolar</a>
: Amit</p>.
```

When you're all finished, your code should match the illustration here.

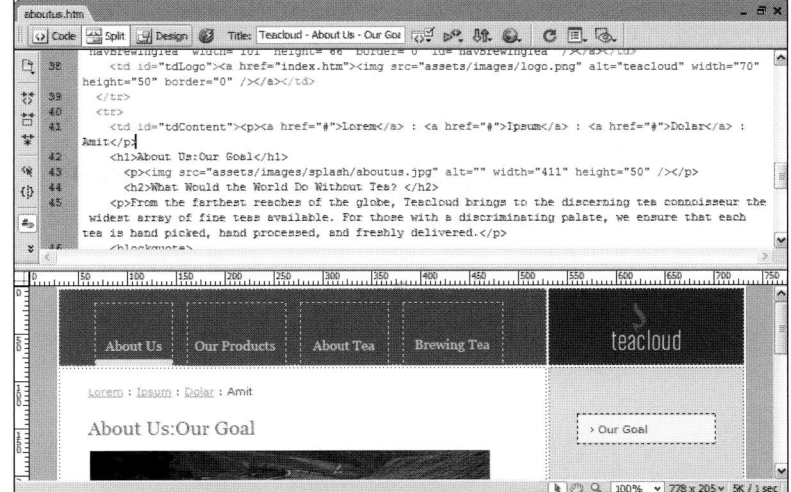

VIDEO:

codehints.mov

The code hinting features in Dreamweaver 8 make developing pages by hand a breeze. Unfortunately, there's just too much dynamic stuff going on with code hints for a few screenshots to do them justice. To learn more about code hinting, check out **codehints.mov** in the **videos** folder of the **HOT CD-ROM** to learn more.

7 Either click and drag to select the entire **<p>** tag and its contents, or click in **Design** view and select the **<p>** tag in the **Tag Selector**.

Either method will work, as long as you get the content and the opening and closing **<p>** tags.

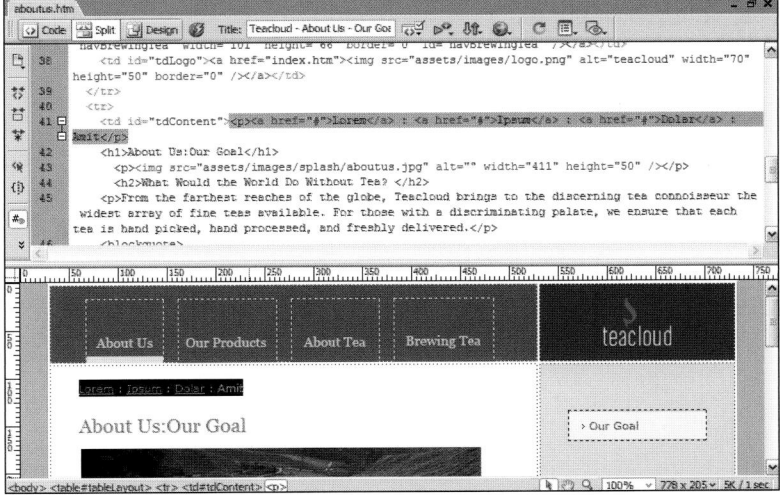

8 In the **Snippets** panel, click the **New Snippet** button to open the **Snippet** dialog box.

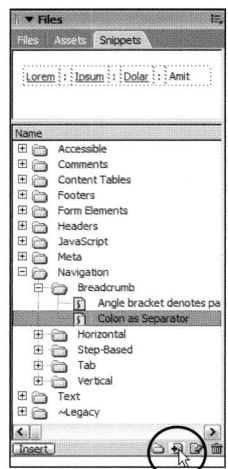

9 In the **Snippet** dialog box, type **Standard Breadcrumb** in the **Name** field. Because this is an entire block of code, select **Insert block**. (If you want to wrap a selection with a snippet, you can select **Wrap selection** and provide **Insert before** and **Insert after** code.) Finally, select **Design** for the **Preview type** and click **OK**.

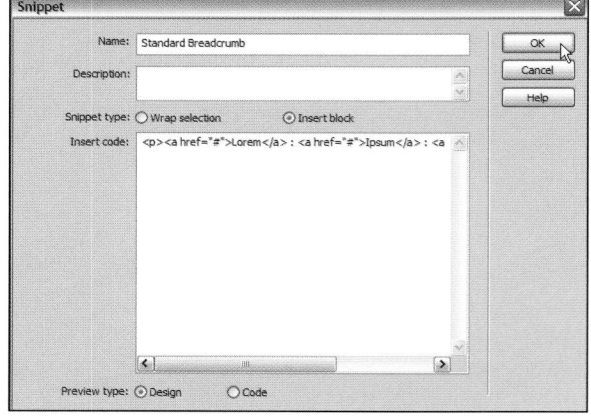

Your new snippet is now listed in the Snippets panel. Click the Edit button to change the snippet, or click the Delete button to remove it completely.

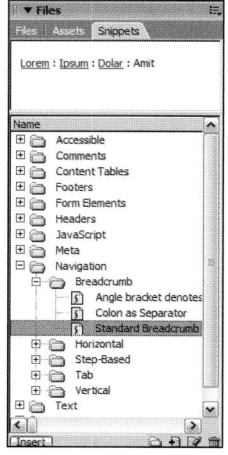

10 Close **aboutus.htm**. You don't need to save your changes

In this chapter, you learned how to work with the Dreamweaver 8 Code view. You learned how to use the Code toolbar, how to use code collapse to make your code easier to read, and how to edit your XHTML code directly in Design view. In the next chapter, you'll learn how to work with forms to collect data from your site's users.

13

Forms

Forms are one of the most important elements of a Web site, because they let you ask questions of your audience and receive answers. Forms can be identical to those you're accustomed to in the nonvirtual world (think IRS, car insurance, or loan paperwork), but they can also be used for more exciting things, such as voting, guest books, interactive poetry, or e-commerce. In general, form-based pages are much more interactive than other types of HTML pages, because they can collect and report information to you and give feedback to your users.

There are two aspects to creating forms: creating the form objects (text fields, check boxes, Submit buttons, and so on) and making the forms function properly. This chapter focuses on the creation of form objects, not on the programming required to make forms transmit data to and from your server. Unfortunately, making the forms operational involves programming that goes beyond the scope of Dreamweaver 8 and this book. At first, forms might not sound like much fun, but they are at the heart of what makes the Web different from paper and publishing mediums of the past.

The Forms Group of the Insert Bar

The objects you use to create a form in Dreamweaver 8 are referred to as form objects. These include text fields, check boxes, buttons, and so on. You'll find all the form objects in the Forms group of the Insert bar.

The Forms group of the Insert bar is the easiest way to access many of the objects you will add to your forms. The following table outlines the different objects available in the Forms group:

	Form Objects	
Icon	**Name**	**Function**
	Form	Inserts a `<form>` tag into your document. If you do not place all of your objects inside the `<form>` tag, your form will not work properly.
	Text Field	Inserts a Text Field object on your form. The text field is the root of all forms. It lets a user type information into a field, such as his or her user name, email address, and street address.
	Hidden Field	Inserts a hidden text field. These fields are used to store information that does not need to be displayed but is necessary for processing the form on the server.
	Textarea	Inserts a multiple-line text field. These are useful for getting large amounts of feedback from users, such as comments on a site or book reviews.
	Checkbox	Inserts a Checkbox object on your form. Check boxes are used to make yes/no-type decisions, such as "Do you love Dreamweaver?"
	Radio Button	Inserts a Radio Button object on your form. Use radio buttons when you want users to select one item out of a list of available options.
	Radio Group	Inserts a group of Radio Button objects on your form, which is just a really fast way to insert multiple radio buttons at once.
	List/Menu	Inserts a List or Menu object on your form. These two objects allow you to make single (menu) or multiple (list) selections in a small area of space. You've probably seen these mostly for choosing the state you live in for shipping something from an online store.
	Jump Menu	Inserts a specially formatted list menu that uses JavaScript to allow the user to select an item from a list and then jump to the URL for that list menu entry.

continues on next page

Icon	Name	Function
	Image Field	Inserts an image on a form, which the user can click. You can use image fields to make graphic-based buttons to submit your form.
	File Field	Inserts a text box and button that lets the user browse to a file on his or her hard drive for uploading. This doesn't mean you can just insert a field and be able to upload though, you need specialized server-side code to handle file uploads, which isn't covered in this chapter.
	Button	Inserts a Button object on your form. A Submit button (or an image field) is required in order to actually do anything with a form. You can also make this a Reset button, which sets all of the form fields to their defaults, or you can set it to not do anything at all, and you can attach your own JavaScript events or behaviors to it.
	Label	Inserts a label into your form. Use labels to attach a text label to a form field to improve accessibility.
	Fieldset	Inserts a container tag for a logical group of form elements. This doesn't affect the functionality of the form itself, but it does allow you to make larger forms easier to read and work with.

TIP: | **Making Forms Function**

Dreamweaver 8 gives you complete control over the layout of your form and the creation of form objects, which is great, but the truth is that there is a bit more to creating forms than just a pretty interface.

Forms are interactive elements that are driven by "scripts." Therefore, when users click the Submit (or similar) button, the information from the form is processed. This processing isn't something XHTML was designed for. So, in order to process forms, you need to use some type of additional scripting beyond XHTML. Although it is possible to process form data through JavaScript or even Java, most Web developers agree the most foolproof way to program forms is through some server-side language, such as CGI, PHP, ASP, .NET, or ColdFusion.

If you have a Web site, chances are very good that your Internet service provider or Web administrator has existing server-side code you can use. Because there are so many variables to server-side programming, and it is outside the scope of this book, it will be up to you to coordinate obtaining the scripts and implementing the processing of your forms.

Here are some online resources:

HotScripts.com, http://www.hotscripts.com

The CGI Resource Index, http://www.cgi-resources.com/

Script Search, http://www.scriptsearch.com/

1 | Working with Text Fields and Textareas

In this exercise, you will get hands-on experience with each of the various form elements. You won't be adding any server-side scripts because doing that would require another book, but you will get everything set up so that when you do want to add some server-side functionality your pages will be ready!

1 Copy the **chap_13** folder from the **HOT CD-ROM** to your **Desktop**. Define your site as **Chapter 13** using the **chap_13** folder as the local root folder. Make sure the **Files** panel is open. If it's not, choose **Window > Files** or press **F11**.

2 In the **Files** panel, double-click **contactus.htm** to open it.

This is the Teacloud contact page, for which you're going to create the contact form.

3 If it's not already selected, choose the **Forms** group in the **Insert** bar.

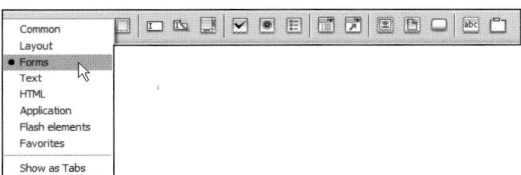

4 Place your cursor in the blank space below **Tell us all about you** and click the **Form** icon in the **Insert** bar.

Before you start working with a form, you need a **<form>** tag. All form elements must be contained inside a **<form>** tag in order for them to work properly with a server of any sort. The only time you don't need a **<form>** tag is if you're using the form elements for display purposes only and won't actually be collecting information from your users.

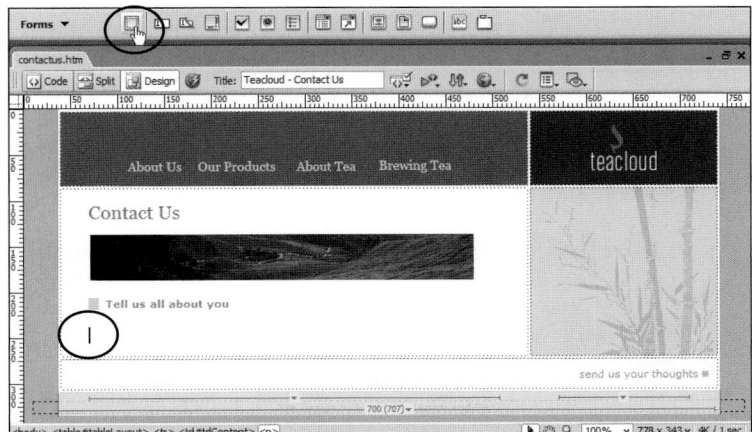

5 Your cursor is automatically placed inside the **<form>** tag for you. In order to organize the form, you're going to put all of your form elements in a table. Choose **Insert > Table** to open the **Table** dialog box.

6 In the **Table** dialog box, match the settings to the illustration shown here to create a table with 10 rows and 2 columns and no headers. Click **OK**.

You may not use all of the rows, you may need more, but 10 seems like a good round number to start.

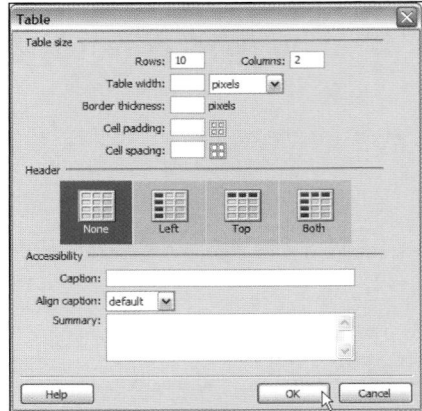

7 Place your cursor in the upper-right table cell and click the **Text Field** button in the **Insert** bar.

---

8 In the **Input Tag Accessibility Attributes** dialog box, type **Name:** in the **Label** field and select **Attach label tag using 'for' attribute** in the **Style** section. Leave everything else at its default and click **OK** to insert the text field.

Notice a new text field has been added to the table, along with its associated label.

NOTE:

The Importance of Labels

Labels allow you to attach a text description to a specific form field. This may not seem like a big deal at first, but labels allow browsers to determine what text description goes with what form field. Labels make it possible for screen readers and other assistive devices to tell a user that the text field in the upper-right corner is indeed intended to be the customer's name.

Labels do a little more than actually describe the form fields; they give users a larger target to hit to interact with a form field. Clicking the label for a text field places the user's cursor in the matching text field. Clicking the label for a check box will actually select and deselect the box, meaning that my grandmother doesn't have to try and aim for that tiny check box to get her bingo newsletter.

Attaching a label with a **for** attribute lets you put a label anywhere on the page and associate it with a specific form element. So the following code associates the label **Name:** with the text field with the same **ID**:

```
<label for="textfield">Name: </label>
<input type="text" name="textfield" id="textfield" />
```

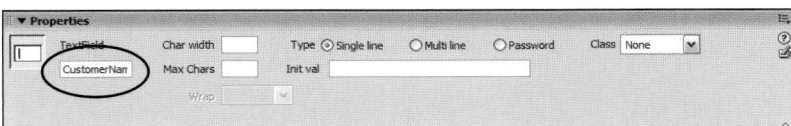

9 Every form field on your page must have a name by which it's going to be referenced. Click the text field in **Design** view, and in the **Property Inspector** set the name field to **CustomerName**.

10 Unfortunately, when you change a form element's name, it doesn't change the associated label's **for** attribute. Click inside the label field next to the form element and press **Ctrl+T** (Windows) or **Cmd+T** (Mac) twice to open the **Quick Tag Editor** in **Edit Tag** mode. The contents of the **for** attribute will already be selected, so just type **CustomerName** between the quotation marks and press **Enter** (Windows) or **Return** (Mac) to commit the changes.

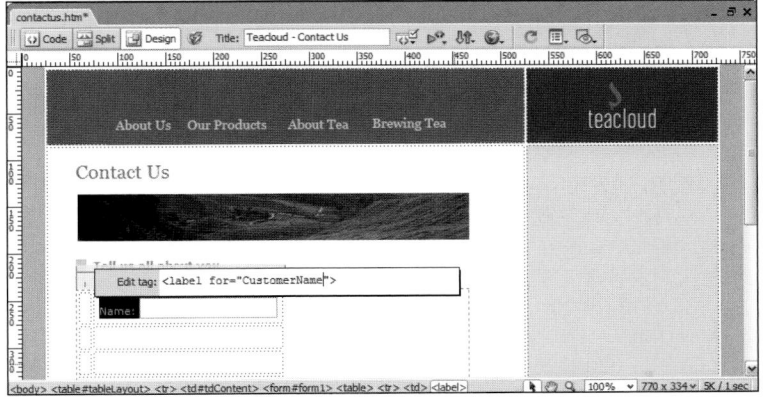

When you change the **for** attribute of the **<label>** tag, make sure that you use the exact same capitalization as the name of the form element. If anything is incorrect, the label won't work.

WARNING:

Form Items Renamed

Generally speaking, Dreamweaver 8 rewrites code for you when you need it to, and leaves it alone when you don't. Unfortunately, when you work with form elements, the default behavior of Dreamweaver 8 is to rename form elements (and their labels) when you copy, cut, paste, or drag and drop the fields. This can be extremely irritating when you start working with labels and form elements and begin to rearrange your forms. You will oftentimes end up with form elements getting renamed when you didn't want them to, and you won't realize it until your client tells you things aren't working properly.

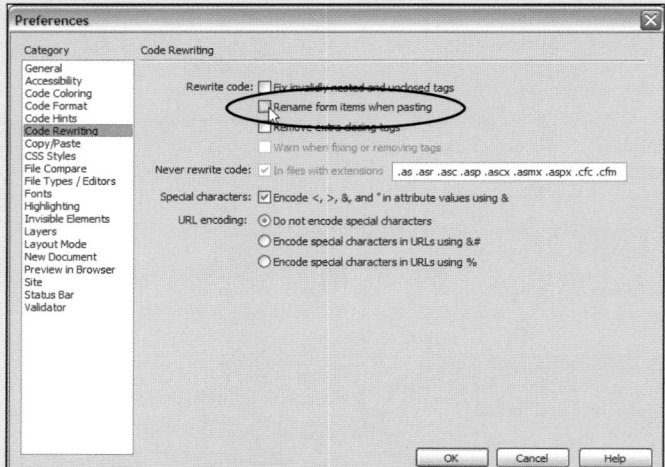

In order to get rid of this annoying behavior, choose **Edit > Preferences** (Windows) or **Dreamweaver > Preferences** (Mac) and select the **Code Rewriting** category. Deselect **Rename form items when pasting** and click **OK**. This is always the first option that we disable when installing Dreamweaver.

11 If you haven't already, be sure to read the previous warning and change your preferences so the form items are not renamed. After making the change to the `<label>` tag, the entire tag is selected in **Design** view. Click and drag the highlighted field from the right column to the left column.

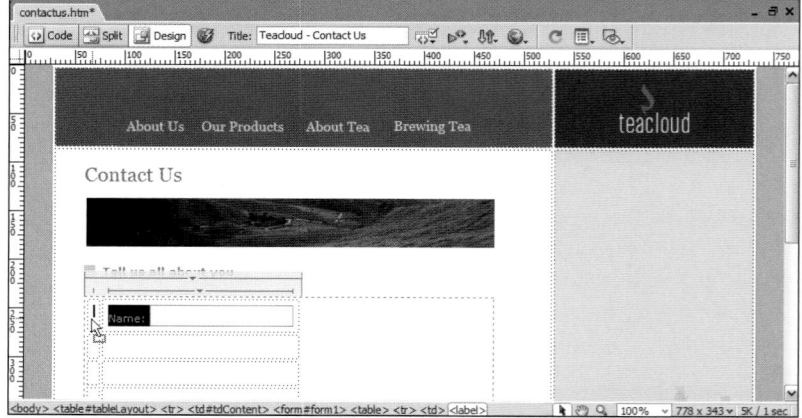

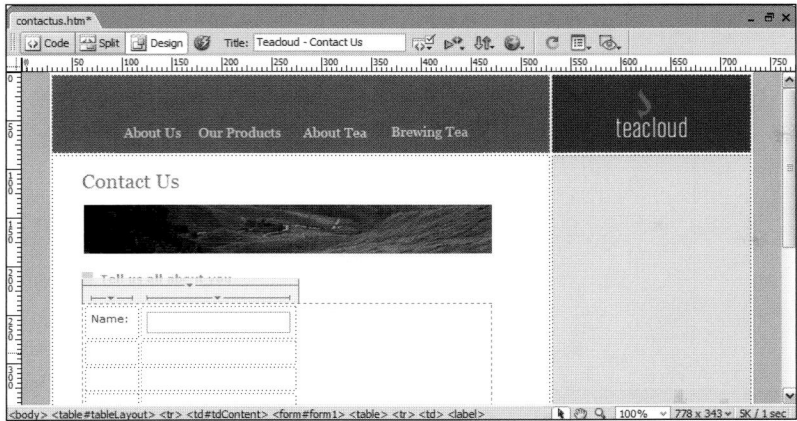

Your page should now look like the illustration here. The label is now in the left column and the text field is on the right. Because you used a **for** attribute for the label instead of wrapping the **<label>** tag around the form element, the *Name* text is still associated with the text field, even though it's in a separate table cell. You'll be setting up the majority of your form elements this way in order to make the form elements line up nicely on top of each other.

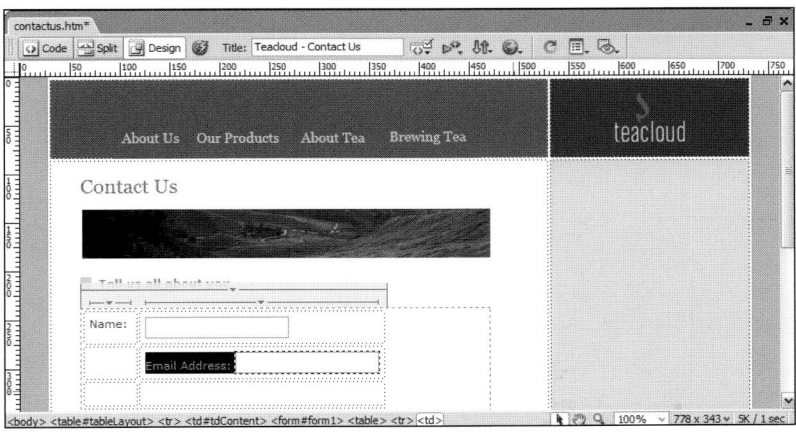

12 Place your cursor in the second row of the right column and click the **Text Field** button in the **Insert** bar. Type **Email Address:** in the label and leave everything else at its default and click **OK**.

13 Set the field name to **EmailAddress**.

14 Set the **for** attribute of the **Email Address:** label to **EmailAddress**.

15 Using the **Tag Selector**, select the **<label>** tag around **Email Address:**, then click and drag the label into the left column of the table.

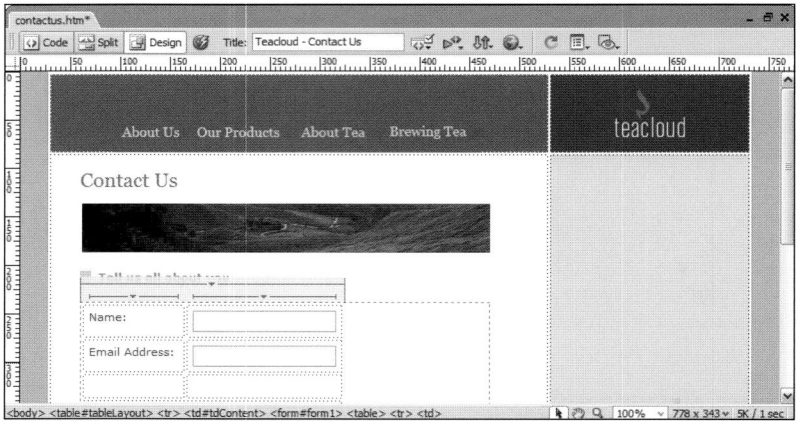

This is what your page will look like after the first two form fields are in place.

16 Place your cursor in the third row of the right column and click the **Textarea** button in the **Insert** bar.

17 Type **Comments:** into the **Label** field of the **Input Tag Accessibility Attributes** dialog box and click **OK** to insert the **<textarea>** tag.

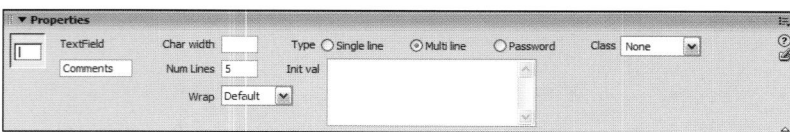

18 Select the textarea in **Design** view, and in the **Property Inspector** set the name field to **Comments** and type **5** in the **Num Lines** field.

If you decide you want a standard text field instead of a textarea, you can simply change the **Type** to **Single line** and Dreamweaver 8 will convert the textarea to a text field for you. If you have a text field and you want it to be a textarea, select **Multi line** as the **Type**.

19 Change the **for** attribute of the textarea's label to **Comments** and move it to the left column using the techniques you learned in Steps 10 and 11.

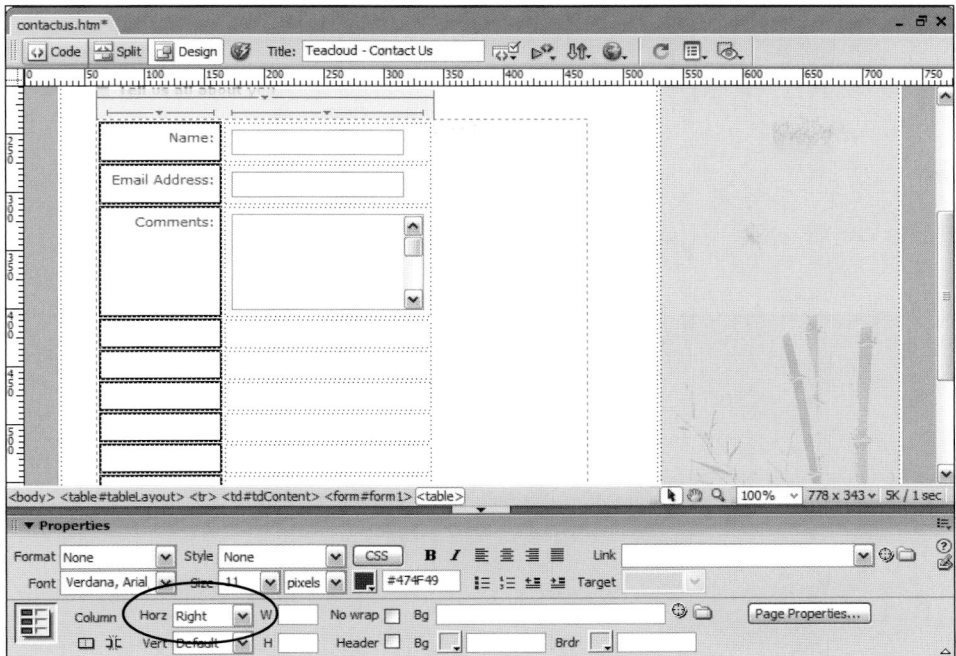

20 Select the left column and set the **Horz** pop-up menu in the **Property Inspector** to **Right** to make all of the labels line up nicely.

21 Save your changes and keep **contactus.htm** open for the next exercise.

In this exercise, you learned how to work with text fields and text areas, as well as how to make sure your form element's labels work correctly. In the next exercise, you'll learn how to work with check boxes and radio buttons.

2 | Working with Check Boxes and Radio Buttons

Check boxes and radio buttons allow users to make decisions in your form. Check boxes are used to make "yes and no" decisions, such as asking users if they'd like to sign up for a newsletter, or if they like the color red. Radio buttons allow users to select one item from a group of choices, such as choosing how they heard about your site, or if red, green, or blue is their favorite color. This exercise shows you how to work with checkboxes and radio buttons.

1 If you just completed Exercise 1, **contactus.htm** should still be open. If it's not, go back and complete Exercise 1.

2 Place your cursor in the fourth row of the right column (below the textarea) and click the **Checkbox** button in the **Insert** bar.

3 Type **Add me to the Teacloud newsletter** in the **Label** field of the **Input Tag Accessibility Attributes** dialog box and select **Wrap with label tag** for the **Style**. Click **OK** to insert the check box.

In this case, you can choose **Wrap with label tag** because the label is going to be listed after the check box, and not inside the left column. Notice that the **Position** is set to **After form item**.

4 Select the check box in **Design** view. In the **Property Inspector**, set the name to **Newsletter**, type **Yes** in the **Checked value** field, and leave the **Initial state** set to **Unchecked**.

Check boxes are submitted only if they are selected. If a check box is deselected, it doesn't have a value, so it's completely ignored. For that reason, the Checked value field should almost always be an affirmative response of some sort, such as Yes, True, or You Bet.

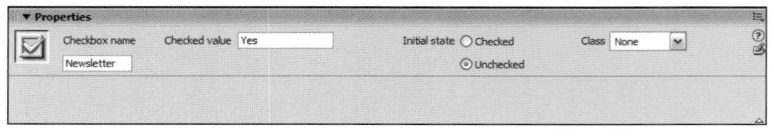

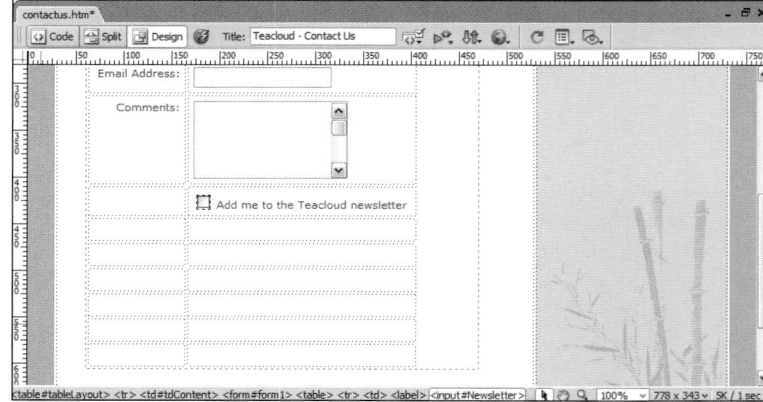

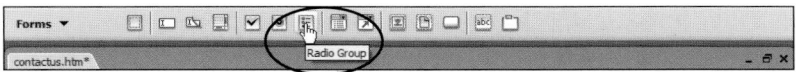

5 Place your cursor in the fifth row of the right column and click the **Radio Group** button in the **Insert** bar.

---

6 In the **Radio Group** dialog box, type **Referral** in the **Name** field.

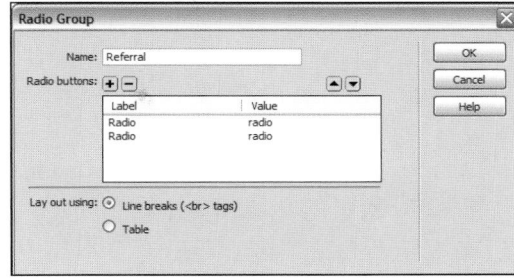

---

7 Click the first radio button **Label** and type **Newspaper Ad**. Type **Newspaper Ad** for the **Value** as well. Type **Friend** for the **Label** and **Value** for the second radio button. Click the **plus** (+) icon to add a new radio button to the list and type **Other** for both the **Label** and the **Value**. Leave the **Lay out using** option set to **Line breaks (
 tags)** and click **OK**.

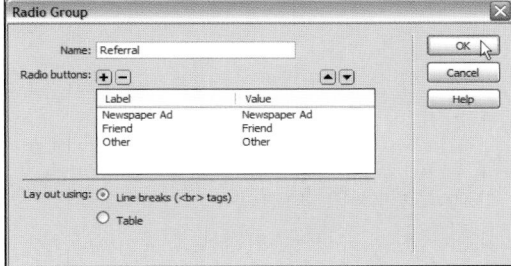

The value of a form field is what will actually be sent to the server when you submit a form. The label is what users will actually see in their browsers. In the examples in this chapter, the two are always the same. If you were working with dynamic data or some other form-processing script, this may not always be the case.

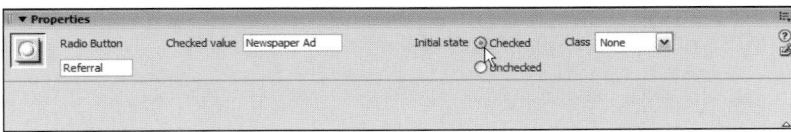

8 Select the first radio button in the group, **Newspaper Ad**. In the **Property Inspector**, select **Checked** as the **Initial state**.

It's always a good idea to select a default value for radio buttons to ensure that at least one of the options is selected. If an initial value is set in a radio group, it's impossible for the user to *not* select something from the group—an option will always be selected.

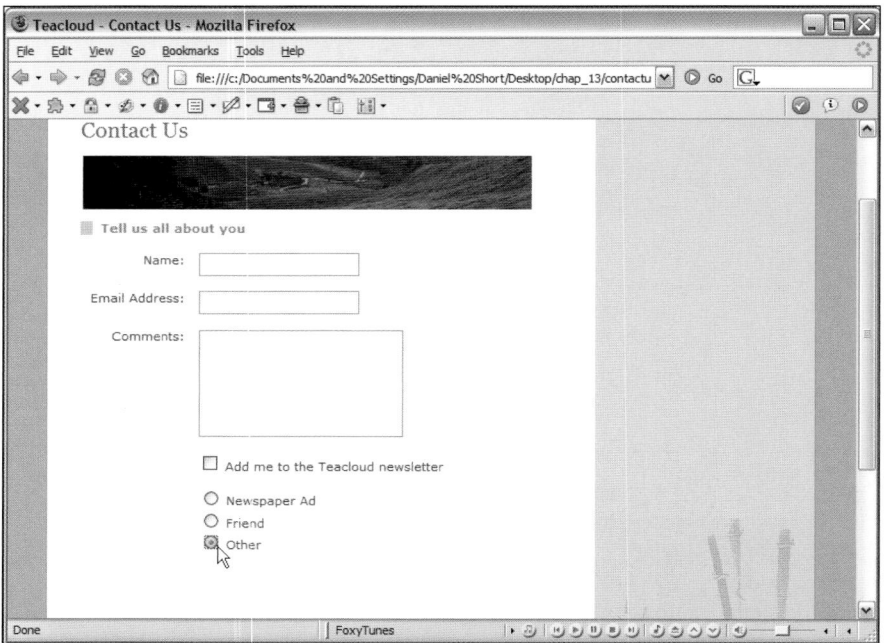

9 Press **F12** to preview the page in your browser. Click each of the radio button options to see how they behave in the browser.

---

10 When you're finished, return to Dreamweaver 8. Save your changes and keep **contactus.htm** open for the next exercise.

---

3 | Working with Lists and Menus

Lists and menus give you a compact way to offer users a large number of choices. These are most often used for letting a user select his or her state or country for mailing addresses. In this exercise, you'll learn how to use lists and menus to allow users to select their favorite type of tea and tell you which Teacloud shops they visit the most.

---

1 If you just completed Exercise 2, **contactus.htm** should still be open. If it's not, go back and complete Exercise 2.

2 Place your cursor in the table cell below the radio button group you inserted in the previous exercise. In the **Insert** bar, click the **List/Menu** button.

---

3 Type **Your favorite tea:** in the **Label** field of the **Input Tag Accessibility Attributes** dialog box and select **Attach label tag using 'for' attribute** for the **Style**. Click **OK**.

---

4 Click the menu (or **<select>** tag) in **Design** view. In the **Property Inspector**, type **FavoriteTea** for the name.

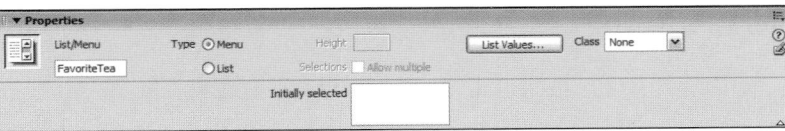

---

5 In the **Property Inspector**, click the **List Values** button to define the items in the menu. Click directly below the **Item Label** field and type **Black Tea**. Press **Tab** and type **Black Tea** in the **Value** field. Press **Tab** again to go to the next row and type **Green Tea** for the next **Item Label** and **Value**. Finally, press **Tab** again and enter **Oolong Tea** for the third **Item Label** and **Value**. Click **OK** to add the items to the list.

6 Change the **for** attribute of the label to **FavoriteTea** and move it into the left column using the techniques you learned in Steps 10 and 11 of Exercise 1.

Your page should now look like this illustration after inserting the menu.

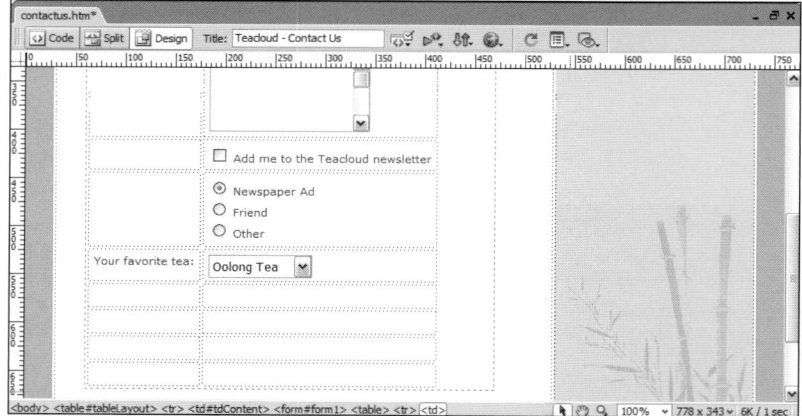

TIP: | **Setting the Initial Value of a List**
When a user views your page in a browser, the first item in the menu will be selected by default. You can change the default selection by simply choosing a different item in the **Initially selected** pop-up menu in the **Property Inspector**.

---

7 Place your cursor in the table cell below the menu you inserted and click the **List/Menu** button in the **Insert** bar again.

---

8 Set the **Label** to **Select your favorite stores:** and make sure the **Style** is still set to **Attach label tag using 'for' attribute** in the **Input Tag Accessibility Attributes** dialog box.

---

9 Select the menu and set the name to **FavoriteStores**. Set the **Type** in the **Property Inspector** to **List**. Type **5** in the **Height** field and select the **Allow multiple** check box.

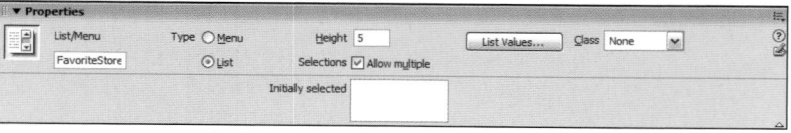

Setting the Type of the menu to List lets the menu show more than one item at a time. You can then specify the height to determine *how many* items are displayed at once. If you check the **Allow multiple** check box, users can select multiple items by holding down the Ctrl key and clicking multiple items in the list. It's normally a good idea to put instructions on how to select multiple items in your form, because users might not know it's even possible.

---

10 In the **Property Inspector**, click the **List Values** button to open the **List Values** dialog box. Add the following store locations to the list:

Anaheim
Beverly Hills
Brea
Ojai
Pasadena
Pomona
Venice

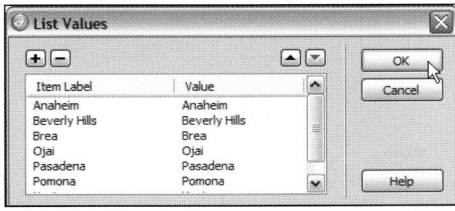

Set the **Label** and **Value** to the same values for each store location, and then click **OK**.

---

11 Set the **for** attribute of the label to **FavoriteStores** and move the label to the left column using the techniques you learned in Steps 10 and 11 of Exercise 1.

---

12 Place your cursor directly after the list and press **Shift+Enter** (Windows) or **Ctrl+Return** (Mac) to insert a line break. Type **Hold down the Ctrl and click to select multiple stores.**

Your page should now match the illustration shown here.

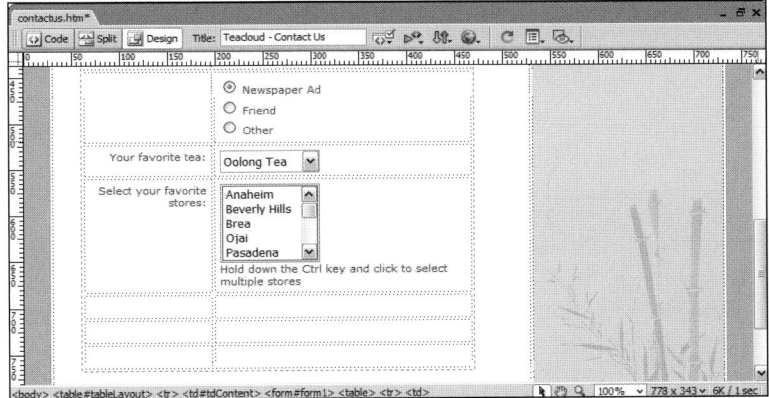

---

13 Press **F12** to preview the page in your browser and experiment with the multiple-select menus.

---

14 When you're finished, return to Dreamweaver 8. Save your changes and keep **contactus.htm** open for the next exercise.

VIDEO: | **jumpmenus.mov**

Want to learn how to create some fancy navigation using list menus? To learn more about how to insert and manipulate jump menus, check out **jumpmenus.mov** in the **videos** folder of the **HOT CD-ROM**.

4 | Submitting Form Results

A form is ultimately useless if you don't send the data anywhere. To get your form to actually do anything useful, you'll need to add a Submit button and have the user actually submit the data to you. This exercise walks you through adding a Submit button to your form and explains how you specify which page the form will submit to and how it will send the data.

1 If you just completed Exercise 3, **contactus.htm** should still be open. If it's not, go back and complete Exercise 3.

2 Place your cursor in the table cell below the favorite stores list menu and click the **Button** button in the **Insert** bar to open the **Input Tag Accessibility Attributes** dialog box.

As a general rule, you don't need to specify a label for a button, because the button displays its value on the button itself.

3 Click **Cancel** to close the **Input Tag Accessibility Attributes** dialog box.

The button has now been added to the page without a label tag. Only the actual Submit button has been added to the document. All buttons that actually submit the form are added with the default Submit text.

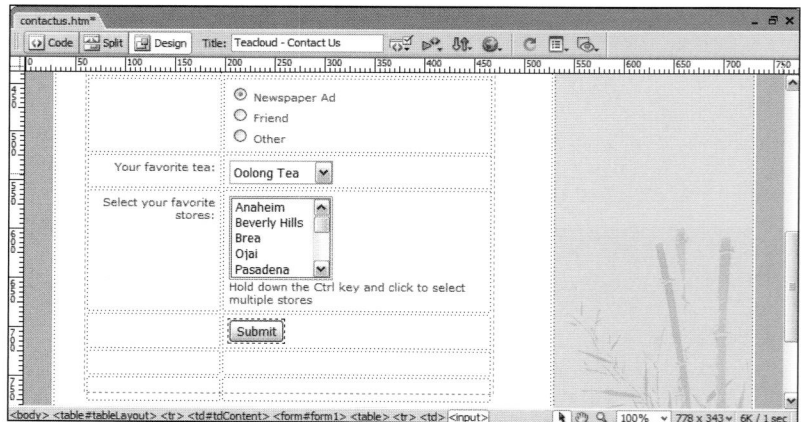

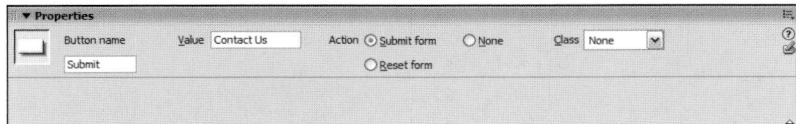

4 With the button selected, type **Contact Us** in the **Value** field in the **Property Inspector**.

There are three actions for a button: Submit, Reset, or None. A Submit button actually submits the results of a form to the page specified in the **<form>** tag (more on that next). A Reset button sets all of the fields in the form to their default values. This is useful for very long forms when a user might want to start from scratch. Finally, a button with an action of None doesn't do anything by default. You can click it all day and it won't do anything, unless you attach a JavaScript event to perform some action.

5 Press **F12** to preview the page in your browser. Click the **Contact Us** button.

Because there is no action set for the **<form>** tag in the document, nothing happens with the form's information when you submit the form.

6 In the **Tag Selector**, select the **<form#form1>** tag and look at the **Property Inspector**. The following table describes the options available for the **<form>** tag.

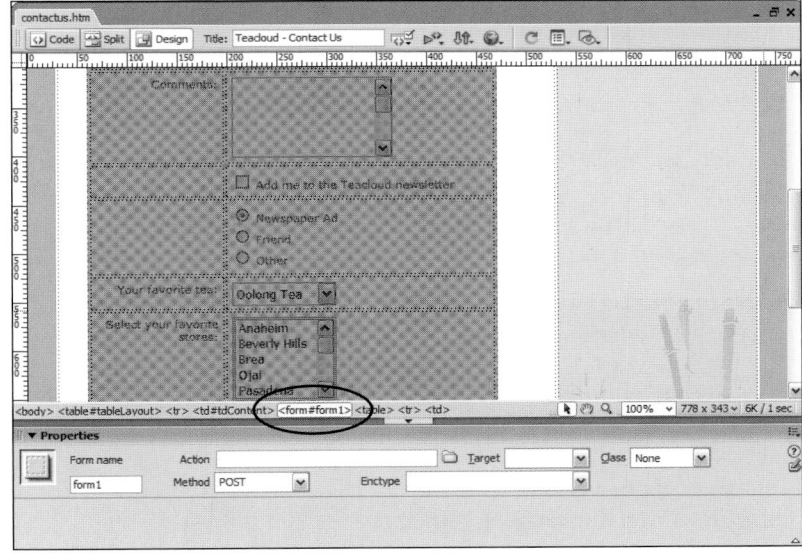

Form Tag Attributes	
Attribute	**Description**
Action	The `action` of a form is the name of the page that will receive the form information. This is almost always a dynamic page of some sort (ASP, PHP, ColdFusion, and so on). This can also be a `mailto` command, which you'll learn about in the following sidebar.
Target	The `target` of a form is used when working with frames. The target specifies which frame in a frameset will receive the form information.
Method	The `method` of a form determines how information is sent to the action page. If you choose `POST`, the form information is sent as an actual form post to the server, and none of the form information will be visible in the browser. If you choose `GET`, each form element on the page will be added to the URL in the browser as a name/value pair.
Enctype	The `enctype` of a form determines the encoding that will be used to send the information to the browser. Ninety-nine percent of the time you don't need to specify an encoding type, but if you're dealing with file uploads or `mailto` actions, you'll need to tell the browser how to submit the form information.
Class	Assigns a CSS class to the `<form>` tag.

7 Click and drag to highlight the last two empty rows of the table and press **Delete** to remove them.

---

8 Close **contactus.htm**. You don't need to save your changes.

VIDEO:  | **formstyling.mov**

You've just finished building a fairly simple contact form. Unfortunately, it's rather bland and could use some styling to make it a bit easier on the eyes. To learn more about form styling, including how to use CSS to style forms, check out **formstyling.mov** in the **videos** folder of the **HOT CD-ROM**.

NOTE: | **Form Elements in Safari**

The Safari browser on Macintosh computers doesn't allow form elements to be styled. Safari uses the OS X built-in "Aqua" form fields and buttons for all of its form elements, and there's no way to override their appearance. So if you depend on a certain style for a form element in order to gain users' attention, just remember that if they're on Safari they won't see your styling, and you need to provide some alternative form of feedback in addition to form styling.

Sending Form Results Through Email

Your form information isn't going to do you much good if you can't actually get the information. One way around complex server-side programming is to send the results through email. However, there are too many pitfalls to make email an acceptable solution. You can set the action of the **<form>** tag to **mailto:you@yoursite.com**, which lets the user send the form data through their own email client, but the problems with this method include the following:

- Not everyone has a default email client installed. (Many people use Web-based email accounts, such as Yahoo, Hotmail, or Gmail.)

- Even if they do have an email client installed, not all have one that supports a **mailto** form.

- If users do have an email client that supports a **mailto** form, it's very easy for them to just not send the e-mail at all, or for a malicious user to alter the form information before they send. They can also see any hidden form elements that weren't intended for their viewing.

- Many browsers and email clients will prompt the user with a security dialog box before they will allow the email to be created, which can scare many users away.

So what are you to do? First, check with your host to see if they have any server-side scripts that will send form results for you. Many hosts will already have a form-handling script set up and ready to go. If they don't, several sites will handle sending form information for you. Two of the most popular are **http://www.response-o-matic.com** and **http://www.formmail.com**. These sites accept a form post directly from your site and then email you the results. You can find more services of this sort at **http://hotscripts.com/Remotely_Hosted/Form_Processors/index.html**.

In this chapter, you learned how to work with each of the different types of form elements: input fields, textarea, select lists, radio buttons, and check boxes. As you begin developing more complicated sites, forms will become increasingly important, and you'll spend a large amount of development time getting those forms just right. Formatting and working with forms is a skill no Web designer can do without. In the next chapter, you'll learn how to use behaviors to add interactivity to your sites (including how to validate forms).

14

Behaviors

Dreamweaver 8 uses the term *behaviors* to describe its prebuilt scripts, written in JavaScript, that extend XHTML to do things it can't do on its own. Dreamweaver 8 ships with various behaviors that allow you to do all kinds of cool things, such as open a browser in a smaller window or detect the version of a user's browser.

The Macromedia Extension Manager lets you easily install and remove additional behaviors (in the form of extensions) from Dreamweaver 8. In early versions of Dreamweaver, you had to download and install the Extension Manager application yourself. In Dreamweaver 8, the Extension Manager is pre-installed and ready for use.

This chapter shows you how to use some of the behaviors that ship with Dreamweaver 8 right out of the box. You'll also learn how to download additional behaviors from the free online service Macromedia Exchange, which houses hundreds of additional Dreamweaver 8 third-party extensions.

1 | Using the Open Browser Window Behavior

Times arise when you just can't cram everything onto a single Web page. As a result, many Web developers choose to open additional, yet related, information in another window. In this exercise, you'll open a new browser window to display larger images of the Teacloud teapots that simply didn't fit well into the main products page.

---

1 Copy the **chap_14** folder from the **HOT CD-ROM** to your **Desktop**. Define your site as **Chapter 14** using the **chap_14** folder as the local root folder. Make sure the **Files** panel is open. If it's not, choose **Window > Files** or press **F11**.

---

2 In the **Files** panel, double-click **kettlesandteapots.htm** in the **ourproducts** folder to open it.

This page has some nice images, but they're simply not big enough. The page itself doesn't have room for the larger images of the teapots, so you're going to open a pop-up window with the larger image of each teapot.

---

3 Click to select the first teapot on the page, the **Teacloud Azul** teapot. If it's not already open, choose **Window > Behaviors** to open the **Behaviors** panel.

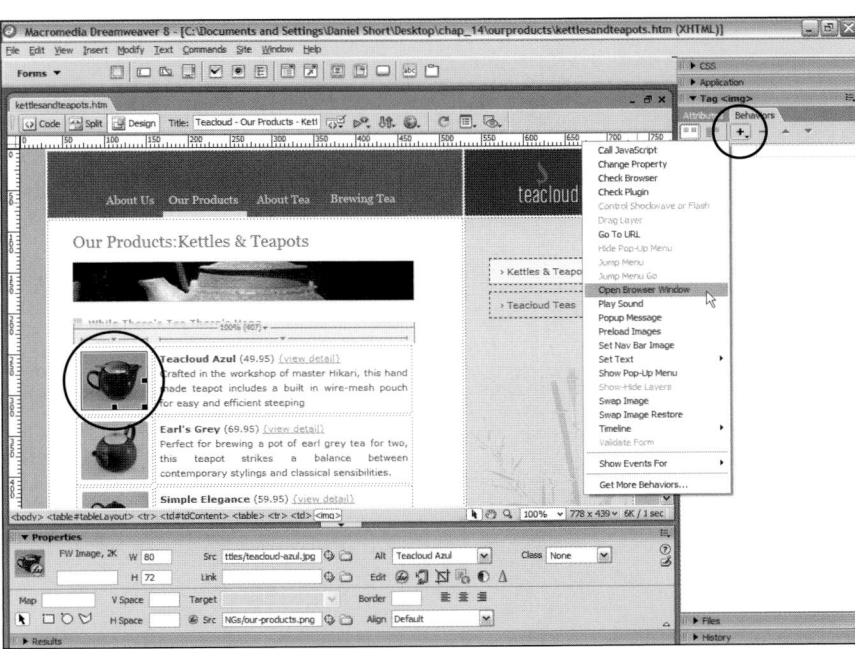

4 In the **Behaviors** panel, click the **plus** (+) button and choose **Open Browser Window** from the pop-up menu to open the **Open Browser Window** dialog box.

---

5 In the **Open Browser Window** dialog box, click **Browse** and select **kettlesandteapots/azul.htm** in the **ourproducts** folder. Type **530** in the **Window width** field and type **350** in the **Window height** field. Select the **Status bar** option and type **teacloudazul** in the **Window name** field. Click **OK**.

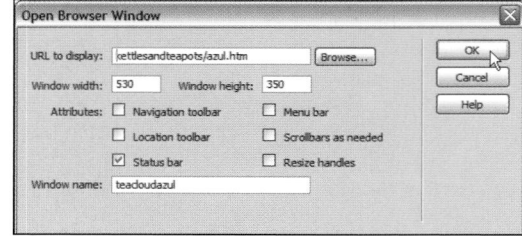

After you click OK, the behavior is automatically applied to the `onclick` attribute of the `<img>` tag, which indicates the pop-up window will open when a user clicks the image.

NOTE:

Open Browser Window Options

The Open Browser Window dialog box contains a number of options you need to understand. The window width and height sets the size of the browser window you want to open. The attribute options affect how the window is created. You can specify whether you want the user to be able to resize the window (resize handles) or if you want a scroll bar in the pop-up, if required to view all the content. The other attributes refer to different pieces of the browser chrome (the elements that actually make up the Web browser), such as the address bar and the Forward and Back buttons. None of the attributes are counted as part of the window width and height, so a window with a height of 350 pixels will actually be taller if you choose to display a status bar, navigation toolbar, location toolbar, or menu bar.

The window name actually provides a JavaScript reference (similar to an ID) in order to manipulate the pop-up window. If you create 10 different pop-up windows and give them all the same name, they would all open using the same window, instead of each opening its own independent window. If you want each pop-up window to open in a separate window, make sure you give each window a unique name.

6 In the **Behaviors** panel, choose **<A> onClick** from the **Event** pop-up menu.

In order to ensure the behavior works in older browsers, and to make sure the hand pointer shows up when a user moves his or her mouse over the image, you need to change the event in the Behaviors panel to **<A> onClick**.

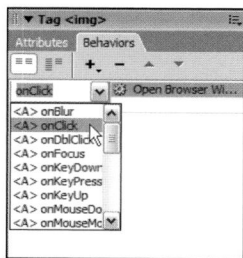

7 Press **F12** to preview the page in a browser. Click the **Teacloud Azul** image to open the pop-up window you just defined.

Notice the pop-up menu has a status bar at the bottom, which reflects the choice you made in the Open Browser Window dialog box, and the dimensions match the ones you specified.

8 Return to Dreamweaver 8. Click to select the **Earl's Grey** image. In the **Behaviors** panel, click the **plus** (+) button and choose **Open Browser Window** from the pop-up menu to open the **Open Browser Window** dialog box.

9 In the **Open Browser Window** dialog box, click **Browse** and select **kettlesandteapots/earlsgrey.htm** in the **ourproducts** folder. Match the **Window width**, **Window height**, and **Attributes** options to the ones shown in the illustration here. These settings are the same as you specified in Step 5. Type **earlsgrey** in the **Window name** field. Click **OK**.

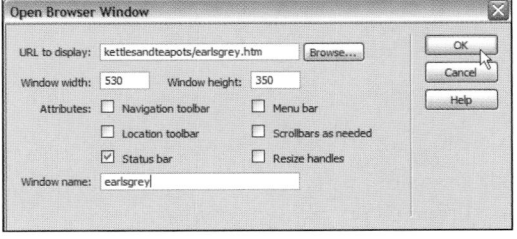

When you create multiple pop-up windows from the same page with similar content, you want to use the same dimensions and attributes so users have a consistent experience. Having pop-up menus with varying sizes and appearances can be frustrating for users viewing the content.

10 In the **Behaviors** panel, choose **<A> onClick** from the **Event** pop-up menu.

11 Repeat Steps 8, 9, and 10 to create a pop-up window for the **Simple Elegance** image. Set the URL to **kettlesandteapots/simpleelegance.htm** and name the window **simpleelegance**.

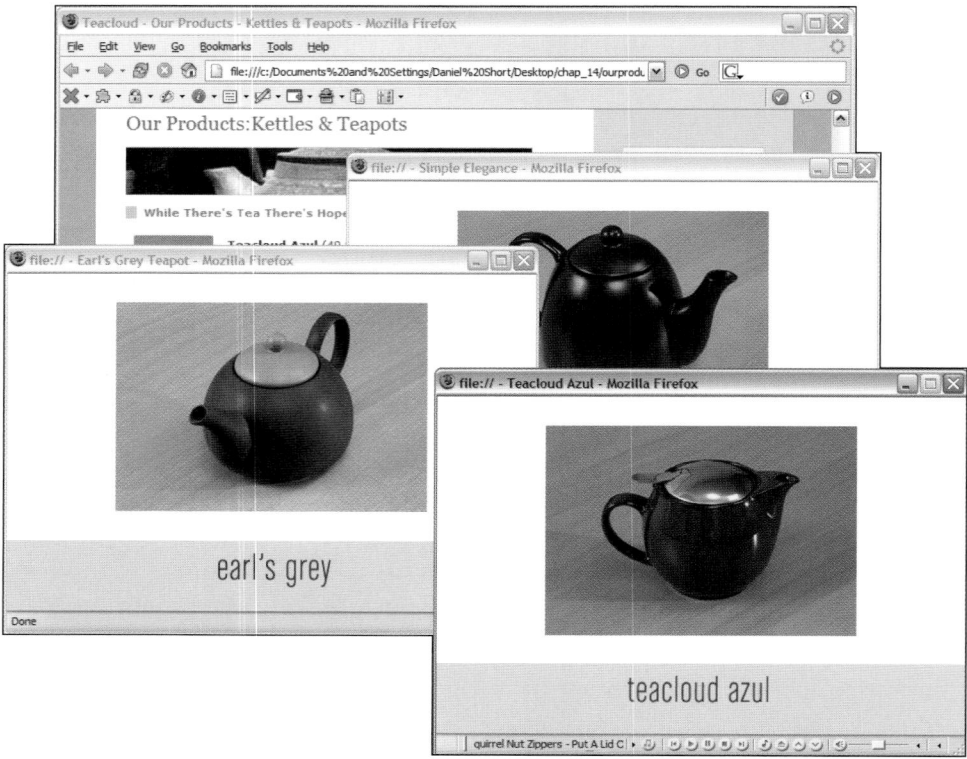

12 Press **F12** to preview the page in a browser. Click each of the images to open the pop-up windows displaying the larger images.

Notice that each image opens in its own pop-up window. As you can see, using a behavior in Dreamweaver 8 made it really easy to create this functionality.

---

13 Save your changes and close **kettlesandteapots.htm**.

VIDEO: | **foolproofpopups.mov**

One problem with pop-up windows is that they're completely unusable if a user has JavaScript disabled and search engines can't follow the links Dreamweaver 8 creates for the pop-ups. To learn how to make pop-up links search engine–friendly and to ensure they work if users have JavaScript disabled, check out **foolproofpopups.mov** in the **videos** folder of the **HOT CD-ROM**.

2 | Using the Change Property Behavior

If you recall, way back in Chapter 11, *"Rollovers,"* you learned how to create a disjointed rollover so you could display text on the home page when a user moved his or her mouse over one of the navigation buttons. In this exercise, you'll learn how to get the same result without using any additional images by using the Change Property behavior to change the contents of a **<div>** tag on the page. The Change Property behavior lets you manipulate nearly every property of an element on the page; in this case you'll be editing the content of the **<div>** to change the text it displays. All of the text styling has already been taken care of for you with CSS rules already defined in the page.

---

1 In the **Files** panel, double-click **index.htm** to open it.

You're going to create the same effect you did in Chapter 11 without using images. So, the first thing you need to do is create a container for the hint text you're going to display.

---

2 Choose **Insert > Layout Objects > Div Tag** to open the **Insert Div Tag** dialog box.

You'll need to create a **<div>** directly after the start of the content table cell, which you'll do next.

---

3 In the **Insert Div Tag** dialog box, choose **After start of tag <td id="tdContent">** from the **Insert** pop-up menus. Type **divHints** in the **ID** field and click **OK**.

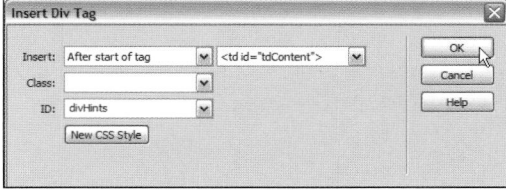

You should now have a **<div>** with placeholder text before the Welcome to teacloud image.

4 Delete the placeholder text and press **Ctrl+Shift+spacebar** (Windows) or **Cmd+Shift+spacebar** (Mac) to insert a nonbreaking space into the **<div>**.

In this case, you need to have some text (even if it's a nonbreaking space) inside the **<div>** so it doesn't collapse. If the **<div>** doesn't contain any text, it will collapse to 1 pixel tall. Then, if you change the text inside the **<div>**, it will expand to fit the text, and the Welcome to teacloud image would shift on the page.

5 Select the **About Us** image in the navigation bar and press **Ctrl+[** (Windows) or **Cmd+[** (Mac) to select the parent tag, which is the **<a>** tag. In the **Behaviors** panel, click the **plus** (+) button and choose **Change Property** from the pop-up menu to open the **Change Property** dialog box.

You need to ensure the **<a>** tag is selected, not the image, so you apply the behavior to the proper element.

6 In the **Change Property** dialog box, choose **DIV** from the **Type of object** pop-up menu. All **<div>** objects with an ID will then be displayed in the **Named object** pop-up menu. Choose **div "divHints"** from the **Named object** pop-up menu.

The Change Property dialog box lets you change any property of any ID'd element on your page.

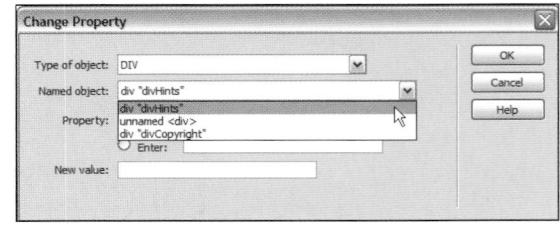

7 Choose **innerHTML** from the **Property** pop-up menu.

The innerHTML property contains all of the XHTML inside the object being manipulated. Changing the innerHTML property will change the XHTML inside divHints.

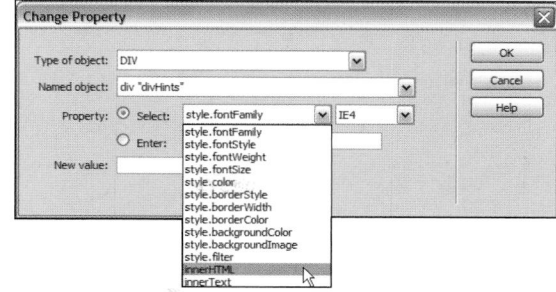

8 Type **Find out more about the Teacloud philosophy** in the **New value** field and click **OK**.

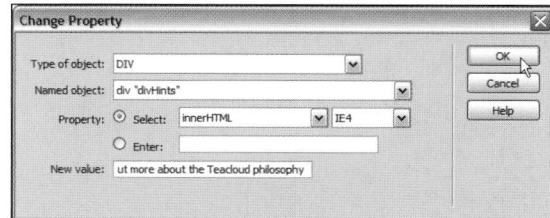

9 In the **Behaviors** panel, click **Change Property** to select it. Choose **onMouseOver** from the **Event** pop-up menu to change the behavior from **onClick** to **onMouseOver**.

Using the onMouseOver event will cause the behavior to fire when the user moves his or her mouse over the image.

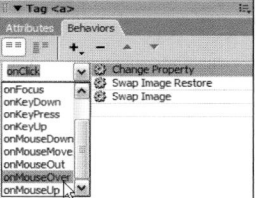

10 Press **F12** to preview the page in a browser. Move your mouse over the **About Us** navigation button to change the text and then move your mouse off of the button.

You defined a behavior to change the contents of divHints when you move your mouse over the button, but you didn't define an event to change it back once you move your mouse off of the button. You'll define this behavior next.

11 Return to Dreamweaver 8 and make sure the **<a>** tag for the **About Us** navigation button is still selected. Click the **plus (+)** button in the **Behaviors** panel and choose **Change Property** from the pop-up menu to open the **Change Property** dialog box.

12 Choose **div "divHints"** from the **Named object** pop-up menu, select **innerHTML** in the **Property** pop-up menu, and type ** ** in the **New value** field. Click **OK**.

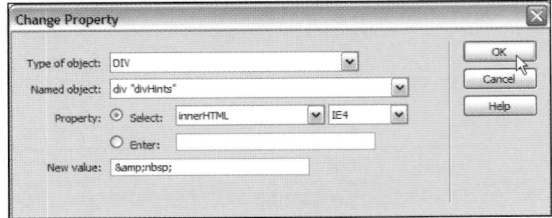

In order to make divHints appear blank and to prevent the content on the page from moving around, you need to set its innerHTML back to a nonbreaking space. The Change Property code requires the content be encoded, which is why you entered   instead of just .

13 In the **Behaviors** panel, click **Change Property** to select it and choose **onMouseOut** from the **Event** pop-up menu.

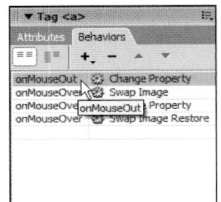

14 Press **F12** to preview the page in a browser. Move your mouse over the **About Us** navigation button and then move the mouse off.

Now the disjointed rollover is working as intended—the text appears when you position your mouse over the navigation button and disappears when you move your mouse away from the navigation button.

15 Close **index.htm**. You don't need to save your changes.

3 | Using the Validate Form Behavior

In the last chapter, you learned all about creating forms. In this exercise, you'll learn how to validate the information users type into the form. Giving users a place to enter information doesn't guarantee they will enter the information correctly. It also doesn't guarantee they will enter any information at all. Using the behaviors in Dreamweaver 8, you can validate, or verify, the type and format of the information users provided before it ever gets into your inbox.

---

1 In the **Files** panel, double-click **contactus.htm** to open it.

This file contains the form you created in Chapter 13, *"Forms."* You're going to be adding validation to the contact form.

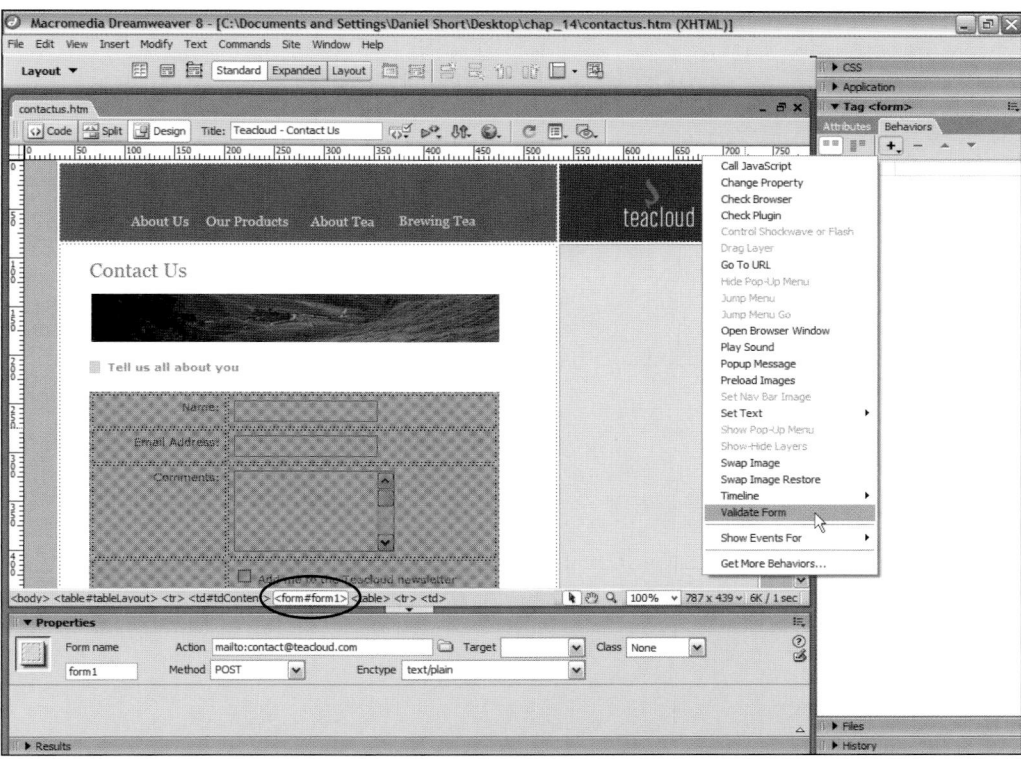

2 Click anywhere inside the table and choose the **<form>** tag from the **Tag Selector**. In the **Behaviors** panel, click the **plus** (+) button and choose **Validate Form** from the pop-up menu to open the **Validate Form** dialog box.

The Validate Form dialog box displays all of the text fields and textareas in your form. You can select each form element and specify whether the field is required and what type of data the field can accept.

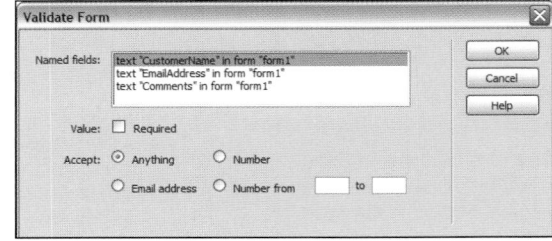

3 Select the **CustomerName** field and select the **Required** option to make it mandatory for users to enter their names.

Notice that Dreamweaver 8 adds *(R)* after the field to indicate that the field is required. The items in parentheses after each field give you a visual cue of what each field requires.

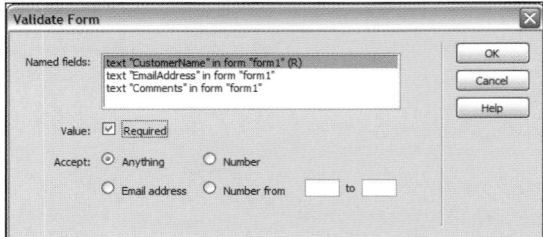

4 Select the **EmailAddress** field, select the **Required** option, and select **Email address** in the **Accept** section.

The email address validation ensures that the user actually enters a properly formatted email address, including the "@" sign and the top-level domain name (.com, .net, and so on).

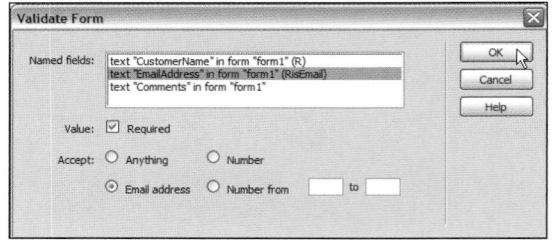

5 Click **OK** to apply the behavior to the **<form>**.

The Validate Form behavior is added to the onSubmit event of the form tag. Regardless of how users submit the form (clicking a button, pressing Enter while in a form field, or submitting the form through a JavaScript function), the validation will be automatically processed.

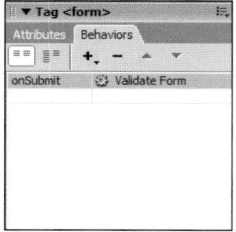

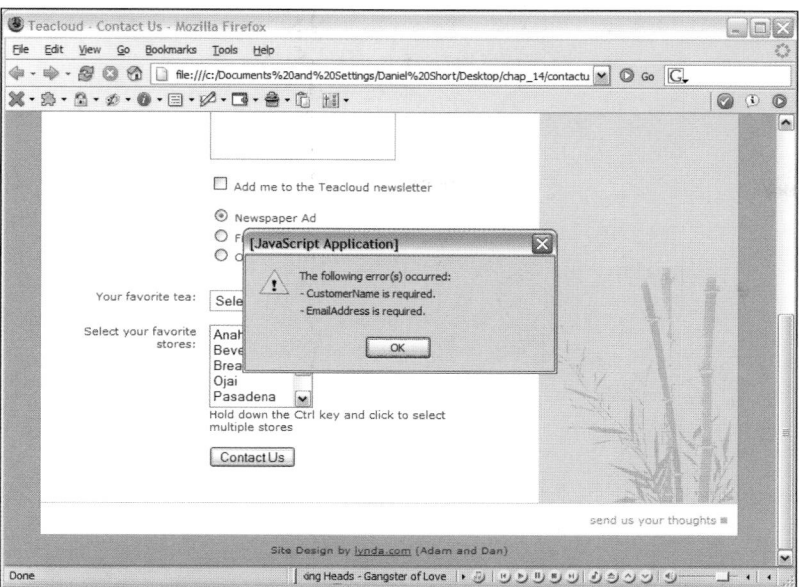

6 Press **F12** to preview the page in a browser. Leave all of the fields blank then scroll to the bottom of the page and click the **Contact Us** button.

Notice an error message appears, indicating the fields that were not filled in correctly. Each of the fields is validated individually, and then the error message lists the errors. As a result, users cannot submit the form until they fill in the information appropriately.

TIP: | **Never Trust Strangers**

The advice your mother gave you as a child still applies today. Never trust a user filling out a form on your site. Your users aren't necessarily computer-competent individuals, and they may misuse your form, or they could be even worse and be looking for holes in the security of your site. For this reason, you should *always* validate any input that makes it to your server. This includes doing client-side validation (through JavaScript) on any pages containing forms.

Unfortunately, the Validate Form behavior is simply inadequate to get the job done. There are far better form validation behaviors out there. The one we use most often is Yaromat's Check Form behavior, which you can find at **http://www.yaromat.com/dw/?t=Behavior&r=forms**.

The Check Form behavior offers far more flexibility and gives you control over check boxes, radio buttons, and lists, as well as the standard text fields.

---

7 Close **contactus.htm**. You don't need to save your changes.

Getting More Behaviors

It is possible to create behaviors that are far more complicated than the ones this chapter describes, such as behaviors that script complex interactions between Dreamweaver 8 and Fireworks 8. However, creating this type of command requires very strong JavaScript skills, which are way beyond the scope of this book.

The good news is that the JavaScript gurus who can create more complicated Dreamweaver extensions often distribute these from their own sites. There is actually a sizable third-party market for Dreamweaver 8 extensions. Read on for information on the Macromedia Dreamweaver Exchange and a couple of the third-party sites we've found most useful. Make sure you also check out Appendix B, *"Dreamweaver 8 Resources,"* for a listing of these sites, and Appendix C, *"Installing Extensions,"* for information on how to install new extensions into Dreamweaver. In addition, you can choose **Help > Dreamweaver Exchange** to access Dreamweaver Exchange, the online community for extensibility developers.

Dreamweaver Exchange

The Dreamweaver exchange contains thousands of extensions for the entire Macromedia product line, not just Dreamweaver 8:

http://www.macromedia.com/ exchange

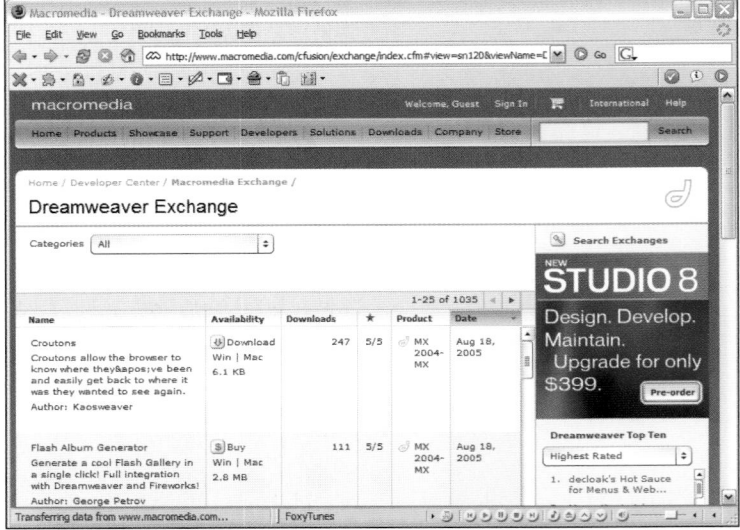

Massimo's Corner

Massimo's is a great Web site for getting some really useful commands and ColdFusion code:

http://www.massimocorner.com

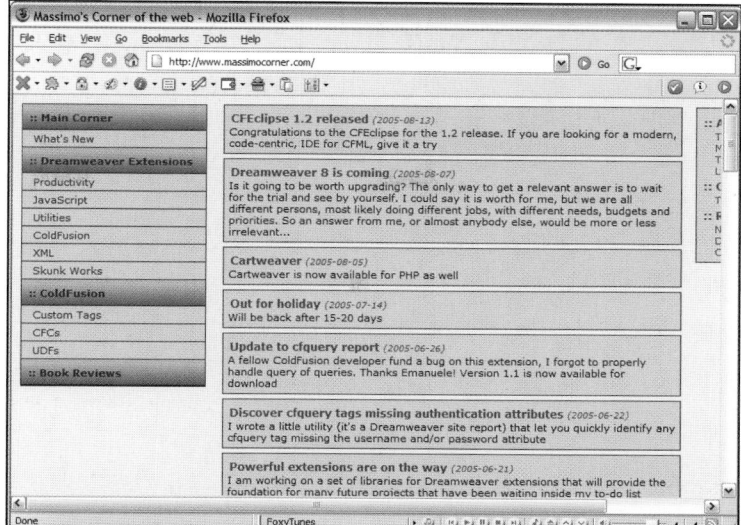

Yaromat

This Web site is another great repository for Dreamweaver behaviors, commands, and objects:

http://www.yaromat.com/ dw/index.php

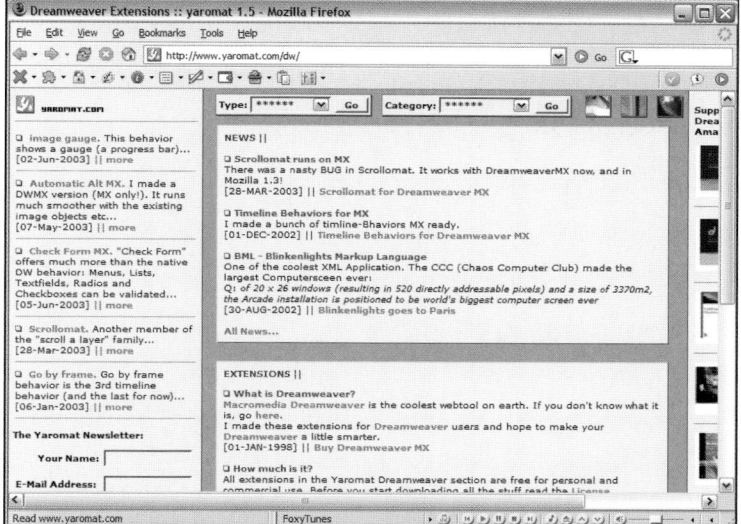

There are hundreds of other Web sites selling commercial extensions, but we'll leave you to find those through the Macromedia Exchange. You can get a head start by checking out the DWFaq extensions list:

http://www.dwfaq.com/Resources/Extensions/

In this chapter, you learned how to use behaviors to open browser windows, change properties of an element on the page, and validate forms. There are a number of other built in Dreamweaver 8 behaviors, and thousands of third-party behaviors, that allow you to do everything from swapping an image to inserting full-blown mini-calendar applications, and everything in-between. In the next chapter, you'll learn how to use Fireworks 8 in combination with Dreamweaver 8 to boost your productivity.

15

Fireworks Integration

Designing and developing Web pages cannot be done with Dreamweaver 8 alone. At some point, you will need a graphics editor to create the various images, buttons, and other visual elements for your pages. You could hire a designer to do all of the graphics for you, but if you want to create graphics on your own, Macromedia's Fireworks 8 integrates beautifully with Dreamweaver 8. When you export images from Fireworks 8, the application places bits of data into a separate document as well as creating the graphic file. The HTML code generated from Fireworks 8 is easily understood by Dreamweaver 8, which makes these two tools work together very well. Plus, if you just need to make some simple edits to your images, Dreamweaver 8 has a great set of Fireworks tools right onboard.

In this chapter, you will learn how to insert graphics into your XHTML pages that were created with Fireworks 8, how to edit images in Fireworks 8 from within Dreamweaver 8, how to use the Fireworks editing tools inside of Dreamweaver 8 to edit graphics, how to insert rollovers created in Fireworks 8, and much more. Dreamweaver 8 and Fireworks 8 have been designed to provide you with a smooth and integrated workflow for designing, generating, editing, optimizing, and placing Web graphics into your XHTML pages. Like yin and yang, Dreamweaver 8 and Fireworks 8 were meant to be together.

The following chart outlines some of the ways that Dreamweaver 8 and Fireworks 8 can work together to accomplish many of your Web design tasks:

Dreamweaver 8 to Fireworks 8 Workflow	
Feature	**What It Does**
Launching Fireworks 8 to optimize an image	Launches the Fireworks 8 Optimize panel in Dreamweaver 8.
Inserting a Fireworks 8 image in a Dreamweaver 8 document	Inserts a GIF or a JPG image that is linked by a MNO file or Design Note to a Fireworks 8 PNG image file.
Inserting Fireworks 8 HTML code in a Dreamweaver 8 document	Inserts Fireworks 8 HTML code into a Dreamweaver 8 document with the click of a button. The HTML code is linked by a MNO file or Design Note to a Fireworks 8 PNG image file.
Pasting Fireworks 8 HTML code into a Dreamweaver 8 document	Places Fireworks 8 HTML code into a Dreamweaver 8 document. The code can be pasted with or without the reference to the file Design Note or MNO file.
Editing a Fireworks 8 image or table	Launches Fireworks 8 through the Design Note, for the purpose of modifying images and tables. Revisions are then updated and sent back to Dreamweaver 8 smoothly by the click of a button.
Inserting an image placeholder	Lets you to create a blank graphic of the right size to fit your design in Dreamweaver 8.
Updating a Dreamweaver 8 image placeholder in Fireworks 8	Launches Fireworks 8 and opens the Dreamweaver 8 placeholder image for design. Then the image is saved and sent back to Dreamweaver 8.

The Importance of Design Notes

Design Notes are a key component to Dreamweaver 8 and Fireworks 8 integration. When you export a GIF or a JPG file from Fireworks 8 to a Dreamweaver 8 site folder, a folder named **_notes** is automatically created within your local root folder. This folder contains Design Notes files, which uses the Macromedia note file extension (.mno). Design Notes contain information about the graphic files you exported from Fireworks 8, such as where the source PNG file is located. PNG is the native file type for Fireworks 8, and the PNG files generated there contain crucial information about the graphic that other formats cannot store. The information from Design Notes is used when you launch and edit a Fireworks 8 table or image from Dreamweaver 8. When you export an image from Fireworks 8, Design Notes are automatically created. When a graphic or table is selected in Dreamweaver 8, the Property Inspector will display the Fireworks 8 icon and the path to the source file.

Here is a Fireworks 8 graphic selected in Dreamweaver 8 with the Property Inspector displaying the path to the source file. Notice how Dreamweaver locates and displays the Fireworks PNG source file—this is all possible because of Design Notes.

The best thing about Design Notes is there is really not much you have to do. All of the Design Notes' magic between Fireworks 8 and Dreamweaver 8 goes on behind the scenes, letting you focus on creating your Web pages.

External Image Editor Preferences

When you install the Macromedia Studio 8 suite, preferences for an external image editor are set for you automatically. Fireworks 8 is selected as the default external image editor for Dreamweaver 8. This is what lets you go between Dreamweaver 8 and Fireworks 8 smoothly and effortlessly. It is these preferences that launch Fireworks 8 when you edit an image in a Dreamweaver 8 document.

If your preferences aren't set properly, you can set them yourself by following these steps:

- Choose **Edit > Preferences** (Windows) or **Dreamweaver > Preferences** (Mac) and select **File Types/Editors** in the **Category** list.

- In the **Extensions** list, you can scroll through all of the extension types that Dreamweaver 8 will recognize.

- In the **Editors** list, you should see Fireworks 8 selected as your primary image editor. If it's not, click the **plus** (+) icon and browse to the Fireworks 8 executable file to set Fireworks as the primary image editor for that extension.

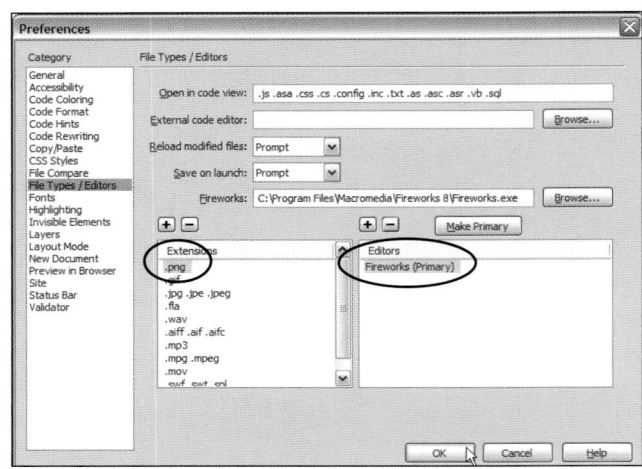

The preference settings for file types and editors in Dreamweaver 8 are shown here.

1 | Inserting Fireworks 8 Images

Now that you have a general understanding of what is going on behind the scenes, it is time to have some fun with Dreamweaver 8 and Fireworks 8. In this first exercise, you will practice the simple technique of inserting a Fireworks 8 image into a Dreamweaver 8 document.

1 Copy the **chap_15** folder from the **HOT CD-ROM** to your **Desktop**. Define your site as **Chapter 15** using the **chap_15** folder as the local root folder. Make sure the **Files** panel is open. If it's not, choose **Window > Files** or press **F11**.

2 In the **Files** panel, double-click **index.htm** to open it.

This is the default index page you've been working with throughout this book, but it's missing the image in the center of the page.

3 In the **Files** panel, expand the **assets** and **images** folders. Click and drag **landing.jpg** into the center of your document. If the **Image Tag Accessibility Attributes** dialog box appears, type **Welcome to teacloud** in the **Alternate text** field and click **OK**.

The Fireworks 8 graphic has been inserted into the Dreamweaver 8 document. You can see this graphic was created in (and exported from) Fireworks 8 because when it is selected, the Src field in the Property Inspector tells you so! The graphic is linked to a PNG file, and this is happening due to the Design Note.

---

4 Save **index.htm** and keep it open for the next exercise.

That was easy, wasn't it? Inserting Fireworks 8 images is no different than working with other images; you just end up with more options in Design view than if you worked with an image that wasn't exported from Fireworks 8.

---

2 | Editing Images with Built-in Fireworks 8 Tools

In this exercise, you will learn to how to edit and manipulate images using the built-in graphics editing tools inside Dreamweaver 8, which can be helpful for those small adjustments that don't require the full set of Fireworks 8 design tools. Once you get the hang of it, you'll see these tools can help enhance your productivity because you can crop, resize, and make other minor edits with Fireworks 8 tools without having to leave Dreamweaver 8.

1 If you just completed Exercise 1, **index.htm** should still be open. If it's not, go back and complete Exercise 1.

2 Select the **landing.jpg** image you inserted in the previous exercise. In the **Property Inspector**, select the **Brightness and Contrast** tool. It's the one that looks like a half moon.

When you click an editing tool, a dialog box will appear warning you that any changes you make will be permanent. If you don't like the way the image looks after you have adjusted it, you can undo the changes (so it's not completely permanent).

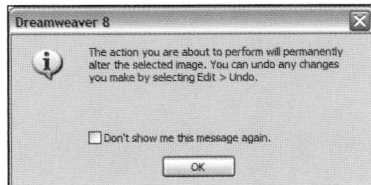

3 Click **OK** to close the warning dialog box. The **Brightness/Contrast** dialog box appears automatically, and you can begin editing the image.

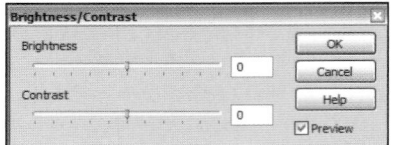

4 Click and drag the **Contrast** slider to the right to increase the contrast. To decrease the contrast, drag the slider back toward the left. When you are happy with the result, click **OK**.

For a simple edit, such as this one, it was easy to make the changes directly in Dreamweaver 8 without having to go into Fireworks.

5 Save your changes and keep **index.htm** open for the next exercise.

Now that you have an idea of what to expect, you can use the following chart to guide you through your experimentation with these tools.

Built-In Editing Tools

The following table outlines the built-in editing toolset in Dreamweaver 8, which should give you a better idea of what each of the tools does:

	Built-In Editing Tools in Dreamweaver 8	
Icon	Name	Function
	Edit	Launches Fireworks 8 for full-featured roundtrip editing of individual images and Fireworks 8 tables.
	Optimize in Fireworks	Opens the Fireworks 8 Optimize panel allowing compression changes to images.
	Crop	Activates cropping handle controls allowing for image cropping inside Dreamweaver 8.
	Resample	Allows scaling of image files to the desired size. Use the image handles around an image to resize it, and then click the Resample button to change the actual physical image dimensions to the new size.
	Brightness and Contrast	Activates brightness and contrast controls, which lets you make adjustments to image brightness and contrast directly within Dreamweaver 8.
	Sharpness	Activates sharpen controls used to increase overall image sharpness directly within Dreamweaver 8.

EXERCISE

3 | Editing a Fireworks 8 Image

In this exercise, you will learn to use roundtrip editing to edit an image that was created in Fireworks 8 while you have Dreamweaver 8 open and active. This lets you edit an image, re-optimize it in Fireworks, re-export the image, and then update the image inside Dreamweaver 8 by clicking just a few buttons. This exercise demonstrates that you can go between the two programs easily.

NOTE:

Fireworks Required

You must have Fireworks 8 installed in order to complete this exercise. If you own Macromedia Studio 8, you already have Fireworks. If you own a stand-alone version of Dreamweaver 8, you can download a trial version of Fireworks from Macromedia's Web site at **http://www.macromedia.com/go/tryfireworks**.

---

1 If you just completed Exercise 2, **index.htm** should still be open. If it's not, go back and complete Exercise 2.

2 Select the **Welcome to teacloud** graphic (**landing.jpg**). In the **Property Inspector**, click the **Edit** button.

In the Property Inspector, notice the Src field beneath the Target option. The source text field displays the path to the source file for the selected image. In this case, it is pointing to the **landing.png** file. This option appears only when you have selected an image that has been exported from Fireworks 8.

You are now in Fireworks 8 viewing the source document. At the top of the window, notice that it says *Editing from Dreamweaver*, which indicates that you opened this document for editing directly from within Dreamweaver 8.

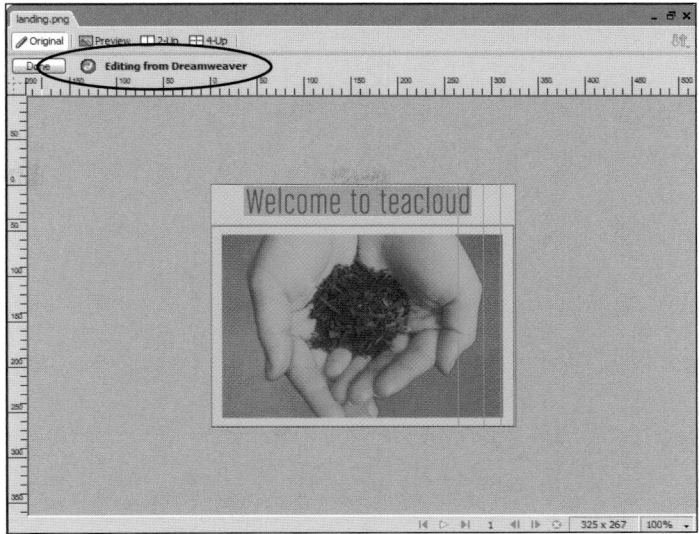

Images Without Source Files

As a general rule of thumb, it is always best to work with the source file for an image, especially if you are going to resize and recompress the image, as will be the case in this exercise. If you attempt to edit an image that doesn't have a source

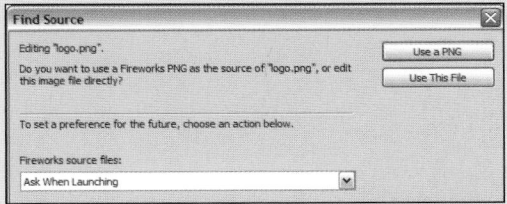

file attached to it through Design Notes in Dreamweaver, you will see the Find Source dialog box when you click the Edit icon in the Property Inspector. If you click the Use a PNG button, Dreamweaver 8 will allow you to browse to a PNG file and specify it as the source for your image. If you don't have the source image or simply don't want to use it, click **Use This File** to open the image directly in Fireworks.

3 Choose **Modify > Canvas > Image Size** to open the **Image Size** dialog box.

4 Make sure both the **Constrain proportions** and **Resample image** check boxes are selected. Set the **width** to **300** pixels.

Notice the height automatically updates to 246. The Constrain proportions option automatically adjusts the height to keep the same aspect ratio as the original image.

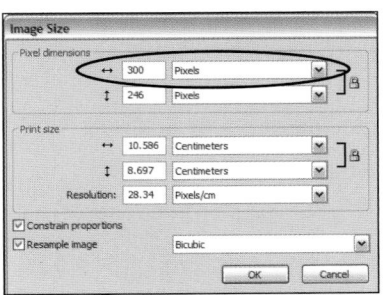

5 Click **OK** to resize the image.

Because you edited the source file, the image will scale perfectly without distortion. This is one reason you want to work with the source file whenever possible because GIF or JPG files do not always rescale without distortion.

6 Click the **Done** button.

A number of things happen after you click Done. First, the actual source PNG file is saved with your changes and then closes. Next, the actual image inserted into the Dreamweaver 8 document is re-exported from Fireworks with the export settings defined inside the Fireworks 8 PNG file. Finally, Fireworks 8 closes and you are returned to the Document window in Dreamweaver 8. All of the changes you made in the source PNG file are reflected in the Dreamweaver 8 Design view.

7 Save your changes and close **index.htm**.

4 | Inserting Simple Rollovers from Fireworks 8

Fireworks 8 lets you create rollover images and export the HTML and images, ready for you to import directly into Dreamweaver 8. As a result, you can create all of your rollover images in your graphics application (where it makes sense) and drop the entire thing inside Dreamweaver 8—behaviors and all.

NOTE:

Fireworks Required

You must have Fireworks 8 installed in order to complete this exercise. If you own Macromedia Studio 8, you already have Fireworks. If you own a stand-alone version of Dreamweaver 8, you can download a trial version of Fireworks from Macromedia's Web site at **http://www.macromedia.com/go/tryfireworks**.

---

1 You're going to start with a blank file this time, so choose **File > New** and create a new basic HTML page.

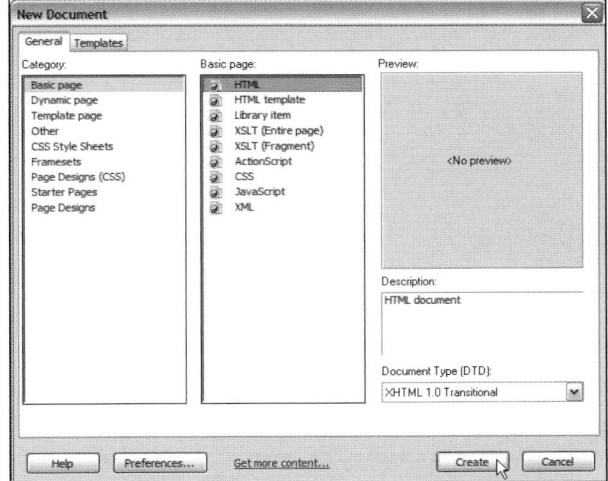

2 Choose **Insert > Image Objects > Fireworks HTML** to open the **Insert Fireworks HTML** dialog box.

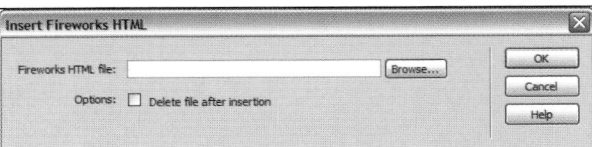

3 Click **Browse** and select the
top-navigation.htm file from the
assets/images/navigation folder.
Click **Open** (Windows) or **OK** (Mac).

This file was exported from Fireworks 8,
and it contains an HTML table to lay out
the images as well as all of the JavaScript
rollover code. You should also notice all
of the images in the same folder as the
top-navigation.htm file. These are all of
the images associated with the HTML file.

You're returned to the Insert Fireworks
HTML dialog box.

If you check the Delete file after insertion box,
the original HTML file you selected will be
deleted after it is inserted into your document. We recommend that you don't delete
the file unless you are sure you don't want to
import it into another page.

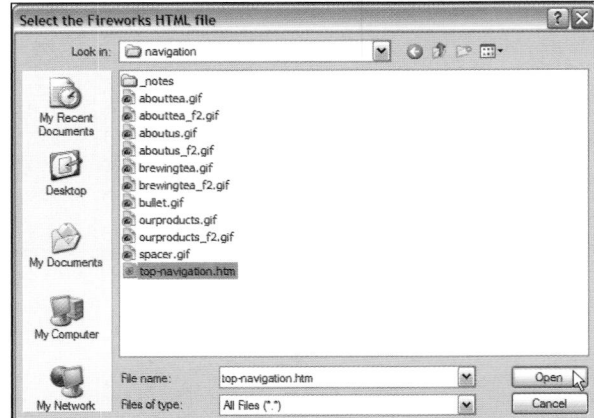

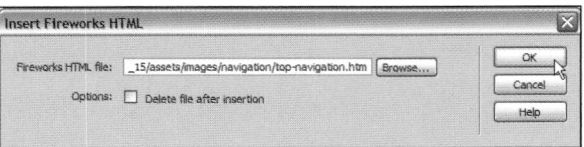

4 Because this is a new document, Dreamweaver 8 doesn't
know how to write the paths to the image files it's about to
insert. When you receive the alert to save your document,
click **OK** and save the file as **fw-rollovers.htm** at the root of
your site.

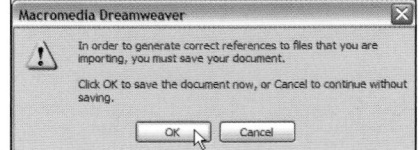

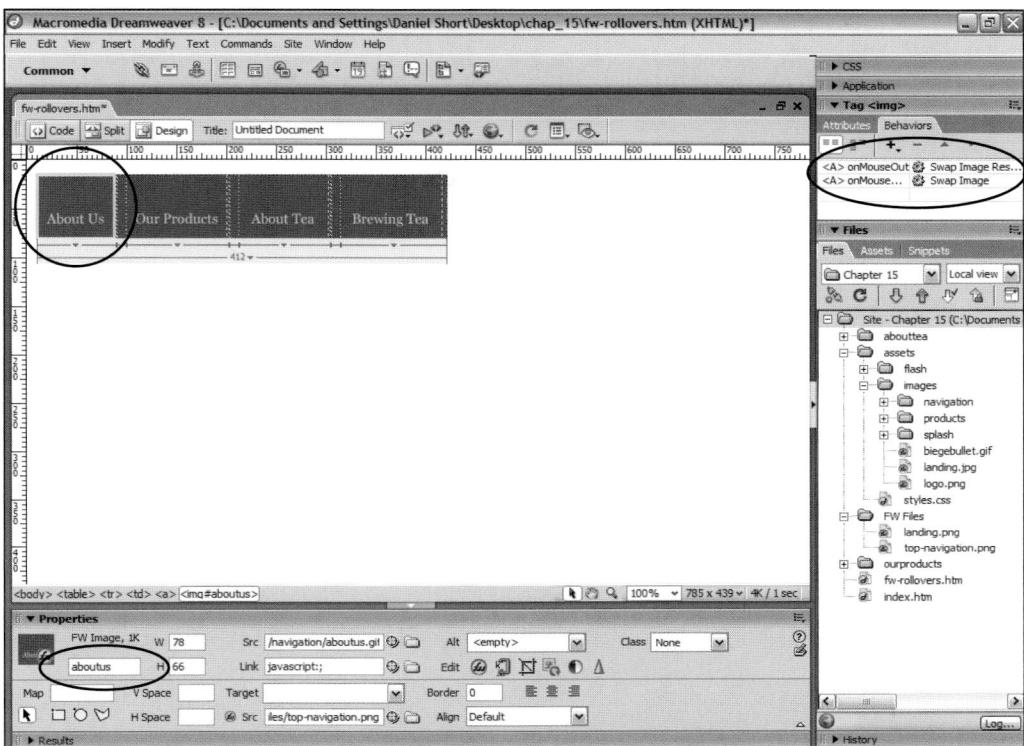

This is what your page should look like now. All of the images have been written to the page, along with their appropriate IDs and all of the behaviors necessary to create the rollover images. If you select any of the images, you'll see the Swap Image and Swap Image Restore behaviors in the Behaviors panel.

 NOTE: | ## Import from Outside Your Local Root Folder

If you try to import an HTML file that is not within your local root folder, you will see the following dialog box. Click **OK** and choose a place inside your local root folder to save the files.

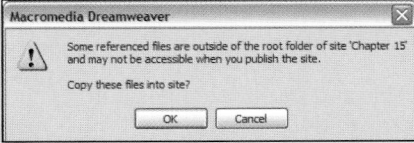

5 Press **F12** to test the rollovers in your browser.

With the click of a few buttons, Dreamweaver 8 imported the images and the necessary JavaScript to make the rollovers function.

6 Save your changes and keep **fw-rollovers.htm** open for the next exercise.

5 | Updating Fireworks HTML in Dreamweaver

Once you start working with Dreamweaver 8 and Fireworks 8 in tandem, sometimes you will want to make changes to the original Fireworks 8 HTML that you placed in your Dreamweaver 8 document. This exercise steps you through the process of applying a simple modification to a Fireworks 8 HTML file that you placed in a Dreamweaver 8 page. In this example, you will modify the navigation bar that you inserted in the previous exercise. You will go back and forth between Dreamweaver 8 and Fireworks 8 accessing and modifying the original Fireworks PNG file.

NOTE:

Fireworks Required

You must have Fireworks 8 installed in order to complete this exercise. If you own Macromedia Studio 8, you already have Fireworks. If you own a stand-alone version of Dreamweaver 8, you can download a trial version of Fireworks from Macromedia's Web site at **http://www.macromedia.com/go/tryfireworks**.

---

1 If you just completed Exercise 4, **fw-rollovers.htm** should still be open. If it's not, go back and complete Exercise 4.

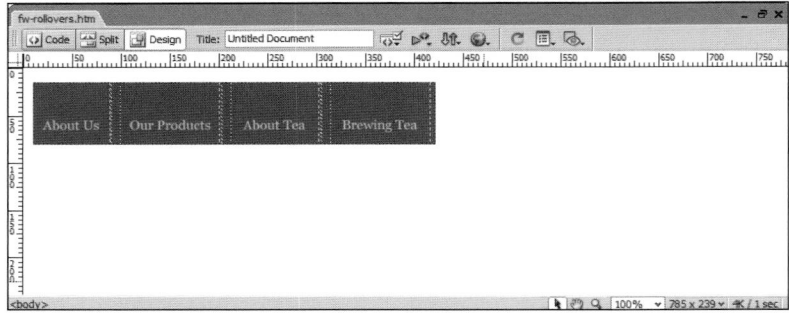

2 Click anywhere in the table and select the **<table>** tag in the **Tag Selector** to select the entire table.

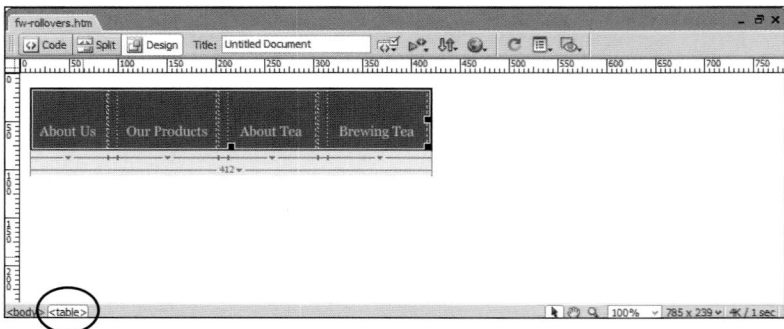

3 With the **<table>** tag selected, the **Property Inspector** indicates you have a Fireworks 8 table selected by displaying **Fireworks Table** in the upper-left corner. The source file for this table is **top-navigation.png**. Click the **Edit** button to launch Fireworks 8 (if it is not already open), which will then open the file **top-navigation.png**. 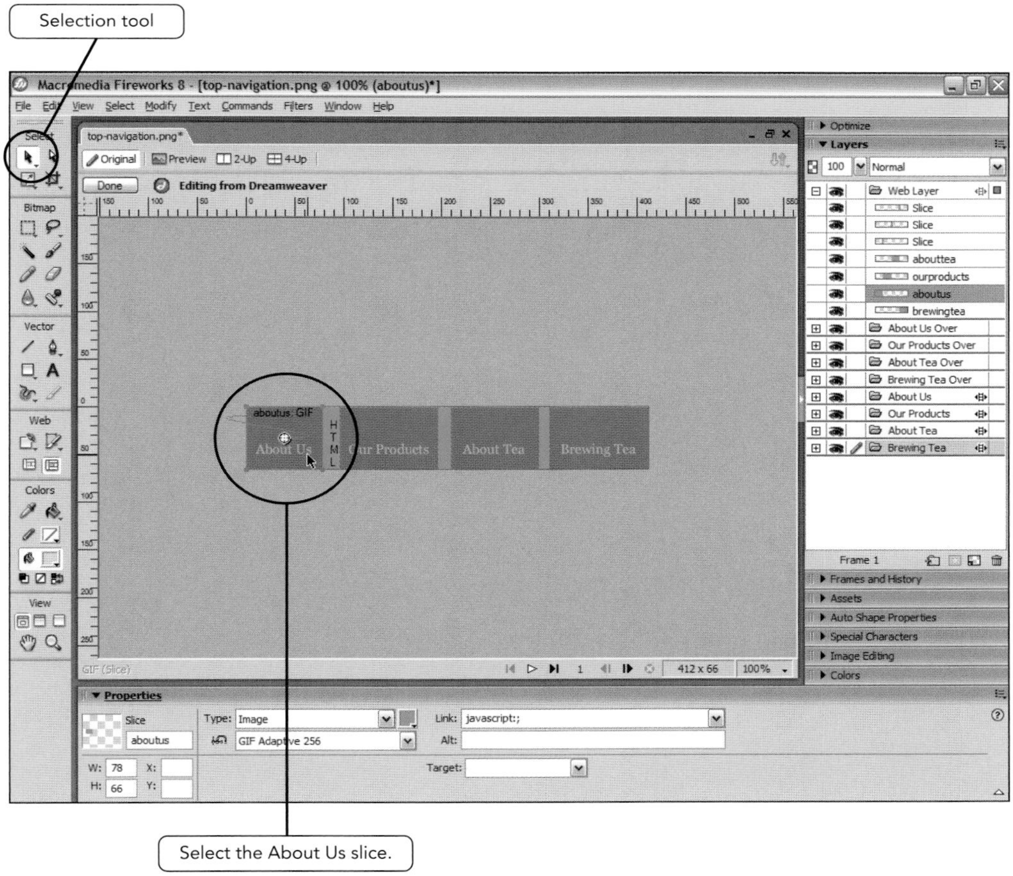

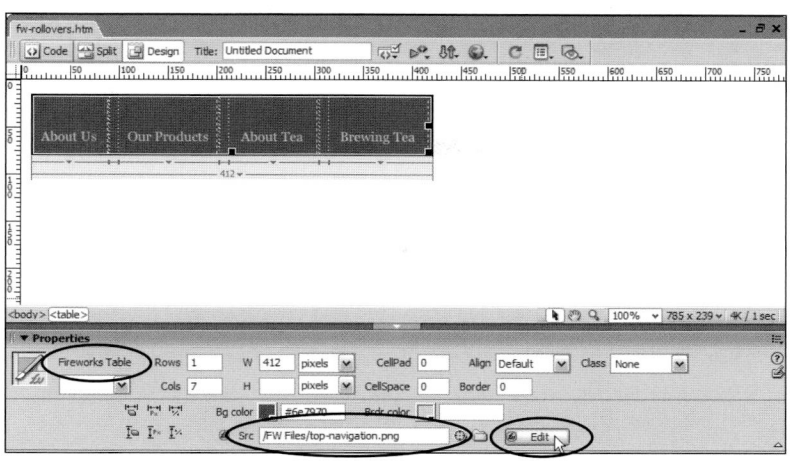

Selection tool

Select the About Us slice.

4 In Fireworks 8, select the **Selection** tool from the **toolbar** and click to select the **About Us** slice.

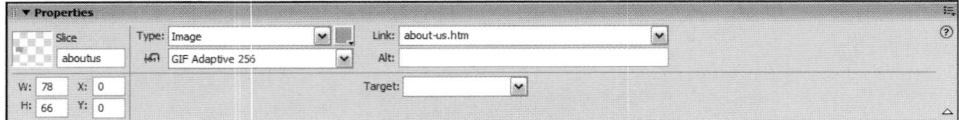

5 In the **Property Inspector**, type **about-us.htm** in the **Link** field.

That's right, Fireworks 8 lets you create links directly inside the application. This means you can easily create an entire navigation bar—links and everything—right inside Fireworks 8.

6 Select the **Our Products** slice and type **our-products.htm** in the **Link** field of the **Property Inspector**.

7 Select the **About Tea** slice and type **about-tea.htm** in the **Link** field of the **Property Inspector**.

8 Select the **Brewing Tea** slice and type **brewing-tea.htm** in the **Link** field of the **Property Inspector**.

9 After you've finished making all of your changes, click **Done** in the upper-left corner of the **Document** window.

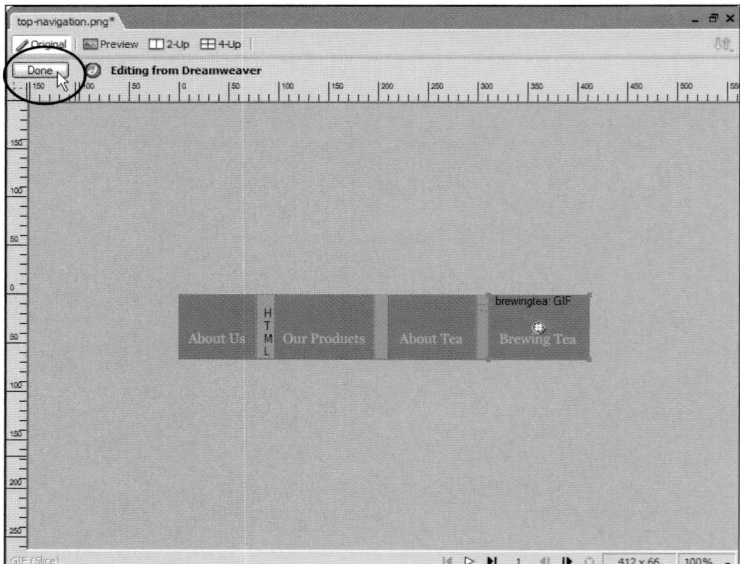

When you return to Dreamweaver 8, notice the navigation bar has automatically been updated. If you click any of the navigation buttons, you'll see the link has changed to the links you specified in the Fireworks 8 PNG file.

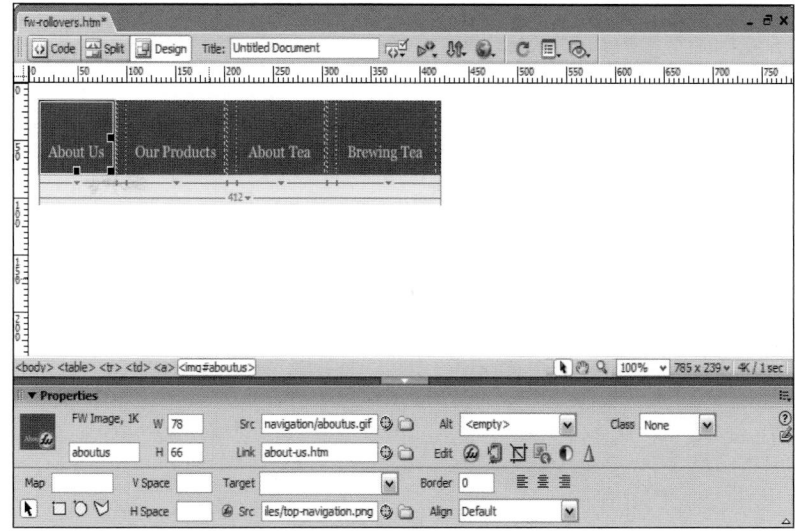

10 Close **fw-rollovers.htm**. You don't need to save your changes.

About Fireworks 8 Export Settings

Because Fireworks 8 lets you export both graphics and HTML, you need to understand how Fireworks 8 controls the export settings.

In Fireworks 8, there are settings that control the type and amount of compression your graphics receive, and there are separate settings for controlling various attributes of your Fireworks 8 HTML.

There is a special layout layer in Fireworks 8 called the **Web layer** that lets you assign interactivity

and HTML information to areas of your document that you designate as slices.

When preparing a document as a Web page in Fireworks 8, you use the Web layer to add interactivity and define page layout. On export, Fireworks 8 uses this information to generate the HTML and JavaScript code that will display and animate your images according to your designs.

6 | Manipulating Fireworks 8 Pop-Ups

Fireworks 8 can create sophisticated CSS-based pop-up menus. Although you can create pop-up menus in Dreamweaver 8, the pop-up menus you can create in Fireworks are far superior. In this exercise, you'll learn how to insert and edit a Fireworks 8 pop-up menu.

NOTE:

Why Aren't You Showing the Dreamweaver 8 Pop-up Menus?

Dreamweaver 8 pop-up menus are slow at best, and completely unusable at worst. They rely on a large amount of proprietary JavaScript and aren't even remotely accessible. In fact, when you start to add a pop-up menu inside Dreamweaver 8 you receive the message shown in the dialog box to the right.

As you can see, it's a pretty strong case for sticking with the Fireworks 8 pop-up menus.

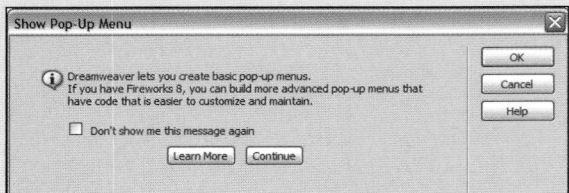

NOTE:

Fireworks Required

You must have Fireworks 8 installed in order to complete this exercise. If you own Macromedia Studio 8, you already have Fireworks. If you own a stand-alone version of Dreamweaver 8, you can download a trial version of Fireworks from Macromedia's Web site at **http://www.macromedia.com/go/tryfireworks**.

1 In the Files panel, open **kettlesandteapots.htm** from the **ourproducts** folder.

You're going to add a navigation bar that contains a pop-up menu.

2 Click inside the navigation table cell and choose **Insert > Image Objects > Fireworks HTML**.

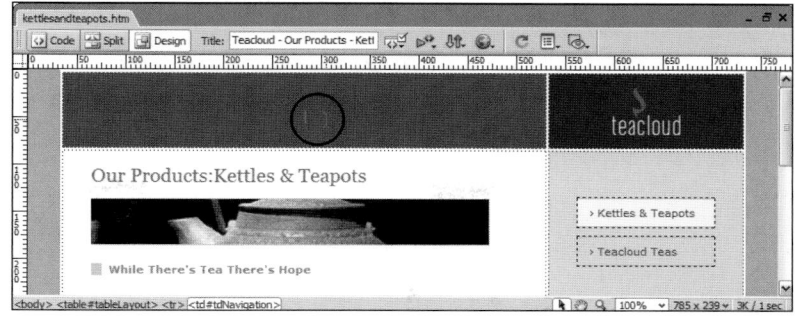

3 In the **Insert Fireworks HTML** dialog box, click **Browse** and select **ourproducts-popups.htm** in the **assets/popups** folder. Click **Open** (Windows) or **OK** (Mac).

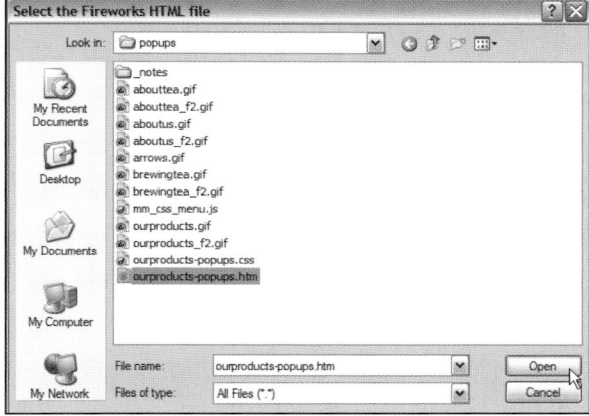

4 When you return to the **Insert Fireworks HTML** dialog box, click **OK** to add the menu to your page.

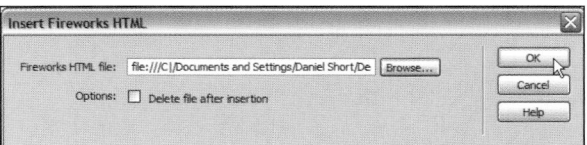

You can see that Dreamweaver 8 has added quite a bit of code to your page. It has added all of the navigation buttons you had earlier in this chapter, but it's also added a large number of **<div>** tags to the page to handle the pop-up menus.

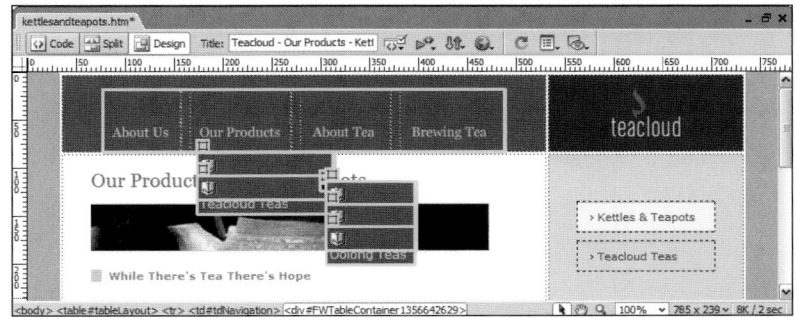

5 Press **F12** to preview your page in the browser. Move your mouse over the **Our Products** button and you can see how the pop-up menus behave.

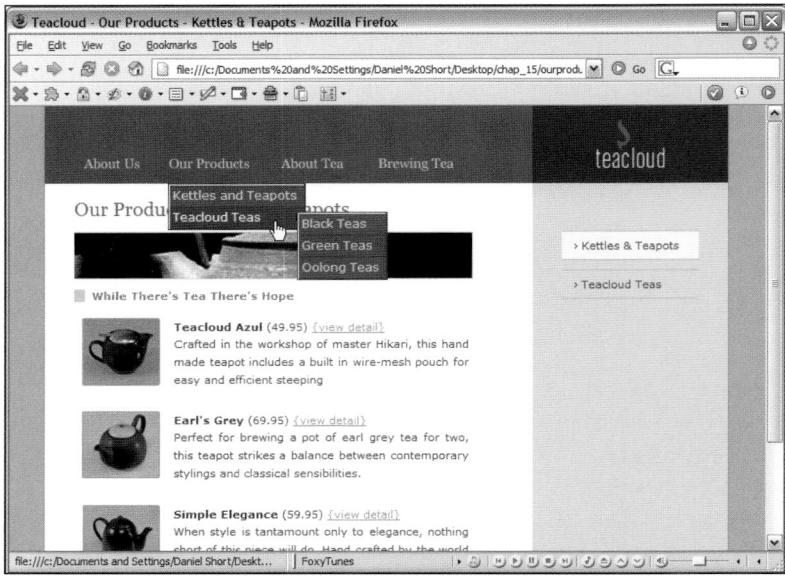

6 Return to Dreamweaver 8 and select the **Our Products** button. Click the small Fireworks icon in the **Property Inspector** to open the **popups.png** file in Fireworks 8.

If you look at the Src field in the Property Inspector, you can see that the image (and the pop-ups) were generated from the **popups.png** file. Clicking the Edit icon in the Property Inspector will open the related document.

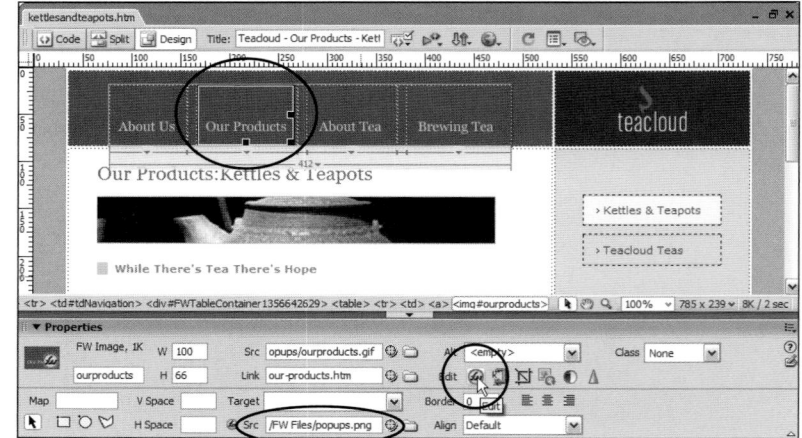

7 Select the **Our Products** button. **Right-click** (Windows) or **Ctrl+click** (Mac) the button and choose **Edit Pop-up Menu** from the contextual menu.

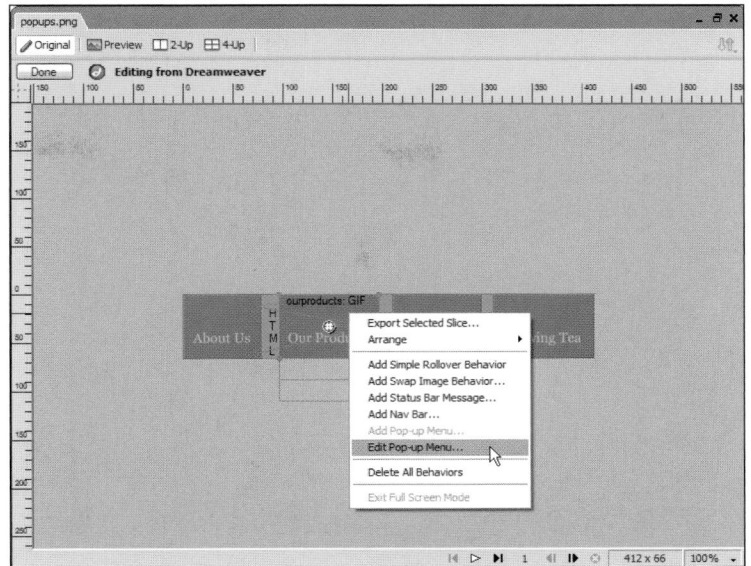

8 In the **Pop-up Menu Editor**, click the **Oolong Teas** entry and click the **minus** (–) symbol to delete it.

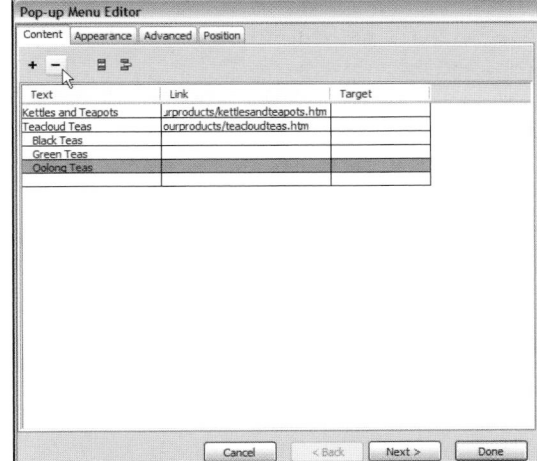

9 Click **Done** to return to the document.

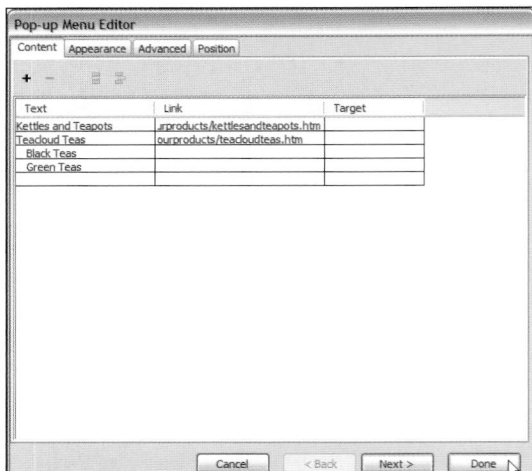

10 In the **Document** window, click **Done** to return to Dreamweaver 8.

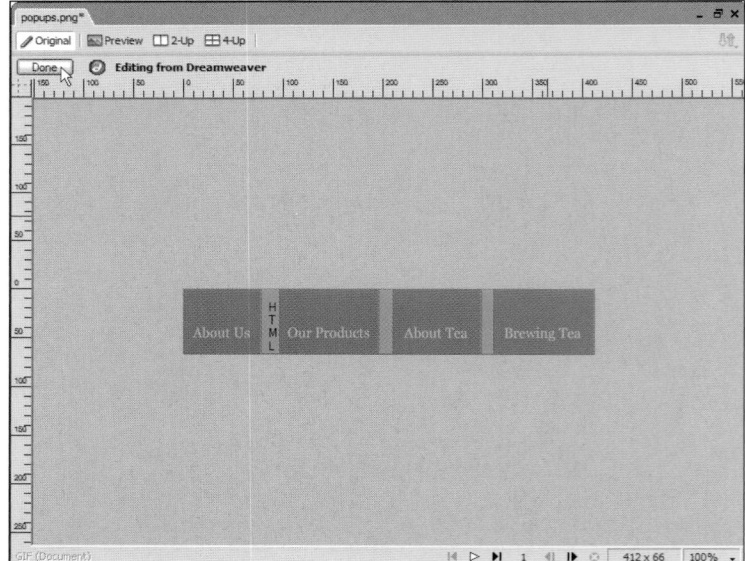

11 Press **F12** to preview the page in your browser.

Move your mouse over the Our Products button, and then the Teacloud Teas menu item, and you'll see that Oolong Teas is no longer listed in the menu.

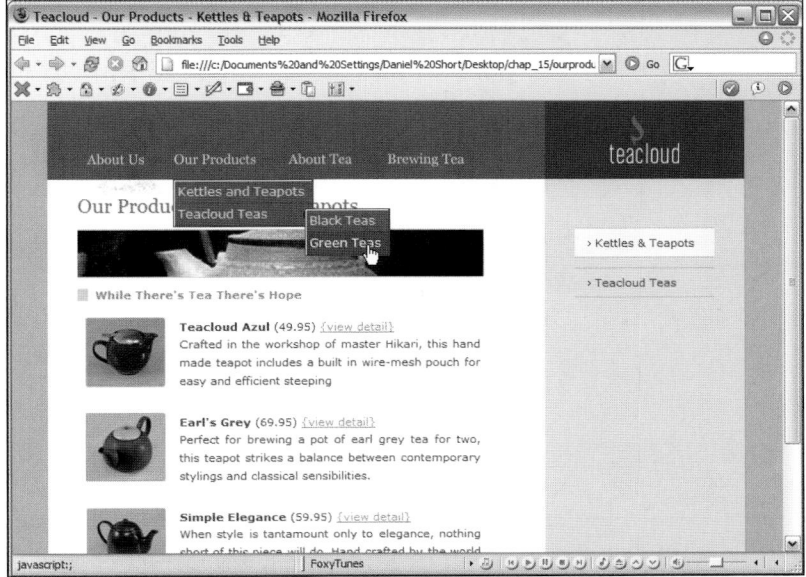

12 Save your changes and close the file.

NOTE:

Learning Fireworks 8

The purpose of this chapter was to show you how to integrate graphical content in Fireworks 8 with Dreamweaver 8. For more information about how to use Fireworks 8, including how to design pop-up menu rollovers, use the **free 24-hour pass to the lynda.com Online Training Library** provided in the Introduction of this book and check out the following video-based training resources:

Fireworks 8 Essential Training
with Abigail Rudner

Studio 8 Web Workflow
with Abigail Rudner

That's all there is for this chapter. You've learned how to increase your productivity by moving back and forth between Fireworks 8 and Dreamweaver 8. You've learned how to edit images directly inside Dreamweaver 8, as well as how to insert and edit pop-up menus created by Fireworks 8. In the next chapter, you'll learn how to work with templates and library items.

16

Templates and Library Items

Two of the biggest challenges Web designers face are making pages look consistent and updating changes throughout a site. Templates and library items can help you meet both challenges successfully because they make it easy to create consistent pages and page elements, as well as automatically update multiple pages when changes are required.

Templates are useful for entire page designs. They can lock in colors, fonts, Cascading Style Sheets, tables, images and even behaviors, while leaving other parts of the document editable. Once you create a template, you can create new pages based off of the template.

Library items are useful for page-design elements, such as a navigation bar or copyright notice. They are little pieces of HTML or text you can drop anywhere in a page (template-based or not). You will soon learn the differences between these two Dreamweaver 8 features by following the hands-on exercises in this chapter.

1 | Seeing Templates in Action

The best way to understand templates is to see them in action. In this first exercise, you'll modify an existing template and see how Dreamweaver 8 locks regions of a template so they can't be edited. You'll also see how easy it is to update multiple pages across your site by changing the navigation and updating all of the child pages that are based on a template.

1 Copy the **chap_16** folder from the **HOT CD-ROM** to your **Desktop**. Define your site as **Chapter 16** using the **chap_16** folder as the local root folder. Make sure the **Files** panel is open. If it's not, choose **Window > Files** or press **F11**.

TIP: | **Templates and Library Folders**

You may have noticed there are two folders inside the **chap_16** folder: **Templates** and **Library**. Dreamweaver 8 automatically creates these folders for you on when you create a template or library item. If you do not use templates or library items, Dreamweaver 8 will not put these folders in your directory structure. The **Templates** and **Library** folders do not need to be uploaded to your server once you publish it to the Web unless you're working with another developer who needs them; they are for use in Dreamweaver 8 only.

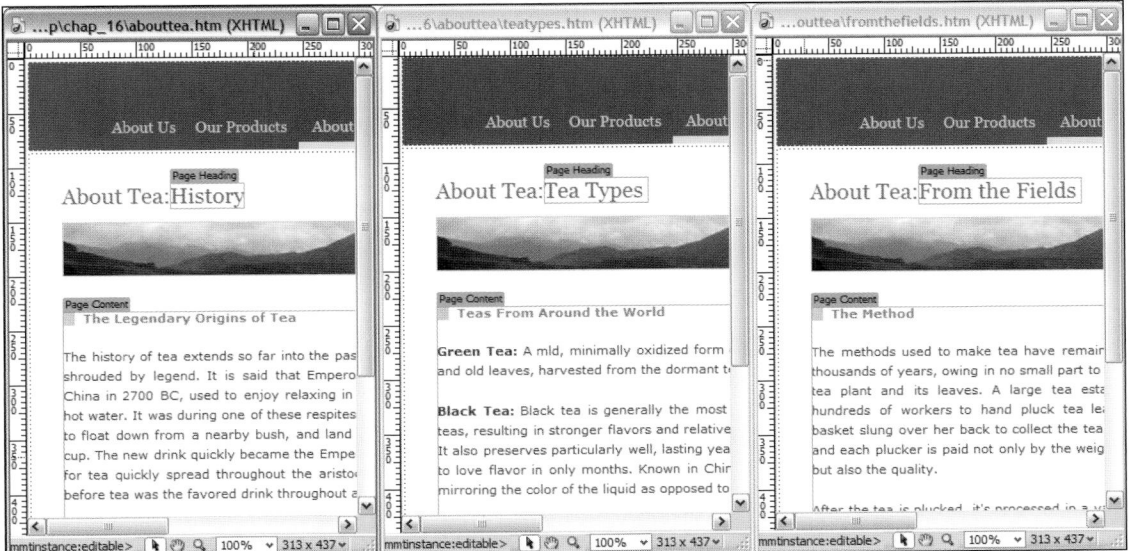

2 In the **Files** panel, double-click **abouttea.htm** to open it. This file, as well as several others inside the **chap_16** folder, have a template called **AboutTea.dwt** already applied to them. Go ahead and open **fromthefields.htm** and **teatypes.htm** in the **abouttea** folder. Notice that they all share the same layout and headings. Close all of the files except **abouttea.htm** before continuing.

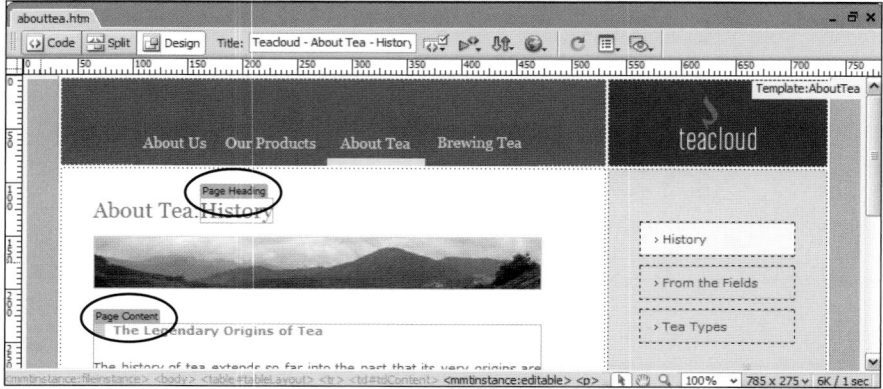

When you open a file with a template attached to it, you will see a tab in the upper-right corner identifying the name of the template file and a tab around each of the template's editable regions. The colors of these areas are set in the Highlighting category of the Preferences dialog box.

3 The **Assets** panel can show you all of the templates in the current site. If this panel is closed, you can open it by choosing **Window > Assets**. Then click the **Templates** button to view the templates within your site.

4 Highlight the template called **AboutTea** in the **Assets** panel, and then click the **Edit** button to open the template so you can start editing it.

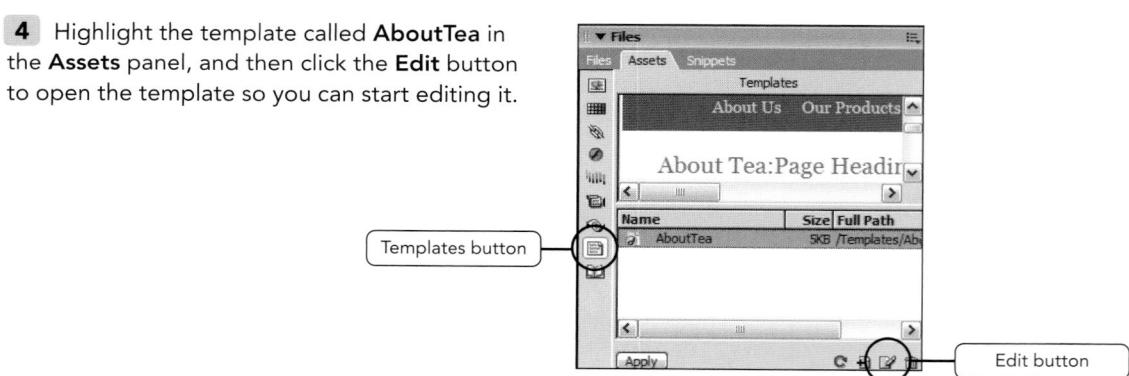

Tip: As an alternative, you can switch to the **Files** panel to open **AboutTea.dwt** from the **Templates** folder. All templates for a site are stored in the **Templates** folder at the root of the current site.

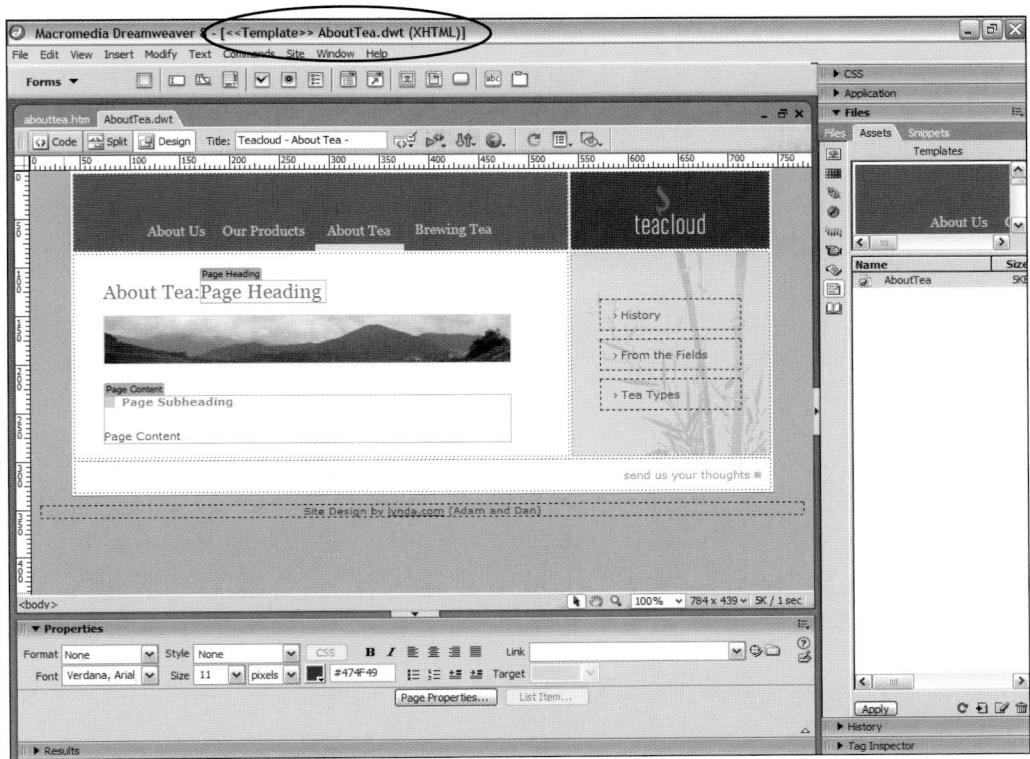

It's easy to tell when you are editing a template because the title bar displays <<*Template*>>, and the template filename. All Dreamweaver 8 templates have a .dwt file extension.

5 Replace the text **About Tea:** with **About Teacloud Tea:**.

Notice the *About Teacloud Tea* text is not inside any of the bordered regions in the document (editable regions). This area of the page is locked down in any page based on this template, and any changes made to the template will be made in the child pages.

6 Choose **File > Save** to save your changes.

You have just saved a change to the layout of the master template. This change affects the multiple pages you viewed in Step 2, which were created with this template.

---

7 The **Page Heading** editable region is inside a **<p>** tag. Dreamweaver 8 will warn you that you have an editable region inside a block-level tag, and it lets you know users won't be able to create new blocks (paragraphs) inside this editable region. Click **OK** to acknowledge the warning and continue.

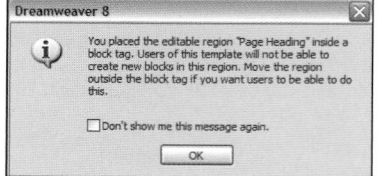

---

8 After you save the template, the **Update Template Files** dialog box appears. Because you want to apply the layout to all three pages, click **Update**. Dreamweaver 8 will update all files associated with this template.

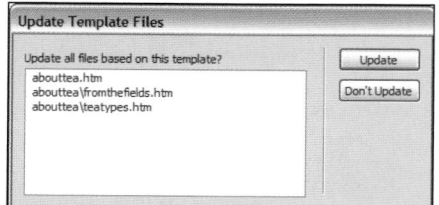

Dreamweaver 8 keeps track of which files are based on which template. Anytime you save a template, Dreamweaver 8 will prompt you to update the files based on that template.

---

9 As Dreamweaver 8 updates each template, it will list the status of all of the pages in the **Update Pages** dialog box. If you don't see the bottom half of the dialog box, select the **Show log** box to see all of the information. In this case, the three files you opened in Step 2 are updated. Once you are finished reviewing this screen, click **Close**.

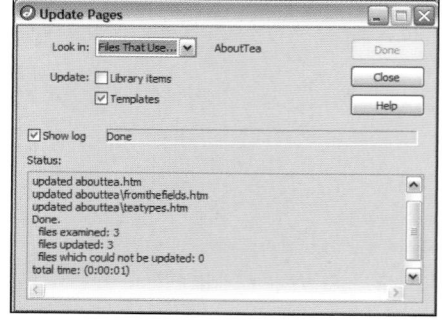

Note: If you have any files open while performing this operation, the page will be updated, but if you close the file without saving the changes, you'll lose any changes made by the template. Make sure you save your changes to **abouttea.htm** (which is still open) when you close it.

TIP: | **Manually Updating Child Pages**

If, for whatever reason, a page doesn't get successfully updated, you can always manually update the page. Open the page that you want to update and choose **Modify > Templates > Update Current Page**. The page will immediately update with the latest content from the template. If you want to manually update *all* pages based on a template, choose **Modify >Templates > Update Pages**, select the template you want to update, and click **Start**.

10 Open **fromthefields.htm** and **teatypes.htm** from the **abouttea** folder. Notice each now has the text change made in **AboutTea.dwt**.

Imagine how much time templates could save you if you had hundreds or thousands of pages that shared the same layout!

11 Close all the files.

Working with templates is an excellent technique to ensure design consistency. The only caveat is that you must create a template file first. How do you do that? Check out the next exercise to find out.

Templates and Teams

Using templates when designing a site on your own can certainly be helpful. It lets you lock down your design and quickly make changes on a large scale. But the real benefit in using templates comes when you're working with other designers or content contributors.

The ability to lock down a design when other team members are working on a site can be invaluable, especially when working with nondesigners. (Would you trust your boss with Dreamweaver?). Giving Dreamweaver 8 to a novice on a team without using templates can be disastrous. Macromedia has done a wonderful job making it possible to control your design while still giving content editors the ability to do their jobs.

Macromedia's Contribute (**http://www.macromedia.com/go/contribute**) allows content editors to work on Dreamweaver sites using templates so that they can add content without being able to affect the design of the site. I've always liked to call Contribute "Word for Web pages," because it lets non-techie editors easily update their sites, just like they'd update a Word document. The technical details are hidden from them, but at the same time, all of the content is accessible.

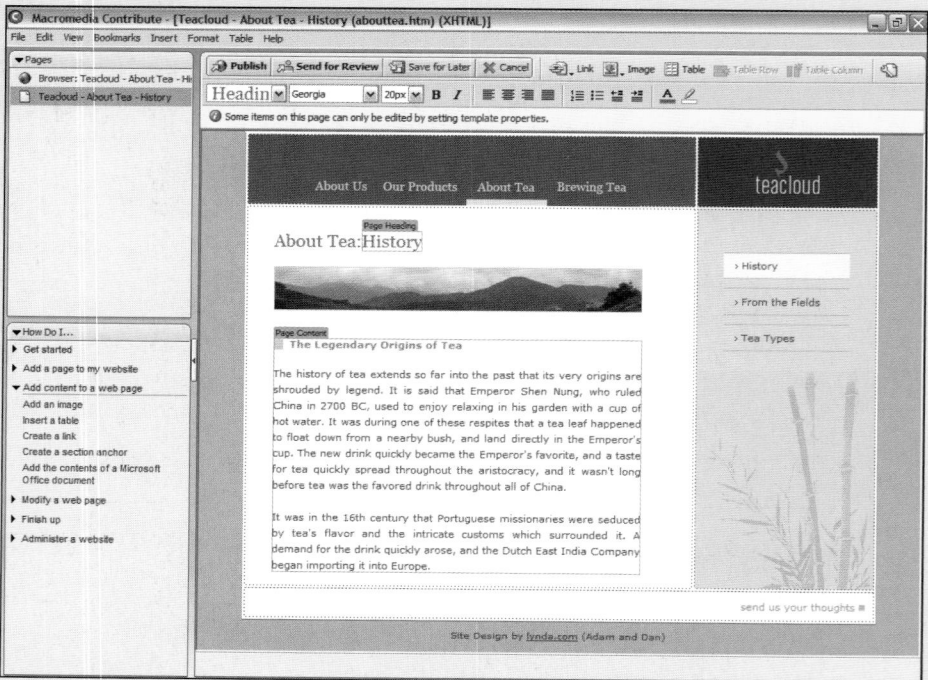

2 | Creating a New Template

Now that you're familiar with the way a template looks and feels, it's time to create your own. In this exercise, you'll take one of the Teacloud pages, convert it into a template, and begin adding editable regions. Editable regions allow you to make some part of your pages editable while locking down everything not in an editable region.

NOTE:

Everything is Locked by Default

Templates work by making *everything* locked by default. Unless you specifically say that something is editable by placing it in an editable region, Dreamweaver 8 will lock it down so that no one can touch it in child pages.

---

1 In the **Files** panel, double-click **ourproducts-base.htm** to open it.

This document was created for you, but the following steps would also work on a document of your own creation. Once you have created the basic layout of your document, the next step is to save it as a template.

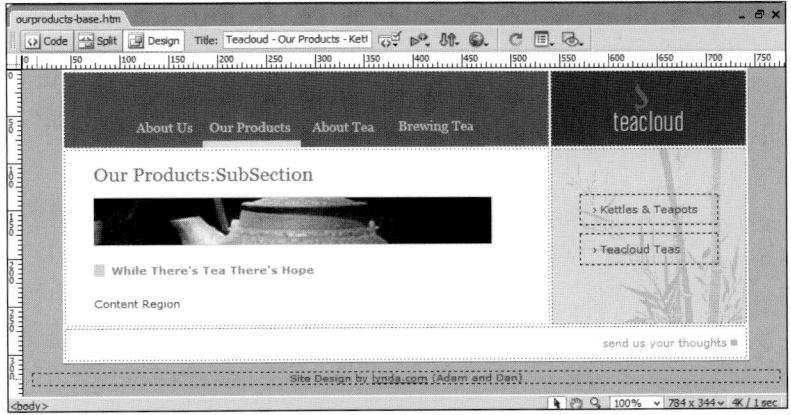

2 Choose **File > Save As Template** to open the **Save As Template** dialog box.

---

3 The file name **ourproducts-base** is prefilled in the **Save as** field; change this to a more appropriate name, such as **OurProducts**. You can also enter a user-friendly description of the template, which is displayed in the **Templates** section of the **New Document** dialog box. Click **Save** to create the new template.

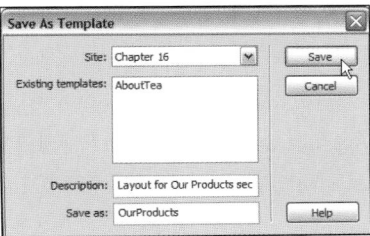

You can see that the other template that you worked with in Exercise 1, AboutTea, is already listed in the Existing templates box.

4 A dialog box appears, asking you if you want to update links. Click **Yes** to close the dialog box and update the links in the document.

When you save a document as a template, Dreamweaver 8 copies that document to the **Templates** directory. When the document is copied to the **Templates** directory, all links (this includes **<img>** tags as well, not just hyperlinks) must be updated so that the template can find all of the assets necessary to display the page correctly. Always click Yes to update links when saving a document as a template.

Your new template appears in the Templates category of the Assets panel. If you don't see the template, click the **Refresh** button in the **Assets** panel. The top portion of the Assets panel displays a preview of the template.

Now that you have created your template, you need to decide which areas you want to be editable and which areas you want to lock. By default, there are no editable regions in a new template. If you were to save the template as is and create a new child page from this template, you wouldn't be able to make any edits except for the page title. You'll learn how to create editable regions next.

5 Select the word **SubSection** at the top of the page and choose **Insert > Template Objects > Editable Region** to designate this area as an editable region.

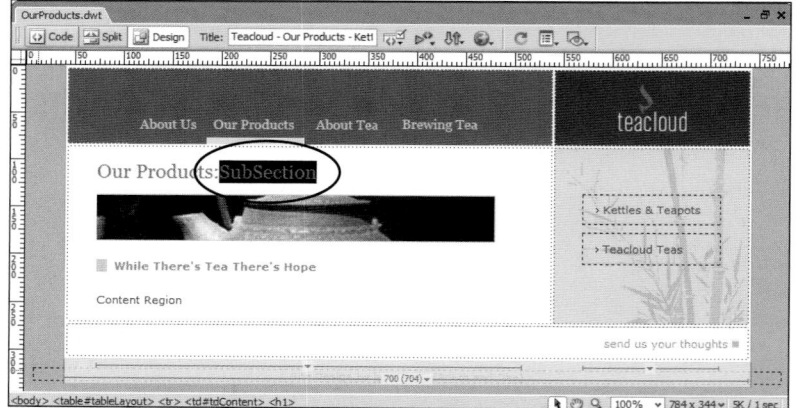

6 In the **New Editable Region** dialog box, type **Sub Section Heading** into the **Name** field and click **OK**.

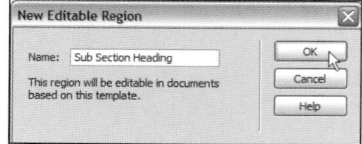

Notice the name you entered appears at the cursor location as a label, surrounded by a highlighted box. This indicates that this area of the template is editable—you or other members of your team can enter information inside this editable region.

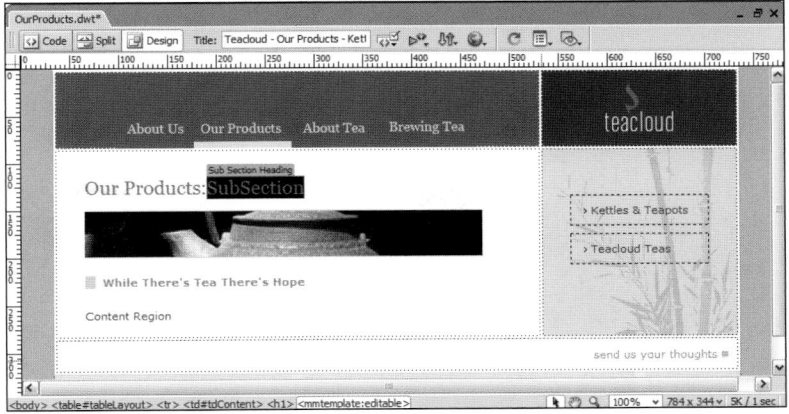

TIP: | **I Don't See Any Tabs!**

If you don't see any tabs or highlighting in Dreamweaver 8, choose **View > Visuals Aids > Invisible Elements**. If you disable this feature, you will not see any tabs or highlighting in your template files. You can choose **View > Visual Aids > Invisible Elements** to turn the tabs on and off whenever you need them.

TIP: | **Highlighting Preferences**

You can modify your document's highlighting colors in the **Preferences** dialog box. By choosing **Edit > Preferences** (Windows) or **Dreamweaver > Preferences** (Mac) and then selecting **Highlighting** in the **Category** list, you can set the highlighting colors to any color you want.

7 Click and drag to select the **Content Region** text. Choose **Insert > Template Objects > Editable Region**. In the **New Editable Region** dialog box, type **Content** and click **OK**.

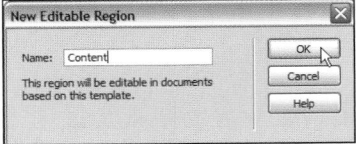

Give your editable regions plain-English names so that others working with the templates understand what should go where. Avoid using special characters, but spaces are just fine.

This is what your template should look like at this point.

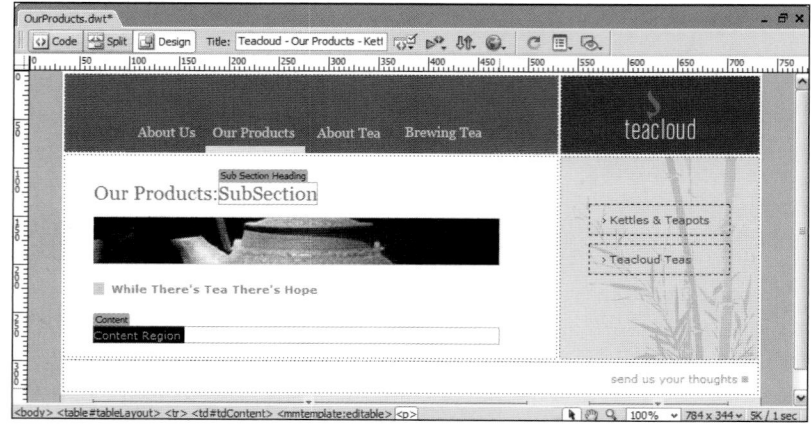

8 Now that you have designated the necessary areas as editable, close this file. When prompted, save your changes. In the dialog box warning you about inserting an editable region inside a block tag, click **OK**.

Congratulations—you have just created a custom template! Next, you will create a new page based on your newly created template.

9 Switch to the **Assets** panel (**Window > Assets** if it's not already open) and select the **Templates** category. You will see the new template in the template list. **Right-click** (Windows) or **Ctrl+click** (Mac) the **OurProducts** template and choose **New from Template** from the contextual menu.

Templates category →

10 After the new page opens, choose **File > Save As** and save the file as **ordering.htm** inside the **ourproducts** folder.

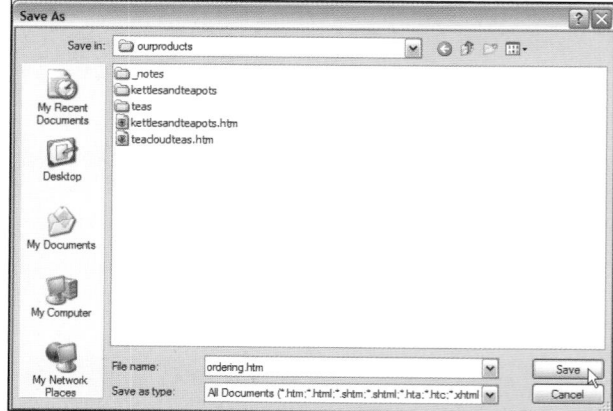

This is what the page
looks like with a template
applied to it. The two
areas you designated as
editable are labeled and
ready to be edited.

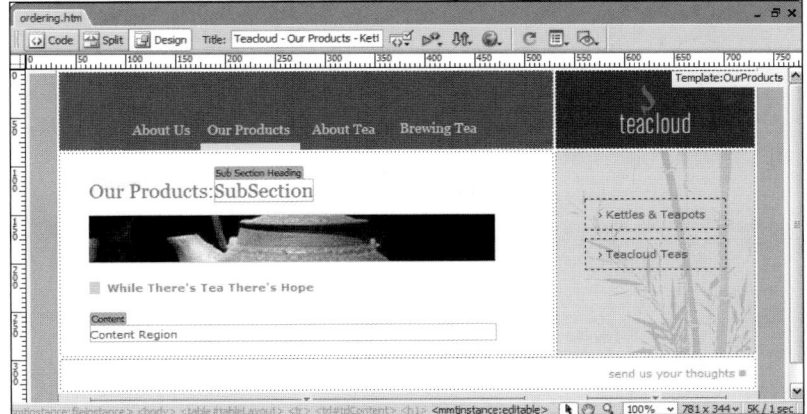

11 Click the tab labeled
Sub Section Heading to
select all of the text in the
editable region. Type
How to Order.

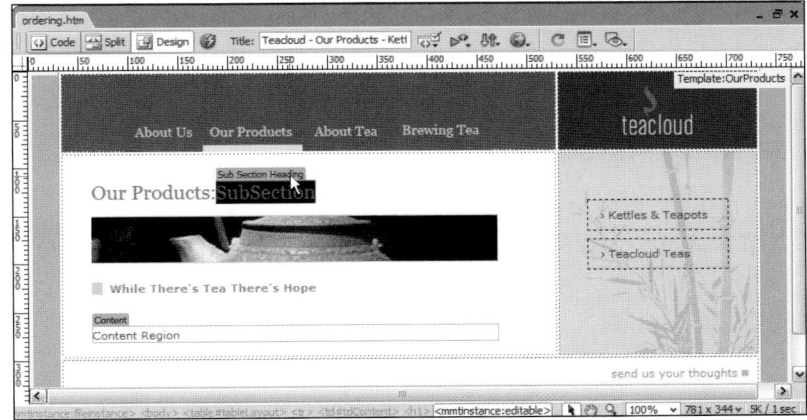

12 Click the **Content** label to select all of the text in the editable region.

13 Open **placeholder.txt** in the **chap_16** folder and copy all of the content from the file. Go back to **ordering.htm** and paste the text into the **Content** editable region.

This is what the page looks like with the content inserted into the document.

---

14 Save your changes and close **ordering.htm**.

TIP:	**Detaching a Template**
	You are not going to detach the template now, but it's good to know how for future reference. There may come a time when you want to modify sections of a page that has a template applied. Because some areas are locked, you can't modify them with the template still applied. By choosing **Modify > Templates > Detach from Template**, you can detach the template from the page and make the entire document editable again.

3 | Applying Templates to Existing Documents

In this exercise, you'll go through the process of applying a template to an existing document. As you go through the development process, you'll most likely not start by developing a template, which is completely natural. Templates can be limiting and difficult to work with when you're constantly tweaking a design to get it just right. But once you get it just right and create your first template, you may need to go back and apply that template to documents you've already created.

1 Open **teacloudteas.htm** from the **ourproducts** folder. This file doesn't have any design at all, just some product descriptions. You're going to apply a design to it using the template you created in the previous exercise.

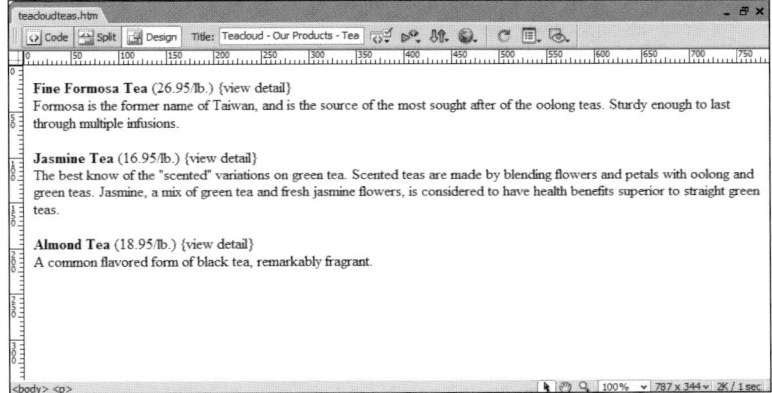

2 Choose **Modify > Templates > Apply Template to Page** to open the **Select Template** dialog box, which lists all available templates in the current site. Select the **OurProducts** template and click **Select**.

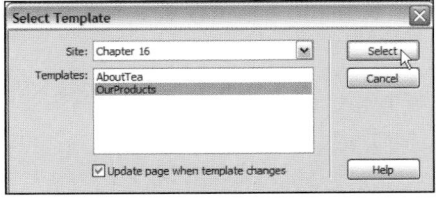

3 When you apply a template to a document, if the editable regions in the document don't match the editable regions in the template you're applying (or there are no editable regions in the current document), the **Inconsistent Region Names** dialog box opens. Select the **Document Body** region (which contains everything between the **<body>** tags in your page) and choose **Content** from the **Move content to new region** pop-up menu. Click **OK**.

The Inconsistent Region Names dialog box can be a bit overwhelming at first. It simply provides a way for you to put your content in the correct editable region when you apply a new template.

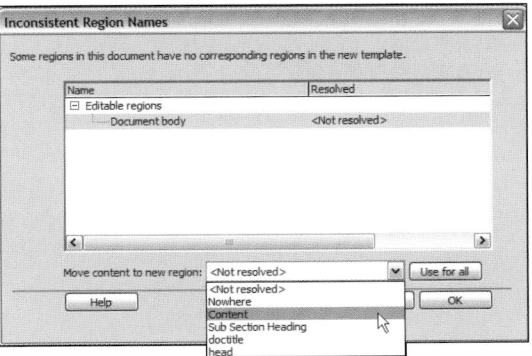

This is what the page
looks like with the new
template applied.

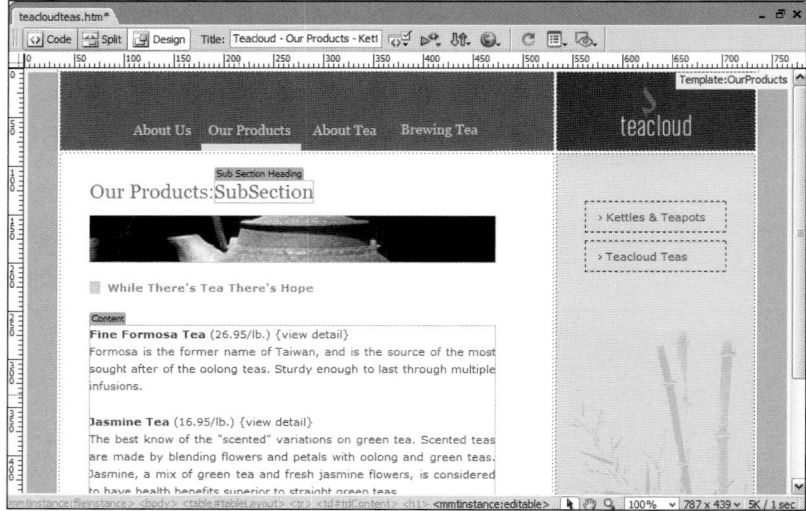

4 Click the **Sub
Section Heading** tab and
type **Teacloud Teas**.

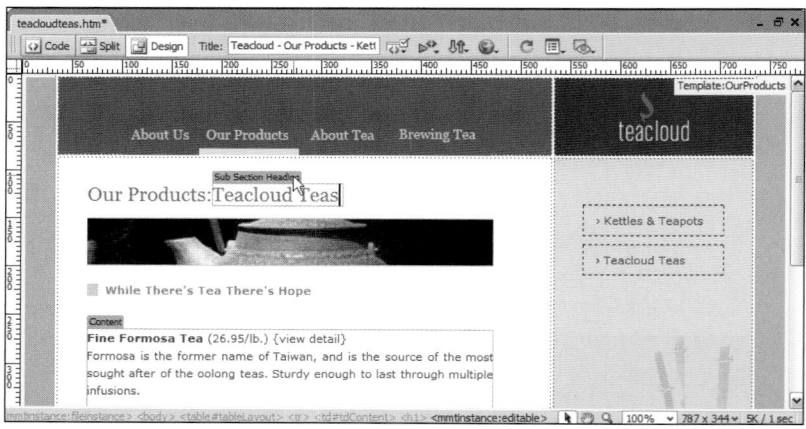

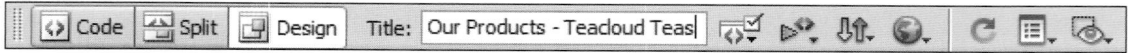

5 One unfortunate side effect of applying a template to an existing document is that you lose the document's title. In the **Document** toolbar, click inside the **Title** field, and change **Kettles and Teapots** to
Teacloud Teas and press **Enter** (Windows) or **Return** (Mac).

6 You now have your new page wrapped up in the **OurProducts** template. Close **teacloudteas.htm**. You don't need to save your changes.

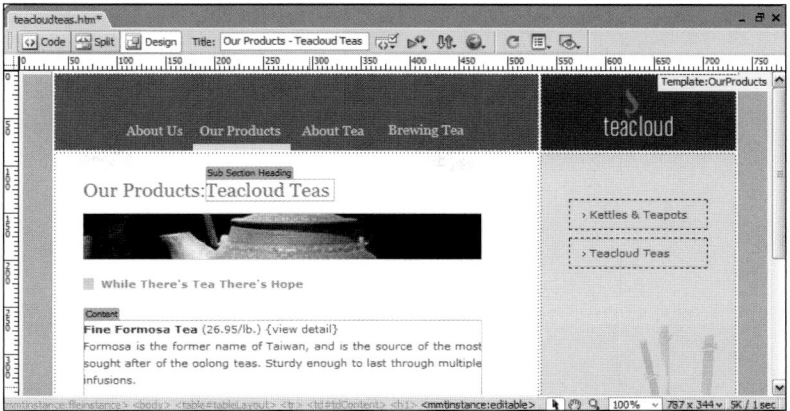

NOTE:

Applying Templates to Fully Designed Pages

There may come a time when you need to apply a template to a page that already has a full design. When the Inconsistent Region Names dialog box comes up and you decide to put the Document body inside the Content region of your template, you'll end up with one design inside another, which is probably not what you were after. The easiest way to make this situation work is to copy the content of your fully designed page, paste it into a new blank document, and then apply the template to the new document. Then just save the new document over the old one. This gets rid of any existing design elements that could break the new template you're applying.

4 | Modifying a Template

Unless you're like us and get everything right on your first try (yeah right), you'll need to go back and modify your existing template to tweak things after you've started working on your child pages. In this exercise, you'll modify the template you created in Exercise 2 to change some text alignment. Once you've made this change, you'll get to watch Dreamweaver 8 take care of the hard work for you by updating all of the child pages based on the template.

1 Before you can modify a template, you must open it from the **Assets** or **Files** panel. In the **Assets** panel, double-click the **OurProducts** template to open it.

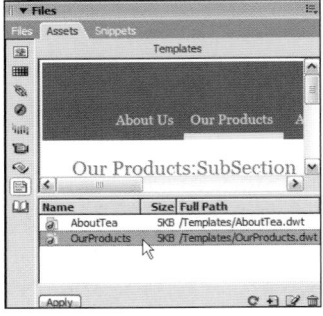

2 Place your cursor inside the **Our Products:** text and choose **Edit > Select Parent Tag** to select the entire **<h1>** tag.

Click here.

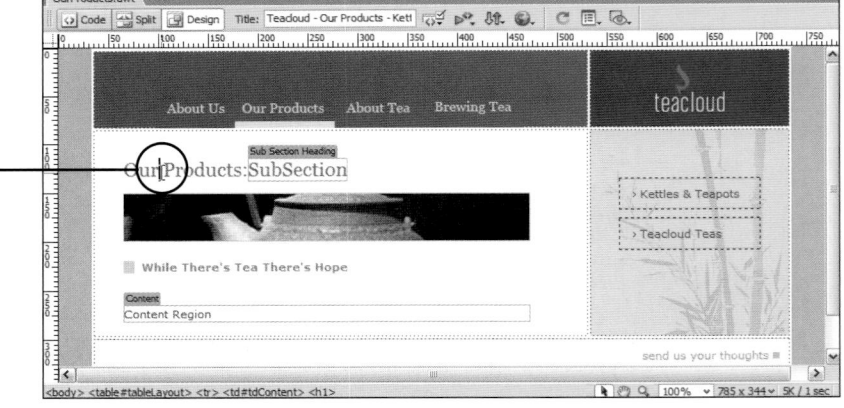

3 In the **Property Inspector**, click the **Align Right** button to change the text alignment.

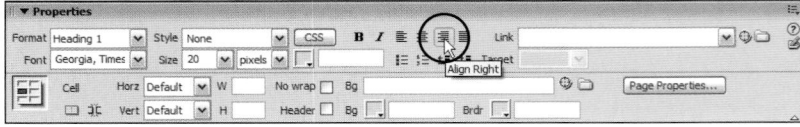

This moves the text to the right of the page.

4 Choose **File > Save** to save the template changes. A dialog box opens warning you about inserting an editable region inside a block tag. Click **OK**.

5 In the **Update Template Files** dialog box, click **Update** to update any files using this template (in this case **ordering.htm** and **teacloudteas.htm**). The **Update Pages** dialog box will list which files were updated. Click **Close** to close the **Update Pages** dialog box and continue.

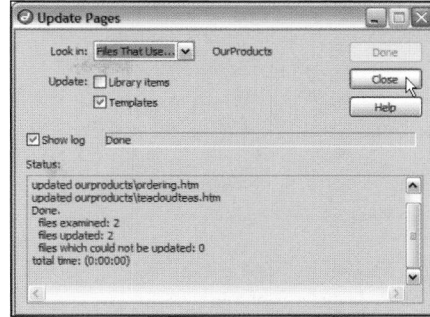

This is what **teacloudteas.htm** looks like with the revised template applied to it. Note that the heading at the top of the page is aligned to the right, just like the template.

6 Save and close everything but **OurProducts.dwt**; you'll be using it in the next exercise.

NOTE: ### Locked Head Content

After you apply a template to a page, you can no longer edit any information in the **<head>** tag that is part of the parent template. You can add additional JavaScript, styles, or behaviors, but you can't modify or remove any JavaScript, styles, or behaviors that were actually part of the template file. If you do need to edit the code in the locked region of the **<head>** tag, you need to remove the template by choosing **Modify > Templates > Detach from Template**. The downside, of course, is that if you make changes to the template, this unlinked copy will no longer be updated.

5 | Adding Repeating Regions

Repetitive work is the bane of many Web designers' existence. We like to design, not enter in the same information again and again. Repeating regions (and repeating tables) let you get rid of some of the drudgery and make entering repetitive data quick and precise. One of the problems with data entry is the likelihood for mistakes. Lock repetitive tasks into repeating regions and you'll cut down on data entry errors significantly. In this exercise, you'll learn how to make the Teacloud catalog pages easier to modify and update by using repeating regions.

1 To begin, take a look at an existing catalog page that's not based on a template. Open **kettlesandteapots.htm** in the **ourproducts** folder.

As you can see, this page is a wonderful candidate for a repeating region. Each teapot is in its own row, and each teapot has the same layout.

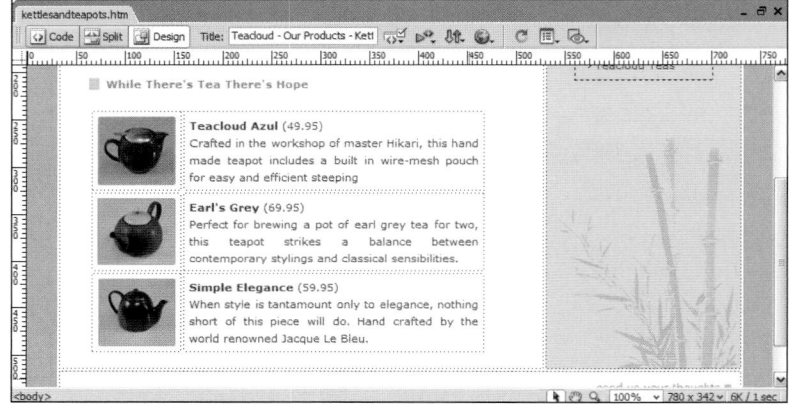

2 If it isn't already open from the previous exercise, open **OurProducts.dwt** from the **Templates** folder.

You're going to add a repeating region to the template you've been working with in the previous exercises.

3 Switch to **kettlesandteapots.htm** by choosing **Window > kettlesandteapots.htm** or clicking its tab at the top of the **Document** window. Select the entire table containing the teapots and choose **Edit > Copy** to copy the table.

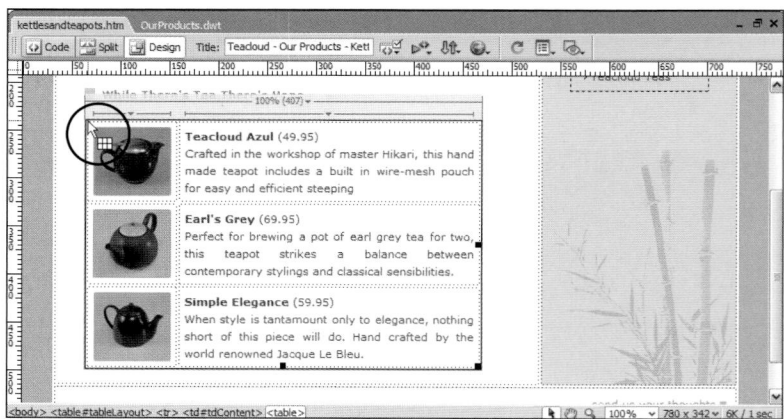

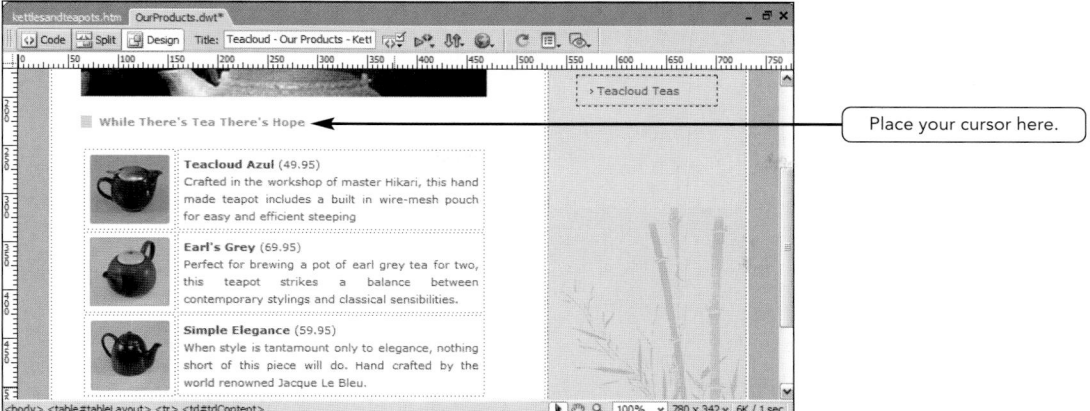

Place your cursor here.

4 Switch back to **OurProducts.dwt**. Place your cursor after **While There's Tea There's Hope** and choose **Edit > Paste**.

The product table from the existing product page is now part of the template.

---

5 Click in the second row of the first column and drag to the bottom right of the table to select the last two rows of the table. Press **Delete** to remove them. You need only one row to create a repeating region.

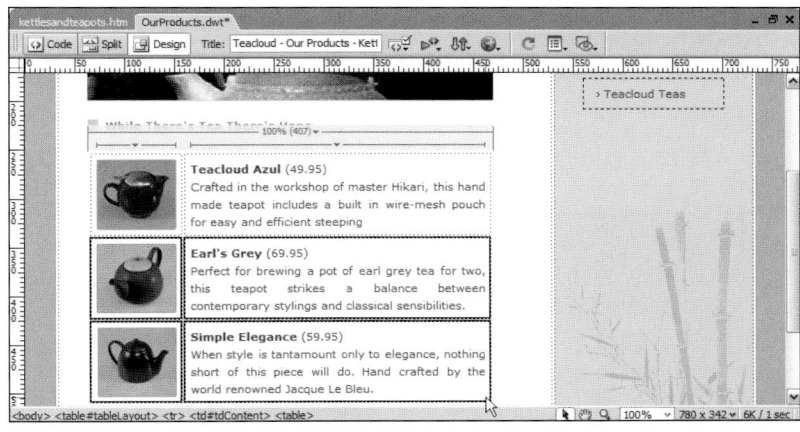

---

6 Click inside either of the table cells in the second row of the table, and click the **<tr>** tag in the **Tag Selector** to select the entire row.

7 Choose **Insert > Template Objects > Repeating Region** to open the **New Repeating Region** dialog box.

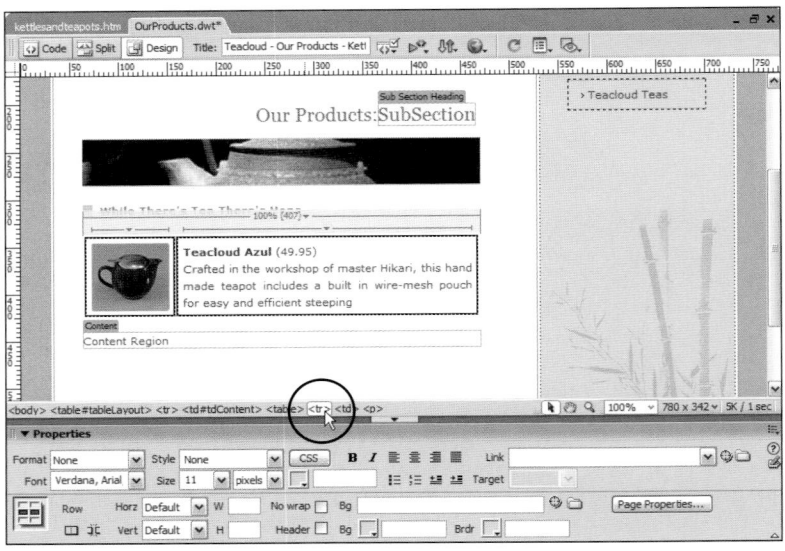

8 Type **Catalog Row** as the **Name** of the repeating region and click **OK**.

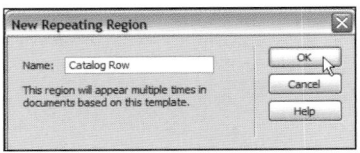

This is what the file looks like after you add the repeating region to the page. You can see a new tab wrapped around the table row, with the label *Repeat: Catalog Row*. This easily identifies this row as a repeating region.

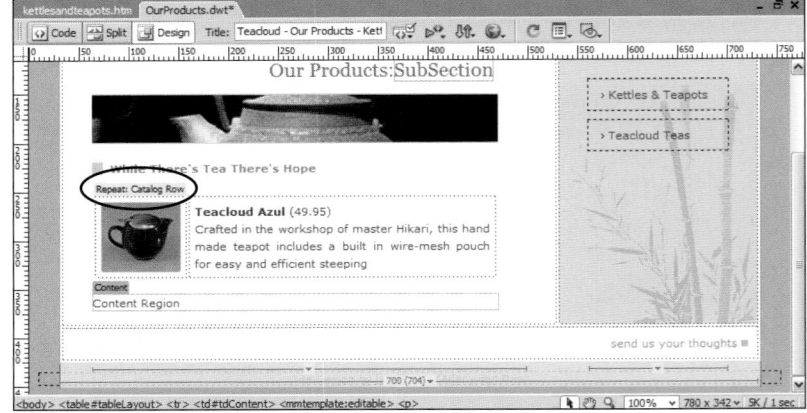

9 Select the image in the first table column and choose **Insert > Template Objects > Editable Region**. In the **New Editable Region** dialog box, name the region **Product Image** and click **OK**.

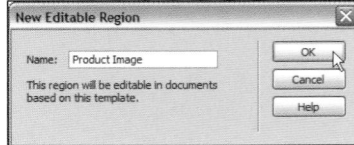

You've added a repeating region, but you need some editable regions as well. If you don't specify any editable regions inside the repeating region, you won't be able to add any content to the rows inside the child pages.

10 Click and drag to select the teapot name, **Teacloud Azul**, and press **Delete**. With the cursor still in the same location, choose **Insert > Template Objects > Editable Region**. In the **New Editable Region** dialog box, name the region **Product Name** and click **OK**.

11 Do the same for the product details and the price, naming the regions **Product Details** and **Product Price**.

This is what your template should look like after all of the editable regions are in place. The product image, name, price, and details are all in editable regions, and the rest of the page is still locked.

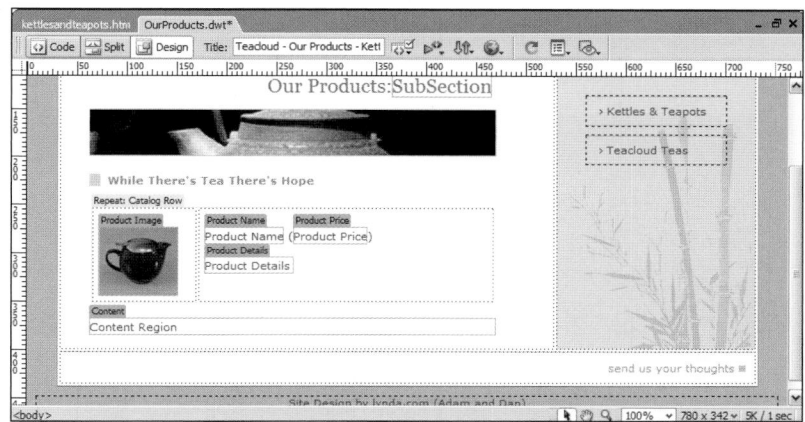

12 Save the template and update all of the pages based on the template. Close any open documents before continuing to the next exercise.

You're probably thinking this is all very unexciting at this point. But now it's time to create a new page and start working with the repeating region! Continue on to the next exercise to learn how to *use* those repeating regions.

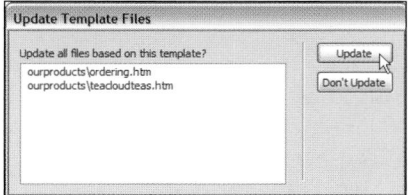

6 | Working with Repeating Regions

In the last exercise, you added a new repeating region to a template. Looking at it inside the template wasn't all that awe-inspiring, but now you get to play with the repeating regions. In this exercise, you're going to create a new page based on the template you saved in the previous exercise, and you're going to add some new catalog entries.

1 In the **Assets** panel, select the **Template** category. **Right-click** (Windows) or **Ctrl+click** (Mac) the **OurProducts** template and choose **New From Template** from the contextual menu. Save the new document as **kettlesandteapots-new.htm** in the **ourproducts** folder.

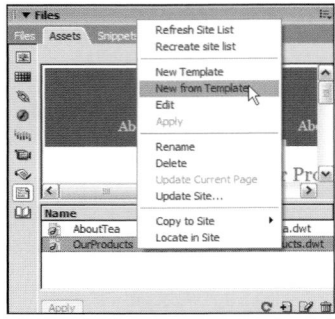

2 The first thing you should notice is the **Repeating Region** controls above the repeating region you added in the previous exercise.

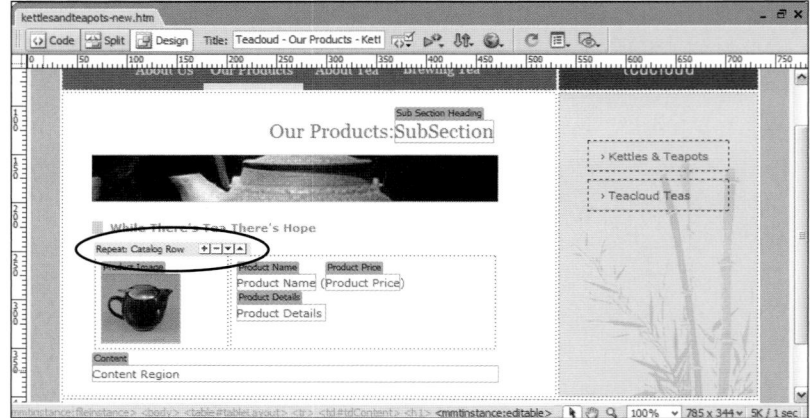

The Repeating Region controls let you add a new row after the currently selected row (**+**), delete the selected row (**–**), and move the selected row up (**up arrow**) or down (**down arrow**). The selected row in this case is whichever row the cursor is currently inside.

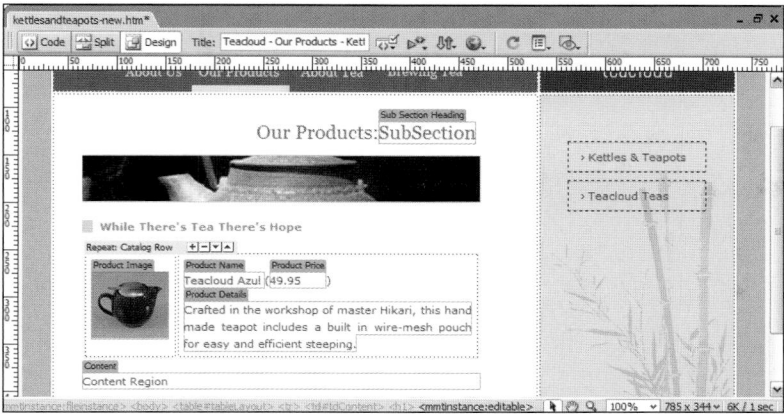

3 For the first product, click the tab for each editable region and type this text:

Product Image: Leave the default image, since it's already the image of the Teacloud Azul teapot.

Product Name: Teacloud Azul

Price: 49.95

Product Details: Crafted in the workshop of master Hikari, this hand made teapot includes a built in wire-mesh pouch for easy and efficient steeping.

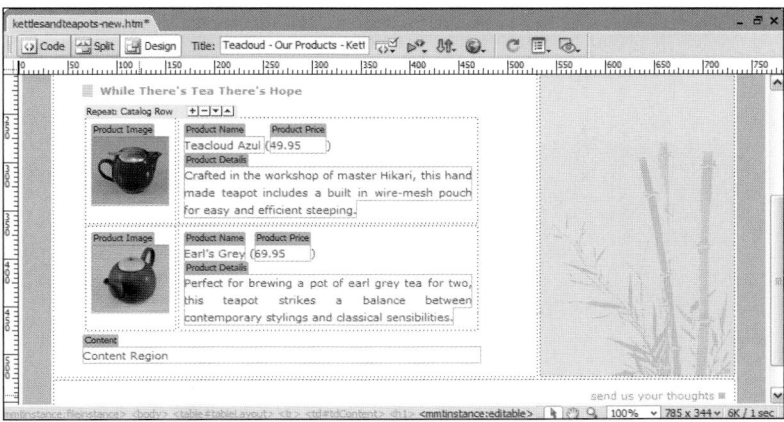

4 Click the **add** button (+) to add a new row directly below the **Teacloud Azul** row. Enter the following text for each editable region in the new row:

Product Image: Set the image **Src** to **../assets/images/products/kettles/earls-grey.jpg** in the Property Inspector

Product Name: Earl's Grey

Price: 69.95

Product Details: Perfect for brewing a pot of earl grey tea for two, this teapot strikes a balance between contemporary stylings and classical sensibilities.

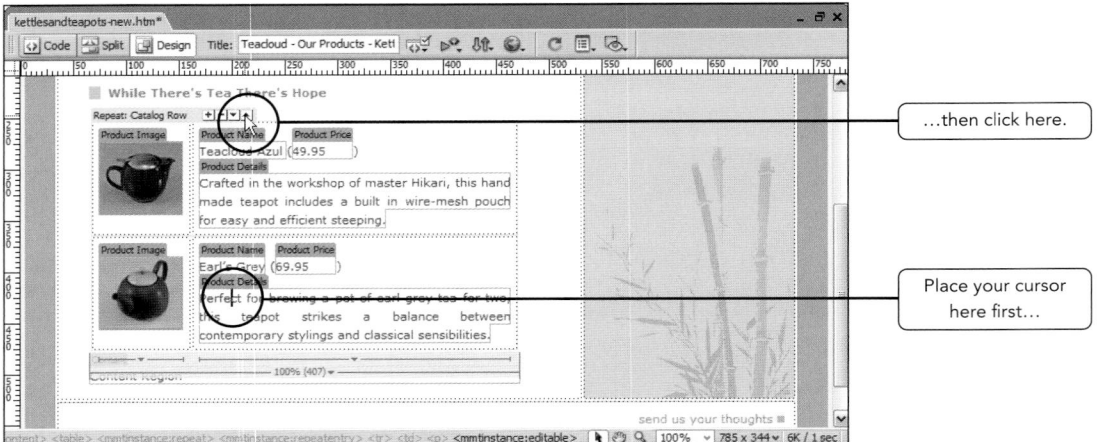

...then click here.

Place your cursor
here first...

5 Now that you have two products set up, you can play with changing the order. Place your cursor in any of the editable regions inside the second row. In the **Repeating Region** controls, click the **move up** button (up arrow) to move the second row above the first.

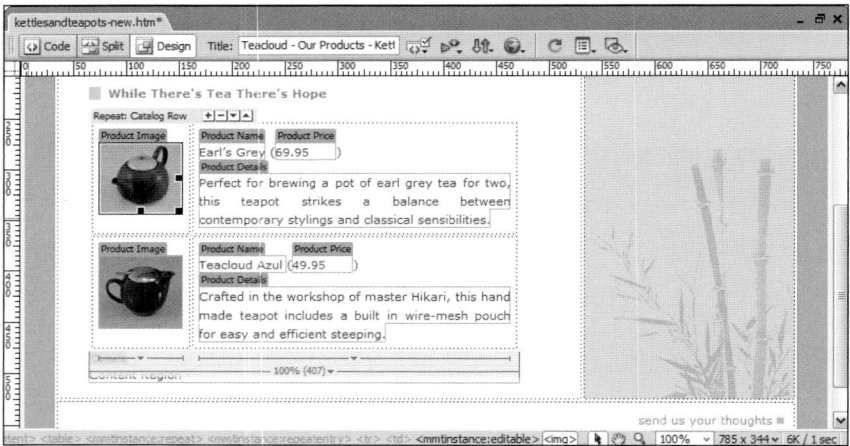

This is what your page should look like after moving the rows around.

In this exercise you learned how to work with the Repeating Region controls to manipulate the repeating region you added in the previous exercise. You can now take your templates to the next level and make sure that others on your team (or your boss who wants to be a Web designer) don't make a mess of the design you spent so much time putting together.

EXERCISE

7 | Adding Optional Regions

There will be times when you'll want to hide or display elements on a per page basis. Using optional regions lets you turn sections of a template on and off using template parameters (which you'll learn to modify in the next exercise). In this exercise, you'll create an optional region that will allow you to easily turn off the product repeating region you added in Exercise 5. The Teacloud Teas page doesn't need the product display, even though it's based on the OurProducts template.

1 Open **teacloudteas.htm** from the **ourproducts** folder.

As you can see, when you added the repeating region to the OurProducts template, it added that repeating region to the Teacloud Teas page as well, an unintended side effect of making the kettles and teapots easier to add.

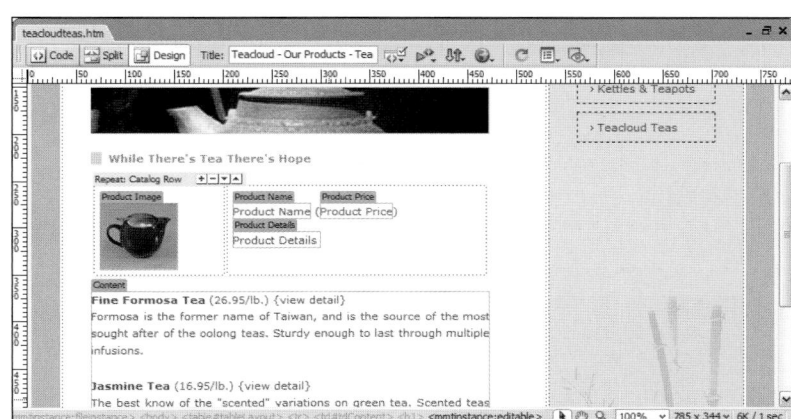

2 Open **OurProducts.dwt** from the **Templates** folder. Click the **Repeat: Catalog Row** tab and choose **Edit > Select Parent Tag** to select the entire product table.

Click here.

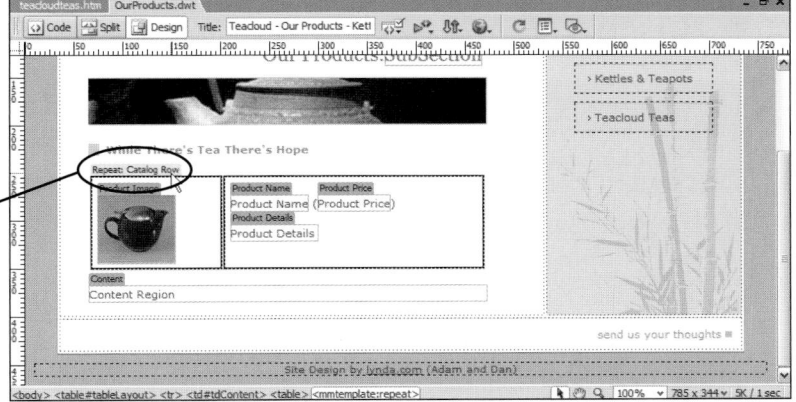

3 Choose **Insert > Template Objects > Optional Region** to open the **New Optional Region** dialog box.

The New Optional Region dialog box lets you give the optional region a friendly name for references in the Template Properties dialog box (which you'll learn more about in the next exercise).

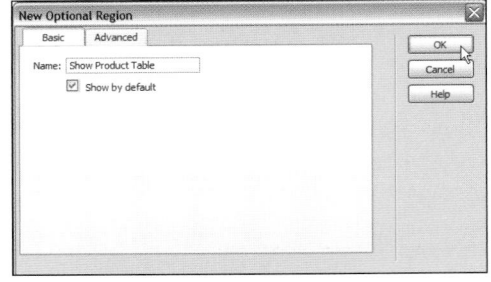

4 Type **Show Product Table** as the **Name** of the optional region, and leave the **Show by default** box selected. Click **OK** to add the new region to the page.

The Basic tab of the New Optional Region dialog box will do everything you need to do for 99 percent of the templates you'll build. You may eventually have need for the Advanced tab, which lets you pick from existing template parameters already on the page, and it lets you enter custom template parameter expressions to decide whether to show a region or not.

This is the OurProducts template with the new optional region added to the page. Notice the new tab wrapped around the product table, which is labeled *If Show Product Table*. This tab gives you a quick reference to let you know that an optional region is wrapped around the content.

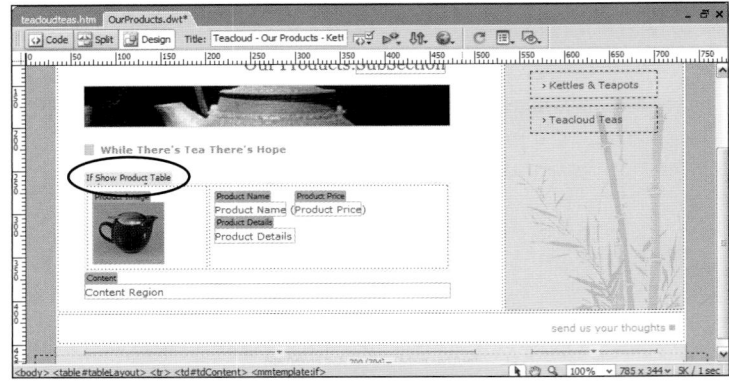

5 Save the **OurProducts** template. When the **Update Template Files** dialog box appears, click **Update**. Click **Close** in the **Update Pages** dialog box after everything has been updated.

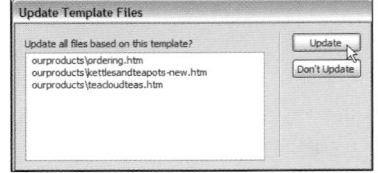

6 Switch to **teacloudteas.htm** to see what's changed. Leave this file open—you'll be using it in the next exercise.

Surprised? There's absolutely no change to the way the document looked before you added the optional region. That's because when you defined the optional region, you left the Show by default box selected, so the optional region is being shown. Check out the next exercise to see how to use the optional region in your page.

8 | Modifying Template Properties

When you created the optional region in the previous exercise, Dreamweaver 8 created a template parameter for you to control the display of that optional region. In this exercise, you'll learn how to modify template properties on your child pages.

---

1 If you just completed Exercise 7, **teacloudteas.htm** should still be open. If it's not, go back and complete Exercise 7. Switch to **Code** view and scroll up to line **35**. (This may be slightly different on your machine.)

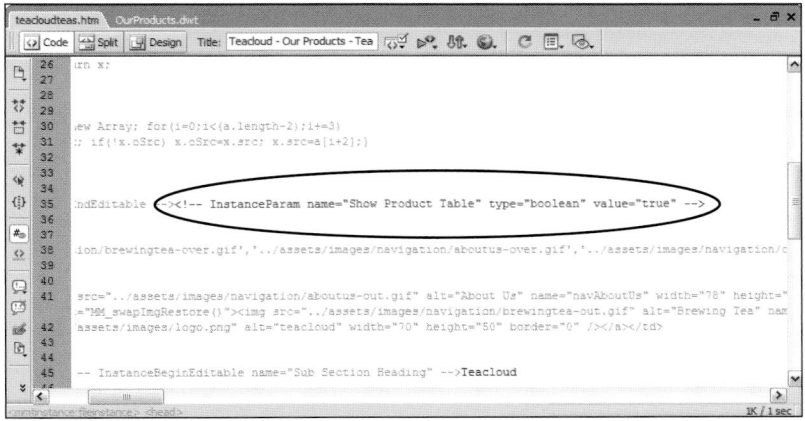

The HTML comment is how Dreamweaver 8 defines template parameters in your documents. Template parameters control any optional regions on your page. As you can see, the name of the template parameter is Show Product Table, just like you defined in the previous exercise, the type of parameter is **boolean** (meaning true or false), and the default value is **true**.

---

2 Switch back to **Design** view and choose **Modify > Template Properties** to open the **Template Properties** dialog box.

---

3 With the **Show Product Table** template parameter selected in the top half of the dialog box, deselect the **Show Show Product Table** box. Click **OK** to close the dialog box and update the page.

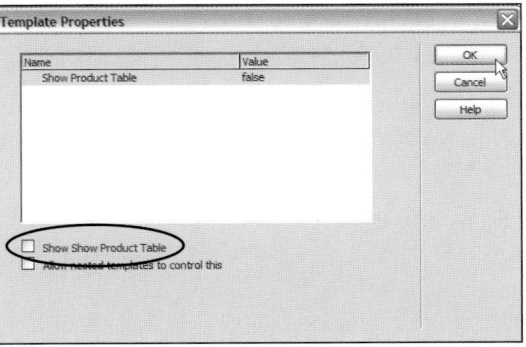

It may seem odd that the dialog box says *Show Show Product Table*, but the default behavior for the Template Properties dialog box is to put the word *Show* before the optional region name. Regardless of the goofy wording, we prefer to give optional regions names that read well with the word *If* in front of them, so they make sense when looking at the labels for the optional regions in the template itself.

---

4 You should now see that the product table is no longer displayed on the page. Save and close all open files.

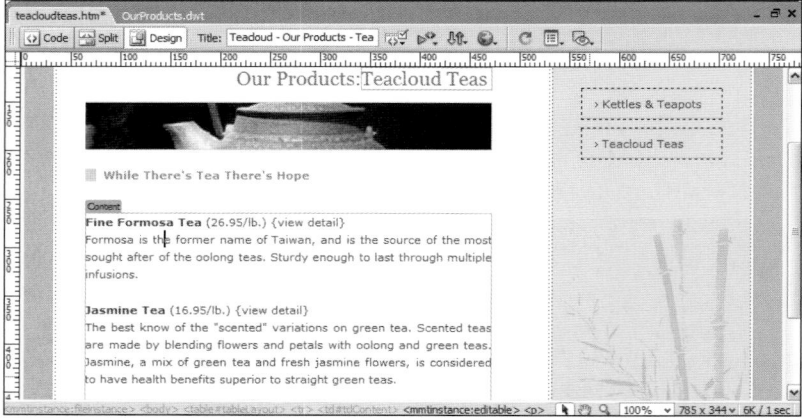

When to Use Library Items

One of the biggest issues with using templates and library items is trying to figure out when to use which. Templates are good for locking down entire layouts, whereas library items let you lock down small reusable pieces of code, whether you're using a template or not.

The best example of when to use library items is with copyright statements (which we'll show you in the next few exercises). In most sites, you'll have two or three different page layouts, perhaps with three or four different templates. You might have pop-up windows that contain copyright statements, along with all of your standard pages. It's far easier to make that copyright statement a library item and include it in each of your templates and pop-up windows than it is to change the copyright every year in each template and each pop-up window.

9 | Creating a Library Item

Library items and templates are somewhat similar in function. Both are used to apply changes to multiple pages with ease. The difference is that templates affect the entire page design, whereas you use library items for individual page elements, both inside and outside of templates. In this exercise, you will create a library item for a copyright statement and then apply it to a page by simply dragging it into Design view in Dreamweaver 8.

1 In the **Files** panel, double-click **index.htm** to open it. Scroll to the bottom and you'll see the copyright statement that needs to be on every page of the site. Click and drag to select all of the copyright text.

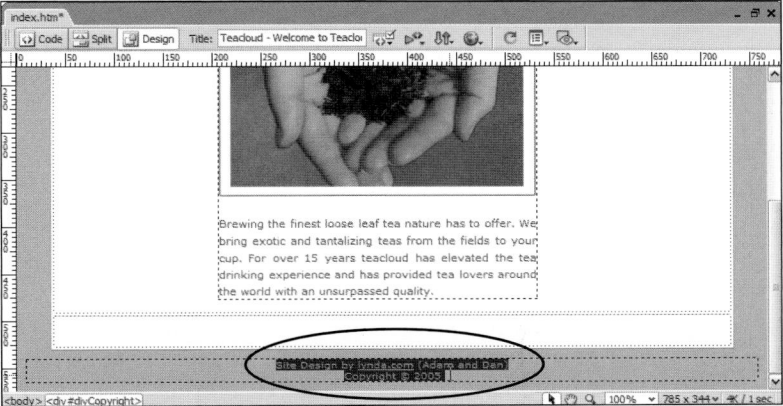

2 In the **Assets** panel, select the **Library** category. Click the **New Library Item** button. Your new library item instantly appears in the category. It needs a name, so type **Copyright** in the bounding box.

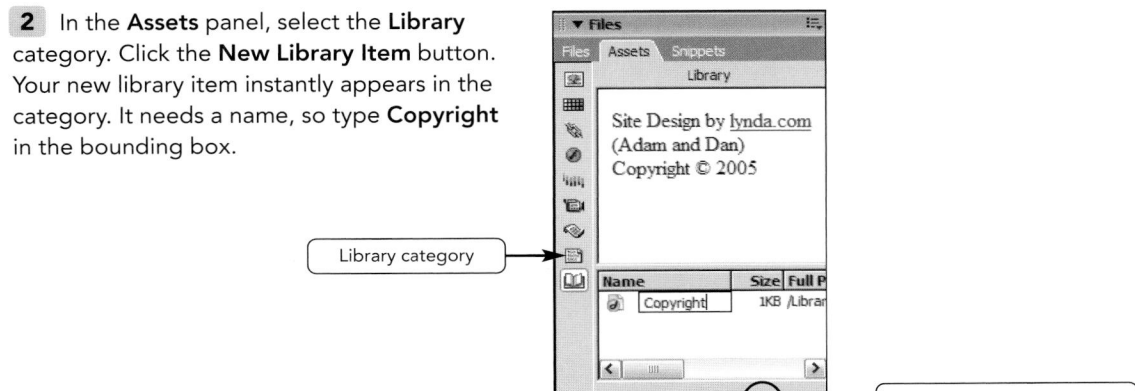

Library category

New Library Item button

When you click the New Library Item button, Dreamweaver takes any highlighted text in the current document and adds it to the new library item. It will then convert the selection in your document into the new library item. If you get a warning stating that the library item may not look the same in other documents, just click **OK**.

Dreamweaver 8 took the liberty of converting the selection in **index.htm** into a library item for you. You can tell that a block of text is part of a library item because of the yellow highlighting.

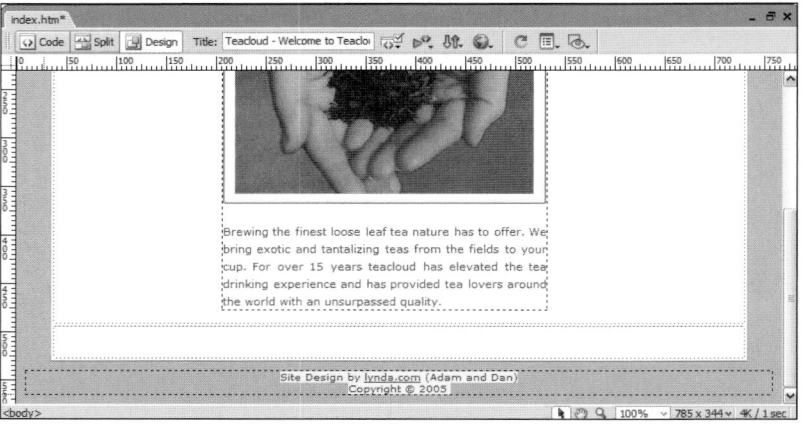

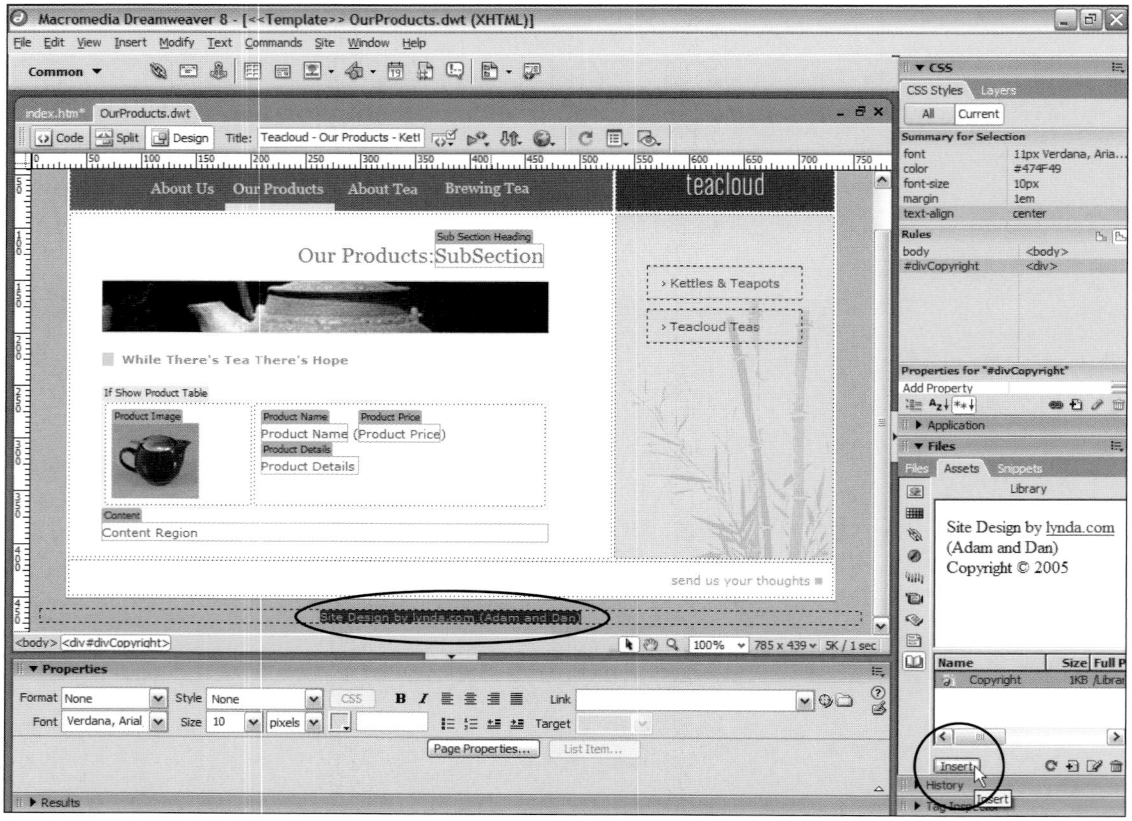

3 Now that you have created your library item, you can apply it to any page in the site. Open the **OurProducts** template. Scroll to the bottom and click and drag to select the text in the footer. In the **Assets** panel, select the **Copyright** library item and click **Insert**.

The template is now using the library item for the copyright statement in the footer.

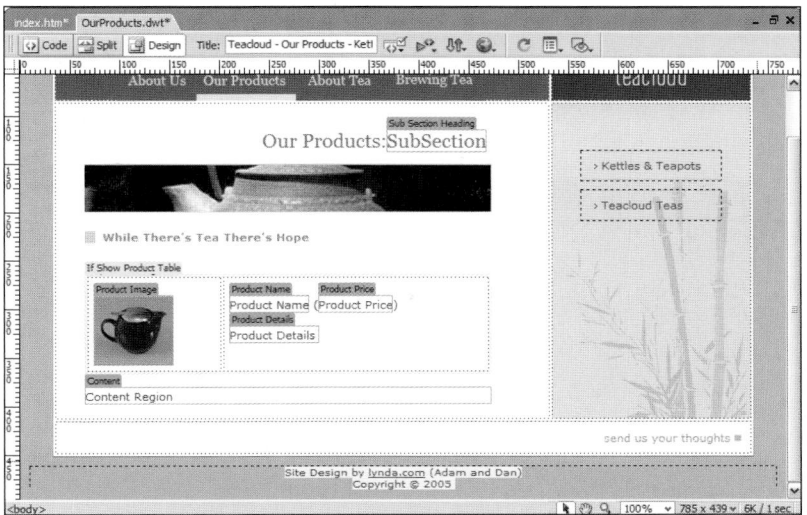

4 Save the **OurProducts** template and update all of the pages based on the template. All of the template-based pages are now using the same library item.

5 Save and close any open documents.

In the next exercise, you'll modify the Copyright library item and see that it's just as easy to update a library item as it is to update a template.

10 Modifying a Library Item

Now that you know how to create library items, you are going to modify the one you just created and then watch Dreamweaver 8 quickly update your page.

1 In the **Library** category of the **Assets** panel, select the **Copyright** library item and click the **Edit** button.

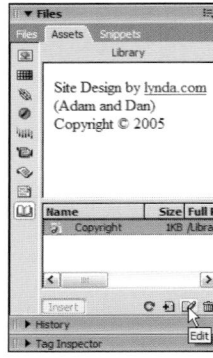

TIP: | **Edit Right from the Page**

You can also edit library items by **right-clicking** (Windows) or **Ctrl+clicking** (Mac) the library item in any page it's applied to. Then just choose **Open Library Item** from the contextual menu.

---

2 Change the copyright statement to read **Copyright © 2004–2005**.

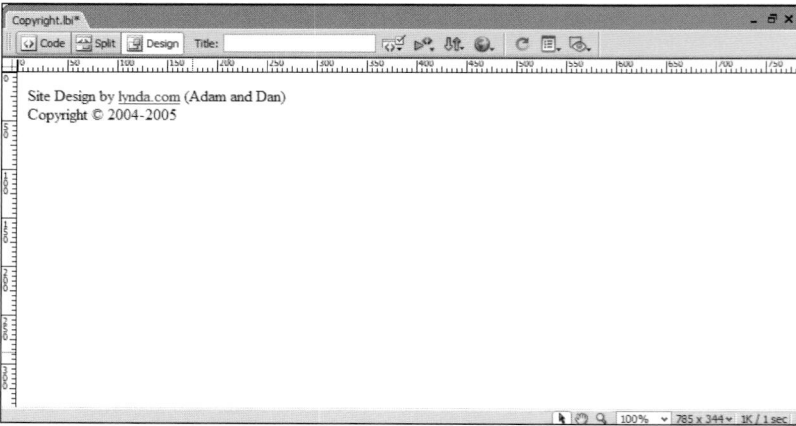

3 Close the library item file, and when you are prompted, make sure you save your changes. In the **Update Library Items** dialog box, click **Update**.

Notice that not only is **index.htm** listed, but the OurProducts template and all of the pages based on that template will also be updated.

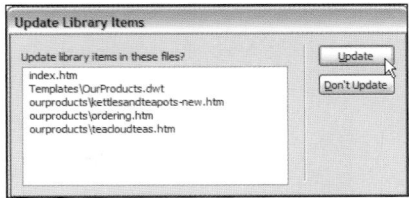

4 Click **Close** to close the **Update Pages** dialog box when you are done reviewing it.

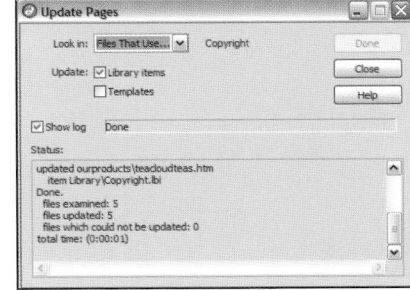

5 Open **index.htm** again and you'll see that the new copyright dates are now listed on the page. Close all open documents.

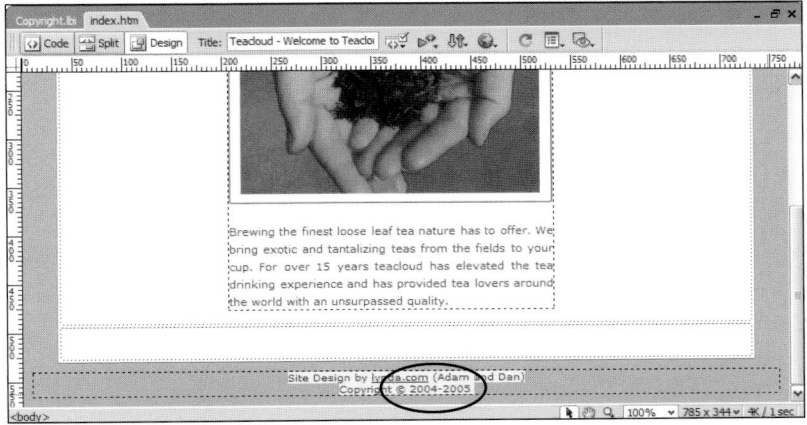

In this chapter, you learned how to work with templates and library items. You learned how to add editable regions, repeating regions, and optional regions to a template to make it easy to manage all of the product documents for your site. You also learned how to lock down smaller areas of a page by using library items. These solutions make it possible to make changes in large numbers of documents all at once. In the next chapter, you'll learn how to use a different type of automation in Dreamweaver 8.

17

Automation

If you design Web pages, you will quickly notice an abundance of incredibly repetitive and boring tasks are required to do your work. Fortunately, Dreamweaver 8 has several features to help you automate many of these boring tasks, such as the History panel and custom objects and commands. In this chapter, you'll learn about the History panel, which memorizes and replays steps you've performed while creating a Dreamweaver 8 document. You can script this panel to replay these steps, which is one great way to automate repetitive tasks. This chapter also introduces you to the powerful Find and Replace feature, which can efficiently make changes to your current page, a range of pages, or your entire site. You will also work with one of the preexisting commands that ships with Dreamweaver 8 right out of the box: Create Web Photo Album.

What Is the History Panel?

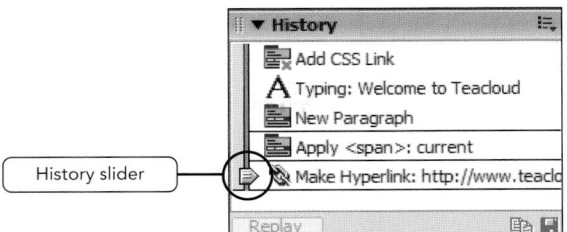

History slider

The History panel displays the last 50 steps (by default) you have performed since you created or opened a file. This offers a nice visual overview of the different steps you've completed. You can use the slider to quickly undo and redo these steps. This visual approach to stepping backward and forward through your document gives you more feedback than pressing **Ctrl+Z** and **Ctrl+Y**

(Windows) or **Cmd+Z** and **Cmd+Y** (Mac). You can copy the steps in the History panel from one document to another, which is helpful when you want to share information between documents. You can also copy steps from the History panel and save them as commands, which lets you replay them at a later time, in any document, with a just single click.

1 | Using the History Panel for Undo/Redo

This first exercise gets you comfortable working with the History panel. You'll learn how to use this panel to repeat or delete operations you've performed. Working with the History panel can be much easier than choosing undo and/or redo multiple times.

1 Copy the **chap_17** folder from the **HOT CD-ROM** to your **Desktop**. Define your site as **Chapter 17** using the **chap_17** folder as the local root folder. Make sure the **Files** panel is open. If it's not, choose **Window > Files** or press **F11**.

2 In the **Files** panel, double-click **contactus.htm** to open it. Place your cursor in the table cell containing the **Name:** label.

To make the labels for the form fields easier to see on this page, you're going to change the formatting for the table cells containing the labels.

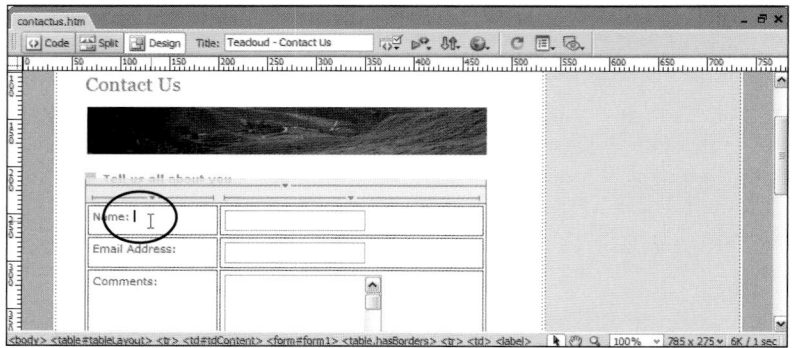

3 In the **Property Inspector**, type **#E3E5DC** in the **Bg** color field and choose **Right** from the **Horz** pop-up menu.

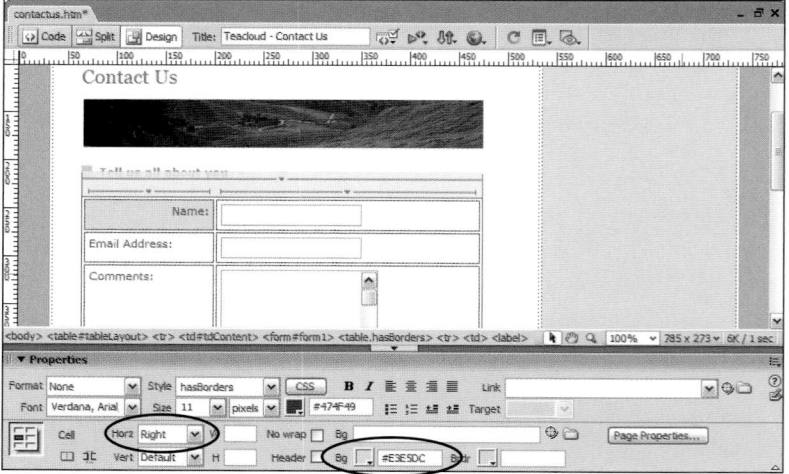

4 If the **History** panel isn't already open, choose **Window > History** (**Shift+F10**) to open it.

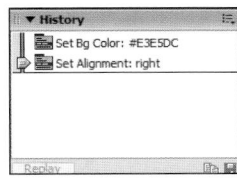

The History panel displays the change you made to the table cell in Step 3. As you continue to make additions and changes to your document, your steps appear here automatically.

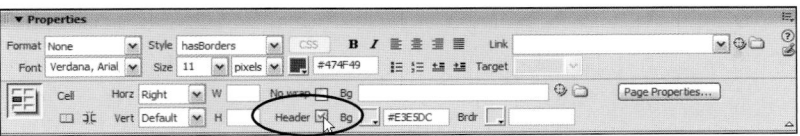

5 With the table cell still selected, check the **Header** check box in the **Property Inspector** to change the **<td>** tag to a **<th>** tag.

Notice the History panel records this step as well.

6 In the **History** panel, click and drag the **History** slider up to the top so the first step is highlighted. This undoes the last formatting you applied to the page, just as though you had used the **Undo** command. Click and drag the **History** slider back down to the bottom of the list to reapply the text formatting.

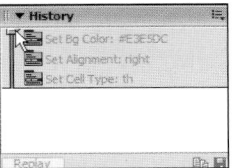

This is a nice way to step through the changes you have made to a document. It beats having to press **Ctrl+Z** (Windows) or **Cmd+Z** (Mac) because it gives you feedback about what change you are undoing.

7 Place your cursor in the table cell containing the **Email Address** label and choose **Edit > Select Parent Tag** to select the table cell.

In order to make sure that the History panel actually applies the changes to the proper element, you need to make sure that the actual table cell is selected.

8 Select the last item in the **History** panel, hold down the **Shift** key, and select the first item to select all of the steps. Click the **Replay** button.

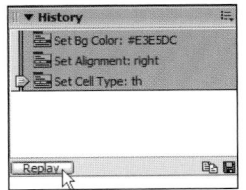

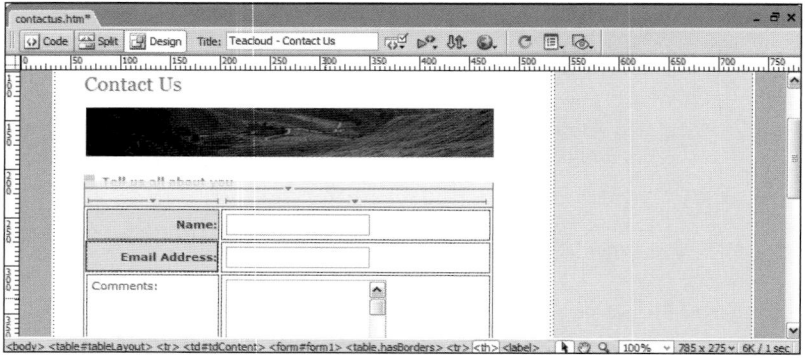

The table cell containing the Email Address label now has the same formatting as the Name label's table cell. As you can see, you can apply or replay the steps in the History panel. In this case, you manually formatted the Name field and used the recorded steps in the History panel to replay the actions to apply the same formatting to the Email Address field. As you can see, replaying actions is a huge timesaver and saves you from repeating multiple steps over and over, which can be tedious and rather boring.

9 Save your changes and keep **contactus.htm** open for the next exercise.

NOTE:

Saving Files and Clearing the History Panel

The History panel does not clear automatically when you save a file. This is great if you want to use it to make changes even after you save the document. If you close the file and reopen it, however, the history is cleared.

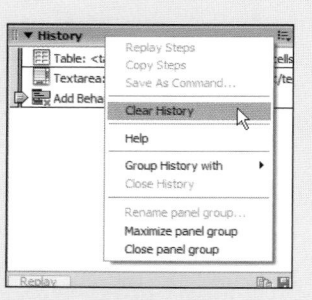

You can clear the History panel at any time. Why would you want to clear the History panel? The History panel uses a lot of RAM if you have made a lot of changes to your document. Clear the history by clicking the **Panel Options** menu in the upper right of the **History** panel and choosing **Clear History** from the pop-up menu. You can't undo this action, so be careful when you use it.

2 | Saving History Steps as Commands

In the previous exercise, you learned how to use the History panel to undo and redo changes. You also learned how to replay the history steps in order to perform repetitive operations. What would you do if you needed to perform those same steps in multiple documents, perhaps hundreds of times over the course of a site's design? Dreamweaver 8 makes it easy to replay steps as many times as you like by saving the steps in the History panel as a command.

---

1 If you just completed Exercise 1, **contactus.htm** should still be open. If it's not, go back and complete Exercise 1. The **History** panel should match the illustration here.

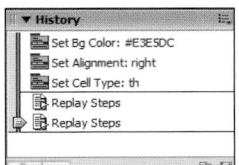

In this exercise, you'll use the existing steps in the History panel to create a command you can use over and over to format multiple pages.

> ### NOTE: | What Is a Command?
>
>
>
> A *command* is a small JavaScript file that records specific functions performed in Dreamweaver 8. These files are stored inside the Configuration\Commands folder. Some commands ship with Dreamweaver 8, such as the Create Web Photo Album command. You can even create your own custom commands, using the History panel, or write them from scratch with JavaScript. For example, you can copy steps from the History panel and save them as a command. Dreamweaver 8 converts the selected steps into JavaScript so that you can replay them from any document. As you can see, commands can be very powerful and can save you a lot of time.

---

2 Click the first step in the **History** panel. Hold down the **Shift** key and click **Set Cell Type: th** step to select all three steps in the **History** panel.

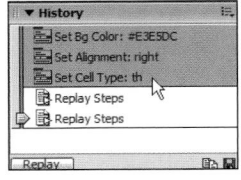

---

3 Click the **Save** button to open the **Save As Command** dialog box.

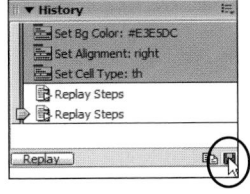

---

4 In the **Save As Command** dialog box, type **Format Table Label** for the **Command Name** and click **OK**.

When you name commands, try to be specific about what steps the command performs. As you create more and more commands, you'll need to remember which command does what. By using a descriptive name, you'll be able to remember what steps the command performs.

---

5 Place your cursor in the table cell containing the **Comments** label and choose **Edit > Select Parent Tag** to select the table cell. Choose **Commands > Format Table Label**.

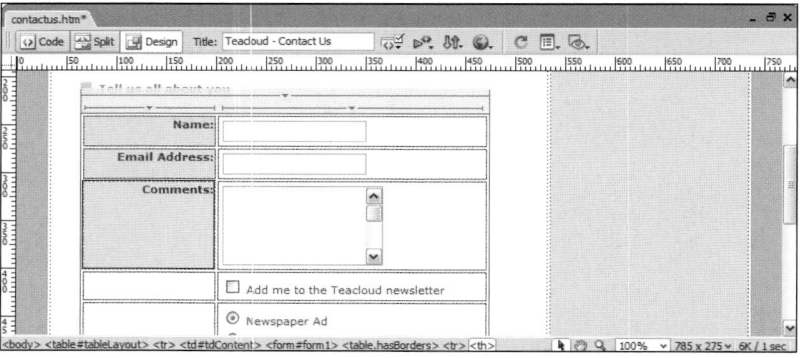

The Comments table cell is now formatted exactly the same as the other two table cells. Saving a set of history steps as a command makes it easy to perform the same steps as many times as you need, and on any page you want (not just documents in the current site).

---

6 Close **contactus.htm**. You don't need to save your changes.

VIDEO:  **webphotoalbum.mov**

Saving your own history steps as a command is great, but commands can do so much more. Commands can do as little as setting some table formatting to as much as creating entire Web sites and pages. Dreamweaver 8 ships with a number of commands, which you'll find useful. One of the commands is the Create Web Photo Album command, which will automatically convert an entire folder of images into a Web Photo Gallery. To learn how to use the Create Web Photo Album command to build your own online photo albums, check out **webphotoalbum.mov** in the **videos** folder on the **HOT CD-ROM**.

3 | Using Find and Replace

One of the most powerful (and least acclaimed) features in Dreamweaver 8 is the Find and Replace feature. With it you can perform what would normally be very time-intensive tasks in an incredibly short amount of time. The Find and Replace feature is similar to the Find and Replace feature in other programs, such as Microsoft Word, but it's geared specifically toward Web development. In this exercise, you'll learn how to use this feature to replace text on a page and how to replace text in the source code of your documents.

1 In the **Files** panel, double-click **aboutus.htm** to open it.

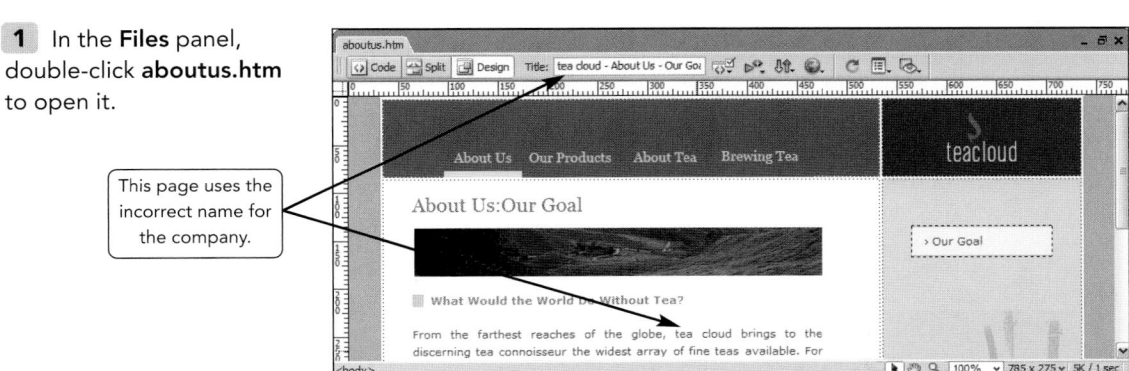

Notice this page incorrectly used *tea cloud* in the page title and within the body text. The proper name for this company is *Teacloud*. Unfortunately, every page in the site uses the wrong company name. You could open each page in your site and make the corrections manually, but that would be a very inefficient way to work. This site has fewer than 10 pages with the wrong company name, but what if you had a site that had a similar problem with hundreds of pages? By using the Find and Replace feature, you can make these changes quickly and accurately.

2 Click to select the **tea cloud** text in the **Title** field of the **Document** window. Choose **Edit** > **Find and Replace** to open the **Find and Replace** dialog box with your selection already in the **Find** field.

3 From the **Find in** pop-up menu, choose **Entire Current Local Site** to ensure Dreamweaver 8 searches all the pages within the current local site.

Take a moment to examine the other available options. As you can see, Dreamweaver 8 lets you modify as little or as much of your site as you wish. You can search in as little as a few selected words, to a specific folder, or the entire site.

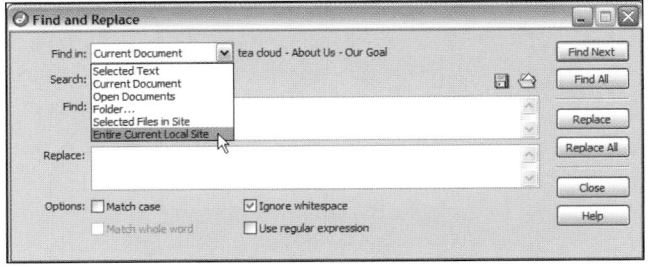

4 Choose **Text** from the **Search** pop-up menu to ensure Dreamweaver 8 searches only the text on each affected page. You can also search through the source code or even specific tags.

5 The **Find** field should automatically contain the text you select in Step 2. If it doesn't, type **tea cloud** in the **Find** field.

6 In the **Replace** field, type **Teacloud**, to define the text that will replace the text in the **Find** field. Click **Replace All** to have Dreamweaver search the text on all the pages in your site and make the necessary replacements.

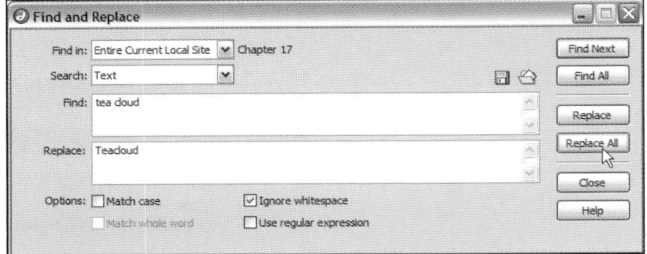

There are plenty of other options, such as making sure that the Find and Replace matches the case exactly. Click the **Help** button to learn more about these options.

7 Because you don't have every page in your site open, Dreamweaver 8 displays a warning telling you that this operation cannot be undone in pages that aren't open. Click **Yes** to continue.

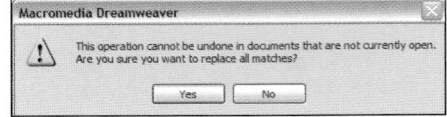

Dreamweaver 8 opens the Results panel, which shows you every replace that Dreamweaver 8 per-formed. This lets you make sure everything was replaced correctly.

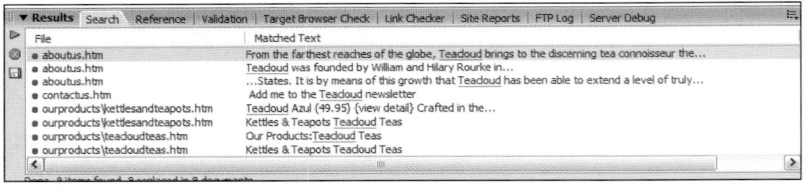

8 Double-click any entry in the **Results** panel to open the page and go straight to the replace text, just in case you replaced something you shouldn't have.

> The text in the <title> tag wasn't replaced.

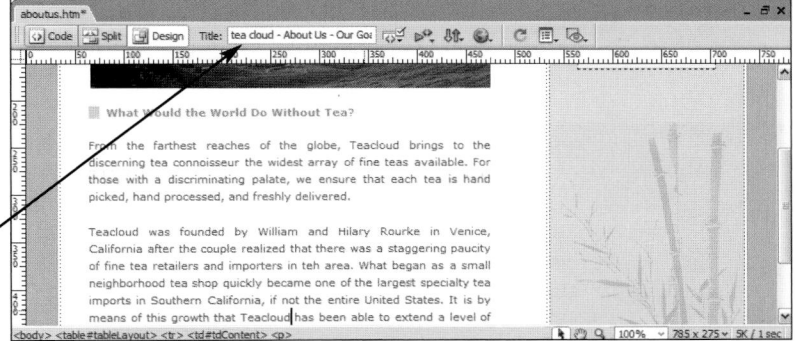

Notice only the text on the page was replaced; the text in the **<title>** tag was left alone. When you set the Search option to Text in the Find and Replace dialog box, Dreamweaver 8 limited the search to the text within the **<body>** tag of the page. Because the **<title>** is outside the **<body>** tag, that text was not replaced.

9 Choose **Edit > Find and Replace** again.

Notice the settings from the last find and replace operation are retained.

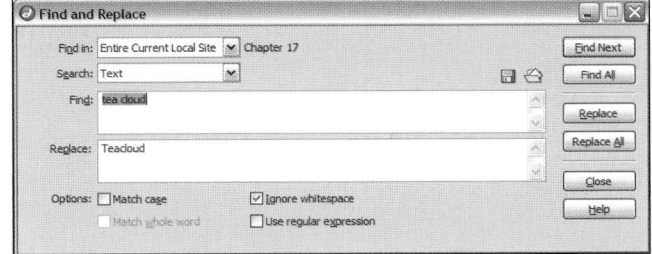

10 From the **Search** drop-down menu, choose **Source Code**. This causes Dreamweaver 8 to search through all the source code on the page, including the **<title>** tag, instead of just the text contained within the **<body>** tag. It will also find any problems with tag attributes, such as a misspelling in an **alt** attribute for an image. Click **Replace All**.

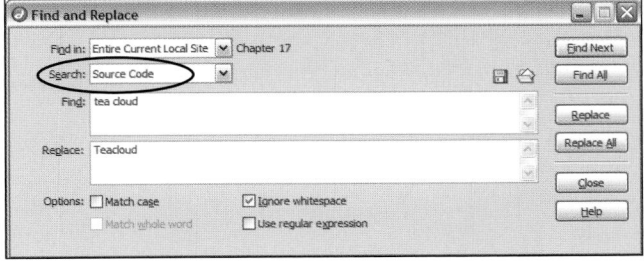

11 When the warning dialog box appears, click **Yes**.

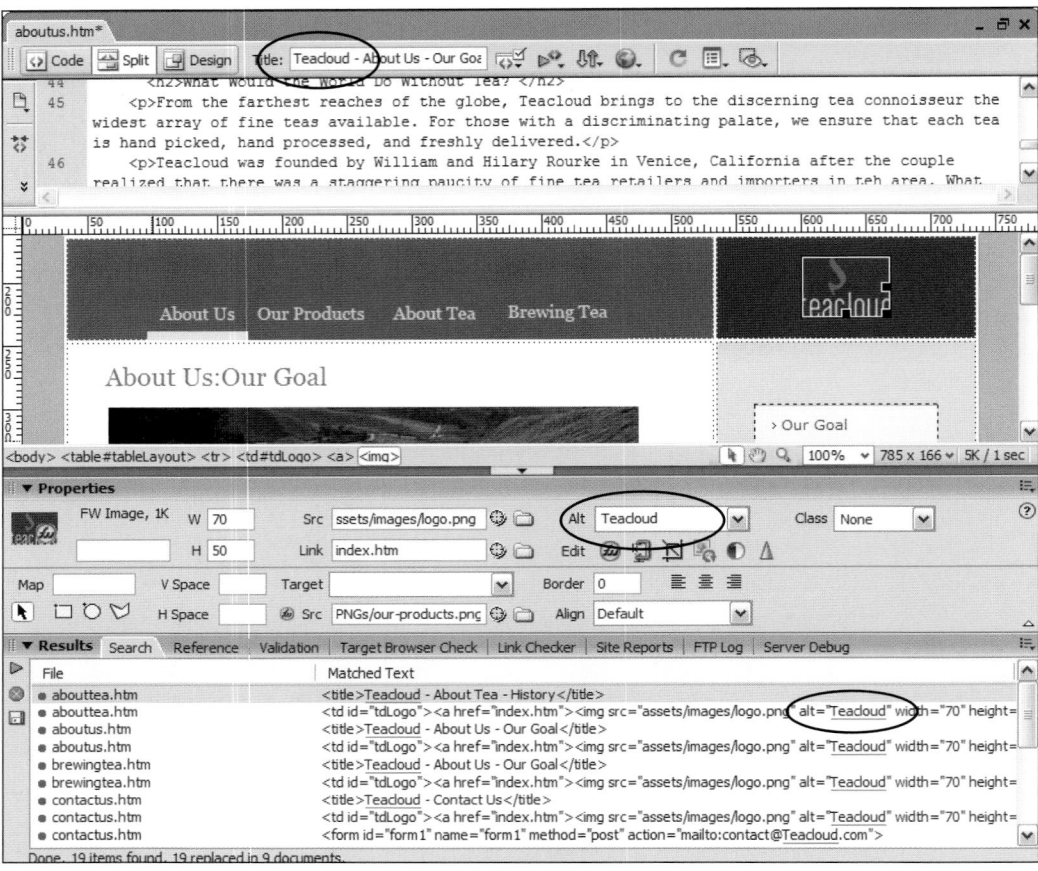

Because you are replacing text in the source code of the page, Dreamweaver opens the current page in Split view and highlights one instance of the text that has been changed. As you can see in this image, the page title has now been properly changed, as have several problems with **alt** attributes.

---

12 Close **aboutus.htm**. You don't need to save your changes.

VIDEO:

findandreplace.mov

There's a lot more you can do with the Find and Replace feature in Dreamweaver. To learn about out how to use the Specific Tag and Text (Advanced) search options (and more), check out **findandreplace.mov** in the **videos** folder on the **HOT CD-ROM**.

In this chapter, you learned how to speed up your development processes using some of the automation tools in Dreamweaver 8. You learned how to use the History panel to quickly undo and redo steps, how to save those steps as a command that you can run any time you want, and how to use the Find and Replace feature to make changes to large numbers of documents at once. In the next chapter, you'll learn how to make your pages more accessible to people with disabilities.

18

Accessibility

Accessibility is one of the hottest buzzwords in the Web-design industry today because it remains one of the most significant issues Web designers have faced in the past few years. Accessibility means making your Web pages accessible to everyone, including people with disabilities. With the passing and enforcement of Section 508 of The Rehabilitation Act, Web designers are now charged with not only making their sites visually appealing, but also "accessible." This law applies mostly to federal and state agencies, schools, and government vendors. Its direct impact on most other sites is expected to be less serious. Regardless, every Web designer should make his or her pages as accessible as possible for everyone.

Before you learn the nuances of accessibility in Dreamweaver 8, it's important to first establish what the term "accessibility" does and doesn't mean, specifically in the context of Web design. In a Web-design arena, accessibility simply means "online content that can be used by someone with a disability." Although this definition is accurate, consider this as one part of the accessibility equation.

Making your Web sites accessible does not mean you make them accessible only to persons with disabilities, but that you make them more accessible to *all* people who visit your site, including those with and without disabilities. For example, if you implement a technique that makes your site more accessible to a person with impaired vision, and it now becomes less accessible to someone who has good vision, you have failed in making your site accessible.

Dreamweaver 8 has a suite of features that help you create accessible Web pages. It even has a great reporting feature that can help you identify accessibility problems in existing Web pages. In this chapter, you'll learn how to use the accessibility features in Dreamweaver 8 to ease the process of creating accessible Web pages. Whether you know it or not, you've already been using several accessibility features as you worked through the previous chapters.

W3C Accessibility Guidelines

To help you create accessible Web sites, the W3C (**W**orld **W**ide **W**eb **C**onsortium) has developed a collection of documents to help you understand accessibility and how to create accessible documents. Don't feel as though you have to memorize these four documents, but familiarizing yourself with what's contained within each will be of great help when you have an accessibility question and no one is around to ask.

These four documents are the *de facto* standard for understanding, creating, and developing accessible Web pages.

Web Content Accessibility Guidelines 1.0
http://www.w3.org/TR/WCAG10/

This is one of the most important documents on Web accessibility. It identifies and explains the 14 guidelines and their checkpoints, and it prioritizes each. This is the place to start learning more about Web accessibility.

Techniques for Web Content Accessibility Guidelines 1.0
http://www.w3.org/TR/WCAG10-TECHS/

This document gives you techniques and examples for making your Web sites accessible. Once you

understand the 14 guidelines of Web accessibility, this document helps you create accessible pages by giving you sample code and different scenarios you might encounter. You might want to print this document and keep a copy nearby.

CSS Techniques for Web Content Accessibility Guidelines 1.0
http://www.w3.org/TR/WCAG10-CSS-TECHS/

This document focuses on (and gives examples for) creating accessible Web pages using CSS (**C**ascading **S**tyle **S**heets). (You can also find examples using deprecated code, which illustrates something developers should not do.)

HTML Techniques for Web Content Accessibility Guidelines 1.0
http://www.w3.org/TR/WCAG10-HTML-TECHS/

This document focuses on creating accessible Web pages using HTML (**H**yper**T**ext **M**arkup **L**anguage). You can probably imagine why this document is so important. Similar to the CSS Techniques document, this one also provides readers with good and bad code examples that illustrate what developers should and should not do.

Setting Accessibility Preferences

The first step is to learn how to turn the Accessibility preferences on and off in Dreamweaver 8, which you'll learn about in this exercise. These options let you create accessible pages as you add content, instead of adding them when the page is finished. This proactive approach saves you time and ensures you don't forget something later. If you learn to work with these options turned on, creating accessible Web pages is no more difficult than creating non-accessible Web pages. Dreamweaver 8 turns all of these options on by default, but you should still know where to find them.

1 In Dreamweaver 8, choose **Edit > Preferences** (Windows) or **Dreamweaver > Preferences** (Mac) to open the **Preferences** dialog box.

2 Select **Accessibility** in the **Category** pane to see what accessibility options are available in Dreamweaver 8. By default, each of the **Show attributes when inserting** check boxes are selected, as is **Offscreen rendering (need to disable when using screen readers)**. Select the **Keep focus in the panel when opening** option if you want access to a panel after you open it; by default, Dreamweaver 8 keeps the focus in the **Document** window.

Note: The **Offscreen rendering** check box at the bottom of this dialog box is available to Windows users only.

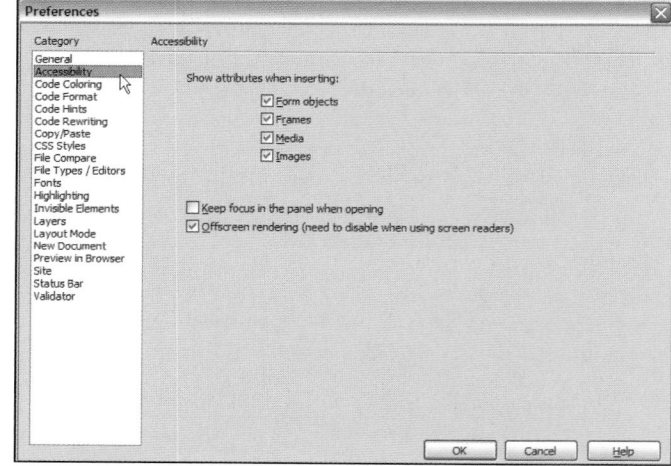

If, for whatever reason, you don't want or need the accessibility options for a particular object to display, deselect the appropriate box. You don't have to turn on all the accessibility options; you can turn on only the options you want. At any time, you can return to this dialog box and deselect any of these options to turn them off.

3 Leave all of the accessibility boxes selected and click **OK** to close the **Preferences** dialog box.

IBM Home Page Reader

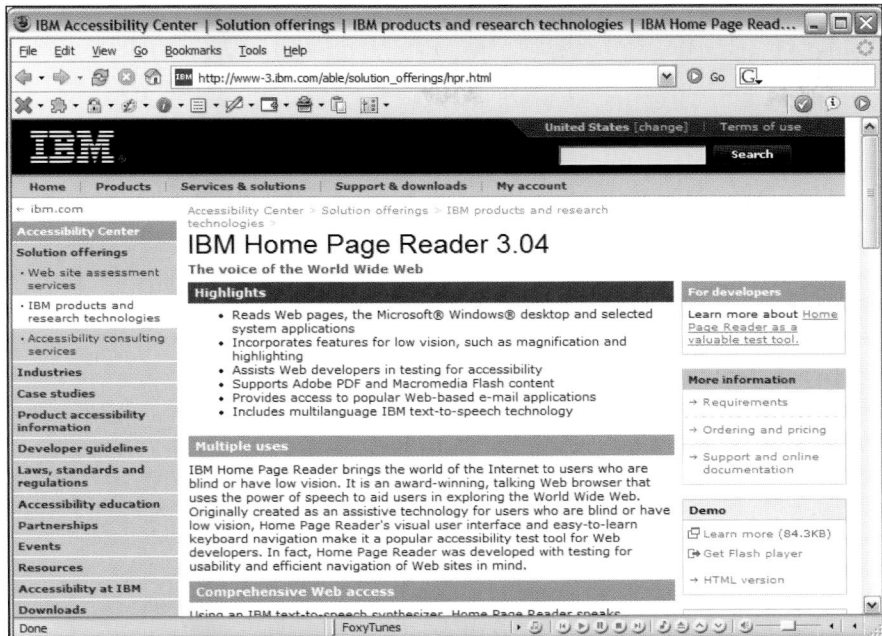

Throughout this chapter, you'll read about screen readers. This refers to all screen-reading software and hardware collectively. One of the most popular screen-reader programs is IBM Home Page Reader 3.0. This program helps blind and visually impaired users surf the Web by reading the contents of Web pages aloud.

Download and install a trial version of the Home Page Reader, close your eyes, and experience firsthand what it is like surfing the Web as a person who is blind or visually impaired. You'll be amazed at how much you take your ability to see for granted. Hopefully, this experience further convinces you that making accessible Web pages is the right thing to do!

You can download a trial version of IBM Home Page Reader at **http://www-3.ibm.com/able/ solution_offerings/hpr.html**. Currently, only a Windows version is available.

2 | Inserting Accessible Images

Millions of people in the world have some type of visual impairment, such as color blindness and partial and/or total blindness. Because the Web is a visual-centric environment, making the images on your pages accessible should be a priority. In this exercise, you'll learn how to add alternate text (**alt** attribute) and a long description for images on a Web page. The **alt** attribute is important because its information is read aloud by a screen reader.

---

1 Copy the **chap_18** folder from the **HOT CD-ROM** to your **Desktop**. Define your site as **Chapter 18** using the **chap_18** folder as the local root folder. Make sure the **Files** panel is open. If it's not, choose **Window > Files** or press **F11**.

---

2 In the **Files** panel, double-click **accessibility.htm** to open it.

This is just a blank page you're going to use to learn more about the accessibility attributes.

---

3 Choose **Insert > Image** and navigate to the **products/kettles** folder. Select **teacloud-azul.jpg** and click **OK**.

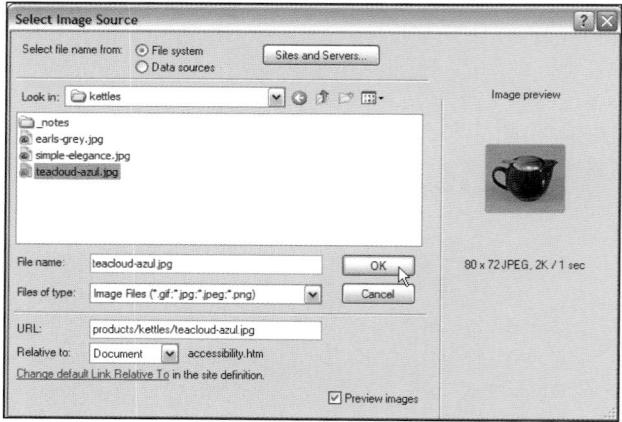

Because the accessibility attributes for images are enabled, the Image Tag Accessibility Attributes dialog box appears automatically. If the accessibility attribute for images is disabled (in the Preferences window), this dialog box will not appear automatically, which means you won't be prompted to add **alt** text. Leave this option turned on so you never forget to add **alt** text to the graphics on your pages.

---

4 In the **Alternate text** field, type **Teacloud Azul Teapot** to add the **alt** attribute to the image tag.

When you're creating the **alt** attribute, keep it short but descriptive.

---

5 Click the **Browse** button next to the **Long description** field and select the **teacloud-azul.htm** file in the **products** folder.

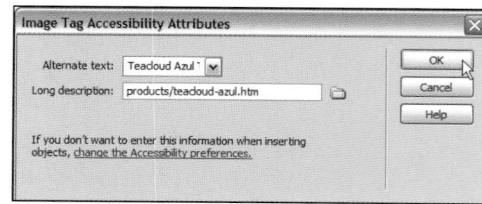

The `alt` attribute helps visually impaired people because that text is read aloud by the screen-reader programs. Additionally, in some browsers, the text appears in a small help tag (tooltip) when the mouse hovers over the image.

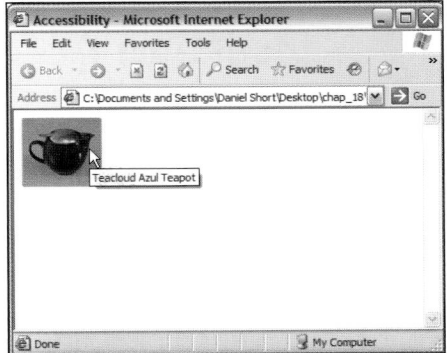

NOTE:

The longdesc Attribute

Adding the `alt` attribute to all the images on your pages is a big part of making accessible Web pages. However, sometimes you may want to offer a more verbose explanation of an image. In these cases, you should use the `longdesc` attribute as well, which lets you link to a text file that contains a longer description of the image. The link is no different than any other link, except it won't appear to people who aren't using a screen reader. If an image has a `longdesc` attribute applied, and a screen-reader program encounters the image on the page, it is read as a link so a person with a visual impairment knows that particular image contains a longer description. Open **products/teacloud-azul.htm** to see an example of a long description file.

---

6 Switch to **Code** view.

Notice `alt` and `longdesc` attributes were added to the `<img>` tag. Dreamweaver 8 added this code when you entered information in the Image Tag Accessibility Attributes dialog box.

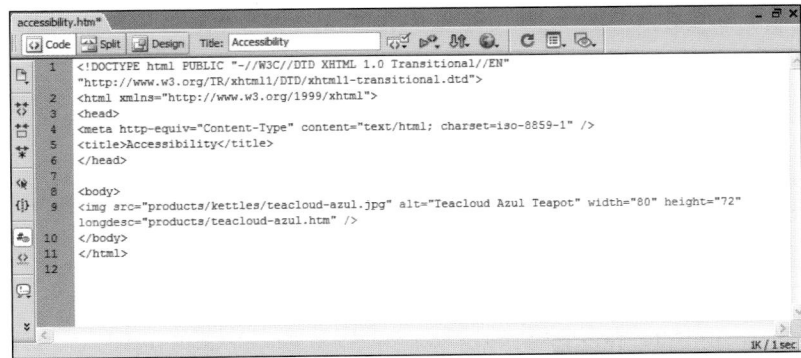

Adding the `alt` and `longdesc` attributes to all the images on your page is one of the easiest and most significant ways you can help make your Web pages accessible to everyone.

---

7 Switch back to **Design** view and choose **Edit > Undo Image** to return to a blank page for the next exercise.

---

3 | Inserting Accessible Tables

The original intent of tables on the Web was for displaying tabular data. The Web was invented by scientists and academics who loved nothing better than a nice long table full of facts and figures. When you're using tables for data in your sites, do your best to make them usable for those with disabilities. This exercise shows you how to add accessibility attributes to your tables and show you what they're used for.

---

1 If you just completed Exercise 2, **accessibility.htm** should still be open. If it's not, double-click **accessibility.htm** in the **Files** panel to open it.

---

2 Choose **Insert > Table** to open the **Table** dialog box. Match the **Accessibility** settings to the ones shown in the illustration here and click **OK** to insert the table.

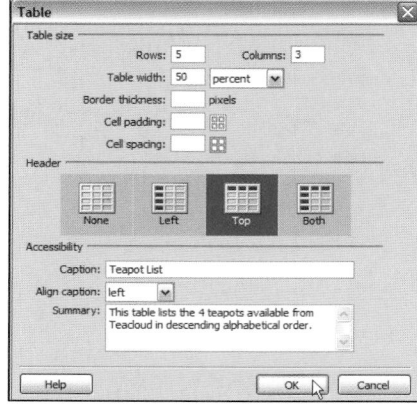

At this point, here is what the table should look like. The caption for the table has been added above the table, but the summary isn't visible.

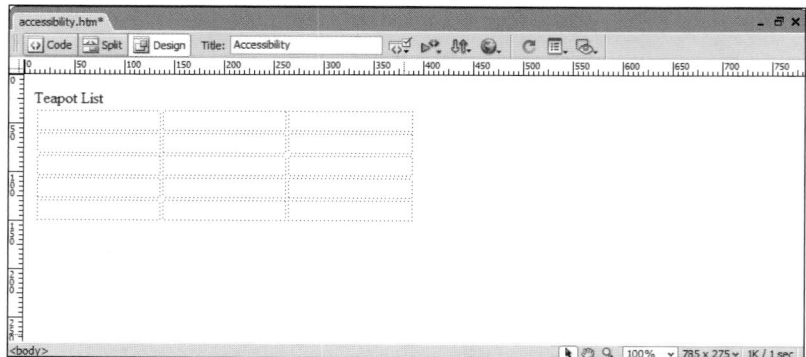

NOTE:

The Summary Attribute and Caption and TH Tags

When you're using tables for displaying actual tabular data (and not for layout purposes), make sure you use the proper supporting table attributes so your table is accessible to those with screen-reading programs. You should know about a couple of tags and an attribute:

- **<th>:** Identifies certain cells as header cells, letting the user know if the information in the table is organized horizontally or vertically and what the major groups of data are. In most cases, the first row serves as the header in a table.

- **<caption>:** Provides a brief description of a table's content. The screen-reading software reads the caption first to let the user know that he or she has encountered a table and what is contained inside the table. For example, "A list of bonsai classes" is an appropriate caption for a table that contains information on bonsai classes. The caption appears directly above the table.

- **summary:** This attribute provides a detailed explanation of the contents of the table. For example, "This table lists the available bonsai classes, instructor, classroom number, and date of class in chronological order" is a good table summary. The summary is not seen in the browser; it is read only by screen-reading programs.

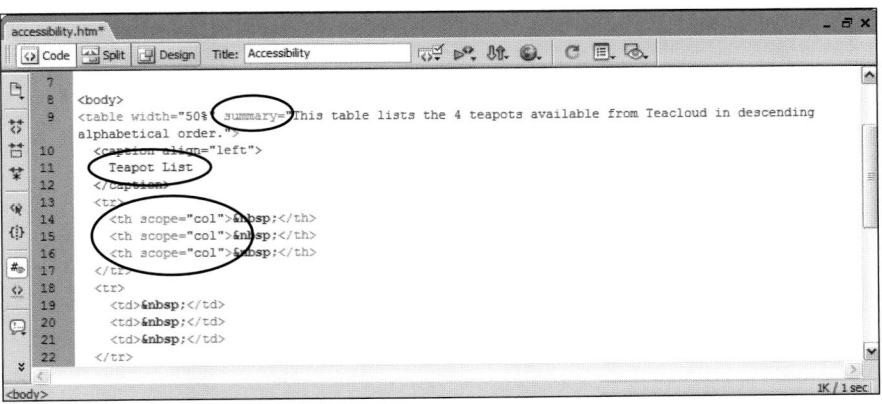

3 Switch to **Code** view to view the XHTML code for this page. Here, you can see the various tags that were added to make this table accessible.

---

4 Switch back to **Design** view and choose **Edit > Undo Table** to return to a blank page for the next exercise.

---

4 | Inserting Accessible Form Objects

Form objects tend to be one of the most overlooked elements on an accessible Web page. For some reason, many people don't know that there are problems with forms and accessibility, as well as good ways to make form objects accessible. Fortunately, Dreamweaver 8 has a feature to help you make your form objects accessible, which is exactly what you'll learn to do in this exercise.

1 If you just completed Exercise 3, **accessibility.htm** should still be open. If it's not, double-click **accessibility.htm** in the **Files** panel to open it.

2 Choose the **Forms** group in the **Insert** bar to display a collection of buttons that lets you add various form objects to your page.

3 Click the **Text Field** button to insert a text field on the page and to open the **Input Tag Accessibility Attributes** dialog box.

4 Type **First Name:** in the **Label** field. This text appears on the Web page as normal text and lets the user know what information should be entered into this text field.

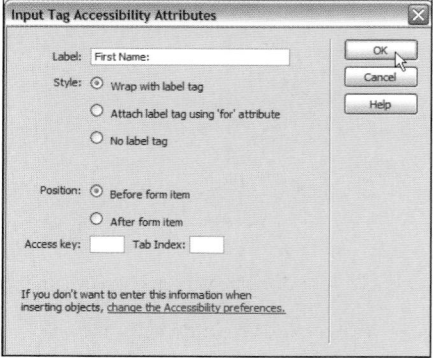

5 Select **Style: Wrap with label tag**.

6 Make sure the **Position: Before form item** radio button is selected. This places the label text before the form object. Click **OK**.

Understanding the Input Tag Accessibility Attributes

The Input Tag Accessibility Attributes dialog box has a number of options. Here's an overview of each:

Input Tag Accessibility Attributes	
Option	**Description**
Label	This text appears next to the form object. Depending on which Position option you choose, the text appears before or after the form object.
Style: Wrap with label tag	This wraps both the label text and form object with a `<label>` tag.
Style: Attach label tag using 'for' attribute	This option uses the **for** attribute to associate the `<label>` tag with the form element it's related to.
Style: No label tag	This option does not add a `<label>` tag around the form object.
Position: Before form item	This radio button places the label text before the form object.
Position: After form item	This radio button places the label text after the form object.
Access key	The key you enter here plus the Ctrl key can be used to select this object in the browser window.
Tab Index	This option sets the tab order of the form objects. This helps you specify how the form is navigated by someone using the Tab key to move from one form object to the next.

7 Click **Yes** when you are prompted to **Add form tag?**.

The form object won't work properly unless it's enclosed within the `<form>` tag. For more information about forms, check out Chapter 13, "Forms."

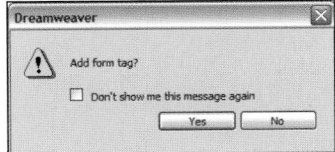

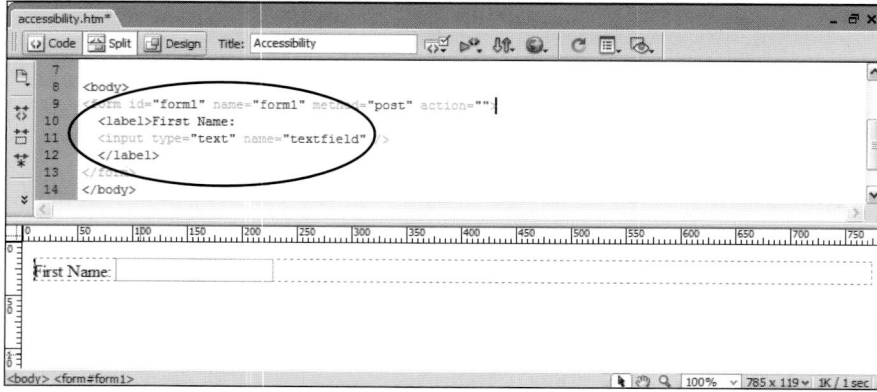

8 Switch to **Split** view.

The label is added to the left of the input field, and the entire block is wrapped in a `<label>` tag. Now, instead of just normal text in front of an element, the label tag allows that text to identify with a specific form element within screen readers. It won't appear any different to other users, but it will be more accessible to those with a disability.

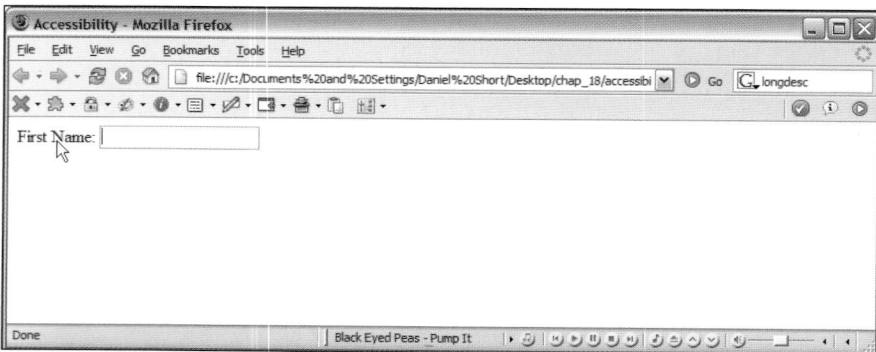

9 Press **F12** to preview the page in your browser. Click the **First Name** text, and your cursor will be placed inside the text field. This lets you know you should enter your first name into that particular text field.

Users can click labels to select and deselect check boxes, select radio buttons, and set lists and menus back to their default selection. Labels are far more useful than simply making it easier for screen readers.

If you want, try adding other form objects to your page. There's no harm in experimenting with these settings, and practice will definitely make you feel more comfortable. We especially encourage you to work with the check boxes and radio buttons to see how the labels affect their use.

10 Save your changes and close **accessibility.htm**.

NOTE:

Accessibility Testing

This chapter showed you how to create accessible Web pages as you created the pages. What can you do if you already have a completed Web site and you want to make sure it's accessible? Dreamweaver 8 allows you to analyze your Web pages and report back any accessibility errors. Simply choose **File > Check Page > Check Accessibility**, and Dreamweaver 8 analyzes the page you have open and provides you with a list of errors.

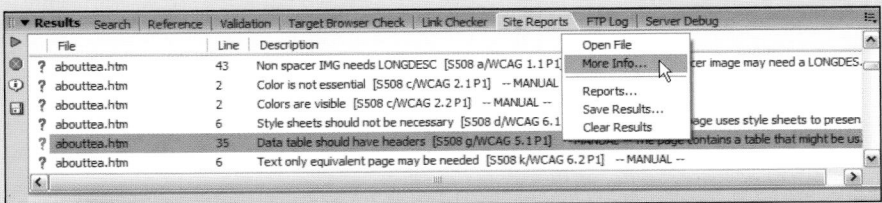

The Results panel provides reports on the Web pages in your site, including the Check Accessibility report. If you right-click one of the entries and choose **More Info**, you can access the UsableNet Accessibility Reference Guide to get more information.

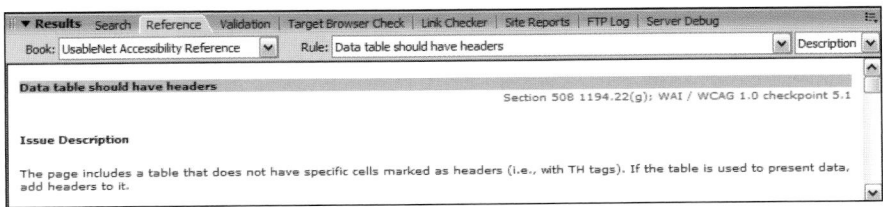

The UsableNet Accessibility Reference Guide helps you make sense of the accessibility errors in the Results panel. This fantastic resource is built right into Dreamweaver 8.

This chapter showed you how to make your Web pages more accessible by using the Dreamweaver accessibility attributes as you work with images, tables, and form objects. In the next chapter, you'll learn how to insert media objects, such as Flash and MP3 files.

19

Inserting Media Objects

You've learned a lot working through this book, but there's still another important Dreamweaver 8 feature to learn about—how to work with media objects. Media objects are items that you add to your pages that typically require a plug-in to play back properly in a browser, such as Flash movies or objects, QuickTime or Shockwave movies, Java applets, ActiveX controls, or other audio or video objects. Plug-ins are special program extensions installed in your user's browser that let the user view plug-in-based content, such as Flash, Shockwave, Real Audio, QuickTime, and so on.

In this chapter, you'll learn how to add media objects to your sites and how to use their associated plug-ins. You will also learn how to set parameters in the Property Inspector to control how and when your media objects play.

As exciting as this may seem, it's also the area of Web development where compatibility issues between browsers really get intense. Not everyone has the same plug-ins loaded to support playback of media objects, and some plug-ins work differently on Macs than they do in Windows. Dreamweaver 8 does a great job of letting you put this content on your site. It's the rest of the Web's limitations that you'll likely have to struggle with!

What Is a Plug-In?

In the early days of the Web, any file that wasn't an HTML file had to be downloaded and required a separate "player" for the content to be seen. This process was a hassle for most Web users because it meant breaking the flow of the browsing experience to view material in an external application. In response to this problem, Netscape introduced the idea of plug-ins, which extended the capability of HTML pages to display non-HTML-based content. Today, browsers ship with a variety of pre-installed plug-ins, including QuickTime Player, Flash Player, and RealPlayer. This chapter focuses on techniques to insert plug-in based content into your pages so it can be viewed directly in the browser, without requiring the use of an outside-player application.

Plug-Ins Require Viewer Participation

As you work through these exercises, you might find yourself being directed to download plug-ins from the Internet or reassign them in your browser preferences. If this seems like a hassle, remember that you ask your audience to do the same thing when you present plug-in-based content to them.

URLs for Downloading Plug-Ins	
Plug-Ins	**URL**
QuickTime	http://www.apple.com/quicktime/download/
Flash	http://www.macromedia.com/software/flashplayer/
Shockwave	http://www.macromedia.com/software/shockwaveplayer/
Real Player	http://www.real.com/player/?src=player_redct

EXERCISE

1 | Linking to Sounds

You can add sound to your page in multiple ways. In this first exercise, you learn to add sound to your page simply by creating a link to a sound file. As you will see, you must consider some nuances when you work with sound files. For example, no standard format for sounds exists on the Web. Sounds are handled differently between browsers and operating systems (as if designing Web pages wasn't difficult enough). Fortunately, by the time you finish the hands-on exercises in this chapter, you'll have a better understanding of how to add sound to your site.

1 Copy the **chap_19** folder from the **HOT CD-ROM** to your **Desktop**. Define your site as **Chapter 19** using the **chap_19** folder as the local root folder. Make sure the **Files** panel is open. If it's not, choose **Window > Files** or press **F11**.

2 In the **Files** panel, double-click **audio.htm** to open it.

You will see two links at the top of the page. These two links point directly to two different sound files. The first link points to a WAV file, and the second link points to an MP3 file.

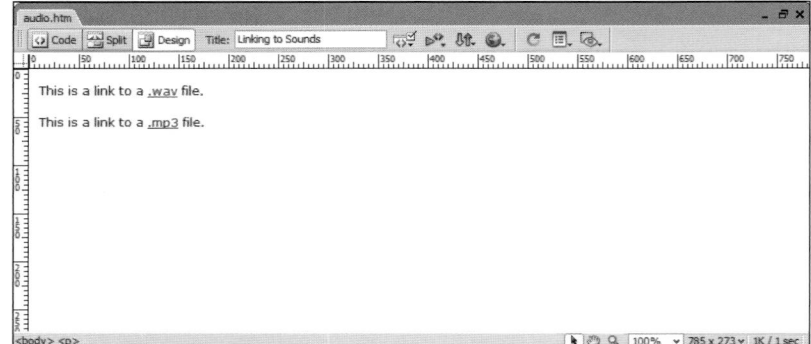

3 Place your cursor in the **.wav** link at the top of the page. In the **Property Inspector**, notice this links to the **timefortea.wav** file in the **assets/sound** folder.

That's all there is to it. When a user clicks this link in a browser, the file will open in the user's default application for Windows Audio files.

4 Place your cursor in the **.mp3** link.

This link points to the **timefortea.mp3** file in the **assets/sound** folder.

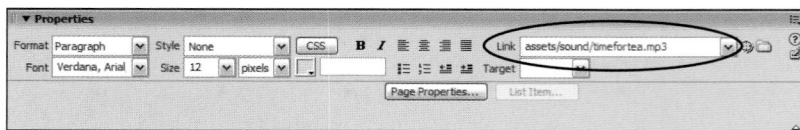

Nothing too complicated about this so far. You are simply creating a link, but instead of pointing to an HTML document, you point to a sound file.

5 Press **F12** to preview this page in a browser. Click each of the links. Clicking either link will play a 30 second sample of music.

Your browser may differ, but in Internet Explorer clicking the .wav link opens Windows Media Player, and clicking the .mp3 link loads the file in the browser through the QuickTime plug-in. Depending on how your browser preferences are set up and what operating system you use, clicking the links might launch different audio players—or none at all! Performing the same steps in our installation of Firefox loads the QuickTime plug-in for *both* of the sound files.

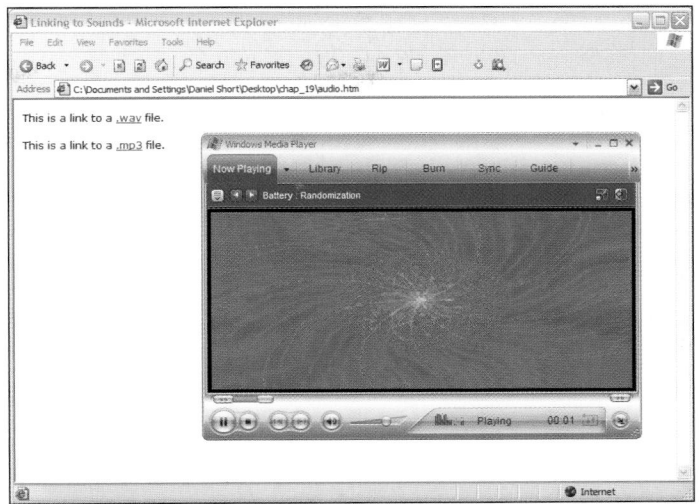

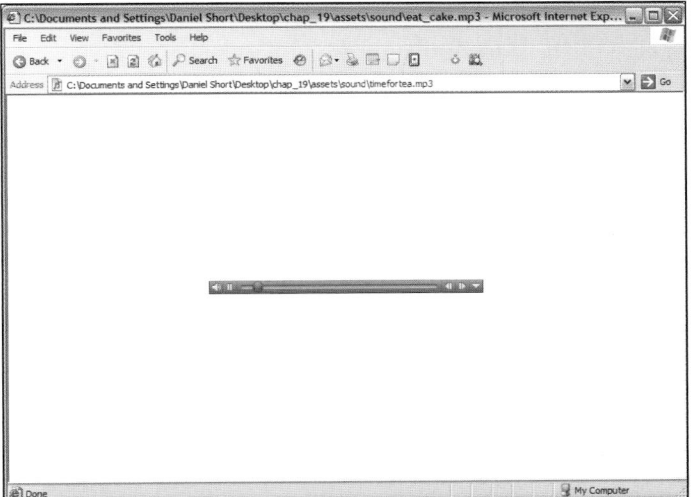

TIP: **Different Sound Players**

Just about every browser will let you choose which application or plug-in plays the audio files you find on Web pages. In fact, you can set a different one for each type of audio format. For example, you might choose to have the QuickTime plug-in play AIF and WAV files and have the Flash plug-in play SWF files. You can control this by modifying your browser preferences. Check these settings if you experience any problems while trying to play sound files. For instructions on how to change these settings, see your browser's Help feature.

6 Return to Dreamweaver 8 and keep **audio.htm** open for the next exercise.

In this exercise, you learned (whether you wanted to or not) that browsers are finicky beasts. You never know what players they may, or may not, open when a user clicks a link to a particular sound file. In the next exercise, you'll learn how to embed the sound directly in the page, so at least the user won't have to load an external application (such as Windows Media Player) to play a sound file.

Understanding Different Sound Formats

One of the problems with adding sound to your Web page is deciding which format to use. Most Web publishers use MP3, RealPlayer (RAM), or WAV files—the most commonly supported audio formats. It is a good idea, however, to be familiar with the other formats that you might run into on the Web. The following chart gives you an idea of what's out there:

Sound Formats	
Extension	**Description**
.au	This format was one of the first introduced on the Internet. It was designed for NeXT and Sun Unix systems.
.aiff/.aif	The .aif (**A**udio **I**nterchange **F**ormat) was developed by Apple and is used on SGI machines. It is the main audio format for Macintosh computers.
.midi/.mid	The .midi (**M**usical **I**nstrument **D**igital **I**nterface) format was designed to translate how music is produced. MIDI files store just the sequencing information (notes, timing, and voicing) required to play back a musical composition, rather than a recording of the composition itself, so these files are usually small, but playback quality is unpredictable.
.MP3	The .MP3 (**MPEG-1** Audio Layer-**3**) format is the hottest audio file format on the Web. It offers superior compression and great quality. This file format is widely used in Macromedia Flash content.
.ra/.ram	The .ra (**R**eal **A**udio) format was designed to offer streaming audio on the Internet.
.rmf	The .rmf (**R**ich **M**usic **F**ormat) was designed by Headspace and is used in the Beatnik plug-in. This format offers good compression and quality.
.swa	The .swa (**S**hock **w**ave **A**udio) format was developed by Macromedia and is used in Flash.
.wav	This format was developed by IBM and Microsoft. This is the main audio format for the Windows operating system, but WAV files play on Macs and other systems.

2 | Embedding Multimedia Files

In addition to linking to a sound file, there is another approach to adding multimedia files to your Web pages. You can embed multimedia files so they play directly inside your Web page instead of linking to the physical file (as shown in the last exercise). This approach is good if you just want to play—not download—files within the Web browser. Embedding multimedia files gives you more control over them because they actually appear inside your HTML files, along with the other content. By modifying specific parameters, you can control when the player starts, how it appears on the page, and whether it loops (continuously plays) or not, as well as several other settings. In this exercise, you'll be inserting one of the sounds from the previous exercise.

1 If you just completed Exercise 1, **audio.htm** should still be open. If it's not, go back and complete Exercise 1.

In this exercise, you're going to embed the WAV file from the previous exercise directly into the page.

2 Place your cursor at the end of the first paragraph and press **Enter** (Windows) or **Return** (Mac) to create a new paragraph.

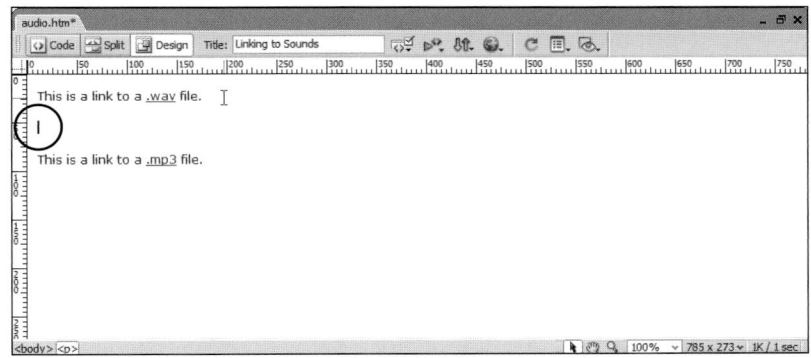

3 Choose **Insert > Media > Plugin** to open the **Select File** dialog box. Browse to the **assets/sound** folder and select the **timefortea.wav** file. Click **OK** (Windows) or **Choose** (Mac).

Dreamweaver 8 displays a plug-in icon on the page to indicate where the plug-in will appear.

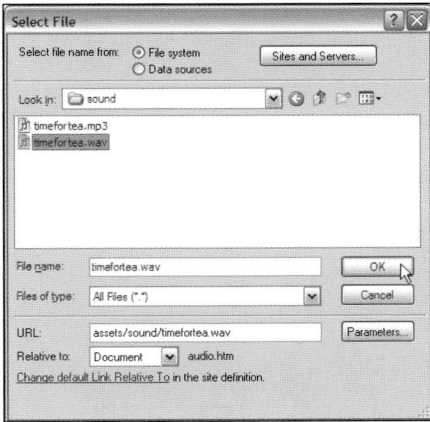

4 Select the plug-in icon and click the **Parameters** button in the **Property Inspector** to open the **Parameters** dialog box.

The Parameters dialog box is where you will insert any parameters and values you need. See the note at the end of this exercise to learn a bit more about parameters.

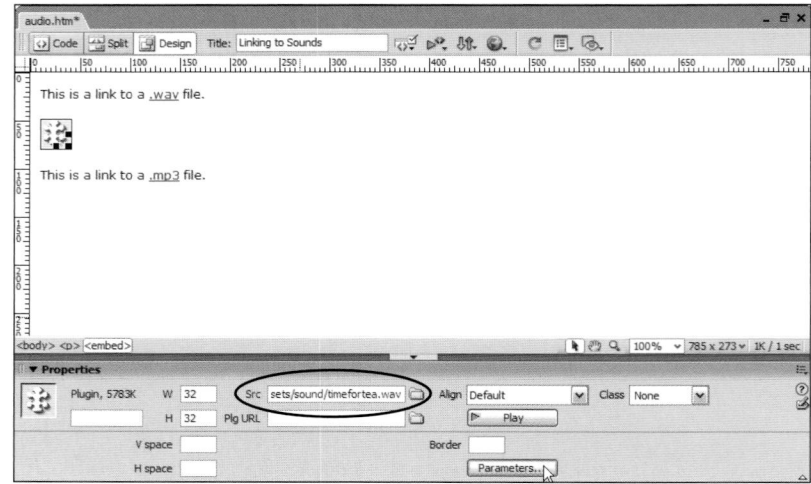

5 In the **Parameter** column, type **autoplay**, then press **Tab**. Type **false** in the **Value** column and click **OK**.

This prevents the sound file from playing automatically; to play the sound file, the user will have to click the Play button.

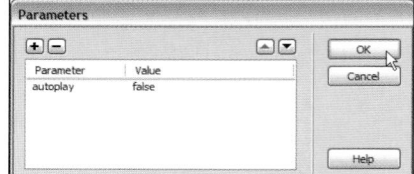

6 In the **Property Inspector**, type **150** in the **W** field to change the width of the plug-in.

You need to widen the plug-in so the user can see all of the play controls (Play, Pause, Stop, and so on).

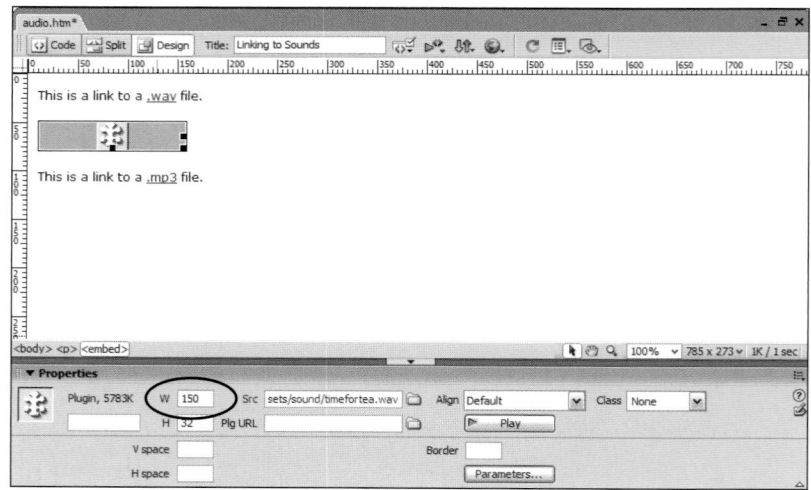

7 Press **F12** to preview your page in a browser. Click the **Play** button to hear the sound. Here, you can see that QuickTime is being used to play WAV files in Firefox for Windows.

Note: If you get a broken image icon, your browser doesn't know what plug-in to use to play the file.

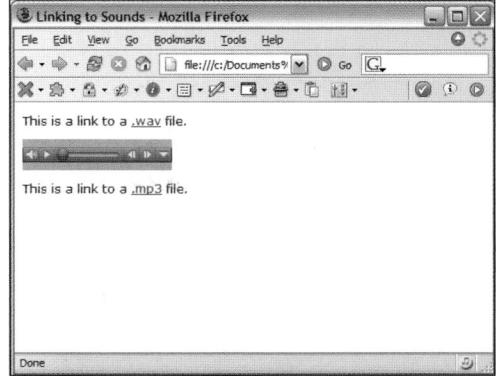

8 Return to Dreamweaver 8. Save your changes and close **audio.htm**.

In this exercise, you went through the process of inserting a sound file directly into an XHTML document. You can insert just about any type of media file that has a valid player associated with it, including QuickTime movies, Windows Media files, RealPlayer movies, and the list goes on. You'll find a MOV file in the **assets/movies** folder if you want to practice inserting additional multimedia files.

NOTE:

What Is a Parameter?

Most plug-in content is controlled by various parameters (sometimes referred to as *attributes*), which are different for each kind of plug-in. A *parameter* is an option passed to the plug-in that tells it how to behave. In Exercise 2, you learned how to set the autoplay parameter to false. That parameter is part of the QuickTime specification.

This chapter covers sound, Flash, Flash Video, and QuickTime, but many other types of plug-ins are on the Web. To learn what all the parameters are for a plug-in, it's best to visit the site from which you downloaded the plug-in.

3 | Inserting Flash Content

Because both Dreamweaver 8 and Flash 8 are Macromedia products, it is not surprising that Dreamweaver 8 supports Flash content. Instead of the generic plug-in object that you used in the last exercise, Dreamweaver 8 has a Flash object all its own.

1 In the **Files** panel, double-click **index.htm** to open it.

This is the same **index.htm** file you've been using throughout the book, but we've removed the image that's been there all along. In this exercise, you're going to replace it with a Flash movie.

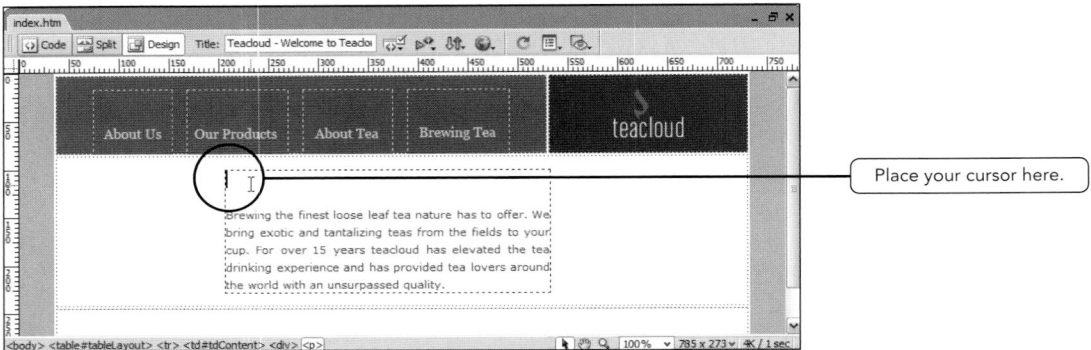

2 Place your cursor above the opening paragraph of text and choose **Insert > Media > Flash**.

3 In the **Select File** dialog box, browse to the **assets/flash** folder and select **teacloud_home.swf**. Click **OK** (Windows) or **Choose** (Mac) to insert the Flash file. If the **Object Tag Accessibility Attributes** dialog box appears, type **Welcome to Teacloud** in the **Title** field and click **OK**.

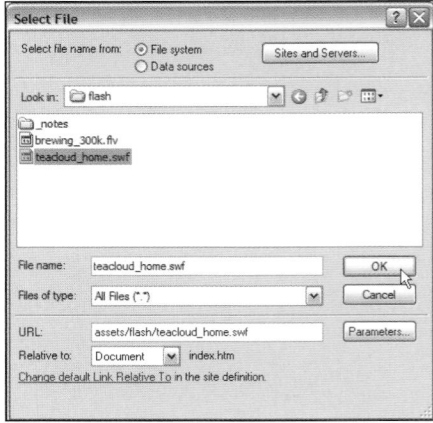

4 Select the Flash movie and look at the **Property Inspector**.

Dreamweaver 8 inserts the Flash movie and automatically determines the height and width of the movie and sets a number of other defaults, such as whether to loop the movie and whether it should play as soon as it loads.

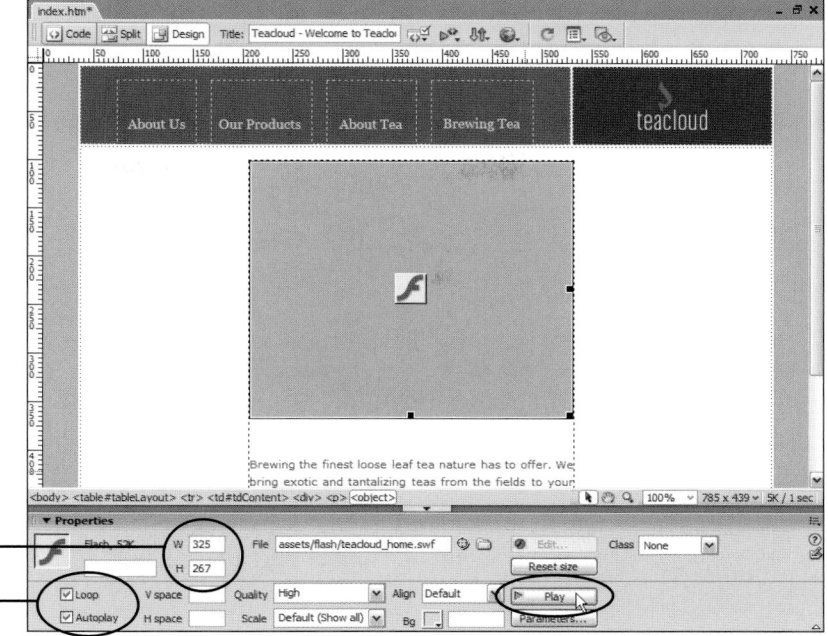

Height and Width

Loop and Autoplay options

5 Press **F12** to view the content in your browser. You can also click the **Play** button in the **Property Inspector**. You can play Flash content directly in Dreamweaver 8, unlike DHTML or generic plug-in content.

6 Return to Dreamweaver 8. Close **index.htm**. You don't need to save your changes.

Inserting Shockwave Content

Shockwave is a plug-in that allows Macromedia Director content to be published online. The plug-in size is over 1 MB, whereas the Flash plug-in is under 200K. Macromedia Director, like Flash, is an authoring tool that supports better animation, sound, and interactivity than HTML pages. The differences between Flash and Director relate to how the authoring tool is structured, how the interactivity is programmed, and how images are formatted for the Web. Flash is installed in more browsers than Shockwave, and many more people know and use the Flash authoring tool. Director is by far a more powerful authoring tool with more sophisticated programming capabilities, but because of the larger download and smaller amount of Director content on the Web, it doesn't have the installed user base of Flash. For more information about the two, visit **http://www.macromedia.com** to read the specifications and features.

Just like inserting Flash content, it's easy to insert Shockwave content. Just choose **Insert > Media > Shockwave** and complete the dialog box. Like with Flash content, you can view Shockwave content directly by clicking the Play button in the Property Inspector. Remember, in order to view Shockwave content, your users will need to have the Shockwave Player plug-in installed.

4 | Inserting Flash Video Content

Macromedia recently introduced Flash Video—a way to provide high-quality video through the Flash Player. This is good for those of you wishing to publish video on your sites because nearly everyone in the entire world has the Flash Player. Dreamweaver 8 makes it easy to insert Flash Video content, and you can even choose from a nice selection of prebuilt playback controls.

1 In the **Files** panel, double-click **brewingtea.htm** to open it.

2 Place your cursor before **1. The Infuser** and choose **Insert > Media > Flash Video** to open the **Insert Flash Video** dialog box.

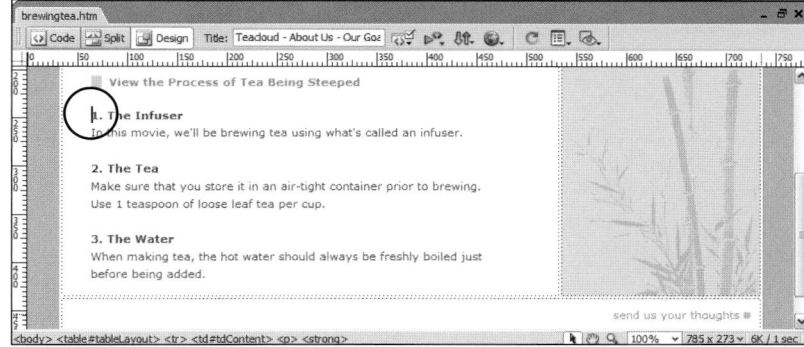

3 Leave the **Video type** pop-up menu set to **Progressive Download Video**. Click the **Browse** button and select the **brewing_300k.flv** file in the **assets/flash** folder. Click **OK** (Windows) or **Choose** (Mac). You can choose any **Skin** you like and it will adjust the playback controls used for the Flash video content. In this case, we chose **Halo Skin 1**, but choose any you like to view a preview of what the skin will look like. Click **Detect Size**, and Dreamweaver 8 will determine the size of the Flash Video file, (205 x 131 in this case). It will also display the total size with the skin included. Finally, select the **Auto play** option and click **OK**.

There's a lot going on in this dialog box. Click the **Help** button to learn more about the Insert Flash Video options.

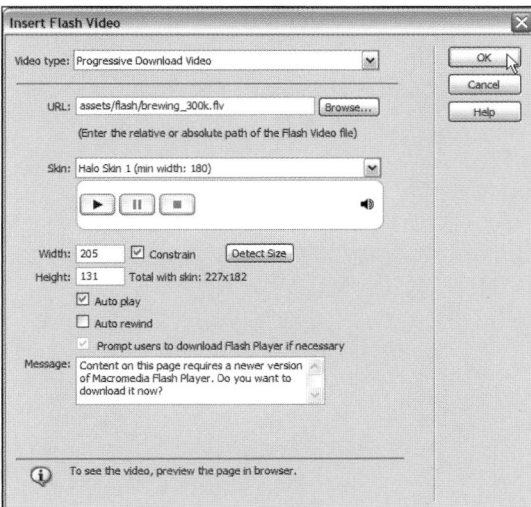

4 Place your cursor directly after the Flash Video placeholder and press **Enter** (Windows) or **Return** (Mac) to put the Flash Video in its own paragraph.

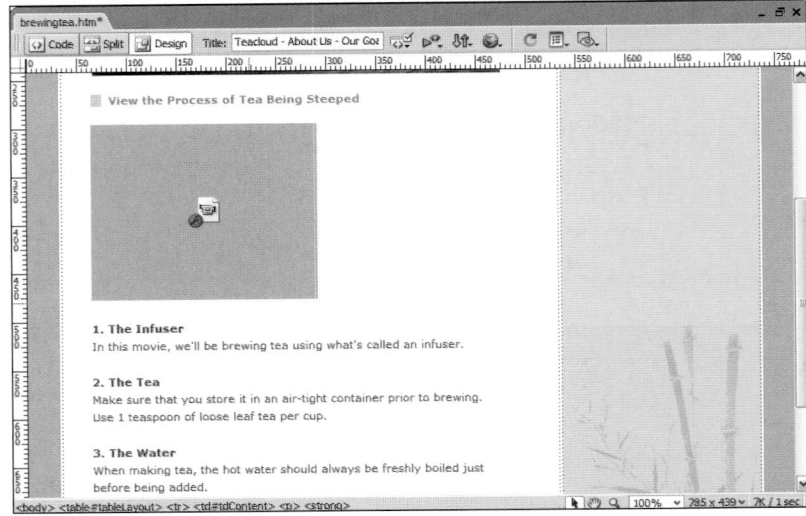

5 In the **Files** panel, notice Dreamweaver 8 has added two files to your site: **FLVPlayer_Progressive.swf** and **Halo_Skin_1.swf**. If you don't see the files, click the **Refresh** icon in the **Files** panel. Both of these files are necessary for the Flash Video to play correctly, and they should always be located at the root of your site.

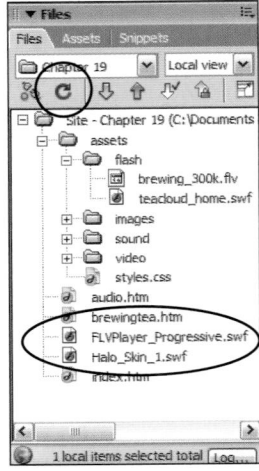

6 Press **F12** to preview the page in your browser.

The Flash Video file should start playing immediately, showing you how to brew a perfect cup of tea. Click the playback controls to play, pause, and stop the movie playback.

---

7 Return to Dreamweaver 8. Close **brewingtea.htm**. You don't need to save your changes.

In this chapter, you learned how to insert multimedia files, Flash movies, and Flash Video. Learning how to work with media objects can greatly improve the visual interest of your site. Next, you'll learn how to (finally) get all of this hard work online so the rest of the world can see it.

20

Getting Your Site Online

It's one thing to design a Web page, and an entirely different thing to get what you've designed online for everyone else to see. One of the features we have always felt was missing from other books was concrete instructions covering how to access, upload, and update files to a Web server. Until now, you were forced to struggle through this process on your own, which could prove frustrating. Fortunately, this chapter walks you through the process of uploading your pages to a real live Web server. This means that you, your colleagues, your family, and your friends will be able to see the results of whatever you publish on the Web.

This chapter shows you how to create a free Web hosting account with Tripod and then use Dreamweaver 8 to upload a Web site so others can view it live on the Internet. You do not have to sign up for the Tripod account unless you want to follow along with the exercises. If you already have a Web hosting account, you can learn to use it by reading this chapter as well. Either way, this chapter shows you how to set up your FTP preferences and upload your site to a Web server using Dreamweaver 8.

Free Web Hosting with Tripod

Tripod is one of many Web services to offer free Web hosting to anyone who wants to sign up. Within just a few minutes, you can have a place to upload your files to on the Web, if you don't already have another spot reserved.

You will be pleasantly surprised by how much you get for free. The Tripod free Web hosting package includes a lot of extras. All you need to complete the exercises in this chapter are the 20 MB of free disk space and FTP access that are provided with the free Web hosting account. The only disadvantage to the free service is that it does include

advertising. It's the perfect place to get started, though, and when you're ready to go "pro" and get rid of the ads, you can upgrade to a low-cost service with Tripod, or seek out other service providers that will meet your needs.

If you already have a hosting service of your own, feel free to work with your own settings in the exercises, rather than those described for Tripod. For the FTP settings, just substitute your own settings instead of Tripod's. You can acquire your FTP settings by asking your own hosting service or the Web administrator for your company.

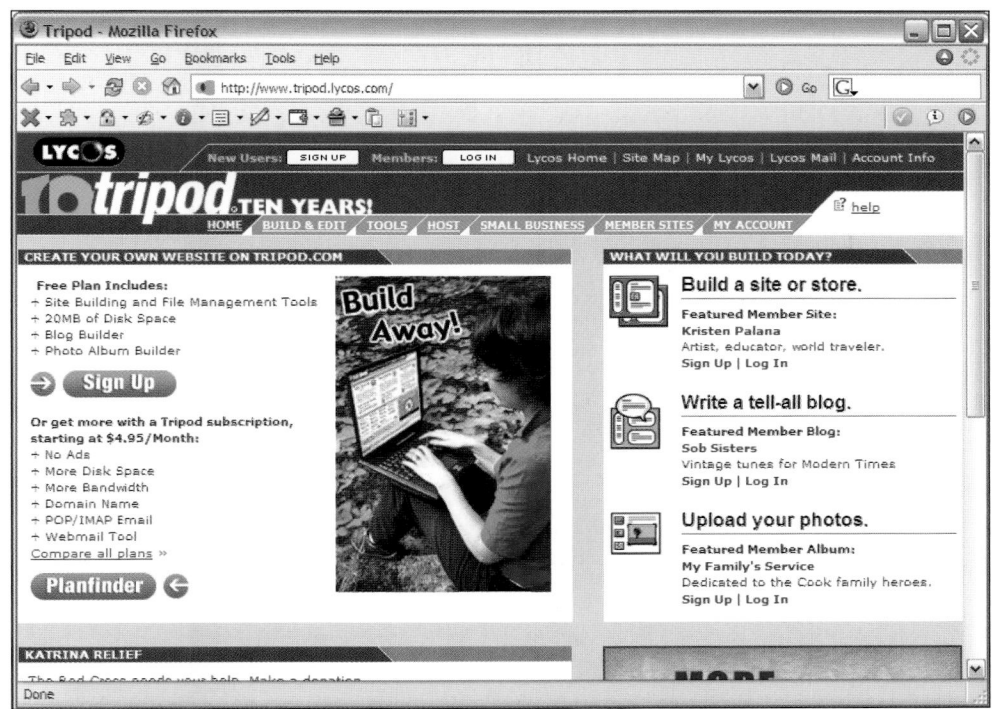

1 | Signing Up with Tripod

The first step in getting your free Tripod Web site online involves filling out a form on their site. This exercise shows you what parts of the form to complete. If you plan to use your own Web server instead of Tripod's, you can skip this exercise.

---

1 Launch your preferred Web browser and browse to the Tripod home page at **http://www.tripod.lycos.com**. Here you'll find a complete rundown on their services.

---

2 Click the **Sign Up** button. This takes you to another Web page where you can create your own Tripod account.

---

3 Complete all of the information requested on the form. Your **Member Name** will appear as part of your Tripod URL. For our ID, we used **dw8hot**; therefore, when the account is set up, our URL will be **http://dw8hot.tripod.com**.

Note: Do not use **dw8hot** as your ID; be sure to use your own unique ID, and make sure to write it down because you'll be using your user ID and password in the next exercise.

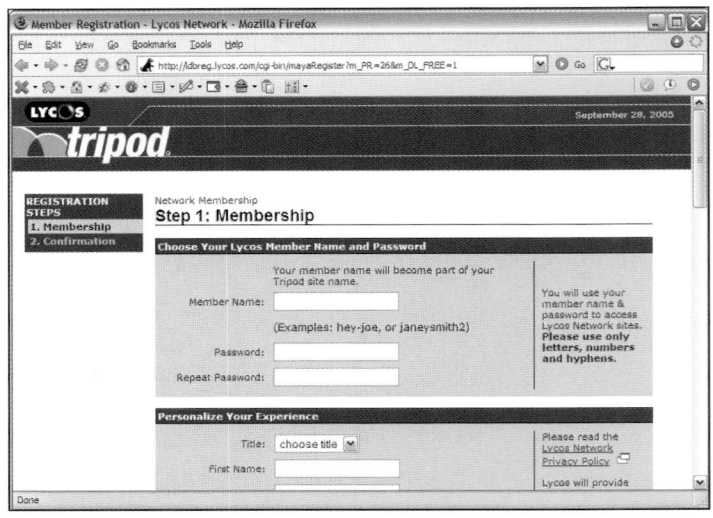

---

4 When you are finished entering your information, click **I Agree** at the bottom of the page to submit your information.

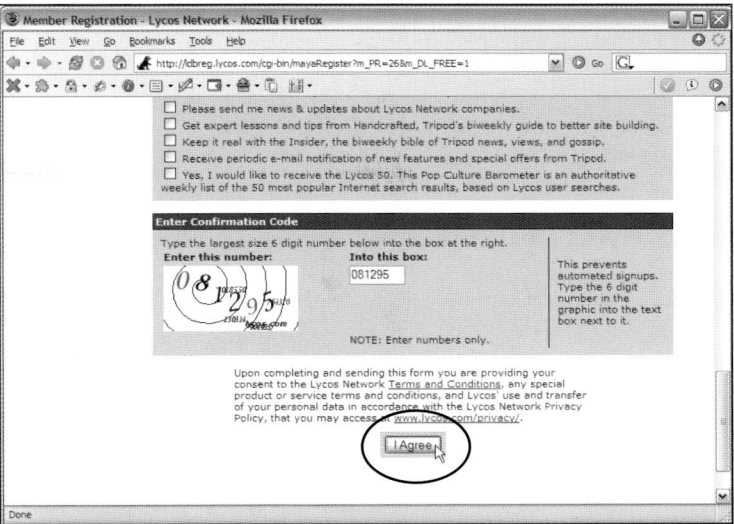

NOTE:

Privacy Policies

Any time you provide personal information about yourself on a Web site, you should be familiar with the recipient's privacy policy. Some sites gather personal information and then sell it to marketing companies, which can result in some extra and unsolicited emails in your inbox. If this is of serious concern to you, make sure you review Tripod's privacy policy (**http://www.lycos.com/privacy/**) before you provide them with information.

5 After you click through the **Special Offers** screen, Tripod will present a few options. Choose **Publish a web site built using other software** and choose **Macromedia Dreamweaver** from the list of software products. Click **Next**.

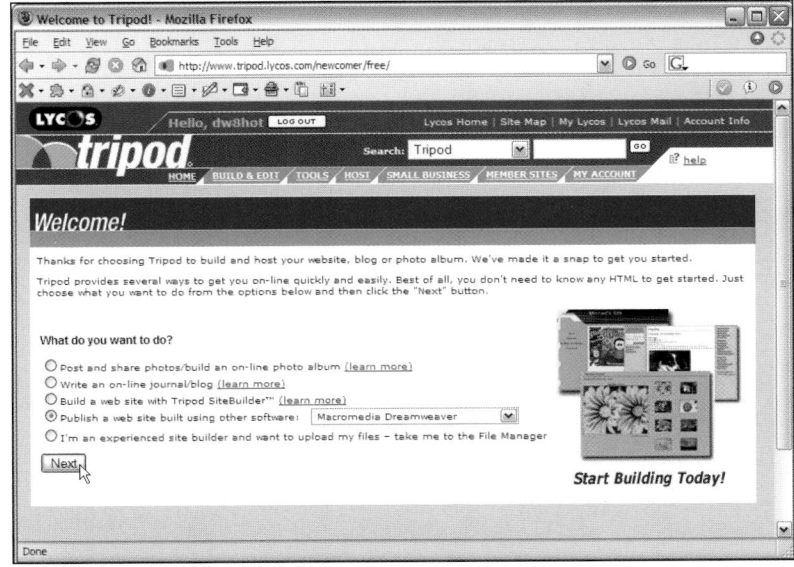

6 You have set up this Tripod account and are ready to set up your FTP preferences in Dreamweaver 8 and begin uploading your site. Quit the browser; you will come back to it later after you have uploaded your site from Dreamweaver 8.

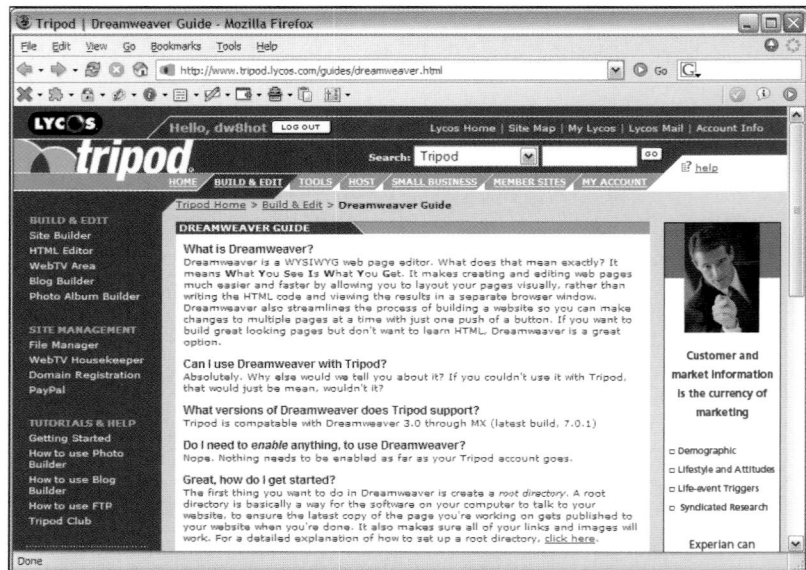

Macromedia Dreamweaver 8 : H·O·T

EXERCISE

2 | Setting FTP Connection Information

In order for your site to be seen on the World Wide Web, your files need to be uploaded to a publicly available (or live) Web server. Most Web developers and designers build pages on their hard drives (as you have done in this book) before transferring their files to a live Web server. In Dreamweaver 8 terminology, the files on your hard drive are referred to as *local files*, and the files on a live Web server are referred to as *remote files*. You can upload your files from Dreamweaver 8 by using the Site Definitions FTP settings.

Note: In order to complete this exercise, you need to know the member name and password you selected when you created your Tripod account, or have the information handy from your own account. If you forgot that information or have not signed up for a Tripod account yet, go back and complete Exercise 1 before beginning this exercise.

1 Copy the **chap_20** folder from the **HOT CD-ROM** to your **Desktop**. Define your site as **Chapter 20** using the **chap_20** folder as the local root folder. Make sure the **Files** panel is open. If it's not, choose **Window > Files** or press **F11**.

2 Choose **Site > Manage Sites**. In the **Manage Sites** dialog box, select **Chapter 20** and click **Edit**.

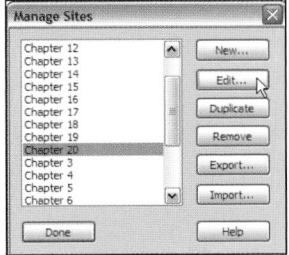

3 Make sure the **Advanced** tab is selected. Select **Remote Info** in the **Category** list, and then choose **FTP** from the **Access** pop-up menu.

Next, you'll modify your FTP settings before you upload files to your site.

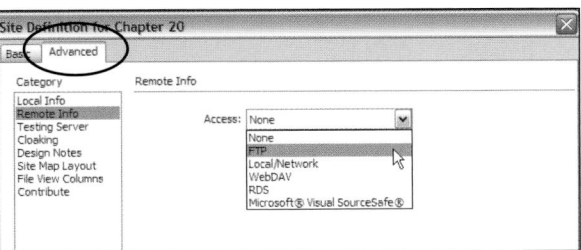

4 Match the settings to the ones shown here, making sure you specify the **Login** and **Password** for the Tripod account you created in Exercise 1. Click **Test**.

If you signed up for the free Tripod account, your FTP information should be similar to the information shown here, except for the Login. However, if you are using your own Web hosting service, enter that information instead.

Be sure to use your own Tripod ID here.

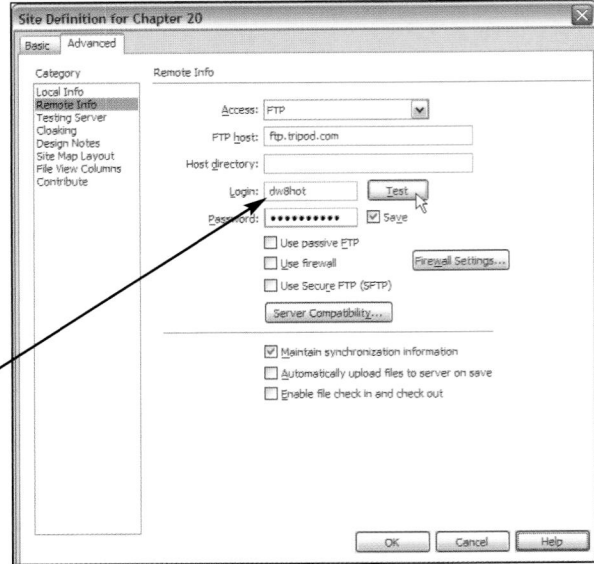

If you set up your connection correctly, Dreamweaver 8 will display a message saying that it has successfully connected to the server. If you receive an error message, you'll need to verify your FTP settings and potentially check with your ISP or network administrator for possible firewall settings you may need to adjust.

5 After you've successfully tested your connection, click **OK**. When you return to the **Manage Sites** dialog box, click **Done**.

What Is FTP?

FTP stands for **F**ile **T**ransfer **P**rotocol. This term is usually associated with the process of uploading files to a server. You will hear this term used as a noun ("I used an FTP program to upload my files") and as a verb ("I am going to FTP all of my files now").

It is important to note that you do not have to use Dreamweaver 8 to exchange files with the remote server. You can use other FTP applications as well,

such as WS_FTP (Windows) or Fetch (Mac). There are advantages to using Dreamweaver 8 over these applications, however, such as file synchronization and site management. You'll learn about these advantages shortly.

Here is a handy chart that describes the FTP settings in Dreamweaver 8:

FTP Settings in Dreamweaver 8	
Setting	**Description**
FTP host	This will typically be an address similar to the URL of your Web site. In some cases, it may begin with the prefix *FTP*.
Host directory	If you have a specific directory on the server where you are supposed to place your files, you would enter it here. This option is not always used.
Login	You will be given a user name or ID to use to access the remote server. It is important that you enter this information exactly as it is given to you, otherwise you will have problems connecting.
Password	In addition to a user name or ID, you will also be given a password to use when accessing the remote server. If you don't want to enter the password every time you connect to the remote server, click the Save check box and Dreamweaver 8 will remember your password! **Note:** The password you enter here is just stored in a text file on your hard drive, so anyone can read it. Don't select the Save check box if security is a concern at your location.
Use passive FTP	The Passive FTP option lets your local software set up the FTP connection rather than the remote server. Leave this option deselected unless directed by your system administrator.
Use firewall	Select this box if you are connecting to the FTP server from behind a firewall.

3 | Putting Files onto the Web Server

Now that you have set up your FTP preferences, you are ready to use Dreamweaver 8 to connect to a Web server and upload your files. Once you have completed this exercise, you will be able to see your Web site live on the Internet.

1 Before you try to upload your files to the Web server, make sure you have established a connection to the Internet. You should be able to browse the Web and look at other sites as a test to see that your Web connection is working.

2 Make sure the **Files** panel is open; if it is not, choose **Window > Files**.

Notice the Connect button, at the top of the panel, is no longer dimmed. Once you specify your FTP preferences, you will have access to the Connect feature.

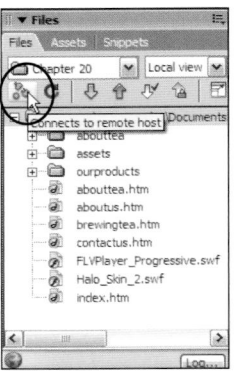

3 Click the **Connect** button. Dreamweaver 8 will attempt to connect to your Web server. If you don't have an active internet connection or the FTP details are incorrect you will receive an error message.

4 With the local root folder selected, you are ready to upload the files for your site. Click **Put Files**.

Note: If you want to upload a single file, don't select the local root folder; instead select the particular file and then click **Put Files.**

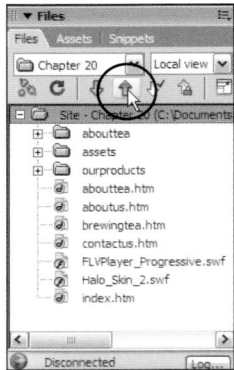

5 You are asked whether you want to upload your entire Web site. Because this is the first time you are uploading your site, click **OK**.

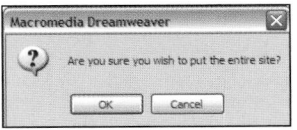

After Dreamweaver 8 starts to upload, you will see the Background File Activity dialog box, which shows you the FTP progress—whether you're uploading or downloading files. If you click the triangle next to **Details**, you can see a detailed list of what's happening on the server. You can also just click **Hide** and continue working in Dreamweaver 8. The only things you can't do while Dreamweaver 8 is interacting with the server is switch to a different site or perform any action that would cause Dreamweaver 8 to interact with the server. Unfortunately, Dreamweaver can only do one thing with the server at a time.

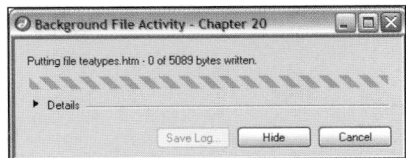

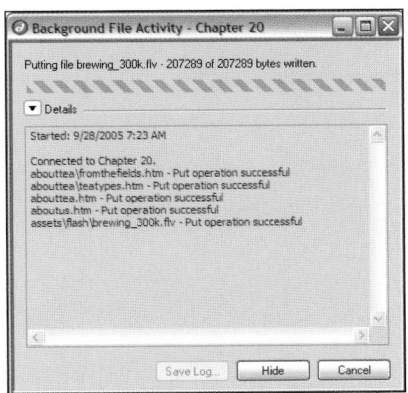

6 After all of the files have finished uploading, click the **Expand** icon in the **Files** panel.

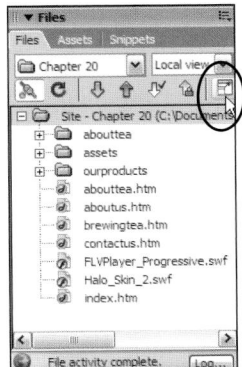

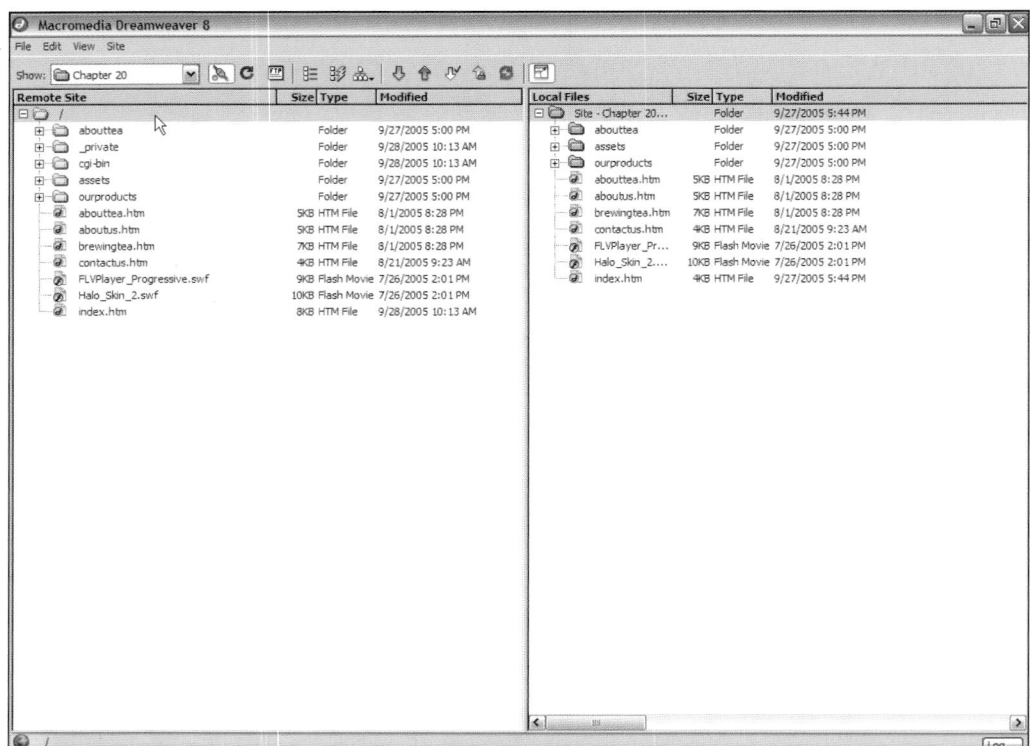

You can now see the remote files (on the left side) are nearly identical to the local files (on the right side). The only differences are the two folders (**_private** and **cgi-bin**) that Tripod adds for you automatically.

NOTE:

The Difference Between Getting and Putting

There are two different ways to transfer files between the local site and the remote site (the Web server). The Get command copies the selected files from the remote site to your local site. This process is referred to as *downloading*. The Put command copies the selected files from the local site to the remote site. This process is referred to as *uploading*.

7 Open a browser and type the URL for the tripod account you created in Exercise 1.

Because our Tripod ID was dw8hot, the URL will be **http://dw8hot.tripod.com**. Of course, your URL will be different. Just replace dw8hot with your own Tripod ID and voila—your Web site is live on the Web! Congratulations!

4 | Running Site Reports

As your sites get larger, you will find it increasingly difficult to manage all of the files. Trying to locate files with missing alt text descriptions, untitled documents, redundant nested tags, and so on, can prove to be a very time-consuming task. Dreamweaver 8 lets you identify and locate files that meet specific criteria. This feature can save you time hunting for the files manually and will make sure your files are in good shape. In this exercise, you will run a report on a finished site and fix some of the problems identified in the report.

---

1 Choose **Site > Reports** to open the **Reports** dialog box, where you can specify the type of report you would like to generate.

---

2 From the **Report on** pop-up menu, choose **Entire Current Local Site**.

This option ensures that all of the files within the current site are processed.

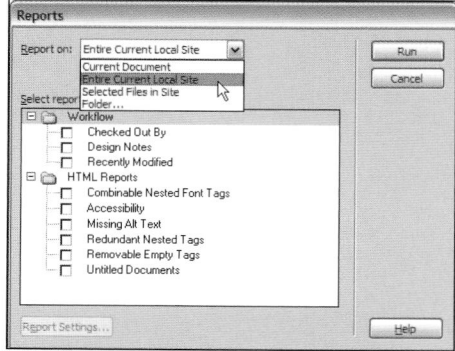

---

3 Select the **Untitled Documents** check box.

This option examines all the documents in your site to make sure each one has a valid name instead of the default *Untitled Document* Dreamweaver 8 uses for each new file. This is a good thing to check because some search engines use the page title as part of their listings.

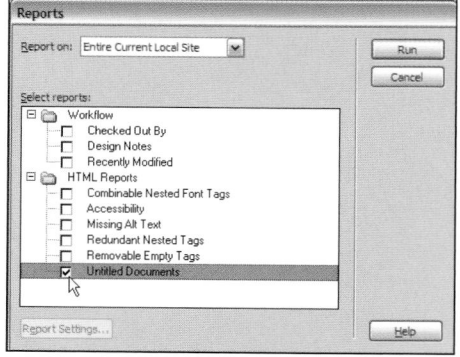

---

4 Click **Run** to begin scanning all the files in your site, looking for ones that have **Untitled Document** as the page title.

When Dreamweaver 8 is finished scanning your site the Site Reports tab of the Results panel will open and display the files that meet the criteria you specified. In this case, you are looking for files that have *Untitled Document* as the page title.

5 Double-click **brewingtea.htm** to open the file so you can correct the problem.

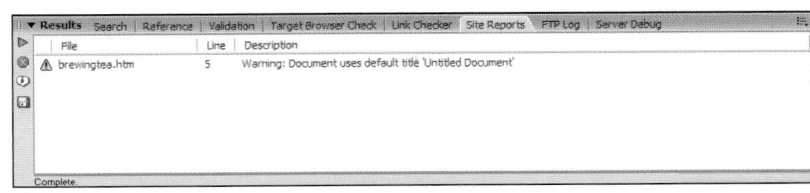

Notice the Title of the document is set to *Untitled Document*.

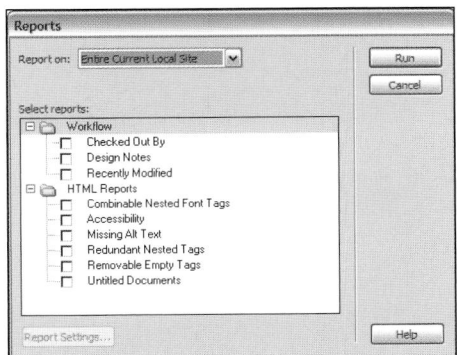

6 Type **Teacloud – Brewing Tea** in the **Title** field and press **Enter** (Windows) or **Return** (Mac).

7 Save you changes and close **brewingtea.htm**.

The Reports Dialog Box

The Reports dialog box offers a wide range of options and flexibility. The following table outlines these options and provides a brief description of each:

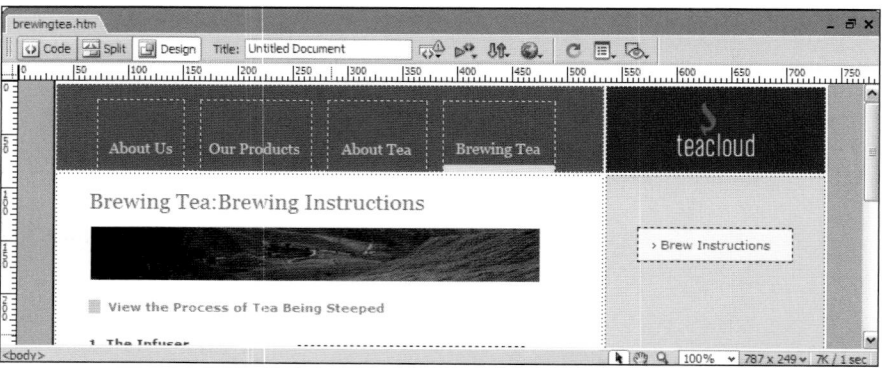

Reports Dialog Box Options		
Option	**Selection**	**Description**
Report On		
	Current Document	Checks only the active document.
	Entire Local Site	Checks every file within the local root folder.
	Selected Files in Site	Checks only the files that are selected within the Site window. You must have the files selected before choosing this option.
	Folder	Checks a specific folder. When you choose this option, you can browse to the specific folder you want to process.
Workflow		
	Checked Out By	Identifies files that have been checked out by a specific user (when using the Dreamweaver 8 Check In/Check Out feature). When this option is selected, you can specify the name by clicking the Report Settings button.
	Design Notes	Searches all of the Design Notes in your documents. The Report Settings button will give you access to specific search criteria.

continues on next page

Reports Dialog Box Options *continued*		
Option	Selection	Description
Workflow (continued)	Recently Modified	Reports files that have been modified within a specified date range. You can click the Report Settings button and check for files that have been edited within a certain number of dates or any other arbitrary date range you wish to review.
HTML Reports		
	Combinable Nested Font Tags	Reports all nested font tags that could be combined into a single **<font>** tag. For example, **<font color= "#CC3366"><font size="1">Hello</font></font>** would be reported.
	Accessibility	Analyzes the Web pages against the Section 508 Guidelines to determine if your pages meet these accessibility requirements. This is a very useful feature and can even help you make existing Web pages accessible. See Chapter 18, *"Accessibility,"* for more information.
	Missing Alt Text	Identifies all images that do not have an **alt** attribute applied to them.
	Redundant Nested Tags	Reports nested tags that can be combined.
	Removable Empty Tags	Reports any tags that don't contain any content, such as empty **<div>** or **<p>** tags.
	Untitled Documents	Searches the document to see if it has a page title of *Untitled Document*.

After learning how to put Dreamweaver 8 to use, you've finally learned how to get that site online. Congratulations! We hope this book helped you get up to speed with Dreamweaver 8 quickly, and you now feel ready to tackle your next Web project. We wish you the best of luck with all of your future projects.

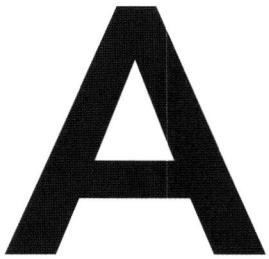

A

Technical Support and Troubleshooting FAQ

If you run into problems while following the exercises in this book, you might find the answer in the Troubleshooting FAQ. If you don't find the information you're looking for, use the contact information provided in the Technical Support section.

Technical Support Information

The following is a list of technical support resources you can use if you need help:

lynda.com

If you run into any problems as you work through this book, check the companion Web site for updates:

http://www.lynda.com/books/dw8hot

If you don't find what you're looking for on the companion Web site, send the authors an email at:

dw8hot@lynda.com

We encourage and welcome your feedback, comments, and error reports.

Peachpit Press

If your book has a defective CD-ROM, please contact the customer service department at Peachpit Press:

customer_service@peachpit.com

Macromedia Technical Support

If you're having problems with Dreamweaver 8, please visit the Macromedia Technical Support Center. To contact Macromedia Technical Support, visit the following link:

http://www.macromedia.com/support/

Frequently Asked Questions

Q When I preview my files locally, I get an error that the file or image cannot be found.

A This is one of the most common problems beginners encounter when creating links in Dreamweaver 8. This almost always occurs when you create a link that is Site Root relative instead of Document relative. Creating a Site Root relative link will cause a / character to appear at the beginning of the path to the file, which will cause images to disappear, frames to not function properly, and file links to break when previewed locally. You can correct this problem by relinking the file/image and making sure you are using the Document relative option.

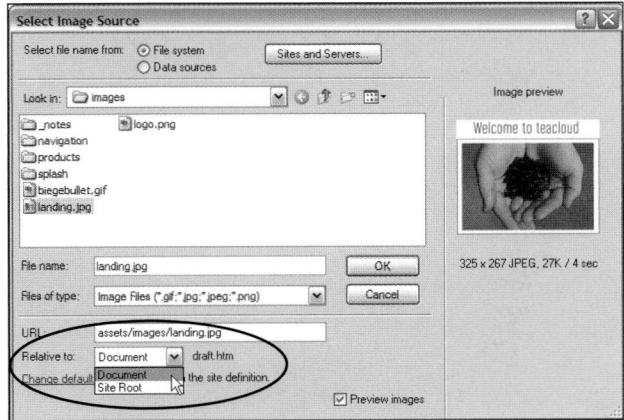

Q I can't find a feature that existed in previous versions of Dreamweaver. What happened?

A Some features found in previous versions of Dreamweaver have been removed from Dreamweaver 8. This was done because these features were obsolete and/or recommended a workflow that is no longer current with modern Web practices.

Q How do I call up the Property Inspector?

A If you can't see the Property Inspector or, for that matter, any of the Dreamweaver panels, pull down the Window menu and click on the one you want to open. The menu also includes a list of shortcut keys that will help you quickly access all of the Dreamweaver panels.

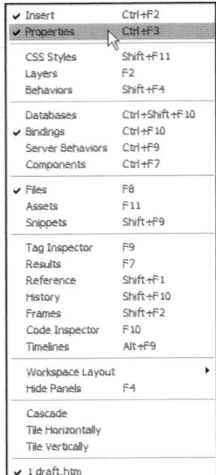

Q I defined my site for a chapter, but files that are listed in the exercises aren't there. What happened?

A When you were defining the site, you may have specified a folder that was inside the chapter folder, instead of the chapter folder itself. Go ahead and redefine the site. (If you need to revisit these steps, visit Exercise 1 in Chapter 3, "Site Control.")

Note: Selecting the correct folder is done differently on Mac and Windows, as shown here:

- **Windows:** When you're browsing to define the chapter folder, and the **Choose Local Folder** dialog box pops up, select the chapter folder. First, click **Open.** After the folder is opened, click **Select.**

- **Mac:** When you're browsing to define the chapter folder, and the **Choose Local Folder** dialog box opens, highlight the chapter folder and click **Choose.**

Q Where's the color picker?

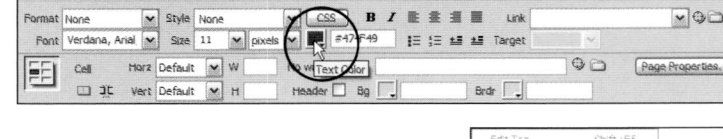

A Because it's context-sensitive, the color picker appears when you click in one of the Dreamweaver 8 color wells. Color wells appear inside the **Property Inspector** and the **Page Properties** dialog box. You can also find the color picker in Dreamweaver's Code view by **right-clicking** (Windows) or **Ctrl+clicking** (Mac) and choosing **Code Hint Tools > Color Picker** from the contextual menu.

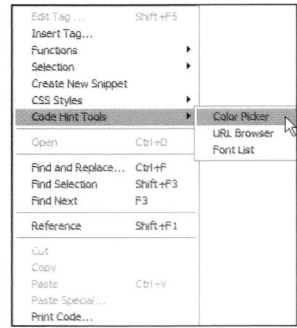

Q I put one layer on top of another! How do I delete it?

A To delete a layer, select it by the handle at its top and press **Delete**. You can also use the **Layers** panel to select the layer, which might be easier in some cases where they overlap. Of course, there's always the universal undo command, **Ctrl+Z** (Windows) or **Cmd+Z** (Mac).

Q I just specified a tracing image in my Page Properties window, but I can't see it when I preview the page in my browser.

A The tracing image is a template to be used for layout in Dreamweaver. It is invisible in the browser window. It's there for your reference only, and your end users will never see it.

Q Why do I get the message, "To make a document-relative path, your document should be saved first"?

A It would be nice if the dialog box simply stated, "Save your file now, or Dreamweaver can't keep track of your files," because that's all it's asking you to do. All you need to do is click **OK** and save your file (inside the defined site), and Dreamweaver 8 will write the path correctly.

Q Why do I get the message that my file is located outside of the root folder?

A Dreamweaver 8 is asking you to move the file into the root folder you've defined as your site. If you work with files outside your defined root folder, Dreamweaver 8 cannot keep track of your links or manage your site, which is counterproductive to the way the program is structured and to your workflow. Though this message is annoying, it is actually helping you maintain a healthy site without experiencing broken links and problems uploading your files when you publish it. **Note:** There are different ways to handle this message, depending on the system you are running:

- **Windows:** Click **Yes**, and Dreamweaver 8 will automatically put you in the correct folder. Click **Save**, and the file will be moved.

- **Mac:** Click **Yes**, and then browse to the correct folder. At that point you will be prompted to save, which you should do.

Q When I try to locate files, why can't I see the file extensions at the end of file names, such as .gif, .jpg, and .html?

A On Windows, you will need to change your Preferences to view file name extensions. See the Introduction at the beginning of this book for instructions on how to do this.

Dreamweaver 8 Resources

There are many great resources for Dreamweaver 8 users. You have ample choices among a variety of newsgroups, conferences, and third-party Web sites that can really help you get the most out of the new skills you've developed by reading this book. Here you'll find a list of the best resources for further developing your skills with Dreamweaver 8.

lynda.com Training Resources

lynda.com is a leader in software books and video training for Web and graphics professionals. To help further develop your skills in Dreamweaver 8, check out the following training resources from **lynda.com:**

lynda.com Books

The **Hands-On Training** series was originally developed by **Lynda Weinman**, author of the revolutionary book, *Designing Web Graphics*, first released in 1996. Lynda believes people learn best from doing and has developed the **Hands-On Training** series to teach users software programs and technologies through a progressive learning process.

Check out the following books from lynda.com:

Designing Web Graphics 4
by Lynda Weinman
New Riders
ISBN: 0735710791

Adobe Photoshop CS2 for the Web Hands-On Training
by Tanya Staples
lynda.com/books and Peachpit Press
ISBN: 0321331710

Flash Professional 8 Hands-On Training
by James Gonzalez
lynda.com/books and Peachpit Press
ISBN: 0321293886

Flash Professional 8 Beyond the Basics
by Shane Rebenschied
lynda.com/books and Peachpit Press
ISBN: 0321293878

lynda.com Video-Based Training

lynda.com offers video training as stand-alone **CD-ROM** and **DVD-ROM** products and through a monthly or annual subscription to the **lynda.com Online Training Library**.

For a free, 24-hour trial pass to the lynda.com Online Training Library, register your copy of Dreamweaver 8 Hands-On Training at the following link:

http://www.lynda.com/register/HOT/ dreamweaver8

Note: This offer is available for new subscribers only and does not apply to current or past subscribers of the lynda.com Online Training Library.

To help you build your skills with Dreamweaver 8, check out the following video-based training titles from lynda.com:

Dreamweaver Video-Based Training

Dreamweaver 8 Essential Training
with Garrick Chow

Dreamweaver 8 New Features
with Garrick Chow

Learning Macromedia Dreamweaver MX 2004
with Garo Green

Intermediate Dreamweaver MX 2004
with Garo Green and Daniel Short

Dynamic Development with ASP and Dreamweaver MX 2004
with Daniel Short

Web Design Video-Based Training

Studio 8 Web Workflow
with Abigail Rudner

Photoshop CS2 for the Web Essential Training
with Tanya Staples

Fireworks 8 Essential Training
with Abigail Rudner

Web Development Video-Based Training

Learning CSS 2
with Christopher Deutsch

Learning XHTML
with William E. Weinman

Learning HTML
with William E. Weinman

Learning JavaScript
with Charles G. Hollins

Flashforward Conference

Flashforward is an international educational conference dedicated to Macromedia Flash. Flashforward was first hosted by Lynda Weinman, founder of lynda.com, and Stewart McBride, founder of United Digital Artists. Flashforward is now owned exclusively by lynda.com and strives to provide the best conferences for designers and developers to present their technical and artistic work in an educational setting.

For more information about the Flashforward conference, visit
http://www.flashforwardconference.com.

Online Resources

Dreamweaver Discussion Group
**news://forums.macromedia.com/
macromedia.dreamweaver**

Web Sites

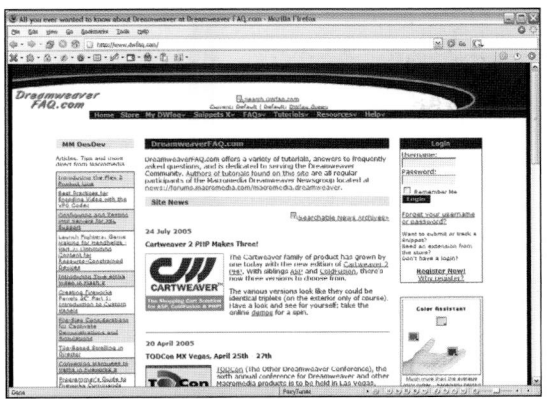

DWFAQ.com   http://www.dwfaq.com

Community MX   http://www.communitymx.com

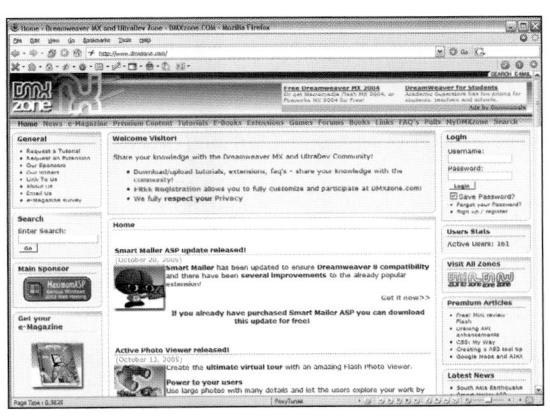

DMXZONE.com   http://www.dmxzone.com

Books

Dreamweaver MX 2004 Killer Tips
By Joseph Lowery and Angela C. Burgalia
New Riders
ISBN: 0735713790

Eric Meyer on CSS
By Eric Meyer
New Riders
ISBN: 073571245X

More Eric Meyer on CSS
By Eric Meyer
New Riders
ISBN: 0735714258

Installing Extensions

Although Dreamweaver 8 is a massive and highly capable application, it simply can't do everything for everyone, and frankly, who would want it to? If Dreamweaver tried to do all things for all people, it would probably fail miserably at most of them. However, the engineering masterminds at Macromedia made Dreamweaver 8 extensible, which means it's possible for a third-party to extend the functionality of Dreamweaver through plug-ins called extensions.

Extensions can add behaviors, commands, toolbars, and server behaviors, and they can even change the way the core functionality of Dreamweaver behaves. Each extension is a collection of HTML, JavaScript, CSS, or even DLLs that create all of this new and wonderful functionality. In the golden age of Dreamweaver 4, you had to handle installing extensions all your own. It was a matter of "copy file A to folder B, and copy files C, D, and E to folder F." With Dreamweaver MX came the Extension Manager, which took care of all of this mess for you.

The Macromedia Extension Manager

The Macromedia Extension Manager is the brains of the Dreamweaver 8 extensibility engine. It manages all of the information relating to extensions in each of the Macromedia products. The Extension Manager handles all of the installation tasks for Dreamweaver 8 (and other Macromedia products) automatically. You simply double-click an extension file (which has an .mxp file extension) and the Extension Manager takes care of the rest.

Installing an Extension

Here's how to install an extension:

1 Choose **Help > Manage Extensions** to open the **Extension Manager**.

2 Click the **Install Extension** button to open the **Select Extension to Install** dialog box.

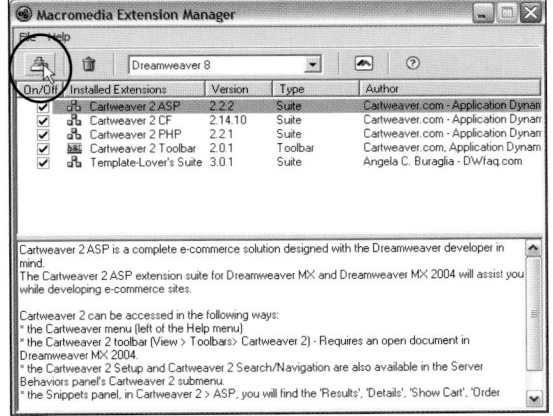

3 In the **Select Extension to Install** dialog box, browse to the MXP file for the extension you want to install. Highlight it, and click **Install**.

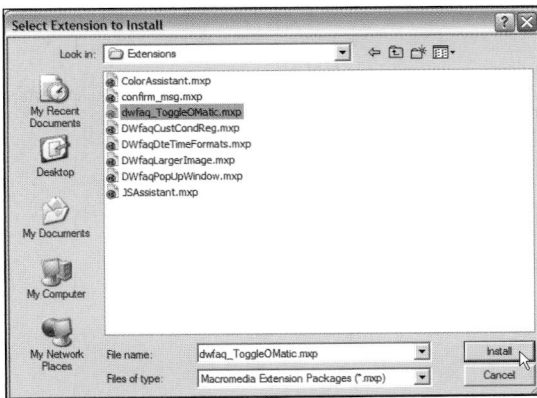

4 You need to either **Accept** or **Decline** the End User License Agreement for the extension. Click **Accept** to continue the installation. (Click **Decline** if you don't want to continue with the installation.)

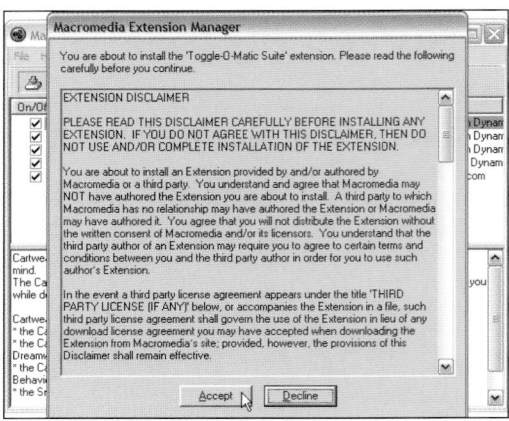

A progress bar shows how much time remains to complete the extension installation.

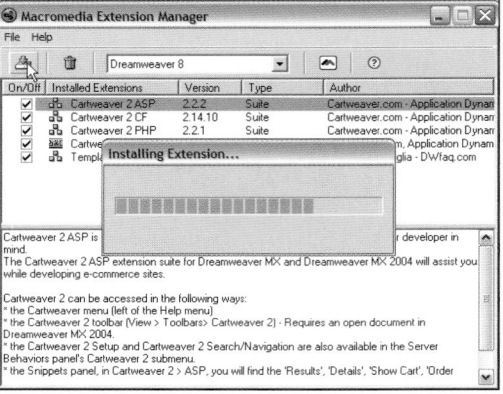

5 After the installation is complete, Dreamweaver 8 lets you know the installation was successful. If you have Dreamweaver 8 open, you may need to restart it before you can use the extension. Click **OK**.

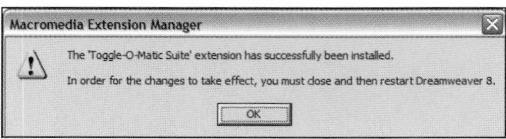

The extension is now displayed in the Extension Manager.

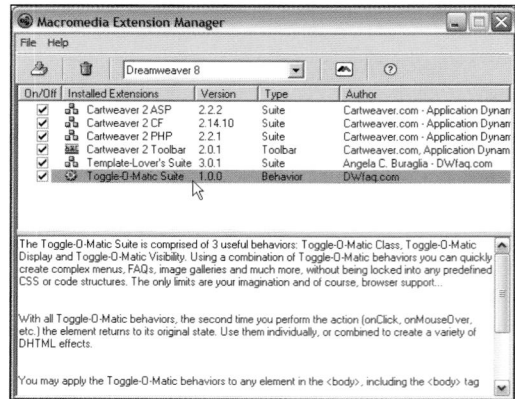

Disabling an Extension

Disabling an extension allows you to easily remove an extension from Dreamweaver 8 and add it back at a later date. To disable an extension, simply deselect the box next to the extension in the Extension Manager, which will leave a copy of the files on your local system for the Extension Manager but will remove them from Dreamweaver 8.

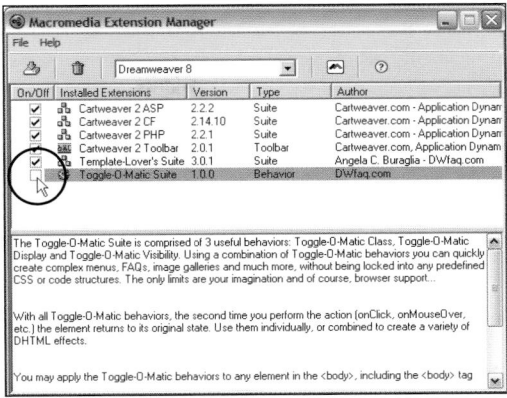

Uninstalling an Extension

1 To completely remove an extension from Dreamweaver 8, and your local machine, select the extension and click the **Remove Extension** button.

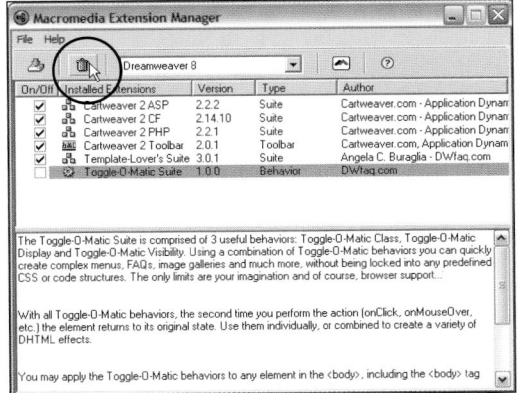

2 The **Extension Manager** will prompt you to confirm removal of the extension. Click **Yes** to permanently remove the extension, or click **No** to cancel the operation.

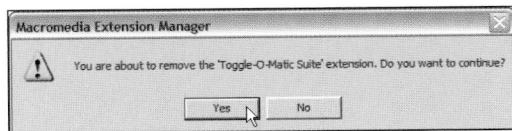

3 After the extension has been successfully removed, click **OK**. If you have Dreamweaver 8 open, close and then restart it to ensure that all of the extension files have been properly removed.

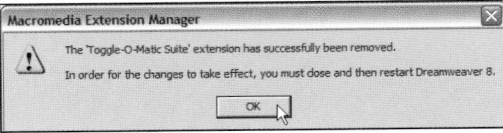

Index

Symbols

% (as measurement unit), 174

A

\<a\> tag, 83
absolute URLs, 40–42
accessibility, 446–457
  formatting text using headings, 168
  inserting form objects, 454–457
  inserting images, 450–451
  inserting tables, 452–453
  setting preferences, 448–449
  testing, 457
  W3C guidelines, 447
Adobe Acrobat, creating PDF files, 105
Adjust Position command (View menu), 251
Align Center button, 71, 185
Align Left button, 186
Align Right button, 186
alignment
  images, 71–73, 187
  table content, 226–231
  text, 71–73, 185–188
All mode, CSS Styles panel, 125–126
alt attribute, 451
alternate text field (Insert Rollover Image dialog box), 290
animated rollovers, 293
Application group (Insert bar), 18
Apply Comment button (Code toolbar), 322–323
Apply Template to Page command (Modify menu), 413
Assets command (Window menu), 62, 402
Assets panel, 62–63
Attach External Style Sheet dialog box, 121

attributes
  alt, 451
  \<form\> tag, 360
  longdesc, 451
  scope, 210
  summary, 453
Auto Indent option (XHTML Code view), 317
automation, 434–445
  Find and Replace feature, 441–445
  History panel, 435–438
  saving history steps as commands, 439–440

B

background images, 252
Balance Braces button (Code toolbar), 322–323
behaviors, 362–375
  Change Property, 367–370
  Check Form, 373
  obtaining complicated behaviors, 374
  Open Browser Window, 363–366
  Swap Image, 296–298
  third-party market, 374
  Validate Form, 371–373
Behaviors command (Window menu), 295
Beyond Compare (Scooter Software), 30
block elements (CSS) *versus* inline elements, 156
\<body\> tag, 6
books (resources), 495
border manipulation, tables
  CSS, 213–217
  XHTML, 207–212
\<br /\> tag, 70
Brightness and Contrast tool (Fireworks 8), 381, 383
Brightness/Contrast dialog box, 382
browser offset, modifying, 251
buttons, 344
  Align Center, 71, 185
  Align Left, 186

F

N

Named Anchor button, 95
Named Anchor command (Insert menu), 96
Named Anchor dialog box, 95
named anchors, 94–101
navigation, tables, 204
Navigation Bar command
   Insert menu, 300
   Modify menu, 306
navigation bars, 299–307
New command (File menu), 55
New CSS Rule button, 130
New CSS Rule dialog box, 130
New Document dialog box, 55–57
New Editable Region dialog box, 408
New Library Item button, 429
New Site command (Site menu), 36
new source files, linking to, 85–89
null links, rollovers, 292

O

objects, media objects
   embedding multimedia files, 463–465
   inserting
      Flash content, 466–468
      Flash Video content, 469–471
      Shockwave content, 468
   linking to sounds, 460–462
   plug-ins, 459
online resources, 494–495
Open Browser Window behavior, 363–366
Open Browser Window dialog box, 363–364
Open Document button (Code toolbar), 322–323
Optimize in Fireworks tool (Fireworks 8), 383
optional regions, templates, 425–426
Ordered List command (Text menu), 190
ordered lists, 189–190
ordering fonts, font lists, 183
original image field (Insert Rollover Image dialog box), 290
Outdent Code button (Code toolbar), 322–323
over state (rollovers), 299
over while down state (rollovers), 299

P

<p> tag, 70
padding, white space management, 181
Page Properties button, 111
Page Properties command (Modify menu), 111, 250
Page Properties dialog box, 111, 116–117, 250
pages
   properties, CSS, 111–115
   structure, formatting text with Property Inspector, 168
   titles
      versus filenames, 61
      setting, 60–61
panels, 25–27
   Assets, 62–63
   CSS Styles, 125–128
   Files, 44
   groups, 25–27
   History, 435–438
   Reference, 115
   Snippets, 337
paragraph breaks *versus* line breaks, 70
parameters
   defined, 465
   templates, 428
Password setting (FTP), 479
Paste command (Edit menu), 305
path structure, 45–47
PDF files, 105
picas (as measurement units), 174
pipe symbol, 69
pixels (as measurement units), 173
placeholders, 85–86
Plugin command (Insert menu), 463
plug-ins, 459
   downloading (URLs), 459
   parameters, 465
   Shockwave, 468
Point to File feature, 81–84
points (as measurement units), 174
Pop-up Menu Editor, 397
pop-up menus, integration of Fireworks 8, 394–399
pop-up windows, 366
preferences, 28–30
   accessibility, 448–449
   highlighting, 409
Preferences command (Edit menu), 29, 208
Preferences dialog box, 28

Preload Rollover Image check box, 293

preload rollover image field (Insert Rollover Image dialog box), 290

Print command (File menu), 105, 275

Print dialog box, 105

Print Preview command (File menu), 275

printer-friendly style sheets, 274–276

privacy policies, 475

product registration, ix

properties, templates, modifications, 427–428

Property Inspector, 18–19

    class names, 170

    formatting text, 165–173

pseudo-class selectors (CSS), 128, 155–159

Put command, 482

Q–R

Quick Tag Editor, 329–331

radio buttons, 343, 352–354

Radio Group dialog box, 353

radio groups, 343

Recent Snippets button (Code toolbar), 322–323

redoing operations, History panel, 436–438

redundancy, interface, 19

Reference command (Window menu), 115

Reference panel, 115

references, CSS, 115

registration, ix

relative links, 47–48

relative URLs, 40–42

remote sites, transferring files, 482

Remove Comment button (Code toolbar), 322–323

Remove Extension button, 499

renaming form items, 348

Render Screen Media Type button, 280

Repeating Region command (Insert menu), 420

Repeating Region dialog box, 420

repeating regions, 418–424

Report On option (Reports dialog box), 486

reports, running site reports, 484–485

Reports command (Site menu), 484

Reports dialog box, 486–487

requirements, Dreamweaver 8, 1

Resample tool (Fireworks 8), 383

resizing handles (layers), 254

resources

    books, 495

    design for multiple devices, 284

    Dreamweaver 8, 492–495

    Fireworks 8, 399

    online, 494–495

    training, ix

results (forms), submitting, 358–361

rollover image field (Insert Rollover Image dialog box), 290

Rollover Image command (Insert menu), 291

rollovers, 286–311

    creating, 288–293

    CSS, creating with pseudo-classes, 155–159

    disjointed, 294–298

    inserting, 293, 387–389

    navigation bars, 299–307

    null links, 292

    rules, 287

root folder, 35

rounded-corner tables, 242–246

Roundtrip XHTML, 3–4

rows (tables), 200

rules

    CSS, 110

    rollovers, 287

S

Safari, form elements, 360

sans-serif font, 184

Save As Command dialog box, 439

Save As dialog box, 58

Save As Template command (File menu), 407

Save As Template dialog box, 407

Save command (File menu), 58

Save dialog box, 50

Save Site Map command (File menu), 50

Save Spacer Image File As dialog box, 267

saving

    documents, 55–58

    workspace layouts, 28

Scooter Software, Beyond Compare, 30

scope attribute, 210

screen readers, IBM Home Page Reader, 449

<script> tags, 325–326

scripts, 344

W

X-Y-Z